Letters to Monica

Philip Larkin was born in 1922 and grew up in Coventry. In 1955 he became Librarian at the Brynmor Jones Library at the University of Hull, a post he held until his death in 1985. He was the best-loved poet of his generation and the recipient of innumerable honours, including the Queen's Gold Medal for Poetry and the WHSmith Award.

As one of Philip Larkin's chosen literary executors, Anthony Thwaite edited the *Collected Poems*, *Selected Letters* and *Further Requirements*. His own *Collected Poems*, drawing on fifty years' work, was published in 2007.

Published in association with the Bodleian Library.

Praise for the hardback edition of *Letters to Monica* (2010)

'To lovers of the poetry, this selection of correspondence that lasted forty years is completely fascinating – not just for the inadvertent light it shines on the poetry but also for the elucidation of Larkin's own taste and his opinion of his own work and worth. The length and intimate nature of Larkin's relationship with Monica Jones gives the letters and the opinions they express a compelling authenticity and almost vulnerable honesty.' William Boyd, *TLS*

'His low-key but oddly forceful personality is one of the things that comes out most vividly in the work – the letters are part of the poetry in that sense – and is a sort of poetic statement in itself.' Derek Mahon, *Literary Review*

'These are the most intimate letters of a major poet . . . Throughout, you can see the poems coming, poems that you know by heart.' David Sexton, *Evening Standard*

'Philip Larkin is the best-loved poet of the past 100 years, and these irresistibly readable letters reveal the life and personality more intimately than ever before . . . He is constantly and inventively funny, concocting parodies and spoofs with loving care . . . the total effect is exhilarating. You feel sorry when you turn the last page. He said of Mansfield's journal that it made readers "more sensitive, more receptive, happier than before". These letters do the same.' John Carey, *Sunday Times*

'As an editor, Thwaite treads softly. His unobtrusive cuts give a shape to the letters, bringing Larkin's clear-eyed observations of love, work and his surroundings to the fore. Fans will find the drafts of his poems particularly thrilling.' Emma Hughes, *Country Life*

'Larkin's letters are affectionate, flirting, playful, even whimsical. There is something of Mass Observation about them – reflections on life, literature, domestic chores and personal feelings . . . one warms to the pair in their decent (if distanced) domesticity.' Iain Finlayson, *The Times*

'Not only are they funny, sad and true; they are also charmingly replete with 1950s detail, evoking a world of curry-powder concoctions, rasping gas fires, and long but civilised train journeys.' Rachel Cooke, Observer Books of the Year

by Philip Larkin

poetry
THE NORTH SHIP
XX POEMS
THE FANTASY POETS NO. 21
THE LESS DECEIVED
THE WHITSUN WEDDINGS
HIGH WINDOWS
COLLECTED POEMS (edited by Anthony Thwaite)
EARLY POEMS AND JUVENILIA (edited by A. T. Tolley)

THE OXFORD BOOK OF
TWENTIETH-CENTURY ENGLISH VERSE (ed.)

fiction
JILL
A GIRL IN WINTER
TROUBLE AT WILLOW GABLES (edited by James Booth)

non-fiction
ALL WHAT JAZZ: A RECORD DIARY 1961–71
REQUIRED WRITING: MISCELLANEOUS PIECES 1955–82
SELECTED LETTERS OF PHILIP LARKIN 1940–1985
(edited by Anthony Thwaite)
FURTHER REQUIREMENTS: INTERVIEWS, BROADCASTS,
STATEMENTS AND REVIEWS 1952–85
(edited by Anthony Thwaite)

PHILIP LARKIN

Letters to Monica

EDITED BY

ANTHONY THWAITE

faber and faber

Bodleian Library
UNIVERSITY OF OXFORD

First published in 2010
by Faber and Faber Limited
Bloomsbury House, 74–77 Great Russell Street,
London WC1B 3DA
This paperback edition first published in 2011

In association with the Bodleian Library
Broad Street
Oxford OX1 3BG

Typeset by RefineCatch Limited, Bungay, Suffolk
Printed in England by CPI Mackays, Chatham

A CIP record for this book
is available from the British Library

ISBN 978-0-571-23910-8

2 4 6 8 10 9 7 5 3 1

CONTENTS

INTRODUCTION

Between December 1946 and April 1984, Philip Larkin wrote to Monica Jones more than 1,421 letters and 521 postcards: about 7,500 surviving pages altogether. Other letters have apparently been lost or have disappeared. He wrote from his parents' house in Warwick, from Leicester, Belfast, Hull, his mother's house in Loughborough, London, Oxford, and elsewhere. Apart from Larkin's family letters, chiefly those written to his mother for over thirty years of her widowhood, they form the most extensive correspondence of his life. Certainly they mark his most important relationship. It was to Monica that the dying Larkin entrusted the fate of his copious diaries ('Make sure those diaries are destroyed'); and indeed soon after Larkin's death on 2 December 1985 Monica handed over the diaries to his former secretary Betty Mackereth, who fed them into the shredder in the Brynmor Jones Library, Hull. However, these many letters to Monica survive, and they chronicle his life and his attitudes more intimately than anything else we have.

In the Introduction to my edition of Larkin's *Selected Letters* (1992), with Monica Jones at that time ailing but still alive for another nine years (though deeply depressed and deeply disorganised), I wrote:

> The ... long and extremely close relationship with Monica Jones, dating from 1946 in Leicester, is shown only fragmentarily here; but, again, apparent losses may later be recovered.

In fact, at my request Monica had earlier searched and had found about twenty letters in the house in Hull she had inherited from Larkin at his death. I used thirteen of them, or extracts from them, in the edition. Later, as Andrew Motion has recorded, he went to Monica's cottage in Haydon Bridge, Northumberland, and found many more (several in a distressed state, affected by water and mould). He drew on some of these in his biography of Larkin, published in 1993.

What I never could have guessed is the quantity of letters that emerged after Monica's death in 2001. These were gathered together, as the property of the Estate of Monica Jones and were sold by that

Estate, through the London specialist dealers, Bernard Quaritch, to the Bodleian Library, Oxford – which is also where all Monica's surviving letters to Larkin are deposited.

Monica Jones and Philip Larkin first met in the autumn of 1946 at Leicester University College. Monica had been appointed as an Assistant Lecturer in English there in January 1946. Larkin arrived in September 1946, as an Assistant Librarian. (The total library staff then was three people.) Both had been at Oxford (he at St John's, she at St Hugh's) between 1940 and 1943, but they had never met there. Both had First Class degrees in English. They had been born in the same year, 1922, and came from rather similar provincial middle-class backgrounds. Monica was an only child: Larkin had an older sister, Kitty, but the ten-year age gap, and differences of temperament, kept them apart.

For the first few years of the relationship, Larkin was involved with Ruth Bowman, whom he had met in Wellington when she was a sixth-former. Indeed, when he returned from his Belfast interview in June 1950, he had a blurred notion that he and Ruth could marry and 'start life afresh in a far countrie' (as he put it in a letter to his old school-friend Jim Sutton). But when Ruth, in exasperation and misery, broke off the engagement, Monica quickly became central to Larkin's attention. He touches on this in a long letter started on 23 May 1951, in which he writes about 'the progress of my misengagement'.

Monica's long career teaching at Leicester University (from 1946 until she retired in 1981) was marked in particular by two things. First, there was the panache of her lecturing, in which, for example, she would wear a Scottish tartan when talking about *Macbeth*. (Some were rather shocked by her. A former student, now in her late seventies, recalled: 'In my then opinion, Miss Jones was very suspiciously blonde, very highly made-up, and talked a great deal without asking our opinion of anything. All that was excusable, but what really upset me was that her tops were much too low at the front.') Second, Monica regarded publishing as a bit showy, and she never in fact published anything during the whole of her academic career. This held her back from any promotion. She agonised about her lecture preparation, marking and the awfulness of many of her colleagues, in a way that is paralleled by Larkin's complaints. They fed each other's misery.

Monica and Larkin's friendship and correspondence began with books and reading. The very first letter partly concerns him lending her a copy of his novel *Jill*, recently published by the Fortune Press, and proofs of *A Girl in Winter*, which Faber were to publish in February 1947. Over the years much else was added to books and reading: gossip and rancour about colleagues; the irksomeness of work; eating, drinking, indigestion; actual and supposed illnesses; sport (chiefly cricket, but also boxing); music; films; planning holidays and looking back on them; and a great deal of affectionate whimsy about their version of the world of Beatrix Potter, embellished with Larkin's skilful sketches.

Their literary enthusiasms weren't entirely the same. Monica was much keener than Larkin was on Walter Scott, Jane Austen and George Crabbe. From early on, and right through, Larkin was fascinated by D. H. Lawrence. They shared a delight in Hardy, and in Barbara Pym. They were equally scornful about many reputations of the time – C. P. Snow, Pamela Hansford Johnson, William Cooper, Marghanita Laski, and dozens of others.

Another running theme is Larkin's feelings about his old St John's friend, Kingsley Amis – about Amis's spectacular success with *Lucky Jim* in 1954, his domestic life, his marital and other affairs, and frequently Larkin's exasperation with the man. Monica and Amis were always wary of one another: she knew he had cruelly drawn on her in his portrait of 'Margaret' in *Lucky Jim*.

As well as Amis, other names frequently recur. There is the Vice Chancellor of Hull, Brynmor Jones, privately mocked by Larkin for his alleged Welsh obtuseness; Larkin's deputy in the Library for many years, Arthur Wood, on whom many painful fantasy humiliations are heaped; Monica's Leicester colleagues, from her first chief (A. S. Collins – on the whole approved of) to later ones (Arthur Humphreys, P. A. W. Collins, both reviled) who are frequently gossiped about. Peter Coveney, for long Warden of Needler Hall, Hull, is mocked too, but his thoughtfulness and kindness, after Larkin's mysterious collapse, hospitalisation and subsequent convalescence in 1961, are taken notice of. George Hartley, founder with his then wife, Jean, of the poetry journal *Listen* and then the Marvell Press, at an early stage is burdened with the derisive title the 'ponce of Hessle'. Robert Conquest, who first wrote to Larkin early in 1955 concerning what was to become the anthology *New Lines*, is much mentioned too. Larkin showed some interest in, and even cultivated a slightly *voulu* jealousy about, some of Monica's 'young men' – chiefly students at Leicester who seemed attracted to her: Bill Ruddick, John Sutherland, and others.

These are discursive letters, full of the sense of someone talking, entertaining, complaining, exchanging bits of shared argot, but often analysing too. 'Life is first boredom, then fear': there is much mention of both. Larkin often itemised his daily rounds and common tasks – changing his sheets, washing his sheets, washing his socks, mending his socks, mowing his mother's lawn when he was staying with her, mowing his own when he eventually had his own house at 105 Newland Park.

The letters are linked by the long-lasting affectionate playfulness of the two of them: he a seal, she a rabbit ('Dearest bun'); the harsh cries, or laughs, or exclamations of seagulls (*ogh ogh, Awwghgh*!) in reaction to the idiots and idiocies they came across. Larkin realised – quite often realised – how the two of them were closely bound, ill-suited in some ways to deal with the world, and yet oddly drawn together. On 26 May 1955 he wrote: 'We are strange correspondents, each sitting in his tiny threadbare uncomfortable life, sending messages of hope and good cheer'; and again, on 26 September 1957, 'We are a queer pair, each with vast, almost complementary drawbacks.' It is clear, at times, that Monica would have been glad to marry him; Larkin, with many guilty twinges, always drew back. His intermittent, very close relationship with Maeve Brennan in Hull caused much grief and much analysis.

It was to Monica that Larkin poured out his fears and miseries – on moving from Leicester to Belfast and then to Hull, and living in successive lodgings, for instance. Solitude – 'peace and quiet' – was much sought by Larkin, as is apparent throughout his life, his letters, and his poems. He was irritated and depressed by the intrusion of noise and noisy neighbours in his various lodgings and flats, a frequent burden in these letters until in 1974 for the first time he moved into a house of his own, by which time his correspondence with Monica had dwindled to almost nothing.

He was burdened by the mess he thought he was making of his job in Hull (though by all other accounts he was a notably successful head of the Brynmor Jones Library). He was terrified by the mystery of his collapse and hospitalisation in March 1961, and poured out this terror in what is one of the longest letters in this collection. Some of the letters, indeed, are very long – twelve or fourteen sides. Almost every letter and card was written in Larkin's clear handwriting. As is apparent from time to time, he was much influenced by the 'feel' of the pen in his hand and its result on the page.

What is particularly fascinating is the sharing with Monica of progress (or otherwise) on particular poems. To begin with, what he shows her are completed poems ('Wedding-Wind', 'At Grass'), and later his privately printed pamphlet *XX Poems*. Later still, he tries out drafts of poems on her, asking for her comments: 'Church Going', 'Myxomatosis' (28 September 1954), 'An Arundel Tomb', and many others. How strange it is that he seemed in serious doubt whether to include 'Church Going' and 'Spring' in *The Less Deceived*.

There are a great number of Christmas cards, birthday cards and greetings cards, often embellished with their private jokes, such as the persona of 'Dr Pussy' ('G. F. Pussy'), a Victorian clubman, a cat fond of fish and ceremony; or signed, variously, 'Ted o' the Pennines', 'Robert "I'm the greatest" Lowell', 'Elspeth McBun', or risqué ones purporting to be from Monica's head of department, A. R. Humphreys. Some cards contain verses, most notably perhaps a birthday card 'after J. F. Gilbert' ('Priam winning the Gold Cup at Goodwood in 1831') on which is written a poem beginning 'Those long thin steeds' (see overleaf).

The two of them shared a sympathy with animals, in the sense that both of them deplored bullfights, vivisection, myxomatosis and pet-shops, and they were much taken not only with Beatrix Potter's inventions (and even with those of some of her imitators and followers) but with real creatures, in particular cats and rabbits; though Monica had a fear of hens, and of some other birds.

After 1972, the letters are mainly shorter and much less frequent. Larkin's mother went in January that year into a hospital in Leicester, then into a nursing home nearby. This meant that Larkin was visiting his mother much more often, and therefore seeing Monica in Leicester more frequently. They also used the telephone more freely than had been their practice; though both were natural letter-writers rather than talkers on the telephone.

In October 1982, Monica fell downstairs in her Haydon Bridge cottage, went into Hexham Hospital, and then convalesced with Larkin in his house in Hull. She returned to Haydon Bridge when it was felt she had recovered. But then, at Easter 1983, when they were both staying in the cottage, she was badly stricken with shingles. When she was released from hospital, Larkin offered her shelter and care in his house in Newland Park, Hull. There, Larkin looked after her until his death in December 1985. They had, towards the end of his life, settled into something close to marriage. Monica hardly left that house in Hull until her own death in February 2001.

Priam Winning the Gold Cup at Goodwood in 1831

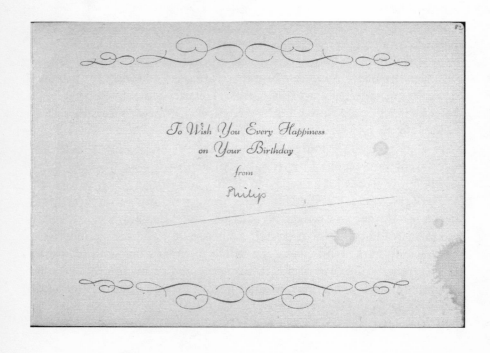

To Wish You Every Happiness
on Your Birthday

from

Philip

Those long thin steeds,
And natural downs
So near at hand,
We cannot see,
Nor that tiny
Excitement share
In the delicate stand:
We cannot be

Elsewhere than here –
And yet, just so
May others stare
On our casual scene,
And cry for pleasure
At the out-of-reach
Enchantment there
Where we have been.

DL

From an engraving by J. Clark after J. F. Gilbert

NOTE ON THE CONTENTS

To keep the book to manageable proportions, I have made many internal cuts, indicated with square brackets, as well as omitting many letters in their entirety. I have, I think, included something of everything, but in some cases I have chosen to give only a few examples of repeated themes and topics. In spite of his professed contempt for holidays ('they seem a wholly feminine conception, based on an impotent dislike of everyday life and a romantic notion that it will all be better at Frinton or Venice'*), it was Larkin who substantially made the hotel bookings, consulted the timetables and booked the tickets; and parts of many letters are taken up with discussion about such arrangements. Accounts of meals eaten, whether self-created ('Spaghetti Pearson Park') or consumed elsewhere, I have often left out. There is a great deal of talk about colleagues, in Leicester, Belfast and Hull, which would require tedious explanation. It was with Monica that Larkin shared the trivial details of his daily life – his hair, his health, his weight, his clothes, his hangovers, whether he needed to wash the car or put it away in the garage, the records he played, the programmes he heard on the radio. (Both Larkin and Monica were keen followers of *The Archers*, but in general I have left out Larkin's reactions to the latest bits of news from Ambridge, because they demand too much explanatory synopsis-writing.) I have included something of all this, but have omitted much.

There are several inexplicable gaps in the Bodleian Library holdings. Between 1946 and 1949 there are only twelve letters (and six postcards), of which I have used four letters. In 1950, there is one letter in January, then nothing until 4 July; in the first half of 1953, nothing except a couple of postcards; and only a handful for much of 1954, until August of that year, followed by twenty-four letters. The present volume includes thirteen letters to Monica, or extracts from letters, which were previously printed in the 1992 *Selected Letters*.

* 'Not the Place's Fault', 1959 (reprinted in *Further Requirements*, 2001).

After the 14 January 1973 letter, the total remaining tally until 12 October 1982 is as follows: *1973* two letters, two postcards, one greetings card; *1974* two postcards, one greetings card; *1975* two postcards, one letter; *1976* three postcards, one letter; *1977* one letter, two postcards, one greetings card; *1978* one greetings card; *1979* nothing; *1980* two postcards; *1981* one letter, five postcards. After the 12 October 1982 postcard and the two letters later that month, the tally runs: *1983* six letters (one included here), five postcards; *1984* two letters (one included here), and the Christmas 1984 card with poem included here.

To make clear the places from and to which Larkin and Monica were writing, Appendix A shows their successive addresses. Appendix B is a biographical glossary, which contains brief notes on most of the people mentioned, many of whom are also identified in footnotes.

From as early as 1950, Larkin adorned his messages to Monica with drawings, from sketches of his room to the raised two fingers at the British Library Lending Division (Boston Spa). We have reproduced only a fairly modest – but representative – selection; but indication is made on the appropriate pages of many more.

Larkin and Monica shared a taste for deliberate, usually comic, misspellings. Examples are: *flithy*, *booldy*, *arl* (for *all*), *anthin* (for *anything*), *scurley* (for *scullery*), *wans* (for *ones*), *human bean* (for *human being*), *yuors turly* (for *yours truly*), *shabbily* (for *Chablis*), *haddock* (for *headache*), *Bow Joe* (for *Beaujolais*), *bogray* (for *buggery*), *Ganniss* (for *Guinness*), *wassups* (for *wasps*), *Wickla* (for *Wicklow*). Some of these mimic pronunciations, others seem gratuitous. I have tried to transcribe them accurately, but no doubt sometimes have failed.

ACKNOWLEDGEMENTS

For many and various kinds of help, I thank the following: Chris Fletcher, Judith Priestman and Kate Longworth (Bodleian Library, Oxford); James Booth (University of Hull); Jeremy Crow (Society of Authors); Judy Burg and Kate Butler (Brynmor Jones Library, Hull); Christine Fyfe (University of Leicester); James Campbell; Ian Duhig; Judy Egerton; Alistair Elliot; John Fuller; Jean Hartley; Monica Johnson; Roger Kingerlee; Betty Mackereth; Michael Millgate; Andrew Motion; Peter Porter; John Sutherland; Ann Thwaite; Hilary Tulloch; Ron Costley, Charles Boyle, Paul Keegan, Katherine Armstrong, Anne Owen (Faber and Faber); the London Library.

LIST OF ABBREVIATIONS

AA	Automobile Association
AEH	A. E. Housman
A G in W	*A Girl in Winter*
ALR	A. L. Rowse
ARH	Arthur Humphreys
AS	All Souls
ASC	A. S. Collins
B	Samuel Butler
BJ	Brynmor Jones
CB	Charlotte Bronte
CC	Cyril Connolly
CDL	Cecil Day Lewis
CQ	*Critical Quarterly*
DHL	D. H. Lawrence
DT	*Daily Telegraph*
EJH	Elizabeth Jane Howard
EMF	E. M. Forster
Ez	Ezra Pound
GBS	George Bernard Shaw
GG	Graham Greene
GMH	Gerard Manley Hopkins
GSF	George Fraser
GW	Great Western (Railway)
HB	Haydon Bridge
H of D	*Heart of Darkness*
JA	Jane Austen
JFK	John F. Kennedy
JCP	John Cowper Powys
JMM	John Middleton Murry
JBW	John Wain
KM	Katherine Mansfield
K/KA/KWA	Kingsley Amis

LD	*The Less Deceived*
Ll. P	Llewelyn Powys
MMcC	Mary McCarthy
NALGO	National Association of Local Government Officials
The NS	*The North Ship*
NS	*New Statesman*
NS & N	*New Statesman* (and *Nation*)
OB	Oxford Book
Obs	*Observer*
OBTCEV	*Oxford Book of Twentieth Century English Verse*
PAWC	Philip Collins
P of H	Ponce of Hessle (George Hartley)
Spr	*Spectator*
ST	*Sunday Times*
ST Col. Supp.	*Sunday Times* Colour Supplement
T and T	*Time and Tide*
TH	Thomas Hardy
The H of the M	*The Heart of the Matter*
TLD	*The Less Deceived*
TLS	*Times Literary Supplement*
TUC	Trades Union Congress
TWW	*The Whitsun Weddings*
UFAW	Universities Federation for Animal Welfare
UGC	University Grants Committee
VC	Vice Chancellor
VSP	V. S. Pritchett
WBY	W. B. Yeats
WEA	Workers' Educational Association
Winter	*A Girl in Winter*
W de la M	Walter de la Mare

Letters to Monica

21 December 1946

Beauchamp Lodge, 73 Coten End, Warwick

Dear Monica,

What a very pleasant surprise your letter was – I was alone in the Library and feeling very sour and disinclined to work, & your letter removed the first condition though the second is a mountain that no faith can move. Yes, Molly[1] finally decided to go – she was helped by a *present* from Miss B.[2] – a pot-pourri, or so I'm told – this made me anticipate one for myself and indeed I prepared a little speech for the occasion – but I didn't get anything!! Probably Miss B. quailed at the thought of buying anything for 'a gentleman' – 'so difficult, my dear.' [...]

In answer to your appeal, I'm enclosing my proofs & the 'lending' copy of *Jill*.[3] On your own head be it! They are both very much first shots: *Jill* perhaps a bit 'firster' than the other. Do not say anything of them if no particular verdict occurs to you: and if you think *Jill* an adolescent bit of rubbish and *Winter*[4] a pompous lifeless platitude don't hesitate to say so.

      Finally, a very happy Christmas & a bright New Year.

      Philip

1 Molly Bateman, assistant in Leicester University College Library.
2 Miss (Rhoda) Bennett, Librarian, Leicester University College.
3 *Jill*: Fortune Press, October 1946.
4 *A Girl in Winter*: Faber, to be published February 1947.

Easter Sunday [6 April], 1947

Warwick

My dear Monica,

I am busy proving the falsity of the dictum that to a well-stocked mind the word dullness has no meaning – it has a great deal of meaning

3

for me: I might almost say the meaning of meaning. I hope this is not so with you. I hope you are doing whatever you like best, a lot.

The tide of fuss consequent on the novel is gradually subsiding and bare promontories of my daily life are beginning to emerge. Very few more reviews have raised their ugly heads: *John O'London* was quite nasty, through the mouth of that broken down old snapper up of orts & imitations, Richard Church.[1] I think we have seen the last of them now, unless the Big Three shd suddenly break their silence. I had a little interview with Fabers, plus a lunch in Charlotte Street: there was a depressing atmosphere of 'you'll have to do better than this next time' about the meeting, as at a tutorial. They say it has sold *circa* 3½ thousand. They should not grumble at that. I bet their old faithfuls don't bring in a comparable figure, after allowance has been made for their names.

Well, all this seems very egotistical, but the Lord forbid I shd speak about the College. We shall be having enough of that all too soon. I am suffering from a sort of cinematic-Tantalus-fixation, that is, wherever I go good films shrink away and leave only dross. This only serves to add irritating emphasis to the practice of bus-conductors: wherever in Warwick you ask to be put down, they put you down at the cinema.

I am reading Kilvert's diaries.[2] Excellent. I shd like the whole lot. Perhaps we can persuade Rawlings to buy them for the Eng. section – after having convinced him that they are such as wd not bring the blush of shame to any innocent cheek or the taint of sin to any home.

Easter greetings! –
Philip

PS. – returning 9th p.m.

1 *John O'London*'s review of *A Girl in Winter*.
2 William Plomer's one-volume edition of *Kilvert's Diary* was first published in 1947. This was preceded by three vols: 1938, 1939, 1940.

4 April 1948

73 Coten End, Warwick

My dear Monica,

Throughout this troubled holiday I've been wondering how you are – whether when you arrived home you managed to recuperate. I do hope so, although I suppose it is simply a case of being fattened for the slaughter, or the arena, once again, isn't it? Why don't people all dislike work as I do? Am I wrong or are they? Is it natural to like work? Then this is another of the numerous cases of what is natural being confused with what is good.

My holiday was rather as I expected – my poor father grew steadily worse & died on Good Friday.[1] Since then mother & I have been rather hopelessly looking at the stock in the house – this morning I shifted 100 lbs of jam – 1945, 1946, & 1947 years – and about 25 Kilner jars of bottled fruit. Seventeen dozen boxes of matches, a shoe box of chocolate – all this from one small cupboard. I don't know what will happen to it all – I don't like sweet things, you remember. Otherwise I have been steadily answering letters of sympathy. It's curious how at the beginning the letters *are* sincere and *sound* sincere, but when I had written twenty or so I certainly wasn't *sounding* sincere and I'm not sure if I was *being* sincere. [...]

It is snowing here at the moment: this accords very well with mood and circumstance, both of which are Hardyish. [...]

1 Sydney Larkin died 26 March 1948. See 'An April Sunday', L.'s poem after his father's death, written on the same day as this letter, in *Collected Poems* (1988).

13 April 1949

The Senior Common Room, University College, Leicester

My dear Monica,

I have eaten the last lunch of the term now, & opposite me Zandy, C. G. Wilson & Taylor are reading: Taylor in particular is reading *Punch* – he read this all yesterday, & has not finished it yet. I mention these things because I always believe in telling my correspondent what is around me in case it seeps into my text. I was glad to get your letter & hear of your anti-religious front. We have moved the religious section right away upstairs & I feel that all religious books shd be taxed about £10 a copy.

Well ... I feel, with my tiny but definite scraps of news, like a town mouse writing to a country mouse: i'faith, cousin, Mr Atten$^{bro\,1}$ does send word that he is on the mend, instead of the make, and that he is being starv'd in consequence of a complaint of y^e Stomach, doubtless induc'd by the matchless Victualling of our Domestick Bursar. Y^e

Herbacitie is greatly forrard in yᵉ Gardens, also Mʳ Knapp's moustache, the effect of wch on his expression I have not quite made up my mind about. A small *Apparatus* has appeared in yᵉ Common-Room, marked 'H2S test – Do not move. L. Hunter'; and dyd occasion a Witticism from me about the no. of bad Eggs on the staff. Mʳ Martin has donn'd a Fair Isle pullover and a curious jacket, cut for riding but made of gents' suiting, that doth in no wise enhance hys amiability. The College Visitor –

But the College Visitor, old J.K.P.,[2] needs modern English, or I do. As you said his play was in your drawer I borrowed it to read – holy smoke. I have never read anything more nauseating than that last act. When his vacuous alert face came round the door on Saturday I felt I wanted to shriek at him what Llewelyn & John Cowper Powys shrieked at Baron Corvo in Venice: 'We're engaged! All the time! Right up to the bloody hilt!' Kingsley[3] was in the building, and I nearly effected an engagement, but I felt so sick of JKP that I refrained from doing anything to prolong the interview a second. However, Kingsley *heard* him, & pronounced him 'a mental chucker-out', i.e. someone to emerge from behind the bar at 10 p.m. and start talking to clear the room. By God he'd do it well, wouldn't he? [...]

1 F. L. Attenborough; Principal of Leicester University College.
2 John Peel, Geography master, Alderman Newton's School, Leicester, and 'College Visitor'; see Appendix B.
3 Kingsley Amis, visiting L. in Leicester. According to Amis, this visit was the *donnée* of *Lucky Jim*. First in his essay in *Larkin at Sixty* ('Oxford and After'), then in the version of this incorporated in his 1991 *Memoirs*, Amis wrote: 'In 1948 or so I went and stayed with him at his digs in Leicester ... On the Saturday morning he had to go into college and took me ("hope you won't mind – they're all right really") to the common room for a quick coffee. I looked round a couple of times and said to myself, "Christ, somebody ought to do something with this." Not that it was awful – well, only a bit; it was strange and sort of *developed*, a whole mode of existence no one had got on to from outside, like the SS in 1940, say. I would do something with it.' As this letter shows, Amis's visit to L. was not in 1948 but in April 1949. Amis's encounter with a 'provincial' university's staff common room was probably his first experience of such a place, since he did not begin work at Swansea until October 1949. In the same essay, Amis went on: 'Jim Dixon's surname has something to do with ordinariness, but at the outset had much more to do with Dixon Drive, the street where Philip lived.'

23 July 1950

12 Dixon Drive, Leicester

My dear Monica,

I have just been weighing my new Journal: it weighs 2 lbs 2 oz. The first little record of my schooldays weighed 3½ oz: how monstrously the ego has flowered since! Before I start it I am going to have *My life and hard times* stamped on the back. In gold.

Thanks very much for your letter,[1] which put me faintly in mind of one K.M. wrote to a young man called Goodyear (who at one time was 'Middleton Murry's best friend') but charitably left unposted:[2] however on looking it up I found it wasn't very like. I'm sorry if my ponderous adumbrations(!) sounded melodramatic: all I meant is this: that our friendship, though successful, has been confined to a narrowish front, and if from that you've constructed an over-favourable image of me I do feel almost bound to say that to my mind you wd like me less – or think less of me – if you had had more opportunity of learning my general behaviour-patterns. Not *le divin Marquis*, nor Captain Hugh, but a good deal more like Mybug[3] or Portia's[4] Eddie – or even Portia's father – than's compatible with your idea of the Good Man. That's all. And I say it in the spirit of one who points out the defects of a thing when praised for being, owning or doing it. Not in panic or in patronage. So there we are, and of course nothing is spoilt. [...]

The Madge visit[5] went off pretty well on the whole. A good deal of one-sided literary praise, though at one point I did find myself saying '*The water from the upper reservoir, Is led into the lower reservoir,* well, when you can say that, Charles, it seems to me you can say anything' – which, though fairly *sincere* on my part, does sound a bit *queer* out of its context, and I shouldn't have cared to see Collins's[6] snarling pipe-ridden face expressing itself at my elbow – some plain good food, a lot of fixations, imagos, transferences, traumatics, functions & so on, a few literary anecdotes (the literary editor of *The Listener*[7] prowls up & down outside the Wellington Barracks daily), two gay uninhibited nippers, a mother-in-law (Irish), very nicely-distempered walls, madder & delphinium according to where you were, & simply awful weather, rain falling all the time. There was a fair amount of high class drinking (i.e. not beer or spirits) & literary fine-talk ('Joyce is the ...... since Shakespeare'). They had a disconcerting habit of whipping off to bed about eleven, leaving me disconsolately shifting a hot glass of

Bournvita from hand to hand & trying to read the beginning of *Mary Barton* in a cold pool of electric light. And that wass my 'oliday. Oh, the only embarrassing moment was when Charles Madge handed me a page of this Mallarmé[8] to read – not poetry, technical stuff about rhyme – & asked me if I agreed. As you know, my French is like Grimes' ('I'll start with some jolly old *huitres*')[9] so I was fairly caught there, you bet. A few of the words I knew, like *et* and *le*, but there was a lot in between, very awkward. Oh yes, & one thing he did say when we were walking along towards a Park was 'I did like … that very (*some complimentary adj.*) poem you sent me … about racing.'[10] […]

1 L.'s letter dated 23 July 1950 is the first (apart from one dated 7 January) to survive from that year. L. is replying to a letter of Monica's, dated 19 July, which evidently refers both to a recent meeting and a recent letter of L.'s, the first of which 'upset' Monica. She comments: 'It would be ridiculous for four years' perfect friendship – it was perfect to me anyway – to be upset by an hour's stupid folly, for that's what it was, I was exhausted & miserable & overwrought, it was hysteria […] You, as a man, will be aware of the valuable & well known & utterly consoling truth that All Women Are Unreasonable (so it doesn't matter how they act or what they say, you need never pay any attention). Well, I claim my sex's privilege. So do stop beating yourself, tho' I'm sure you take a perverse pleasure in it, but goodness, I really should be upset if I thought we were going to be made melodramatic […] I value you very much. In fact I believe I like you better than anybody I've ever met, but just as usual, just as always, so *don't* read things into what I say or write, do feel secure that all's the same as ever it was.'
2 Unposted letter from Katherine Mansfield (dated 4 March 1916) to Frederick Goodyear, serving in France with the Royal Engineers.
3 In Stella Gibbons, *Cold Comfort Farm*.
4 Portia in Elizabeth Bowen, *The Death of the Heart*.
5 The poet and sociologist Charles Madge had written to L. about *The North Ship*, which he admired. Madge visited L. in Leicester (see letter of 4 May 1950 to J. B. Sutton in *Selected Letters*), and then L. visited Madge in Birmingham.
6 A. S. Collins, Monica's head of department at Leicester.
7 J. R. Ackerley.
8 Years later, L. referred to this 'page of this Mallarmé' in a letter to Anthony Thwaite (see *Selected Letters*), 17 October 1981: '… Larkin as Mallarmé, and so on … Funnily enough Charles Madge, who had been shown The NS … by Enright when they were both in B'ham in the Forties, invited me for a weekend on the strength of this, and floored me by handing me a wodge of (prose) Mallarmé and saying "What d'you think of that?" My plume-de-ma-tante French wasn't up to it, so I suppose I flannelled a bit, and he looked disappointed and said he thought it was what I wanted to do or say or what not …'
9 Evelyn Waugh, *Decline and Fall*, Chapter 12, 'The Agony of Captain Grimes'.

10 Charles Madge was evidently referring to 'At Grass', completed 3 January 1950, which L. had sent to Madge on 7 May 1950 (see *Selected Letters*) along with a dozen other poems.

1 October 1950

The evening star rises in front of my window!

Queen's Chambers, Queen's University, Belfast

My dear Monica,

Well, here I all too indubitably am – the first day in Ireland.[1] My reactions? B to B –, the whole shoot. But best start from the beginning.

My train dashed through the weeping quarries of Derbyshire to the most dusk-ridden ruinous vision of Manchester imaginable. There I had tea & ham rolls (not real ham). Train to Liverpool, 'bus to docks, walking through endless warehouses to find the *Ulster Duke*, which left at 9.30. In the meantime I had eaten fish & chips and 2 hyosin tablets, cowled in my duffle coat. I let them fight it out while I sat on deck, watching the long bare quays move slowly backwards. It took a good hour to get out of L'pool. Then I went to bed. Waking at 4.30 am. I looked out of my window & saw seas running swiftly but not high: I never felt at all queasy, for which God be praised. Before I went to bed I finished *August folly* (very good reading).

This morning I came here by car, to find Queen's Chambers is 3 large Dutch fronted houses (red brick) knocked into one.

Q.   You are pleased with your room?

A.   Frankly, no. It is large enough, & has a nice view, but there's *no carpet*, *nothing* but that horrible rubbery green lino the whole place is floored with.

Q.   At least the paint is fresh?

A.   Fresh grass-green. My candles will clash. The whole place reminds me of certain 12/6 hotels I have stayed at in London.

Q.   The food is surely not too bad?

A.   Surely not too good, either. The roast beef at lunch was as pedestrian as a centipede. And I don't like the admitted absence of any kind of food after about 7 pm. I'm going to be hungry.

Q.   The Warden however, would seem –?

A.   The Warden's all right if you like dried-up little historians who have a Jane Austen cult & play chess. No, heark 'ee, cully, this room is grossly underfurnished, the lampshade is made of brown paper, the bulbs are too weak, the noise from the trams tiresome, the sixpenny meter for heat will prove expensive, the students ubiquitous, the servants iniquitous (where's the strap from my suitcase?). Michael Innes speaks somewhere of the combination of refined luxury and barbarous discomfort that is the Oxford don's life: it is the Belfast don's life, too, except for the refined luxury.

Q.   There *is* hot water.

A.   Yes, there *is* that. (*Curtain.*)

A brief walk into Belfast this afternoon (after milkless Nescafé with the Warden) confirmed my memory of it as a wide and cobble-streeted town, lined with frowning buildings in the late Victorian manner & some indifferent shops. I'm already fed up with anything called Ulster, Northern, Victoria, etc., also with the Irish male face (craggy, drink-flushed, with greasy black curls & a too-tight collar) & the Irish female face (plump, bad-teethed, pinkly powdered, with a diamanté lizard on the lapel).

However, despite all this I'm calling all my native artistic insensitivity to my aid & I suppose shall endure. But Digby! but Beaumont! Really, dear, what I had in mind was much nearer the truth than your arts & crafts stuff. This armchair has wooden arms, by the way. There are 3 large Presbyterian churches in this square mile. Ah, quelle horreur! But I might also add that but for a blunder on the part of the porters I should be in No. 18, a worse room, & not No. 25. A Mr Graham should be in this room by rights.

How nasty my writing looks.

Well, I'm afraid you won't have had the distraction of novelty to take your mind off our parting. This will be meeting you on your return & I hope it will take the edge off seeing your old colleagues again: I hope too your room doesn't look sad & lonely now my lethargic cadging figure isn't in it. Truly I shall always remember the fireplace & the cricket-bin & all the battery of things on the mantelpiece, Fifi & blue Neddy & the flowered lamp. Your life there has come into extremely sharp focus for me now: heating milk, singing in the kitchen, drying stockings, etc. You make it seem quite unusual and fascinating. ('Huh' – 'at the whiskey again'). I loved every time I visited you, & do want to thank you again & again for being so kind, so gracious & so generous. All three of you.

In a short while now I have to go to dinner with Graneek,² so I will try to do something about my shoes & my hair & post this. Work tomorrow, ha ha ha. Grow old along with me, The worst is yet to be. The adjective I shd choose so far is 'drab'.

Goodbye, dear Taurus. Tell me what has been happening, & what you are doing. What of your Flanagan & Allen turn with A.S.C.?

Affectionately yours, Philip

An *honour* to be in this place, Christ! It's like a prison & Rugby in 1840. The town smells of horse dung.

1 L. had arrived in Belfast to take up his new job as Sub-Librarian, Queen's University, Belfast.
2 Graneek: Librarian at Q.U.B. (See Appendix B).

10 October 1950

Queen's Chambers &c.

[...] I'm sorry my thanks went down the wrong way: truly I meant no harm. I was only trying to say that I didn't take you for granted. Of course I can see dozens of ways in which thanking would sound nasty. But you must remember that there's absolutely nothing of the confident male about me: it'd be better perhaps if there were.

And the Yeats was only obvious because I'd heard you say you wanted one an evening or so before. I had a great love of him when I was 21–22 which has since waned considerably. Now I can't stand the fervent unreal atmosphere of all his moods, his wild-old-man stuff, his arrogance – he is the very antithesis of D.H.L. & Hardy. However, he can write. I haven't got the full edition: mine stops at *A woman young & old*. I don't think you'd find in him any of the *perçant* quality you talk about. He is all much too unreal. For me that emotion is always connected with the past, and usually with love: and the person who whispers most immediately past my guard is the great dealer in those two things, Hardy. *Not a line of her writing have I, not a thread of her hair, If it's ever Spring again, Spring again*: at these first lines my spine contracts & a shiver runs over my ribs. And as another random example I do quite see what K.M. means with *Le temps des lilas et le temps des roses*, & the clear voice, in her *Journal*, don't you?[1] [...]

Tonight I was hurrying along the dusty narrow stack when my practised eye (ahem!) noticed a book seemingly misplaced, & I pulled it out ... It was in fact not misplaced, but looking at it I found it to be called *Love's looking-glass or, spectrum amoris* – an anonymous book of drivel dated 1895. Opening it 'at random', as they say, I hit a poem 'To M. B.-J.': now that's a strange thing, a queer one, isn't it?[2] Not a very good poem, though: full of bounding & fillets & Artemis & so on. But a book like that – no author, no merit – I find extremely evocative & wd sooner pore over than over Chaucer, Spenser, Shakespeare, Milton, Dryden, Pope, Blake, Keats, Shelley, Byron, or 'AE' (George Russell). [...]

1 *Le temps des lilas*, by Maurice Bouchor (1855–1929); Katherine Mansfield, *Journal*, 29 February 1920.
2 M. B.-J.: Monica's initials were M.M.B.J.

14 October 1950

Queen's Chambers

Dear Sacred Cat,

Sometimes there clings about your letters a faint redolence of perfume – whether from your hand or from the place you keep your notepaper I do not know. If there's a faint redolence about this one, it'll be of an orange I have just eaten. It is Saturday night and I am pleasantly tired. Well, tired. This afternoon I got my bicycle out again & cycled to Carrickfergus. This is about eleven miles up the Antrim side of Belfast Lough & used to be a port when Belfast was nothing at all: the road runs by the sea all the way & is therefore at sea-level: *no hills*. The wind blew me there by about 3.15 and I sat miserably on the esplanade, then walked round the castle & round the squarish drab harbour where Wm of Orange landed in 1690. The weather was clouded windy & cold, & Carrickfergus reminded me of what I imagine *Scotland* to look like – stone ugly houses, hideous churches & chapels, & an air of moral unbending discomfort everywhere. So I ducked into a cafe with a coal fire & asked for egg & chips – 'Naw eggs' – & sat reading your letter through again. When I'd finished the sun was out, & I felt inclined to return home though I had thought of staying the evening, having dinner at the one hotel, & reading *Wuthering Heights*. But the ill-concealed *dullness* of that, coupled with the prospect of riding home in the dark, decided me against staying & I pedalled back against the strong wind. This gave me time to look at the view which before you get near Belfast is good: the Lough is wide and choppy, the hills on the landward side green & with sudden smoke-coloured shadows. The sky was full of changeable sunlit clouds as it nearly always is: if England is a brewer's advert, Ireland is a railway poster. At Whiteabbey I thought of Trollope, who wrote his autobiography there, & just before Whitehouse (yes, it's really called that) I found a *peacock*, yes, a live one, standing on the margin of the road, looking a bit disgusted with the 20th century. Where it had come from I can't think. Belfast greeting me with its fearful cobbled streets, making me realise how saddlesore I was: in all I'd done about 25 miles. It was very misty & *Odd man out-ish*:[1] louts kicking a football about on wasteland, the goal chalked on a wall reading NO POPE HERE, DOWN THE FEINIES, WE'RE READY FOR THEM. I bought some more cherry cake & oranges, & got in about six. A nice outing, though rather a lonely one. [...]

You'll be amused to know that your *Portrait of a G.B.*[2] had me quite at a loss till I was eating my tea. I *couldn't* think what G.B. stood for: 'Girl Bride' kept elbowing its slightly-questionable way out of my unconscious & being crammed back again. Do you mean, when you say it's too depressing to endure, that you are racked by the crucifixion of a fine spirit? Or that you simply can't stand reading about such people? Till I'm sure which you mean I'm not able to make much comment: I think his life was depressing from one angle, but I don't think he thought so, & indeed was so scathing on the subject of suffering & unhappiness & pity that one's a bit chary of dropping one's quite-sincere tears on his grave. And C.C.'s remark is misleading: Lawrence HATED Galsworthy's novels. He thought they typified everything he disliked: where Galsworthy failed was in not hating his characters as much as D.H.L. did, according to D.H.L. Hence the 'almost' a great novel. Galsworthy knocked them down but didn't wipe his boots on them: hence his failure ...

Still, don't let's have any literary criticism. If you're still feeling fed up with your life, I sympathise & can say I shd feel just the same. Let us admit quite freely that any sort of enthusiasm for salaried employment is quite foreign to both of us. Before very long I can see that I shall be giving a paper to the Northern Irish branch of the ALA – at least, I can't *see* it, it's just not visualisable. But you know the kind of thing. Salaried employment is the norm, the *status quo*: now I have always felt quite out of touch with the norm & the *status quo*. The idea of entering into it & being successful in it & *caring* about it – fantastic. As you say, *c'est pour les autres* ('I never said any such affected thing!'). As for the Crabbe chapter,[3] it's quite a dilemma, isn't it? How does he *mean*? Would it be *openly acknowledged*? Could you do it if you said you would? (If that

13

sounds ungracious, you must remember that writing is by no means an act of will with me: I'm so used to *not* writing.) If you can do it *easily* – well, I don't know, I was going to say, do it, but I see your point about being associated with A.R.H. The Cambridge Jnl would be better than that, really. Do you think you *can* refuse? I know all one wants is to be left ALONE: God, if I had anybody sniffing after my 'work' ... [...]

1 *Odd Man Out*: novel by F. L. Green (1902–53), made into an impressive film (1947).
2 *Portrait of a Genius But ...: The life of D. H. Lawrence,* by Richard Aldington (1950).
3 The Crabbe chapter: A. R. Humphreys had suggested she contribute a chapter on Crabbe to, possibly, what was to become *The Pelican Guide to English Literature*, vol. 4, which contains five essays by Humphreys, as well as one by their colleague A. S. Collins, two by P. A. W. Collins and one by C. J. Horne.

21 October 1950

Queen's Chambers

Dear White-and-gold,

[...] I don't know the poem *you* quoted either: what is it? Mine about Mrs P. was from Auden's *Dover*. I read his collected shorter poems recently. Not expecting to be impressed, I was impressed: by the liveliness and the variety. How clever these people are. I also happened on a poem called *Dublin* by MacNeice & that also depressed me by its extraordinary talent. Despite all we say about them, Auden & MacNeice have *talent* whereas the tiny fish have not. Poetry is like everything else: if you're not ⅔rds of the way there already, it's not worth starting. Regarding literature, I was interested by your D.H.L. remarks: any judgments on him are to me like a stick incautiously poked into the cage of a tiger: I bound to savage it. Yet in these days I grow more & more unwilling to try to say anything about D.H.L.: he is so enormous, so shifty, so deceptive, fascinating, & evanescent – also I get the odd feeling that I am *inside* him, staggering helplessly from aspect to aspect, & quite unable to see him as a whole. Or objectively. He has always meant so much more to me than any other writer. I have adopted his conclusions so uncritically, that half the time I have been living in a sort of interchanging dream, where I am him & he is me. There are times when I belittle him & really get him down, then find what I am shaking so furiously is a little stuffed puppet of myself, & he is far away. Then sometimes I relapse into abject hero worship & can only think of the humiliating abyss between his value and mine. Then again his sheer inconsistency infuriates my orderly mind: I want to chop him into shape: I demonstrate his inconsistencies to myself, & feel satisfied for perhaps $\frac{1}{2}$ an hour, but then a dreary reaction begins & I think that consistency is not much of a virtue beside the tough rich sense of life Lawrence, preeminently among writers, can give me. After all to a materialist that is the main thing: it's what I look for in every writer – Hardy, Ll. Powys, G. Eliot. And what's more, *life as I see it*, and with an eye that ranges so far – from historical generalisations, & speculations about cultures & civilisations & the genius of different nations to the smallest of domestic details – Mellors' dog wanting its supper, old Morel frying bacon on the end of his knife & spelling out the paper early in the morning, before drawing the curtains. He does seem to me to include *everything* – just as his language has its grand style (& it can be irritating enough at that) & its quick slangy but wonderfully exact impressionism, his mind seems to be able to relate any given part of life to the rest of it: he shows a scene, a piece of behaviour, & in a touch relates it to the person's whole life, & the state of their world. (You'll think I have been swallowing an awful lot of bunk.) Then again his moral judgments seem to me so devastatingly accurate – you remember when Kate has run away from the bullfight, the young American who has stuck it out for the sake of the 'experience' comes boasting about it afterwards – 'He looked wan, peaked, but like a bird that had successfully pecked a bellyful of garbage.'

However! rereading all this makes me think it sounds like the outpourings of some Swedish girl you have had over for the summer, & who has just discovered 'Daysh Lawnce'. If I might add a word about your remarks, I think Lawrence was a complete egoist in the sense that he felt how beautiful life could be *if he had his way*. He'd never make the compromise required to settle in society. After all, we agree ourselves that work is quite boring & people quite tasteless, but I at any rate haven't the courage or the energy to do anything about it. You can get away from the Acacias & the office if you have sufficient wits to earn money otherwise & sufficient resilience to do without the balms of familiarity & custom & the benefits of the herd. D.H.L. had both & I admire him enormously for it. Abroad he was not happy (don't forget his health kept him out of England) but he was at least Lawrence. At home – well, I don't know what he wd have been. I just can't imagine. For the rest, he was painfully ingenuous about this leading business, almost totally dependent on Frieda (which doesn't surprise me, since the greater yr capacity for loving the greater yr dependence on the object of love), and condemned to second rate people since first rate ones wouldn't abrogate their personalities to him as everyone had to do. As – finally – for ambition, he was ambitious in a conventional way when a young man: ('I s'll make a thousand a year!') & also snobbish ('My wife's father was a Baron'): later on he wanted to use the powers he felt he possessed for the benefit of mankind: but having been kicked in the teeth several times I think he gave up any idea of self advancement, & only wanted to be let alone & to leave Frieda enough to live on when he died. Anything like Arnold Bennett's yacht or James' Collected edition or Walpole's knighthood – or – well, I can't think of anyone with a house-fetish, but all that was quite foreign to him, & I think you get him quite wrong if you think of him – at least after 1918 – as wanting any kind of 'social acceptance'.

But I could – as you're no doubt uneasily aware – go on about him for ever. Now it's a quarter to 6 & I must cross the busy dusky road for supper. [...]

26 October 1950

QCB

Dearest M.,

The *Belfast calendar 1950–1* describes me as an Assistant Libn., much to my annoyance – Graneek assures me it is a mistake.[1] Considering he *read the proofs* I think this is a poor show. Graneek is extremely nice without being at all my kind of man: he is a pusher, a mover, a coherer, an urger, a carer: I am a leaner, a stopper, an analyst, a discourager, a scoffer. Nevertheless he is extremely nice & I can't imagine him in a bad temper.

Bought *Mrs Dalloway* on Wed. 2nd hand & 3/6. The woman looked at it & at me, then said 3/-. I have been reading it since – 'You write so well, Virginia, so *damned* well': who said that? K.M. – well, yes, but there is much wooden & dead in V.W. Any 'real people', any 'psychology' comes off very badly. She spins her vision of life, & does it well. But she has not the depth of that KM story about the canary, or Ma Parker, or *The Daughters of the late Colonel*. The difference between V.W. and K.M. is the difference between E.M.F. and D.H.L. It is discouraging to reflect on KM's experience & apprehension of pain &

suffering & to reflect how little she has become 'known' by it – I mean to say 'Mansfield!' suddenly brings to the mind's eye a bright Russian-doll-childish person, not the lonely Shakespeare-annotating invalid of the *Letters*. You – or rather the *Sunday Times* – would never call her a mistress of the human heart, so little did all she 'went through' express itself in full. Do you see what I mean by all this? I feel there is small hope for less gifted ones. [...]

1 L. was Sub-Librarian at Queen's University, Belfast – senior to 'an Assistant Libn.'

28 October 1950

Queen's Chambers, Belfast

Chère chatte sacrée,

[...]

Regarding poems, the fundamental reason I am shy of sending them is that they're not very good. If I were sure of a generous ration of congratulations from you I'd send them like a shot, but – well – They're not all like *At grass*, you know. In fact only *At grass* is like *At grass*. The others are far more modern & less polished. For all my nightly labours under my lamp looking out over the tramlines I have only done one since arriving. I will write to Horne's friend[1] this coming week, or do something about it, anyway. It would be rather amusing to use my farewell gift money to pay the printer's bill – out of good cometh evil. Only then everyone'd expect a free copy, which would be most retrograde to my desire. 'Horses – mm – hah – *old* 'orses eh? Ha – er – he was – er – always in and out of that place, mm – what? Along with that faller Collins—'. [...]

1 Not known. C. H. Horne was a lecturer in English at Leicester.

1 November 1950

Queen's Chambers

[...] What news? Well, I wrote to two Belfast printers about my poems: one sent up a representative, the other said they only published commercially, which didn't include poems, but that A, B, or C should do a good job for me. The representative came from D. He was a short-haired man, & dropped my letter in the precincts of Queen's, so that it was picked up & *read* by numerous people before being handed back by a pink-faced shining-eyed office-hag: he required more details before giving an estimate. So there things rest for the moment: I shall have to type the whole thing out first of all. A powerful deterrent is the shouting mediocrity of ¾ of the pieces in question: well, private publishing really is the end, of course. *Thrice holy is my Garden now Since it is sown by Thee* kind of stuff: *O Man! thy purblind eyes are sightless yet!* type of tack. *On seeing Lucinda with her hair in curlers* ('Say, pretty Nymph'): *Parting: a sonnet sequence* ('We did not say goodbye: shunting, the trains') – oh, & all the rest of the printed-for-the-author-at-Oakdene-Swedenborg Road-Beckenham-Kent atmosphere. Humiliation's final dregs. And in *New writing 40* I find James Michie, John Wain, Alan Ross & Michael Hamburger[1] merrily bashing away, & even Kingsley has got $25.00 out of *Furioso* (U.S.A.) – a good title for anything K.W.A.[2] publishes in, don't you think? – for two poems. [...]

They tell me Shaw is dead – I never see a paper, except the *Belfast News Letter* ('Ulster Protestants Telegraph Rome – Pope Warned'). If I had a black tie I'd wear it: he has given me much pleasure at odd times. A world without Shaw seems definitely a postwar one, doesn't it? He has been there, & nearly the same age, ever since I can remember. I always meant to *see* him, too, by some means, but now he's gone & I haven't done. Ah, well. [...]

1 James Michie (1924–2007), John Wain (1925–94), Alan Ross (1922–2001), Michael Hamburger (1924–2007): all Oxford contemporaries of L.
2 K.W.A.: Kingsley Amis.

5 November 1950

Queen's Chambers, Belfast

Dearest M.,

Not on the whole a very satisfactory day. It's ten to five. I'm lying on my bed, having cleaned three pairs of shoes, still dressing-gowned from a stupifying bath earlier on. You can guess how warm the rooms are: I never have the fire on but I can lie in only my dressing gown and not feel cold. Very little has been done today. I spent this morning writing home, a job that becomes extremely difficult sometimes. In fact I expect it lies at the bottom of the day's unsatisfactoriness. My mother's patient attempts to find someone to live with so that she need not bother either of us make me very uncomfortable. When I lived with her I was consumed with desire to get away – it seemed a prime necessity, like breathing – but now I *am* away it seems very shabby & callous of both of us that she shd have to be bothering her head about advertisements and pretending to like people when really the ordeal of setting up house with a complete stranger will be as miserable to her as to me. I long to tell her to stop troubling & bring everything over here, but I know that it would be final self-destruction as far as I was concerned. It seems to me insulting to do anything else, as well as selfish and ungrateful, and it's no use not helping people when they need help on the grounds that someday it'll be possible to help them enjoyably ... I do sincerely think that life with a really sympathetic personality wd do her more *good* than life with myself or my sister, but there are very few chances of finding such a person, & many more of finding cadgers, bores, mean spirits, & so on who will be difficult to displace once they are installed.

Well, that's enough about that particular aspect of my affairs: it will all boil up again at Christmas, as you can well imagine. I quite dread it: selfish again. O flames! Forgive me for bothering *you* about it.

I shall have to start dressing for supper in a couple of minutes – 5.45 on Sunday. I am wearing a suit today – gloomy conformity to local tradition. But most of the students here dress up on Sunday & look so neat that I get shamed: nearly every day of the week they wear semi-stiff white collars, the kind I wouldn't wear for a bob a day, & after all they are doctors-to-be & therefore I suppose quite well off. When anyone falls ill they are all on him like a pack of vultures. Sometimes drunks are brought in to be resurrected medically before being sent home to their landladies.

Must dress. It's been a beautiful day but is now misty & coldish, & growing dark. [...]

I'm so glad you like Barnes, & you are certainly welcome. I dislike telling people my likings too, but if anyone really agrees then my pleasure may even increase. He is a strange writer, undistinguished for many pages and then suddenly becoming not only *good* but *subtle*: don't you think that of say *The wind at the door* (I don't mean the rhymes)? But I still don't know him very well yet. Hardy, Barnes & the Powyses: what a splendid team from one county.[1] I'm glad too that your work is more under control now: I grinned at 'the usual half-interest in it has returned'. How well I know it. [...]

Monday. Awake, my soul, and *without* the sun &c. I've finally assembled 20 poems[2] – representing 'all I wish to preserve' since 1945, and am typing them out. I know them all so well now that they are like old friends, hopeless old friends whom you know will never get a job. The difficulty will be knowing what to do with them – I haven't more than 10 friends, & I doubt if I can give away more than another 30 to reviews & great men: I can see myself sending parcels of them to Blackwell's instructing them to give one free to anybody who says 'please' when speaking to the assistants. This all depends on my having enough money to foot the printing bill. The main concern will be *keeping them out of Belfast.*

I trot over the misty road to breakfast now: am getting tired of eating with the students. It reminds me that the meadbench must have been rather like that – boisterous & noisy. [...]

1 the Powyses: John Cowper, Llewelyn and T.F. – all from Dorset, like Thomas Hardy and William Barnes.
2 *XX Poems*, privately printed in Belfast by L. in April 1951.

20 November 1950

Q.C.B.

Dearest Monica,

Herewith the six anticlimaxes.[1] The printers say £14 a hundred, which is all *right*, but still quite a *lot*, as I have about £45 still outstanding in various other ways. Of course I expect I shall end up by accepting it, but I wish they were a little more confidence-inspiring – the poems, not the printer. [...]

O dear! I do seem to have created a bad impression lately: I'm awfully sorry about 'hostility' – [*sketch of war mask*] – it's quite unintentional & must spring from being a bit rushed & my natural sub-sarcastic way of talking sounding much nastier when written down. But trying to remember what I wrote doesn't enable me to recall any real hostile intention, quite the reverse. I thought recent letters had been confidential and affectionate.

About Christmas – I'm awfully late and must rush to breakfast – I should certainly like to see you & hoped to do so: should we stay somewhere two days 21–3? I expect I did sound a bit hesitant, but there are all sorts of reasons, mild & bitter, none of which being that I don't want to see you. I envisaged somewhere within reach of Liverpool, Leicester, & Stourport[2] – Shropshire? Ludlow? I don't know that area well. Welsh marches?

> Sorry for being grim. A kiss for Cinderella.
> Philip

1 The poems L. sent Monica on 20 November were 'Wedding-Wind', 'Spring', 'Wires', 'Coming' ('On longer evenings …'), 'Modesties' ('Words as plain as hen-birds' wings'), and 'The Dedicated'. She commented (21 November):

> I like best *Wedding-wind* & *Spring*, & I don't like the Wild West one at all – it's all right, but I don't like it at all … *Wedding-wind* I like *extremely*, it's a lovely title, breathing Hardy & Housman; and, marvellously, breathing a genuine rusticity – that's a horrid word for it – a real countrified air, like you was bred & born in it. Stables, horses & chicken-pail anyone could do; but candlelight, floods, the girl's apron – these are the real close intimate touches […]

2 Stourport: Monica's family home.

25 November 1950

Queen's Chambers, Belfast

Dearest Monica,

Tonight is the night before the poll:[1] Fighting Tom Teevan has organised a 'monster rally' to burn effigies & generally impede the progress of civilisation. I had been meaning to go to this, but at the last minute the Wilson – Williams combine asked me to go *with them*, & my refusal has prevented my going alone. A pity: I should have liked a glimpse of Irish politics, as the nearest thing I shall ever see to the drawings of Mr Hogarth. How often in life is one offered one's desire, on conditions rendering acceptance impossible! (Opening my dictionary to ensure I had spelt effigies right – yah – I notice what seems to me rather a good definition of 'eighteen': 'one more than seventeen'.) […]

The two English lecturers are Braidwood & Monaghan. Both are men, 30–40, Braidwood a pipe-smoking, garden-digging, kiddy-loving moustached Scot: Monaghan a redfaced, owl-eyed, entirely humourless & graceless Irishman. Gone are the days when my real place was in the English department! Really I doubt if my real place is anywhere here: but if anywhere I suppose it would be the book-house. Here I have been grimly repressing my desire to crack jests & so on, but it's wearing a bit thin: I wasn't born to be stern & unbending. On the other hand I am definitely or at least officially past the age of indiscretion, & I had better keep my mouth *fermée*. I am an old man who makes a lot of trouble with his mouth.

Wednesday morning. Sunlight pours in: I present to it a sullen face. My dear boys didn't go to bed till 2 last night: it really isn't their fault: they made no serious noise after about 12.45, but once the train of insomnia has been lighted in me, there it is. The warden tells me they have applied for single rooms, & may get them. But will their successors be worse or better? *Je me demande*. Two docile negroes, in bed sharp at midnight – that's my ideal ... (following yr practice of annotation I may remind my future editor that I'm talking about the ideal occupants of the room above). In reply to your query, When beside Wednesday do I have off? *NEVER*: well, every fourth Saturday morning. That's all, that's all, that's all, that's all.

As I read Savage[2] for pleasure I naturally can't reproduce his arguments coherently, and yet they aren't arguments but assertions: however, he does say: 'The incompleteness & indeed the reversibility of Forster's moral symbolism is shown in his "realistic" confusion of the attributes of the "good" and "bad" types ...' That's something of what you remarked, isn't it? But the answer he gives is that 'the life of the irresponsible, moneyed, parasitical bourgeoisie is false, because it is based on social falsehood, and nothing can ever be made really right within it.' 'The life of Forster's characters ... is based on falsehood because it is based on unearned income ...' I can't envisage yr rose-chiselled lips saying such monstrous things, as Oscar would say. I obtained & read *Oscar Wilde & the Black Douglas*[3] recently: do you know, despite all this obvious *amende honorable* we are seeing today, I can't help feeling I should have been shouting with the loudest, like Pickwick? I try to imagine how I should feel if Ken Tynan, or Peter Brook, or any other of the sexual ambivalents of my decade at Oxford were after a career of ostentatious brilliance, lagged by the heels and put through the hoop – and I can't help admitting that my feelings would be, to say the least of it, very mixed ... And all this about Oscar's 'horror of coarseness' etc. merely irritates me as a sort of hypocrisy. Actions are coarser than words. However, I can't see that he had anything to grumble about: he had a jolly good time, & anyone who chooses to bring a libel action against a speaker of widely-known & easily-verifiable truth is sticking his neck out so far that he might well be taken for a giraffe, though what one would take a giraffe for I do not know. One remark I noticed: 'He (Lord A.) apparently goes to the races every day, and loses, of course. As I wrote to Maurice to say, he has a faculty of spotting the loser, which, considering that he knows nothing at all about horses, is perfectly astounding.' It's hard to grumble at the source of such as that.

12.45 p.m. Sun still shining: yet I am left with a faint sense of dissatisfaction, hard to analyse. I had my hair cut, & changed my liberry[4] (*Life of A.J.A. Symons*), & had coffee, & looked round the shops, buying a copy of Wild Bill Davison's *Tishomingo Blues* that so insinuatingly wound itself into all last summer; but a sense of having been rebuffed remains with me, perhaps because the cow in the record shop wouldn't let me – or didn't want to let me – look through a pile of *Jazz collector* & *Tempo* records she had just unpacked – cow of Hell! I have never seen any before, & Belfast is the last place I expected to find them: I'm sure they will never sell them. They are the Real McKoy, fantastic private dubbings of entirely irrevocable records: the Malone Society Reprints in terms of Jazz. [...]

Thursday night. Instead of having supper tonight I went alone through driving rain to see *Gone to earth*,[5] then ate out, then called on the Warden for tea & 'good talk'. I have now recovered from the yearning discontent aroused in me by this as by nearly all films: my mind is a pool: if stirred, it grows muddy. That is to say, if the frosted artificially-sealed bivalve behaviour of my life is fissured, disquieting fumes of emotion rise through the cracks. I get a faint idea of what I suppose other people are feeling all the time: also I have a sense of looking down into the struts of things, seeing the pretty-nearly-objective truths about things like family life, death, having children, & all the appalling veracities I try for the most part to exclude from my daily life. My gingerbreads (miserable scraps they are too) become very guilty and I feel once more a sense of psychic cripplehood: not extraordinary, of course: just someone in whom desires are not strong enough to break shells of convention, habit, fear, custom, & form new patterns of its own: it's always very strong on me, this desire to do a certain set of things I least wish to do, & of course it induces fatal & damaging shillyshallying, as *Gone to earth*'s low Shropshire hills painfully reminded me. Was it good? No: but I'm sufficiently Webbite not to mind, except that a good film *could* have been made: at the start I really thought it was going to *be* good: the opening sequences are simply Hazel searching for Foxy, finding

23

her, & then sensing 'the death pack' & running home: a quick impression-
ist sequence of little animals seeking shelter & some brutal destruction
riding out at large: striking the correct note, which wasn't sustained,
of the cruelty of the world as symbolised by the foxhunt. The end was
effective, though perhaps not good: Hazel & Foxy go down the earth-
work at the climax of a long chase. Dead silence: the hounds clustering
over the lip of the shaft, shot from below: then the sunset (still no music)
& a long unnatural human hunting-cry 'Gone to earth' followed by the
sound of a horn. Still silence, a blank black screen, & *The end*, as quick
as that.

> Westminster's crown has gained a special jewel –
> A fat, deceitful, vulgar, Irish fool:
> 'The heart of Churchill & the wit of Wilde?' –
> Teevan touched pitch: the latter was defiled.

The above not very coherent epigram sprang unwatched from the
contemplation of this inset.[6]

Kingsley wrote again, grumbling about the amount of work he has to
put in, & saying that he had a 100-minute session with 'Professor Lrd
David Cecil' & A.N. Other about his B.Litt. thesis, at the conclusion of
which they told him that they thought he had not borne out his main
contention. No final decision yet, of course, but straws show which
way the wind is blowing. There is a vacant English lectureship here, but
it won't be filled this year. If you want to change nonentity-Professors,
& exchange a pair of pleasant colleagues for a ditto of unpleasant ones,
WATCH THIS COLUMN.

Midnight & I must lie down.
Bradley on Saturday.
O God.
  Loving wishes:
  Philip

1 Local election in Belfast.
2 D. S. Savage (1917–2007), author of a collection of critical essays, *The Withered
Branch* (1950).
3 *Oscar Wilde and the Black Douglas* (1949), by the Marquess of Queensberry.
4 Library book – one of L.'s many facetious spellings, shared with Monica.
5 Film version of novel by Mary Webb, 1917.
6 L. included a newspaper photograph of Thomas Teevan, who was elected as the
Ulster Unionist Party MP for Belfast West on 29 November at the age of twenty-three.

26 November 1950

Queen's Chambers, Belfast

Sunday night. 10.45.

Dearest M,

[...] Grateful acknowledgements of your mild judgments on my six things (as Kingsley would call them: somebody – Browning, perhaps – always spoke of his poems as 'his things'; since when K.W.A. has also done so, with comico-sardonico-ambiguous effect): you are very lenient. Not of course that I am not prepared to raise my hackles in defence of my chickens, illogically: however, I won't, because it's all a question of ear, really. The *prairie* one[1] was the only Belfast one – written straight off before breakfast in pyjamas. *Wind* is about the oldest – 1947 or so. *Dedicated* is fairly old, too. The other 3 are all Dixon Drivers,[2] *Spring* last spring. On the whole I think *Wind* is the best: I wish I could write more like that, fuller, richer in reference: I am quite pleased with the to-me successful use of the floods & the wind as fulfillment & joy. Shouldn't write like that now! Then I like *Modesties* & *Long evenings*. *Spring* is 'smart'. *The dedicated* is just but faint. And the *prairies* – well, just a little verse: no wings. I do tremble, though, to think of your getting your claws on the real rubbish! Part of my delay in putting the booklet *in manuas suas* is that I hope I can write a few substitutes for the more egregious weaker sisters ('Surely God teaches us with sunrises' 'O give me the road, the turning road, the yearning road, the burning road, That runs from Bishops Stortford to the sea'). FOURTEEN POUNDS is a lot of money to spend on the like of that.

I had another session with maps, hotel guides & Bradshaw on Saturday, in an effort to find a suitable place in Derbyshire, but really there's nothing that I can see, unless *Buxton* – and it would be extremely cold up there. These Peak places must have hotels but I can't find 'em. My reading of Bradshaw finds a train leaving Liverpool at 8.45, *arr.* Shrewsbury 10.39. Then a 11.55 train must get to Ludlow at about 1.15 – d'you agree? My plans for this brief 10 days are a kind of circular trip, going from Swansea to Liverpool on New Year's Day, as I'm assured can be done: a round ticket, to save money. Like most of my holidays, it will probably leave me feeling I have gone the distance with Jack Gardner.[3] However, you will have my freshest attention, & it would be extremely nice if you could meet me half way: could you get to Shrewsbury by 10.39? If you have to stay a night, that wouldn't really do, or at least there'd be as much point in your coming to Liverpool, wouldn't there. For some reason I have got Ludlow on my brain. *Could* we try for there? I should I suppose find *some* way home. Living at Loughborough might make it easier to return by another route, though I agree it won't be easy. Still – to save time – could you write to Ludlow? I suppose The Feathers is the best – can we afford it? I shall be being milked rather hard this Christmas – but I expect it will be all right. If they're full there is an A.A. place called the Charlton Arms, Ludford Bridge, Ludlow. I only ask this because you so kindly offer it.

I had a social evening out at an economists on Friday – Mr & Mrs Cuthbert. Two young economists & their young wives also attended; also the Professor of Economics, his wife & young daughter. The Professor of Economics is a grizzled, humorous, sports-jacketed, pipe-smoking, daughter-towsling old Barriesque daddie: dislike of his wife sprang fully-armed from my head, like Minerva from the head of Zeus. She hated housework & liked doing pottery, and had a talent amounting to genius for misunderstanding what I said. She also runs the staff dancing class. Add to this the pince-nez'd querulous appearance of a country subpostmistress, & boy, you got sump'n. Came home bristling as usual with non-cooperation, 'queer-ness', & so on.

If you *seriously* don't remember who said 'What genius' &c., let me tell you that it was said by an Irish ecclesiastic after he had gone dotty in the 18th century.[4] He wrote a book about little men, and horses. [...]

Saki says that youth is like *hors d'oeuvres*: you are so busy thinking of the next courses you don't notice it. When you've had them, you wish you'd had more *hors d'oeuvres*.

Think I'll post this tomorrow, to prevent you being disappointed & quicken up the Xmas booking. Tendernesses, Philip

1 *prairie* one: 'Wires' (what Monica calls 'the Wild West one').
2 Dixon Drivers: written when L. was living in Dixon Drive, Leicester, 1948–50.
3 Jack Gardner: boxer.
4 'Good God! what a genius I had when I wrote that book'; Jonathan Swift, of *The Tale of a Tub* (in Walter Scott's *Life of Swift*).

28 December 1950

Kings Head Hotel, Loughborough, Leics.

Dear Skirted One,

Now Christmas is over, the Residents' Lounge is unheated ... Well! I'm shamed by the arrival of your letter this morning: from my point of view Christmas Day & Boxing Day were spent in the bosom of the family, & yesterday over at Lichfield, or Another part of the bosom, as you might describe it. O dear! I did like your present, but you would have laughed at my expectations: as soon as I handled it, I thought: I know what this is – it's *The ordeal of Paul Cezanne* by John Rewald (Phoenix House, 30/-), & a slight pang of apprehension went through me, despite the quite genuine pleasure I should also have felt, at the thought of the ordeal of Philip Larkin that would come from reading it. So fixed was this idea in my head that when I unwrapped it in the dining room on Christmas morning my eyes yearned out on stalks – *Wind?* – Wind in the *what*? – Wind in the *Willows?*[1] – and all the *Salon des Réfusés* & *impasto* & Degas & *Le Chef d'Oeuvre* rolled away like a bad dream & I was safe with Ratty & Toad & all the rest of them – animals all, as you quoted so very aptly. I'm very pleased to have it & certainly shan't pass it on to my dear little niece. The illustrations are of course quite new to me: I don't quite like his idea of Mole – too *hairy* & rather reminiscent of Beckett's T.C.D. friend – but the others are delightful. I like especially the caravan one, & Rat & the wayfarer, & lost in the Wild Wood, & the picnic. There is also a headpiece of Toad asleep in the hollow tree that is very charming. Thank you very much – thank you too for the large & very pretty card. I opened that as soon as I got home.

Not much of a haul this Christmas! A laundry bag (asked for), a 10/6 book token, a second-hand tie, & a pair of expanding cufflinks enamelled in blue with large 'P's in cursive script on them. That's all, that's all, that's all, that's all. Shan't get very fat on all that, eh? Not even a card from my sister: I am left with a powerful sense of having given rather than received, & the 4 above-mentioned articles. The family so far has not been so bad as I feared – *plenty of time yet* – but the utter comfortlessness of the spiritual slum my sister inhabits is not cheering. Nor do I think I am very good with children. However I did think of you on Boxing Day especially, as the Quorn Hunt met in Loughborough Market Place & I attended. Don't think I can really describe it all at length – I felt very sorry for the first arrival, a plumpish girl in a bowler hat, whose horse, finding itself alone in a large oval of people, promptly waltzed the length of the market and back as if wading invisible obstacles. However, eventually the pack arrived – a forest of wagging tails & servile ears – & four pinks, & a man in horn goggles like a great tophatted toad: drinks & sandwiches were brought out, & there was much tail switching & breathing & hat-touching: nearly everyone was under forty-five, I should say: a very young meet. At last they formed up & moved off with a parp on the horn – silly little squeaker-thing – & the Council street sweepers closed in with their shovels & barrows, & the crowd, wearing its tartan scarves & new gloves, slowly dispersed, leaving behind it an aura of Christmas King Sixes.

Of yesterday I'll say only that the return from Lichfield was hampered by a missed connection & a consequent fearful long busride, & that I met my Canadian cousin, who was in the Mounties for 5 years, & who urged me to 'make a trip over there' next summer. This I should quite like to do, except for the fare (c. £125) & having to live with him.

[...] All this seems very much centred on my own immediate doings – yes! Ludlow was delightful, & I shall always remember your plaid coat & golden hair moving fearfully through the heavy pewter-coloured light of St Lucy's Day in Ludlow Castle. Don't be alarmed: I am quite well, & I expect was making a fuss about my influenza: anyway any relapse now will be due to Lichfield (Lyk-field: we are all buried there: I said 'A bigger family gathering in death than ever in life') & Burton on Trent.

How awful, your falling over. Don't do it again. Are you fairly recovered now? And for my part I always find home depressing, not for *its* fault entirely, but entering it is to leave the harmless universe of make believe I inhabit & encounter the real world where children are reared & are a nuisance but will be alive after you are dead, & where people grow old & have to be looked after not because you like them but because they are *breaking up*, & where style in words & behaviour counts for nothing at all. But what I dislike about my bunch is that they are PHYSIOLOGICALLY AND PSYCHOLOGICALLY INCAPABLE OF ENJOYING THEMSELVES. They have nothing nearly so wrong about them as you say yr Mother has, yet they go about thrashing themselves into deeper ecstasies of misery till I want to shake them till their teeth chatter. I am extremely distressed at your news: I hope with all my heart that things will get better. Such troubles are more depressing than any other kind, and can't by any stretch of the imagination be described as imaginary.

Now I'd better put my coat on & look round the shops & call on my family. I have found that I'm fond of Hollands gin. Wish you were here to be stood one. Wasn't the Test Match maddening! Oh dear, I don't much want to return to Belfast. Take care of yourself, Great Skirted Grebe. Philip

1 Kenneth Grahame, *The Wind in the Willows*, edition illustrated by Arthur Rackham, first UK edition 1950.

6 January 1951

Queen's Chambers, Queen's Elms, University Road, Belfast

Feast of the Epiphany, '51

Dearest M,

By virtue of the 3rd progr. I am partly in York Minster, listening to the Epiphany Procession, but I am also in the S.C.R. of this place, before a large coal fire. Have you ever seen this paper before?[1] I use it because I happen to have it here, not because I like it; the crest amuses me, particularly the Alsopp's Brewery Hand which means, If you're thinking of coming here – DON'T! They say it's the red hand of Ulster, but Ulster must have been caught red-handed often enough not to boast about it – e.g. Teevan. The book is shaded over because we don't care much about books here, & the harp because it is reminiscent of Eire. As for the sea-horse, I don't know: perhaps symbolising the impossibility of getting fresh fish in Belfast.

The house is empty except for myself, & will be so till Monday, so I am spending long hours alone, sometimes happy, sometimes depressed. I feel worse now than I did at the end of my first spell, but then I had the holiday to look forward to, the thrilling journey, & the lit cavernous streets of Ludlow, & the holly-freckled Feathers. No! nothing to look forward to at all like that.

(This Epiphany Service is really splendid – but I expect it's small chance that you can hear it.)

I have just finished Gaskell's *Life of C.B*[2] (I know I took it out in October, but I only started to read it yesterday) & enjoyed it extremely. I have an unbuttressed belief that Mrs G is a great writer, but let that go. I'd forgotten her dislike of Jane Austen, which is all right, but not to boost *George Sand*, oo dear no. From this life Emily emerges as the one you're most curious about. She would have scared me to flight: the most inhuman of them, by a long chalk [...] I feel so strongly that when you agree with my complaints & say that life is hard & that I shd read the Rambler that you are too indulgent: life *is* hard: disease, disappointment & the big snuffer of death hold all the cards: but what I rail against is my sense that for want of – what? courage? initiative? love? – I am losing the few chances of happiness it does offer. And that the cure for this is probably to be put to work in a Lyons, or be struck a few shrewd blows about the *health*, or run by the slack of my pants into the Army. Your comfort & agreement are for people who have had real misfortune, not a tail chasing impostor like myself. Or at least that is what I feel when I have been reading about the Brontës. Pack, clouds, away! The organ is growling & shrieking and nasaling, & the Epiphany is over. I will pick this up later in the evening.

Now it's Bach's *Christmas Oratorio* Part 5: my kind of music – o the oboes, harpsichord, cello, & shrieking emotionalism, as Kingsley calls it! He made me listen to some of his Mozart on Sunday, & I had a chance to reaffirm that insofar as he affects me at all he affects me adversely. Still, enough of that. [...]

Now it's getting on for 11.30: I have spent ages producing the following two lines:

Always too eager for the future, we
Pick out the festivals ten weeks away

– which now seem aimlessly undistinguished. A maid brought me a cup of cocoa & 2 biscuits: what I feel I should fancy most is a pint of cold light draught beer and perhaps three or four real ham rolls. But nothing now till breakfast ...

Just now I counted the blankets on my new bed – there are six. But this won't be any too many in that bleakness: nevertheless it's something of an achievement to have got them just by guiding the conversation round to cold rooms in general.

I've also been starting the day with Test Scores – wish they'd been more exhilarating, too. Archer & Hassett waste as much time as Hutton & Simpson but there'll be no Miller to pitch into the Australian 4, 5 & 6, will there?

Now I shall go to my bed & read *Death on the Nile* & *The reverberator* – most of this letter seems to be fairly cheerful, but I'm getting a *little* resourceless – at least, my legs feel as if they need exercise, & don't at all want to go to bed. But I hope wherever you are you are surrounded by hot water bottles and not Eileen's dear little children – Or hasn't Eileen got children? My 1950 diary with all that information isn't here, & I may make all sorts of bloomers like pairing off Yvonne & Jean Christophe, setting up Histle as a guest house owner in Northumberland & Mary ... Mary ... *was* there a Mary? Perhaps she had all the children. Good night. Four minutes to midnight.

Sunday 7. Jan. About 5.30 pm. Though this has been on the whole a nice day, food is still occupying my mind: I'm wondering in short if I'm going to get any! After Sunday lunch nearly everybody goes away, not to return till bedtime, so ... But otherwise today has not been too bad [...] But this is the last stretch of peace I shall have for Heaven knows how long: tomorrow it's back ta worruck, & the students begin to reinvade this place – And at that point the groaning tray came: at least, I did the groaning, as it was only a small Welsh rarebit & three slices of bread. Having wiped them off the face of the earth, & finished *The reverberator* & *Death on the Nile*, I feel a bit flat. Can it be a frustration of my societal instinct, as Lawrence wd say? No: I think it's just another example of the danger of looking forward to things, which was what my poem was going to be about. I think I'll revert to it, & see if I can add two more lines. There's some more Christmas Oratorio at 9.30.

– Listening to it now. The fire smoulders under the bucket's last grit, dust & scraps. In the meantime I have read some *Wuthering Heights*, played a game of patience, & of course the poem, but it is all no good. I expect you wrote me a letter for this weekend, did you? but of course it didn't arrive. [...]

I have just been adding up my accounts. I wrote about £79 worth of cheques in December, & there's still Income Tax, & Clarke & Satchell's, & January ...

O this Bach! how the programmes can talk about Mozart being the music of the angels when there are such passages as this one. *Quilts* of voices, trumpets going like a *sewing machine*, so *exciting*, as exciting as jazz ... However, I'm aware musical criticism isn't my 40. So I'll shut up.

Perhaps I had better shut up altogether, and post this off to you. The kind of letter I should write if I were in prison, with nothing to distract me. Well, work tomorrow, which won't I suppose be very cheering. I'll try that poem again.

Good night. Do try to let go of your hot water bottle before it gets too cold.

P.

1 Letter written on headed paper with 'The Queen's University of Belfast' on the left with shield in roundel.
2 Elizabeth Gaskell's *The Life of Charlotte Brontë*.

13 January 1951

Queen's Chambers, Belfast

Dearest Monica,

Well, what a blow,[1] what a mean job – heavens, I do sympathise with you: talk about being shaken down like a cobweb! It's quite the most unpleasant thing I have heard of for a long time: the thought of you *not* in the White House is not really conceivable, and to lose that splendid room where you are able to live your own life and be relatively private and comfortable is a tragedy. To be ejected from filthy lodgings is never wholly unpleasant – one thinks of being free of the old fool's cooking or conversation – but to lose a room I always felt you'd made a part of yourself (apart from its initial advantages) seems too much to be borne. Is there no redress? Is there no alternative?

You say that the prospect of action prevents you from feeling the full diapason of horror: ah, to my mind it's the unsettledness that's so upsetting. The first notification is like the first blow of an axe at a tree. All savour is gone from life until the ground has stopped quaking from under one's feet, which isn't till one's setteled again, with fire & reading lamp – my two essentials. But that's an additional misery I certainly don't want to foist on you. Oh dear, it's not easy to know what to say, except that I'm very sorry, more than sorry, and know you must feel quite flattened – cut off at the knees as D.H.L. would say. Who broke the news? What is the general feeling? Any hope of any objections? Who'll be wardening the place when it *is* a hostel? Is there any indecent scuffling for the job? ... Well, there'll be no more married quarters, if that crumb of satisfaction affords you any pleasure. O dear. It's all sad. The keenest memory of your room – not so much *as* a room but as a *mise-en-scène* – I have is on the day of the Evans wedding. You boiled me an egg. I fetched your spray. That day ranks very clearly in my mind, perhaps because of the film: really I wouldn't mind seeing that relic again. (But do you think that it will always be an unmixed pleasure to them? – don't you think a time will come when time regained so vividly will be a pain? Simply to see oneself young when one's old oneself? (I feel that sentence would be very difficult for the foreign student.) No, memory may be cruel but that sort of thing is much crueller. (At least to my way of thinking.) The other time I remember your room is the tea-time when I fetched in some logs. That must have been since 1948. It would be in my journal somewhere: it was a very cosy hour or two.

A few facts: thanks for the books. They arrived Friday 12th, as did your letter. Only the letter was later. I fell on *The rock pool* like a man athirst, & found two funny things I'd never noticed before: I also read *The naughty princess*, which made me laugh a lot. I'm not sure which I thought the funniest: Presents for princesses, perhaps. But they all had good moments: 'I'm the mirror. Name of Bannister' made me grin, among many others. [...]

I think there were one or two misapprehensions of my last: certainly I don't want to be bucked up with little talks on the Duty of Happiness. I was just saying that most of my miseries didn't deserve the solicitude you show for them. And my poem was really an attempt to capture my feeling on returning here: a sense of amazement that what we wait for so long & therefore seems so long in coming *shouldn't* take a proportionally long time to pass – instead of zipping away at the same speed as everything else:

it's

No sooner present than it turns to past

We think each one will heave to and unload
All good into our lives, all we are owed

For waiting so devoutly and so long:
Right to the last

We think each one will heave to and unload
All good into our lives, all we are owed
For waiting so devoutly and so long:
But we are wrong.

Only one ship is seeking us, black-
Sailed ...

Undistinguished-looking stuff, now I write it down in longhand. I suppose it is my equivalent of your dismay at finding yourself back. It certainly seems more final. The first term was a joke (conceivably), but the second term isn't. I had a powerful sense of distance, coming the second time. Before Christmas I thought we might move the house here: now I don't know, it does seem a long way for Mother if I am going to return to England in a few years. Of course I do understand your misery – at least, I can understand it in part – oh, I am so sorry. Deeply, deeply sorry.

I can hear it raining – you realise my room sticks out like a promontory, like the front of a ship, catching all the weather that's going. But the blessed quiet! I can go to bed at midnight now, & know I shan't hear that booted ape blundering about overhead. Sleep! Sleep!

Your lemon soap is still an ornament. I love it.

[...] This afternoon I had afternoon tea in a sombre silent lounge of the Grand Central Hotel – 3/-. The silence could have been cut up & weighed on scales. I was reading a book called *Make you a fine wife*, by Yolande Földes, that I found lying about the Chambers: I was rather shaken by its apathetic immorality. I thought the cheap Hutchinson novel was the guardian of morals and happy endings: in this one the good man ended up married to a careerist bitch & the woman he had lived with all through the book went off to be a good deal happier with his son. No happy ending, no good ending happily & wicked ending unhappily – what is fiction coming to? It rather plunged me into gloom. I'm afraid the country is in a terrible state. For a moment I felt like an old nurse with a Union Jack pincushion and a pot of strong tea on the hob – not a familiar feeling for me. [...]

1 Monica had been asked to leave her lodgings in Carisbrooke Road. She moved to 6 Westgate Road.

34

16 January 1951

Queen's Chambers, Queen's University, Belfast

Clever Little Lamb,

[...] I do like corduroy weskits, but can't afford one. This, as some-one or other said, is a period of retrenchment. [*drawing of L. digging a trench*]

I am keeping my eyes diligently away from the sales, & trying to build up my current account to print the poems. But now I can't think of a title: originally I'd thought of *20 poems for nothing*, but Kingsley shuddered at it: said it was like Roy Campbell. Now I can't think of another: do you think that is so bad? Apart from all the impossible kinds of title, I don't like the drab kind (*Poems*), or the self-denigrating kind (*Stammerings*), or the clever kind (*Stasis*). There'll be about 22 now, or even 23: I want something unaffected & unpretentious – for Lord knows there are few to pretend anything about. *Speaking from Experience*? – sounds like 'Twelve broadcast talks by the Radio Padre'. No, it defeats me. And I don't *ask* for advice because in such matters I should be extremely unlikely to take it.

Rain again! I love hearing it against my newly-cleaned windows. Eddie is back from a ski-ing holiday in Austria: signet ring flashing on chocolate finger, his boots strike sparks from the stones (I know that's not grammar). The chap in my old room can't understand why I left it. [...]

Thanks for the account of my mother, by the way! When she got the dress home she thought it was not too bad after all, so I shall not

 make fun of it. Of course I don't knowingly tease you about your skirt. I like it very much. How do the checks go?

That's it. All I say is that it arouses the worst in me – which isn't very bad, of course, but still, it *is* the worst. That right 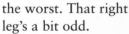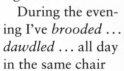 leg's a bit odd.

During the even-ing I've *brooded* ... *dawdled* ... all day in the same chair from dream to dream and rhyme to rhyme I have ranged, which is probably why I have this rash. Or

35

perhaps I have measles. Eventually I read some of *The Great Gatsby* & *Nocturnall: upon S. Lucies Day*, which I haven't done for ages.

Study me then, you who shall lovers be
At the next world, that is, at the next spring ...

I always admired that. If my agents succeed in screwing some £30 out of Albatross Books, I'll get my booklet done, even if I have to call it *Poetical Pieces*. I'm afraid this isn't a very long letter, but my life hesitates at present. Mother is very sorry about your misfortunate moving future: so am I. Tell me any more news there is about it. I expect just now (12.7) you are looking very long & sacred.

Affectionate greetings
Philip

18 April 1951

Queen's Chambers

Dearest Monica,

Lawks! and lawks again. 'And the fatigued face, Taking the strain Of the horizontal force And the vertical thrust'[1] – though thank the Lark there've been no vertical thrusts: in other words, Kingsley has gone, leaving me just able to support the horizontal weight of my salaried employment, but only just. He certainly dropped plenty of plates around, though only 10 of my 15 pounds. On Saturday we went to Dublin, drinking all the way there, there, all the way back, and back: I am only just about recovered. He left me as usual feeling slightly critical of him: despite his organised self defence, I detect elements of artlessness? – no, what I mean to say is that despite his limpet-grip on life, terre-à-terrish & opportunist, there are times when I fancy I can see further than him in his own way. More of that, if needed, when we meet. However, he also intensified my predominant sensation of being a non-contiguous triangle in a circle – [*diagram of triangle within circle*] the inner life making no contact with the outer. Buried alive! He also went off with two of my irreplaceable books: how lucky he doesn't like DHL or KM or any of the Powyses.

Tonight the house is full of cries, affected laughter, thunderous feet. *Plus ça ne change pas, plus suis-je la même chose.* (I'm sure that's all wrong). Ooh! one thing I must relate: we had supper on the boat before he left, and, as we began our soup, a Voice that sounded as if it were coming out of a treacle-well – or a plum pudding well – requested that its bill be brought. We exchanged glances & turned round: there was in person the author of *Perelandra*[2] ... On subsequent enquiry I find that he is 'a Belfast man', Kingsley promised to 'get talking to him', but I bet he didn't. [...]

I started to read Rowse on the Elizabethans,[3] but dear me, even if I were a Tudor fan I'd feel a little out of love with the age – don't you hate his *proprietary* air towards all these tombs & big houses? Makes me want to draft him onto night shift. For all that he'd deny it he doesn't approach it as a poet – rather as a journalist. If only he were more of an artist, even a Guedellan or Stracheyan artist. Wouldn't you like to hear him on Blenheim Palace?

Jim Sutton has returned the two DHL books I bought in Oxford & they remind me very strongly of that light-coloured slant-roofed room & the Symonds razor towels. And the snivelling wind. Do you remember our search for one of old England's log fires? And what we found?

Photographically lined[4]
On the tablets of my mind

– I suppose that is Gilbert, but it sounds like Hardy a little, sort of

– Why the steps, and the sea,
   And the distant Nore should be
   Photographically lined
   On the tablets of my mind –

But now you cannot tell, you cannot tell!

   O the noisy *fools*! (That's me, not Hardy.)

As you can tell by my handwriting I am feeling very withdrawn & austere at present, & rather extravert after orgies of self inspection. At lunch time I go into the Botanic Garden hot house and inhale the thick summery air: the flowers are not remarkable but it's a wonderful experience among these chilly mountainpasses of air. I have CORRECTED MY PROOFS[5] and returned them to Mr Hennessy, whom I did not dare ask how long the wait would be. Truthfully, they looked neither especially nice or especially nasty, but very *bitty*, scraps, motley, no cohesion or wealth, wch is I suppose natural enough. I could not be *proud* of them.

How horrible, relatives & television! I do sympathise. Perhaps to some extent they'll cancel each other out.

Quiet thoughts from blunderland –

Philip

1 W. H. Auden, poem beginning 'Between attention and attention'.
2 C. S. Lewis.
3 A. L. Rowse, *The Elizabethan Age*, vol 1: *The England of Elizabeth: the structure of society* (1950).
4 'Photographically lined ...': from W. S. Gilbert, 'The Story of Prince Agib' (*The Bab Ballads*).
5 Proofs of *XX Poems*.

23 May 1951

Queen's Chambers, Leicester [*sic*]

Dearest Monica –

I can neither stand, sit nor lie, think, feel or intuit – the toothache with which I closed my last letter has blossomed & this is the morning of the second day looked at through the red spectacles of pain. Like dockers' unions other teeth are coming out in sympathy. This morning I went to a pleasant but ineffectual young dentist, a friend of Piggott's, who has *taken the filling out & put a dressing in* – ass! As if that will do any good! If I like I can go back this afternoon & he will *kill the nerve* – ha! X-rays at the Royal are also spoken of: but I know my teeth: if I get toothache it means an extraction. I shall look odd without it.

All this is extremely disorganising. I sat miserably in the cinema last night watching an awful film about racing cars, then tried dousing myself with drink with the idea that alcohol is anaesthetic (*vide* 18th century surgery), but it didn't work. Aspirins are the only thing, but my stomach this morning was queasy with aspirin & oil of cloves, a disgusting combination.

How odd! It has momentarily quietened. Perhaps because I stopped thinking about it for a bit. I'm sure that only in this effete century would it be regarded as a reason for demanding special consideration. But it does divert my mind a little from the attentive acknowledgement of your long letter. I should say one of the longest I've ever received, about 7000 words, the length of a couple of short stories or half a dozen *Times* leaders. O flames! This is the last sheet of paper. Dig for some more ...

More found. I forgot to say that after I left the dentist I went to buy some painkiller at a chemist's, & on emerging saw the dentist slipping out of his door with a dog. That shook my faith in him terribly: not that I had much anyway. He had also *seen me to the door*, another bad touch. Oh for my old Coventry dentist, with his Ronald Coleman smile, tank of fish to look at, expensive equipment, and overflowing appointments book!

I'm afraid *teeth*, & *dentists*, & *white coats*, & *canines*, & *nerves*, will play a largeish part in this letter. They bulk incredibly large with me at present. Do you ever go to the dentist? I seem to remember your going once or twice, but not unless driven.

This letter has not really got under way yet: the time is after twelve & I must go to the bank before lunch. I think I'll leave it till I get a chance either at teatime or after I come off work at night. Don't take it that I didn't enjoy getting your letter: I did, really. O curse! my tooth has started up again. *All along the upper jaw, in and out the molars ...* What a bore I'm being.

5.10 p.m. Am just feeling like something out of one of Kipling's more pain-conscious stories – 'Larkin had for so long hung shuddering on the skewers of pain that he lifted his hand involuntarily as McConachie took out a toothpick' kind of stuff. It is a little red thread that runs down the tooth, apparently, & was inflamed & infected. So the next thing to do is get the beastly thing x-rayed for abscesses. If there *is* a sizeable one at the root, what happens next is too terrible to contemplate: it makes you realise what books entitled *Oral Surgery* are about. These dental boys are itching to graduate from the drill & to start *cutting the bone about*. Disappointed doctors, all of them, sidetracked into dentistry by incompetence or desire for high wages.

My face has not yet unfrozen, so I can't tell whether the pain is less, the same, or more. It might be a *little* less. But not *spectacularly* so. Dear, dear! Progressively blinder, & balder & more toothless! And now I live, & now my life is done!

Now I must have an early tea & work 6–9, when I should really like to sit very still in this chair, perhaps snoozing, looking at the shifting greys of the sky. More at 9.0 p.m. – I am still not unfrozen, & feel that we haven't finished with the beast yet. Dentist again tomorrow at 10: X-ray on Friday at the Royal. O miseries.

11.40 p.m. – Safely in bed. Pain bad all evening but suddenly slackened about half an hour ago. I *do* hope they don't have to bore into my gum.

I can hear Bill stoking the furnaces: long swishes as he drives his shovel into the coke. Now he is talking to his dog. It's a wettish night.

I'm sorry you felt low when you wrote, and think you have every right to be: sorry too I omitted to say how much I enjoyed your visit and how pleased I was that you should come at all, knowing your hatred of travel & ships & water. The weather had turned coolish & wet here – no, I don't think it broke immediately you went, but it's broken now. (My stomach is *ticking*.) I haven't your letter by me now, but I'll turn to it tomorrow. Hope you are just vanishing into the burrow of sleep . . .

Thursday evening Thank you for reminding me about Empire Day. Queen's flew a flag & I was nice to a nigger. The dentist changed the dressing & I am much better off now, though the x-ray tomorrow still holds good – that will be an expense of spirit in a waste of time. Now I sit at peace between my two windows, seeing the brand-new shift of the trees in the sun. Peace at last, and welcome.

I think what I did mean about not having talked much was that I felt we were not making much *contact* – plenty of talk, in fact, but almost an increasing strangeness. I feel I am not good at making contacts anyway. Not that I'm *awkward* or *reserved* ... You'd under-stand better what I mean if I could describe the progress of my misengagement[1] – not that I want to describe it – but I found I was able to develop simultaneously what would pass for friendship & love along with a more definite detachment than ever before. Not that I acted insin-cerely: it was the first time I have had anyone to please and I found I enjoyed it, but the affair – or my side of it – moved if I pushed it, so to speak; if I made no effort it didn't move. I thought that a point would come when the partition between myself and the whole situation would break down and I should be carried away by it, seeing the point of everything. It didn't; all I felt was that I'd irretrievably committed myself to the other side of the glass while being forced to remain separ-ate. That wd have been dreadful, a kind of waking death, so I had to uncommit myself, which wasn't pleasant either, except that fundamen-tally I was getting what I wanted, despite all my crocodile tears & poems ... Of course, all this is commonplace and might be described in simpler terms: it did leave me feeling, though, that I was a monster of egotism, a psychic cripple, etc., etc., and that instead of helping me to 'know myself' it had quite upset all my ideas of how to behave. I knew simply that if I behaved in the way most natural to me it led to disaster, for no easily-discernible reason, & so I had better behave in no way at all – i.e. not behave at all – or – well – no, my ideas on the subject are all very confused. At any rate, I feel very much back in my shell. My nature, perhaps, is rather like a spring – it can be stretched out straight, but when released leaps back into a coil. Well, this has wandered a bit from making contact, but something like that I felt like saying – I mean, do you *know* it already? have you made up your mind about it? Or have you just thrust it out of mind? It is quite the most important thing about me, or part of it. You surely can't regard my sealed-off ineffectualities as anything but failure, or think that I regard them as anything but failure.

Brrr! Comes that chilly backwash that always succeeds talking about oneself. Like Pernod, it has the quickest lift, but it drops you as far. Let's talk about something else. [...]

Nature hasn't been taking the pen from my hand at all – haven't written anything for ages, except a bad sonnet[2] & a bad unfinished poem about a march[3] on Sunday afternoon. I gave the Warden a copy of *XX poems* – he knew 'I wrote' (God! God! God!) – and the ones he picked out for brief commendation were III & the road-between-us. I asked him if he didn't like XX, & he said yes, but the last two lines reminded him of The Best Poems of 1924, which I thought pretty smart, for him. O by the way – 'sicken inclusively outwards' means to spread outwards, like a spot of disease growing, taking in more and more of the surrounding surface. 'Meaning's rebuttal' really is clumsy: I mean (in my simple way) that each of the technical terms intoned by reality (terms that seem denotative not connotative, scientific not emotive) in fact for all their seeming precision are Janus faced & mean also the opposite of what they mean. This was an attempt to describe my own bewilderment whenever I try to think clearly. A wish for instance may be a simple wish – I want bread. Or it may be a cover wish to conceal the wish for chocolate. Or it may be a direct expression of the hatred of bread, which for some reason can't be confessed. I know this will sound all nonsense, but if you can conceive 'wish' treble-yolked with three meanings like that you will see what I 'mean'.

O dear I did feel sorry for you waiting for a night of high wind – please don't feel like that. Your life is awfully hard, I do realise – much harder than mine. Lord knows how you manage, doing everything alone & single-handed, but you do it *well*. I mean you always look nice & don't breakfast off pilchards-in-tomato or live among Scottie night-dress cases. Is that any consolation?

Bed now. I think it is raining. My teeth are stirring, uneasily.

Much love
P.

1 To Ruth Bowman: See Appendix B.
2 Presumably 'To My Wife', completed 19 March 1951.
3 'The March Past', apparently completed 25 May 1951.

7 June 1951

Queen's Chambers, Belfast

Dear graminivore,

I'm not sure what you are *doing* in this picture except preparing supper. However, I'm sure you are comfortably off. Do you think you should have whiskers, or not? My whiskers are an integral part of me.

However. I am feeling very *June-like* tonight, that is, a pulp of my ordinary self. Hay fever has opened an offensive without throwing all its troops into battle but quite nastily enough to keep me busy.

There is quite enough drawing here already. Enough! Seriously I felt very dead today, slept at lunchtime & dragged about all afternoon. Yesterday however I had the morning off, & after completing a few commissions in town & being unluckily *collared by Bradley* for coffee, I got my bike out and rode up the Lagan towpath. The weather was hot and splendid, & the river-side deserted except for a horse-drawn barge. It's almost entirely unspoilt, no houses anywhere, only lock gates &

occasional refreshment-stalls (shut). I saw something I imagined to be a magpie, *heard* waterrats clopping in & out of the shallows, & hardly sneezed at all, being free to wonder at the unbroken blue sky, cliffs of wood shadow descending to the water, & the thick anonymous dust that softly powdered my pedalling shoes. After going some miles, I came up onto the road, & stopped at a small licensed house near Ballyskeagh I'd noticed before. An old man came in from the garden to serve me, & the pub was another minor 'find', being strangely *English*, with a dartboard & Albin (Aldin?) hunting prints on the dark walls, & behind the counter ancient mirrors inscribed with proprietary brands of spirits dating from about 50 years ago, and a vast collection of regimental badges. Resting on top of the 'reredos', as you might call it, was a German helmet – not the kind we know, but the real old 1914 Uhlan spike-topped variety, its gold chain tarnished, but still carrying an aura of *evil* as in the early pages of illustrated war histories, Louvain Cathedral mouldering, etc. After that I proceeded to Lisburn, a small town, & failing to find anywhere to eat bought bread, cheese, onions & an apple, & sat in the gardens, reading *I leap over the wall*.[1] The tar was oozing on the roads, & altogether it was a happy few hours. It is surprising how one's whole attitude changes on being released from *work*. My step was firm, my eye buoyant, my voice unfaltering; I wasn't thinking about the grave, or how miserable my lot was; no, I got up early, embracing the day eagerly like a groom his bride, and sang like Toad to the noise of my wheels – & all because I had *a few hours to myself*. I very soon found out in my life how I resented Ringmaster Work putting his jackbooted foot through each fragile paper hoop of time! God we shall not live for ever! as Ll. Powys wd say. Jim Sutton is the man, living on bread & tea in his cottage sooner than indulge in such grim farce: at the thought of work his broad keen good humoured face takes on a look of overpowering disgust. 'I couldn't …'

Well!

I have just read that John Brett's painting *The stone breaker*[2] is in Liverpool City Art Gallery: I must go & see it. Do you know it? I'm sure you do. It's probably in Gaunt's *PreRaphaelite Tragedy*.[3] I've never seen it in colour but it *looks* to me like a perfect picture, utterly timeless. The next time I'm in Liverpool I'll go & see it.

Friday.
Interruptions! I must post this instantly if you're to get it. Your letter was very nice & interesting – today you go to Fred's?

Today I feel I'd like to go to bed!

Finis!

Kind thoughts
from Philip

1 Monica Baldwin, *I Leap over the Wall* (1950).
2 John Brett, Pre-Raphaelite painter: his *The Stonebreaker* was one of L.'s favourite paintings. See p. 57.
3 William Gaunt, *The Pre-Raphaelite Tragedy* (1942). It is not illustrated there.

19 June 1951

Queen's Chambers, Belfast

Dearest Monica,

A word. I sit at nearly 10.30 pm, reading lamp perched on my side-ended travelling-trunk, looking out of my west-facing window, where the redness of the sky has subsided to grey – the low meandering solid grey of the hills, and the watercolour streaky grey of the sky. An evening spent adding a page to a dull little article my conscience is bullying me to write, followed by the Ganniss and the reading of *12th night* & some scorching hot chips, mouth-blistering. Hay fever hovers around. Waves of sadness occur, like the fine breath of a garden. A tablet of Goya 'Blue moss' is perfuming the room. Why has it so strange a name? *Blue* moss? *What* blue moss?

The Warden excelled himself last night, the mean little schoolboy of Hell – 'Are you going out tonight?' 'Oh no – not at all – saving money you know—' *'Then come & listen to the devil's disciple on the wireless!'* Caught in the oldest trap in the book! He (like all self centred people) is *slightly deaf* so the wireless was on *very loud & off station*: the play I think *rather tedious*: he shamelessly *cadged* some cigarettes off me (that's to say, gave one & took – ASKED FOR – three) – I don't know. If it's not one swine it's another: Bradley or Beckett. I took beer along too, *being decent*: he greeted it: 'O good: we'll drink yours first' – I should be *ashamed* to act as he acts. Well well. Well well. Mustn't lose our tempers must we. WHY MUSTN'T WE

Bateson[1] seems to have stuck in your craw! I must say I forget most of it, as I always do, but I remember I couldn't agree with him about the audience side of it. Have you ever understood the line that a poem does not exist until it is read? It has always seemed illogical to me. If a man writes a poem it exists whether anyone sees it or not, the same as Gauguin's pictures round his Pacific shack. Will it exist any more if a thousand W.E.A. classes chant it every Friday night?

I think the prosaic quality you censure in verse is beautifully exemplified in a bit of Spender which I *believe* runs

For you are no Orpheus,
She no Eurydice:
She has truly packed and gone
To live with someone
Else ...[2]

At this point the poem falls blubbering to its knees. I expect I do it sometimes, though I don't find it at the spot you indicate in *At grass* – would you prefer a comma after *sky*?[3] Truly I have no theories about poetry at all, but I do think that most fascinating effects are got by playing off the rhythm and language of speech against the rhythm and language of poetry. *They are not long, the weeping and the laughter*[4] – *And when she wakes she will not think it long*[5] – *Everybody else, then, going, And I still left where the fair was?*[6] – such lines are so successful to me that some other poets fade to nothingness beside them in entirety. Talking about rhythm I see Ridley[7] insists that we say:

Cóme away cóme away déath
And in sád cypress lét me be láid
Flý away flý away bréath
I am sláin by a fáir cruel máid

Of course I dare say he is right: all the same it would be rather nice to lengthen 2 & 4 to iambics. However, I must not be a-pudling in these matters. And by the way I send no poems because I do not find any I have the face to make known to you. They are all just dull, or frivolous, or incompetent. And there is *no* social conscience about them!

Tonight is threatened to be a drunk noisy night, so I am armed with patience. *The entry of the drunks*, march of the Queen's University Air Squadron. [...]

1 F. W. Bateson, *English Poetry: A Critical Introduction* (1950).
2 Spender, 'No Orpheus, No Eurydice', from *Ruins and Visions*, 1942.
3 Monica had written (16 June 1951): 'That sort of easy lazy flatness you must watch – you could easily find a better way of saying it. Even the beautiful *At Grass* has its tiny threat of that sort of weakness, as I thought when I first read it & still think – it is the 1st half of stanza 3, & the uneasy feeling comes on at the second run-on line: 'against the sky' is all right until 'outside' picks it up again; then the stanza recovers so nicely that it doesn't matter & is nothing serious, but if it *has* a weak spot, it is there. Do you see what I mean?'
4 *They are not long*: Ernest Dowson, '*Vitae summa brevis spem nos vetat incohare longam*'.
5 *And when she wakes*: Christina Rossetti, 'Rest'.
6 *Everybody else, then, going*: Thomas Hardy, 'Exeunt omnes'.
7 M. R. Ridley, Shakespeare scholar.

27 June 1951

Queen's Chambers, Belfast

Dearest M.,

Many thanks for your long letter – it is a wonder, this effortless writing of 14 pages: dammee if I can do it. It takes me ages to write anything: even a simple letter goes to the typists scored over like a MS. of G. Flaubert. Maybe if I could I'd write something in the literary line. You must not mind if I don't write much. I mean I write home once a week, & other letters as they arise – about one a week – it is really fantastic to write twice to you from the point of view of *output* – though that sounds a shade unchivalrous. I thought the dual-purpose brassière was a winner, & under your guidance have begun Hensley Henson.[1] He seems to get to the top very quickly! One minute he's saying that how the poor live makes him indignant with the life of a rich churchman: the next he's a canon of Westminster. So far I've not formed much impression of him. Another book I'm reading is DHL's *Movements in European history*, which I find Queen's possesses: a hack book done for the O.U.P. during lean years. His conjunctival sentences drive me crazy: 'So the Emperor Charlemagne rallied to the cause. For above all he inherited the idealistic strain of the Franks. And many of the barons were quick to side with him. But some did not' etc. A sort of continual buttonholing of the reader for fear he will get away.

Good night!

Sweet dreams.

Thursday night. Slowly my room is reaching a climax of untidiness – I 'move' to this ghastly Presbyterian hostel on Sunday. I looked in there today – noise of a wireless came bellowing out of a door marked 'Quiet Room'. *My* room is about 7' × 7' × 7'. 'Roughing it'. Still, it'll be cheap – about 50/- a week. This house is full of Dublin tennis players & American athletes – the Yale & Harvard boys who got pasted by Oxford & Cambridge. I have an ulcer or sore place inside my lower lip – radium needles! social diseases! Most painful.

Today a copy of *The long divorce* came from Crippen,[2] as Kingsley calls him: and I have read it. Not very mysterious, but rather freer of *bêtises* than heretofore. He sends his approbations of *XX poems*, naming for praise 2, 3, 5, 7, 16 and 20! Dear Bruce. His letter was so cordial and self-deprecatory.

Warden has *gone*. SPLENDID.

I'm afraid this is not going to be the proper letter I promised after all. Really I haven't the *generosity of spirit* at present to write a proper letter – I am pressed down, but not running over. Do not think I neglected your enquiry about your clothes! But I honestly should not say anything about the way you dress. You have style, and that is sufficient: it would be quite unwarrantable for me to suggest you alter anything. I can only speak of general effects: beware of too-tightly done hair, or tight jersey *and* skirt *too* often. It looks very neat and business-like, but after a while it seems like a never-relaxed tension, as if you had no softness or luxuriance to fall back on, and that insensibly tires the observer. This sounds impossibly precious! But it is all I can say. You know far more than I of the possibilities of fashion & cut & material: I can only try to describe the 'psychic effect'. And that is probably a lot of nonsense. [...]

1 Hensley Henson (1863–1947), Bishop of Durham, controversial liberal Anglican.
2 'Crippen': Bruce Montgomery, pseudonym Edmund Crispin.

12 July 1951

The Library, QUB

Dearest Monica,

Sorry about this paper. It was all I could buy at the Botanic Gardens Post Office. It really reminds me of painful letters written in large pencil script – 'Dear Mum, I got here in time for Tea. Cook ad taken up my bag and ared the Bed, it is not a bad Place so far, I ave a Room over the Stalbes.' *etc*. Don't you think so?

Well, Orange Day or whatever they call it is nearly over, & no one can say I haven't done my duty by the North. Breakfast over, I took my bicycle out in light rain & pedalled slowly out of the town on the University side towards the village of Finaghy, where a huge procession eventually arrives from Belfast to form up on a field there and be addressed. Most people were straggling out in that direction, with headscarfs and tottering children & lunch in a bag: in fact it was rather like a scene for a modern 'road to Calvary' with orange stalls & mineral waters & sudden overpowering stenches of vinegared chips. Finaghy is just a nasty little suburb, & in the end I met some Queens people who took me into their house out of the rain & let me park my bicycle & made tea. We got back to the road in time to watch the procession. This is a procession of the Loyal Orange Lodges. I don't know what precisely these are – they're clubs, of course, partly social, but mainly intended to keep up the Protestant & Unionist ascendancy, & therefore a considerable political force. Each Lodge was preceded by its banner, a big silk picture the size of a sheet held up on two poles; and also by a band. Then the members walked in slouching fashion – you can't call it *marching*. The banners were incredibly diverse. Mostly they were pictures of Ulster history: King William, King William landing at Carrickfergus, the Battle of Aughrim, Protestants being drowned in the River Bann (this was a rather fetching one of plump naked ladies up to their waists in water being gesticulated at by Puritanical-looking fellows in green); or even in the same antique old-china style the Normandy landing or some incident from the Somme. Then there were the iconographical ones: Disraeli (yes!), Queen Victoria, General Gordon, Lord Carson, George V, & a host of local celebrities in dog collars or military garb. Then the miscellaneous: Britannia & a lion, the crown, sceptre & Bible, Ridley and Latimer burning (very popular, that), and strange symbolic scenes of young women on rocks, clutching at a huge cross

48

('Our sole Hope & Refuge'), all done in this pink-yellow-and-purply High Church postcard style.

The bands were various, too: fife & drum, pipe & drum, brass, & even accordion, all keeping a strong beat that slightly disagreed with the one behind & the one in front. As for the Lodges themselves ... I said afterwards that it reminded me of a parade of the 70,000 Deadly Sins. Take a standard football crowd (soccer), cut a fringed orange anti-macassar in two and hang one round the neck of each man: give him large false orange cuffs & white gloves to emphasise the tawdry ugliness of his blue Sunday suit, & clap a bowler hat on his head – then you have a Lodger ready for marching. Most of the anti-macassers were orange edged with purple, but some were purple edged with orange: certain members ('Sir Knights' or 'Provosts') carried shiny & curiously-repellent symbolic swords & axes – not real, but silver-plated. The dominant impression from this endless tramping file of faces was of really-depressing ugliness. Slack, sloppy, sly, drivelling, daft, narrow, knobby, vacant, vicious, vulpine, vulturous – every kind of ugliness was represented not once but tenfold – for you've no idea how *long* it was. They started coming by at 12 noon: at 12.45 I was expecting the end, but no! we left for lunch at 1.15 & the parade didn't finish going by till 2. About 20,000 men in all shambled by, or 280 Lodges. It was a parade of staggering dullness (every face wore the same 'taking-himself-seriously' expression) & stupefying hypocrisy ('Civil and religious liberty' was a catchphrase much repeated, like Ridley & Latimer). Having seen it, I shall *not* see it again. But the drums go beating about the town all day.

I do hope that hasn't bored you! It *was* boring, of course, but interesting, in a macabre & sordid way. Much more *thrilling* was Sandy Row, the Protestant Quarter, on Wednesday night – bonfires at every street corner blazing up house-high. I strolled down about half past eleven (drizzle coming down as usual) & was fascinated by the cardboard arches across the streets, the thick waves of Guinness, War Horse tobacco, & vinegared chips, the dancing crowds, & the pairs & trios of gum-chewing young girls roaming about wearing paper hats stamped 'No surrender', 'Not an inch', & various Unionist catchwords. Police stood uneasily about in their raincapes ...

Friday How tiresome this letter is up to date! but I must finish & post it now or you won't get it for Saturday. Dear, I sympathise really deeply about your *burrow* problem: but, without whimsy, it certainly is the devil. Still, don't do anything hasty! Better a week or so in Cravenhurst than a cycle of a house where someone is learning the accordion. No, noise doesn't *hurt* me, but it introduces a spasm of claustrophobic rage: also I can't relax as long as noise is going on. Half my muscles remain automatically tensed.

Send me as many wails as you like, if it helps, though I hate hearing of things hurting you. Jumpers: those sound lovely, but I need length – 24″ from bottom of neckline at least. If you think they'd have the length, I'm sure my chest isn't nearly 36″.

What a good Test Match! What a good Robinson–Turpin fight! What good leaders of the championship! Sport is looking up!

I have *put in for a flatlet*!!! More about this later.

I think I shall arrive quite early on Thursday – before lunch, as things look at present.

Loving thoughts: keep ears up. Philip.

11 August 1951

7, College Park East, Belfast

Dearest M,

This is the first letter I have ever tried to write in an aeroplane. We are about to leave *terra firma* & no doubt when we have done so my writing will be more legible. At present we are 'taxi-ing': a full plane, not readily distinguishable from an ordinary 3rd railway carriage as far as personnel goes. Now for it! – No, not quite. Now? Rain sweeps, driven by wind & propeller-blast. Long wait, to enable one to grow nervous. Brrr! It really is a vile morning. Another plane has just gone: perhaps we were waiting for it, but still we stand. Now? Yes!.....

And we are now *up*, & not so smooth as I'd hoped. If *this* is going to be a rough passage, I shall be *quite cross*. Now we are up in the clouds & I expect will shortly emerge into the sun. Dense cloud. Visibility nil. People lighting cigarettes – not yrs truly!

Well, since seeing you borne backwards into wet Exeter, I have had 4 nights in Swansea,[1] 1 in Loughboro' & 1 in B'ham as I had said I was going to (just then I had a spasm of panic for fear we *hit* something: we are still flying in this dense cloud), & I don't know that I greatly added to my store of happiness. The Madges[2] are freshest in my memory, & they did seem pleasant & I wasn't quite so nervous as on first encounter. There wasn't an omelette: only cold chicken & ham, & a bowl of lettuce rinsed in vinegar, with a pear to follow. One of the children had chickenpox, so in 2 or 3 weeks (if I survive this flight – I *do* wish we'd emerge from this fog of vapour) I may develop it myself, for to the best of my recollection I've never had it. The only 'taker' for 20 *poems* reported by C. Madge so far is D. J. Enright, a Cambridge man as far as I remember, who wants – or says he wants – to notice them in *The month*, a paper I don't know.[3] Eliz. Lake is just finishing a novel about her convent education & so is very full of the subject. I asked them about 'Charlie boy' & Madge said that he had known both Burgess & McLean at Cambridge but hadn't seen them since – his guess was that they had gone to U.S.S.R. to spill some Washingtonian beans. However!

Beastly clouds. I'm scared. Suppose we knock into another plane?

The night in Loughboro' was less of a success. I'm afraid the house situation gets worse instead of better, & what the solution will be I don't know, but have an uneasy inkling – involving the transport of a certain party to N. Ireland.[4] Tears etc were well featured on both sides, along with phrases like 'cracking up', 'breaking down', 'end of tether', 'can't go on', and other merry catchphrases of both sides of the house. I begin to think it unlikely that Mother will ever take a house alone, or find anyone to take it with, or escape from the mechanical mousewheel of exhibitionistic depression that at present contains her. As for my sister, a plague on her! The south fog light on her, & make her By inchmeal a disease[5] ... while there I bought Mother – or made her buy – a little Bush radio set, which I was quite sorry to leave.

Swansea was as big a contrast to what came before it or after it as could well be. (Oh dear! *suppose* we hit something?) The contrast to our 2 days of planned exploration was profound. Sluttishness, late hours, drink, squalling children & (*Here is the flight bulletin. Over Liverpool going about 160 m.p.h., 10 mins. behind schedule.*) poor, insufficient food. Nor did the compensations for these seem as sufficient as in days of yore. I was read nearly ALL *Dixon & Christine*,[6] & suggested it should be called *The man of feeling*, an idea wch Kingsley quite took to, but will probably not entertain finally.

I was very pleased to hear you had a good Sunday in Exeter, but the trip home sounded *beastly*. My trip across the Bristol Channel was *none too good* – there was quite a *swell*, & certain parties were very ill indeed: not me, though. On the whole I'm rather a bad sailor, I think. The story about the man in the lounge was funny because your excuse was *true*, & he probably wd think it wasn't. It sounds like an ultra-skilful hand-off. This reminds me that in Swansea I met Kingsley's ex-'mistress', a curious dark crooked-mouthed prognathic girl whose scarlet cheeks & burnt-cork eyebrows reminded me of Tod Slaughter made up for some villainy or other. Truly one man's meat is another man's buttered parsnips.

Well, I think I will have a little read now: still foggy, with glimpses of the sullen sea far below. I will add to this if anything occurs to me later.

12.30. Clouds cleared: Isle of Man far below. Tiny boats on sea ... Sun ...

12.45. Crossing Irish coast. Visibility good. Churches surrounded by white specks – gravestones. Much woolly drift. *Bumps.* We are probably losing altitude now. Goodbye till *terra firma* ...

1.0. Safe! Sitting in bus, awaiting transport to city.

3.50. And now I'm sitting in Q.C., having dumped my bags into 7 College Park E. & disliked the look of it intensely. Belfast doesn't look very nice to me: a good thing tomorrow is Sunday and there is *no work*. At such points in life a holiday becomes like a hallucination: I hardly feel I have had one. We did walk to Fingle Bridge, didn't we? Yes, of course. But what a straw in the scalepan against months of *boring work*! The right sort of straw, but *only one*.

If I post this now, you may get it on Monday morning. Thank you for your birthday card: you *have* an eye for these things. I had: socks, handkerchiefs, booktoken, record. And some chocolate cake. A grey day.

Much love, Philip

1 L. stayed in Swansea with Kingsley and Hilly Amis.
2 L. stayed in Birmingham with the poet and sociologist Charles Madge and his wife.
3 Enright's review, the only one of *XX Poems*, appeared in the Catholic journal *The Month*, in November 1951. Enright had been a pupil of F. R. Leavis at Downing College, Cambridge, and a contributor to *Scrutiny*.
4 'Loughborough ... transport of a certain party to N. Ireland': L.'s fear that he would have to move his mother from Loughborough to Belfast, to live with or near him.
5 Shakespeare's *The Tempest*, Act 2, sc. 2.
6 Earlier version of what became *Lucky Jim*.

26 August 1951

7 College Park East, Belfast

Dearest Monica,

A putty-coloured fit of torpor on me this weekend – the sinful sort, the deadly sin. Truth is that my holiday lasts just about a fortnight, then I fall backwards . . . So any hint of spinelessness will be due to that. I sit in my room like Miss Havisham, about whom I have been reading this week. Better the Dickens you know than the Dickens you don't know – on the whole I enjoyed it. But I should like to say something about this 'irrepressible vitality', this 'throwing a fresh handful of characters on the fire when it burns low', in fact the whole Dickens method – it strikes *me* as being less ebullient, creative, vital, than hectic, nervy, panic-stricken. If he were a person I should say 'You don't have to entertain me, you know. I'm quite happy just sitting here'. This jerking of your attention, with queer names, queer characters, aggressive rhythms, piling on adjectives – seems to me to betray basic insecurity in his relation with the reader. How serenely Trollope, for instance, compares. I say in all seriousness that, say what you like about Dickens as an entertainer, he cannot be considered as a real writer at all; not a real novelist. His is the garish gaslit melodramatic barn (writing that phrase makes me wonder if I'm right!) where the yokels gape: outside is the calm measureless world, where the characters of Eliot, Trollope, Austen, Hardy (most of them) and Lawrence (some of them) have their being. However, as I say, I enjoyed much of *G.E.* & may try another soon. [...]

Since starting this letter I've begun to read *Bleak House*, with pleasure, again. More like a real book. *Punch* have not acknowledged my poems. I sent a bit of doggerel to Bateson[1] – a sort of splenetic A.P.H.[2] poem about novel-writing – but whether he will print it I don't know. He replied sympathetically, asking for 'a critical article'. I replied thanking him but 'I know I shan't' (didn't say that!). [...]

It seems extraordinary to think this is still August – it feels like late September to me. If I had nothing to do but sit about & write poetry I'd do a series of impressionistic poems on the months of the year, but being a working man I can't afford the time. To *not* work! Have you ever thought how delightful? 'Do? Oh I'm afraid I don't do anything.' Better £300 unearned than £1000 earned! [...]

1 L. sent 'Fiction and the Reading Public' (written 25 February 1950) to Bateson, who published it in *Essays in Criticism*, January 1954. It later appeared in L.'s *Collected Poems*.
2 A. P. Herbert, writer of light topical verses.

1 September 1951

7 College Park East, Belfast

Dearest Monica,

Saturday afternoon. Stupid with a huge unhealthy lunch. Reginald Foort has just rendered Handel's *Largo* on the B.B.C. cinema organ, leading me to reconsecrate my life for the 100th time – how I do love Handel, and how very English I feel he is: along with me how many J. B. Priestley characters were listening in tiny houses in rigid streets beneath the factory chimneys on both sides of the Pennines! how many of them will be hurrying along to the mulberry & lime coloured brick chapel these autumn evenings to sing the *Messiah*! What other artist has caused a king to leap to his feet? Or mesmerised the cautious heart of Samuel Butler? Though I don't think he wears as well as Beethoven or Bach, there is something enormously simple & appealing about him: big white clouds, blue skies, classical columns, sheep feeding quietly, and some nymph or younger son advancing to sing an aria of such wringing beauty that you can't imagine why everyone isn't supplied with a record of it free, why it isn't as well known as *Ave Maria* ... But I grow verbose. Understand, though, that it was the *Largo* that began it. What does *Largo* mean? Where is it from? Tell me these things. Ah, splendour! [...]

Who should turn up on Thursday but Colin & Patsy Strang! ('Who should come in but Higgins!')[1] The letter announcing their impending arrival reached me on Friday afternoon (Heysham strike) so it was a great surprise. They have come over to look for a furnished house, and already know more about the topography of Belfast, though they have no house. Colin is a queer amalgam of Bruce & Kingsley & Peter Oldham: not a strong character, he has been deeply impressed by all three & listening to him is like hearing a composite record of all three. [...]

Another thing that turned up on Thursday was a proof from D. J. Enright of his notice, which turns out not to be a separate notice but one in a crowd. After puncturing Robert Wilberforce, Wm. J. Grace, Vera Barclay, F. J. Friend-Pereira, John H. F. McEwen, Lynette Roberts, Lawrence Spingarn & Haro Hodson, he says 'It is Mr L's that is, immediately (Pox take *immediately*! How crept *immediately* in!), the most impressive of these collections.' After a graceful & I must say pleasing reference to *A G. in W.* he says I persuade words into being poetry & don't bully them. He then quotes in entirety the Mayhew poem about the ruined girl.[2] The review then closes with a special – I mean his voice changes – notice of W de la M. And you are quite right about the R.C. aspect! It is definitely & officially Catholic, edited probably by Father O'Jasus in a chalky soutane & biretta covered with candle droppings. O well! it's nice to hear an *official* kind word, & Enright *is* a Cambridge man of the Scrutiny caravan. [...]

I see what you mean about marrying all other married folk, but that isn't what puts me off marriage – or at least what lies at the bottom of my frothy denunciations of that state – I rarely see myself as behaving like everybody else: or if I do it's only as a trick to throw what I consider extraordinary features into better relief, or as a means of storing up energy by living the easier way. I find it more puzzling to know what people *think* they are doing who get married. To me the strain would be the constant lack of solitude, the never-being able-to-relax, not at midnight, or 3 a.m. or any time of day at all. But the single life of course has its demerits. Is it better to die of disintegration or of continual watchfulness?

Beckett turned up for a day recently & I thanked God I was not to live with him further: faint embers of my dislike glowed in me, ready to flap to flame. He had had an absurd *American* haircut, & looked like the top boy of his Grade whom his mates called 'Professor Radium' or 'Atom Brain'.

Tonight I believe I accompany the Strangs to the Graneeks: social life is better than private disintegration, but not than private creation.

I burst out laughing the other day on inventing a facetious misprint: 'It was soon apparent after the tea interval that Hutton & Lowson had decided to go for the buns' —

[...] I am pushing on with *Bleak House* & like it much better: also Allott's book on Gr. Greene,[3] which is not all that good so far. After the evening out last night I couldn't sleep well & awoke with the horrors – I felt a *kitten*, or some *light* thing, moving about on the bed. Needless to say, when I crept shuddering to the wall-switch, arms wrapped across my face for fear of running into a *bat*, there was *nothing in the room*. What queer things do happen at three in the morning. [...]

1 James Joyce, *Dubliners*, 'Counterparts'.
2 'Deceptions'.
3 Kenneth Allott, *The Art of Graham Greene* (1951).

6 September 1951

7 College Park East, Belfast

Dearest Forepaws,

[...] The Strangs have gone now, after getting a house. I quite genuinely enjoyed their visit. In a sense I'd sooner have them here than the Amises: Kingsley is closer to me, but he takes a lot out of me that I'd sooner were left in (as he would say himself). They made a great hit with the Graneek-Strangeways group: 'so alive'. Well, they certainly did

56

stand out like velvet rubies against Belfast, even though in the circle of Montgomery-Oldham-Amis-Larkin they are the stooges, the dogs things are tried on. They will *hate* the people here! Patsy already says that one of Colin's colleagues tells you everything the second time he meets you that he told you the first time he meets you. Not Beckett, either! [...]

15 September 1951

Florence Nightingale Hall, University of Nottingham, Nottingham, Nottinghamshire

Dearest Monica,

It is a long time since I wrote you a letter – deployed and unprompted – this *will* probably turn out to be one, at least I intend it to. As you see from the superscription 'the Conference' (dread words!) is settled in Nottingham's newest hall of residence – a tall sumptuous echoing building positively *le dernier cri*. [...]

Well, after arriving at Liverpool yesterday I hung about until the Art Gallery was open, then I rushed in shrieking 'The stonebreaker! the stonebreaker!'[1] & was shunted into a room containing the heaviest PreRaphaelite fancies – 'The finding of Jesus', 'Isabella and Lorenzo', 'Dante's first sight of Beatrice' & hundreds of others, and there was the picture I was looking for in a corner. The reproduction gives no *idea* of the exquisiteness of it. Everything is glowing & thrilling with most sensitively-rendered light & with that almost surreal sharpness of detail they were so good at. This card I sent you is merely a pale washed-out greenish memory. Anyway, having gazed at it for a long time, I went off to the Library & the curtain really descends then until now, the horrid interim being filled with librarians, jolly ladies with hearing aids, awful seedy-looking men with sidewhiskers and wet teeth who look as if they ought to be employed ghosting hack biographies of royal mistresses in the B.M., and thin young men in new chocolate brown suits & Brylcreem who resemble engineering apprentices. Everybody knows everybody else better than they know me & obviously this is the social event of the year for most of them. Just as two years ago at Birmingham my comfort & stay is K.M.'s letters – her effect on me at Birmingham was visionary: the world glowed with imparted radiance, but this time the letters are not so striking – they are *similar* to each other in a way that the extracts were not. *The* fact about them (how nasty my writing is this morning) is that they're love letters – 'all I write or ever will write will be the fruit of our love' – and so instead of a series of brilliant 'sketches' you have the whole plant, roots, stalk & flowers. In a way the 'love' doesn't get over to me – inhibited, I suppose, by knowing that it's J.M.M. who's the recipient – but alas there *is* something suspect about it – it's perfect, & therefore untrue, of the imagination only – but I long to know what you think of them: you may see them more clearly than I. But being given the whole plant makes me critical – or is it just that it's Murry at the bottom of it? If the recipient were the young Hardy, or Edward Thomas (for a good writhe one day you should read Helen Thomas's books about him), I should perhaps take it easier. I don't know. [...]

1 *The Stonebreaker*, painting by John Brett, Pre-Raphaelite.

19 September 1951

Further North than I have ever been dans ma vie – i.e. The Dunelm Hotel, Durham

My dearest M. (there was a cinema in Hull called 'The Monica'!).

Back from *a library evening*, all colleagues together – now if I'd had *this* in Leeds or Hull, it would have been much more welcome. But to start at the beginning: it seems ages since I posted your last letter among the turning Nottinghamshire leaves. Walking back from the post I picked up a pair of acorns for my buttonhole. The same day as I said I went home, & found mother hesitating on the brink of buying a house that she quite liked insofar as she likes any house – quite a nice 4-bedr. house in the same road as my sister, for £2500. I'm afraid I *offered* £2,350 & then departed, leaving the rather nasty remainder to her – I like the house, but the act of really pushing mother out on her own gnaws at my conscience. My life is so entirely *selfish* that mirages of unselfishness torment me. I long to abandon myself entirely to some-one else. The peculiarity of my character is that I never feel that there is *any* mingling – either I don't 'abdicate', & the other person loses, or I do, and I lose myself. A monstrous infantile shell of egotism, inside which I quietly asphyxiate. To read K.M.'s dreams of a shared life with Murry – this perturbs me greatly. He who shall save his life shall – or the other way round, anyway. To live quietly and complementarily with another would be extraordinary – almost impossible – I don't know, it's only the fact that I do nothing for anybody that promotes these self-searchings. Let's get back to Leeds, where I arrived a bit after seven & had a long search for a hotel that would take me, pounding past lighted Monty Burtons and suspicious loitering bobbysoxers. Eventually I got a room at The Griffin Hotel, a dingy stale huge horror of a place full of brewers' rubber mats & commercials, had a bath & went to quite a clean and comfortable bed.

The next day I viewed the library – the Brotherton Collection was superb: I had only a few minutes there and almost at random was handed one of the little books made by Branwell Bronte as a child – the Glasstown stuff, something-anger, you know & dozens of Charlotte's letters. A v. superior young man named Humphries (!) showed me round, not caring about any of it.

Then on to Hull, 1½ hrs in a railway carriage with a 75-yr-old Bradford man who'd made a fortune selling second-hand pianos. He talked *non-stop*, until nearly at Hull some young engineers got in & he switched onto them. This prevented me from reading or dozing or recuperating or anything. At Hull the hotels were full up again, & I fetched up *chez* Mrs Hunwin, in a spotless 'attractive modern home', very nicely looked after & fed (dinner bed & brkfst for 17/6), & went to see *Tom Brown's schooldays* & the Turpin fight with a traveller in detergents & a young man who works for an oilcake company. *Tom B's s* was pretty feeble. No 'No thank'ee, said George, diving his hand further into his coat tails.'

To the U. College in the morning – uncannily like Leicester – the same *aura* – the motto of the place 'Lampada ferens' – a *pun* on Ferens the magnate who set them up. Lawks! but I felt in a way reconciled to Queen's – the bright 'modern' pictures on loan from the Art Gallery etc. etc. [...]

Sept. 20 1.30 p.m. In a Cafe Thanks for letter!! Yes, I got it all right, & on the whole I think it's as well you have decided not to join me – the trip is very rushed & temporary, & the hotel business would be even more tiresome if we were seeking 2 singles. I can't say I think you'd have liked Leeds & Hull, but this town[1] pleases me quite a bit. I hardly did more than put my head into the Cathedral, being so hurried, but I noticed the plaque to Livingstone – was that the name? – mentioned by H.H.?[2] The Library is nice I must say – almost as small as U.C. Leicester – *no* science, *no* medicine, *no* law – just arts, economics & maths. And divinity of course. And of course an antiquarian library of no small order (how affected that last sentence sounds – I mean, they've a lot of old books), & the possessors of some modern stuff too. Did you know Wordsworth was an Hon. D.Litt of Durham? I didn't.

I'll post this now, and write more. *Later* House worry! for all my protestations of last night, I've advised purchase at full price – well, if it doesn't work out we *will* alter it. O dear! Love, Philip

1 Durham.
2 Hensley Henson.

6 October 1951

49 Malone Road, Belfast

Dearest Ears,

Soured by my evening meal, heavy with gas fire fumes, I take up my pen in general despondency, having about reached the limit of rewriting a first page even for me and being thereby confronted with a fresh example of my incompetence in the field my competence in which I use to excuse my incompetence in other fields – I mean, the field of CREATIVE WRITING, subject for study in the universities of America. [...]

I'm glad the Letters[1] arrived safely – I had visions of their falling into the hands of some wandering Megan or Myfanwy from the valleys. Your spegglechib strictures amused me[2] – of course that did remind me of you, quite often, & so seemed more human, though I shouldn't really use it myself, or if I had a private language it wouldn't be an infantile one. I like her quotations from songs better. But the spegglechibs, like Edinburgh, I'd thought would be things you'd *like*! How mistaken you can be – I mean I can be. And I don't think I really agree about the stories v. the personalia – I don't know, perhaps I do: but I wd sooner read her journals etc than many of the stories. However just at present I wouldn't criticise anybody who had succeeded in writing & finishing anything. I have a perfectly good novel in my head, divided into 4 parts: one told by a pushing intriguing university wife, one by a Welsh rogue on the run for helping to peddle obscene books: one by a holy fool, sister to the first; and one by an exasperated cerebrotonic Professor, husband to no. 1. The background shd not be beyond me. But I simply *can't write*. When I say 'told by' I mean more seen from the *standpoint* of. Perhaps I ought to say told by: perhaps that wd be better. 'It all began one afternoon in the Michaelmas term. Alec was in his study: I was writing out invitation cards . . .' But my primary trouble is that above all that kind of writing SICKENS me: anything I produce seems awful magazine mediocrity: I begin to long for any eccentricities of style or vision. I've always thought that expression was easy, but 'inspiration' hard, but really they're just the same.

Above all I detest any kind of cooperation with the reader, the 'you-know-what-I-mean' attitude, *knowingness* whether about the world or food or travel or housekeeping or sex or business. Yet the contrast of *fausse simplicité* is as bad: 'A woman with yellow hair came into the room and sat down in a blue chair' – no, everything has been done, and only a blind high-threshold charging insensitivity can find new ground, and that I shall never possess. Alas! It may be that I am not trying to write about what *really* interests me, like not being able to write about what really interests me for instance. O well. I had a note from Watt yesterday: the Swedes are still buying *Winter*,[3] though not in sufficient quantities to make me any money. Seven years ago – seven lean years – no, it's not seven really. 1944–5, I wrote it.

I've another letter of yours to acknowledge – a long one of Oct. 1 p.m. Your remark about footworn stones made me want to dig out and quote that not very original but heartwarming sentence of Hardy's about a worn stone step meaning more to him than scenery. What a miracle of feeling Hardy was – in a sense much rarer than a genius of expression, a particular set of responses that can never be repeated. You've no idea how it irks me to be failing to write – not only on my own account (I mean egotistic reasons) but it is so galling to be forbidden to express what these people like Hardy have shown – to be denied the privilege of saying 'Don't read me, read Hardy' or 'Read Lawrence' – the feeling that I was in the smallest way in the same line of business. God knows I've no desire to be in the same company as Dewey or Edward Edwards.

Oh & yr mention of Kipling reminded me that at Durham they showed me many Kipling mss., among them *The wish house*, a story I think good. Do you know it? And lookee here, do you *really* like Kipling? *All* Kipling? *'The makin's of a bloomin' soul'*? Really I am not quarrelling with his opinions but the 'texture', the 'feel' of his verse is as efficient & insensitive as linoleum to my nose & ears, refreshing though it initially is.

Paws.

61

Sunday. After lunch. This morning was beautiful, bland benevolent sun, the dying leaves rustling, the sky a soft blue sheet dabbled with chalky fingermarks (I mean very high clouds): I wrote home, & read *The end of the affair* (Grum Grin)⁴ which Bruce says marks the end of GG and Kingsley says marks his final advance beyond mortal criticism. Me, I think it's good, better than *The H of the m*,⁵ but spoilt & I don't mean marred – by an entire lack of proportion concerning religious matters. The novel to me is the artform in which we show *what happens* in human life. 'Miracles' do *not* happen; 'belief' does *not* happen; or if they do all we are interested in is how they affect the non-miraculous non-believing world & its characters. This book entirely breaks up into a lot of rubbishy 'miracles' that turn it all to nonsense. The idea of a jealous lover putting a private detective onto his mistress, only to find that the man she is visiting is a Hyde Park atheist who is preaching unbelief to her & thereby slowly converting her to belief in God – that's good, that's quite all right. But when she dies of pneumonia & when the atheist cures himself of a disfiguring birthmark by sleeping with a lock of her hair & praying – that is all silly religious nonsense & wrecks the book. It is all spoilt by lack of sense, lack of tact, lack of knowing simply what is literature and what isn't. It even carries a kind of whiff of Catholic miracle-literature that is most displeasing.

And talking of nonsense what a poor review of KM in the *NS & N*.⁶ Quite inarticulate with incomprehension. All this stuff about hate & rancour makes me wonder if they've got hold of the same book as I. Haven't they ever been cross? Haven't they ever let off steam? If KM is hate whatever is DHL? The review made me quite angry: surely KM was only a simple case of passionate imaginative energy & love, damaged by a typical disease & by 'loving' (not to enquire into that word more than necessary) a slippery emotional character like Murry, who played up to all her all-for-love two-children-holding-hands line of talk but was quite content to live apart from her & indeed found actual cohabitation with her a bit of a strain. It takes her a long time to realise this discrepancy but when she does she immediately starts to shorten her lines, to be independent, & this entails *curing* herself. Murry is a little obtuse about her desire for complete cure. As long as she is ill she will be dependent & dependence must be banished: therefore she *must* be *quite well*. Something along these lines wd have been better than all that stuff about Mrs Thrale, and 'sensitivity'.

More paws.

Monday – Egad! I feel more cheerful tonight. I've had another go at p. 1 and actually finished p. 2, & that's the only thing that gives me deep self satisfaction these days.[7] Maybe tomorrow I'll do p. 3 & p. 4. Oddsfish but it's not time to lie down in the dirt just yet. Last night I was out at a country doctor's house, whose charming wife wrinkled up her Presbyterian nose at the mention of *The rock pool*,[8] and today I hear the flats are promised for Thursday. We draw our kit on Wednesday night. I have got the very high rooms, with almost no windows at all.

[*drawing*]

I didn't really finish telling you that I enjoyed your previous long letter. I was struck again by the genuine quality of your pessimism: I play at pessimism but you really are a pessimist, or if that seems an unkind word – hell! shuffling through the letter I believe I have the wrong one. I mean I moan & groan but I believe everyone *else* is having a good time, & that there's a good time to be had, boys, if only you aren't cursed at birth – this is the Byronic or psychoanalytic fallacy. In my case it is shot through with periods of insensate elation such as I feel tonight.

I showed Leo Japolski over the flatlets, & he looked in the little ovens & said solemnly 'There's just room to get yr head in' which made me laugh so much I've repeated it to all and sundry.

Rereading this page I find it sounds fearfully out of character – a letter from Rupert Brooke at Rugby or even Ll. Powys at Sherborne. Someone terribly young & impulsive. I feel it is not very likely to be of comfort to you in your new and sorrowful situation, but believe me I do think of you and sympathise through every day. A new place is always disastrous, I've come to accept that as almost axiomatic, but I do hope that when some of the first shock has worn off you'll be able to spread yr wings a little, and find that the dogs don't look so lost. What can one say in such circumstances! Of course I sympathise with the mattress & the *swindling* & old Bunface. Such things strike at the very root of life, of daily living & peace of mind. All I can say is that if it doesn't seem better by end of term *think about changing for the better*. I know mother would certainly house you for the interim. It's not so bad at L'boro except in the evening, getting back. That *is* tiring.

Did you see Nicolson's[9] gibes at A.L.R.[10] in the *Sunday Times*? Good stuff. And did you see the rabbit, here enclosed? 'Chelsea Bun'.

Goodnight, dear. This is a letter I enjoyed *writing*, but it may not read very well.   Ph.

1 Of Katherine Mansfield.
2 Monica had written (4 October 1951): 'That baby manner becomes a bit too cute for me, sometimes – but in the stories, of course, that something childish about her is part of what makes them so fresh and beautiful.'
3 *A Girl in Winter*, L.'s second published novel (1947): the Swedish translation.
4 Graham Greene,*The End of the Affair* (1951).
5 Graham Greene, *The Heart of the Matter* (1948).
6 By K. John, *New Statesman*, 6 October 1951.
7 Another attempt at his never completed novel, *A New World Symphony*.
8 *The Rock Pool* by Cyril Connolly (1936) was one of L.'s favourite novels.
9 Harold Nicolson.
10 A. L. Rowse.

15 October 1951

c/o The Library, Queen's University, Belfast

Dearest,

I had better seize the chance to write for I haven't written recently & I have yr letter to acknowledge that arrived on Saturday. I suppose to some extent this will resemble the first letter of a newly wed to her married friend in the sense that what before the weekend was just a vague unformed conception – sometimes delightful, sometimes threatening – is now a precise reality, neither delightful nor threatening, and only promising better things in the well worn consolation 'You'll enjoy it more when you're better at it' – anyway, here I am, fed (though not very well) and comfortable in my pair of rooms at the top of No. 30, Elmwood Ave.

There's no chance at all of explaining all the things I've done & bought consequent to moving. Suffice it to say that Colin & Patsy saw me in and fixed the electrical things and bought a good deal of kitchen equipment and food, cooked and ate a dinner of filleted pork, and left me dizzy and untried to face Sunday.

Reflections on cooking: what can I do with a Pyrex dish & top? Can I cook meat in it? It seems to get dry when I grill it. Why do my potatoes come to pieces? No, what I think you should do is send me a simple recipe every week suitable for an evening meal that won't take more than 90 mins to prepare, eat, & wash up. I have oven, frying pan, 2 saucepans, milk saucepan, pyrex dish – & only room for 3 things to boil at once: a ring, & a long boiling grill that turns over to form a grilling grill. I grilled some chops very well, I thought, but I had to keep one for today, & it was a bit tasteless warmed up. My potatoes unwreathed themselves like something at a seance and the Spanish onion went on boiling & boiling until *that* had to kept until today too, & that was pretty tasteless. However, it seems so miraculous to be eating anything at all that I don't grumble. Not much, anyway – not at all, really, for my 2 little rooms are so charming & (fairly) quiet that I am quite proud of them. In the sitting room I have a gas fire, a radiogram sent up on approval, and – well –

(skylight!)

carpet

[...] John Wain's poems have arrived.[1] They are quite readable, intelligible, & one at least I wouldn't have minded writing, but the shadow of Empson & to a lesser extent Auden falls across the pages. Not much personal feeling about it, & a certain amount of conventional invocation of mushroom clouds (Hiroshima), Anglo-Saxon terminology, & contemporaneity (For Harpo Marx): if they haven't many virtues they at least avoid the worst faults.

As for my poems I have 3 only written since the collection. None is good, but to prove it I send one.[2] You don't have to be nice about it! I know it's quite all right as far as it goes but its fault is in not going far enough. [*at bottom of page* *having just endured typing it I'm not so sure] I'm still fighting a death-struggle with my story – pp 1–6 are now extant & consecutive: a tremendous victory! G. Greene's latest hero says he wrote his books by doing 500 words a day – breaking off regularly in the middle of a scene or description – this has inspired me to do the same: 500 words is very little, only two foolscap sides. Just think of making a living by doing that! 500 words a day would produce an 80,000 novel in 160 days – a bare half year! What bliss! How near Paradise lies to our hand, if we could but lift it! You could write the stint in oh, an hour, easily: even supposing you completely rewrote the thing you could do a book a year. [...]

Later. Five to midnight: I've had a bath and reached p. 8. My writing is sib to the writing done in asylums that the warders destroy every morning – writing for the sake of writing – to sustain a conception. As a matter of fact I suspect one trouble is that the first key-character is quite unsympathetic to me and I should do much better with any of the others. But this is a mere quibble, a get out.

How are you getting on with K.M.? I've read Ezra Pound's *Letters*, that Leavis was so nasty about, & find them not so bad as I expected, but still bad, especially the nearer you get to the present day. He amuses me by calling Robert Bridges Rabbit Britches but perhaps I am easily amused.

Kingsley writes, grumbling about 5 lectures a week & 4 teaching hours ...

Goodnight, paws ears & powder puff
Philip

1 *Mixed Feelings* (1951).
2 Typed poem, 'March Past', enclosed.

1 November 1951

30 Elmwood Ave., Belfast

Dearest Monica,

Here I am with a few hours free for once (Monday carousing, Tuesday recovering, Wednesday working & more carousing): I had fried my sausages & they spread all over the pan, & parboiled (? I mean partly boiled) some vegetables, a few of which I hooked out and mashed but which I hope will form the base of some kind of stew. And drunk a glass of milk & a cup of coffee. And played my new records – six unsuspected sides by Muggsy Spanier, Pee Wee Russell *et al.* discovered by me in *Tempo* lists, 6/6 each. I ordered them blind, & played them trembling, fearing lest they should be a fearful let down – but they weren't: not a dud among them: six sides of aggressive attacking jazz, touching greatness only here & there, but what John Hewitt would call 'good bread'. They date from Feb & March 1945: already 'history', really – wartime. My great prayer now is to have scooped Kingsley over them, wch I'm almost sure to have done.

Well, Bruce[1] has now gone, & his friend Mary, & the Strangs & I am settling back into our normal sloth. Bruce manifested his usual inability to stay still & we drove down to Dundalk on Sunday night, just over the border, ate half a sheep each, & returned very late. The meeting was successful on the whole, the Strangs serving as a buffer between Bruce & myself, absorbing a good deal of the shock of his powerful personality which so prostrates me, but it did for all that leave me somewhat discontented with my condition &c. How much stronger my friends are than I am! sheer stamina that absorbs double gins, late hours, fat cigars, and so on and so on. '*Par delicatesse, J'ai perdu ma vie*' ('By delicacy, I have lost my life') – *Verlaine*. On the whole, I most resemble Patsy Strang, who 'bores easy' and is terribly mercilessly clear sighted about whether she is enjoying herself or not, relapsing into yawns & slumber very easily. [...]

The sex boys are cut down to a very short ration this week, eh? Only divorce. Not very interesting. I don't know about 'morning sickness', naturally; so much is said these days about the concomitants of pregnancy & child-birth being entirely unnecessary figments of the modern imagination that ignorant laymen no longer believe or disbelieve anything. I think – though of course I am all for free love, advanced schools, & so on – someone might do a little research on some of the *inherent qualities* of sex – its *cruelty*, its *bullyingness*, for instance. It seems to me that *bending someone else to your will* is the very stuff of sex, by force or neglect if you are male, by spitefulness or nagging or scenes if you are female. And what's more, both sides *would sooner have it that way than not at all*. I wouldn't. And I suspect that means not that I can enjoy sex in my own quiet way but that I can't enjoy it at all. It's like rugby football: either you like kicking & being kicked, or your soul cringes away from the whole affair. There's no way of *quietly* enjoying rugby football. That is the kind of thing our panel of experts might have suggested. If we straightened out all the kinks caused by ignorance & superstition, would the resultant article be a shining paragon? And further, should we expect it to be, considering the enormous & dirty job it has to do – CARRYING ON THE RACE – any more than we can expect a front line soldier to be decorous & genteel? Now I expect you will pluck out yr fur-bound English Book of Common Prayer and repeat this entire passage from some ceremony I have never become acquainted with.

I'm not quite sure what you mean about Hilly,[2] but nothing you said ruffles me – 'course not – what I *remember* saying was that Hilly must regret marrying Kingsley so early when she sees her sister married to a respectable husband who will (very likely) go far. Patsy's reaction to this was simply 'What's the use of a respectable husband going far if you don't like him?' which is true enough, I suppose. If I did say that Hilly regretted 'missing fun' I expect every married woman does, and probably everyone else too.

There will be a library job advertised here soon – graduate £350–£500 – discourage Molly from applying! The successful candidate will be directly responsible to me & will be one of my numerous right hands: the Lord knows what kind of people we shall get. One wrote in this week from Antrim saying that she had no degree & no experience but had 'intelligence & a conscience': who does that sound like? The young Carlyle? Or had he a degree? Another one rang up this afternoon to try 'the personal approach'. I want the ability of Henry Ford plus the docility of Cinderella & the social assets of Sydney Smith.

Yesterday I cleaned my room up. I think I'll always do my sitting room on Wednesdays & my kitchen at the weekends, so you can imagine me scuffling round or hauling the Abhorrence ('Nature abhors a vacuum') after me (not an original joke, but I'll leave you to find where it comes from). Cleaning I like. Cooking (so far) I don't *much* like because the results are so disappointing. I had an awful experience with some pearl barley not long ago, that stuck to the pan and *burnt*. I nurse stews like a candidate nursing a constituency. [...]

I had a *frightful* evening out last Saturday – paper games & charades, did I tell you? And tomorrow 'Professor Boyd's for coffee' & on Saturday the Strangs to dinner, & on Sunday lunch with the Warden, & Miss Webster & Miss Leach to tea (stern daughters of the voice of God) ... My 15 pages are so much waste paper. Dear, I can't write, it's all a fantasy: a kind of circling obsession. I believe in inspiration. If I am not inspired, nothing will ever be done. If I am inspired it's all as easy as running downhill. I know, I've never written anything it wasn't a pleasure to work at. All this 500 words a day stuff is so much bilge. I feel full of blackest disappointment. Sort of, anyway. [...]

1 Bruce Montgomery.
2 Hilly Amis.

12 November 1951

30 Elmwood Ave, Belfast NI

Dearest Monica,

At present half my attention is bent upon a reading of R. Graves new poems on the 3rd progr., but they will soon be over.

Now it is over: Graves I am always prepared to like – his ideas, his practices (except all this White Goddess stuff) – but I can't stand his words, his images & properties. These were no change, except for one or two poems, *The cordwainer* & another one that might have been called *The portrait*: they sounded good, but the BBC have a habit of putting the women's speeches into women's voices, wch I don't much like. It's like having beer changed suddenly to cider while you're swallowing. [...]

Yesterday I spent most of my time with the Strangs – a fearful Sunday, spent almost entirely in the seated position, smoking, drinking, eating off plates on our knees, & hearing the radio, except for a dash out in the car. (*to exercise the dogs) At the end of the day I feel I understand Patsy's complaints about life in Belfast. She is (have you met her?) a large, pale, weak stomached girl, very nice, very charming, but a bit dependent on being with amusing people or in London, which means she spends a lot of time knitting & eating sweets which isn't good for her. She's a doctor. I mean if they go on like that when alone no wonder they hate Belfast. I only marvel that they don't hate everywhere else too. But I don't want to deride them as at least up to yesterday their presence has been a great help. I don't care for their great boisterous dogs either, very much, at all, very much, much, as Kingsley wd say. [...]

Kipling. Where I quarrel with him temperamentally is in his predilection for expressing public themes, common emotions in the sense of conventional newspaper ones; I am at odds with him in his role of 'singer of the tribe', laureate of the Empire. I dislike his subservient playing of Beetle to Kitchener's Stalky & Lloyd George's M'Turk (I know that's a bit out!) It is entirely opposed to my conception of the poet. I feel that however sincere his emotions they can all be found in the leaders of the *Daily Mail*: that further they are 'literary' ideas in that (I'd say the same of Henry James) they are not real situations he has experienced but things he has heard about or thought about & thought exciting. I am not *arguing*, or despising him – what I've said goes for a great many writers after all – but I cannot *like* any writer who hunts with the pack like Kipling. To me in time of war one had better shut up. (There is nothing to be said of war as war, unless in the Owen way – 'But cursed are dullards whom no cannon stuns'.) No, I feel about Kipling as I feel about many writers: they are not sensitive enough, their windows aren't clean, they are yarn-spinners, Wide World magazine readers and writers, the club inkslinger, the school verse cobbler who circulates poems about the unpopular masters. I know Kipling *is* sensitive personally, but he belies it in his general *persona*.

While writing all that, I noticed a *brown mouse* creep out behind the fireplace & edge along the wainscoting – not very nice! First time I've seen him. He *scuttled* back on realising he wasn't alone. This depresses me rather – Beatrix Potter's all very well in print but ... [...]

I'm glad you like – or think well of – Ll. Powys.[1] He *is* irritating – they all are – and frequently I catch myself wondering what I see in his Rationalist Press-John o'London attitudinising, but then I fall under the influence once more of his self-dramatising tricky honesty – awfully hard to pin down – his literary eye – and intensely literary humour, in a way, or at least my enjoyment of it is 'literary' (cf. R. Kipling). I always have a special liking for Letter 320 – did you notice that someone said recently that Ll. Powys' *Advice to a young poet* was a darn sight more sensible than Rilke's *Letter to a young poet*? I have a liking for 161 as well: Lulu laying down the law for the Yank society woman, or whoever she is. A *little* pompous, I agree, but my heart warms to him, doesn't yours? Perhaps not.

I think I shall try to stuff up the mouse's mode of *in*gress, & then to bed.

Yesterday Piggott lent me *The well of l.*[2] which I've just finished. 'Interesting', but rather windy & hysterical. I'd never read it before. [...]

1 L. published an introduction to Llewelyn Powys, *Earth Memories*, in a 1983 reissue. See *Further Requirements* (2002 edn).
2 Radclyffe Hall, *The Well of Loneliness* (1928).

22 November 1951

30 Elmwood Ave, Belfast

Dearest Furry-Face,

'If Shaw embeds his plums in such cake as this, then they must stay there. I cannot trouble to pick them out' – G. K. Chesterton? Robert Bridges? Thomas Hardy? Samuel Butler! Yes, indeed. I'm just reading the new *Selections* from his notebooks, & enjoying them no end. You know, for all that I am hard to please, the things I do enjoy I feed on like a grub feeding on a leaf. There are some passages about his sisters, written in such a flat glancing way that they make one want to scratch: first chop.

Tomorrow night I am on a Queen's Brains Trust – did I tell you about this? When they asked me to oblige I remembered Lang & his house-keeper: 'What's this?' 'Them's brains – you 'aven't 'ad any of them for a long time' – and if I get half a chance I shall start off by telling it. [...]

Regarding Enright, I thought he had chosen that one[1] because it showed a bit of interest outside myself – a rare thing. I don't think it well written: rather lumpy – it arose from reading Mayhew, of course, but also from a recurrent idea of Hardy's 'Tragedy is true guise, Comedy lies' – in other words that the only comfort in misery is knowing that you're not being kidded; that this is the truth. But I'd sooner he printed it than some of the others. There've been no letters from publishers.

You know more about Kipling *and* Dryden than I do, but it wouldn't have occurred to me to compare them – or to liken them to each other – as public writers, because something seems to have changed between 1680 & 1880 – Dryden seems to be speaking only to his peers,

71

the ruling gang, Kipling is – well, writing for the press, the penny (or halfpenny) press at that. A process of vulgarisation has set in & gone a long way. Therefore I find Dryden only dull, not outrageous as I sometimes do R.K. No, I haven't read *R & F*[2] – I was desperately trying to remember which one you'd recommended, but could only think of *P of P's H*[3] – which seemed to be out. As for the War, I always mark down Wells & James (among others) for their ridiculous burst of war hysteria in 1914 – have you ever read anything more sickeningly pompous than the anecdote about H.J. ringing up Marsh to enquire about British citizenship – 'Eddie, how does one – ah – do it?' I mean that was all he said. Eddie guessed what he meant, I suppose through knowing the old bore's verbal tics. And all the people who thought Shaw was antiChrist for writing *Common Sense About the War*. [...]

Did you say the Strangs have a much lonelier life or a much lovelier life? No, all right, I'm being deliberately exasperating: I suppose it was lonelier. Patsy gets v. depressed sitting indoors all day, & has to be taken to the cinema by Colin at night. She says she will have a baby in May, which in part explains it, I suppose. I hope it won't mean they'll go. But I expect they will. I didn't make a very good job of hearing the news, but she didn't seem to mind. I feel like a bald vulture sitting on a crag, while the broad tide of human life goes further & further out ... [...]

1 'Deceptions', in Enright's review of *XX Poems*.
2 Kipling, *Rewards and Fairies*.
3 Kipling, *Puck of Pook's Hill*.

27 November 1951

30 Elmwood Ave, Belfast

Dearest,

Having extricated myself from a coffee evening (10.15) I patter back upstairs. I fancy one reason for the hasty quality of my letters recently is your very agreeable remark that even my short letters have character – fatal! now I fancy myself G.B.S. who could cram as much onto a postcard as most people into a letter. It is very wrong of me & I'll stop it forthwith. No, of course your feelings don't offend me: what an idea. If they affect me in any adverse way it is precisely in that I show such poor return: I reel onwards, day in day out, living entirely off the surface of my reactions, spending too long chattering & so on, immersed entirely in the present – then when I am at last alone, I rake about among the ashes of the day and find a very meagre personality left. You are nothing like this, & in contrast I feel myself superficial, insensitive, somewhat vulgar, somewhat even, well, I won't say cruel, but inconsiderate. And as well – which takes away any sub-Byronic halo – self-deceiving in the sense that all this fine social gaiety & independence depends on not being ill, or not taking on any responsibilities material or emotional, or doing any real work, or being genuinely good to anyone at the definite expense of myself. This is all hard to describe, but true: I am cowardly, fleeing not only others but myself too. It's not a question of tender snailhood – would that it were.

[drawing of snail]

About my literary criticism – rereading it I found it gruff & a bit overbearing: I meant don't mind its being gr. & overb. Answer it by all means. I hate differences as much as you do, serious ones I mean of course.

No, stepping back to feeling for a moment, often I experience moments of violent feeling of I suppose a rather mawkish pitying sort, but instead of grappling with them as a real writer wd I avoid them, averting my eyes, thinking if anything that they are too awful to be written about: I couldn't bear to stir them up or peg them out for investigation. If I think of certain aspects of my mother's life, for instance, or of my father when he was ill, a sort of roman candle of anguish goes off in me & from which I hurry away as soon as I can. They are moments mixed with guilt at my own selfishness, and with horror because I feel they are *true*. ('Suffering is exact' – 'Tragedy is true guise'.) I feel rather as K.M. felt when she heard of her father's being robbed of his wallet – 'I hope to God people don't suffer as we think they do: if so, it's not to be borne.'

If I had said: Mother, come & live with me in Belfast, or told my father the nature & hopelessness of his disease, this facing of the facts would surely have lessened what I feel at present. I don't know. Of course it is no use worrying about these things, nor is it seemly to do the wrong thing & then claim credit for worrying about it – but that's me all over. Well, something too much of this. [...]

2 December 1951

30 Elmwood Avenue, Belfast

Dearest,

> 'You in your sheep's wool coat,
> Buttons of bone,
> And me in my furabout
> On the warm hearthstone.'

Know this little verse, & whence it comes? W. de la M. I like furabout.

You have been much in my mind this evening for having laboriously cudgelled out 4 sides for Peter[1] (don't feel like writing today OR ANY OTHER DAY). I had to search for the address you gave me, & this entailed rereading all your November letters. Only when I'd reread them all twice & put the whole lot in order since June did I remember your Willie Winkie card propped on the mantelpiece. Of course it was on that.

The third thing to remind me of you is D. Wordsworth's *Journal* which I was moved to look into tonight (do you hate the phrase 'dip into'? Sheep dip. I never use it myself: if anyone from Desmond MacCarthy downwards says a book is good for 'dipping into' I know (1) the book is no good (2) the speaker is a fool (3) the speaker *never* reads the book. 'Browse' I'll speak of some other time); I think it's hard to read such things without being shamed by the observation and quickness of spirit. To my mind K.M. is right about her. If I have any wish in life it would be to 'express' or 'render' life as I have known it, but it is such an enormous task I admire more & more people who achieve the smallest success in that line. '*[October] 17th, Friday.* A very fine grey morning. The swan hunt. Sally working in the garden. I walked round the lake between $\frac{3}{4}$ past 12 and $\frac{1}{4}$ past one ...'

I suppose I could express my day in similar terms, but it has not felt a very 'holy' day – I missed shaving and changing my sheets, but I wrote home, did my laundry, made lunch (macaroni cheese & cauliflower). In the afternoon I went out to the Strangs' house to fetch my bicycle where it has been nearly all this term: they were out, but the garage was open & I cleaned my bike & rode it home. The air was chilly, growing misty, & the sun was setting about four in a great orange mass. Well-wrapped-up children tottered home clutching little hymnbooks.

74

After coming in & having tea I cleaned the kitchen, wch tired me rather, even though I didn't polish the floor, cleaning the stove instead. Then I fell asleep after hearing a Mozart symphony – the 'Haffner': good for once, I thought – scorching in front, freezing behind. The draught in this room is shocking! After waking I wrote to Peter, & here I am. I think I'll stop now & make Horlicks – it's 10.20, & there's a programme containing some Handel at 10.30 p.m. – Heard it now. They announced it as Bach, but then played Handel. I really can't say I noticed the mistake: I thought it was very 'free' for Bach, but I didn't recognise the water of the pure fount as I ought to have done. Talking about music, I suppose you didn't hear the 3rd art of the Am. negro progr. this week on the blues? I heard it twice. Very interesting. I expect McLeod heard it, & did not leave you unenlightened. Rereading all yr recent letters made me realise how many points I leave unanswered – really I should start a short-answer tailpiece to my letters when the highflown stuff is finished. But just now my eyes are starting to ache a bit & I think I had better let this lie till tomorrow, beastly Monday. My successor – no, I mean my right hand – will be either a rolling-stone Haileyburian or a Scotch girl. We interview them on Dec 12 I believe. The girl is favourite.

O & in case you wonder if I saw the S. Africans yesterday, the answer is yes. Ulster played very well, & during the first half looked almost equal, but were hopelessly outweighted. But right to the end they'd have scored if given a chance, & they kept rolling these huge van so and sos & Pieters and Pauls over like so many butterfat rabbits. Better than the Scots! And talking of Scots I grinned at yr picture of Ivory, rocking away.

Goodnight!

Next day Now it's about 24 hours later and I have just wasted an evening, entirely wasted it, to my great annoyance: I mentally pick up ideas for poems, and turn them about, but 'poems are written with words',[2] and no words come. Nor have I written any letters. The rain's fallen all day: I have taken it pretty easy at work, but stayed late. My reading has been in & around Samuel Butler recently: I wonder if you'd like him – I suppose insofar as he is an ancestor of the E. M. Forster school you wouldn't like him, but I do, in my uncomprehending reasonless way. There is a little book by P. N. Furbank that's very good in its way, but S. Butler's *Notebooks* are *le vrai homme*. I expect you read the profile on Forster in *The Observer*? My Sundays are complicated by Alfreda Leach, a Scotch R.C. Welfare Officer, who genuinely likes doing things for people, *will* bring in some Sunday papers on the way back from Mass & leave them outside my door (not always the right ones) – this means I have to pay her during the day (& probably stay to tea) & *give her the papers back*, or some of them, which annoys me as I like reading the papers up till about Wednesday, and anyway I wrap things up in them. The Sunday papers are the only ones I get & so my *entire political education* depends on them & being able to read them at leisure. How hard it is, to be forced to the conclusion that people should be, nine tenths of the time, *left alone*! – when there is that in me that longs for absolute commitment. One of the poem-ideas I had was that one could respect only the people who knew that cups had to be washed up and put away after drinking, and knew that a Monday of work follows a Sunday in the water meadows, and that old age with its distorting-mirror memories follows youth and its raw pleasures, but that it's quite impossible to love such people, for what we want in love is release from our beliefs, not confirmation in them. That is where the 'courage of love' comes in – to have the courage to commit yourself to something you don't believe, because it is what – for the moment, anyway – thrills you by its audacity. (Some of the phrasing of this is odd, but it would make a good poem if it had any words ...)

Hope you enjoy the *Messiah*. They are doing it here somewhere. I look forward to hearing your *Largo*. Pardon short letter –

loving thoughts. P.

1 Peter Oldham.
2 Mallarmé: 'Ce n'est point avec des idées que l'on fait des vers: c'est avec des mots.'

11 January 1952

30 Elmwood Avenue, Belfast, N.I.

Dearest Monica,

At this very moment I am listening to *Man and superman*, but that has no connection of any kind with the fact of my starting to write to you. No, I haven't heard it all the way through tonight; but I had about the last third still unheard, as since 8.15 I have been listening to all the long winded speeches. I do think it ought to be played *faster*: old Esme Percy ought to be joggled up and down until he abandoned his infuriating up & down slow motion over-the-waves intonation. I think one of my hells would be to sit through a two-part play, enacted by Esme Percy and Robert Newton. Groo. My throat constricts with an involuntary motion at the thought, at the very thought.

The weather here is horrible: there's a pair of large damp patches on my ceiling that the Buildings Officer says he has given orders about, but they go on growing, and nobody comes to see about them.

Now the final agonised explosion 'Talking!' has sounded and the play's over. Now I can think more consecutively. If I dare say anything about it, don't you find it bubbling over with creative good humour? I think that's one of its most attractive features: it is such a good tempered play, sunny & energetic & extravert. Especially as it is so full of generalisations, making everything simple and not requiring further consideration. To me it's the very best of Shaw, free from all his faults, his sort of inverted Barrie-ism, by which I mean characters like Candida; verbal sadism; historico-political argufying; and the I'm-giving-you-my-own-naturally-very-original-but-extremely-penetrating-interpretation-of-a-historical-figure stuff. Along with it I should put *Pygmalion*, *The apple cart*, and *You never can tell*. Plays I should put at the furthest remove are *Heartbreak house*, *Caesar & Cleopatra*, *The devil's disciple*, and *Getting married* (wooch!), apart from mere sillinesses like *Androcles & the lion* and *Too true to be good*. Oh & right up alongside the first lot I put *Village Wooing*. Am I boring you? This shall cease straightway, but Shaw pleases me inordinately on his day.   I shouldn't really be writing as it is nearly midnight, but your letter today seemed especially pleasing. Thank you for it. Possibly at the bottom of this impression was your long acclamatory passage of me as a food & wine man – & woman man – wch it never occurred to me not to take seriously until you said not. Of course it bears little or no relation to the facts of life, but then nor do my visions of myself. I was trying to think of the number of women who had been in my rooms alone, & apart from Miss Leach the Welfare Officer, Mrs Farrell the caretaker, & Patsy I can't think of any. Talking of the last-named I heard from Colin this morning that their return wd be delayed by Patsy's having suffered a miscarriage. I tell you this to close the record, so to speak: I'm very glad I've told no one else except K.W.A. I'm really extremely sorry. She will probably be a lot more miserable this term than last – and that's saying something. What a difficult letter of sympathy it is to write, to be sure. [...]

4 February 1952

30 Elmwood Ave, Belfast

Dearest,

I feel full of brightness now, having read J. Isaacs' *Twentieth century literature* tonight – he calls himself the Counsel for the Defence; God! reading him is like having a great dog come bounding up &, putting its paws on your shoulders, lick you all over. Everyone is very, very fine & wonderful. Everything is going to be all right. They were the Broadcast Talks ... 'nuff said. Though I am cheered by some things ('1910–1930 may well become known as The Age of Lawrence') I am depressed by others ('Philip Toynbee's prose is full of the evocative precision of poetry') & am aware that although he apologises for not doing more than mention I. Compton Burnett, L. H. Myers, Henry Green, André Malraux *etc etc* he does not even apologise for *not* mentioning any Powys. A queer book. I have only read it very sketchily & even patchily, but I did find it strange that he should insist that this is *The age of Anxiety* while equally insisting on its eminence or even preeminence in imaginative creation. I'm sure it's in your Library. If not, you could do yourself a bit of good by proposing it.

Keep Ll.P. if you like him – this is a poor situation to put you in, I know; I mean I shan't mind if you keep him or not: the only thing I *shall* mind is if you return him if you want to keep him, or vice versa. It's a spare copy I picked up, knowing it would come in useful. I am delighted that you find something in him to like, & think on the whole you have hit on a fact about him when you say he will not be bothered to think. Only I'm not quite sure whether you mean by 'think' describe his emotions accurately & in detail, or 'assess the value of his emotions and build from them a set of values and a philosophy'. I have forgotten all Wordsworth's 'thought', but my prevailing impression at the time was that it was unsatisfactory: that arose I thought because he ventured beyond his brief. We know what we feel, & what sets off our feeling, but no more. In these days it is not so easy to be a literary philosopher, and it must be remembered that Ll. P. was a materialist, he simply did not credit feelings with any further significance than their pleasantness or unpleasantness. The idea of explaining the vividness of a child's sensations by the fact that it was 'fresh from God' would have seemed unnecessary to him: it is simply part of being a child. A second great point about him is that he is a great *dramatiser* – dramatiser & self-dramatiser. Thus he is more concerned with making his effect than with ferreting out the truth. His religious beliefs really boil down to 'If any supernatural world existed, our senses would inform us of it', but what exquisite gusto he has in propounding them, all the gusto of an invalid clergyman's son hallooing for roistering blasphemy. On the other hand he is far from insincere: he has always in mind the great touchstone of *Death*, & consequently life is always judged as how far it fits us, or compensates us, for ultimately dying.

But enough of this. 11.5 & I must to bed. I get up at 7.30 these days, & write from 9–10, or 8.45–9.45. Starts the day better – if I manage it.

I was very sorry you felt ill & lonely, and can only say that your well-bred courage showed through particularly strong. Perhaps that isn't a thing to covet acc. to your lights, but it is a remarkable thing about you. I have kept Lapinova[1] out & look at her occasionally. Very nice. I hope by now the snow has gone, & your 'trembling spine', & all the other miseries. The other night I started up, seized (in the dark) my water-carafe, & emptied it over my pillow, all in one pure reflex movement. Truly in sleep one's soul walks strange escarpments. [...]

Tuesday. Toothache, curse it. I went to my dentist yesterday & he again dressed my 2 bad teeth, a little more permanently, but one has taken it badly and has ached all today. I can see myself losing it – necrosis – sepsis – infection – poisoned while he slept, etc. There's no nerve left in it so I don't quite know what can be hurting. But it augurs ill. If my teeth hurt I always have to lose them. This one started by aching, a year ago nearly.

Bruce wrote today, saying that his last book had fetched only half the normal dividends, & he is going to have to pull up his socks.

Also I have a cold starting, gibber gibber gibber. But this savours of Sam. Butler's letters to Miss Savage, him giving her details of his mild asthma & she refraining from mentioning her incurable tumour. I hereby banish all complaints.

Wain sends me what Ll. Powys wd call a 'foolishly facetious' letter. I find that Ll. for all my belittling of his mental equipment is good at such condemnatory phrases – 'insincere worldlings, religious fanatics, or unpleasant moralists'. I love that highly-dignified letter (p. 164–5). [...]

Meat is shorter here. The butchers are actually marking our books now, & I only got 2/- of pork on Saturday. Half of that I spoilt too. Today I had a sudden 'mad feeling' to emigrate down South – live on my name – get any old job – turn RC – holidays in Wickla – G'day yer Rivrence! – incompetence, poverty & porter. But I shan't of course. No fear!

Hope it is warmer for you, & that you're feeling better.

Lovingly, Philip.

1 Figurine of rabbit.

15 February 1952

30 Elmwood Ave, Belfast

Dearest Poll,

With my instinct for effect I select a piece of this funeral paper to write you a short note on – not altogether meretriciously, for I have been listening to the Funeral Description[1] & remaining within doors, though in no very religious frame of mind as these public occasions always lift my hackles a trifle. But one is impressed in spite of oneself: the quiet simple man I think of as the King gets submerged in a majestic orgy of emotion – there's no other word. The broadcast from Paddington, where the Processional and the Royal Trains were being filled & pipe bands and Guards played alternately, became almost unbearable. Partly it was so *slow*, so harrowingly *slow*. Partly because of the music: after some religious piece by Bach and *The flowers of the forest* we had to endure – during the interval between the departure of the train of guests & the departure of the Royal or Coffin Train – the Coldstream Guards playing Handel's *Largo* slowly & extendedly. Proud though I was that dear Handel should appear at such a time I did not know where to look & was thankful I wasn't there in any responsible position. Then the train departed to the Funeral March, & the commentator. Who had been giving. A very slow. And not very well-phrased. Commentary. At about this speed. Said unexpectedly something like 'And so. The Royal Train. Leaves the station. Bearing away from London. For ever. King George VI.' The sudden simplicity of the last three phrases can only be appreciated if you had chafed earlier at the many cushion-words & kennings which littered his descriptions. If you heard it you will I'm sure agree with me.

Every sentence began 'And so ...' 'And as ...' 'And now ...' [...]

In a way I rather wish I had been seeing the papers this week: but I haven't. I asked one fanatical Orangeman photographer if he'd seen the headline *Duke of Windsor at the Bier*. 'Dad ye see *art ur arn*?' he enquired with hideous emphasis. He doesn't like Edward. [...]

1 Funeral of George VI, who died on 6 February.

12 March 1952

30 Elmwood Ave, Belfast

Dearest Loppit,

[...] Set-back! No berths from Dublin – Liverpool on the Saturday! I think we had better stay here. I'll try to get berths back to L'pool from Belfast. After all, there is plenty to see in N. Ireland. And we can always rest! like Vanya & Sonya, is it, at the end of *Uncle Vanya*. On Sunday I had the most thrilling experience of seeing, from the coast between Cushendun & Fair Head (get your atlas out! [*drawing*]), the Mull of Kintyre, Scotland, a great paw of rock couchant in the still evening water, absurdly near. I wonder if we could manage to see that? It is one of the most thrilling sights I have seen here. [...]

Dear, though I feel sure I wrote between 19/2 & 5/3 I have been remiss enough since. It is partly getting over Jimmy's visit[1] – how I do agree about *time to oneself*: it is *necessary*, you are quite right: if I am deprived of solitude, I become fatigued, famished, tense, like a man deprived of an essential element of diet. I dislike saying so, because it sounds like a 'line' – 'Man can live 3 days without bread, but not one without poetry' – gibber gibber gibber, gobble gobble gobble. Recently I have not had time even to go shopping. Also my novel has broken down, & is finished in the kaput sense, & this causes me the usual depression. My writing has nothing to do with literature. It is a perfect instance of a mental mania, a private raree-show of humiliation & despair.

Thursday – And at that I fell asleep in my chair, a frequent occurrence these days, until Bradley awoke me to come & join a merry party in his room, which I hurriedly declined, & hopped into bed, reading Auden's

Nones. Also yesterday I read *Cheri* and *The last of Cheri* by Colette, & have since been fired with transient longing to be a gigolo & live on strawberries & Pommery & wear silk shirts. Hey ho! [...]

1 Following James Sutton's visit on this occasion, L.'s letters to Sutton almost ceased, after a friendship that began when they were at school together in Coventry in the 1930s and continued regularly by letter until this point.

23 March 1952

30 Elmwood Ave, Belfast

Dearest,
[...] Well, I expect you are safely at home now: I didn't tell you much about Dublin when I was there, did I: the only *new* thing I saw was the Zoo & Phoenix Park, & in the Zoo the only things worth notice were three tall, cool, tan-maculate giraffes, and two jolly sloth-bears, who put on a comical catch-as-catch-can turn for us.

That was on St Patrick's Day: *no drink sold*, and a dreary procession trailing through the town of biscuit wagons, Guinness wagons, tinned vegetable wagons, Electricity Board wagons – all the paraphernalia of a little Republic. There *was* a wagon belonging to the Anti-Partition League, with four little chaps being clubbed steadily by six R.U.C. boys, but though this was being paralleled exactly at the time in Derry nobody apparently paid it much attention.

Returning, Wain occupied my attention for the rest of the week: dear me, how you would have disliked him. A curious personality, with whom it's hard to feel you are holding a serious conversation at any time. He remembered you & said he liked you – this because he happened upon that photograph of you in the British Restaurant: he liked the picture too. [...]

25 March 1952

30 Elmwood Ave, Belfast

[...] John Wain was *funny*, but it was hard to know when, if ever, he was being serious. He was loud in approbation of Empson, whose latest book I am now trying to read. *I* chiefly liked his approbation of my attitude to my gas fire – something for me to tell you about. 'Pshaw! My Ga-ard! Well, Christ!' I do feel somewhat surprised at his success, if it is at all as he describes it, because he seems to me to be impressive only insofar as it must take enormous sang froid to behave, act, speak, look & dress like he does. My eye slid over him when I met the boat – I thought he was one of the crew. [...]

8 July 1952

30 Elmwood Ave, Belfast

Dearest,

Slowly life returns to normal. Slowly fatigue passes from the bones & sinews. The lungs breathe normally again. The light goes off at 11.55 p.m. Meals are taken at customary times. I can even consider mending & cleaning again. No, there is no one like our K.[1] – mister-my-friend – for prostration & etiolation: no one like him for irritating me either: why doesn't he carry a nail file? a fountain pen? notepaper? stamps? since he appears to need these things daily? Well, well. Today I haven't shaved. Tomorrow is Graduation Day: a day off. *Splendid*. I shall devote it to cleaning both my rooms. [...]

1 Kingsley Amis had been to stay with L. in Belfast.

24 July 1952

30 Elmwood Ave, Belfast

[...] Seriously, I think it is a *grave fault* in life that so much time is wasted in social matters, because it not only takes up time when you might be doing individual private things, but it prevents you storing up the psychic energy that can then be released to create art or whatever it is. It's terrible the way we scotch silence & solitude at every turn, quite suicidal. I can't see how to avoid it, without being very rich or very unpopular, & it does worry me, for time is slipping by, and nothing is done. It isn't as if anything was gained by this social frivolity. It isn't: it's just a waste. [...]

21 August 1952

30 Elmwood Ave, Belfast

Dearest,

I feel like some 'case' in a social worker's case-book: 'Mr. L., of university education, was living in one room, where he cooked, ate, washed and slept.' Next door, a sea of rubble obscures the once-bright boards; finger-marks stand out black on the walls: to the south stands the gaunt deal-wood frame of the window, with tarpaulin over it, wind & rain doing their worst. It seems hard to think that it will be neat, clean and furnished again. But when it is, I can see that it will be marvellously elegant. I'll send a photograph when it's finished: but after the carpenter comes the plumber, and after the plumber the plasterer, and after the plasterer comes the glazier, & finally comes the painter – that is the Trade Union's dancing-figure. In all, it will take about three weeks. [...]

11 September 1952

30 Elmwood Ave, Belfast

Dearest,

Tired! Wow! I am in bed, after an evening of polishing and furniture-moving. I'm not back in the living-room yet, but I've put the carpet down & moved in most of the books. And set up the candles, ashtrays, cat & bears. At the heel of the hunt they repainted the whole room – good of them, don't you think? so I needn't have worried about all the finger marks. The curtains will be the big delay. [...]

I'm just finishing a course of revising Kingsley's novel[1] – not word for word, but telling him what I think is wrong with it, & scribbling rude comments in the margin. He is prepared to go to endless trouble, & I think if he could get it accepted he'd die happy, but he has little instinct for writing once he gets outside a sentence. And he has no idea how people talk: in the margin I scribble repeatedly 'People don't talk like this', 'Ladies don't use words like this', 'I have never heard people talk like this'. It is however full of 'laughs', and would amuse many people – not unlike Anthony Powell. [...]

1 Revision of what eventually became *Lucky Jim*.

14 September 1952

30 Elmwood Ave, Belfast

[...] I feel a bit sad today, really because my mother has returned home & I know she's alone: really it gives me a most unpleasant twinge to think of her taking her dinner from the oven and eating it alone, because I know how she hates it. She is pre-eminently a person who will do things for others but not for herself: alone, she enjoys nothing. Well, if you feel like that about it, why not do something to help her? Why don't you? Why don't you? Why don't you? Part of sick life's antidote my foot. Unsavoury humbug. Unsavoury humbug. Unsavoury humbug.

Monday. End of a hard day's work. Book slinging most of the time, with short spasms of being directing intelligence to six or seven Ulster labourers. I'm glad, by the way, that you are fighting the cause of animals in your circle of life. I talked to Kingsley about the animals Hilly keeps, & she promised not to keep anything that cannot fend for itself, but I don't know. So many of their things just *die*, & I'm sure they shouldn't. Hilly is an ass, too.

Have you read *Antigua, penny, puce*?[1] I'm just reading it again & it strikes me as extraordinarily clever, & funny too in a gentle way. [...]

Well, dear, unless anything crops up I don't suppose I shall write again. Lancaster Castle station at twenty three minutes to 8 on the morning of Saturday September the Twentieth. Look for one pale and pinched from labour, ay and o'er-watched too, painfully so, for the channel of our blessed St George beats monstrous high at the season's turn, like to toss foolhardy mariners to the moon. Mittens will be worn, & mouse-skin purses carried; marmots will be met (but only of the right sort) ... Philip

1 Novel by Robert Graves (1936), one of L.'s favourites.

9 October 1952

30 Elmwood Ave, Belfast

[...] Yes, it was a nice holiday, wasn't it? Dominated I think by Sawrey & all its associations,[1] and none the worse for it, either. I don't know what I shall remember clearest – perhaps the train journey from W'mere & yr imitations of Mrs Luttrell![2] or perhaps strolling about by Ullswater, until those frightful thudding feet came up behind us. I'm so glad you enjoyed it all. I wanted you to, for your life ... no, I don't mean yr life, I mean you need a holiday, more holiday than that, even, but I wanted you to enjoy that much, at least.

I really am going to meet Forster: I thought I shouldn't, but apparently the old boy E.M.F. is staying with remembered my name & I am bid to John Hewitt's at 8 tomorrow. Shall I ask him if he's a homo? It's the only thing I *really* want to know about him, you see. I don't even care why he packed up writing.

Dear, I must seem very pompous & huffy, with my portentous hints and veiled criticisms of you, & I wonder you are so patient. It's nothing very frightful, but I feel so loth to arrogate the superiority to the thing criticised that every critic, even temporarily, assumes, that I'm always too shy or ashamed to say what I think. It's nothing very dreadful! only I feel that the best person to say it is the person on p. 57 of *The pie*³ – some very motherly & matter of fact old cat, talking to its kitten – not me. It's simply that in my view you would do much better to revise, drastically, the amount you say and the intensity with which you say it. You are vaguely aware of this already, aren't you? You say you 'chatter like a jay' – do you remember saying that, standing on a corner of Clarendon Park Road, after closing time, before catching your bus? – and that you talk 'tediously & unnecessarily': I don't say that exactly: what I do feel is that you've no idea of the *exhausting* quality of yourself in full voice. Perhaps I am unduly (morbidly?) sensitive, but it does affect me just in that way – I feel quite unable to answer, just that I want to go and be quiet somewhere. No doubt you can recall times when I seemed a bit grumpy at Grasmere! Well, this sounds very nasty in cold blood, but it's *not* meant nastily: I mention it only because I'm getting to the point where ... well, where my refusal to say that I do feel this *very strongly* is constituting a major falsity. I know you don't mean it (whatever it means) – I thought for years that you did – & I think you've never emerged from the time when you either talked all the time or sat dumb; I also think that you may come from a noisier house than mine. But for all that, I *do* want to urge you, with all love & kindness, to *think* about *how much* you say & *how* you say it. I'd even go so far as to make 3 rules: One, *Never* say more than two sentences, or *very rarely* three, without waiting for an answer or comment from whoever you're talking to; Two, abandon *altogether* your harsh didactic voice, & use *only* the soft musical one (except in special cases); & Three, don't do more than *glance* at your interlocutor (wrong word?) once or twice while speaking. You're getting a habit of *boring* your face up or round into the features of your listener – *don't* do it! It's most trying.

You notice I don't say anything about *what* you say – I don't mind about that – these simple points of technique are what I want to urge on you, because I've thought about it for ages & finally've decided that my feelings are abstractly just & not a personal foible. I think you'd get on *much better* all round if you took yourself in hand in this direction. To be honest, I don't think other people mind it as much as I do – they may not want to get a word in edgeways as much as I do! – but they mind it *a bit*, I'm sure, and I mind it *strongly*. Oh dear, how rude & embarrassing all this is. I write it instead of saying it, as I suppose I ought, because I really don't think I *could* say it out loud to you, unless drunk. Please don't *mind* what I say. Look at the picture on p. 57, & imagine she is saying it to you. And don't think I'm making a mountain out of a molehill – I mean I *know*, that as a fault, it's not at all serious: hardly a *fault* at all – a *surface* fault – but that does mean that one's tripping over it all the time. Anyway. To things pleasanter.

I have returned a set of coupons to Vernon's, so when I win we'll go sailing over the sea with a £5 note etc. My curtains are to be delivered tomorrow. There's nothing much else in my mind to worry about, except the general feebleness of my scribblings on reperusal. Poor old captain.

I wonder if you've read any of the Sassoons? If so I do hope you like them. I may have overpraised them, but the 'colours' are very pale in them and not instantly striking. Perhaps you find *him* uncongenial?

Bruce and Kingsley wrote. You heard about the Coronation Ode, didn't you? Like Hookham & Neustadt collaborating – well, no, that's unfair. I wonder if it will ever be performed. Goodnight!

Friday. Your letter this morning ... I wish you weren't goin' away this weekend, because unless I don't send you anything *at all* this will be what greets you on your return, & it's hardly cheering – I've just read it through & think it sounds priggish. But hearkee, I mean it wery pleasant and kindly, not snappish, & you may regard it as a lengthy conversation peppermints if you can. ...   Well, I will send this. Many kisses, yus yus. Fine day here.   Philip.

1 L. and Monica had been on holiday in the Lake District, visiting Sawrey, Beatrix Potter's village, full of pleasant Peter Rabbit and other associations for them.
2 Wife of Claude Luttrell, Lecturer in Old and Middle English at Leicester University.
3 Beatrix Potter, *The Pie and the Patty-pan*.

12 October 1952

30 Elmwood Ave, Belfast

Dearest,

I'm stunned by a huge lunch, a joint for once, cauliflower & potatoes, & tinned grapes, and it's a very wet day: do I think correctly of you bashing back through the rain in bus & railway train? I feel curiously glad that you live at S on S [Stourport on Severn] – to think you are within the orbit of the Midland Red & the unemphatic country of my

early years – I thought S on S very nice, what I saw of it, & the river & pub *thrilling* – so I remember it! Is it nearly right? It's supposed to be night, with the lamp burning ... 'Crouched in the ditch, I felt the Growler's fingers tighten on my arm. Sharpened by the nearness of water, there came the sound of a clinking chain.

'He's a-lockin' up! whispered the Growler.' ... Wilkie Collins? Yurs yurs yurs.

I met old Sell-Soul,[1] as you call him, on the Frida.[2] Sprawled on a sofa, an untidy aged Billy Bunter with a toothy grin, he received us gracefully in rotation, about 10 or 15 minutes each. In my case it was a series of gambits declined on both sides: Cambridge Gambit Declined, Nature of Inspiration Gambit Declined, Light Fantastic Gambit Declined, Have You Read My Book Gambit Declined, and finally silence; from him, Forrest Reid[3] Gambit Declined, Are You Writing Gambit Declined, Yours Must Be A Very Interesting Job Gambit Double-Declined, and finally silence. He wore a boot on one foot and a shoe on the other. I suppose I could have done better, but I always feel about talking to famous men that it doesn't matter what you say to them, like leaving litter on Everest: in any case it is up to them to be gracious & witty to ignorant youth. (I didn't ask him what I wanted to!) [...]

1 E. M. Forster.
2 One of L.'s habitual 'Ulster' spellings, mimicking the pronunciation.
3 Northern Irish writer (1875–1947), some of whose work L. admired. He was a 'boy lover'.

16 October 1952

30 Elmwood Ave, Belfast

My dear,

Well, I think you took all my uncouth and loud-mouthed criticism very gently: I really hadn't thought that someone could be *not* silent through shyness: mine was always the other kind – at least one did not draw attention to oneself that way, which was all I asked. [...]

Do my friends talk more than I do? I suppose they do. No, it's not *talking* I mind at bottom: it was the sort of laying-down-the-law tone with never a chance to reply that grated on my nerves, coupled with a feeling that what you were saying with such exaggerated insistence wasn't *worth* the effort you were putting into it – that I think anyone would notice. However, I've said my say and shall say no more; and having said it doesn't mean that I think I am a Crufts prizewinner – Elmwood Emperor III – while you are only an alley tabby, good for mousing. Rather the reverse if anything. As I said, yours is only a fault in technique. My faults are weaknesses and dishonesties. As for my friends, good Lord, no one minds hearing his friends denigrated a bit. [...]

The Strangs came plunging back – nowhere to live – dogs to the kennels – and stayed with the Davies – George is a fearful Scots bore & Elspeth won a prize in *the Observer* Christmas story competition – & paints.[1] Patsy says their house is *filthy*. I pressed her: 'As filthy as Kingsley's?' 'Kingsley's is an *Ideal Home* in comparison!' But then one of Patsy's guests once told Colin (when drunk) that he thought the M.O. of H.[2] should see *their* house ... so you see we are getting pretty low. A, who is filthy, thinks C is filthier than B. How filthy is C? However, they are on the verge of getting a flat now. They seem less fun than they did. Hum! [...]

1 George Davie was senior lecturer in Philosophy at QUB; Elspeth was a writer of short stories.
2 Medical Officer of Health.

23 October 1952

30 Elmwood Ave, Belfast

[...] Isn't it strange, I had a premonition of worry when I took the envelope from the rack: because you don't usually write for Thursday,

I suppose. Well, anyway, I'm glad you wrote – worries are always better shared, especially such formidable ones;[1] but *really*, I must say I think the chances are *extremely* slender & remote of there being anything in the air. To my certain knowledge I was never within a mile of endangering you, and it's only a disinclination to tempt fate & the fact that I don't know much about such things except generally that prevents me from saying flatly that it's out of the question – you do understand that I *personally* think it *is*. I'm not surprised you feel sick, with all the worry & gins and salts. Surely it's not unknown to miss a time? especially if you are worrying about missing a time? Now please don't torment yourself any more: just go on ordinarily, & give up all these specifics & things. I'm sure it's quite unnecessary. Keep me posted, of course, & talk about it in letters if you want. Patsy of course would be more authoritative, but I'm sure you don't want her to know. [...]

1 Monica feared she was pregnant – but not for long.

24 October 1952

30 Elmwood Ave, Belfast

Dearest Bun,
I'm so glad you're out of your worry! So now you can go about your lavender-drying with a cheerful heart. [...]

5 November 1952

30 Elmwood Ave, Belfast

Dearest rabbit,
Well, I am sitting in a somewhat collapsed condition – 9 a.m. – I got up at 7.30, simply because I was awake. With the 9 a.m. news has come the news of Eisenhower's victory – I *knew* he'd do it. The era of American generosity is at an end. With a military man in charge we are one move nearer the next war. This is Old Larkin's

Almanac, prophecies seen through the bottom of an empty glass, like Gubbins. [...]

Evening. Ah, more peace now. I have finished up some curry & eaten bread & cheese. Today I spent mostly lettering a large notice – very badly – but it was an enjoyable change. (Just at present I am listening to the recorded voices of Stevenson & Eisenhower. Interesting. It's a somatonic victory, a cerebrotonic defeat – or, cutting out the jargon, a victory for the short fat noisy men over the tall thin brainy ones – & confirms my forecast that U.S.A. is tired of trying to be civilised, & is due for a period of barbarity. I must say I think war is a bit more likely on account of it all.) [...]

I'm reading *Jude* myself too now. It confirms my memory of it as a spare keen book – very little turgidity or Gothic. The other thing that strikes me is how old DHL might have sketched some episodes. I'd forgotten the leader writer. 'Sue Bridehead, of course, thrills from the thoracic, sympathetic centre. Her stunt is to act directly on the nerves of any man unfortunate enough to be on her wavelength, such as her cousin Jude (ah, those close relations, like Poe & his Ligeia!), or the poor devil of a consumptive she frays into the grave. The trouble with such women is not that they are badly-disposed, but that they *cannot* act from the lumbar ganglia, the dark *sightless* solar plexus. It is meaningless to them, even antipathetic. And if you force them to it, they set their teeth and send out waves of sheer hatred to numb and balk you, as poor old Phillotson found out ...'[1] Well, I see my love of mimicry has wasted another half page, but there's any amount of that tack in *A study of Thomas Hardy*, & I must say it still colours my judgment. You see the story *as* a story. To me it still has the aura of a Lawrence tract – I suppose I must be practically alone in feeling that! What did Hardy think of Sue? To me, she forfeits a good deal of claim to sympathy by her coquetting about with emotions (e.g. the walking down the aisle with Jude before her marriage to P.) but skedaddling whenever there's a hint of being taken seriously. All this no-you-mustn't-love-me-well-perhaps-if-you-like-you-may stuff. And I presume Hardy foresaw that she would. I wonder what he thought he was doing exactly. [...]

1 L. is parodying D. H. Lawrence. Lawrence's *A Study of Hardy* appeared in his *Phoenix* (1936).

8 November 1952

30 Elmwood Ave, Belfast

[...]

Sunday night – No: it wasn't that I couldn't have written, but it wouldn't have been much of a letter. Now it is twenty five to eleven, & I am by accident listening to a recital of poems of bereavement by Margaret Rawlings – O dear! she is reciting C. Rossetti's *Echo* – 'Speak low, lean low'; dear me, & now a passage from *The woodlanders* – what good does this sort of thing do? Do you think that even C. Rossetti, even Hardy, should be read over the radio at times like this? What good does it do? I sincerely hope my mother isn't listening. And now *Remember me when I am gone away*. Do you think such orgies are cathartic? Or just a tearing of the sutures? (Now Bishop King's *Exequy* or *Obsequy* or whatever it is.) To me, since death is the most important thing about life (because it puts an end to life and extinguishes further hope of restitution or recompense, as well as any more experience), so the expression of death & the effects of death are the highest planes of literature (now *Death be not proud*) and should not be lightly loosed upon the populace. (Now *I think continually* ...) I know it might be said that death is about as important as the final whistle in a football match: that (finish with Vaughan – *sweet peas sits crowned with smiles* – & our Lord Jesus Christ) it is what happens before that matters. True, but after a football match there are other football matches; after death there's nothing. I don't think death can be fitly compared to anything in life, since it is by its nature entirely unlike. [...]

You sound rather as if – no, let me see, my last letter would arrive Friday, wouldn't it? You sounded a little unlettered. And of course I like getting letters from you: only I feel so guilty about replying so baldly, & because my shallow mind is always in a whirl I never touch on more serious matters. I have almost given up *Jude*; really it's too much: I have accompanied them to Christminster, but really, I just *don't want to look*, like at a street accident. I expect you are right about Sue. It's funny: one starts off thinking one is shrinkingly sensitive & intelligent & always one down & all the rest of it: then at thirty one finds one is a great clumping brute, incapable of appreciating anything finer than a kiss or a kick, roaring out one's hypocrisies at the top of one's voice, thick skinned as a rhino. At least I do. That's why you must never think I criticise *you yourself*. You're always right, even when it's not pleasant to be right. Now a day's work – Lard!

Love from the sty.   P.

16 November 1952

30 Elmwood Ave, Belfast

Dear one,

A quarter to 11. Have spent the evening in from about 7, listening first of all to an I. Compton-Burnett novel adapted for radio (and, for once in my life, I thought it a darned good idea, a resounding success, & worth repeating & exploring), then toiling away at my own nonsense. You, I expect, in free England, have been tossing away the ale, opening your mouth unnecessarily wide, in some smoky little bar parlour in the depths of the country, with the great grey Mr Collins, who, despite all tales to the contrary, had rather a fondness for children. Jolly good show, jolly good show. *Carpe diem. Nox est una perpetua dormienda.* Etc. [...]

I called myself a rhino because I feel daily thicker-skinned than you, & indeed (as in the drinking-writing phrase) seem thicker-skinned *towards* you, and towards my mother, while maintaining a Stiggins-like veneer of exquisite remoteness. This is a trick I'd like to pillory in a novel one day. As for your being right, I mean of course that you're right even when it would be pleasanter to be wrong, & probably harmless. It strikes me how often it *doesn't matter* whether you're right or wrong: only occasionally is the matter brought to the test – by you I mean one, of course. Can I think of an instance? Well, say, Miss A chucks Mr B, & Mr B goes round thinking (and saying) that he chucked Miss A. Wrong, but never brought to the test, & ∴ harmless. And so on. [...]

The time approaches 11.30 & I must go to bed. Read *Macbeth* today: good. I do long to make a film of it. But I still read very carelessly, without taking things in. I really ought to screw myself up to finishing *Jude*, but I honestly shrink from it. [...]

Yes, do ask mother to tea. I don't know whether she'd think what you suggest – quite likely, for she has a simple mind, somewhat gross & common in such things – takes after *her* mother. But she'd be genuinely grateful to be handed over to Leicester, & she *does* like you. A wave of a frozen paw. Philip.

28 November 1952

[postcard]

Very many thanks for the books, and much as I like J. Puddleduck it is the other that at present wins my heart. If you are sure you can part with it that's probably the one I'd like – though I'm not at all clear in my mind at this distance why you *shd* be giving me a Potter! Re my mother, I understand she has *refused* your invite – of course, I didn't ask her if she'd accept, I just thought she would. I'd forgotten about her fear of late nights & the dark & sundry sandy-whiskered gentlemen. That's all it is. I know she likes going to Leics. in daylight.

Have refused an invite for Monday (Francophils: French Consul: Utrillo: crumbs) & Sunday, so hope for more time soon. Scribbling progresses. Much good it is too. Regards. P.

29 November 1952

30 Elmwood Ave, Belfast

[…] The real hero of *J. Townmouse* charms me completely. He is quite my kind of person. I shall know what to say to Kingsley (or Bruce) now: 'Oh yes, yes, you have been most kind; but I do feel so ill.' His account of how he spends his time in the country is lovely, & I think his leaf-umbrella most sensible. O yes, yes: you have been most kind: this is the one for me. The picture of him carrying in grass-cuttings!

I had a sort of difference of opinion with P. Strang about the Potter books: she condemned them as 'anthropomorphist': further, she accused me of not liking animals at all, only Potter ones & ones on my mantel-piece. I was somewhat at a loss. I do sometimes feel ashamed of liking these sweet little bunnies, but the emotion is there & she touches it. I know that by 'animals' she means Twinkle, their stupid obstreperous sheepdog, & that in a sense it's true, but of course I've had no chance. I was never the intimate of cats like you! I never paid calls in the loft! 'Good afternoon Mistress Tabby! Yes I should love a cup! What a sweet kettle-holder! Mouse-skin, is it? Did you cure it yourself?' etc. etc. That was never my good fortune. Of course I'm not going to *stop* reading Potter, because I can't defend myself, & I don't take my inability to do so very seriously anyway.

Thanks for the other books: I'll be delighted to read them. I have a good deal of reading piled up at present: at present St John Irvine's *Oscar Wilde*, a fantastic book, full of the ramblings & out-bursts of this old 'character' – my God, surely nationalism is the surest mark of mediocrity! By p.200 we've been twice told that *Pelagius* was an Ulsterman. *Pelagius*! And 'AE', born, I admit, at Lurgan, Co. Down.

But still! Now 'Irish' claptrap is subsiding, 'Ulster' claptrap comes into its own. But he's amusing enough when he fulminates against better-praised Irish writers: Yeats who 'while applauding every slum patriot who shot a peeler in the back for the honour of Ireland ... was pensioned by the British'; Moore: 'singular mixture of fop and gifted fool ... became a vain and mean and envious & quarrelsome old man'; Robbie Ross: 'that small, bunched-up sodomite' – my next book is *Robert Ross, Friend of Friends*,[1] so I shall be able to judge what I think of him. But the Wilde book is quite readable. You know, his story *is* a remarkable one: it is one of *the* stories: it is almost a parable. Compared with his life the lives of Shaw Wells Bennett Chesterton DHL – bah, nothing. Wilde's life will be read till the end of reading, don't you think? And not only by his 'camp', either. I *must* buy that *De profundis*. [...]

1 *Robert Ross, Friend of Friends*, ed. Margery Ross (1952).

3rd December 1952

30 Elmwood Ave, Belfast

[...] How very interesting about Snow.[1] You don't say what he's *like* – is he fearfully ugly? and noticeably homo? He hadn't got old Pam H.J.[2] with him – you should hear her on the Critics – had he? The fun in listening to her is trying to spot the places when she draws breath. Well, I can't be sarky about JW[3] at present because he *says* he has talked GS Fraser into accepting some of *XX poems* for an anthology[4] – 'envelopes should be marked *Springtime* & sent to me at' – wch after all is not bad of him, decent of him to take the trouble, & all that. I was looking through them again & shivering a bit.

Well! so that's the line he's on, is it? I must say that any literary theory that leads to the elevation of Marghanita Laski should be greeted with hideous skirling uncontrollable laughter – though really I must read *The village*. It certainly does seems a bit Procrustean – if there could be such things as Procrustean pigeon-holes – curiously enough I lay on the rug last night and recited (read) aloud to myself the closing 3 pages of *The waves*, if he is talking about deadness of that author. Enjoyed it, too. After all, say what you like about Virginia Woolf, she was a *writer*, & the daughter of a writer, and not a jumped-up little scientific civil servant. Do not pay any attention to him. The thing that matters is talent: form matters only secondarily. If to him talent means Marghanita Laski, Pamela Hansford Johnson, Richard Church, C. P. Snow, P. H. Newby (as I'm sure it does: perhaps even Norman Collins), well, he had better get back to his testtubes *aussitot que possible*: he disturbs the order here. There is bad in all good authors: what a pity the converse isn't true! All one can say is, fashions change. Experimental writing *as a form* may be temporarily exhausted. I shouldn't be surprised. But give us fifty years of C. P. Snow & *transition* will be coming back *au galop*. The talents writing during the 50 years though will not be either better or worse than they would have been at any other time.

Time! scribbling time!

Later. Back from scribbling & my evening drink. Feel a bit queer – think it is pesky cold out & it may have affected me.

Thanks for your ps about liking, or not liking, animals. I feel, though, that with the question of things being attractive in books that are not so in reality we are on dubious ground – ground I am always unhappy on (like a rugger ground!). It's a very old question, I expect – probably in Aristotle, certainly in Morgann[5] – and I must confess I always mark down an author who does it – *lying*, I call it, as the old Scotswoman described the profession of RLS. DHL did it with his *Plumed serpent* killings, for instance. Of course all this is a long way from our friends the Flopsies.

'Wm Cooper's' real name is Hoff[6] – have forgotten the initials. I fancy he did research during the war: his subject I imagine is physics, or physical chemistry; he is short, dark & bouncy, married to a clergyman's daughter I think he said, in attack rather a bounder, or at least the Strangs thought so: I was too dazzled by his status as 'a writer' ... This is all very conditional! I don't suppose he's in *Who's Who* but he'd be in *Whitaker*. Nor do I know the school he taught at, but Collins would know. Did he take his 1st degree at Leicester? He well might. [...]

1 C. P. Snow.
2 Pamela Hansford Johnson.
3 John Wain.
4 *Springtime*: anthology of new writing ed. G. S. Fraser and Iain Fletcher (1953).
5 Maurice Morgann (1726–1802), political writer and Shakespeare critic.
6 William Cooper: *nom de plume* of Harry Hoff.

13 December 1952

30 Elmwood Ave, Belfast

Dearest of burrow-dwellers,

I feel a bit better now. My hands feel queer still, but the sensation of being about to *collapse* has departed. I've spent an enormous lot of money today on food and drink: a hock is boiling in the kitchen, & a pork fillet waiting for the morning. This afternoon also I bought 1/- worth of mistletoe & have hung it over my door – the golden bough! Isn't the world full of interest? I should never have thought of doing that a year ago. Walking home I noticed everyone looking at me as if I might be expected to break out into priapic licence immediately, & grinning, & I grinned inwardly, & felt very jolly & like the reformed Scrooge. It's nice to think that the druids' branch, the slow moongrowth of sluggish waxy berries, guards my door. Do you think it will keep away unwelcome guests? [...]

21 December 1952

30 Elmwood Ave, Belfast

My dear bunny,

Well! What a magnificent & useful present. It turned up on Friday, just as I was going to Dundalk for a meeting of the Irish Philosophical Club. Of course I was not going to 'keep it for Christmas' – anyhow a telepathic jump told me what it was – so I set off for the south in a haze of gratitude. Really it is very thick & fine, and I shan't suffer any more in the small hours when small goblins seem to be blowing their streams of cold air down the bed-clothes at your neck, & in at the sides, & pouring buckets of cold air over your head. Thank you, thank you, thank you! Your present from me is dull in the extreme – entirely lacking in inspiration. I find that all my presents this year are like that: just like anyone else's presents. 'A Book of Beauty'. A box of chocolates. And so on. I think I shall keep it till I see you ... which leads me to say that we are reserved at the Woolpack Hotel, Warwick, for the nights of 29th & 30th Dec. This is the hotel I remember: I don't know whether it's any good, but it's not on the main street & should be a bit quieter than the larger ones where Civil Servants were during the war. I shall enjoy showing you the town, such as it is: I wonder if we could get into the castle. It's quite pleasant. [...]

24 June 1953[1]

30 Elmwood Avenue, Belfast

[...] Now you will be wondering what I thought of *The secret garden*,[2] which I read between 4 and 5.30 a.m. (all but the first 50 pages) on Tuesday morning when I couldn't sleep. Well, I thought it astonishingly good. I can't imagine how I've never come across it before. But what surprised me above all was that I was expecting a book whose dominant effect wd be ... how shall I put it? ... *fairy-like*: not in the whimsical sense, more like the light that never was on land or sea, whatever that was: crooked boughs, dusk, memories, moths, pale flowers – avoiding Burne Jones, but perhaps Rackham ... And now you present me with this paean of delight in life! these crusty loaves, best butter, syrup in porridge, the sunshine, the smell of earth, the slow modelling up of flowers, the doxology, the wonderful cry of 'I shall get well! And I shall live for ever and ever and ever!' If it has any message, it's surely that – well, I can't put it in a sentence, but it's that life is strong and joyful enough to push up & overturn the strongest and heaviest morbid fancies and fears: it calls on everyone to put aside distrusts and shrinking-back, and live to the utmost while life is for the having. You'll think this fantastic, perhaps, but the author I was most reminded of was my old friend Ll. Powys. Now *don't* run away with the idea that I'm just carelessly glancing at it & dropping it unappreciated into the well-worn *glory of life* box. This sort of thing has been said so often it's bound to sound debased: if it makes it clearer or more acceptable you can think of K.M.'s vivid exultance instead of L.P., but I do want to get across that my chief impression was a deep one, *punched* by the expression of delight in natural life. But did I *like* it? I hear you querying suspiciously. Yes: there was hardly anything I didn't like: I thought all the Yorkshire side of things masterly, and Martha & Dickon exquisitely drawn. If I object to anything it's the two extreme edges of the book: if we say the tone stretches from fairytale through to Ll. Powys (I'm just labelling, you understand) I took a little exception to the extremes of the pathetic fallacy, as they call it, at the one end, & the sort of Rudolf Steiner 'Magic' atmosphere at the other – a sort of Xtian science feeling. I don't know if what I've said is going to upset you. I remember you described it as exactly the sort of book we can share: I can't remember your saying anything about the book itself, because I hadn't read it, but you said it made you cry: I was more *excited*, I really did find it exciting, & any tears that came to my eyes were of excited happiness. But there's more to say about it than I can well put down now.

Thursday Wuuurrrghgh. I owe you 21/1d I think – 24/11 plus 1/2 minus 5/- Shall I pay you when I see you, or send a #? The BBC are paying me 6 gns for the 38 lines of XIV – I can only count 24, so maybe John has added a conclusion.³ But I daren't object, as it is 4 gns for 24, then 1 gn per 12 lines. Isn't it funny? Feel poor today, head like a peppered watermelon. Fondest thoughts.   P.

1 This appears to be the first letter surviving since 21 December 1952.
2 Frances Hodgson Burnett, *The Secret Garden* (1911).
3 L. read 'If, my darling' (XIV, in *XX Poems*) in 'First Reading', compiled by John Wain. This was broadcast in the Third Programme, 1 July 1953.

28 June 1953

30 Elmwood Avenue, Belfast

Freed rabbit,

It's lateish on Sunday evening, and I am collecting myself slowly after a very *dispersed* weekend – very hot here, yesterday & today the finest of days, and I've been moving round slowly, dazed by heat and hay-fever. And of course this test match is a great time-waster – and Saturday afternoon was spent in hearing the worst, & the evening protracted to 4 a.m. by bridge. As I lay preparing for sleep I heard a bird beginning to sing in the garden below – o! how that does ravish me, I think I cd listen to it for a small eternity (who said that, of what ?): it's one of the most wonderful moments of any day. If I hadn't felt tired I'd have got up there & then & seen the dawn. I know you don't like birds, but the cool shapely twitterings that rise before daybreak remind me of the dewy tents of leaves they are hidden among, the flowers folded in the darkness, the beady eyes glancing about – 'sleep all night with open eye'¹ – and the sense of running into a new day, adventurous and triumphant. I hope these purple passages don't embarrass you. By the way! don't let anyone take you to a 3D film, as one – I've forgotten the title: *Man with a question* or something similar – includes a disturbed bird flying *straight out at you*. [...]

1 Chaucer, *Canterbury Tales*, Prologue.

1 July 1953

30 Elmwood Ave, Belfast

Dearest,

This is being written in the Reading Room, of all places, where I am filling a gap for ¼ an hour. I'm sure my letters are too scrappy these days: the fine weather unsettles me, I go strolling round the avenues at night, sensing the vertiginous romance of other lives, when I should be writing to you, or at least attacking my ms. But the gorgeousness of the weather draws me out.

Well, we agree well enough about *The S.G.* – I'm thankful you accept my reaction & Powys comparison: I was almost sure you'd say 'Great God! can't he ever see over his own fence, I give him this exquisite poem of childhood, & all he can do is jam it into the same drawer as that overgrown ranting public schoolboy—' The K.M. was really an attempt to propitiate you! I agree she's much less apt. I expect a point where it scores with *you* is its 'sensibleness' – I am not all that *sensible* – however much I may applaud Mary, temperamentally I remain a Colin, and that may account for a hesitation about my 'really liking' it, even though I approve & admire. I thought it remarkable how she managed to achieve a steady cumulation of emotion, while having only the one string to her bow: I mean she never really scored except with this wonderful evocation of the returning spring & of growth – it was like having the volume control turned slowly up – and I was amazed how successful she remained. In fact I found it technically very clever: the idea of two children neither of whom has ever seen the spring is extravagant in theory, but how easily accepted in practice! and I felt a faint satisfying sense of irony in the fact that the secret garden was really – in essence – so very universal, so extremely *unsecret*, in point of fact: I mean, there *was* a garden, but it is only a symbol: once it has been worked out the garden is everywhere – the moor, everywhere. Isn't it? I've bought 2 copies now myself. Yes, of course I shd have 'expressed' it to *you* if I'd read it by accident. As a matter of fact I thought of you the moment I saw the cover: I'd heard of it, faintly, before, in the way that one's heard of, say, Mrs Molesworth; the cover scored heavily, & I thought: if the inside's as good as the cover that wd be just what the Dr ordered for Monica, a quick glance assured me that it was – I mean in the sense of style, of quality. Of course the cover is misleading otherwise, it leads you to the Rackham error. And I am really delighted to have made so successful a gift! All for half a crown! And to think my eyes were roaming dispiritedly over Connoisseur books at 45/- – *Some English makers of porcelain*, etc. etc., the *Victoria & Albert Collection of Bedroom China, edited by John Summerson with an introduction by James Laver* – you know the kind of thing. Oh! and one more literary parallel: can't you think of another lady[1] whose regeneration was symbolised by the adoption of dialect? [. . .]

Evening – And damn me if I haven't begun the SG again, & read to p. 141. I *do* like it. 'Tha knew how to build tha nest before tha' came out o' th'egg.' 'Ay, this is tha supper, tha needna look as if tha wouldna get it!' You know the first: the second is Oliver Mellors talking to his dog. In fact, the book I keep being reminded of, in a distant oblique underwater way, *is Lady C*. I don't know if you know this book, but the theme is very much the same, rebirth, resurrection: Constance is 'yellow', and a bit scraggy, like Mary, & feels she *must get out* in the spring, and does: I can't quote much, because Lawrence is not quite so concentrated, but as I expect you know she finds on her walks the hut where the keeper is rearing young pheasants, and how she keeps going until they hatch. To amuse her he draws one out very carefully from the hen's feathers and puts it on her hand: 'there it stood, on its impossible little stalks of legs' – and as he is looking at it in amusement he sees a tear fall on her wrist. And so it all starts. There *is* something about this, and about the conclusion 200 pages on in Mellors' last letter ('But never mind. All the bad times that ever have been haven't been able to blow the crocus out: not even the love of women. So they won't be able to blow out my wanting you, nor the little glow there is between you & me. We'll be together next year. And though I'm frightened, I believe in your being with me. A man has to fend & fettle for the best, and then trust in something beyond himself. You can't insure against the future, except by really believing in the best bit of you, and in the power beyond it'), there is to my mind a faint kinship between them & the S.G., though not of course to be pushed too far, for in L. there's all the grownup things to muddy the course of the fable, and L. is occasionally a shoddy or careless writer, whereas F.H.B. is at worst conventional or a bit hackneyed. But the comparison can to my mind be made, & an odd one it is, too, I suppose. [. . .]

1 Lady Chatterley.

7 July 1953

30 Elmwood Avenue, Belfast

Dearest,

Hmm! ... I've just visited old John Wain briefly, but left him before any word of mine could be spoken. This isn't affectation (if it matters whether it is or not): it wd cause me severe embarrassment to hear any of those lines.[1] I don't know if you wondered whether it is addressed to anyone in particular: as it isn't, I don't mind saying it isn't, though I was a good deal exercised in my mind at that time about my ex-fiancée. I did get a copy of the *Church Times*, thanks. Did you see that *The Listener* pointed out that springime or no springtime I (and some others) are in the early 30's? This reminds me of a joke in the *New Yorker*: 'I think it's cruel to call anyone middle aged just because they're not young any more.' Anyway, there's nothing to look forward to now except the cheque for 8 gns. & the autumn number of *Essays in Criticism*, which is reputed to have a short jeering poem of mine in it[2] – again written in 1950. And, of course, *Lucky Jim*. [...]

1 BBC *First Reading* broadcast of 'If, My Darling'.
2 'Fiction and the Reading Public'.

13 July 1953

30 Elmwood Ave, Belfast

[...]

In bed. A lowering day, but not as wet as yesterday: the orangemen marched as usual, & for the first time I met a little lodge marching through the country lanes with banner, band & bowler hats. I should think all the roman catholics must pray fervently for rain on these days, the processions must be so irritating.

My laptab *has* come: whether it's really worth the money or not I don't know. I suppose it is, only I can't sit cross-legged now as I usually do, & shall have to get into a fresh habit. I seem to be spending money wholesale these days: I owe sundry small sums too. Do you think there will be beer in Scotland?[1] I can only imagine us putting down peaty-tasting whiskey while rain drives down outside & the sea is shrouded in mist. How well we shall get to know the antlered stag in the hall!

The picture of Glencoe on the stairs! the crossed claymores in the bar! [...]

1 L. and Monica were going on holiday to Scotland, and that was immediately followed by L. taking his mother to Weymouth.

26 July 1953

Royal Hotel Esplanade, Weymouth

[...] There's a great deal here that wd delight you: the statue of George III, glaring heavily along the front, is *coloured*; and everywhere in the town one has only to lift one's gaze from the garish fronts of Saxone, Melias & so on to see the pretty round shallow bow windows & the colour-washed plaster. The harbour & old town is delicious. [...]

I can see that this week is going to be very different from last – split between my want to go off exploring alone & doing my duty by my mother. But then nothing could be very like Mallaig, could it? I'm sorry we never got to Rum & Eigg. I shall never forget the Chinese geese, & the sense of perpetual drizzle, & the day on Skye which was so like being the only people in Paradise (except for your relations) and was so beautiful. It was a lovely holiday. This half will be much less eventful, but I may finish Rousseau.

Love & kisses

5 August 1953

Flat 13, 30 Elmwood Avenue, Belfast

[...] If we'd got as far as the birthplace,[1] I was going to pick a flower or a piece of flowering grass for you to press, but I didn't think you'd want anything from the churchyard. It's the most *hidden* church & churchyard I ever saw, &, when approached from the road, almost invisible. It was utterly silent and withdrawn, as if belonging to the past, or as if its vicar was someone from T. F. Powys. I took a few photographs, but they haven't yet been developed. You'll be touched, too, by the extreme simplicity and even poverty of his belongings in the museum – the three horn & steel push-pens lying tumbled together on his desk, & marked 'Tess' 'Jude' & 'The dynasts' – to show wch they wrote! I was a bit disappointed with the MSS. on show – not as interesting as the lot I saw previously. The only poem MS. is his earliest, according to the card: 'Retty's phases', but I can hardly believe it *is* his earliest. Perhaps it's the earliest surviving MS. only. [...]

You know, I'm sure you'll hoot, but what prompted your remarks about politics, my thoughts on't?[2] Did I *say* 'wood of conservatism'? Or *write* it? I can't place it at all – what was it in connexion with? *Wood*? Babes in the? Bowls? Beer from the? Really, I know I say my poor old brain is, etc., but I hope I'm not forgetting something of *the last 14 days*. No: or perhaps I'm turning into the type – the Montherlant type – who 'does not forgive, but forgets – *really* forgets – ...' I hope not. Anyway, I don't mind what you say: all reasonable enough, surely, & the idea of my brooding and fretting over your *political opinions* is enough to make a Staffordshire cat laugh. You know I don't care at all for politics, intelligently. I found that at school when we argued all we did was repeat the stuff we had, respectively, learnt from the *Worker*, the *Herald*, *Peace News*, the *Right Book Club* (that was me, incidentally: *I knew these dictators*, *Marching Spain*, I can remember them now) and as they all contradicted each other all we did was get annoyed. I came to the conclusion that an enormous amount of research was needed to form an opinion on anything, & therefore I abandoned politics altogether as a topic of conversation. It's true that the writers I grew up to admire were either non-political or left-wing, & that I couldn't find any right-wing writer worthy of respect, but of course most of the ones I admired were awful fools or somewhat fakey, so I don't know if my prejudice for the left takes its origin there or not. But if you annoy me by speaking your mind in the other interest, it's not because I feel sacred things are being mocked but because I *can't reply*, not (as usual) knowing enough. Like Ambrose, I don't know the index figure for a family of four. Oh dear, this is an enormous subject: & I could talk about it for ages: if I've ever evinced irritation when you've been talking politics, it's been due to a great many reasons, some dependent on me, some on you, some stretching far beyond the question in hand, and it wouldn't, I feel, be fair to mention some without the others. And that would take pages, even if I were sure enough of the rightness of them to advance them as true.

By the way, of course I'm terribly conventional, by necessity! Anyone afraid to say boo to a goose is conventional.

I've written a tiny little poem since returning, hardly a poem at all:[3]

What are days for?
Days are where we live.
They come, they wake us
Time and time over.
They are to be happy in:
Where can we live but days?

And to seek where they join
Brings the priest and the doctor
In their long coats
Running over the fields.

Don't take it seriously, but it's a change from the old style.

Wednesday I shouldn't think there's much danger of yr taking it seriously, having just re-read it, but I can't rub it out. Talking of poetry, Kingsley sent me a whole bunch of typescript saying that as he was having a book of poems done by Reading would I like to select them, improve them, arrange them, & think of a title? I did the first, & I don't expect he'll like my choice. I left out the ones about the atom bomb, & left in the comic ones like *Ode to the East-North-East-by-East wind* ('Jacking my hair up in one leaning spike ...'), and *Something nasty in the bookshop*. [...]

1 L. and his mother on holiday in Dorset, in 'Hardy country'.
2 On 30 July 1953, Monica had written from Stourport: 'As for yr complaint – I might as well deal with it once for all & never no more – about "the wood of my conservatism" as you call it, if you really can't stand a bit of that, you need never hear it again [...] I certainly thought you didn't care either way, & imagining that speech was free thought you could equally well hear me talk as anybody else; I certainly *never* knew you fancied yrself a Socialist, & I must say you've kept it pretty dark ... It seems to me that either you've intended to conceal it or you don't know much about it, for you certainly don't *talk* like it. All politics preys on the basest sides of human character, relies on it, brings it out; I don't *like* it any more than you do [...].'
3 'Days'. Line 7 later revised to 'Ah, solving that question'. 'Days' was not published until *Listen* (Summer/Autumn 1957), and then in *The Whitsun Weddings* (1964).

7 August 1953

30 Elmwood Avenue, Belfast

[...] Weymouth was 30/- a day for Mother (4th front) & 28/6 a day for me (4th back). 1st fronts were 40/- a day! The food was quite passable: quite uninspired of course, but I could eat it well enough. And on our last day (Friday) they graduated us to the window: we could there look down on the passing multitudes like the fellow in Clough's poem.[1] I think Mother enjoyed it. I told you how I was variously estimated as her brother & her husband, didn't I? We had a pleasant walk to 'Mellstock': Hardy played a part in my parents' courtship, & it astonishes me to hear her repeat snatches of his poems she learnt simply to please my father – *We kissed at the barrier*, for instance (as apparently they always did). Of course my father was grabbing the books as they came from the press, in the nineteen-hundreds. O frigid inarticulate man! He met my mother on the beach at Rhyl. He was there for 3 days only, on a cycling tour, but before leaving he had a picture of them taken together & exchanged addresses (I agree this doesn't sound especially fr. or inart.!), & despite a separation of several years his intentions didn't alter. I find all that very strange & romantic, partly because unlike the father I knew. He must have been as intensely idealistic as a young man as he was nihilistically disillusioned in middle age. [...]

Travelling on Sunday was queer: I arrived at Heysham to find it more or less deserted except for crowds of young folk who were inundating the station bar, where men drink from the ships. They seemed an unsavoury gang of juvenile delinquents, fast, flashy, yet curiously intimate – were they some youth-club, some junior razor gang & its molls taking a holiday *en masse*? Later I discovered they were all part of a variety show called 'Taking off tonight' booked for the Empire this week, and got talking to the producer, a wheezy Cockney in an Anthony Eden hat. 'The agents won't give you a single booking unless you've got a posing act' he assured me. I couldn't see any of the phthisical gum-chewing girls who looked worthy of the job. No doubt they look better across the footlights. [...]

Birthdays[2] are a time when one stocktakes, wch means, I suppose, a good spineless mope: I scan my horizon and can discern no sail of hope along my own particular ambition. I tell you what it is: I'm quite in accord with the people who enquire 'What is the matter with the man?' because I don't seem to be producing anything as the years pass but rank self indulgence. You know that my sole ambition, officially at any rate, was to write poems & novels, an activity I never found any difficulty in fulfilling between the (dangerous) ages of 17–24; I can't very well ignore the fact that this seems to have died a natural death. On the other hand I feel regretful that what talents I have in this direction are not being used. Then again, if I am not going to produce anything in the literary line, the justification for my selfish life is removed – but since I go on living it, the suspicion arises that the writing existed to produce the life, & not *vice versa*. And as a life it has very little to recommend it: I spend my days footling in a job I care nothing about, a curate among lady-clerks; I evade all responsibility, familial, professional, emotional, social, not even saving much money or helping my mother. I look around me & I see people getting on, or doing things, or bringing up children – and here I am in a kind of vacuum. *If* I were writing, I would even risk the fearful old age of the Henry-James hero: not fearful in circumstance but in realisation: because to me to catch, render, preserve, pickle, distil or otherwise secure life-as-it-seemed for the future seems to me infinitely worth doing; but as I'm not, the entire morality of it collapses. And when I ask *why* I'm not, well, I'm not because I don't want to: every novel I attempt stops at a point where I awake from the impulse as one might awake from a particularly-sickening nightmare – I *don't* want to 'create character', I *don't* want to be vivid or memorable or precise, I neither wish to bathe each scene in the lambency of the 'love that accepts' or be excoriatingly cruel, smart, vicious, 'penetrating' (ugh), or any of the other recoil qualities. In fact, like the man in *St Mawr*, I want nothing.[3] Nothing, I want. And so it becomes quite impossible for me to carry on. This failure of impulse seems to me suspiciously like a failure of sexual impulse: people conceive novels and dash away at them & finish them in the same way as they fall in love & will not be satisfied till they're married – another point on which I seem to be out of step. There's something cold & heavy sitting on me somewhere, & until something budges it I am no good. I hope you don't think me pompous for writing this paragraph. I felt I must explain why though I'm very touched by all the nice things you say of me I can't do more than shake my head gently, and raise one paw in mild protest – not, I suppose, that you expect me to acknowledge them like a newly-crowned champ! Finally, don't think I haven't *tried*: I have tried. Will power can do nothing unless the impulse is there first. Enough! no more. [...]

1 A. H. Clough's *Dipsychus*, sc. V: 'How pleasant it is to have money'.
2 9 August 1953: L.'s thirty-first birthday.
3 By D. H. Lawrence.

14 August 1953

30 Elmwood Avenue, Belfast

[...] By the way, was it *Alton Locke*[1] you were advising me to read? I've got about ⅔rds of the way through and not found anything special to enjoy ... *was* it *Alton Locke*? Or am I misremembering? Since finishing *Under the greenwood tree* I haven't found a decent book to read: still struggling on with *Restless house*,[2] wch isn't very interesting, but I can see how Zola appeals to Angus Wilson: all the unreal 'satiric side'. What killing satire on the middle classes to describe a quarrel between husband & lover during a wedding, so that bride & groom are only half attending in their anxiety to hear the details! And the priest doing the same, so that he bungles the ceremony! Yes, killing, if one believed it for a moment. Zola is one of these people who aren't a bit like they're supposed to be. I expect Balzac is the same. You'd like a book I was looking at called (I think) *British game*, by Brian Vesey Fitzgerald: it's another one in the Collins New naturalist series. Readable, & with nice pictures. But I chafe, ignorantly I suppose, at the cheerful assumption that game is game, and that naturally people want to 'shoot lots and lots of grouse, grouse in hundreds'. They live on *Calluna* shoots, which is heather – the grouse, I mean, not the people. And they need a lot of grit – quartz grit suits them very well. So I suppose that's why they live in Scotland.

No, I don't mind what you say about D.H.L.[3] Loyalty binds me to him, but for a long time I've outgrown – or detached myself from – his personality: much about him appeals to me and always will, and I don't side with the people who laugh at him, the Catholic crew & the philosophic crew and the political crew, but one only has to imagine placing any *reliance* on him ... And much of his coyness strikes me as awful bad taste. I suppose I haven't the *breadth of temperament* to appreciate the faults of genius: just a narrow-gutted *bourgeois*, I suppose. I like Ll. Powys better these days. I was reading *The 12 months* & quite exulting over it. I should love to analyse his development as a writer, how he gradually improved his original horrible Rabelais-translator's jocularity by *original observation* – O blast! no more paper: have to dig for it.

Here we are. I kept Elizabeth *well informed* today concerning the Test Match. She did not react much, wch is all right if she wants me to stop doing it.

I don't think you quite catch my meaning about what-is-the-matter: I agree I can keep out of jug & earn a living & enjoy myself – it's only writing, or not writing, that irritates me. 'You can't do anything if you want to badly enough' – my version of Butler's dictum. And, if you want to know, what I think the matter is is that I have no great opinion of my creative springs, since they appear to me to be corrupt and laughable. In fact you point it out, in a way, in your letter, over this past business. I do love the past. Anything more than 20 years back begins to breathe a luminous fascination for me: it starts my imagination working. Why? Because it *is* past, I suppose, & leaves my feelings free to get to work on it. Do you think I should trouble my head about a prostitute down in Amelia Street, and not safely tucked away in Mayhew? This is one example of one aspect of the 'Working of the creative imagination', which in my experience is generally contemptible and absurd, and forms a vast confidence-trick, an elaborate system of avoidances & compensations. Now any worthwhile writer never thinks of *questioning* his imaginative excitements. Do you see what I mean, O lop ears, O silky jacket? [...]

1 Charles Kingsley, *Alton Locke* (1850).
2 Translation of Emile Zola's novel *Pot-Bouille* (1882).
3 In a letter dated 2 August 1953, from Stourport, Monica had written: 'I've been reading some more Lawrence ... On one page he says men hate competent women, on the next he's hating submissive ones. What he's really *asking* for is a sweet old-fashioned little dear, who shams yielding wifely stuff & tough as steel underneath deceives & manages him for his own good; a *Woman's Page* person & he really deserved one.'

14 September 1953

30 Elmwood Avenue, Belfast

[...] Thanks for your picnic card this morning: glad to know you are getting on all right. I arrived safely on Sunday morning after a tiring journey & in no very good state of health, having a large & painful inflammation on my right leg, proceeding from & to I don't know what; 'Tangent's foot[1] has swollen up & turned black': amputation: 'it's bound to recur elsewhere': 'why didn't you come to me before?': 'now come on Mr Larkin, upsadaisy, let's see if we can leave one crutch at home today, shall we?' Monopedal fantasies haunt me. If I have a wooden leg I should like a Long John Silver one, & a parrot, & a patch over one eye. Avast, ye lubbers! Skeered of a capful o'wind? 'A seafaring man with a wooden leg ...' Which has the most exciting beginning, *Treasure Island* or *The invisible man*? Perhaps when you come we can decide.

I must say that *Lucky Jim* is now, to my mind, one of the funniest books I've ever read, at least I *think* so. Only a printed copy can settle the question finally. But I don't think anything can stop it being a howling success: it seems to me so entirely original that my own suggestions really pass unnoticed, as they were for the most part concerned with structure & plot. I don't myself think anyone has been funny in this way before, and that even if he never writes anything else it will remain as a landmark. [...]

1 In Evelyn Waugh, *Decline and Fall*.

Christmas night, 1953

21 York Road, Loughborough

My dear,

Well, the worst of it is over now: it's nearly bedtime and once again the professional uncles of the BBC and all the rest of it have driven away what Christmas feeling I had. However, in this short time between the nuts and mounting the stairs I feel like sending you a special greeting, allied to the sharp stars and dropping rime and curled-up animals and fires ageing into ash and the wind going quietly along the lanes as it's accustomed to do and meeting no one – factors which every year are driven away by the *spirit of Christmas presents* – a ferret-faced man with a new corduroy cap on his head & a yellow muffler smoking a King Six. In short, thank you for your presents and I hope you did not have too bad a day. I wore my cat bow all day: oh, it's obviously *good*, I think, & I like it tremendously. It really reminds me of the kind of thing one finds at the back of a drawer in a deserted room, in fact I could quite imagine a story about it, or a play. [...]

Saturday. Dreary day. Home, I think, might be defined as the place where one is bored and irritated – and, of course, embarrassed, too, sometimes – or perhaps the place where reality is strongest, which is very much the same thing. [...]

Sunday. Been to church, where the archdeacon had a stab at interpreting the beginning of St John's gospel. It's a fine day here, but I am revisited by fear concerning the feeling in my chest. I think, again, that home breeds fear as well as boredom and the rest. Can one cause cancer by thinking about it? Can one cure it by not thinking about it? How does one not think about it? [...]

30 December 1953[1]

21 York Road, Loughborough

[...] If I were a titled eccentric I should devote my life to writing a study of *Men and animals*: a history of the animal in society. As Food; As Property; As Game; As friends; As Gods (that should come earlier); As Philosophical concepts (pre- & post-Darwin). There's six fat volumes! And I'd pack into 2 & 3 every monstrous outrage I could find authenticated, whale hunting, seal slaughtering, bullfighting, bear baiting & all the Bertram Mills stuff, lineal descendant of the 'mad bull covered with fireworks & released in the market, 3 p.m.' However, as I'm not a titled eccentric I suppose I shan't. [...]

1 After this letter, there is an inexplicable gap until August 1954.

3 August 1954

30 Elmwood Ave, Belfast

Well, dearest bun,

You were certainly yanked away quickly enough at the heel of the hunt! I stood till you had gone out of sight round the corner, then returned to work, where I was clapper clawed by old bagface about all the 1000 & 1 little things she can worry about when the boss is away. I wasn't in the mood for it, I can tell you. Dearest, what kind of a flight did you have? I thought of you, when I was eating my lunch, soaring through the large cloud-littered sky.

Now I have eaten most of the things you left, & the birds have discovered your crusts, & the cleaner has cleaned up my room (without finding your pen), so the holiday is fading rather horribly quickly, as far as outward show is concerned, but I was very dejected this morning when no rabbit came to my bedside to thump its drum! Slept badly, too.

One thing I feel is that even if you didn't have many outings you had plenty of interesting books to read: in fact it was quite a Summer School for you! I don't think I have ever seen you laugh at anything so much as at that passage in Mary McC. about the young man whose shirt has shrunk. I was quite alarmed; you would have been surprised if I'd thrown the week's water at you.

As you see, I'm enclosing a copy of the churches poem,[1] & hope you'll let me know what you think of it. I'm afraid it is not entirely effective, but you must judge for yourself and let me know. I could write plenty of 'background' stuff about it, but you had better read it unsupported first: do remember, however, that I write it partly to exhibit an attitude as well as to try to arouse an emotion – the attitude of the 'young heathen' of whom there are plenty about these days – the first line, for instance, is designed both as sincere statement of fact & also as heavy irony. [...]

1 'Church Going' began to be written on 24 April 1954. Its final draft appears in notebook no. 4, dated 28 July 1954.

10 August 1954

30 Elmwood Ave, Belfast

[...] Thanks for all the nice things you said abt my poetry, but I think you put your paw on the flaw in *Churchgoing*, a lack of strong continuity – it is dangerously like *chat*, 4th leader stuff. The most important emotion – the church as a place where people came to be serious, were *always* serious, & all their different forms of seriousness came to be intermingled, so that a christening reminded of a funeral & a funeral of a wedding: nowadays these things happen in different buildings & the marvellous 'blent air' of a church is growing rarer – this emotion I feel does not come out nearly strongly enough. However, I don't know what can be done about it now.

Am reading Wyndham Lewis's *Self-Condemned*. It bears a remarkable resemblance to *Kangaroo*: K. with all the response to Australian scenery left out, & also the politics. [...]

Thursday. Orangeade & the last of your marble cake. [...]

Finished Wyndham Lewis. I haven't read all his novels, but this one, like *Tarr*, carries a feeling of a man trying to convince himself that things that hinder or disturb him are wrong. This is a tale about a professor of history who beats it to Canada before war breaks out (he 'sees through' history, but why he can't see through it & remain in England isn't explained) & lives there in self-imposed horrible conditions, hating the savage mediocrity of the place. Then he & his wife start making friends, & he gets to like the place, writes a column in the local paper, meets local university people, visits Ottawa ('where he found the excellent library in the Parliament Building of the greatest use'), gets to like the radio ('American radio, with all its wonderful gusto'), & finally accepts a Canadian chair, 'history' having presumably become opaque again. His wife, seeing that he will never leave, kills herself because she hates Canada yet can't return to England unless he does (no money). The last 40 pages show him trying to throw off his sense of remorse at this by a variety of arguments, & in the end succeeding ('she just set herself to obstruct everything ... her death was her last act of obstruction'). The reader is left longing to draft him into the nastiest division in the American Army for a long spell of latrine-fatigue. I don't think W.L. is any good. His sexual sensibility is measured by the calendar in my kitchen (see the Tarr-Anastasya chapter in *Tarr*, & 'worse than pinning up *Esquire* in his room, he maintained a live *Esquire* colour-block', i.e. his wife), & his literary sensibility sees fit to employ cliches in a jocular fashion for purposes, presumably, of humour – but it is this, sometimes, that reminds me of D.H.L. – and the purpose of his book seems, as I said, simply to get his own back on people. Otherwise, it seems pointless. However! [...]

16 August 1954

30 Elmwood Avenue, Belfast

[...] Kingsley sent one of his letters recently, not very good:[1] *Church going* didn't interest him, though he was quite polite about it. He wants the inversion removed from the 1st line of the last verse, also 'blent' (both these on the grounds of poetic archaism) & objects to the 'historic present' of the 1st two verses. Not a word about the poem as a whole, except that he 'doesn't feel as I do'. No word of any kind from the Dolmen Press. Poem by Lerner in the *New St.* Article by Kingsley in the *Spr.* about the Eisteddfod, quite funny. The thought of Kingsley going about with a button in his buttonhole marked 'Press' in Welsh (' "You're a bloody English bags," says your man in Irish') is just one more fantastic thing, don't you agree. Says he is too poor to buy me a birthday present, on the previous page having detailed expenditure on records to the extent of £4, & told me some of the things he has seen on television. Still, I didn't buy him a birthday present either. [...]

Am getting on very well with *Bleak House* – I do like it. There is more to thrill, & less to irritate or bore, me than in any other I've read. I've just reached those wonderful pair of lines I'd use for a book of ghost stories if I wrote one – ' "As to dead men, Tony," ...' Do you remember it? In the chapter called *The appointed hour*, or something like that. And every Chesney Wold paragraph is splendid, & every Inns of Court paragraph too. I am enjoying it. It's as if someone had said to Dickens, Charley, I want a good long novel with plenty of dry old lawyers, and a miserable country house in Lincolnshire where it's always raining, and a mysterious affair about a girl, what everyone knows a bit of but no one knows all of – might make her tell part of the story – oh, this sounds awfully Dickson Carrish, but I'm sure C.D. got it in a flash, & fitted the Jellabys & Smallweeds & Turveydrops in later. They aren't nearly as stirring as the rest, or (to me) interesting. [...]

1 See Letter of 11 August 1954 in *The Letters of Kingsley Amis*, ed. Zachary Leader.

23 August 1954

30 Elmwood Ave, Belfast

[...] There was such an interesting programme on the radio tonight – some Canon giving a recital of street pianos, playing popular songs of the '90s, & interspersing them with gossip & jokes of a sort of old-wag order. Very nice! It conjured up to me the sunsets, the mouldering brick streets, the open public-houses full of soldiers off to South Africa, the endless jingle & trot, the children playing with hoops & chalking the pavements, & the old people sitting at their doors on wooden kitchen chairs (a steel engraving of *The death of Nelson* visible on the wall behind their heads), and from round the corner the sound of this twangling hymn, like the harping of Cockney angles. There's a sentimental passage for you! But seriously I think you wd like this, & much that is on the radio: I do pity you, forced to attend to television night after night. [...]

The only person I can think of who saw the poem you speak of[1] without knowing of my ups & downs with Ruth is Collins. Are you distressing yourself on his score? Nobody else saw *XX poems*, & it was never reprinted. I really don't see where the agony comes in, if you mean people wd take it as applying to you. However, I'm very sorry that it did. 'It was all rather silly really', to use one of those classic phrases suitable for labelling almost any activity in retrospect. [...]

I suppose I like decisive people if they've decided what I've decided! not otherwise. But really you mustn't keep thinking of me as clever by any real standards – I shdn't be a librarian if I weren't incapable of *any* kind of serious thought – I know nothing, read nothing but novels, think nothing – no, really! Prrrff! I always try to comfort myself with Keats' remark about 'irritable reaching after fact and reason', & the unsuitableness thereof, for a poet. [...]

Handel, who is 'This week's composer', is playing on the radio at present, & makes me wish you were here, covering the carpet with long alien golden hairs (I still find them, now & again, in all sorts of places – shut in books, for instance). [...]

1 'If, My Darling'.

13 September 1954

21 York Road, Loughborough

[...] Depressed myself slightly tonight by reading some scrappy journal entries (all right, diary entries) for the first half of 1941 – I didn't remember myself as such an awkward young fool, but there we are. A terrible time, just trying to cross from being a schoolboy to being a – well, I don't know. The depression mainly came from the thought that all I have learnt to do since then is avoid 'conflict situations'. Even that is something, I suppose. But I am no more master of my destiny than a tomcat is master of the *Queen Mary*. The only entry that made me genuinely laugh recounted how I unwrapped a Swiss roll and fitted it over someone's door handle – can't remember the man or what happened, but it wd be a queer thing to take hold of after dark. Also reminded myself of something I had quite forgotten – opening the diary of a man I despised and finding some strictures about myself, ending with a remark to the effect that he had been 'severer with me lately' & was pretty sure I had 'felt' it – a sort of classic entry for people to find in other people's diaries! God, I behaved stupidly. And the distressing part is that so often I really haven't altered in the slightest. Most of the 'writing' avowals, or vows, are what I say, or at any rate act on, now. But why should my judgment be any less immature in matters of literature? Journals – diaries – are two-edged weapons! I really must arrange for mine to be destroyed when I die. Nearly bought a will form in Cheltenham, but can't think of anyone to make executor. Suppose it will have to be the bank. [...]

23 September 1954

30 Elmwood Avenue, Belfast

[...] My return was not marked by any great portents: there was a letter from Donald Davie inviting me to his 'Fellowship' dinner in T.C.D. & also saying that he heard nothing very encouraging about the Dolmen Press! So that may be going down the drain. [...]

The Librarianship of Hull is vacant: sounds not a bad place in many ways, but do I want a headship? Damned if I think I do. Member of senate ... Committees ... all that rubbish. Branch librarian of Bridport is more my line, really. I wonder if I shd ever have the courage to do anything like that? (Of course, I don't mean the Hull job is *mine for the asking*: I'm sure it's not: but one has to think such things over as if they were.)

Friday Evening coming in. Made a saucepanful of 'savoury rice' (rice, chopped bacon, curry powder, butter, milk) & blew myself out. I'm reading Fothergill yet again. I must say I do like him, though his humour is insufferable at times & I expect he was something of a toady. His unswerving devotion to 'what God wants' & his *hard work* earn him all my respect.

Talking about insufferable things, I found a foul article in *Punch* (15/9) by that poetic-play fool/swine Ronald Duncan called *Fewer rabbits, more men*. Written in the witless Wodehouse-and-water style of a naval station's magazine, it celebrated the arrival of myxomatosis at the writer's village ('when the first bulging-eyed creature was discovered ... it was drinks all round at the pub that night'). I read it very carefully to see if it could be intended satirically but I don't see that it could be. I therefore wrote a protest to the editor, very mild really, pointing out how unamusing, disagreeable & shameful it was.[1] He is bound to have had others. And if I may – entirely without rancour – say so, it is this sort of thing that makes me look down on *Punch* (you remember you once scolded me for it). It may be the backbone of England, but the *New St.* wd never offend in that way, and I judge them accordingly. [...]

I remember thinking, at Xmas 1949 or 1950, that if in 1945 someone had forecast that my first 3 Christmas cards in 5 yrs time would be from Charles Madge, Faber & Faber, & a girl called Jane Exall I mutely admired at the time, I shd have formed a very optimistic & erroneous picture of 1950 ... Now, today, I feel that if in 1949 someone had told me that the T.L.S. would, in its leading article, reproach the P.E.N. *New poems 1954* for not including me among its pages I should have thought the future held nothing but gold ... In fact it lists about thirty writers, myself included, from Amis to Watkins, & passing Hartley, Heath Stubbs, & Christopher Logue (who's he?), so I don't feel unduly flattered. From internal evidence, too, I guess the author to be G. S. Fraser, which isn't encouraging, but not so serious since the article isn't signed. The only ones in of 'our gang' (God) are Wain & Davie, indefatigable self advancers. Oh, & Elizabeth 'Everywoman' Jennings, of course. Apparently she works in the Oxford Public Library in Blue Boar Street. [...]

1 Letter to *Punch*: evidently not published.

28 September 1954

30 Elmwood Avenue, Belfast

Ha, my bonny bun,

Have about 20 mins to spare before Alec[1] is due with MY RECORDS – don't know yet what they are or in what condition. I thought of you last night when I was finishing an 8-line poem:[2] it began as a furious diatribe in response to filthy Ronald Duncan, but it finished as a very casual little anecdote: I've sent it to the *Spectator* along with *Church going*. Larkin goes propagandist. I feel shy of showing it to you. I'm afraid it will seem vulgar, or melodramatic, or not savage enough – too much of a literary little 'human' verse; not rabbity enough ... But who could be rabbity enough – D.H.L. I suppose, but he would be of unpredictable sympathy – 'I *hate* rabbits! I'm *glad* they're dying! I wd like to kill a million, *two* million rabbits!' etc. Hardy, I suppose, in a funny grotesque way ('blest champaign'). But I am rather ashamed of my little effort – knowing, that is, that *you* are what you are – except, of course, that I have seen *no* poem on this topic except a bit of silly facetiousness by A.P.H. I do think somebody might have written something. [...]

I have sent a covering letter saying that both of them are based on subjects that have cropped up in their pages recently so they *may* make up in topicality what they lack in the eye of eternity. I hope they pay me more than the usual measly 2 gns for the long one. I was staying with Kingsley when he got a cheque for that dreary stuff about the noble-man's son who couldn't see through it all, & *he* certainly got more than 2 gns. – & that was before he published *LJ* & became 'famous' & joined their staff. Still, 'I am content with what I have, Little be it or much . . .' and I don't like the notion of chaffering for money for poems anyway. 'If you think it's worth sixpence, pay that . . .' – No, I'm afraid this page is rather insincere, but I did take a long time over that poem & I do feel it's worth more than something done in 3 evenings. I know Schwartz wd tell me it was worth no more than what people wd pay to have it . . .[3]

Have you seen the Randall Jarrell excerpts in *Vogue* (October)?[4] I read some of it in *Partisan Review,* or one of these papers, & thought it quite good, but not nearly up to the M. McC. Rather *jollier,* more *à la* Robie McAuley ('absolutely rotten highballs') – but good stuff all right. – Ah, here is Alec.

Wednesday. Here indeed . . . didn't get to bed till near 3.30 a.m., $\frac{3}{4}$ drunk on red wine & some Bourbon whiskey he brought home, very nice, much nicer than ordinary whiskey. But o tragedy! he brought me BLP7003 Sidney Bechet vol. 2 when I'd asked for BLP7002 Sidney Bechet vol 1![5] You can't *imagine* how disappointed I was, though I pretended it was all right & what I'd asked for. It meant instead of 6 tracks of which I could forecast 4 superbs & 2 fairs I get 6 tracks, 2 'absolutely rotten', 2 fair, 2 good . . . so I *haven't* got his 1939 12" *Summertime,* on which the band are reputed to burst into spontaneous applause of him at the finish, or *Blue horizon,* or *Dear old Southland* – and all the session-mates I have of them are so good. O well. He brought me a tie in addition, very nice tie, mauve, long narrow thing, made by 'Fruits of the Loom'. I thought that very kind of him. His stories of America sound much what one expects – he says he didn't sleep properly ever all the time he was there, partly due to radio-controlled taxis booming about the streets all night, partly due to the heat. [. . .]

1 Alec Dalgarno, Lecturer in Applied Mathematics, QUB.
2 'Myxomatosis', completed 27 September 1954, published *Spectator* 26 November 1954.
3 George Schwartz, Economic Adviser, Kemsley Newspapers, 1944–61.
4 From *Pictures from an Institution* (1954).
5 L. completed his poem 'For Sidney Bechet' on 15 January 1954.

2 October 1954

30 Elmwood Ave, Belfast

[...] No word from the *Spr* about my deathless verse.[1] I should say that *Churchgoing* should be worth a fiver to them at present, arguing as they are about churches & their decay, preservation, sale, etc. – see Betjeman's poem this week? Lucky he doesn't pitch on my subject: do you know, as I say I think he's easily the best English poet today, except me, & we're not after entirely the same game. I think much of *Chrysanthemums*,[2] well, a bit trivial, but *some* of it is quite (i.e. absolutely) admirable – *House of rest*, this is a great favourite of mine; *I.M. Walter Ramsden* – this reminds me of a favourite picture I've long carried in my head & never quite formulated: it's an old photograph, taken in a college (very dark archway) & there are some young men in straw boaters talking together, in the general costume of the S. African War period ... I was to bring it into a novel, but never did; *Variations on a theme by T.W.R.*; *Business Girls* – I can see excellences in others, but these are the ones from which I get the strongest poetic vibration. And then we're given *Station syren*, *Hunter trials* & *Phone for the fish knives* for good measure! Damn' good, oh jolly good. He is due to write about the reviews his poems received in next week's *Spr* – feel like writing to say how highly I think of his work, as I suppose most people have been rather condescending. [...]

1 The *Spectator* had been sent 'Church Going' and 'Myxomatosis' by L., both of which they were later to publish ('Church Going', 18 November 1955; 'Myxomatosis', 26 November 1954).
2 Betjeman, *A Few Late Chrysanthemums* (1954), reviewed by L. in *Q* (literary magazine of QUB), Hilary term 1955. See *Further Requirements*.

10 October 1954

30 Elmwood Ave, Belfast

[...] The situation in Dublin was to some extent embarrassing about my poems.[1] Davie was for them (he said) & the two Irish (young fellows, they were) against. They thought them 'too self pitying' (I offered Davie this phrase & he gladly accepted it) and 'too sexy' (his own words). He was very apologetic, but I think the collection hadn't pleased him as much as he had expected. He did tell me 4 (out of 12) they all liked, but I can't remember them now, except *Triple Time*. The one he praised most was *Latest face* (classes in T.C.D. have been analysing this); the one he liked least *Wires* – in fact he thought it 'very feeble'! So there you are. I was disappointed at the time, but not now. O, another one that aroused general displeasure was *To fail*, but I think perhaps I made an error of judgment in including it. It really is very personal indeed. Somehow I don't think I shall see a book of my poems published unless I pay for it myself.

The bells are ringing through the dark. It's just half past six.

8.45 p.m. – Have just finished and typed a poem,[2] not good: slangy, unprofound. As a matter of fact I went a walk today & my head buzzed with ideas, ideas for short poems, that is. Pray the Good Rabbit that I succeed in doing so. [...]

1 Donald Davie, Thomas Kinsella and Liam Miller had been considering L.'s poems for publication by the Dolmen Press in Dublin. They were turned down. 'Triple Time' (completed 3 October 1953), 'Latest Face' (February 1951), 'Wires' (4 November 1950) all appeared eventually in *The Less Deceived*. 'To Fail' (later called 'Success Story') was completed 11 March 1954, appeared in *The Grapevine* (Durham University), February 1957, but did not appear in book form until the *Collected Poems*.
2 'Places, Loved Ones', 10 October 1954.

18 October 1954

30 Elmwood Avenue, Belfast

O, dear bun,

Half past nine. Have been fiddling around since eight with a new poem, a 'panoramic' poem of a kind I'm not very proficient at (*vide Sex: oils*) but like. My sleek head is fuller of Hull than of poetry at present, though not to any useful end. Graneek has read my application and made one or two remarks. Tomorrow I shall get the typist to 'roll it' (14 copies required) & Wednesday send it off. I fear I have not much chance against what Graneek calls the black-jacket-and-striped-trouser brigade. There must be so many eager young subs with wife & nippers 'whose crying is a cry for gold',[1] who will put up a better show than me. Of course it will be all up if any of the committee has read *Toads*[2] – *Listen*[3] is printed practically IN *Hull* – I can imagine some dismal Jimmy reading verses 1–6 aloud for the benefit and discrete *Myrthe* of ye assembld Companie. I wish I'd paid more attention to the place when I was there in '51. I'm glad your verdict was on the whole encouraging: I shd have hated to feel you didn't approve. [...]

'My attention was drawn' today (by Lerner)[4] to the letter by swine Higham[5] in the T.L.S. – really, to be teamed with that crowd just because I didn't send anything to New Poems '54! What a life! The *Spr.* have said nothing about C.G. & the rabbit one: makes me suspect the Golden Age is over. Davie said they'd returned 3 lots of his 'stuff'. O well. Silence, patience & exile. All this drivelling 'movement' business will ensure that we sink together, never to rise again. [...]

1 Tennyson, 'The Daisy'.
2 L. was evidently thinking of the selection committee's likely reaction to the notion of 'work' being like a toad, and all that follows.
3 The poetry periodical run by George and Jean Hartley in Hessle, a suburb of Hull, 1954–62. It published several of L.'s poems, including 'Toads'.
4 Laurence Lerner: see Appendix B.
5 Charles Higham: Australian poet and editor, at the time resident in England.

22 October 1954

30 Elmwood Avenue, Belfast

Bun dear,

Wuff! rather poor temper tonight, due to failure in the poetic line – curse it, I haven't written anything good for ages. What was the last? Hell, I don't know. How hard it is! You pick a good subject, or *have* a good subject, and start it off after a fashion, & then you realise you haven't the slightest interest in it, & can't muster up the least coherent & living sentence. [...]

Did you see that rave review of Randall Jarrell[1] by John Metcalf today? Silly ass. It's downright dull in too many and too extensive places to be any real good, whereas I doubt if there's a dull page in *The groves*. How incompetent the literary world is! How vile! How silly! Look at Richard Murphy in the correspondence page – whur ders he *mean*? Look at that tyke the TLS reviewer – Enright, Davie, & Gunn! Hack, spit & gob. Has any of them ever written one seriously-good poem? No! Well, then. I will not bother rabbit's ears any longer with such churlish spite.

By the way, I found a poem about a snail recently. It begins

She goes but softly, but she goeth sure;
  She stumbles not as stronger creatures do . . .

and has the lines:

She makes no noise, but still seizeth on
  The flower or herb appointed for her food . . .

Know who it's by? Guess –

John Bunyan! If you didn't know, I expect you were thinking of Cotton or Herrick or Walton or Gilbert White: I should have. Don't you like it? The rest is quite good, but irritates by an illogicality later on. Only 12 lines: 1686, *A book for boys and girls*. [. . .]

Just now I really have little news to report: Kingsley doesn't write to me, so I don't write to him, nor that fat self-indulgent fool Bruce. The *Spr.* says nothing about my poems, which does not argue that they are very anxious to print them. I don't myself feel any great spirit rushing in me like a wind. The only live subject of thought I have is this public humiliation in Hull, hypothetical humiliation I should say, since no one has replied to my fat envelope yet.

Monday. Ah! letter from you today. I'm not one of the save-it-to-read-in-the-apple-tree school. I tear it open instantly and walk slowly upstairs reading it, not taking off my scarf & raincoat till I've finished. Very nice! We both seem a bit drab at present, witness this letter to date, you with reason, me without. How dreary & depressing this room-hunt is! Everything looks its worst when seen in such circumstances. [. . .]

You and your bottom – you never believe me when I say that while there certainly is a point of no return in that quarter, you haven't anything like reached it. I lay in bed one morning last week remembering one after-breakfast time when you were looking out of my kitchen window, and let me tuck your skirt up round your waist to be admired. You were wearing the black nylon panties with the small hole in! In consequence of this memory I was guilty of what I believe the Confirmation Books called 'impure thoughts', and, worse, late for work. Anyway, better than *Ganymede*, what? Yes, I always thought India to Forster was what Berlin was to Isherwood – somewhere where he could really go to town at last without any fear of 'what the neighbours would say' (or, worse, do).

– Got dragged out at that point, a matter of fuseboxes and keys, wch I didn't like & didn't manage to solve. Wuff! Hope the above paragraph doesn't sound, what was it you called it, *coy*.

Had a form from Blackwell's today asking for '1 Larkin. Poems' – don't know what this is supposed to mean, but shall send them a XX, & charge 3/6d. I like to think of some poor crazed creature[2] paying over his/her money ... But, honestly, I was looking at that XX last night, & I thought that only one, namely XV, had gone quite dead. Most of them were leppin' around still. People never say anything complimentary about IX, but I don't think it's so bad as I used to, & certainly says more about me than anything else (except *To fail*). The last line is 'exactly me'.[3] [...]

Hull have acknowledged my application – their acknowledgment had been lying under a pile of periodical-post for a day or two. I don't think Graneek is guilty of any *arrière-pensée*: I may have reported him wrong. He believes in going in for things 'irregardless', but I dare say if Hull *want* a respectable citizen they won't consider me. I shd say I'm too young anyway, since at this distance since demob there are bound to be some pretty impressive candidates about. £1300 will soon whistle the boys in. No, I may get a trip to England from it, but that's all I'm expecting. [...]

1 Of *Pictures from an Institution* (1954), which L. contrasts with Mary McCarthy's *The Groves of Academe*.
2 Almost certainly Anthony Thwaite, who ordered *XX Poems* from Blackwell's in Oxford at this time.
3 Poems from *XX Poems*: XV, 'Who called love conquering'; IX, 'Waiting for breakfast, while she brushed her hair'.

30 October 1954

30 Elmwood Avenue, Belfast

Beloved rabbit,

Arthur[1] looked in just before 5 while I was cleaning the windows (not done since you did them, honey) & playing George Lewis' *Burgundy Street blues*, the nearest approach to jazz Timmy-Willie-Music, and left me the new K.M. journal & the old one, to compare them. He often does this, buys some delectable book on Friday or Saturday, then lends it to me *before he's read it* so that it shan't interfere with 'his own work' on Sunday. It is of a size with the J.M.M. letters, but thinner of course (336 p). It has a beautiful frontispiece, the beloved grandma & her husband when young, quite exquisite. Have I read it? Well, only scraps: there is some previously unpublished Carco stuff, and plenty of cut sentences ('J. and I were lovers after supper') – but for the most part I've read what

I knew before, and it has done me good – I mean I feel more sensitive, more receptive, happier, than before. O, I daresay there'll be a few jeering reviews (some dirty mick in the latest edition of Dublin *Studies* says that K.M. was to V. Woolf what Priestley is to Fielding(!) – and quotes VW's opinion of *Bliss* to prove it!) but she is *all right* . . . I do think that she is one of the few people (Hardy is another) who set things moving, swinging, quietly, harmoniously, inside one, as if some thaw was taking place. And again it makes you dreadfully miserable, since you apprehend life more keenly, and since you know (or I know) that she's so far ahead in unselfish observation and transcription. I'd forgotten she quoted 'O crocus root', & liked to read again that French poem

Le temps des lilas et le temps des roses[2]

Ne reviendra plus ce printemps-ci . . . ('. . . in my mind I heard it sung in a very pure voice to a piano . . .') which seems much nicer than any other French poem I've ever read, in fact, it seems the ONLY French poem I've ever read that *is nice at all*. Then 'Be not afeared, the house is full of blankets.' 'Why hath the Lord not made *bun* trees?' And her cats – 'his whole complete little life side by side with ours' – I'm sure Colette is miles away. 'Every umbrella hides a warm bud of life.' Oh, & speaking of umbrellas, she adds a ribald note after *there ain't going to be no tea* to the effect that Helen Schlegel must have been got with child by Mr Bast's umbrella. What a thing to cut!

KM's *Journal* can hardly help arousing questions within oneself of a disagreeable nature:

Q. What is your aim in life?

A. Oo-ah-

Q. Ten years ago you were determined 'to write', weren't you?

A. Yes.

Q. What's happened to that determination?

A. Oo – ah – well –

Q. Have you replaced it by any other worthwhile aim, such as doing your job well, or helping people, or being 'rooted in life'?

A. Can't say I have.

Q. In fact, you're just drifting, doing nothing that might entangle you with your amniotic environment?

A. Well, look at old –

Q. Haven't you always said that the most important thing about people is the kind of environment they are trying to create round them?

A. Yes.

Q. How d'you fancy you show up, then, with your nancy-boy's job and Billy Bunter books and sex no nearer than your Bessie Smith records?

A. Oh go and boil yr head.

– actually, that exchange doesn't really make my point about K.M., that she is enormously dedicated, from page 1 ('I mean this year to try and be a different person ...') in 1904, to p. 334 ('to be rooted in life ...') in 1922, she was enormously aware of things unquestionably more pure, more significant, more beautiful than she was herself & of the problem of translating them by means of art, by catching hold of their tiny significant manifestations ('Charles sat darning socks ... When he took up the scissors, the cat squeezed up its eyes as if to say "That's quite right", and when he put the scissors down it just put out its paw as if to straighten them ...'). This seems to me to depend enormously on the fact that she did not distinguish between life and art. This is of first importance: no 'stupid life at its bungling work', as in H.J. Art is good insofar as it catches life, and, really, the opposite is true too, in KM. These attitudes are not inclusive, but exclusive – a continual refining, a self-purification. She never said, as I'm afraid I do, well, this is bloody dull, but it's life, life's like that; nor, well, this is fine, splendid in fact, but of course it's only a book, just imaginary. The first would be instantly discarded in favour of the second. And of course you *have* to think like that to be a writer, just as you have to believe your soap is the best in the world if you're a soap-seller. If you don't believe art is better than ... no, wait a minute, that isn't what KM thought. If you *don't* believe that good art is better than bad life, then bugger off, there's plenty of room for your sort in the civil service. If you *do* believe it, then stay and try to convert *the whole of life into art*, until the smallest action is a ritual, an *auto da fe*, rejecting what you can't transmute. 'And out of this ... I want to be writing.' This is leading *me* into raving, but I feel at present that the 2 things to consider about K.M. are the art-life business as sketched out above, & the question why (generally speaking) are her stories so unsuccessful ('a charming talent – but not great! Why say great?' D.H.L.)

It gave me a queer sensation to find that she wrote J.M.M. a letter 'to be opened after her death' on Aug 8th 1922 – the day before I was born! I can't see this letter has ever been published.

I'm sure the envelope won't hold all this. Good night; bless you, dear paws. S.[3]

1 Arthur Terry, Lecturer in Spanish, QUB. See Appendix B.

2 See note 1, p. 12.

3 S. for Seal.

6 November 1954

30 Elmwood Ave, Belfast

[...] Have also bought the K.M. *Journal* – I was so interested in the things you said about her & it, though I forget much of what I said that you are replying to.[1] Do you see what struck me? The incessant harping on the conviction that the *aperçus* in which 'life' seemed most piercingly summarised (e.g. 'On the wall of the kitchen there was a shadow, shaped like a little mask with two gold slits for eyes. It danced up and down') put on her not only an artistic obligation to record them, but a moral obligation to 'live up to' them. This is stressed again & again & again. *I* think (but of course I've never been a girl) you do her less than justice in implying that 'wanting to be a different person' was only self dramatisation. In its numerous contexts it reads to me more like the ordinary reaction of any person who sees anything beautiful – a wish to return thanks, or to – this is more like it – to struggle towards a state of mind in which such perceptions would be more common, and in which they wd be of some practical use. After all, that is what one feels about such things, if only one could rely on them for help, seriously! Of course, I only bother about this idea because her noticings (is that the English equivalent?) are so extraordinary. I am quite sure nobody has ever written to touch her, not even Lawrence. That sentence, or pair of sentences, about the shadow on the wall, seems to me to contain such a lot: the suggestion of a gaiety, sinister because heartless, at the very centre of life – yet only a mask! What looks through it is still a mystery.

Of course I don't deny there is a lot about her I don't care for. The childish racket, & its element in her marriage & in her writings (worse!). The fits of temperament – but of course she was ill. The self will – yes, but after all, she knew that if she could but get away she could do something, left to herself. One doesn't get rid of one's family by being a decent person. The crankiness & mystic notions & dramatics. I don't know! Perhaps if I went through the *Journal* marking the bits I like you could follow pointing out how attitudinising they were. But I shd like to look into this conversion of life-into-art business, & also the Journal v. Stories business. [...]

Sunday. A quiet day: bright & frosty in morning. I've spoken no words to anyone except the paperman. After a meagre lunch I cycled round some of the back ways, but the day was dull & even slightly damp by four o'clock so there wasn't much to enjoy. After reading the papers this morning I put on my huge radio & couldn't understand why there was nothing on the home service except the noise of a large silent audience. Then I looked at the clock ... I had been unwittingly transported to the Cenotaph. Hastily I tried to collect my thoughts, looked at my poppy, thought of Sassoon at the hydro in Scotland, and *They shall not grow old, as we that are left grow old*, then a thump of gunfire released me from my effort. *Though poppies fade In Flanders fields* – who wrote that? 1914–1918: that drab patch on our century, grey-green, green-brown, the colour of churned mud, how really it is trembling with emotion if you look closely! A silly sentence, but you know what I mean. 1939–45 will never stir me as much: I don't think the reason's entirely in me, either.

Yes, the Hon. Pat[2] did get to Paris: she's a student at the College Franco Britannique. Corbiere is now vilipended, but after all he's served his purpose & got her there: he can be abandoned now. She sounds as if she's enjoying herself, except for an Embassy party, where she seems to have been sat on rather. God knows where Colin is – Newcastle, I suppose. [...]

Monday after lunch Light drifting skies, rain seeming to be wafted up from the ground, making an umbrella useless ...

Thought to have finished this last night but didn't, brooding over useless poem – *très mouvement*! Kingsley reports the popular belief that we are all G. S. Fraser's catamites. You don't know how I should like to write a different sort of poetry altogether! but when I try, I just can't produce even a *bad* poem. [...]

1 In a letter dated 3 November 1954, Monica wrote: 'I'm touched and amused to see how, always, a little of KM shakes a letter out of you to me – it does, doesn't it? [...] I do hope I'm not getting tired of her [...] I feel I know too much about that kind of writing-in-a-diary: naturally in those days I called it a "journal" too. I can smell it out in her absolutely – *I* know when she's writing the truth & when she's making it up, I've done it all myself ... It seems awfully presumptuous to say this, when she *did* do something & I never do & never will, that I wouldn't say it to anyone else for anything[...]'
2 Patsy Strang.

14 November 1954

30 Elmwood Ave, Belfast

[...] I'm not keeping 'the rabbit one' from you: it's only that in it I kill the rabbit, which makes it totally out of character & rather like a piece of journalism. I'll transcribe it:[1]

{Blind   {sightless
{Caught in the centre of a   {soundless field
As hot, inexplicable hours go by
What trap is this?   *Where were its teeth concealed?*
You seem to ask.
                    I make a brief reply;
Then clean my stick. I'm glad I can't explain
Just in what jaws you were to suppurate:
You may have thought things would come right again
If you could only keep quite still and wait.

It's not much of a poem. But of course I *felt* strongly enough about it. I hardly dare ask what you think of it. I strove (queer word) to give the essential pathos of the situation without getting involved in argument. Give me your opinion on sightless/soundless. I believe rabbits are both blind and deaf, so either wd do – a field with no sights or sounds in. Oh dear. Is this 'using' the rabbits? Honestly, my motives are really good – better than the poem, I'm afraid. [...]

Dear bun, I know what you mean about turning life into art – I sometimes have you with me for long stretches, noticing things together – actually that sounds *horrible*, but yesterday I walked up the Lisburn Road, a *very dull* road, for about 2 miles, a road nobody would ever walk along for pleasure – rather like, say, the Melton Road in Leicester, but *I* enjoyed it & so wd *you*, & I thought as much at the time. Simple pleasures!

You look a bit worried, trying to keep in step! Rabbit's hay. [...]
Letter from Kingsley, having apparently recalled how nice it is
to get letters from me, and outlining plans for a Fantasy anthology
(him, me, Wain, X, Y & Z). Letter from Hartley confirming that
Fraser is putting us all in some anthology of Fabers[2] – perhaps even the
FBMV,[3] 3rd ed. Postcard from the Imperial Hotel, Hull,[4] saying a room
is reserved ... [...]

1 Variants in 'Myxomatosis', which L. appeared to have completed in its final form
on 28 September 1954.
2 G. S. Fraser's *Poetry Today*, which included Amis, Conquest, Davie, Enright,
Gunn, Holloway, Jennings, L. and Wain, appeared from Faber in 1956.
3 *The Faber Book of Modern Verse*.
4 The hotel where L. stayed at the time of his interview for the Library job in Hull.

23 November 1954

M.V. Irish Coast

Dearest Bunny,

Well, I have got as far as the boat, after hellish dull wet journey
through Sheffield, Penistone, & Manchester, & have eaten a fish
supper, & 2 Kwells[1] to help me keep it down. I feel really quite
blank and scared/exhausted. To give you the details, simply: there
were seven of us, me, the deputy, & the librarian of the Hull Institute
of Education; then 4 others, Roberts of Manchester, Cox & Clark
of Leeds, & Jolley of R.C.S., Edinburgh – or R.C.P., I never can remember. Little chap like a pocket E. M. Forster who was offered my Belfast
job but had accepted the Edinburgh one. They *started* at 11 in alpha-
betical order, & got through about 1.30 p.m. Then there was a long
wait. Then they called   in[2] & offered it to me. So I accepted. I'm
now (I fancy) the youngest University librarian in G.B.[3] Much good
may it do me.

The place seems well enough, but I can see that the go-ahead
professors – equivalents of Simmons & Sykes – are fed up with the
library and want some drastic action. I don't think I'd care to make
friends with those chaps, but I shall have to do business with them.
All in all I feel *woundy scared*, & shall have to start learning up my
work, & Graneek's work, & every-bloody-body's work, & forget all
this modern stuff. [...]

Wednesday Home again. Bright frosty morning. Feel very low, & as if I had agreed to command NATO forces in Europe. O bun! Hugs. Seal. [...]

1 Anti-seasickness tablets.
2 The blank is filled with a tiny self-sketch of L. as a seal.
3 L. was thirty-two.

28 November 1954

30 Elmwood Ave, Belfast

My dear,

[...] Your letter helped me to dispel some of the misery that hung about me like indigestion in the middle of the week. I was absolutely rigid with terror all Wednesday. Graneek said he'd never seen anyone react to success like it. Success, forsooth! It has been a whirl of congratulations, & Ashby pulling off his glove to shake hands, & nothing-succeeds-like-success, & *resigning* (brrrr!), & noting various reactions. They all seem fairly friendly about it, except a fat fool of a law professor called Montrose – a Billy-Bunter Roman emperor – & I thought I detected signs of chagrin in Brian Tate. But this is accompanied by *no word from Hull*: it might all have been a dream, or a nightmare. Suppose it was? Should I mind? Well ... in a way – with the strong sensible bit of my mind – I should. But there's a feeling strong upon me of penetrating further and further into the wrong kind of life. O to be a Controller of Stamps![1] I can't reconcile this career stuff at all: perhaps it is Yeats' 'theatre business, management of men', or my 'mask'. Or perhaps I am blindly following a pattern laid down by my father. Or perhaps it's just the way things happen: I want to move, & the only move is upwards. I'd sooner move sideways, like a crab! [...]

Did you notice the rabbit poem, tucked away in *the Spr* on Friday?[2] Wonder if I shall receive any letters about it. I don't like the broken line: the first half has insufficient carry-on from the first 3 lines; the second is rather stupidly enigmatic, suggesting a farcical interpretation, like a belch or something of the sort. But I like lines 5 & 6, & lines 7 & 8 are vitiated only by the unspoken 'Yes, & you may *not*' hanging about them. I should have done better to choose something more incontrovertible for my *finale*, but the thing was written in such a tearing hurry

I didn't stop to consider such niceties. I do hope you find it respectful to the awful state of yr nation. I should hate it if you thought I was just earning a couple of guineas from their sufferings. [...]

Monday My hat, I felt bad today – couldn't sleep last night, and cut the library after lunch till about 4.15 pm. I felt *ghastly*, also depressed and scared. What a hopeless character mine is. In 1950 I ran away from England & the problems it held, but really they're still there unchanged & now I'm *going back* to them ... Five years older, five years poorer, five years colder, five years ... can't think of a rhyme. Surer? Surer of what? Brrr. [...]

1 L. is thinking of a title given Wordsworth, and in effect a sinecure.
2 'Myxomatosis' was published in the *Spectator*, 26 November 1954.

7 December 1954

30 Elmwood Ave, Belfast

[...] I feel be-etter now: of course your letters cheer me up, make me feel wherry full of beans! I am all right, scared about Hull of course, but ready to shorten my lines to almost any extent to meet it. Really, the fat salary is the *only* attraction. Let me explain the family situation – last Christmas & Easter were hell at home: I don't know what was wrong, possibly Mother was trying to bounce me into 'doing something' – anyway, I told myself 'You must never come back to England till she is dead and gone if you want a quiet life.' But my sister grumbled that things wd be better if I could come home oftener, & that she had it all the time, etc., which seemed reasonable to me, hence my return, at length. But M. now drops hints of 'sharing a house' or 'dividing a house into 2 flats' for herself & (hypothetical) companion, & for me. This was not what I had meant, at all. On the other hand I don't want to hock my weekends so that I never get any peaceful recuperation, 10 hours' travelling in 3 days, great stuff. But again I don't imagine that any companion would ever be found so that I shd be tied as at Leicester, if the other course were followed.

At Christmas all this will no doubt be thrashed out. I'm not looking forward to it. Honestly, I don't know what I want – but I do know what I don't want! I find the presence or company of my mother largely depressing. It fills me full of a sense of guilt & motheaten pity & wormeaten fear of responsibility and age and death. These things are uncomfortable. Of course, they may also be justified and salutary. [...]

Faintly, on the gusty wind, a brass band playing *Once in royal David's city* ... Christmas is coming! *If Christmas were what Christmas were what Christmas seems, And not the Christmas of our dreams* ... Now *Christians awake.* And the rain is *pelting* down. *Rise to adore the mystery of love* ... Did I tell you how all last Armistice Day I could not get from my head the line *Tranquil you lie, your knightly virtue proved?*[1] It repeated itself time & time again, seeming to hold the whole spirit of the day. That day ... It positively sends shivers down my spine. Like August 4th 1914: the overheard clink of the milkman's measure as he filled the jug, & the words 'We're going in' – so the sudden repeated exclamation 'They've signed! They've signed!' and, in the distance, cheering ... 'Not knowing what to do, like, we followed the crowd up west, but when we got to Admiralty Arch we couldn't get through, and had to go round ... Everyone was makin' for the Palace ...' O rabbit! do you understand all this? O life! O England! 'And bugles calling for them from sad shires ...'[2] O tripe! O Noel Coward! O Cavalcade! [...]

1 Words from the hymn 'O Valiant Hearts', written during the First World War by Sir John Stanhope Arkwright (1872–1954).
2 Wilfred Owen's 'Anthem for Doomed Youth'.

15 December 1954

30 Elmwood Avenue, Belfast

[...] I am suffering pangs of conscience about buying my mother a pair of *fur gloves*. She asked for them. I ought to have refused, really. If this sounds lavish, it's because Bruce suddenly sent me ten iron men for reading his proofs, just about five times as much as I had decided to ask for. So look out for misprints in '*Best sf*', published by Faber & Faber.

As for your strictures about my mother,[1] no, of course I'm not offended, but I think yr language rather turgid – John Middleton Bunny. I don't know whether I agree with you or not, really; but, of course, if one starts blaming one's parents, well, one would never stop! Butler said that anyone who was still worrying about his parents at 35 was a fool, but he certainly didn't forget them himself, and I think the influence they exert is enormous. I've told you before that the only characteristic I can't trace directly to one or other of them is hay fever! What one doesn't learn from one's parents one never learns, or learns awkwardly, like a mining M.P. taking lessons in table manners or the middle aged Arnold Bennett learning to dance. I never remember my parents making a single spontaneous gesture of affection towards each other, for instance.

Of the present situation, well, again I don't really know what to say. Admitted, my mother is nervy, cowardly, obsessional, boring, grumbling, irritating, self pitying. It's no use telling her to alter: you might as well tell a sieve to hold water. On the other hand, she's kind, timid, unselfish, loving, and upset both by losing her husband rather early & by being seventy (next month) with both her children showing *marked* reluctance to live with her. Balanced intelligent people, I know, can adjust themselves and find compensations, but she isn't balanced or intelligent. It seems to me a vicious circle. If she were more attractive she would have a more interesting life: on the other hand she won't get it until she's more attractive. Am I, ultimately, on her side? God knows! In my heart of hearts, I'm on no one's side but my own.

You seem to suggest that I've yet to throw off my mother & grab myself primary emotional interest in a woman my own age. This may well be true – it sounds true – but it's not a thing one can do by will power. It's all too difficult for me to write about: I never got the hang of sex, anyway. If it were announced that all sex wd cease as from midnight on 31 December, my way of life wouldn't change at all. I tremble to think what mafficking most people would throw themselves into! (Of course I don't *welcome* this trait in myself!)

Think I'll have a bath now. I always feel I need a bath more when I'm wearing my blue suit. Can't explain this . . .

Later – Duly bathed. I don't mean, of course, that I don't like making love with you: that wd be *inaccurate* – I only mean I don't take girls to dances or out or that kind of thing – Chwist naher – and I suppose that's not healthy, i.e. not normal. Still, let's drop all this, till we can talk about it. I feel much better since having the bath – much be-etter! – and writing verse 2 of my poem.[2] *Reasons for att.* earned the censure of the

Dolmen Press boys – too sexy, I suppose, for the priest-ridden crooked little lice. It's not up to much. [...]

1 In a 20-sided letter dated 7 December 1954, from 8 Woodland Avenue, Monica had written: 'Forgive what may be a terrible page to read, but don't be robbed! don't be robbed of your soul! I don't mean by that exactly, simply, don't live with your Mother; if you could do it without being robbed, that would not count, but can you, can you even live at all without it; can you? I would say, *make* the effort, *do* it, but it isn't a matter of effort. Anyway, forgive me, & say you do please ...'
2 This is likely to be verse two of the following, which appears in Notebook 4, after October 1954, though itself undated:

How we behave, I find increasingly,
Depends on something like a sense of shape,
Not on ambition or ability.
What shapes our comfort? What decides
Long before policy has woken up,
The manly square, the lucky seven-sides?

Quarrelsome diamond? dangerous triangle?
Designs more intricate and twice as sharp
Direct us; we adroitly disentangle
Person and place and impulse that will best
Illude us we are there safe in the loop,
Bright in the star, and chuck away the rest.

20 December 1954

30 Elmwood Ave, Belfast

[...] George Hartley of *LISTEN* – 'Lissen' – writes to ask if I wd like to 'kick off' a series of volumes of poetry he wants to publish – in Hull!! Have written temporising. If only he lived in any other city! 'Luke at that, Mister Chairman. Luke at that word. Used to write it oop in you-rinals when I was a nipper. Now they call it poetry.' [...]

Christmas 1954¹

Christmas

No traps are set that day; there are no guns;
    Dogs do not bark.
Even our oldest, even our youngest ones
    Hop out by dark.

Yet none can tell why such a respite should
    Each year come round,
As if, that day, some mighty Rabbithood
    Peered above ground.

A rhyme and
a present,
with all love,

From Philip

To Monica
for Christmas
1954.

1 On 20 December 1954, Monica wrote to L.: 'A Christmas poem for me! I love
it. Don't you, aren't you very gravely pleased & proud? A secret present for me –
for a secret reason. I can't say how much I like it. It is better than *The Oxen* for
Christmas; your little poems! they are being good ones, in the pretty cards, aren't
they, don't you think so yourself?'

28 December 1954

21 York Road, Loughborough

Dearest Monica,

Yes, I ought to have reported my safe arrival, but as we didn't *sink* I hoped you'd guess I'd got home in the end. [...]

I sat looking at your parcels for ages. I *couldn't* think what they were. The one that rattled I put down as shaving soap (wch I didn't want!) & the book I finally decided was that O.U.P. illustrated edn of nursery rhymes (wch I quite wanted to look at, but not much more than that). I was quite enchanted with the soap – what luxurious pellets! so far I haven't used it, but it smells so fine and unusual I know I shall enjoy it when I do. Then I got some of the wrappings off the book, & seeing the grey jacket & dark blue binding I thought '*Oxford editions of the poets*! Great God! Who is it? Landor? Shelley? *Vaughan*?' Then I saw the words *Brewer's dictionary* & I really thought you'd gone ravers: 'yeast is yeast, but waste is waste', I muttered – then I got it all out & could see that your reason hadn't dismounted from its throne, & that in fact I had a good sensible present, the sort of luxury (as you say) I shdnt buy for myself but am very glad to have, to set beside my other works of reference in my small bookcase. I too thought we had it somewhere, but I can't find it. It is a curious work. Like others of its kind it's better at telling you things it knows than things you don't know. I tried it with several things – B.V.D.'s,[1] making the fig, jessie (Scotch for pansy-boy) – and got no or unsatisfactory replies. On the other hand it was informative about *bunny*, & *harrowing* about cats – the awful barbarous cruelties practised on cats, all because they were connected in the popular mind with witches ! – and just by reading about I've found many entertaining things – the last words, yes,[2] also the taverns & giants. And it's nice to have the jeroboam – magnum stuff tabled, & the months-&-jewels, & the Bibles, & many more. I should like to set you a baby questionnaire:

1. What is *jerked beef*?
2. Would you fetch a rick mould if asked to?
3. What or where is the Brisbane Line? Has it anything to do with ships?
4. What's the French for *April Fool*?
5. You have eaten lots of shaddocks in your time. Why were they called that? What are they called now?

The other two things I noticed are, how *proper* it is (*talking cock*, I mused, but found no elucidation; likewise … but enough!), & how valiantly it tries to keep up with jazz – but no *bop* or *cool*, the latest words. Their explanation of *raspberry* I find Bowdlerised to the point of irrelevance. Well! Thanks! I shall, leave it at home for the present, but when I have anywhere to put it I shall like to have it by me. […]

1 Underwear, 'better ventilated drawers'.
2 Monica had evidently suggested that L. should read the entry on dying words from Brewer.

8 January 1955

30 Elmwood Ave, Belfast

[…] Have been brooding on my poems.[1] There was a letter from Hartley waiting for me when I got back, saying that the book wd be printed in London & promising not to sell it in Hull, saying that in fact it was impossible to sell poetry in Hull. His description of the book – 9" × 6", either Garamond or Ultra Bodoni type – doesn't sound very appetising, but I've rather come round to the view that 'there is a tide in the affairs of men', if this is a tide. It's not a very powerful tide! Fantasy Press are *paying* Davie.[2] This will take care of my poetry for about five years: render it impossible for me to publish another book till I've written a lot more. But I think this is a good year to strike. I've made a list of probables and find 23 suitable ones. I think it's important that there shouldn't be any dud among them, or ones I myself am not sure of. I can't decide about *Churchgoing* – it's one of the 23, but I'm not sure. What do you think? This assuming a standard that disqualifies *Poetry of departures* & *To fail* & *Spring*. I should like it for its length!

Another thing: I am always at a loss about a title. I'd *like* to call it *Such absences*, to draw attention to my favourite poem! only it doesn't make sense, since my poems aren't *really* 'attics cleared of me', far from it, in any way that makes sense. Can you see any way in which it would make sense? Otherwise, I shall have to think of some other title. Can you suggest one?

Lastly, how about dedicating it to you? I don't mean any great fanfare of trumpets, just a note 'inscribing' (rather than dedicating) it to Monica Jones. No subordinate clauses about 'remembering that sundrenched auberge in Picardy where we drank that exquisite bottle of Chateau Margarine ...' Or wd you sooner have Monica, M. Jones, M.M.B. Jones? Or wd you sooner not have it at all? Some of them, the poems I mean, are coarse fare, as you know: I shd quite understand if you'd prefer not to be associated with it. Or if you'd sooner see them all before deciding, I expect that can be arranged. Will you let me know what you'd like?

I see the latest selection by the Poetry Book Club is called 'Kites' Dinner'[3] – shall I call mine *Snake's Dinner*? That makes me grunt with laughter, like a pig, but again I can't see how to explain it. There seem no alternatives to the priggish (i.e. *Poems*, *23 Poems*, *Poems 1946–1955*) or the smart (*In the same breath*, *True to life*, etc. etc). [...]

1 L. is brooding on the contents and appearance of what became *The Less Deceived*.
2 Oscar Mellor's Fantasy Press, at Swinford near Oxford, had since 1952 been running a series of small poetry pamphlets, the Fantasy Poets. Elizabeth Jennings had been no. 1, and later ones were by Gunn (16), Davie (19), Larkin (21), and Amis (22). Jennings's first full-length book (*Poems*, 1953) came from the same press, followed by Gunn's *Fighting Terms* (1954) and Davie's *Brides of Reason* (1955). L. was evidently irritated that Davie had been offered an advance.
3 *A Kite's Dinner*: book of poems by Sheila Wingfield.

16 January 1955

30 Elmwood Ave, Belfast

Dearest,

'So we are at last separated for the first time and I can't tell you *how* strange it seems to be without you and how much I miss you in every-thing *all day long*.' Who wrote that to his brother? No, not J.C.P. or even Ll. P., but Prince Albert Victor (Duke of Clarence) to the Duke of York (later George V) in 1883; not that it's very unusual, I suppose, but I'm struck by the curiously warm, feminine character of the princes, rather like the Powyses, and especially George, who of course I always thought of as very forbidding. In other words I've started Harold Nicolson's *King George V*: good reading. Good for telling. It has given me a line I think simply enormous in context – the last entry in the diary he had kept since 1880, on January 17 1936 – 18 years ago tomorrow! It runs:

'A little snow, & wind. Dawson arrived this evening.
I saw him & feel rotten.'

Give me that, & you can take *Mistah Kurtz: he dead*[1] *avec le plus grand plaisir* ...

Well, this has been a mixed day. More snow, but very sunny. I went a walk between 3 and 5 – it *is* keeping lighter, you know! – and turned down New Forge Lane and back along the towpath. There was snow everywhere and the river was frozen, hard enough to hold bricks. Birds were darting about looking for anything eatable. The sky seemed rosy or even mauve. The snow looked blue, as in that Pissarro in the Leicester Art Gallery. When I reached Stranmillis the street lamps were just coming on.

My dinner was ready about 5.30 & I found it disappointing: steak awfully tough & dry although I had done it quite lightly. Had to *leave* half of it! Meal was redeemed by real cream & a tin of raspberries. Then I washed up & returned to my room for *Take it from here* & laundry. When that was over, I made up my collection for Hartley. In the end I left everything *in* except *Spring* & *To fail* (now called *Success story*):[2] it makes 26 in all. Provisionally I've called it *Various poems*. I hope he is honest and efficient, by God! because it's quite a good set and it will take me a long while to write as many more. I've put in 'To Monica Jones', again provisionally. Provisional *form*, I mean! Not person!

I have been looking up the poem that feels like the ancestor of *Times, places, loved ones*[3] – that is, the first poem in *The Collected poems of T.H.*[4] Do you see what I mean? I did not expect you to find it sympathetic, really, but it's not *very* personal – I only start from 'my own case' in order to make two generalisations. They are the important parts. Anyway, I never read *one* poem by Hardy: and really as Keats said of Shakespeare 'I think I shall never read any book as much' – remember:

I am the passer when up-eared hares,
   Stirred as they eat
   The new-sprung wheat,
Their munch resume ...

        (p. 799)

and:

So, bran-new summer, you
   Will never see

All that yester-summer saw!
Never, never will you be
   In memory
Its rival, never draw
Smiles your forerunner drew,
   Know what it knew!

(779)

This is the third & last verse echoing a first verse, and really, don't you find it *terribly affecting*? I am blinking seal's tears as I write – oh to be able to catch that Hardy note, that rough conversational approach behind which lurks the clearest of voices, fresh as rain, far off and sad! He is *enough*, enough for me anyway. I must read him more, much more.

And that calm eve when you walked up the stair ... (647) And what about *The whitewashed wall?* (648) I like it, but the first verse is wrong, too over-written, if she did no more than look it would be better. Now I've come upon *An ancient to ancients* (658): this is the kind of success Hardy has, isn't it; the quite-original form that could never be used again by anyone, but can be used once well by him. How the reiterated 'Gentlemen' calls up a group of game old birds sitting round a table! It's the after-dinner connotations, I suppose. And the way it stands alone, over and over again, gives a sense of *staunchness*. Imagine the 'Gentlemen' just tacked on the ends of lines! And in the last verse how deftly it is turned to mean the younger generation, just to round it off. I wonder if *The carrier* (670) is the same idea as *Woak Hill?*[5] If they were both thinking of the same story, I mean? And I've not noticed *Green slates* (675) before. But this could go on all night. [...]

1 From Conrad's *Heart of Darkness*, and the epigraph for T. S. Eliot's *The Waste Land*.
2 'Success Story' (formerly 'To Fail') was dropped from the contents of *The Less Deceived*.
3 'Times, Places, Loved Ones' eventually became simply 'Places, Loved Ones'.
4 *Collected poems of Thomas Hardy*: the edition used by L. and Monica was the 4th edition (Macmillan, 1930), and all their page references are to that edition.
5 'Woak Hill': William Barnes ('When sycamore leaves wer a-spreaden /Green-ruddy in hedges ...')

29 January 1955

30 Elmwood Ave, Belfast

[…] I hear the Myxomatosis Committee says it will rage again this year. If this is so, I don't want a holiday in rural England. It would be *quite dreadful* to be afraid to go out lest we shd happen on any pitiful stricken ones. This Christmas was quite enough for me. Do you know, it is absurd – & I mean that – but I keep thinking of them in terms of Owen's *Exposure*. 'Is it that we are dying?' And they looked so like a battlefield – some newly dead, some old, all so terribly abandoned. And of course it was so cold, that day! By the gor I do like Owen, though. Just a small amount: not all. Perhaps tomorrow I'll look some up to quote.

But now – oh, my eyes ache & I feel, 'ow you say, lowzee. Goodnight, furry one. […]

I'm not sure I like this 'poor, poor fellow' line of yours about D.H.L.[1] – it grates on me rather, like an utterance of some moral pocket-handkercher brigader, and I'm not clear about the 'wish to outrage "the human spirit"' – but Lawrence is not really a living subject with me. He died, quietly, about 1950. I really don't know what you mean. And as regards cruelty, except when he was in a temper Lawrence's cruelty was so much literary daydreaming (like Llewelyn's sex). Compare him with a person like Hemingway, for instance, who really enjoys bullfights and big game shooting. I'd sooner have Lawrence: he does less damage. Murry's book, apart from being hideously written, is also very much dramatised, isn't it? As with Keats, he has made up a story of it, but I'm sure it was never as open-&-shut as that.

As a matter of fact, I think the key to Lawrence, or one of them, is his gift of mimicry. Nothing he says can be taken seriously: he is always 'doing' passion, 'doing' prophecy, 'doing' love, 'doing' insouciance, 'doing' blood-brotherhood – what happened if you took him up on them? Oh dear. His petulance at being taken seriously is almost embarrassing. His need to keep pretending necessitated a complete vacuum, hence no job & almost continuous travelling, to evade the barnacles of people & circumstances. To deflate Lawrence you had only to take him seriously. This explains his marvellous writing, too – he could 'do' life, superlatively. I think it explains the fact that nobody took him seriously for a moment, except 'women & mad people'. And he preferred it that way.

Or, at least …

Midday, Monday. Aren't the M.C.C. making heavy weather of things? Do you listen right from 7 to 8.30? I do, but fall asleep sometimes before it's over. Mind you, it's thrilling whatever happens, but I thought that when English journalists were crowing over Australia taking a day to score 160 they should wait & see what pace 'House-on-my-back' Hutton imposed on his New Elizabethans. To hear Cowdrey & Compton cowering at the crease made you think that they imagined that runs appreciated on the scoreboard like money in the bank, if you could only leave them there long enough. What's the use of staying in 3 days if you don't get any runs?

Evening Are you listening to *Sosarme*?[2] I am, and have just spent half an hour hootlessly fronting through Butler's *Notebooks* for the passage saying 'If people must believe in something, let them believe in the music of Handel'. But I did find a passage claiming that music 'improved' up to Handel, & declined since, wch is very much my own feeling though I don't damn Scarlatti & Bach as he does.

By the way, Molly[3] & Arthur are officially to get spliced in June. News broke this afternoon about five o'clock: Joan was about as bowled over at Molly's news as Molly was at Liz's news. (The Davies'[4] eyes are also popping, having 'heard' from the future Mrs Murphy:[5] 'an I-er-ish pawut!' George kept repeating. 'Gud Gaud!') About three people have suddenly got engaged recently in the library, leaving Graneek reeling.

Which leads me on wery properly to say[6] that if I left you with the idea that I was looking to the wallbars of matrimony to strengthen my character on them it was accidental and must have 'shone through' what I was saying, which was that it seemed to me that if we were going to get married this would be a good point to do so. I have a living wage, you want to pack up your job, we both want – or think we want – the same kind of life, we know each other well enough, etc. And we are ageing! I would sooner marry you than *anyone* else I know, and in any case I don't want to lose you. The sort of thing that gives me pause (paws) is wondering whether I do more than just like you very, very much and find it flattering and easy to stay with you instead of, well, behaving as folks do, rushing after other people who take their fancy – of course, very few people *do* take my fancy; the ones that do are 'quite impossible'; & in any case all that kind of thing wears off, being based on illusion & deprivation. Is it fair to marry without feeling 'quite sure'? But am I the kind of person ever to feel 'quite sure'? And anyway, *don't* I feel 'quite sure'? How should I feel if you wrote & said you were going to marry Norman Scarfe?[7] As in my old dream? Sure enough, anyway. Surely!

I agree about the horrors of pretence! But it's a rare marriage that doesn't have them, I feel.

'My publisher' writes to say the book is 'on' – he wants to put in *Spring* & *Since we agreed*, both of wch I'd left out.[8] What do you think? After all, it's your book. He says that everybody in the office of the Business Manager bought *Listen 2* for *Toads*! He praises *Church going*, too.

Tuesday Uurrgghh. Bagface off: I do her evenin' duty. Feel exhausted – this 'flu' is certainly the lingering kind, & rising at 7 has taken its toll, as well. Still anyone's game, isn't it? but I should have preferred a few more runs from England. If Evans can score 42 in 30 mins., why should Cowdrey score 16 in 100 mins?

Graneek had a soppy letter from my successor, signed 'Robert', & talking about the 'smiles & happiness extended to him' when he was here. Wish I'd extended 2 fingers from a bunched fist to him. I'm glad I'm going. This library is breaking up as a team, esp. if Molly goes. Shall I send you a LISTEN?[9] then you can read Mr Murphy. Afraid this is a scrappy letter – am enclosing a blank cheque for socks, rail fare, shirt? Huck huck. Ark ark. Affec. thoughts, P.

1 In a letter dated 22 January 1955, from 8 Woodland Avenue, Monica had written: 'If I thought you liked DHL for all his ideas, his attitudes, his moods – well, honestly, I think I'd be almost afraid of you, I think of it sometimes & then I think of *you* & I know you aren't like that [...] But O, the cruelty, the lack of any central stability in himself wch makes him lash out so pitilessly at people – his one thing, that underlies so much of his work, just the *wish to hurt* – it is pitiful, I am always so sick with pity when I read *about* him that I can hardly go on; when I read *him*, I am more sick with shock. And yes, he *is* obscene, I'd call it that, tho' not for the reasons he was banned for – if he *could* have been just simply obscene in that way it might have helped him – but it *is* obscene, the wish to outrage "the human spirit"; he wishes to outrage, to degrade, to destroy, poor, poor fellow [...]'
2 Handel opera, *Sosarme re di Media*, 1732.
3 Molly Sellar, assistant in QUB Library, later to marry Arthur Terry, Lecturer in Spanish.
4 George and Elspeth Davie: see Appendix B.
5 Patricia (Patsy) Strang, *née* Avis, was about to marry Richard Murphy, Irish poet.
6 Also in her letter of 22 January, Monica had written: 'Look, then, would you like me to say a few of the things I have thought about what you said about marriage? I'll only give you a few at a time, then if you don't like those, I can stop, if you like – anyway, too much at once is tedious & the sort of female letter that makes a man groan "O God!" Well, for one thing, a first thing, you can't marry just because

you think it's a sort of moral duty & a nasty one, a punishment that you ought to take – my dear! what a motive! you *can't*. (One thing that does make me feel we are "suited" is that you can discuss such an idea with me, & that I can hear it without the least offence, & even with understanding – I do see what you mean. But being "suited" & actually wanting to marry is another thing again, too) & indeed I wasn't even hurt, not a bit, just interested & sympathetic, really. Well, that's not a valid motive for marrying, but don't ask me to list what I think *are* valid motives. Another thing, & a question for you, is this. If you *were* marrying (forget the motives for the moment) would you rather marry me than anybody else? I don't mean just the people you possibly *could* marry – than anybody you've seen?'

7 Lecturer in History, Leicester University.

8 'Spring' was included in *The Less Deceived*, as was 'Since we agreed' under the title 'No Road'.

9 *Listen*, Vol. One, No. 3, Winter 1954, contained L.'s 'Poetry of Departures' as well as 'Sailing to an Island' by Richard Murphy and poems by Donald Davie, Kingsley Amis, George MacBeth, Jonathan Price and others.

10 February 1955

Belfast

Dearest,

Sunshine ... distant voices of children ... a dog barking ... the sense of distance ...

This week has got out of hand. I'm suffering from too little sleep & too much drink: my evenings are given over to writing a review of *Chrysanthemums*[1] for the student magazine, not very well either, be it said, or 'going out'. So I'm afraid this will be shortish; I hope you'll forgive me just this once. I'm wearing the yellow socks at present, and they're very gay, though nobody has commented on them. Have you filled in my cheque? I dread seeing 'fifty pounds' scrawled on it in an unambiguously rabbit hand – very trusting of me, giving a blank cheque to a rabbit! Their moral balance is none too reliable. A vision of all the fun to be had for £50 passes over their brains & before they know where they are the thing's done. Great hats with feathers in, velvet coats with pearly buttons, days out on the river – oh, what fun. Then in a few days the stoat policeman comes looking for one of them, and there are many shufflings and lyings and rabbits being bundled out of one warren into another for a few days – oh, yes! Never a conviction. It's the most difficult thing in the world, getting a conviction at River Bunny ...

Evening. Just signed the end of the Betjeman scribble – phew. Hack journalism, except that it's *unpaid*.

The plans of my library came today – how glad I am that it's seven-eighths planned! I have very little feeling for these things. I study tiny cubes and rectangles marked 'Librarian's room' and 'Librarian's secretary' & 'Librarian's Lavatory' & wonder if it will ever come to pass. What a farce! The days are racing by, O Lard! Beverley & District PEN Club. Bradford Oddfellows. Hull Chamber of Commerce. All clamouring for a talk on *Books & you*. O put your furry paw in mine.

I took some photographs of Molly in her giraffe pullover the other day, & have one or two that may enlarge somewhat. There's not much news on that front, after the grand flare up: they're both quiet and undemonstrative. Arthur grumbles 'Molly seems to have as many relations as the people in *War and peace*' – Molly doesn't grumble at all, just carries on falling against people and enjoying attention and so on. The news is gradually spreading, to the accompaniment of good natured guffaws. Most people like both of them, though tend to find them rather comical.

I did enjoy your letter. *Spring days* is nice to have. I'm sorry you felt low, but don't not tell me, please! Describing things does help to get rid of them: hence literature. If you are not dull to me, what care I how dull you be (not very grammatical)? Everybody is several degrees worse in company: if you are dull, then I am hypocritical, chatting about Saxon red-glaze pots or heraldry – you know. I'm sure you would think less of me if you saw me on some evenings – and anyway you are much better sitting alone than I am *wasting my time*.

As regards TEL,[2] I think of him as being a reveller-in-suffering, chiefly his own, rather than a homosexual – I miss in him the *outgoing* feeling necessary for any sort of sex. Homosexuality is surely much more like heterosexuality than it's like anything else, don't you think? But I grin at old EMF, muffled up on the touchline, still cheering the game on.

Really you couldn't say anything more to my way of feeling than that you don't like the idea of *getting* married. I dare say I could go through with it, but the bitter envy & self-reproach that would spring up if I heard of anyone else getting married, say, *in the lunch-hour* indicates where my sympathies lie. I remember saying to Kingsley ages ago that I couldn't stand the idea of 'a decent wedding'. He replied that 'you'd never marry a girl who wanted a decent wedding. So it's all right, you see.' Everything you say I agree with. I think what frightens me most about marriage is the passing-a-law-never-to-be-alone-again side of it.

I expect you've seen K. by now: like you, I can't think how he manages these jaunts. How does he behave in public? I've never seen him at it. Did he say anything of how his latest novel is progressing? *Wants pulling together*, I expect. I'm sure Ada wd find him better amusement than John Wain, though: much less of a swank.

It's after midnight now: must to bed! and finish off this page in the morning. I think of you, curled up in your flimsy nightdress ... *Friday*. Or not too flimsy: snow on the ground this morning! Brrr. This afternoon I must go to see about *removing*: my last week here will be frightful, with nothing in the flat except what belongs to Queen's – no w.p.b., no books, no coffee pot! I wish we were going out this weekend to some interesting place. I think I am 'booked' on Sunday night to one of the people who've never asked me out before &'ve just heard I'm going, a brilliant one called Jope[3] – in 1970 you'll wonder how you ever didn't know of him. I pull your long ears gently – much love P.

1 L.'s review of John Betjeman's *A Few Late Chrysanthemums* in *Q*, 11, Hilary 1955: reprinted in *Further Requirements*.
2 T. E. Lawrence.
3 E. M. Jope, Professor of Archaeology, QUB.

15 February 1955

30 Elmwood Ave, Belfast

[...] 'Nobody writes to me nowadays' – at least, I don't *mind*, exactly, but I get peevish at seeing nothing but Vernons Pools & the Devonshire Laundry. I have 3 regular correspondents – you, Mother & Kingsley, & Kingsley never writes. I shouldn't be surprised if he were fed up with me, in a shoulder-shrugging sort of way: I am of him, except as you say 'the dog is so very comical'. I was interested to hear the book[1] had gone to Gollancz – oh please God, make them return it, with a suggestion he 'rewrites certain passages'! Nothing would delight me more. And I refuse to believe he can write a book on his own – at least a good one. Still, we'll see. In a sense he has behaved more consistently than I have: I sought his company because it gave me such a wonderful sense of relief – I've always needed this 'fourth form friend', with whom I can pretend that things are *not* as I know they are – and pretended I was like him. Now I don't feel like pretending any longer, & I suppose it looks like 'turning against him', although it's not really. None the less I write back much more quickly than he does & wd remember birthdays, etc., if he ever showed signs of reciprocating. And as you say he's not like us. The idea of Kingsley *loving* a book – or a book 'feeding' him, as K.M. wd say – is quite absurd. He doesn't *like* books. He doesn't like *reading*. And I wouldn't take his opinion on *anything*, books, people, places, anything. Probably he has been mistaken, to himself, about me.

I finished my Betjeman article, badly, saying really nothing. Don't know if they'll print it. One thing I didn't say was how much more interesting & worth writing about Betjeman's subjects are than most other modern poets – I mean, whether so-and-so achieves some metaphysical inner unity is not really so interesting to us as the overbuilding of rural Middlesex. I didn't say it because I don't believe in judging poets by their subjects, but I feel it. I prefer the mother-of-five to the golden smithies of the Emperor, or whatever they are. [...]

I don't know that I find you lacking in romance & little ways – at least, that wasn't what I meant, I'm sure. And incalculability – well, I remember writing in a little *débat*[2] some four years ago 'I don't want somebody's daughter who's "two people really" and demands a row and a reconciliation every weekend' – is that the kind of thing you mean? No, I love & admire you for being free from that: there's no surer anaphrodisiac. You're a wonderful distinguished rabbit like that. On the other hand it *may* have something to do with – I mean, whatever I said (forgotten it now), I meant that final conviction (even if temporary) must spring from the sense of being complemented without being hampered by an overdose of what you yourself lack – I think we are much alike, but not exactly complementary. I feel especially that we are both shy, you speechless, me talkative-terrified, and can't in consequence give each other the release from shyness that would mean so much, like the little things (some weeks back Eth complained that Ron[3] touched her hair as he passed her chair when he had been putting coal on the fire) – this sounds a bit horrible, & I can hear you saying: Oh, 20 damns to your great pigface; but I'm sure you understand what I mean. [...]

1 Kingsley Amis, *That Uncertain Feeling* (1955).
2 *Round Another Point* (1951), in *Trouble at Willow Gables* (2002).
3 Eth and Ron: characters in the radio comedy series *Take It from Here*.

8 April 1955

21 York Road, Loughborough, Leics.

Dearest,

A letter with a pen for a change! I think part of my fed-upness in that disastrous letter[1] came from having nothing to write with but that rubbishy ball-point thing & a 2H pencil. I'm awfully sorry about that. You wondered how the memory of Saturday could be so completely eradicated from my mood, didn't you? Well, it was partly mother, who was sickening for influenza all Sunday (she was in bed the next 10 days, on and off) with the customary fall in spirits (& rise in my general worriedness), and partly leaving my pen behind, (only a tiny part, of course) & partly returning to that awful hall where I felt simply rent by the stupid insistence of the various noises, wch were especially notice-able after being at home. These things, or the first and last of them anyway, simply drove out good emotion with bad, as you might say. By Monday night it all seemed months ago, more's the pity! and I was in that state which produced the silly letter. Really, I am sorry. I wouldn't have sent it if I'd known it wd upset you so. Poor dear! Of course I enjoyed Saturday very much, and am sorry it had to end with the 6.50 or whatever time it was, and the consequent rush.

I'm not sure I really *like* this pen. It might suit you better. There's very little 'give' in it.

Well, I am home, and though there's no actual *casus belli* the general tenor is sombre as usual. I wish I could feel with Jim Dixon[2] 'but then it had always been that'! I suppose I do in a way. I wish I could give some idea of my mother's character, because I think you regard her as a *conscious* nuisance, whereas I don't think she can really help it: she has no power of controlling her feelings, which is a pity as they are usually uncomfortable ones. She is a kind of defective mechanism, wch, left alone, stays helplessly in one spot boring into itself, and yet by expressing this misfortune and the misery it causes exhausts the cap-acity (which would accumulate rapidly enough in most people) for doing anything about it. Her ideal is 'to collapse' and to be taken care of, but (and this is an awfully dangerous thing to say!) I think she is continually dissipating her power to collapse, as a real hysteric would, by talking about it. In life, as in art, talking vitiates doing. In fact it is practically impossible to get her to do anything. I wanted to fix her up at a nearby country hotel for a week's rest to recover from the influenza,

148

but the ordeal of staying anywhere alone is too great – in prospect, any-way – so I've dropped the idea. For her the daily round is hideous with traps, and dangerous with hidden ambush and calamity: it is all she can manage to creep through it unscathed. She has no interests or hobbies and spends the time thinking about next summer's thunder-storms, gas taps, electricity switches, dark clouds, & I don't know what. I'm afraid I'm drawing her as a pathological type, but so she is up to a point: what is so noticeable about her is her inability to free herself from these obsessional fears, or even to drive them out by normal interests. She's hopelessly in their power, and will remain so until someone takes her in hand & devotes their entire life to her, or at least gives her a sense of security, which at the moment (as Henry Reed wd say) she has not got. It is all a frightful situation & will get (like most things) worse. Next year she will be 70 and I do wish she cd have a peaceful old age, though not at the cost of giving me a wretched middle-age (expect I shall get smashed up in a train going back for that!). As you can imag-ine she would be a frightful responsibility: I should have to do every-thing, buoyed up by a non existent desire to set up house with her; find the house, find the 'companion' (if I was to have any independence at all), try to keep her from leaving, etc. etc. And all for something I don't want! This doesn't mean I'm going to do it. But what sort of reason is it to refuse to do something unless the person doesn't need you to? 'To him that hath' (since this is Good Friday) 'shall be given, but from him that hath not shall be taken away ...'

This generally sombre mood has been shot through with flashes of pure hatred for my bitch-sister. She is an absolute mean-spirited self-centred little swine of Hell, and I can't retail her latest, it would enrage me too much: ask me when we meet.

My Uncle Alfred has also died: he of the china & flowers. This was last Monday & has contributed to the gaiety here – he was of course the last of my father's brothers left alive. Grand old buck. I shall always remember his red face & blue eyes & white moustache & lopsided bow & great pendulous chops & green felt hat & Northumberland tweed clothes.

I've been concentrating on my library plans, drawing emended versions to scale in Indian ink, & shall have to write a memo explain-ing them ready to be duplicated & send round before the committee on the 19th. By this means I hope to cut the hideous argument & misunderstandings. My main worry is whether I can get the plans duplicated in time, for the memo. will be useless without them. All this labour will probably be useless, as the local Fred & Martin will cook it up with the architect after I've staggered away limp with 4 hours' talking. [...]

Hartley wants me to give titles to *all* my poems, so that he needn't number them & so would save space. I *can't* think of a title for the Mayhew one. Do you think *Less deceived* or *The less deceived* wd do? ('I was the more deceived …')[3] It is quite a good point to title the poems because you can't number *only* the nameless ones, you have to number the lot, & a number *and* a title wastes too much space at the head of the page. I am going to supply him with a sucker list soon. You don't want to go in the back, do you? since you'll be in the front. Any of your friends like to? The results of this sucker list will interest me a very great deal: there'll be a clause whereby people can opt out of appearing if they prefer.

In bed, last thing. To church tonight, not very interesting, but they have put up a board in the porch bearing 2 (bad) verses in sentiment not unlike *Church going*.

Spent much of today trying to draft 300 words of 'poetic aims' for this Japanese anthology,[4] & failing rather.

Last night rooting about among papers I found a letter dated 1902 appointing my father as Junior Clerk at £30 a year in B'ham Finance Dept. – it was his first job. It gave me a queer feeling. How little our careers express what lies in us, and yet how much time they take up. It's sad, really. [...]

1 Apparently missing.
2 In Kingsley Amis's *Lucky Jim.*
3 'I was the more deceived': Ophelia, *Hamlet,* Act 3, sc. 1.
4 *Poets of the 1950s*, ed. D. J. Enright (Kenkyusha, Tokyo; dated 1955, but in fact early 1956). This included all the 'Movement' poets except Thom Gunn, and preceded Robert Conquest's *New Lines* by about six months.

16 April 1955

Holtby Hall, Cottingham

My dear,

I'm back from Beverley now: it took me 35 mins to cycle home in the dark. After posting your card I went to the hotel and had a pint, reading *Under the net*[1] which I'd bought for a shilling in Boots.

No *G. of A.*![2] Though there was an *S. of E.*[3] Then I dined, melon, steak & a kind of raspberry-apple tart, with a glass of burgundy, & went on reading *Under the net*. The hotel was obviously doing a roaring trade & when I left (unchaining my bicycle from a dustbin up the yard) there was the sound of practice-arpeggios from a saxophone & the tapping of a snare drum, so I expect there would be a dance. Beverley didn't make a great impression on me: I went into the Minster, & also into the Parish Church (nearly as big), but did not really grasp much. The parish church had a lovely painted roof, with all the early kings of England (or so I imagined them to be) over the choir. There was also a beautiful street of mansions & chestnut trees called North Bar Without. But the town was too busy for my liking, & had no bookshop. (I confirmed this by verbal enquiry.) I don't think I really want to live there: too far and too large. It's funny how one sometimes has a very quick & definite impression about liking a place, isn't it? [...]

It was very good of you not to 'fly out at' me for my nasty letter. I've already said something about the way my feelings get overlaid and flurried, but I've an uneasy feeling that there's some truth in what you say about my writing 'distantly' after a meeting. It's not deliberate of course, but sometimes I can feel myself doing it and try not to. It is awful and I will try to stop. What it springs from I don't quite know, perhaps a sense of being, no, of having my 'hunger', shall I say, for you satisfied temporarily, and so having a duller edge than when we've been separated for a time. I don't suppose this explanation is a very endearing one either! but I'm not putting you back in your place, anyway: it doesn't mean that. As regards my mother & so on, I hate to think that anything I say cd be construed as meaning however hard a proposition she is, you're much worse – now, really, I *don't* mean that! I'm not quite sure what to say about her and be quite sure at the same time I'm really right & unbiassed. No doubt she has a strong hold on me that it would be silly to try to ignore, but it's not that that makes me contemplate living with her: it's her consistent & continual misery in her present situation – I reckon she & my sister between them make it much worse than it need be, but all the same it's tiresome to have to go somewhere else to sleep every night, especially in cold winters like this one, and she doesn't much like 'living alone' & misses someone coming in at regular intervals – and her apparent inability to do anything about it. I don't really blame her for not being able to do anything about it: I don't suppose I could myself. Her general suggestion (not, as you may imagine it to be, reiterated day in day out) is that she should buy a house, here, & that I should live in half of it, & she, with a companion-help paid out of my rent, in the other. This is a reasonable enough suggestion, but I feel certain that the business of finding the c-h wd fall to me, & that any such would never stop, as my mother is not a pleasant person to live with by any standards, and by conventional ones her life is dull & dreary – no theatres, trips to London, etc. No, what *is* reiterated is her perpetual misery & state of fear: she is a bottomless jar in which to pour sympathy, common-sense, & understanding. You may make a supreme effort one evening, say, to 'talk it out', to banish the demon, & so on, putting out all your unselfishness and concern for her – but in the morning you'll find nothing has altered. After all, why should it? In the first place, action is needed, not words; in the second, my mother's nature generates, by living, a certain distress that must be drawn off by grumbling & depression. I do not remember a time when this wasn't so, and I doubt if external circumstances change it to any great extent. And in the third, I sometimes wonder if anybody can do anything for anyone!

You must realise that there's no comparison between living with her, which would be a duty, & living with you (better call it marrying) which would (or should) be undertaken not as a duty but as a pleasure, that is in the expectation of being happier than I am now. Of course there is the connection between them, that to do either will annoy the other, or at any rate be interpreted as a sign that I don't really want to bother. Marriage in one sense is the most complicated, since it has been known for mothers to live with married sons, & I couldn't ask her to do so without giving you the idea that I'd married to provide my mother with a home, or not ask her without giving her the idea I'd married to get away from her. You see? 'All theorising is flight'⁴ and I avoid offending either by doing neither, and perhaps that's my basic desire, since what people do is what they want to do much oftener than is supposed, but it's a web and a worry. Is this all known to you, or have I made things any clearer? Somehow I *don't* think I shall live with her alone again: I have only to read my diary for that time to dissuade myself from such chivalrous notions. [...]

1 Iris Murdoch's first novel (1954).
2 Mary McCarthy, *The Groves of Academe* (1952).
3 Mary McCarthy, *A Source of Embarrassment* (1950).
4 From *Under the Net*: 'All theorising is flight. We must be ruled by the situation itself and this is unutterably particular.'

25 April 1955

Hull, about 1.45

Dearest Bun,

Here's a note for you when you get back! I am back on my rock again – a seal, yes, but also Andromeda. 'My Chairman' was in bright and early, full of businesslike talk & prognostications of vaguely alarming character, 'opposition to fight', and all the rest of it. This, and leaving you, and coming back, & a bad lunch, has contrived to put me in 'no very good yummer' as Kevin Carroll[1] wd say. The post was unremarkable except for some wedding cake from Colin Strang of all people. Barbara Carr is the name, or was the name.

I did hate seeing you borne away, waving your tiny hand.[2] You seemed very frail and lovable, not your York-self which was dazzling and bold. I comforted myself during the nasty lunch, at which I sat next to the H of D of *German* & stared gloomily out at a view of several lines of washing, by thinking that you would have reached Birmingham, and would be feeling, at any rate, that you were nearly home. Home only to depart again, though!

Well, this will await you to say what a nice time we had: despite old sewer-throat, & the hotel washed down with beer, & that revolting bar – there was the museum, and the walls, & Whisker & Sons, & Hopper, & Leaper Bros – many Bros.! I expect I shall be writing to you again before very long – tonight, perhaps. Oh desolate fishing-port!

My dearest love,
Philip

1 Former Belfast colleague, rendered in L.'s version of his Ulster accent.
2 L. and Monica had spent part of the Easter vacation together, visiting York ('the museum, and the walls'), and enjoying their rabbit fantasies ('Whisker & Sons, & Hopper, & Leaper Bros').

27 April 1955

11 Outlands Road, Cottingham, E. Yorks

Very dearest,

A mild, windy, rainy evening: I am sitting in my armchair, smelling the curious *fusty* smell that arises when I have my small electric fire on.

Today has been an eventful day in which I went to look at a flat! and a lovely one, too: absolutely everything for 4 gns a week, in a near-at-hand respectable quarter. Trouble was, it was vacant for 6 months only – out on my neck in October – and it was *too big*. The living room or lounge was *enormous*, there was a dining room, hall, 2 bedrooms, kitchen & bathroom. Really, I suppose I funked it – I just couldn't imagine myself in such a vast suite of rooms – and who on earth would keep them clean? Oh dear. I was considerably flustered by the whole business, and am unhappy at the prospect of more such journeys. All the same if it had been permanent I'd have taken it. But with no security, no time to spread oneself, & one month off during the six anyway, I felt it just wasn't worth it, though I remembered all your advice about my station in life.

I'm afraid I'm not a natural house hunter. The awful impermanence of life sweeps in on me and I just grow wretched and silent and want to get away & bury my head somewhere. Ostrich! And I felt, funnily enough, how horribly lonely I should be there. No sound would ever have penetrated its walls. I should have sat in one corner of the lounge (a little larger than Jock's Bar) glancing over my shoulder nervously & wondering how soon I could go to bed. A poor showing. I don't feel enlivened by the incident.

How we did walk in York! Round and round, and all interesting. I shall never forget you being so solicitous when I was cold & sulky on Sunday night, instead of hoofing me out in a dudgeon. There's something makes me less good than I ought to be, and I wish it didn't. When I'm away from you I think: Next time we'll really clear away some of the webs between us – & yet when we meet it doesn't happen: I grow stiff & silent, and never move off the ground of rabbithood, which is all very well but which prevents discussion of the real situation, don't you think? I don't know if it's my fault, or yours, or nobody's: I think it's true to say that I do to some extent seize up, automatically, when we meet – but don't take this badly, dear: I'm honestly only trying to explain myself, or even explain it away, if that were possible. I mean, obviously there must be something, or we should long ago have settled things. If we are so similar and get on so well & should like the same things, honestly, then I don't see what is stopping us. Do you see what I mean, o wise rabbit? It's not really fair of me to make this 'parade of extraordinary honesty & frankness' – I don't like it myself – I wish I could decide things, fiercely and for good, and say them – instead of this almost-Russian verbiage, concealing I don't know what, probably nothing but funk. I know you are careful not to 'crowd' me, from motives of decency & pride, and heaven knows I don't want to be crowded, and yet it does to some degree play not into *my* hands, but into the hands of whatever lies under my delay. I wish I had not started writing this. It was really to apologise for dodging issues at Selby. I feel sometimes that every time we part is a fresh insult to you. 'Anguish of indecision, nine times out of ten, is caused by a decision struggling to be recognised' – that is a quotation from Camembert (fl. 1698) I have just made up.

Had a letter from Enright, saying he was going to regale the Japs with 8 of my pieces, to the tune of £7. I suppose it will turn up in *yen* or something.

Oh the wireless – gabble gabble gabble. I have the usual wool in my ears, but it doesn't help much. Apparently Sam the negro[1] enquired of Farrell why I left Holtby! Farrell made some jesuitical reply.

This letter is losing its concentration since the ruddy wireless came on: I'll leave it aside for a moment. Both the people Charles Madge told me to watch out for here – his friends – are filthy Commies, serious ones.[2] Brett[3] said today he didn't believe in *travel*, wch made me like him a bit more.

Few minutes after – No, I really can't do anything *at all* – it really is *disgusting*, I feel tearful with rage – why must she leave her door open so that her filthy radio *floods the whole house*? It's quite loud enough to be unpleasant as it is. Why must the *fool* have *all* the downstairs doors open, ensuring that it is *twice as bad*? It really affects me strongly: a kind of spiritual claustrophobia – I can't get out, & can't get away, there's no way out, I can't stand it! Oh *hell*. How long will this go on, wasted time, wasted wasted wasted – I've done nothing this year so far, certainly nothing since coming to this godforsaken dump. Whenever will life take a turn for the better again? *How can it*?? I shall *never* find anywhere quiet, there just aren't any such places for *single men – they* don't want quiet, serve them right for trying to get out of the 20-yr plague of children! *There are no such places.* – What a hideous phrase that is, single men. I've had a chilly bath, washed hair & my one brush, & am back again now. The wireless is reduced to a low grumbling of music, overlaid with voices. Quarter to eleven. Oh, it's so silly, so hysterical to go on like that, I know; you must think me an awful fool. O rabbit! (I must drop back to it for a moment) I wish we were somewhere quiet. To me quiet means quiet – to you it means absence of strife, doesn't it? Do try to forgive all this – perhaps you are upset too, though, and this won't cheer you up. Do you remember patting me on the nose to stop my mewing?

(They seem to be having a row, downstairs.)

The quarrelling & the radio have sunk to a lower note still. *Good.* This letter is a pathological document, I'm afraid – honestly, I should never patronise anyone, I'm much too silly myself. What should I do without you? Goodnight, my dear one – I had all this coming to me, I know. And of course it isn't much. It could be much worse. Goodnight, dear rabbit, goodnight, sweet rabbit, goodnight, goodnight, goodnight.

Thursday morning – Had better send this, though it's a rotten letter and I apologise. O dear rabbit don't hold it against me.

I am to go out to this wretched dinner tonight – don't look forward to it.

I think of the half hour we spent overlooking the square at Selby. How nice it was! That fellow in a bad way praying against his motor bike.

I hope your return hasn't been accompanied by any nasty shocks, except insofar as the whole business is a nasty shock.

Hugs & kisses,
Philip

1 Inhabitant of Holtby Hall, Cottingham, the Hull University hall of residence which L. had just left with relief, to escape the noise etc., only to find things even worse in 11 Outlands Road. (See Appendix A, which relates 11 Outlands Road specifically to 'Mr Bleaney'.)
2 These 'friends' of Charles Madge probably included John Saville, long-time lecturer and professor at Hull University, who was an active Marxist historian and who, with L.'s encouragement, built up an impressive Labour history collection.
3 Ray Brett: see Appendix B.

1 May 1955

11 Outlands Road, Cottingham, E. Yorks

[...] Feel more cheerful today – can't think why. I'm not 'getting on' with people very well yet, but feel a comfortable they-can't-stop-paying-me glow at the pit of my stomach. My mother sent me a note today, too, sounding more cheerful – I think I had sounded cast down on Friday. Ordered *Satchmo* (Louis Armstrong) in the College bookshop – created a fine effect, like a Bateman drawing.

No doubt all this will be dispelled tomorrow if I pick up many replies to my advert: 'Dear Sir I can offer you too nise rooms with coking facitiles nine guinness a weak yours respectively Sarah Glum'. Hey? What about that? [...]

Yeats's *Letters* are greatly improved as he ages – he is rather a humorless young bore, much taken up with the 'movement', but in age he is playful and amusing, recounting how his baby daughter says 'Thine is the kitten, the power and the glory' – but as the kitten grew up she altered it to 'Thine is the cat' & c. [...]

Later. Cheerfulness somewhat dispelled by Mrs D. putting the price up, and asking 'how long I was staying' etc. in quite a reasonable way – & quite reasonably putting up the price for these days – but it felt like a tiny shifting of the foundations, wch is disturbing. Oh dear! You are right when you say we both dread change & prefer to 'sit quite still and wait'. I'm afraid I do, but can't now. Feel quite cast down – no real reason why I shd be, any more than 6 hours ago, but you understand, don't you? Marriage wd be a huge change, wdn't it – I fear it for that partly. Partly, again, I'm very self-centred, and I fear not being able to support the change to *basic* unselfishness I feel marriage entails – I don't mean I'm used to having the biggest egg and so on so much as that I've usually taken great comfort in solitude and not being bothered to consider other people. I should tend to be snappish if I didn't watch out. And partly I'm afraid of the bigness, the awfulness, of marriage – 'till death do us part'. Of course I feel that now, sometimes, even without being married, and more keenly insofar as I haven't done for you what I could – take you away from all these trying people & the hardship of having a job. I'm sorry about the letter I didn't answer. I expect I left it till I could talk to you, & then that time didn't come. Of course you can speak of such things! As far as my making things clear from the first, didn't I say that I'd just got out of a fearful tangle that wouldn't have arisen if I'd not let things drift? Of course that's a long time ago now. But it made a deep impression on me, my unfitness for 'romantic attachments', & since it entailed so much distress I thought that above all I must never let it happen again. You *mustn't* think of me as one who, 'having once known love, can never more' etc. I am more like one who, having once got into the soup, dare nevermore, etc.

Oh dear! must go to bed. The household is retiring. Feel tired and confused. Tomorrow I shall meet the awful world of accommodation again – I wish I moved naturally among these things, but as I said, they just make me curl up inside. Goodnight, dear rabbit: dear Monica: many kisses [...]

3 May 1955

11 Outlands Rd, Cottingham, E. Y.

Dearest,

Back from the Binns's[1] – him & her, & Prof Brett & his wife: that's all. Not quite a predicted evening: house in a new estate, but quite un-Eaglelike: one huge room instead of 2 small ones. The conventional appurtenances of ivy up the wall, those lampshades, & curious ornaments. Frightening knowledgeableness on everyone's part, especially Binns, who speaks Chinese & whose post as Eng. Lang. lecturer apparently embraces the whole of Scandinavia & therefore the fishing industry in Hull. Did *you* know that the reason coke-scoops corrode is that rain through coke forms weak sulphuric acid? I shan't be 'such good value' here, I can see that. Still, I set the wives hunting for flats.

There was drink: Aqua Vita(e?), mint-smelling Scandinavian spirit which Mrs Brett pronounced as 'like Bols' & I *fancy* Mrs Binns added 'or Kummel' – both a bit wide of the mark, in fact. Then Beaujolais, 49, darned good too. An' ciharettes for further orders. Large talk about yachts and croquet & motor-mowers also was bandied about, & laying out gardens, or getting the War Ag.[2] to lay out gardens (*market*) – all very frightening to a poor worm trembling between lodgings & the deep blue sea. Life, life! Inexhaustible appetites.

I found a charming bit in the Yeats letters,[3] about how he had chanced to find one night an erotic drawing of two lesbians, and 'it got into my dreams and made a great racket there' – don't you find that funny? In fact his letters show him up very well: light, fragrant, wholesome, humorous. Almost never spiteful or self pitying or pompous. [...]

Back again. Well, I am nearly committed to Mrs Squire, rightly or wrongly I don't know. Hallgate (not Northgate) is the central street in Cottingham, & I walked along it from no. 1, my nerves getting worse as the shops started. Then just in time they stopped, and I found a high wall with a door (wooden) bearing no. 200 and a polished-smooth plate on which the name Squire could just be seen. Opening it, I found a long orchard-garden, and an old-fashioned house at the bottom. Mrs Squire met me, a decent old party of 77, well spoken, & showed me 'my kitchen' & 'my room'. The first is a small one at the foot of the stairs, not noticeably good or bad, with a gas stove & I suppose a sink, though I'm ashamed to say I didn't notice it all as sharply as I should. The 'room' is simply a medium-sized bedroom, with a gas fire, 2 armchairs, a little bay window with a table in overlooking the orchard-garden, and some hefty Victorian furniture. There is a large modernised bathroom next door, for the whole house – her, & her niece & husband, whom I didn't see. The general look of the room is hideous, but it was upside-down with a mattress etc. airing for the people coming in tomorrow. I liked it on the whole, chiefly for the orchard-garden, the fact that it was so central yet so secluded, & because *it is the right kind of house – Potterish*. Mrs Squire had a Potterish look too. Rent 38/6 a week, and a meter for the gasfire. I enquired closely into the radio-problem, & it isn't perfect, it is in the room beneath, but I asked her to put it on while I listened, and if it's never worse than that it isn't too bad. The other thing is it may be cold in the winter. But *on the whole* I thought it quite good. *It is near the pub*, and of course very near all the shops, & the bus terminus. People won't think much of it, I can see, but it will no doubt do for me. No room for books of course. I was influenced by the thought of having breakfast in the bay window, looking over the trees, but I may be mistaken. It will mean a lot of running up & downstairs with a tray – I must get a big tray.

Phew! I feel exhausted. You have had a round-by-round description of one of the most gruelling days of my time here. In the pictures during the advert-shorts there was one advertising, well, I don't know what, dog food perhaps, but the scene of a little girl hugging a retriever was laid in a pet-shop, & in the background was a hutch of rabbits. Tears started to my eyes and began rolling down my cheeks in a very silly way.

I think one thing I can say about the progress of our relation is that I've grown tired of all my friends except you – all my close friends, that is: not many really. This is worth mentioning because you have often felt that you were in a different camp from all sorts of points of view, haven't you? 'Socially, politically, morally' as one might say. I kept you apart because I know, myself, that I acted a different part with them from my behaviour with you, and since I couldn't do both at once it was well not to try. And in any case I couldn't *see* you mixing into, nasty phrase, life as it was led at Kingsley's house or the Strangs'. Therefore I kept them away from you, and as I did myself still enjoy their company I suppose I was keeping part of my life hidden from you in a suspicious way. But when I met Kingsley in Cheltenham, & the Strangs on Boars Hill, & Bruce in Abingdon, I thought on each occasion: I'm through with this. Basically. You have shown me better things!

I suppose I shall see K. & B.,[4] at least, from time to time, but not with the same ruthless keenness. Reading this through, it sounds mawkish & self righteous – I mean, perhaps, things better than the role I was acting – I don't know! No, I *am* quite genuinely hard & nasty, in some degree, & need doses of it occasionally, but not often.

I quite genuinely have tummy-ache at the moment. Has your headache gone?

Thursday 7 a.m. in bed. Brilliant morning. Awake somewhat depressed. Corners of people's houses! Why do we live in them? That place will be too small, I shan't be able to have the new record player I'd planned to buy. I don't know, I feel basically distressed at living & its problems, a fundamental *je ne suis pas heureux ici* feeling saddening my whole outlook – and not only not happy but not competent, not skilled, practised, adroit: I have no house no wife no child no car no motor mower no holidays planned for Sweden or Italy: I feel them all sucking greedily at the marrowbone and my own insufficiency strikes me. And perhaps it is only fear after all! I dread being one who only at 50 gains what everyone else has had since they were 25. Well, at least we can have a holiday, can't we? I've felt too bothered to think about it. What do you think? I've asked everyone here to settle their dates at least provisionally by the end of this month.

Well, dear, this strange document will be your birthday letter, and by rights should express nothing but celebration of the day when little rabbit was deposited on the unfeeling crust of the earth, to find its way about for seventy years? oh dear, as I write this tears overflow my eyes and I don't know what to say: I wish I could hold you closely and try to forget this silly wretchedness. It *is* only the weather & the miles! [...]

When I stop writing to you I feel bereft, but I *must* get up. Oh my dear! What absurdity it all is!

My dearest love,
Philip

1 A. L. Binns: see Appendix B.
2 The War Agricultural Committee, created to maximise domestic cultivation for food.
3 L. was reading the recently published edition by Allen Wade of *The Letters of Yeats* (1954).
4 Kingsley Amis, Bruce Montgomery.

9 May 1955

11 Outlands Road, Cottingham, E. Yorks

[...] I've tried *ordering The G. of A.*,[1] just as new – have you ever tried that? Feckless bun, if not. I brought my copy back with me, and revel, positively revel, in it. I *do* think it better than *A S. of E.*,[2] richer, more verbally farcical. She is the most adroit writer of our time, unless Evelyn W. goes neck & neck, & of course they're very different in technique – she could never do 'busted tester's leg for 'ee'[3] etc.

Very tired! Up at 6.30 – woke at 4.30 to hear the 'charm' & the cuckoo – lovely birds, with no clocks or newspapers, shouting for delight. Am in consequence v. tired, and must to bed, but I just wanted to give you a few words. Good night!

Tuesday morning Up and dressed and breakfasted: the radio heaving away downstairs & also into the son's (empty) room next to mine, by loudspeaker. Have just finished verse 5 of the poem I thought of with you in York[4] – do you remember? (You said with some bitterness that the rush of the thrush was all you ever got.) It is 'only light'.

I do feel like talking to you much more, but I had better put my shoes on and go to work. Work is a kind of vacuum, an emptiness, where I just switch off everything except the scant intelligence necessary to keep me going. God, the people are awful – great carved monstrosities from the sponge-stone of secondratedness. Hideous. And there's nowhere else to lunch, within easy reach anyway.

Blackburn Rovers! Did you see that one of the Scilly Isles has black rabbits on it? In the *Observer* last Sunday? It sounded v. attractive. What think you? – Samson Island. Black rabbits. Do read the article.

It's evening now, and very cold. I've spent it in 'my room', adding verse 6, & reading the beginning of a life of John Galsworthy. Written in a horrible style by H.V. Marlot. [...]

Wednesday. This letter isn't being as solid as its predecessors – must start changing soon for this Senate Dinner. [...]

After the dinner. Groogh! These affairs are barely worth the drink they serve. Prof Brynmor Jones (the articulate Colwyn-Williams) much in his element – took me aside, gripping me by the elbow, to explain his 'tactics' tomorrow – he is sitting on the fence, as Pro Vice Chancellor, between the Vice Chancellor, who wants new halls, new halls, & the rest, who want a new library. He sounds as if he is going to advocate both, with what results I don't know. I was introduced to the Chairman of the UGC who looked like a successful broadcaster – young, round faced, shining – & moaned my moan, or tried to. I honestly think that Hull is making too much of its library deficiencies, and they may provoke a retort instead of agreement. Actually they should never have appointed me, I am quite the wrong man since I don't care 2d about it all. We shall see. I would much sooner kiss your pretty measurements than worry about Stage I, interim accommodation etc.!

Dear me, must to bed now. Glad you liked the little verse.[5] It came 'straight off' – used up the lower part of the page left blank by your Christmas poem, which also came 'straight off' – would you like that page? Wallyble manuscript – 2 Larkin poems as they boiled over from the seething brain, both meant for you alone. Say if you would.

To bed, to bed! XXX

Thursday evening. Feel exhausted. Day began badly by my getting in late – V.C. had been ringing up, they wanted to start much earlier than had been arranged. Anyway, I arrived & before long was showing Sir Keith Murray round, like a social worker showing a new councillor a distressed area – 'one water closet per three families!' The reason I was in late was I had lost my little tooth – had put it down somewhere last night (only on the dressing table as it happened) but I *couldn't* see it. *Thought I'd swallowed it*: was already imagining where *the incision* wd have to be made. [...]

Friday. Must round this off, and send it off to you inside a gift I wot you will be right glad to receive. Your nice letter this morning – how much more coherent than mine is. Woke early this morning & felt depressed and frightened at this huge million-book library I am saddled with, then fell asleep & slightly overslept. Yes, I liked the red suspender belt. I have rather lost the thread of what I wanted to say about ourselves, but perhaps over the long gloomy weekend I shall be able to say more. Nobody has invited me out this weekend, yet, so I ought to have plenty of time. I'm glad you liked the shears – I *felt* they were good.

Much silky love   P.

1 Mary McCarthy, *The Groves of Academe*.
2 Mary McCarthy, *A Source of Embarrassment*.
3 Evelyn Waugh, *Scoop* (Book III, 'Banquet').
4 'Mr Bleaney', completed May 1955.
5 Not known.

3 July 1955

200 Hallgate, Cottingham, E.Y.

[...] You'll see I enclose a subscription form for this book:[1] I was round at Hartley's last night & they were busy sending them out, so I collared a few, about sixty. He had 600 printed, & is busy finding 600 people to send them to. This upsets my idea of dining with Landor & with Donne,[2] my idea, that is, of having just a select few friends in the back, since all the people imaginable are getting them, nuns, military men, alcoholics, feather-bedders, sexual deviants, impostors, people like Dannie Abse & C. A. Trypanis & George Fraser, not to mention all the poor crazed creatures who are subscribers, or have sent poems, to *Listen* ... So what I am working round to is that if *you* have anyone you'd like to receive a form, either send me the name & address or I'll send you some forms. The general effect of the evening was to depress me, slightly: I hate to think of the publicity involved. As for the form, well, it's the type that will be used, but not the paper: I don't care for the type. 'The Marvell Press' is H's idea, God knows why. M. was born at Hull, or died here, or at any rate was an MP here. The asterisked clause is my idea, though I don't know if it's a good one. Some people may prefer not to be listed, though I can't think for the moment who they'll be. Hartley is off to London now to learn window-dressing: his wife keeps on the business still. She has far more sense than G. H. He is complacently sending forms off to 'Herbert Read Esq' and 'C. Day Lewis Esq', sodding fool. I have given him the names of A.S.C.,[3] Horne,[4] &, I can't think why, Mollie[5] at Leicester. Oh, & the Evanses. So you know where you are. It will be of tremendous interest to me to see if anyone responds.

Well! having got that out of the way, let me ask your advice on one point – do you think 'to provide an object' wd express the sense better than 'to create an object' in the last verse of *P of ds*?[6] It seems that people understand *object* to mean just a thing, an entity, not as an ambition as I intended. [...]

1 *The Less Deceived*.
2 From W. B. Yeats, 'To a Young Beauty'.
3 A. S. Collins: Professor of English, Leicester.
4 C. H. Horne: Lecturer in English, Leicester.
5 Molly Bateman: assistant at Leicester University College Library.
6 'Poetry of Departures': 'to create an object' prevailed.

12 July 1955

200 Hallgate, Cottingham

[...] Had a letter from Jean Hartley this morning, reporting that 41 copies have been subscribed for so far – by Sunday. This doesn't mean 41 people, as some will have taken more than one. First in the field was someone called Stanley Chapman, who subscribed before I'd sent the MS. She mentions as well Madge, Winter (2), Horne, Hoggart, Norman Nicholson, Leishman, Flew, J. D. Scott, Philip Oakes, & a few more – the Murphys, Japolsky, & one or two Belfast people along with people I've never heard of – John Cotton, Lawrence Clark![1] I think as a response it's not too bad, but I hope it is followed up by others. Norman Nicholson is the big surprise as far as I'm concerned: I shall have to start being respectful about his bunk. I feel surprised and pleased by the thought of people bothering to answer & *send money*. How do you feel? And lo, Miss Rabbit's name led all the rest. [...]

For the last week or so I have been repeating Hardy's lines in *A bird-scene at a rural dwelling* – it's just like where I live here, at present. (p.665). Not that anyone comes out at five, but the garden is so close and agreeable. It is always a pleasure to walk down it to the gate, under the trellis-arch that goes all the way & has things growing round it. You'd like it, though it's rather a wilderness. I think you're right about T.H. when you say he isn't a beginners' poet. I think one has to attend closely to what he's saying, because he's very accurate and often his 'awkwardness' comes from choosing a particular word – now I have been trying to find an example, but have roved on reading for pleasure. I don't remember seeing *The faded face* (420) before! And I am a reader in much the same style as you – don't think of me as a Lerner, knowing 'how to read a poem'. Hardy has his quirks – how about *The conformers* (213)? Nearly all express my feelings – except some of the ballads. How about *The curate's kindness* (194)? [...]

Mrs Squire gave me some strawberries tonight: she's a rarely-kind old thing. Never a cross word. But I don't know! this place won't really do, if anything else offers itself – but of course things don't offer themselves.

I've quite abandoned any head of dept dress; I loaf about in sandals, bow, carnation shirt. I've just got a new telephone system in the Library: great fun, in a way. Gives the illusion of things being done. If I press the buttons in a certain way we can all talk at once & hear what each other is saying – haven't tried it yet. Scotland wd be gorgeous now,

I agree. My hayfever isn't too bad, I must admit – not so frightful as of yore. Just a great nuisance sometimes. I ride to work every morning, gradually learning every peculiarity of the road as I used to know the roads to school. I always had a gift for *surfaces* – Manor Road, Park Road, Station Road, Warwick Road, they were all differently-surfaced, or so I felt: well, they were, I suppose. [...]

1 Stanley Chapman, poet, designer, 'pataphysician', who designed some of *Listen*'s covers; Charles Madge, poet, Professor of Sociology, Birmingham; Winter, unknown; C. H. Horne, Leicester University; Richard Hoggart, then Staff Tutor at Hull University; Norman Nicholson, poet; J. B. Leishman, Fellow of St John's, Oxford; Antony Flew, philosopher, Reading University; J. D. Scott, literary editor, the *Spectator*; Philip Oakes, poet and journalist; Richard Murphy and Patsy; Leo Japolsky, lecturer in French, QUB; John Cotton, poet and schoolmaster; Lawrence Clark, unknown.

22 July 1955

200 Hallgate, Cottingham, E. Yorks

My dear,

I sent a very dull letter today, & yet if I begin another it's really only to anatomise my dullness. It's so intense as to be a little frightening. I come 'home', eat a rough supper in my room so as to be away from the horribly-close noises of the household, & then sit ... Nothing to do. The room seems airless. I don't want to do anything, not to try writing poetry, not to write letters, not to go out – where is there to go? I just sit & shudder at the noises of the household. Reading doesn't attract me. I've no friends. Really I feel like a plant in a pot that nobody waters. There's a horrible piano jangling somewhere – sounds too faint to be in the house, but too loud to be outside it. I feel: 'You've properly done for yourself, now.' It's all very horrible. The inhabitants of the house seem very close tonight: there is continual talking. Have they visitors? Someone to stay? I shrink in every fibre of my being. Some are upstairs, some down. They call to each other, in horrible flat voices, short unintelligible questions and answers: half of them are addressed to dogs. Another voice is rumbling, the piano is still going ... altogether the house sounds as if in five minutes a large family is to leave for its summer holidays. Oh dear! I can't disentangle my different strands of feeling: part nausea (only half accounted for), part boredom, part hatred of my surroundings, part terror of the future, and even of the present, part tiredness: all play their parts. I don't know why I shd write it down for you. It's not interesting, I know. But ...

Pause to eject a horrible wriggling leggy thing *with wings* – lucky for it it fell on its back & couldn't get up. This made it easy to throw it from the window. This is about the first *action* I've performed for several hours. I hope it won't come back.

Another pause, this time to have a bath. The household seems to be 'making for bed' – I am living among the lower classes, I fancy. Lower, not lowest. It wouldn't give Orwell a kick, & it doesn't give me one, either. My object is to get out. But how? Abandon the ideal of Cottingham? I don't care all that much about it, to be honest. But what's the procedure – *advertise*? Oh god. *Agents*? double god. Oh hell. 'Let us off & search, & find a place Where yours & mine can be natural lives ...'[1]

It's 11.15 p.m. Better to bed. One absurd thing I did when at home was order a tweed hat. I had gone in a shop that couldn't give me anything I wanted so in despair I ordered a tweed hat. I bet I look a fool in it. I can wear it on Sark. Perhaps no one will notice there. [*drawing of seal wearing hat*]

Saturday God: the house seems full of people – this is the kind of 'quaint' life people have when they're young and adventurous, not when they've got £1500 a year. Curse it all. Must dress now & go to work – that's another evil thing.

After lunch. Ugh! That's my reaction to life at present. The sun is shining brightly & it's very hot, real heat-wave, but I am really nearer the state of mind I was in when I came here than I've ever been since ... Horrible lunch alone, & back to this filthy hovel, which smells horribly of hot meat & god knows what else – & is over-populated: I don't know who else is here but there is someone here ... Oh *God*. Filthy lowerclass swine. Fool that I am. *Ugh*. I had meant to stay here till after the summer, but I wonder whether in fact I shouldn't get moving right away, while I am relatively free to go round looking at places. I can't come in the front door without my stomach contracting in disgust. What a fool I am. I think I ought to start ringing up agents, or something. My being shrinks from it, & I don't know what I want anyway. O how stupid & hateful it all is, & how utterly fed up I am. There is some lower-class oaf *singing* on the stairs ... dear bun, I feel quite hysterically frightened at my ... of my circumstances, I must calm myself. I ought to go out, I suppose, but that's only a palliative – my dear, I do feel absolutely sick at heart, my blankness has been goaded into revulsion & I am up in arms again, sufficiently fed up to start moving again, back at the point when not moving is worse than moving. And I can't *do* anything, not now: I must endure the weekend, & all next week, & ... This state of mind is different from my earlier howls: this is a kind of nausea, as if life were some milk-skin clinging to my lip. I don't, at the moment, see how I'm going to endure it, it's all so frightful – I really had better go out.

9.50 p.m. I went a long bike ride in boiling weather, enjoying it in snatches, but obssessed (oh, how do you spell that word?) with the contents of this letter and the circumstances that produced it. I went to Beverley in a roundabout way, had tea at the Beverley Arms, then went west in a long arc round the villages and wolds to Kirk Ella & Hessle, for the sake of calling on Jean Hartley to see what the position was now. But she was out & the filthy sluttish mother-in-law merely shouted at me through the window – why is my life in the hands of the workingclass? By the time I got back I must have done nearly 20 miles & felt tired. The house was quiet when I came in, but somebody came in after me & I don't think things have altered. In Beverley I went into St Mary's and found the rabbit (see enclosed leaflet). I like this church: I hope one day you'll see it. The rabbit is not a very attractive one: I should say it is sneering rather, and some of it has broken away. Then again it might be a hare, I suppose. But it is certainly wearing a satchel. What evidence there is for the Lewis Carroll story I don't know. The only guide I have says nothing about it – doesn't even mention the rabbit. Still, it is *there*, a lone invader of a hated ecclesiastical stronghold. I expect the satchel contains carrots. Looking into a small papershop for cricket scores I found a pile of Beatrix Potters, & read Apply Dapply's Nursery Rhymes – especially the present of carrots put down on the stair. It made me wish you were with me – or rather, it reinforced my wish that you were with me. I thought a lot about you as I rode, about your mosquitos (I don't think I notice mosquitos as such) and your garden – glad you used the secateurs. You have a closer grip on things than I. My life is tourniquet'd at every point: I am too exhausted to wail about it – & the immediate stimulus to do so, mercifully, is lacking – but it is so, yes indeed. When you exhorted me not to sound so bored with everything in London I reflected that I probably do sound bored a lot of the time – I'm horribly lacking in 'outgoing' feeling.

About Norman N. – well, I don't care for him, I must admit, from what I know. I find his poetry rather 'smart', & his regionalism & Christianity I'd sooner infer than have crammed down my throat. Still, I'm very glad to have his six bob & his name in the back.

This ride has tired me out, & I'd better prepare towards bed. At times my whole body was wet as I rode, as if I'd gone through a waterfall: the air was so hot. Even now the waistband of my trousers is damp. I felt most envious when I passed boys swimming in a river, most horrified when I passed a tannery, most pleased when I found the rabbit, most ... oh! awyawyaw! More tomorrow, darling bun. Or is there some scoundrel in the bathroom? I never know how many people there are in this house.

Sunday. My uncertainty persists. Where is that music coming from? those voices? My *Observer* didn't come this morning. What am I doing here? I agree last summer seems an impossible dream – Belfast does, altogether, though I had my depressions there. Oh hell, why can't I stop being miserable and complaining? Why is the wireless so loud? Why does it seem to alter in volume from minute to minute? Who are all those people talking? I don't know who the extra swine were, but I think they all went off yesterday afternoon to some wretched caravan-site: heaven alone knows when they will return or how many of them. Someone comes in to sleep, therefore, & numerous people throng in all day – curse the whole crowd.

Are you fed up with all this? Or does it seem no more than the murmuring of bees to you in your garden? Did you like the scarecrow I drew?

Had better go & have my horrible lunch – & it really will be horrible.

4.15 p.m. It wasn't too bad. But this is an afternoon almost sinful in its dullness. Here am I, with nowhere to go & nothing to do. Outside the sun shines, the children shout ... I'm lying on my bed. The room is airless. Oh my dear! My life is all wrong. I have to go out to awful people tonight – this afternoon is the only time I have. And I do nothing. Someone is sawing outside. I feel thoroughly down, & slightly sick. It would be such a beautiful day to be with you, and we're miles and miles apart, separated by the filthy Humber & all the rest of it.

Monday. Evening. Cooler today. I was so pleased to get your letter this morning, & only sorry that the one you had from me was so spiritless.

Not that this is much better. I am not sure what the position in the house is, but I think the usual swine are back & I believe the extra swine are here too, though I haven't done more than hear them. They aren't a nuisance, yet, though something queer is going on in the bathroom – talking, & a strange chemical smell, as if they were ... well, what? Washing a dog? I don't know. Anyway, I can't get in.

It is a consolation to know you were thinking of me at 3 yesterday: I was thinking of you too, as you can guess, but not quite in the way indicated – I was trying to approach a poem for you. I didn't succeed, but I didn't try hard, as I didn't feel in the mood quite, & I didn't quite know what I wanted to say. – Ah! a strange man has gone down the garden, carrying a bag & wearing an overcoat. A good omen, though no more than that so far.

Your handwriting sometimes turns me into a boxer – I stare wonderingly round, trying to think why you should be reading *The Aeroplane World*, & why it shd remind you of me. *Daimler Test New Goblin Jet at Farnsworth* – eh? *RAF Have Answer to Mig XII* ... Then I 'twigged'. I had intended to bring it to Sark for you.

I managed to hear the close of play scores tonight – I do hope they stick it out tomorrow. One can hardly envisage a win, but I have a feeling that if they just try to stay there they'll lose. I gathered May & Insole were doing well at the close. Compton is never any good when he tries to go safely, is he? How long is a day's play – 6½ hours? A long time – 390 minutes, is it? and they want 366, is that right? No, they'll never do it, not without the help of Jess-hop & Thumper [*drawing of seated rabbit*] no! hopeless. He is *sitting down*. Very bad – have altered it.

Library a little worrying today – I can't seem to do any *work*, & a complaint has arisen from one girl about her salary, which I doubt my ability to put right. More & more I feel my position here a dangerous farce. The people I visited last night – the local Bishop & his French, separate-salad-serving wife – weren't as bad as I feared, but full of yarns of doublecrossing & so on, wch sent shivers down my back. *I am frightened, sweetheart, that's the long & short of it* ... – do you know who wrote that? Applications have started to come in from people for this job I've created – *real people, graduates, with degrees*, as M. wd say. Brrr. Holy God. Larkin made a mess of Hull. Bad appointment, that.

Just eleven. I think the house is back to its normal population. Felt horribly tired today – I wake up at 6 a.m. & then feel tired all day. Wish I didn't.

I'm sorry about your aunt – what an awful chain-reaction this visiting is. How long will she stay?

> Must go to bed –
> goodnight, aquarius rabbit!

Tuesday. No great improvement in morale. Letter from Jean Hartley, reporting another 17 subscribers (26 copies) – Bateson, Pinto, Enright, Lerner, Trypanis & co. Judy Egerton has opted out of the printed list – the only one to do so. I wonder if she thinks it's the done thing? Or perhaps I've annoyed her by not going to Donegal.

I'm wondering if I should do any booking for our Sark trip. Certainly the position about the connection *to* Sark should be investigated, from Guernsey. Should I book 2 plane seats from London, if it is all right? Leave you to make yr way to London?

Good day, dear one. I'm sure I've no comfort at present except you.

> All love
> Philip.

1 Opening lines of Hardy's 'The Recalcitrants'.

3 August 1955

200 Hallgate, Cottingham, E. Yorks

My dear lonely rabbit,

'They don't mind getting in a hole' (7) was a down clue in the *Times* this morning. ***B*T* ... I got it eventually, after Flopsyish delay. Well, here I am, back. I ought just to bring you up to date – I went home on Saturday afternoon, 1.30 to Grantham – a lovely run, the scorched land misty with heat, like a kind of *bloom* of heat – and at every station, Goole, Doncaster, Retford, Newark, importunate wedding parties, gawky & vociferous, seeing off couples to London.[1] My literary pleasure in this was damped by missing the 4.8 connection at Grantham: however, by a stroke of luck I asked the way to the bus stop of a man who was about to drive to Melton Mowbray. He was a farmer & a little gruff – and with a horrifying habit of covering his face with his hand(s) when trying to remember something, the Rover leaping along at around 50 m.p.h. the while. Anyway, he put me down in M.M. about 5 – next bus to Loughborough 5.55 (the train would have got me in at 5.51), arriving 6.46. So I had quite a good tea at the Anne of Cleeves cafe & caught it in good (i.e. 20 mins wait) time. I thought what a nice place M.M. was. The bus journey, again, was awfully enjoyable, though I recognised nothing. I was marvellously free of hay fever, & looking forward to going home, so all presented its best aspect in gorgeous weather.

So I was at home Sunday, Monday & Tuesday, doing nothing but pore over a poem, play records, & go walks with M – short ones, of course, because there might be a storm. I must say home is where the records are: I should love to play you the pieces I have by 'Muddy Waters', a blind singer. And my Barber sides,[2] or 'tracks' as they're called on LP, sound good, despite our disappointment at Wembley. They played about 5 pieces on Monday, *South*, *N. Orleans Hop Scop blues*, *Jailhouse blues* (with Ottilie), *High Society*, & there may have been one other, I don't remember. They had only 15 mins INSTEAD OF THE USUAL THIRTY, so there was little enough time. *Jailhouse* is the rising *Lord, Lord, Lord* number.

Otherwise I turned out my wardrobe & sorted a few letters. Home is a mixture of bad & good at present. – Oh! before I forget: I dyed 3 pairs of white socks *mauve*. Not your terylene ones, but old ones I shall never wear. They came out blindingly bright – don't know if I shall ever wear them now: perhaps they'll set off my *tweed hat*, when I get it. If that has any colour it is mauve, or heather. The dye was dylon, from Boots. They have a large range of colours. They are far brighter than your dress you are wearing in the 'studio portrait' I took of you! Far, far brighter! It does seem that the way to get bright coloured socks is to buy white ones & dye them. The dye might be diluted in the interests of subtlety.

– However, as I was saying, home is a great mixture of nice & nasty, though having said it I don't really feel able to say anything more than that the balance shifted as the days went on, rather paralysing me. By 'nasty' I mean of course Mother's constant distress & complaints – & the unhappiness they cause me, not merely guilt, indecision & co. but real sympathy. There seems no answer, short of hiring someone to be with her night & day, & that isn't a very safe solution. She goes from neighbour to daughter to fake psychologist to real psychiatrist & gets comfort from none, or not much. Very disturbing. We went out to tea with the batty secretary of the College Principal – that was pretty trying too. I wasn't expected, so she produced a third sundae glass & scrabbled juiceless pineapple chunks from the waiting two glasses to make up the third – with her fingers. Hum. The sandwiches were ham & fish.

Coming back I felt low – I bought *1984* & reread it with pleasure, thinking how like Hull it all was. 'The hallway smelt of boiled cabbage and old rag mats.' However: contrary to my expectations, work was nastier & here pleasanter. Two impossible applications for this job arrived, & the only possible one of the previous two withdrew. Farrell says he wants to apply for a job at Leeds. Had disagreeable conversation with electricians, & the Head Porter, a fair swine to my way of thinking. When I got back to Hallgate the niece offered me some chocolates on the grounds that it was her birthday, & there was a 5 page letter from K. grumbling about Portugal.³ He is a fool. Anyone could tell him that taking 3 children to a privately-recommended place abroad would be awful. It's the place that's the real trouble – small, dirty, & swindling. They're going to move. However, it seems *LJ* is going to be filmed *and* broadcast (18/- a minute), so he can stand it. One letter I 'sorted' at home was from Kingsley, thanking me for the schedule of Chapters 1–7 & containing 2 pages detailed questions for 8–15. ('I see what you mean about the lecture, though I don't know if I can do it.' I told him how to do it. He did it. Oh well. No more signs of the 'little present'. I hope *That uncertain feeling* gets a good scragging. He is now planning a new one, *Pay up and look pleasant.*) He has met a man called Tyrrell with a Goanese wife, who pronounces 'bottle' as 'mwontle'. This makes me laugh.

I'm glad the results went your way, especially Craik's girl. I've thought of a phrase to introduce the things you want to say at departmental meetings: 'Look, I don't want to rock the boat, but—' – and then whatever it is, Swedes, colonials, Spenser, proof correcting examn papers, etc. You can file it with 'What's on your mind, Arthur?'

Yes, I agree about the cool sitting-rooms. My ideal is a large first-floor room, with a carpet & a large sofa, a wall of books with the bottom shelf partitioned for & filled with records, and a large record-amplifier pulsing in the corner, bringing out the bass very clearly. It overlooks a garden with fields beyond. I am lying on the sofa, sipping a gin drink.

I'm very excited to find that the Botany prof. here, a man called Good, was born in Dorchester about 1900 & was brought up there. *HE OFTEN SAW HARDY WALKING ABOUT.* I'm going to force him to invite me round. He's off now to Fleet, behind Chesil Beach, near Chickerell, where Meade Falkner's *Moonfleet* was apparently set. Isn't that thrilling? Trouble is, he's not very bright: thinks Hardy is like A. E. Housman. But he told me a striking story – after Dunkirk,

Dorchester was full of soldiers, lying about exhausted all about the grass verges of the streets, *sleeping it off*. During these two days, a meeting was held at the Hardy statue to commemorate the 100th anniversary of his birth (2 June 1840) – *with the soldiers lying around snoring*. He saw it as 'This England' – NS & N – but I see it as pure Hardy. How he'd have *felt* it! Talking about England, did you see *Henry V* is to be shown at the Academy, Oxford St.? *I want to go*. When I was at home I looked into Ll. Powys briefly & set myself chuckling.

Pity we didn't find *The Bun & Bush*, isn't it? Wish I'd known which it was. I expect it used to be called *The bun & bush*, and was run by Cicely Parsley.[4]

Today is Thursday. I'll put this in the post as I have to go & waste my evening with my pop-eyed little deputy at his rotten little house, rot him. I should like to feed him into a haychopper.

I have been wondering about Scarborough Cricket Festival. There are 3 games, M.C.C. v. Yorkshire, Gents v. Players, & T. N. Pearce's XI v. S. Africa. (Hutton is down for the first 2.) They run from 31 August – 2 Sept., 3 Sept – 6 Sept, & 7 – 9 Sept. respectively. I'm wondering if we could see any of it, around the end of August, the first 3 days of Sept for instance, round about there. I have to be 'in the saddle' from Sept 5th as the others are away. Does it appeal to you at all? We might have to stay outside Scarborough – it might be hard – but I'm told one can walk into the actual cricket. I've seen the list of teams for the games, & they're all the Test match boys, if fit.

Lunch today at The Good Fellowship – 4/-, greasy, circling flies, sauce bottles, commercials, pretty dreary. Still, 'It makes a change'. But how dull this part of the country is! How dull life is here anyway!

I enclose Mary's form. Hope your visitors aren't causing too much trouble. Stroke ears.

Love from

---

1 This appears to be the germ of what eventually became 'The Whitsun Weddings'.
2 L.'s recordings of Chris Barber.
3 Amis had chosen Portugal as the place in which to spend his money from the Somerset Maugham award.
4 Beatrix Potter character.

6 August 1955

200 Hallgate, Cottingham

My dearest,

Saturday morning, nearly a quarter to nine. I have been 'upstairs' since about half past five, feeling none too happy – reading plays by Terence Rattigan. I have read *French w. tears*, *Flarepath*, *The Winslow boy*, & one whose name I've forgotten – *While the sun shines*. All quite enjoyable. The theatre's terribly moving, isn't it? Like the pictures. I always remember a record the Egertons suddenly put on one night, a scene between Noel Coward & Gertrude Lawrence from *Private lives*. You can imagine the kind of thing, yet it was astonishingly 'moving' (silly word that is – emotional, then). After hearing it I saw just how N.C. had been good & why he'd been successful. Of these plays I read, *French* & *Sunshine* were the best. I shd think they must have been about equally funny to see, though 'redolent' of war-time atmosphere, & *Winslow* just boring because it had no real plot. You don't know who *did* steal the 5/- & you don't really care. There's only one good scene in it & that only because cross-examinations are natural drama, aren't they.

Had a letter from Robt Conquest this morning. He writes a letter every time he doesn't feel like work, which is about twice a week in my case & no doubt is the same in about 15 other people's cases. He is a great gossip. He says that John Wain has gone off with his wife Marianne, who has just decided to divorce him, & has (i.e. John has) another girl, a psychology student, also called Marianne, who has been sterilised; also that every single character in *L. in the p.*[1] is crudely drawn from life – the nastiest being Hilary Corke. The 'awful family' has already written to complain. I'm not sure John is the decent man I take him for. Still, gossip is always exaggerated. [...]

Sunday. Evening. People pour into the house, doors slamming, dogs barking ... I went a walk this afternoon. People had told me to 'walk to the Wolds' or the Dales or something, but when I got about a third of the way there I thought 'this is enough for me' and turned back through Rowley and Little Weighton. It was a fairly sunny afternoon but there were cloudy intervals. Near home I stopped and watched half a dozen Jersey cows. How lovely they are! like Siamese cats, almost: the patches of white round the eyes and the soft way the coffee-colour melts into the white underbody. They were licking each other affectionately in pairs, on the chest and along the neck. When one stopped the other would begin licking back! The Peaceable Kingdom! In the end I found I'd walked about 11 miles – long way for a seal. But never a rabbit did I see, alas. I ought to write a *Lament for the rabbits*. My head is full of ideas for poems, these days, but they vanish as soon as I sit down. [...]

Will write more tomorrow. Well, when I was young I used to make these nights[2] occasions for prophecy, but I don't now. They were usually of the order *Shall write a novel, shan't have a woman*, or occasionally vice versa, but they grew so negative in the end that I abandoned them. My mother used to have a jolly litany of 'You'll never be sixteen/seventeen/eighteen again', thus early implanting in me the fear of time. [...]

Tuesday – is it? No: *Wednesday*: groogh ... Today's worry is that Mrs Binns (remember her?) rang up to draw my attention to a flat advertised by postcard outside the local newsagents. This says it's in one house, apply to another, after 7 p.m. The house it's in looks quite impossible, contriving to look at once small-modern & ancient-battered. If *I* had seen the card I'd have done no more about it, but as someone else has drawn my attention to it I feel I ought to follow it up. *Don't want to*. I feel it's impossible to have any sort of flat in that sort of house. And yet – and yet – ... It is the *certainty* that I shan't like it, coupled with the fear that it will be just not bad enough to make me wonder whether, when I've settled down, I shouldn't prefer it ... It *sounds* good, of course: but it *couldn't* be, in a house that size – not even a third floor as you have. Oh I do feel so sick about it all! It's back on the Hull side of Cottingham again, horrible dreary area, near Outlands Rd. Farrell says he has heard it's 4 gns (fur'd) and no good – people zip in & out as fast as they can. Oh *God*. The front gate is *off*, the front garden is all weedy. Yet the smell of food floats to where I sit: I remember all I've said about this place, & how *impossible* it'll be in winter, really impossible, & yet I do nothing – what can one do? Pester agents? Reverting to your letter, & the first page written on 31 July, I don't know whether I have any ideas any more about how to live; certainly not the camping-out ones, or not as *ideas* – I do shrink rather from commitments in any sphere, which would tend to make me shy of houses, but hell, sometimes there's worse things than commitments. As for *houses*, I'm afraid I'm just not practical enough for it to be anything but unmitigated torture – I *couldn't* have a house, all alone. (Oh this filthy smell of fried potatoes! Let me light a cigarette, sick though it will make me) Who would clean it? And a house means neighbours – and what sort of house – semi-det.? And yet really I *ought* to go, & 'enquire', or it will offend the Binnses, who did take the trouble to let me know about it ... I know! [...]

I really must post this tomorrow – I do sympathise with your impatience with your life. I feel the same, only more rage at myself for not having the *brazen energy* to live properly – to find a place by *brute force* – not just tamely exist in the least horrible way I can find with the least trouble. Fool, fool. Do you think if we married we should be the same, & live in a semi-detached house called 'Oakdene' & advance 'sound parish views'? That wd be awful, wouldn't it? There would be a piano next door, played by someone who changed the treble but not the bass. The bakelite handle of the 'french window' ... The kitchen audible in the lavatory & vice versa ... but this is a horror story. I'm sure we'd do better than that. Must get ready for bed now. Goodnight, dear bunny.

1 *Living in the Present*, John Wain's second novel (1953).
2 The nights before his birthday.

15 August 1955

200 Hallgate, Cottingham

Dearest,

A drearyish evening – very *hot*, for one thing. Am worried also by Mrs. S. having discovered my programme[1] – she is bound to listen & *Mr Bleaney* is included. Of course it doesn't apply to this house, but it isn't calculated to inspire confidence in any landlady. What else? Oh yes, insects – one of those shiny black buzzing things, *hard*, most hateful. You can't *see* them because they're so dark, but you can hear them knocking into things. And finally I have *hired* a wireless, which for some reason makes me uncomfortable – why, I'm not quite sure, but it definitely does. It's not here yet. I felt really terrified in the shop, just at the prospect of signing an agreement. Oh, a properly disturbed seal – as when is it not? Fool. Anyway, I'm bound to have the thing for 2 months anyway. What hellish knots I tie myself in, over nothing. [...]

Thank you for your letter – I'm afraid you are equally miserable, poor dear. I *am* sorry. I feel it can't go on, & yet it does, from term to term and landmark to landmark, on & on, never getting any simpler or easier or even duller. I mean we do not feel it less. Our lives are not as good as a play. Perhaps other people's aren't, either – yet one wonders. [...]

Heard from John today – he says next term is definitely his last.[2] Ah, *si sic omnes!* 'The air outside the pigstye smells cleaner to me, and I'm going outside to prove it.' Outside the university, that is. He tells me to get *Interpretations*,[3] edited by him, when it comes out, for the Library: 'if the English department refuse to have it on the grounds that it would show up their own incompetence, tell them not to worry, as their incompetence is not the closely guarded secret they imagine.' He ends 'ever thine'. How corny can you get?

Wednesday Nearly zero hour. Feel *fairly* nervous. I hate these occasions. I suppose RM will know only what Patsy has told him about me: nobody I know has known RM. Mrs. S. is at the ready below! I wonder if you are similarly waiting?[4]

Well, while I have drawn that, the relevant part of the programme has passed. I liked the reference to 'Francis Chelifer'[5] – he was, you remember, editor of *The Rabbit-Fanciers' Gazette and Goat-Keepers' Guide*. But God knows what Mrs S. is thinking down below! or *my staff*, or the V.C., or Brett. I thought he made me sound rather a dreary devil, didn't you?

Have just been down to see Mrs. S., & find her quite unperturbed – doubt if she 'took in' much of it. She is really a dear old thing. Says she was born on the Isle of Wight, 77 years ago.

I suppose for that matter I am rather a dreary devil. I must say I thought Roethke's poems sounded good. If I could only understand what he is on about I shd like him. *Mr Bleaney* went down the best I thought: *Elsewhere*[6] seemed to lack the odd rhythm I hoped it had – I don't think he understood it. *Departures*[7] of course has its own 'tune' in my head wch they didn't reproduce – there should have been much more tone-colour & drama in the reported speech, or the direct speech, is it. Oh well. 28 guineas for yours truly. Scandalous of course. Think what *he* gets. [...]

1 Broadcast by Richard Murphy on BBC Third Programme, *Three Modern Poets*, drawing on L., W. S. Graham and Theodore Roethke, was later published in the *Listener* (8 September 1955).
2 John Wain: leaving Reading University to freelance.
3 *Interpretations*: critical essays on poems, ed. Wain.
4 In a letter dated 18 August 1955, Monica wrote: 'Reception was so bad that I couldn't hear the one poem of the 3 that I didn't know, or hardly. That's one you haven't shown me, tho' you told me about it, or not about it but its title & that he was using it for this programme. *Mr Bleaney* sounded so very like you – yr catalogue of the room's shortcomings! Like you & like me – I smiled at the radio as if I were smiling at you as it was read. And I like your poetry better than any that I ever see – oh, I am sure that you are the one of this generation! I am sure you will make yr name! yr mark, do I mean – really be a real poet, I feel more sure of it than ever before, it is *you* who are the one, I do think so. Oh, Philip – I don't know what to say! You will believe me because you know it doesn't make any difference to me whether you are or not, I shouldn't think any less of your value if yr poems seemed to me bad & if everybody said so; and because I've never said to you this is magnificent, this is greatness triumphant, in yr hands the thing becomes a trumpet' [...]
5 Character in Aldous Huxley's *Those Barren Leaves* (1925).
6 'The Importance of Elsewhere'.
7 'Poetry of Departures'.

19 August 1955

200 Hallgate, Cottingham

Dearest bun,

The heat, the heat! Simply frightful – there's almost certain to be a storm somewhere near before long. Felt ghastly this morning, due no doubt to my old enemy tomato-skins, but am improved tonight. Of course, it may have been reading Betjeman's review of *That uncertain feeling*[1] (insipid title, to my mind) – *summa cum laude*. There is also a simple-minded review in the *N.S.&N.*, though I suppose favourable. I'm surprised no one treats Kingsley as a master of words, of style, of syntax: that is where his main strength lies. I am longing for my copy: hope to get it tomorrow (paying for it, of course) – publication day isn't till Monday. What the *NS & N* terms a brilliantly funny opening scene in a public library is, I am prepared to swear, taken from one of my Wellington letters. *I remember writing it*: 'a sample encounter with a borrower.' Really, I do find it irritating – of course, I'm not in possession of the text, or of my own letter of ten years ago, but I do dislike being used *to open the show*, to put everyone in a good humour, to make them think 'Ah, this is going to be just as funny as the other one' – see what I mean? It irritates me powerfully to see this stuff, small though it may be, used for his credit & advantage, when I wrote it just for my & his amusement. Well, I seem to be getting rather 'psychotic' about one little scene – but I'm not sure that will be all, and I think I do well to be irritated. Don't you? I mean, though it stands to reason that K. couldn't write a scene like that without help, nobody will think of it that way – it'll just be 'a brilliant opening scene'. Oh, well, I suppose it's no great matter. Damn me if I don't lay my tongue round him when I write, though.

I've gone back to the Archers again, now I have a wireless. They haven't changed much!

It's some time since I read *W.H.*[2] I never know what to think of it. In a way I don't appreciate the emotion of Heathcliff's love, or his hatreds – it doesn't 'come over' to me: I think the novel splendidly constructed and written, but the central emotion doesn't quite touch me, not like the emotion of, say, *Lady Chatterley* or *Mr Weston's Good Wine*[3] or *Tess* or *Jude*, to name a few well worn okay works – only at the very end, when H. isn't eating anything and doesn't know if he's coming or going, that part I like. Are people 'moved' by it, as by *Lear* or *Othello*? I don't think I am. And Gothic – yes, but not Italian: German, isn't it? Heathcliff to me is a sort of sprite of the bergs, a cousin to Mary Shelley's monster, a creature of the northern mists, a gnome. [. . .]

Sunday night The house is full again, & smelling of hot meat: the usual two are back, plus somebody's son & somebody's grandson – God! This has been an utterly dull day. I secured Kingsley's book yesterday, & have been reading it at intervals since: I was piling it on about the first scene, really, though there are spills & spars of a dialogue of mine in it. I contribute about 4 other gags in the course of the book, but they've mostly been adapted. On the whole I found it very funny, but it's more irritating than *LJ* – more inverted Angela Thirkellism[4] about the lower classes, Churchill, Tory governments, upper classes, etc. I think Toynbee whacks it on the head well and truly in *the Observer*. You, I venture to predict, will find it rather heavy going. But there are some extremely funny things in it. [...]

1 Kingsley Amis's second novel.
2 *Wuthering Heights*.
3 Novel by T. F. Powys (1927).
4 Allusion to the popular novels of Angela Thirkell, 1890–1960, who (according to her biographer, Margot Strickland) wrote 'middle-brow novels for middle-brow tastes'. She had produced a novel a year for the previous thirty years when she died.

7 September 1955

200 Hallgate, Cottingham, E. Yorks

Dearest Byrne –

Well! this isn't Monday, or Tuesday, but the evening of Wednesday. I fell slackly into my horrible life here, unable to face writing about it for at least 48 hours, but now Farrell's wedding is over & Conquest has agreed to meet us in the S.P. at 9 p.m. next Tuesday night I feel I have at least that much to say, as well as moans. 'O more than moan'! Conquest's proofs came today:[1] *Maiden name*, *Church going*, *Latest Face*, *Skin*, *Born Yesterday*, *Triple Time*, *I Remember*, and *Photograph Album*. Jolly nice they looked, too, on the whole, but they are not quite my favourite sort of poetry. I am struck by my ease and deftness of expression and rhyming, rather than by any depths of feeling. Still. The book is for 'early next year'.

The Farrell wedding[2] was nice but boring. The colourful bright little church wasn't bad for an RC establishment, very light, not overdecorated or smelling of incense. As it was a mixed marriage (I hadn't known that) the ceremony was of the simplest & was very effective. After the photographs and so on we went off to the Beverley Arms – the fine weather was splendid – for insufficient drink, dreary food, &c. Farrell looked unexpectedly well in morning clothes (I wanted to say *wear it always*), and Alex had a nice dress but an undistinguished head-dress.

Coveney was an usher, & looked like Oscar Wilde. Wood carried gloves, & was so more correct than I. I didn't look very well, and didn't feel very interested in my surroundings. I had been put next to my secretary (match-making?) whose attention was soon claimed equally by the littlest bridesmaid squalling on her other side & an eager serious-looking young man opposite who passed her from his wallet a photograph of the highest W.C. in the world (in the Brenner Pass) and contrived in other ways to introduce, as F. O'B. would say, an element of smut into the proceedings. He turned out to be the Borough Librarian of Bromley, M.A., LL.B., F.L.A. After the orgy of confetti-sadism the guests sulkily dispersed. The youngest bridesmaid's dress had had a great hole burnt in her dress by someone throwing a lighted match at her – jolly good idea, wish I'd thought of it. No one knows where the couple have gone, but Italy is suspected. There were a great many elderly relatives (including an old man rather like T.H.) but none of them burst into those great baying embarrassing sobs so common to these occasions. Well, enough of it! The service was enlivened by wandering wassups. I thought of you.

There's 'such a nice' piece of music being played just now from the Three Choirs Festival: it will interest me to find out what it is. Vaughan Williams, perhaps. [. . .]

– It was Elgar's *Symphony 2*, in mem. Edward VII, & I don't think it was the 3 Choirs. Anyway, I'm glad it was something I'm not ashamed of liking. Don't you like Gertrude's description of music as *experiences in pure duration*?[3] Generally speaking I agree.

Pause while I consider a nearly-finished poem. [. . .]

There's a perceptive review of TUF by Maclaren-Ross in the *Listener*: but of course he's not much judge – Bloomsbury boozer. But he makes a good point about the *muddledness* of the book in general. [. . .]

1 Proofs of L.'s poems to be included in *New Lines* (1956).
2 John Farrell was a member of L.'s Library staff.
3 The allusion is to Jarrell's *Pictures from an Institution*, in which 'She would go on to say that, emotionally speaking, there was no difference between the *Manzoni Requiem* and *Tales from the Vienna Woods*, and would finish with a blank, fanatical, considering stare: "They're both *essentially* experiences in pure duration." (And, truly, for her they were.)'

10 September 1955

200 Hallgate, Cottingham

[. . .] Conquest writes to ask if he shall bring Anthony Hartley on Tuesday: I've agreed, but he may not come, and I rather hope he doesn't.

Conquest's letters are those of a cheerful idiot, with a taste for school-boy smut, so be prepared. [...]

Colossal noise downstairs, like a pub. O God! I should like to lob a 'pineapple' among their riot. Yes, I try to draw comfort from our holidays, but a Leopardian mood (nothing to do with leopards) sits on me & I can only think of their ending: you remember his poem about the night before the festival, & how he thinks that people are happier in their expectation than they will be at the festival.[1]

Sunday morning I lay in bed listening to the omnibus Archers – how dull it is! Wish I could have the writing of it for a week – Carol Grey wd seduce Christine, who wd turn into a prostitute in an effort to atone for the lapse, Jack Archer wd be run in for watering the beer, W. Gabriel wd be gored *to death* by a bull, T. Forrest would be caught in one of his traps all night, Dr Cavendish would appear in the *N of the W* as running a highclass brothel-cum-abortion clinic – the possibilities are endless. Don't you think?

Well, 6.4 p.m. at Kings Cross ... *Can't* finish this poem,[2] drat it.

> My dearest love
> Philip

1 Leopardi, '*Il sabato del villaggio*' (The Village Saturday Night).
2 Probably 'Ignorance' (completed 11 September 1955).

26 September 1955

200 Hallgate, Cottingham, E. Yorks

Dearest,

> Back to this dreary dump,
> East Riding's dirty rump,
> Enough to make one jump
>   Into the Humber –
> God! What a place to be:
> How it depresses me;
> Must I stay on, and see
>   Years without number?

– This verse sprang almost unthought-of from my head as the train ran into Hull just before midday. I'm sure no subsequent verse could keep up the high standard. *Pigs* & *digs* rhyme, of course, likewise *work* & *shirk*, & *Hull* & *dull*, but triple rhymes are difficult. Anyway, it gives an indication of how I'm feeling. Fearful change from life as it was lived on the island. [...]

I suppose in sum I miss you, and the happy life we led on Sark, & dislike being back at work & in these sluttish surroundings, and having said that much (!) I should really pipe down, rather than list feeble grumbles. But o, 'tis true, 'tis true.

27 September. God – that radio is on again, so that I can hear every word. What a bore. Am just in the middle of trying to write to Hartley, putting a few *points of business*. First the news, then a boxing match. Hell!

– It went on till about 10.10 – that's about an hour. I think it's the niece who plays it now – the one who washed my shirts. I didn't manage to write to Hartley after all. [...]

Mother went off on her ride & sent me a postcard from Buxton. She didn't seem in very good spirits though home was quite amicable. She watches both my sister & myself very keenly for any change in our circumstances: in a way I think she'd welcome my getting married if it led to her having part of any house I lived in. It irritated me in a way, but there you are – if people don't like their lives they are expected to be on the lookout for ways of altering them. Anyway, I don't expect it's *real* planning: but the concept serves to prevent her doing other things. [...]

Wednesday. So pleased to get your letter this morning, when I had overslept & was feeling anything but good – you express very much what I feel about the 'human' side of the holiday, though I remember it always used to be so on 'family hols'. The last afternoon was glorious, especially the PR scene and the kitten & dog: I regret my ineptness but I am always feeling we should be – well, what? I don't know: I want to bring us closer together without self-deception ('not wont to wear Life's flushest feather'[1] – remember that poem?) yet am so cautious about measuring the rice & raisins that it must seem a sort of gratuitous mental cruelty – for want of something better to do, almost! You are a true rabbit in wanting to ignore trouble: I a true seal in rhapsodising romantically over the more melancholy side of things. I'm writing this in the Library & must end – you may like to have it – but I'm awfully sorry you've suffered from the inhuman dampness of our rooms, & hope it stops quickly. You know those Hyde Park rabbits were more rabbity than the Hampstead ones, weren't they? More *natural*, somehow.

Lots of hugs & rabbit kisses   P.

1 Hardy, 'Between Us Now':

Between us now and here –
  Two thrown together
Who are not wont to wear
  Life's flushest feather –

2 October 1955

200 Hallgate, Cottingham, E. Yorks

[...] *Work* ('the toad work') is not too good at present – I am *making a balls* of certain high-level negotiations wch will no doubt redound to my discredit. Curse the whole crowd. There's a Senate meeting this afternoon & I had better try to acquaint myself with the minutes & so forth. Then tonight I will go on writing to my dear acquaintance.

– Yes, but I didn't. I went to the bookshop and ordered *The Art of Beatrix Potter* on approval (84/-). It looks lovely – all her drawings. Then I found items on the agenda that I ought to have thought about! Really, I must read at least the agenda in future. [...]

I was glad you tried to reply to my remarks about us,[1] and of course I see what you think about me sometimes: I'm thankful you don't think it more often. As if I could ever hate or despise you for anything! I dare say you are right about the low ebb of our relations around '51 and '52, and I did behave rather shabbily. I *was* rather dazzled by Patsy in those days, though I didn't realise it went on so long.[2] Since then I *have* changed, but I think my great worry has remained fairly constant – that our relation did not seem to contain the force that would turn it into something else – marriage for instance, or affair-and-parting – and worrying whether it was my fault or your fault or just nobody's fault, whether it did & I was trying to pretend it didn't, or *vice versa*, or whether it was just my fault for being so self centred – and in any case what I ought to do about it. That is the sort of worry that leads me to makes these occasional outbursts. If they have any 'spurious' quality it's that they *are* emotional outlets to some extent, as well as being attempts at apology for prolonging a state you must find rather wounding, no matter how nice about it you are & anxious not to seem possessive. I hate leaving you at the end of a holiday, as if all that was over now and the toys were being put back in the box, yet the impulse to make it real and permanent doesn't seem strong enough to shift me off the sandbanks – or if it is then I'm too feeble to obey it – And all this absurd havering revolts me too. I really mustn't do it, on paper anyway. [...]

1 In a letter dated 28 September 1955 Monica had written: 'I think you have changed more than I have in the progress of our "relationship", I think perhaps & for some time I did not seriously mean much to you, and as you've never *said* that you've changed, I have not known what to believe or where I stood, & being not willing to presume, have not asked [...] And I don't mean that it entered my head to think that there was "anything between" you and P., I can truly say that never occurred to me so don't think I mean that; no, it seemed even more depressing, just that any pair of casual friends whom you cd see any time, still had to have their 3 days kept intact, if you could "manage" an extra day, 2 instead of 1, for me, that had to be taken off yr time at home. Don't mind this *now*, do you: I'm only explaining how it did look as though you didn't much care about me [...] Dearest, dearest, *I* feel very close to you to be able to say this – please be pleased & feel close to me too, you ought to be, & not troubled at all, & I'm sure you see ...'
2 L.'s affair with Patsy Strang went on intermittently between June 1952 and the autumn of 1954.

9 October 1955

200 Hallgate, Cottingham, E. Yorks

Dearest,

I'm sitting in my, for once, overheated room, listening to *Porgy & Bess* from Brussels, but it's a hell of a bore except for the two famous tunes, neither of wch have been played yet. This is the only sheet of paper I have here – at least, I can't see any more, & I know I left a pad in my desk at the Library. Well, to give this place its due, the weather has been splendid yesterday & today. I have been quite transported by the sun, warm air, bees still burrowing into late flowers, the beautiful chill mauve blue of Michaelmas daisies in the churchyard; and in the villages, when I rode out this afternoon, the thick stacks behind the warm brick farmhouses. The sky was pale blue, with the immoveable small curly clouds of autumn in it. Yesterday – after a degree congregation and luncheon of *surpassing* foulness – the village seemed quite lovely. I went to the local library & strolled very slowly back up the main street, pausing to buy two teaspoons & a root of celery, feeling contented with the content that comes from feeling that the world is all right, even if I am all wrong. The pavement outside the Union Hall (over the Cooperative Stores) was scattered with confetti, & inside they were dancing & drinking & sing-ing *Let the rest of the world go by*. Mrs Squire's garden is tidied for the autumn, but still littered with squashy wrinkled plums, with wassups rolling in them, and apples of various sorts, including tiny little shiny *toy* apples, the like of which I haven't seen before. I had my celery for tea, & an egg, & real coffee (since returning I've been too dispir-ited to have anything but *Nescafe*). How good the real coffee tasted! For once I felt insouciant, like a tramp, in my horrible kitchen, reading a library book. [...]

I thought your analysis of our 'lack of force' very acute, and it's very good-natured of you to take my words seriously and not as offences – not that they're *intended* as offences! but as you know, or have guessed, I am always, emotionally, 'on the hop' (!) by feeling bound to 'explain' *why*, if you mean so much to me, I don't 'prewve it'. I always feel so defensive about this. That was the basis of the toys-in-the-box remark – feeling how it must seem from your side. And of course I regret the lack of force in a way (the way I don't regret it being, o well, perhaps the way you don't – shrink-ing from it instinctively as something a bit vulgar) – it is 'the glory' of existence, no matter what messes it leads to. In 1951 I remember writing a peevish, rather 'young' and coarse *Dialogue*[1] on sex as a companion to the one you read about writing. I don't suppose I'd support it nowadays. [...]

1 'Round Another Point' in *Trouble at Willow Gables*, ed. James Booth (2002).

22 October 1955

200 Hallgate, Cottingham, E. Yorks

[...] I've written to Watt[1] again, telling him the position, & asking him what the hell I am to do now. Expect he'll find some new way of confusing the issue – what you bet me he'll reply saying that if he were me he'd agree to Hartley's terms? I shouldn't be surprised. Then where's toad? I do wish I'd handled it better in the first place. 'Larkin, who had an utter indifference to money, never made a penny from any of his books.' [...]

Sunding – ! there's a perfect example of my unconscious habit of writing the beginning of one word and the end of the next. Anyway, Sunday morning. I overslept till 10 p.m., dreaming of Hartley & similar nightmares. The day looks mild & damp. I don't look forward to this week one little bit – it culminates in this awful visit of librarians on Saturday. What is so awful about it is that I can't think of anything to *show* them – we haven't *got* anything, no interesting editions or manuscripts or anything of that order: and if we had I shouldn't know which they were, or why they were 'interesting' (unless they were signed 'Will Shaxpur' all over). [...]

1 A. P. Watt, L.'s literary agent for *A Girl in Winter*, at this point looking into George Hartley's proposed contract for *The Less Deceived*.

26 October 1955

200 Hallgate, Cottingham, E. Yorks

[...] Wednesday evening ... aches in the legs & back. Rain most of today, chilly at night. The day given over to 'business' and 'administration', mostly unsuccessfully – chat with dynamic Vice Chancellor J. H. Nicholson,[1] chat with pop-eyed openmouthed bird-brained Deputy Librarian Wood, on The Institution and Administration of a Satellite Library, chat with Miss Brennan[2] on how the binder I've changed to isn't as good as the old one, & how she never gets any help because Miss Chambers takes all day over the accessioning ...

But I'm writing this tonight because who should ring up last night to fix a meeting tomorrow night but my old friend and *soi disant* publisher Geo. Hartley Esqre, of the Borough of Hessle. He sounded a bit uncertain and said nothing about any agreement, but said that the volume was now at the binders & wd be out in a fortnight bound in pale green. So what will transpire between ye 2 of Vs, I *knoe* nott. Anyway, I'll let you know before I seal (!) this up. I wrote to Watt, but he's away on holiday: I've also lined up a pair of solicitors called Pearlman & Rosen, geniis I shall never dare to invoke. [...]

I don't know about authors! I think I shall never go off ... Who? – Whom? Hardy's poems & novels? Llewelyn Powys? Those two, I think.

They are the two for me. Lawrence: I've got as far with him as I ever shall. As for people who may come to mean more to me – Dickens, perhaps? I don't think so. I was telling Coveney that the essays by Ed. Wilson & Geo. Orwell on Dickens were very good complements – the Yank seeing one side, the Limey the other. He didn't agree – he likes the 'social side'. I asked him if he thought Dickens was like 'real life', & he said he did. I said I didn't. Coveney is a bit of a fool, but very nice & a great help here. [...]

I took out my rabbit story last night & looked at it: it looked jolly good, but I've forgotten how I meant to continue it – just the next chapter, I mean. They're still underground, at the back of beyond. (Did you see the new glazed-pipe advertisement this morning? The children's nursery?)

Poor *dear* bunny, scrabbling at its horrible papers – I felt very sad at your analysis of your position: it would have happened to me – I believe that – if I'd gone into teaching. I can't read, or think, or write nowadays. It's a sad thought, the 10 years – I can't say anything about it, it is just too sad. I don't know that you're much more ridiculous than I am. You at least adopt a motto of 'Non Serviam'. I with my schizoid reeling from Vice-Chancellor to rabbit-story, living like a pig on £1500 a year, am quite as absurd really. In fact I don't think you're absurd *at all*. [...]

Thursday. 11.40 p.m. Groogh! Back from Hartley's. Well, it has been resolved, after a fashion, in an atmosphere awkwardly amicable: a time-limit on the option clause, for only one book; 'profit-sharing' instead of 10% (this *should* mean 50% of profits: hope it does) and anthology rights from publication day, which is a point in his favour, but still. I feel not exactly content, but too tired to argue more, & shall have to stand by it. Took a car back – 12/- ! Filthy robbing knaves.

Oh my dear, boredom, exhaustion & fear are not unknown here – these awful librarians on Saturday! O for a sudden attack of influenza! On Saturday night I shall be just prostrated – but relieved, too, I hope. Curse the whole crowd.

I enclose a copy of *Listen*[3] for you, so that you can see how the world wags. I think the cover is about the best they've had yet. Quite a good number, except for notorieties like Holloway & Alvarez. And all produced for nothing! [...]

1 Vice-Chancellor of Hull, 1954–6. Brynmor Jones succeeded him.
2 Maeve Brennan: her first appearance in these letters.
3 *Listen*, Vol. One, No. 4, Autumn 1955: cover by Quatrezoneilles (pseudonym of Stanley Chapman).

29 October 1955

200 Hallgate

Sweet Bun,

All over, thank God. My 'talk' sounded very gauche and nervous to me: in the audience were *three* people who had been *in for my job*, wch didn't improve matters. But the visit went off with some success – I think 'my staff' enjoyed it, curiously. In a way it 'brought us together' more. Tomorrow I must go in & clear up, curse it – lifting great sheets of glass, & moving chairs.

I've spent this evening listening to *The Archers* & *The heat of the day*; & writing a business letter or two. Ah, sweet content! I feel a great weight off my mind. All clear, till the next time, wch will be the Hull Literary Club in all probability. 'Books and you'. Oogh. Ugh. Cloop, sloop. The Archers were interesting as usual – Dan is talking of retiring! Phil has got his corgi pup. Paul has asked Chris to marry him: she's still thinking it over. John Tregorran's voice still makes me want to drive a tractor over his face, & Carol's voice still makes me think she shd be interested in Chris. Ah never shall bun that morrow see! [...]

Were you surprised to hear me this morning? You sounded quite clear, but not as near as you said I did. I've never rung you up before from that room, my room as it's called. I wondered whether to start off asking you if you could give some Basuto students extra coaching on Friday evenings, but forebore. [...]

Monday. Very cold here – large frosty moon, spilling chill light over the lifeless leaves. Mrs. S. very poorly again – she appears to have been retching all day & is quite broken down by it – she is still coherent but very feeble. I tried to sit with her tonight, but she dismissed me in order to retch better. She gave me her right hand to shake. I do not like the look of her at all.

Hartley was on the blower at 11 a.m., asking for a blurb for the jacket ('the bull on the jacket') to be put in the post tonight – I have done this in the intervals of attending Convocation & so on. Coveney is still in a stew – gave his chief ringleader – solecism, solipsism, or whatever it is – a talking-to tonight, & was rewarded by an organised chant of 'We want salad cream' under his window after dinner tonight – I was there, I heard it. Poor bastard. So you see there are circles of hell below mine. Today, also, I received (what a busy day it's been) a cheque from the Bank of Tokyo for £7.4.0 for my contributions to *POETS OF THE 1950's*[1] – this is the last money I shall ever receive without Horrible Hartley getting half of it off'n me. On the strength of this I ordered second-hand copies of *Innkeeper's Diary* & *Confessions of an Innkeeper*,[2] half price from Heffers, and a volume in the Fur, Fin & Feather series entitled 'The Rabbit' (1898).

That's my day – quite an exciting one. The yellow chrysanthemums put in the Library for Saturday were frost-bitten this morning. As I write this I'm listening to one of the best *Just Fancy* programmes I've ever heard. I put it on really to drown the sound of retching from below, which is really upsetting, groaning & noises similar to those utilised by persons in the article of death. Now it's over, & I'll have to switch off. Can I write any – Whoops! Just heard Princess M. *isn't* going to marry Group Captain Fiddlesticks – well, what a frost! And at 6.15 p.m. tonight I was saying that any announcement wd be bound to be of an engagement, since you couldn't announce *nothing*. Well, apparently you can. How curious & strange. Well, well. What a romantic incident. Christian marriage. Well, well. [. . .]

Thursday 'The niece' tells me that the doctor wants to move Mrs Sq. to a hospital as he thinks she has cancer – I must say this seems likely enough to me. Something obviously has her by the throat. In the circumstances I shan't be sorry to get away.

I haven't seen *Essays in crit* – it's harder to come by them here – but I shall do in the course of the day. Yes, K. is very silly about his style of writing.[3] One day I'll tick him off about it.

You didn't say anything about my poem – didn't you like it?

– Have just read the *E in C* review: to a quick glance (all I've time for) it seems muddled and ill advised, I agree. He can't say all that & then say he isn't saying all that, can he? [. . .]

1 D. J. Enright's anthology, published in Japan.
2 *An Innkeeper's Diary* and *Confessions of an Innkeeper*: John Fothergill.
3 *Essays in Criticism*: Kingsley Amis's 'A Point on the Cultural Graph' was a contemptuous review of C. *Day Lewis* ('amiable and undeviatingly minor gift'), a British Council pamphlet by Clifford Dyment, 1955.

12 November 1955

200 Hallgate, Cottingham, E. Yorks

[...] Thank you for your letter – you do sound a poor bunny, and I wish I were there to cheer you up, & vice versa. When you curse yourself for inaction, I see what you mean, but you may not realise what *enormous dignity* it gives you! Supposing your letters were full of 'On Monday I heard the LPO do the *Jupiter* and *Tales from Hoffmann* – I'm just mad about Sergeant – then on Tuesday Father O'Jabers came and talked about the Christian Mystery in history, and I went home thinking that our machine-made agnosticism may be all right, but after all it doesn't explain everything, and "there are more things in Heaven and Earth, Horatio!" On Wednesday we had our rehearsal for *Electra*, and tonight I'm going round to Joyce's for a good old natter. Tomorrow we're decorating the church and I expect I'll be turning out to yell for the old Tigers if Tubby's car is on the road again ... Have you read *H.M.S. Ulysses*, I think it's simply stunning, it made me weep buckets' – no, this is getting too far from any relevance, but you do see what I mean? I don't say I love you for doing nothing, but I love you for not doing any of the things available. Suppose you wrote poems I couldn't praise! Suppose you read authors I suspect! Suppose you entertained well-assorted parties – the PAWCs, the Hunters, Miss Moody, Barker! No, you are much better as you are, a simple dignified person, nobody's sucker, an enigma.

Mentioning poems leads me to say that in my opinion my poem[1] *was* wrong, but in this way: the subject of it was being brought into communication again with my mother to a record made when any such loss of communication wd have been unthinkable: and the oddness thereof. But the poem wd have come better from her! I shouldn't regard our relationship where I was one as 'a loss' but I suppose she might. In a sense it is written from her viewpoint, or my imagination of it. Coveney wd nod his plump head at all this – he is a lifelong Freudian – but, whether he wd be right or not, the poem is only papered over cracks too deep for me to think highly of it. [...]

1 L. had sent Monica a copy of 'Referred Back' (later 'Reference Back'), and she had replied on 5 November 1955: 'I thought it good enough as a *poem*, but I thought it was about something that didn't exist. Not *literary* criticism at all, but I thought you'd written the wrong poem. I wonder if you see already what

I mean? I mean, that in my judgment (& I do know I could be miles wrong, I'm not setting up my judgment) I did not believe that yr Mother's remark meant that she *liked* yr record: I don't think she specially did. I don't think she specially likes anything for itself, & that is largely her whole trouble's source. You were away from her, with yr records, & she wanted to establish communication again. And *that* is what the poem ought to have been about. There certainly was a poem in the incident, but you wrote the wrong one. If I don't misunderstand both incident & poem!'

24 November 1955

200 Hallgate, Cottingham, E. Yorks

[...] I am simply longing to know what you think of the book,¹ & whether copies have arrived for Horne & Collins, & whether Master Humphries has had his shock yet. I went down to the Hartleys on Monday, & found Jean doing all the work as usual, but I had a note from 'Bob' Conquest today saying he'd received his copy so I expect some at least have arrived. I can't really think of anything fresh about the poems, but as a book it pleases me very well except for the spine & the 428 mill endpapers, & I like the price. Six shillings is the right price for poetry, isn't it? The 1939 price. And yet, you know, there *is* an absurd misprint! I've just this moment checked it, & am furious with myself; in *Absences* it shd be *Rain patters on a* SEA ... How 'floor' got in I don't know. I should never use the same word twice in two lines like that. Oh curse! Do alter it. Isn't it annoying? [...]

Friday. Things fall on me like collapsing masonry – letter from John Pudney (Putnam's)² saying he was particularly impressed by *C.G.*³ & wd I like to submit a collection? Just suppose *The Spr.*⁴ had published it *when they had it* ... Hartley need never have entered my life. [...]

1 Monica wrote on 25 November 1955: 'My real look at your book [...] Again, how nice *Church-Going* looks! I wish you cd have altered "that much" – it is a blemish on a lovely stanza of a lovely poem – a bit of grit that scrapes every time [Monica disliked the ambiguity of the demonstrative pronoun, in the fourth line of the final stanza of "Church Going"] [...] I wish *Myxomatosis* were followed by something other than *Toads* – if I'd seen page-proof I'd have thought so at once; because *Toads* makes clear at once that the toads are "symbols", the transition is rather awkward, & may even make *some* fools think you don't mean real rabbits, or mean something else besides real rabbits, something they think is of "deeper significance", social or personal according to their own batty bias, & that wd be an intolerable thing [...] *I remember* makes yr "friend" sound a perfect horror! it's

quite good in the poem, so long as you never let on it was me in the train with you! I am always proud to see my one contribution, the only one in yr work.

(Fl lazars, em. Rabb. losels & subs. edd.) [Monica had evidently suggested "losels" – rather than, in L.'s earlier version, "lazars" – in stanza three of "Toads", and is parodying the academic convention for indicating emendation in a text.] I shd laugh if some owlish critic picked on this as example of the academicism of the Movement – the University Wits. Ha, ha, laughter down below.'

2 The poet John Pudney was literary adviser to the publisher Putnam at the time.

3 'Church Going'.

4 The *Spectator* first published 'Church Going', after a long delay.

20 December 1955

200 Hallgate, Cottingham, E. Yorks

[...] I hope Chichester[1] is nice & Dickensy. Writing that bit has awakened certain longings in me, certainly irrepressible feelings, very jolly & heartwarming, about snow, and rising suns showing werry orange over frosty hedges, and kitchen fires, and chimney-pots, and deep lanes, and the swift dusk of Christmas afternoon, coming up the steel-coloured sky towards the few little golden bubbles of cloud down the west at half-past three, and animals ... Oh! England! [...]

1 It was in Chichester a little later that L. and Monica saw the 'Arundel tomb'.

7 January 1956

Loughborough

Dearest,

I'm in my own room at 21 York Road, wearing scarf & overcoat & wrapped up in my eiderdown. Two radiators are trained on me, but one is very feeble. The room won't really be warm until I'm ready to leave it, I shouldn't wonder: I'm along here partly to get away from 53 York Road,[1] partly to hear the omnibus Archers, wch is on at present. [...]

I came up from London this morning, feeling pretty tired and fed up after another glimpse of the rich life of the Amis household. It's not his *success* I mind so much as his immunity from worry and hard work, though I mind the success as well. But there's an enormous amount I could tell you – do you know, for instance, that he 'doesn't go in' on *Monday & Tuesday*? I went to the hospital feeling like hell & didn't really enjoy the visit, though mother was 'as well as could be expected', I suppose. [...]

The 'big news' in London was that J. D. Scott has got the push from the *Spr.*, for reasons wch were not altogether clear to me, but they seemed to make up the general charge of not giving his whole mind to the job. Kingsley was asked, in my hearing, if he wd accept it (that was when all these details of his duties emerged), but he said he wouldn't. So I don't know who they'll get. John Wain wd love it, of course, but I gathered that he is on the verge of getting the push too. Working for *The Observer* constitutes a breach of his contract; & in any case the *Spr* think he's no good now, or now think he's no good. It was an interesting glimpse of a very different world. Anthony Hartley is a rather dreary creature, shy perhaps. Don't know. Don't care. [...]

1 53 York Road: home of L.'s sister, brother-in-law and niece.

11 January 1956

200 Hallgate, Cottingham, E. Yorks

Dearest bun & only,

The worst has happened. B.J. is Vice Chancellor!¹ This is the most awful blow, & I'll tell you all about it in due course. Most people are very sick about it, as you can imagine: me as much as anyone. Think of it! It's as if they made Neustadt Principal of Leicester, almost.² [...]

Plenty of letters awaited my arrival: I'll never answer them all. John Wain is reading *Church Going* over the 3rd on Sunday night – another 19 gns into the pocket of GH. Shall be interested to know what he says about it. GH, or The Ponce of Hessle, rang up today, to say that nearly all the 300 LDs are sold, & he's telegrammed for the other 400 to be bound. What will happen when the reviews really start I don't know. [...]

Murphy's book, *The Archaeology of Love*,³ arrived today – 8/6. 'For Patricia': and mainly about her, too, I suppose, though not recognisably. The poems aren't very striking, though adroit enough, I admit, if you like the kind of poetry that sounds like a translation from some other language. [...]

I'm trying to write a poem on something we saw in Chichester. Can you guess what? [...]

As regards Kingsley's life, well, I'd certainly like to work 3 days a week six months a year, & THE REST NOTHING. He & Hilly struck me as a pair of DIRTY RICH CHILDREN – they have no worries, they REFUSE TO SUFFER; no jealousies – Hilly tells me how Kingsley was 't'rrifically necking old Miggy' (i.e. Margaret, her sister) on New Year's Eve, and so on & so forth – not enviable *as such*, but I envy him his lazy life & his absolute refusal to do or worry about *anything* 'nasty'. No wonder he can write. A pity he didn't marry a virago, but then he never wd, he's far too clearsighted, though he couldn't have foreseen the money. Well, this is stupid jealous talk. [...]

1 Brynmor Jones, appointed Vice-Chancellor of Hull University, had been Professor of Chemistry and Pro-Vice-Chancellor.
2 Ilya Neustadt, Professor of Sociology, Leicester.
3 Richard Murphy, *The Archaeology of Love*, Dolmen Press (1955). 'Patricia': Patsy Strang (see Appendix B).

26 January 1956

200 Hallgate, Cottingham, East Yorkshire

[...] It was extremely cold on arrival in Hull and I wasn't at all surprised when I awoke next day to find snow on the ground. Nor pleased.

Nor was I pleased to find a letter from the P of H saying he had 'arranged for me to record' three poems for his filthy programme on

the 3rd. I have now put a stopper on that. (The three in question are dregs & throwouts: *Waiting for breakfast*, *Referred back*, & one you've not seen called *Ignorance*, v. poor & short, about knowing nothing.) I bet this will be Hartley's first & last appearance on sound radio.

I was somewhat mollified by the news that the Royal Society of Literature had asked for a copy, in connection with the Wm Heinemann Award. Don't suppose anthin will come of it. What I'd *really* like is the Queen's Gold Medal for Poetry! Heaven knows how you get in the running for these things. All the first binding has now vanished, like the sugar on high table at a provincial university. Only

300 of course. Another relief load of 150 is expected next Tuesday, then the rest as soon as may be.

– How time goes. I laid down my pen at 9 & picked up my pencil:[1] now it's 11. I've added 6½ lines,[2] but only 4 are 'firm'. It's nice & quiet up here – almost all it is nice &   . [...]

1 L. almost always used pencil for writing in his poetry work-books.
2 Of 'An Arundel Tomb'.

12 February 1956

200 Hallgate, Cottingham, East Yorks

Dearest,

I'm absolutely *sick* of my tomb poem,[1] & thought I wd send it you unfinished as a token for St Valentine's Day. Not that it's in any sense a valentine, but to give you something special from me on that day. It's complete except for the last verse, which I can't seem to finish: but I can't feel it is very good, even as it stands. It starts nicely enough, but I think I've failed to put over my chief idea, of their lasting so long, & in the end being remarkable only for something they hadn't perhaps meant very seriously. Do let me know what you think of it. I hope you don't find any grammatical solecisms, any 'secret shagging split infinitives' (Ll. P.)[2] nestling among the inflexible lines. [...]

1 'An Arundel Tomb'.
2 Llewelyn Powys.

21 February 1956 (postcard)

Time has transfigured them into
Untruth. The stone fidelity
They hardly meant has {grown / come to be}
Their final blazon, and to prove
Our almost-instinct almost true:
{That what survives of us is love. / All that

Comments please. Spent most of yesterday writhing with indigestion – cleaned the silver at night. Went to the M.O. again who doesn't think

196

I'm bad, but advised against the Senate dinner: *good*. Letter from the millionairess[1] saying she likes the *LD*, especially because she can understand it! Both Wood & Farrell[2] announce they're 'putting in for Sheffield'. Am going to cut out Needler dinners[3] for a bit & eat small things here. Isn't the snow fearful! See rev. of ARH's twaddle in new RES![4] P.

1 Dorothy Una Ratcliffe.
2 L.'s deputy and sub-librarian.
3 At Needler Hall, university hall of residence.
4 A. R. Humphreys, in *Review of English Studies*.

26 February 1956

200 Hallgate, Cottingham, East Yorks

Dearest,

Just up & breakfasted – dull morning, still not much warmer. I was just reading *The Apparition*[1] in the *S. Times*: first I thought how good it was ('colloquial') then I tried to imagine myself writing it, & it seemed *silly* – the two *lies* in the first line, for instance, and the general silly-little-boy atmosphere, the 'since my love is spent' *lie* – if it were he wouldn't waste time writing the thing – unless the whole thing is a joke, a Iape, a merie *Ieste*, which it might be, I suppose. Did he get 3 beats out of *solicitation*, I wonder? I hadn't realised that before: it makes it rather heavy.

I read John's article casually yesterday (in '20th')[2] and thought he was right enough half the time, saying it was nonsense to expect students to be critics, but wrong the rest of the time, saying that research should be done (yf I doe *interpret* hym aright) in the realm of critical judgments – are research students any more capable of such judgments than ordinary students? And anyway I'm sure research students aren't tied to such small factual details such as he invents. I should have thought the typical research subject was *The Hegelian Basis of Thorkelin's Transcript B* or *The Elizabethan tragedy of revenge in Henry James*, which gives plenty of scope for the plaie of *Intelligaunce*, or so it seems to me. [...]

Evening. I went out walking after lunch: dull day. Passed a mental hospital. A man was shooting pigeons in the fields: I found two fairly-new cartridge cases, some degree longer than a Bucktrout cork, though about the same width. Called on Coveney, who is back, for tea, then came home. Last night I wrote a few lines about lambs: wish I could finish them off as a companion-piece to the *Pigeons* I *still* haven't sent you. As I sit I feel rather hungry, & not in v. good fettle. [...]

Coveney showed me Cynthia Asquith's biography of Barrie wch contains an account of a visit to Hardy, at Max Gate. She stresses what an awful nuisance Wessex was!. He only quietened down after Hardy began reading aloud (from Charlotte Mew). Barrie reported that Hardy had taken him out to show him where he would like to be buried. The next day he took him out again to show him where he would next like to be buried! According to the account the only difference was a few inches nearer one wife or the other, though since one wife was still unburied then I don't quite see how this could be. I may be remembering it wrong. This leads naturally onto love being stronger than death: I expect I'm being rather silly, but it is a sentiment that does seem to me only justifiable if love *can* stop people from dying, which I don't think it can, or not provably. One might say 'Penicillin is stronger than death, sometimes' with fair truth, but 'love is stronger than death' reminds me of that slogan 'Britain (or London) can take it', wch irritated me in the same way. It surely meant that people can stand being bombed as long as they aren't bombed. If A says 'we can take it', & B is hit by a bomb, then clearly B can't take it, so A's statement only means 'A can take B being bombed': similarly 'love is stronger than death' means 'A's love is stronger than B's death', which is self-evident. A's love is not stronger than A's death. At least we've no reason for thinking it is. Does all this sound very Bertrand Russellish? Perhaps it is not as logical as I think. Of course love is not just a word: I don't mean to be 'cynical' about it. Nor do I want to enlist myself under it because, again, it isn't just a word, & I can see clearly that my life isn't governed by it. Some bright lad (E.M.F.?) said the opposite of love wasn't hate but individuality (personality, egotism) and I've been feeling increasingly that it is this that keeps me from love – I mean love isn't just something extra, it's a definite acceptance of the fact that you aren't the most important person in the world. Here again I feel a fallacy lurking: if A isn't the most important person in the world, then why shd B be? The better conclusion wd be that if A wasn't, then nobody is. Of course I'm not speaking of love as an emotion but as a *motive*, that leads to action, which seems to me the only real proof of a quality or feeling. Do I sound like some horrible young don, half-Jewish, at Birkbeck College? Don't let me. There isn't anything very new about my remarks: obviously people who think themselves the most important person in the world are 'immature' – part invalid, part baby & part saint, as I wrote.

I suppose most people have spells of abrogating their own importance, & spells of trying to get it back, until they settle down into some way of living that ensures it isn't abrogated or reclaimed too often, because most people not only want but must have their cake and eat it as well.

Later – I didn't mean to break off there, but I had another go at the lambs, & finished them. Here they are, & the pigeons, rather corrected I'm afraid. What do you think of them? Do you think the lambs come off? It was written dangerously quickly. Should I send the pair to Lehmann along with the tomb, or keep them (with *Ignorance*) for the next comer? The P of H will print *Ignorance* if I'm not careful, I bet, in his filthy rag.

I've about finished the tomb. I don't feel very pleased with it, some-how. The end of v. 4 now runs

> The air, changing to soundless damage,
> Turns the old tenantry away;
> How soon succeeding eyes begin
> To look, not read. Rigidly they, &c.

verse 6, 4–6:

> Of smoke in slow suspended skeins
> Above their scrap of history,
> Only their attitude remains.

verse 7:

> Time has transfigured them into
> Untruth. The stone fidelity
> They hardly meant has come to be
> Their final blazon, fit to prove
> Our nearest instinct nearly true:
> All that survives of us is love.

The 'almost' line wouldn't do if the last line was to start with *All*: I didn't think it pretty, but it was more accurate than this one, & I felt an ugly penultimate line would strengthen the last line. Or rather, a 'subtle' penult. line wd strengthen a 'simple' last line. Sea-water mean?[3] [...]

1 John Donne poem.
2 John Wain in *Twentieth Century*.
3 TSS of 'Two Winter Pieces' ('Pigeons' and 'Lambs') attached, with L.'s changes, plus 'An Arundel Tomb' with holograph changes.

5 March 1956

200 Hallgate, Cottingham, East Yorks

Dearest,

Great God! I've just read through Randall Jarrell, & found 2 poems I don't mind – good ideas spoiled – & through 40 pp of Kathleen Raine & found nothing that rouses even a *flicker* of interest. I'm scared stiff. Whatever am I to do? Not a single idea on the subject of poetry occurs to me, or not constructive repeatable ones, at least. Have you seen any poems in periodicals since Christmas that are any good? I never see any, really. I suppose I might leaf through *The Listener*, & so on. *You* wdn't like your Flopsy Valentine read, I s'pose. God, I'm desperate. [...]

After working late (7 pm) I came home, had a tin of beef broth, & a custard made by my landlady, & listened to TIFH¹ & (for once) the Goon Show, which (for once) I thought very funny, it being a mock version of 'The wages of fear' called 'The fear of wages' & was extraordinarily cleverly written. Then I wrote a paragraph of 'my talk'. Holy God. I start with a quote from Laura Riding, & if this isn't allowed I'm up the creek. Of course it is all nonsense, theorising, and inefficient theorising at that, but Hell, it's only the Third Programme, as Hartley once said – Hartley! My God! Wait'll I tell you: I've had two pieces of Hartley news today. The first is that romantic Mitchell² (sounds like someone out of WB Yeats) met Danny Abse at a party who said he had got some poems of mine from Hartley for an anthology – I'd know which one? I do not! This is the first I've heard of it. Hardly had I finished typing my letter when Hoggart called, & we had a long chat, during wch he revealed that Hartley is 33, & MAD, a well known local psycho-boy, BEEN UNDER THE TRICK-CYCLISTS, TRIED TO COMMIT SUICIDE, *UTTERLY BARMY* ... actually, it's the 33 that horrifies me. If you knew Hartley you'd see why. He looks about 24 *at the outside*. I've been MAKING ALLOWANCES for him, as AN OLDER MAN, all that kind of thing. I feel just about floored by it all: all I can say is, well, it'll make a good story for the biographers, & (b), as they say, it proves I *am* nice & simple & good and can fall for rogues like the next man. What do you think of it all? Isn't it mad? Aren't I in a spot? Haven't I been a fool? And *he* has the rights of *Church going*, *At grass*, all of them. What a nonsensical indignity.

I can't get over his age. I feel he is a sort of monster, like Dorian Gray. The Ponce of Hessle. My God. [...]

1 *Take It From Here*, BBC radio comedy programme.
2 The music critic and scholar Donald Mitchell, whose initiative brought L. to review jazz records for many years on the *Daily Telegraph*.

11 March 1956

Cottingham

[...] You will be amused & perhaps a little irritated, in a kailyard way, to know that I have been brooding over 'that much' again,[1] but have decided not to change it. The crux of the thing is that, to me, 'that much' implies a definite amount, 'so much' implies a lot. I know you are *right* & I am *wrong*, but there it is. 'So much' ought to mean 'just so much', but to me it does suggest the other meaning, 'so' in the emphatic sense, as if I mean that what will never be obsolete is really quite a lot. I expect your whiskers are agitating in rather a huffed fashion, and I know 'I can do as I like' & that it's a blemish, but I'm afraid my ear is so degenerate that it sounds odd enough to upset the conclusion, so that even though I hate the thought of being grammatically wrong I have in the end left it as it stands. [...]

Conquest has begun wasting F.O. time & paper writing to me again – says A. Hartley *is* reviewing me, but has been away in Germany.[2] (Why?) When I see you I can show you Enright's Japanese anthology, replete with page-long confessions of faith from us all.[3] This is rather a swindle because I don't think I ever realised the page was to be printed: I thought it was just giving Enright ideas. In consequence mine sounds v. brash & 1955. Kingsley sounds butter-soft, Conquest a bore, Davie quite sensible, Holloway rather good, Jennings very church-mousey to the point of affectation, & poor old John in the grip of latter-day paranoia ('I tried to direct the attention of my contemporaries to the poetry of Wm Empson ...'). Poor old John. [...]

1 In the final stanza of 'Church Going'.
2 A. Hartley eventually reviewed *The Less Deceived* in the *Spectator*, 8 June 1956.
3 *Poets of the 1950s*, ed. D. J. Enright (Kenkyusha, Tokyo, 1956). Enright invited, and published, brief statements ('confessions of faith') from each of his *Poets of the 1950s*: Amis, Conquest, Davie, Holloway, Jennings, Larkin, Wain, Enright. L. always

maintained that he did not suppose Enright would actually publish these, but only use them as material for his introduction. L's statement was reprinted in *Required Writing*.

8 May 1956

192A Hallgate,[1] Cottingham, E. Yorks

Dearest,

Very flat, being back. I've done nothing tonight but make up my laundry and finish *A charmed life*,[2] very quickly at top speed, the way I always read books. Is it good, do you think? It doesn't seem nearly so 'thick' to me as earlier works: more readable than *A s. of e.*, less funny than *G of a* – I don't know. I don't think she really 'gets' Miles: I almost feel Warren is the roundest character in the book. And the tale, the theme? And why Dolly? I liked much of it: the beginning, & the scene where Warren sells or doesn't sell the picture, & the *Berenice*, & the love scene & the court scene – esp. Mrs. V. – but the end part left me fairly cold. Judgment suspended, however, until I've read more of it. [...]

Had a letter from a Mrs Fouracre today – in Withernsea, nastily near – saying that *The unplanted primrose*[3] went straight to her heart & enclosing a poem about golden rod. S.a.e. enclosed. Yesterday I heard from Carne-Ross,[4] a very nice letter, saying that my programme had been much liked 'in matter & manner' (kind!) & how about another, etc. – not a definite proposal. That's a consolation. I wish I could write lots of poems, then they could do a programme about me. But I know I shan't, or can't. I've *no* inclination to write at present. [...]

We ought to have talked about holidays more – how little time we have together! I was reading about the Carlyles tonight in V.S.P.[5] 'Their worst agonies seem not to have come from their common hypochondria, her jealousy or his monstrous selfishness, but from not getting letters from each other on the day they were expected when they were separated.' Do you think people will write like that about us when we are dust? My dear rabbit! [...]

1 192A Hallgate: L. had recently moved into this, the top flat of his colleague Ronald Drinkwater's house.
2 *A Charmed Life*, *A Source of Embarrassment*, *The Groves of Academe*: novels by Mary McCarthy.
3 Hardy poem included by L. in his 18 April 1956 *New Poetry* broadcast on the Third Programme.

4 D. S. Carne-Ross, BBC Third Programme producer.
5 V. S. Pritchett in the *New Statesman*.

12 May 1956

192A Hallgate, Cottingham, E. Yorks

[...] The Hartleys cheered me up, in a queer way: George is 23, not 33, he says, wch makes me like him more. Also he returned my *North Ship*, which I fancied he was trying to pinch. Again large gestures were made towards paying me, but no actual money was forthcoming. He says that he reckons I am due for £25 from the sale of the book, which isn't bad I suppose: if I had a royalty of $12\frac{1}{2}$% and he'd sold, what, 600 at an average of 7/-, I should stand to get about £26. So it's about right. All I've got to do is get it! *They* seem more in the money: Jean has a new dress, George has new shoes & a new typewriter like mine, & they have a new bowl in the outside, i.e. the only, lavatory. Isn't it all funny? I suppose *in a way* it's 'romantic', & nice to steer clear of the book clubs & awards & so on. As I've said before, if there *were* a good poet in this age, he probably would slip clean through the fingers of the Poetry Book Society. [...]

I'm reading Robt Graves's *The crowning privilege*,[1] & enjoying it, to my surprise. I don't remember anyone saying, in a review, how exciting it is, in the sense of evoking a thrilling sense of vocation in the reader – the jokes, the insults (all unfair), the sagacity ('necessary poems are rare; and poems in which the original necessity has not been blunted by unskilful elaboration are rarer still'), the quotes (*The Fawcon hath born my mak away*, Skelton, Byron's *Letters*, Swift, an indecent parody of *Oriana*) – all highly exciting and rousing. It makes me like him more than anything I've seen of his for a long time. And of course the kicks in the rear he donates to Yeats, Pound, Eliot, Auden, & Dylan Thomas are richly earned. [...]

1 Robert Graves's Clark Lectures (1955).

31 May 1956

192A Hallgate, Cottingham, E. Yorks

[...] Had a single-side letter from Patsy, announcing the birth of 'Emily'. Her desire to tell me had just about overcome her being offended about my ignoring the invitation at Easter. On Tuesday the Farrells had a daughter too. Farrell looks thinner, & luminous with delight. It was had at home, as Mrs Farrell is an ex midwife. Like E. W. Swanton going out to bat!

That's all the news really, except that Sandy's pictures are pretty awful. Three are impossible: a fourth looks like a fleshy-mouthed Himmler, a fifth like a timid balding bulbous-headed bank clerk. I've asked for a print of the letter: God knows what it'll look like. The *S. Times* rang up to say they wanted to print *Deceptions* as part of their 'poetic heritage' ... Fancy that! me along with Geo: Herbert, D.H. Lawrence & James Kirkup. [...]

The ponce called last night, to do his drawing, & did it – a bold enough effort, in art student's Wyndham-Lewis, & missing, *I* think, the character of my face. It has the look of an ageing balding pansy, rearing with prim lips as a hated enemy enters the room. I haven't yet decided whether to censor it, or whether it wd look better than the photograph by Sandy, Himmler with the soft centre. [...]

26 August 1956

Loughborough

[...] O dear! I'm afraid I can't do much more than grouse about Swansea, but at least I didn't wreck my health.[1] The amenities of the guest room don't include the making of one's bed or a light one can switch off without getting up again. Every morning at 9.10 Housewives Choice bellows its idiocies through the house, banishing sleep. By the time one goes down the formica covered table is spotted with tea, milk, marmalade and so on from the children's breakfast, & the *Daily Mirror* (the only paper taken in the house) is in several pieces & well buttered etc. Breakfast, except for a first disastrous crop of heat-rigid fish fingers, was a boiled egg. Other meals varied in times, sizes, temperatures, & so on. No signs of higher standard of living were evident, except for an artificial sun-ray lamp. My general impression of Kingsley is much as before, that he is really not interested in much more than showing off, and that once he's shown off sufficiently to oneself he's ready to discard one in favour of the most dreary second-raters. Anything clever or funny one says is liable to be jotted down to be passed off as his own in future. However, I spent most of Friday watching the test match without cavil, K. having exhausted his exhibitions by that time, & that was some consolation, though Friday's play wasn't brilliantly eventful. I must say I think that when each of seven England batsmen fail to score more than five apiece, & five score NOTHING, there's no grounds for any kind of congratulation.

However, Swansea struck me as a nice town, pleasantly diversified with hills & residential areas of nineteenth century houses. We went near the sea once or twice but not to any great purpose, but it was always nice to see the bay sparkling in the distance. The children were there quite a lot: Philip & Martin quite nice little boys by now, Sally *ingeniously loathsome*. [...]

1 Post-mortem on a visit to the Amises in Swansea.

10 September 1956

192A Hallgate, Cottingham, East Yorkshire

My dearest,

I've pretty well abandoned the *Ode*.[1] Funny, for it was a good subject, but I couldn't get on with it: it couldn't be made 'serious', was too much of a flight of fancy – 'life' as a floating, hindering, beckoning, despoiling ideal: you'd say it was just my subject, I expect, but it won't cohere & jump (Viola). Perhaps it is too *true*: I often feel poems have to have some falsity in them, like yeast, or they won't 'rise'. But in writing it I found myself bothered by the whole concept: first I spoke of it as something distant and distinct, like an island in the sky, then I wanted to say it was a kind of duplicate of this world, like the margin round the shapes on a blurred photograph – and that seemed too hard to explain, in view of the first idea. So there's a lot of time wasted. [...]

1 This appears to be a poem which L. began on 6 June 1956. In his poetry notebook number 4, it seems to start with the title '*There's not the life*', but then '*Ode to the life*', and begins:

Four-letter fable, lucid as a park,
Within you stroll the splendid crossing-points
All clobbered up like masher, buck and spark:
Under the castles of unresting leaf
Beside the water's lowly tenements
They stalk in a continuous calm excess.
Your air is victory. Is happiness.

There then follow 21 pages of drafts before the poem is abandoned. What follows in notebook 4 is an early draft of what became 'Love Songs in Age', not completed until 1 January 1957. L. later uses 'unresting castles' in 'The Trees'.

18 September 1956

192A Hallgate, Cottingham

[...] Quarter to midnight! I looked at the *Ode* again, stimulated by hearing *Photograph album* read on the BBC (repeat: Saturday 10.5), but didn't add much. I wish I could write differently. Or just write, for that matter. Kingsley & I knocked out a bunch of feeble parodies of 'the movement' in Swansea, & he thinks he can get Spender to print them in *Encounter*. *Moi, je le doute*. This is a dead secret, of course, as they are supposed to be anonymous.[1] But they're so feeble I don't think they'll ever achieve print. The one of E. Jennings is quite good: flat as a mangled pancake. But the rest are so characterless anyway that there's simply nothing to parody. [...]

1 See 'All Aboard the Gravy Train: Movements among the Younger Poets, by Ron Cain', in *The Letters of Kingsley Amis*, Appendix B, ed. Zachary Leader (2000).

27 September 1956

192A Hallgate, Cottingham, East Yorkshire

My dear,

I've spent the evening doing my Merwin/Nott review[1] – tripe about tripe – and a vague melancholy clouds me. [...]

The flat is a trial.[2] Nothing seems likely to *come*: one carpet has arrived, but the North-Eastern Gas Board are hopelessly entangled in the problem of my fire & cooker & meter, there's no sign of the bed, one chair & one carpet are 'unavailable at present', and I don't want to embark on curtains & all the numerous details till I'm *in* the place & have finished with workmen. I really don't know *when* I shall *get* in. If I can get the bed, the kitchen table, the other chair & the gas things I shall move in, & do the rest from there. I went down at lunch, & felt displeased with it all. The front door rattles. The children below were *audible*. The stairs are supremely squalid. Hum. Ha. [...]

Last night – no Tuesday – I missed a N. region review of *N Lines* by N. Nicholson,[3] who was apparently complimentary. I didn't know it was on. The ponce's Holloway book is a Poetry Bk Soc. *Choice* – he knows how to do it, *now*.[4] This means about 750 copies *guaranteed*, wch irritates me as H. is no good. I feel utterly divorced from poetry at present, which I suppose is 'just a phase'. Hum. Ha. Ah, don't talk about our lives and the dreadful passing of time. *Nothing* will be good enough to look back on, I know that for certain: there will be nothing but remorse & regret for opportunities missed not only for getting on the gravy train but for treating people decently.

> The local snivels through the fields.
> I sit between felt-hatted mums
> Whose weekly day-excursion yields
> Baby-size parcels, bags of plums,
> And bones of gossip good to clack
> Past all the seven stations back.
>
> Strange that my own elaborate spree
> Of fourteen days should thus run out
> In torpid rural company
> Ignoring what my labels shout.
> Death will be such another thing,
> All we have done not mattering.[5]

This was the parody of myself I wrote for the group I mentioned earlier, so you see my mind has been running on these lines. Do you like it? It has an air of the train from Rabbithampton, to my *ears*. (Incidentally I *know* that country people wouldn't *buy* plums, especially in the next town, but I was too lazy to alter it all.)

> I sit between fat lop-eared does
> Whose weekly day excursion yields
> Three-decker novels, garden hoes ...

That would be a nice picture to draw, wouldn't it? I'm glad you like the cards. There are 2 more yet. I buy them when I see them, & hoard them up.

The brief summer seems to be over here: coming back over the Pennines we met mist & it hasn't been the same since. Tonight is windy & I expect rainy, though I haven't looked out. Autumn, autumn! It comes quickly in these parts. I wish that poem I once wrote hadn't been such a flop.[6] I long to do *The Seasons*, though I never can write set pieces. It would be my great ambition, like the 4 *quartets*. But I know I never shall. Do you like the idea? I doubt if it would *interest* me enough to get finished, & it wd be hard to avoid being corny – typing up various ideas with each season, like *Ulysses* (autumn – dissolution – middle age – resignation – twilight of W. civilisation, etc.). [...]

1 Review of W. S. Merwin's *Green with Beasts* and Kathleen Nott's *Poems from the North*, for the *Manchester Guardian*, 16 October 1956. Reprinted in *Further Requirements*.
2 L. was in process of moving to 32 Pearson Park.
3 The poet Norman Nicholson reviewed *New Lines* for BBC radio, North Region of the Home Service.
4 John Holloway's *The Minute* was the first book after L.'s *The Less Deceived* to be published by the Hartleys' Marvell Press.
5 L.'s self-parody, one of a group written by Amis and L. See note 1, p. 206.
6 'Autumn', written October 1953.

27 October 1956

192A Hallgate, Cottingham

[...] No, you *misjudge* me about public speaking – it's the desire of the cripple to ice-skate, the asthmatic to sing in opera – I long to wait for the laughter to die down, & then recommence. 'But the motion before us, Mr President, Sir ...', my crisp firm voice reaching effortlessly to the back of the hall, my buttonhole, my evening dress, surrounded by eager pompous young faces. Ah! *La rêve*! [...]

13 November 1956

32 Pearson Park, Hull

Dearest,

There's a hair on this pen – dreadfully difficult to dislodge. It's lateish, nearly 10.30, after a rather depressing evening – nothing much done, except a quantity of draught-excluder applied to the area near the window, with no perceptible effect that *I* can feel as I sit here ... and I think I found woodworm in the window-frames. Then I 'nodded off', wch means a nasty awakening, & I still can't write poems – not since March – which always lowers my spirits. It is just the same as 1946,

1947, 1948 – horrible years when I could do nothing. Growl growl growl. Still, I have had my hair cut, which is something. But I am in a low-pressure state, which means I have no gusto for anything. One keeps thinking it will be better in whatever the next season is. But it isn't.

After listening to some *very* nice music this morning I am wondering whether *Orlando* Gibbon wasn't a sort of Elizabethan Dr P – a large Tortoiseshell gentleman in a lace ruff, a Hilliard miniature in a locket round his neck, and jewels, and a cloak, and embroidered slippers, and a sword ... I don't want to build him up, indeed I couldn't, but he occurred to me. He might be Dr Pussy's third favourite composer.

I had one or two occupied nights recently, and in the meantime slaved at a bad review of Kingsley, Durrell & Sassoon[1] – I find it awfully hard to say enough about the actual *books* with the space available, or quote enough. On reflection I found Durrell pretty thin; K. I puff a little shamefully, & Sassoon I tried to praise but sound a bit among-silent-friends in doing so. [...]

Thursday Fell asleep again at that point!

I bought today G. M. Young's *Early Victorian England* – you know that 2 vol thing. It used to be 42/- & is now 63/-. This set was 50/- & rather shop soiled, for wch he declares he will make a reduction. It's the kind of book I ought to buy for June 2nd, isn't it, really? Which reminds me that I'm coming to the end of *The R. of the N.*[2] The *middle* is good: I was quite thrilled at the general to & froing on Egdon, & the gambling, & of course the scene of the little boy & Mrs Yeobright, which seemed to have that gruesomeness said to be found in 'the ballads', but not by me. 'Your face is white and wet, and your head is hanging-down-like.' But for all this, the characters aren't interesting. Thomasin is colourless, Clym ditto & priggish, Wildeve a nonentity. Eustacia & Mrs Yeobright are the best, but even they aren't especially memorable. I suppose 'the hero is Egdon, ay, and the villain too', but a long tracking-shot of it at first wd have helped. (Perhaps there is one, but I don't remember it!) In the *Dynasts* vein. Next I'll try the one I meant to read – *Far From the Maddening Crowd*, as my father used to say one of his friends always said. (The figure of my father, the shy, not over-robust, Edwardian clerk pressing T.H. on all his friends, is unlike the man I knew. I think he was a terrific romantic; & my mother was the equivalent of Emma Lavinia Gifford. Poor father! My heart bleeds for him. What a terrible fate!) I think there's something quite frightening about all the widows, living effortlessly on, with their NH specs & teeth & wigs, cackling chara-loads of them, while in the dingy cemeteries their shadowy men lie utterly effaced – I want to write a poem on this called *To my mother & the memory of my father*, but can't/daren't. [...]

1 The review was published in the *Manchester Guardian*, 30 November 1956, as 'Separate Ways'. It appeared in *Further Requirements* (2001).
2 Thomas Hardy, *The Return of the Native*.

4 December 1956

32 Pearson Park, Hull

[...] Flurry of insults in the December *Encounter*![1] I'm afraid Conquest isn't much of a champion in any case. And an 'ignoramus' in the *Listener*![2] Well, well. The Irish 6d[3] was meant as a comic compromise between GIVING NOTHING and giving REAL MONEY – like the Musical Banks. Well, I wd sooner be insulted by Tom Scott[4] than praised by Pamela Hansford Johnson – poetry a public activity, oh go and boil your stupid opinionated Scotch head, you haggis-fed clown. [...]

Talk about making the sun run: we certainly filled Sunday afternoon well & pleasantly. I liked the pudding & the sauce, very much, too. Does that sound funny? I expect it does. And that quite remarkable gold turf of cloud filling half the sky when we left. I expect you think I behave one way one time and another another. This isn't the place to go into it all, and I'm not sure I could anyway – not without talking for several days, for fear of seeming to lay more emphasis on one thing rather than another – but I am always worrying about what I want for you, for mother, for myself – or think I want. Of course worrying is all cant. Action is the thing. But don't think I think 'everything is all right'. [...]

I may let the university magazine[5] have *Tomb* this Christmas, in wch case I'll let you have a copy. I don't, myself, like it very much: it belongs to that period after publication when one tries to write *ideas* of poems instead of real poems. In fact I think it's embarrassingly bad! and I fancy you will too when you see it again. Real poems have more bite to them. *Mr Bleaney* is more real. *Lambs* is not bad: better than *Tomb*. [...]

1 A dismissive review of *New Lines* in the October issue by David Wright was followed in the December issue by letters, including one by Robert Conquest.
2 At this period most book reviews in the *Listener* were anonymous.
3 In 'Church Going'.
4 Combative Scottish poet who wrote much in Scots.
5 L. means the Leeds University *Poetry and Audience*, to which he had earlier contributed two poems and a book review. 'An Arundel Tomb' had already appeared in the May 1956 *London Magazine*.

8 December 1956

32 Pearson Park, Hull

Dearest, (perhaps you didn't like 'dear old bun, jolly old bun'. To me it sounds warmer than 'dearest', wch reminds me of Little Lord Fauntleroy, Freddy Bartholomew, C. Aubrey Smith, & a massive St Bernard.)[1]

I feel low today – that *awful* Thwaite Hall[2] dance last night: these things are the *extreme* of boredom: the awful toiling hours between 11 and 1 ... the punch, lukewarm, then cold, like a sort of medicine; the eternal tunes you can hear bumping & hallooing from afar; things like *The Dashing White Sergeant,* that I'm sure doesn't exist anywhere but among these 4 halls: BJ, flinging himself about like a warhorse ('Ha! Ha! among the strumpets') and quarrelling breathlessly through inability to understand: the *conversations* I have to put up with in lieu of 'not dancing', my God ... [...]

I'm sorry if I neglect to answer things in your letters – to some extent I've 'always' done it: my parents, & Kingsley, complained similarly. There may be several reasons – carelessness, forgetfulness perhaps, tho' I *always* write with your *last* letter beside me (some may get missed thereby). I've always tried to avoid the 'I-was-interested-to-hear-you-had-been-to-Sevenoaks-you-would-find-Uncle-Edgar-very-changed-I-can-just-see-you-trying-to-appreciate-the-roses!' kind of letter, a sort of repetition of the one received. Sometimes I don't answer because I can't think of anything to say, or anything 'profitable' to say. These will no doubt be the cases you chiefly complain of. But *never* am I trying to squash you, or cause you uneasiness or pain. Quite the contrary. (*Tuesday.*) I shouldn't think you could be 'too intimate' in that way – and in any case it wd be the height of bad manners to believe you could, since you are otherwise so close to me. [...]

I was very glad to know what you feel about (this sounds like Wolfenden) love-making, or relieved, I shd really say, since often I'm quite uncertain whether you are feeling anything or not, and it seems so unfair if you aren't. It isn't that you seem uninterested (disinterested), but that you rarely *seem* to like anything more than anything else. I think, if you analysed it stroke by stroke, my – or anyone's – way of making love is directed as much towards pleasing you as pleasing myself, and probably it grows by learning what you like – so if you don't give any definite signs in this direction, it makes it a little – a little what? Less straightforward? Less confident? Anyway, if you like most things, there's nothing to worry about, is there. I don't reckon I 'understand' you at all, even if I do sometimes! Doesn't it always seem cheek, 'understanding' people? Do you reckon to 'understand' me? Sometimes you seem to, but sometimes I feel you 'trust' me rather than understand me – curious feeling, like finding a rabbit has crawled into one's overcoat pocket when you take it down from the peg. You try to lift it out, but it is determined to stay, so after a while you leave it, though for all it knows you may be going to the kennels ... This is 'just a thought', not meant as a parable or allegory, but for your *Diverfion*.

Probably not comprehensible! [...]

I'd very much like you at least to *see* this place, but as I once tried to explain it's hardly possible for you to *stay* under the same roof & though there's a hotel across the park it seems rather miserable for you to stay there. It might be best for you to look at it & then both of us go on elsewhere. (The people underneath aren't going away at Christmas.) What an awful long way I am from everywhere. [...]

1 Bartholomew played Fauntleroy and C. Aubrey Smith his grandfather in the film of F. H. Burnett's novel.
2 Hull University hall of residence.

25 January 1957

32 Pearson Park, Hull

Dearest,

What a week: hardly an hour to call my own – Monday, Needler;[1] Tuesday, some jazz films; Wednesday, Condon; Thursday, the Hartleys. And now fresh invasions on the weekend. Oh! Oh! Groans, cries, wails, barks. One is lugged through life by the ears. I know nobody lugged me on Tuesday & Wednesday, but still, it all mounts up. And when I do have time I waste it. And such sad thoughts come.

The Condon evening was too strange to describe fully – there were two 'houses', each an hour Lyttelton, an hour Condon[2] – or supposedly. The first was almost empty: the second almost full. Condon was a little neurotic-lipped man, like a jockey retired by age & drink, with a drunkard's careful movements. W. Bill was a fat fiftyish Jack-Oakie College-Humor man, who chewed gum & clowned about. I couldn't adjust myself to the thought that these were the friends of Bix, and that WB had been driving the car in 1932 when Teschemacher was killed. They played fairly routine stuff, not as good as their records, though WB did some of his notorious tricks of tone. I was on the front row: Condon sat playing his guitar about 6' from my head. The Lyttelton group was as usual, Johnny Picard blowing away manfully & very well. But it was all very odd. A lone shop girl sat beside me, who'd never heard a jazz concert before, & never heard of Condon. I admired her resolution. [...]

A pile of stuff turned up from the MG today, including *Mavericks*,[3] the anti-Movement anthology – no doubt you'll hear enough about it, in due course. Both D. Wright & A. Cronin are included, my detractors. I'm afraid it's no good, worse than *New Lines* in fact, but their charge against us is not being no good, but that we have nothing in common but for the sake of publicity pretended we had. Well, that's probably right, & the fault of old John & the feeblewit Conquest. No doubt there will be the usual sham-fight about it all in the weeklies. [...]

1 Needler Hall: Hull University hall of residence, where Peter Coveney was Warden.
2 Eddie Condon, Humphrey Lyttelton: jazz musicians.
3 Anthology edited by Dannie Abse and Howard Sergeant, intended as a countermove to *New Lines*. Reviewed briefly in the *Manchester Guardian* by L., March 1957.

29 January 1957

32 Pearson Park, Hull

My dear,

I'm sitting on my couch for once, & uncomfortable it is too – as uncomfortable as *out of doors*, which is saying something. What a relief to have an evening in! I am an old sloth. [...]

[...] I too return to work. Several large-scale things loom up that will mean heavy and concentrated work – plans to be finished in detail by August 1st for instance. I could work myself into the ground over this alone, & am wondering whether to abandon ideas of any holiday before that date. The *MG* pelts me with books: *Thomas Cranmer*, a verse play by Anne Ridler (containing the line 'I do not see my father as a rabbit' & a proverb I just can't fathom 'Like lettuce, like lips'); *Collected Poems of E. St V. Millay*; a stack of whining poetry – Holloway, Pound, Trypanis, the Lord knows what. Another girl said she was engaged today – a good one – & intends to leave in April. Hell. I thought it was all too good to last. No sign of little liftcadger[1] hitting the trail. I'd like to hire an eagle to come down & carry him off. I can just imagine the expression on his face. Had a committee yesterday: all right, but I slipped a couple of items into 'any other business' that were really too important not to be agenda'd, and BJ may object when he sees what went on after he left. Wurrgh. Wurrgh. Wurrgh. [...]

Thursday – 10.10 After telephoning I came home, fighting a pain inside probably due to a banana for lunch; drafted a review of *Mavericks*; sped to the bathroom once or twice. So I feel sombre enough to sympathise with your mood. Arid & barren, that's what I be: a huge wash-up after the Farrells last night, wch was a failure as far as food was concerned. The icing of a cake I thought 'wd do' (left from the Hartleys) had turned pathologically sticky & couldn't be served. Biscuits were soggy. Ugh! I must get some tins. [...]

You know, I *know* I shd be just as panicky as you about the flithy work – one wants *to do nothing* in the evenings, certainly not spread rotten books around & dredge for 'a line'. It must be like still being a student, with an essay to do after a week's drinking, only you haven't had the drinking. Quite clearly, to me, you aren't a voluntary worker, from the will: you do it by intuitive flashes, more like an act of creation, & when the flashes don't come, as of course they don't, especially when the excess energy of undergraduate days is gone, then it is a hideous unnatural effort. Of course you aren't stupid, what an absurd question: you are very quick, lively, sensitive. I can tell you I wish I could attend your lectures! I'm sure you put over more of the 'sense' of the writer in question than a thousand value-sifters, that the writer was a person in a particular time & place with faults and worries. I shd imagine you don't seem thorough or exhaustive: your 'idea' of a writer comes quickly &

214

whole, & isn't built up by 1000 bits of evidence from the 38 volumes of his collected works. You could read all 38 & still have no 'picture' of the man, or you might read 1 & have enough & not need the other 37. Is this all raving? Perhaps: but you are *all right*: I've seen your comments on essays: they're sensible, very good: you know a lot they don't know, & by they I include ARH[2] & CJH[3] & the rest. The only way I think you are failing is by not building up a mass of lectures – oh my stomach! A fearful griping ache – that make work progressively easier. Still, I know it's *not* bearable, & *not* 'all in your mind', & if I think of your awful life I wish I cd howl like a dog to express the misery I feel for it. Believe me when I say I do have awful spells of panic for both of us – don't you see that when I say 'liberated' I don't mean 'liberated' in the sense of cloudy sensual euphoria, like a novel by, well, who, I don't know, but – ow ow, more aches – set working so that I could save you from it all, & from age, & my mother too for that matter. How can I say I love you, if I won't help you? It seems such humbug. I am like the girl in *The acceptance world*[4] who didn't like men – or girls either: 'just keen on herself'. And nothing to show for it. Ow, ow. Not working towards anything, even silently. Just playing the fool in the worst of the provincial universities, about to waste a quarter of a million of the taxpayers' money. I think we really ask each other the question *What is wrong with me*, don't we? Since we're so alike I'd say the answer, whatever it is, is probably the same. The 64,000-carrot question! [*drawing of rabbit*]

Oh dear, is this what you call 'jaw'? [...]

1 Arthur Wood, L.'s deputy.
2 Arthur Humphreys.
3 C. J. Horne, Lecturer in English, Leicester.
4 By Anthony Powell (1955).

10 February 1957

32 Pearson Park, Hull

My very dear bun,

I don't suppose you'd ever credit how I waste my time, these weekends – the slow rising, the lethargic meals, the hours spent staring and worrying and fidgeting uneasily as vague sensual ghosts perch about the room; the dreary laundry-doing and bed-changing ... Lord knows I have enough to do: bills to settle, letters to write, books to read – and why don't I go for a walk, or a ride, this fine weather? Only at 10 p.m. do I feel a little less bewildered and adrift, and start to try assembling ideas about 'engagement' for the *London Magazine*, which is holding a silly symposium on this subject.[1] But I didn't get far, & indeed only spurred myself on by imagining contributions by Colin Wilson, Lawrence Durrell, etc. [...]

The day seemed somewhat overshadowed by Kingsley's piece about the Condon concert, & the money he'd get for it, & the money I paid for his seat, and so on. I don't find any sense of justice in money matters in Kingsley. He is generous enough about things he likes – buying wine & food with his friends around him, and so on – but there's no fun about paying me for his seat, so he doesn't do it. Then again, he's very good at deciding what *you* ought to do: because you saved a hotel bill by staying with his friends, then you shouldn't worry about his seat-money. And so on. Still, to hell with him. Actually, his piece was very good, as regards judgment. I'm damned glad somebody grumbled about 'curtailment and short weight'. [...]

Monday Very busy day, yarning with the Ass. Registrar (Works) and dictating long memoranda to the Architect. The former says 'I'm as depressed as you are about this building now'. Still, action, as usual, has made me feel better, even though the building will be a freak and there'll be a lot of what-dyou-expect-with-a-poet-in-charge-haw-haw. Holy God.

Did you feel this earth tremor they speak of? I didn't, though in retrospect I think I heard a growl about the right time. I'm sure you'd feel it, and so would my mother. Did all the surface-dwelling rabbits hesitate with one paw lifted, as if some mighty Rabbithood were shaking the world for its vileness towards them? Dr Pussy thought someone was fooling about with his double-bass, and went flying down the stairs to the closet, but there was nobody. Mkgaoww! Strange! He went back to his version of *La Boheme* – he has just got to Mimi's 7th death. Much more scope, oh yes. But the act is getting rather long.

I've been hacking at this fearful 'engagement' thing – I can't do it at all. One is either ponderous or flippant. They want it by the end of the month, too. Curses! I have too much to do – at least 2 reviews, & this ghastly talk, only a short one, but still. And ordinary work is quite trying enough.

Sorry I don't know enough about Hazlitt to appreciate what you say about him fully – Maugham likes him, if that is anything to go by, & it probably is – but I see what you mean about *going* to a *fight*. I'll try him one of these days. I hardly read anything – never have a book on the go, like I used to. I just re-read 'old favourites' – 'silent friends' – Butler's *Notebooks* in bed at present, & *Summer Lightning*[2] in the kitchen. *Nothing*[3] in the sitting room.

I see *The Boy Friend* has got a new Polly, in its 4th year! I do hope we can see it again – do you think it'll still be on in the summer? I wonder. I must say I was thinking about Sark yesterday. I did enjoy that holiday – just like abroad, without any of the trouble and dysentery and swindling and embarrassment. The bathing & the teas! And, of course, the beautiful lonely scenery. I don't suppose I could get you there again. Have you any other ideas? You know I like the south & west. [...]

I think it's one of yr fantasies, that I like 'womanish' behaviour – I'm sure I don't. I had enough from Ruth to last me for ever, but I was so simple minded in those days that I took it all seriously. However, a hard irreducible core of good sense saved me. (His View of Himself – reminds me of Montherlant's *Analysis of the Fight*: 'I was saving myself for the third round. You see, class tells!' (what the French for all this is I don't know.)) Womanish behaviour *might* 'liberate' me, I suppose, but it wd be more likely to 'drive me back into myself.' Of course I don't think you have designs on my feelings when you are unhappy – of course not! I can't avoid what I think the implications are, though.

10 to 12 – must to bed. The roaster is on. Goodnight, dear.

12 Feb – Tuesday Hoo. Hah. Have been struggling with 'engagement' all night, spurred on by irritation at Lehmann's farcical questions. The Rosenbergs! Hungary! And I feel you at my elbow, frowning whenever I write 'a lot of', 'a bit of', 'get', 'pretty', 'rather', or any of the Kingsley words – I frown myself, too. But the alternative seems to be sounding like a *Times* leader. [...]

1 In the *London Magazine*, May 1957, reprinted in *Further Requirements*.
2 P. G. Wodehouse, *Summer Lightning* (1929).
3 Henry Green, *Nothing* (1950).

12 March 1957

32 Pearson Park, Hull

[...] Good Lord! Murry dead![1] I feel (just hearing it on the 10 p.m. news) quite shocked by it. That is a link gone with a vengeance. He never really existed after 1920, did he – the brief flash during the 1914–18 war by being associated with D. H. Lawrence & Katherine Mansfield, & running that magazine, or those magazines. Then there was the spell with Keats – I still think that must have been a good book: at least, I swallowed it whole – then the Peace Pledge Union, Dick Sheppard period before the 1939 war, but I doubt if that added much to his name. A funny fellow: he was certainly clever enough to be a bigger influence than he was. I suppose he enjoyed his life. He ended up on a farm, didn't he? I wonder if there is a sardonic reunion in Elysium tonight.

George Allison, too.[2] Would you remember his football commentaries, in the old square-4 days? He was the most exciting one I ever heard: his 'It's a goal!!!!' was the most abandoned shriek-roar we shall ever know.

One of the quainter quirks of life is that we shall never know who dies on the same day as we do ourselves.

Proof of my engagement rot turned up today: it doesn't look quite so infantile as it did in typescript, but is dull & elementary & confused. Do you bet that other more showy birds will expose the poverty of my maunder? I wonder who they will be. Not K. – I heard from him on my return. *Surely* not Colin Wilson? Everyone must be sick of him by now. Perhaps W. S. Graham! I was reading his well known *Letter V* on the way to work & thinking how good it was.

Well, it *does* display a remarkable 'new tone', & it wasn't as hard to understand as it might be. I'm sure you felt it was a conseederable honour to be acquent with such a bonnie maker yowow whoop. Seems to have shut up now though. Like me.

Thursday Windy & rainy today. No news. I overslept & started the day badly in consequence. I seem to walk on a transparent surface and see beneath me all the bones and wrecks and tentacles that will eventually claim me: in other words, old age, incapacity, loneliness, death of others & myself ... Wasn't there a George Robey song with a refrain *In other words*? I've opened Hopkins to find fine simplicities to draw your attention to: but I admit they're few and far between. Still, that makes them more effective.

1. Lovely the woods, waters, meadows, combes, vales,
   All the air things wear that build this world of Wales:
2. Sometimes a lantern moves along the night,
   That interests our eyes
3. Some candle clear burns somewhere I come by.

4. All life death does end and each day dies with sleep.
5. To seem the stranger lies my lot, my life
    among strangers.

– I've just noticed in a letter that 'My grandfather was a surgeon, a fellow-student of Keats'! Of those I list I admire 2 most, don't you? I agree G.M.H. isn't really like this, but he does it on occasion. [...]

1 John Middleton Murry, 1889–1957.
2 George Allison, 1883–1957, radio sports commentator.

9 April 1957

32 Pearson Park, Hull

[...] Tonight I heard a few yowling settings of Hardy by some guy called Finzi,[1] wch made me look at the poems again. I shan't believe I am insensitive to poetry as long as Hardy can make me tingle all over like a man menaced by a *revenant*. But they sadden me as much as anything, sadden & frighten. I'm terrified of the thought of time passing (or whatever is meant by that phrase) whether I 'do' anything or not. In a way I may believe, deep down, that doing nothing acts as a brake on 'time' – it doesn't of course. It merely adds the torment of having done nothing, when the time comes when it really doesn't matter if you've done anything or not. Do you understand this? Perhaps you take more naturally to doing nothing than I do. [...]

It's cold and blustering here today. The MG wrote saying that they'd received an 'intemperate' letter from Dannie Abse grumbling about my review of *Mavericks* – it appeared last week. Apparently they gave the price & the page numbers wrongly, & *I* said there were 10 poets when there are only 9, & he characterised one of my remarks as 'blatantly untrue'. The 'engagement' *London Mag* is out, my thing looking awful, worse than any except John Osborne. I can just see the '17/20 See me' on the bottom of the faint-ruled page. Ugh. Literature. Still, I'm glad I chopped at them nastily. [...]

I hardly know what I do in my evenings – doze, write letters, listen to the radio, think about you, or certain aspects of you, wonder if I could start reviewing a book or writing a poem. My cast of mind is very odd. I don't want to learn anything: I have no interests: in fact I *defend my mind* against things: I just go from circumscribed sensation to circumscribed sensation. If anyone tried to turn his life into a womb, that's me. It's all very bad. I don't feel a bit creative these days. Just go on hurling money away & eating hardly anything. [...]

1 Gerald Finzi, English composer, 1901–56.

4 May 1957

32 Pearson Park, Hull

[...] I've spent some time reading Holloway's book,[1] for the first time, & find it not quite what I expected. The poems read like the work of 2 people, one with 'something to say' that could quite well go into prose, & the other 'a poet' who's being dragooned into 'saying' it, but who manages to get a few of his own remarks in on the side. Metrically it's all very rough, & no poem ever succeeds. (He has one line where 'fire' appears twice, once as a monosyllable & once as a disyllable.) However it's not such a frightful book as I supposed. One day I'll have to review it. [...]

Ranging back to your earlier letter, it seems ironic that two such articulate beings shd understand each other so poorly. My remark that it seemed I was bound to hurt *someone's* feelings was my comment on thinking that it was funny that by trying, perhaps unnecessarily, to save my mother's feelings, I shd have hurt yours. Do you see? I was remarking on it, more surprised than anything else, or sardonically amused perhaps. It seemed to me that if I didn't get it one way I got it another. Do realise that I hate causing people distress: you seemed to laugh at me for it not long ago, but there it is. I don't claim any virtue for it: it's rather like avoiding arguments. Have you never thought that my cultured-lacquered good fellowship is a positive version of your timid silence? I'm sure I hate conflict as much as you do. Still, begone dull care! Truth is so unattractive that I no longer wish to establish it.

I've got a copy of *Bertie's escapade*,[2] wch has joined my Potters after a reading. By rights I should back it up with the Shephard *Willows*,[3] wch I have never possessed & hardly ever seen. Much as I like the Rackham, I think Shepherd (I expect he's called Shephard or Sheppard really, isn't he?) may be in better key with the homely & forthright note persistently struck throughout, except for the 2 chapters. Rackham could do the wayfaring Rat *very* well, & no doubt some huge shaggy vision of Pan, but for the atmosphere of River Bank, or Mole End, give me Shephard (can't be bothered to extricate myself & look). [...]

1 John Holloway, *The Minute* (Marvell Press, 1956).
2 Kenneth Grahame, *Bertie's Escapade*.
3 *The Wind in the Willows*, edition illustrated by E. H. Shepard.

24 May 1957

32 Pearson Park, Hull

[...] I've been thinking about Keats rejecting Milton in favour of Shakespeare, & how Yeats and Hardy are the two comparable poles today, and how I at any rate reject Yeats. No doubt people wd say that you can have both, but they seem opposites to me, like Disraeli & Gladstone. Yeats seems to me an utterly artificial poet, dealing in make-believe, arid, ultimately stifling. And so dull! I doubt if another poet has ever had such dull subject-matter, often none at all.

Yeats	Hardy
Abstract	Concrete
Artificial	Realistic
Two faced	Sincere
Egotistic	Modest
Celtic	Saxon
Mad	Sane
Boring	Interesting
Literary	?can't think of opposite
Worried about diction	Not worried
Wrote slowly	Wrote easily
Politician	Lived quietly
etc	etc

I look forward to the collapse of his reputation, into 'utter non being'. Of course I agree with all you say about symbolism! How could I not? My mind is stodgy as usual tonight, but I know I'm with you there, like a rabbit huddled against a warm pipe outside the greenhouse on a frosty night. As soon as you start meaning one thing by saying another you open up a gap & the thing sounds hollow. Rabbits wouldn't understand symbolism. [*drawing of rabbit*]

If I knew more about such things I dare say I shd find it lay at the heart of old Eliot's 'objective correlative'. It's *wrong, wrong, wrong –* *all* modern thought & practice is *wrong*, except the general idea that D.H.L. was a good writer, & the general vilipension of people like Bridges & Chesterton. The 'achievement' I speak of is to set a solid set of works against it all, and it irks me that I can do nothing, & have done so little. I wanted to write such a lot – novels particularly – about 'the way things turn out & the beauty of the natural world'; but it doesn't look as if I shall: and I wanted to do it not for *my* sake but for *its* sake – responsibility is always to the *thing* & not to yourself or the filthy reader. I feel the only thing you can do about life is to preserve it, by art if you're an artist, by children if you're not. Otherwise *it flies forgotten, as a dream Dies at the opening day*.[1] When I think of everything I've seen & felt, & how little of it I've managed to pin – about 3 days of my whole life – then I grind my teeth. Consider people like Trollope & how *much* they did. Of course all this is an idealistic & probably unreal conception of writing, but some people seem to have carried it out, or acted as if it were a fair statement of the facts. [...]

1 cf. Isaac Watts, 'O God Our Help in Ages Past' ('Time, like an ever-rolling stream, / Bears all its sons away; / They fly forgotten, as a dream / Dies at the opening day').

6 July 1957

32 Pearson Park, Hull

My dear,

Saturday night, and a storm brewing – I've been round shutting the windows, and drawn my sitting room curtains so that I can't see the sheet lightning blinking over the near-at-hand trees. Nearly 10. I've been in since shopping, listening to the endless cricket commentary, reading another wretched book, eating supper, snoozing. I went out & bought 2 bottles of wine & some sherry, for no very good reason except that since cutting down my smoking to 1 per day I feel a stronger craving for drink. I wish there were some really nice drink. After gin & Italian and gin & orange I'm trying sherry, but it's not specially agreeable.

A very interesting day's play, I thought, but how they do miss Lock. I can't think what their intention was in leaving him out. I took my portable wireless in yesterday & had it muttering among the shelves as I checked art books. This is a fortnight when we all check. I don't think Wood likes it, has to do some work for a change instead of the sort of thing that makes me want to batter his head in is that on Saturdays in vacation when there's no coffee he goes & sits reading the papers for about 25 mins just the same. Slack little sod! World wd come to an end if he didn't 'cover' *The Times* (4d), *Manchester Guardian* (3d) & *Yorkshire Post* (?) every morning. Little jumped-up sawn-off sod!

I think I can hear it raining, now, but it's still rumbling in the distance. The storm last Sunday put the Guildings' radio out of action – it was a terrific flash, right on top of Pearson Park.

One funny thing I've recently discovered is that there are some university rabbits! Apparently a family lives (appropriately) under the Sanctuary, a shed given over for religious purposes, & gambols about by night. You know the university site is quite large & still fairly wild in parts: I wish I could see them. I was told that one came & looked through the windows of the Union refectory at the graduates' dinner last Saturday. Doesn't it all sound preposterous?

I yielded to the temptation of buying an anti-perspiration atomiser today, partly for the fun of squirting it about, but whether it will be of any use or not I don't know. They seem valuable dodges, & I'm surprised nobody markets them for men – I lingered longingly over 'Body Mist' but lacked the courage to buy it. Peeheeple sahay Ai have goald laights in my hyah.

Oh dear! Storm much nearer, crashing about overhead. – Some time later: I think it's all quietened down now: it was really frightening for a time, like someone flicking a vast electric light on outside the house, and grinding pieces of coal together before chucking them down a 60-ft shaft on to the head of a tympanum. Anyway, now I'm settled down with a fresh glass of sherry & a stack of LPs on the player. Wouldn't it be rather romantic to turn into an alcoholic? 'About half way through 1957 he began to drink much more heavily ...' Appearing drunk at work – taking a poke at Wood ... Kneeling on the table at lunch: 'Oh, I know you think this is only a gesture ...' [...]

Sunday night Stewed again: a bottle of *Graves sec* under my belt – I feel I ensconce myself behind successive lines of defence – drink first of all, then layers of microgroove platters on the player, then *The Poetry of Experience* (for review)[1] on my lap, & what nasty thought can possibly reach me? I think of Hart Crane, his whiskey & his Victrola. Today was rather a splendid day. I went over the Park for a pint at 12.30, & afterwards walked round in a state of suspended ecstasy – the sun shone, the wind blew: I studied the statues of Victoria & Albert, and sang as I walked. After lunch I cycled to the university and played the huge Bechstein in the Assembly Hall. Then outside I met the space-man head of the Dept of Psychology, who asked me to tea, where I eventually met his Boxer, Mitzi, whose comprehension of me was slow in the extreme. Her *grandfather* was good enough to be in a book about the breed. Apparently they are a cross of bulldog & mastiff, wch I didn't know before. In Germany they used to clip their ears, & may do so still, but yis Barbarous practice is illegal in England, good show. All day I felt that one just needs somewhere to be – my flat for instance – & one doesn't want to be rushing off to Venice or somewhere.

Did I say that Miss Browne-Wilkinson had taken a job in W. Africa? She bobbed in for a week & has now gone. It all rather appals me – like a conventional symbol at the end of a Forster novel for BEING SNUFFED OUT. However, her Prof. will be M. Mahood – didju know *that*? – so I suppose it can't be too Graham Greene. Anyway, she's only got a second.

I am just about within an inch of finishing the *Graves sec*: I start it with a full tumbler to my spaghetti, then finish it off during the hours before bedtime. Only 9/6. When I said in a previous letter that monsterism arose from an inability to face life, I meant of course a sustained and unprejudiced contemplation of the passage of time, the inevitability of DEATH, the onset of incapacity and impotence. I think that as soon as – no, I mean that how one regards these facts settles one's whole life: if they seem distant & almost irrelevant then you are O.K.: if they seem closer to you than the name stitched on yr underwear then you have had it, nothing else can possibly win yr concentration. Wch reminds me that recently I read *Under the Net* again – good, I thought: a charming, happy, virile book. I wanted to rewrite it, or ring her up & say I admired it. It really is awfully good. It gives the illusion of a talent strong enough to be careless & even incompetent. I could quite see what she meant by 'Mr Mars' even though it wasn't over-well done. I'm sure she is a perfect fool. But I do like that particular book.

I seem to be building up a fine store of unanswered passages: mostly because they are so hard to answer. My dear, whatever I think or say, or however I behave, it isn't because I think myself superior to you: I'm always aware how much more equable & just and intelligent you are (end of the *Graves*), & of how well you treat me: I mean, to be quite explicit, I notice and am thankful for the absence of the so-called 'feminine', i.e. bloody silly, qualities in you – at least, not b.silly, because men deserve them & anyway they frequently succeed – but anyway the absence of 'tactics' and that. If I am nasty to you, then just answer back, & you will see me collapse like a stoned fig. You must always remember that I have much more chance to get sated of, or irritable with, you than anyone else, because I see you & write to you much more often. And also of course I feel that people think 'This is what he likes' & am specially careful of you. Just conceit of course. But, of course, well, well, there are always sidelines, complications, conflicts. I feel my head sinking forward like a melonful of lead shot. The Murphys wrote (2 letters in 1 envelope) urging a visit – the older I get the odder people seem. Are they each other's idea of the good life? Why? If not, why did they get married? Beats me.

Tuesday, is it? Red wine tonight, a 9/6 Beaujolais (Bow Joe Lay) exported by M. Lebeque, and really awfully good, fresh & flower tasting. $\frac{3}{4}$ of a bottle with my spaghetti, the remaining $\frac{1}{4}$ at my elbow.

My dear (this is a sort of Pecksniffian red flag before the guns go off, isn't it), I quite see what you are getting at as regards our farcical, or non-farcical, efforts. It does rather put it back at me, I agree: I don't mind, in that it seems reasonable enough in a way: what I can say I don't know: if you feel you need 'emotion' in a 'personal' sense, I see what you mean, but it wd be faked emotion as far as I'm concerned: I just don't feel personal at that time. I don't want to be personal, to think of you or me as people. If I do we go off on to quite a different tack. God knows I don't set myself up as a grand sexual columnist, like Marghanita Laski (why *gh*?): I should think I am as incompetent at sex as at algebra, dancing the galliard or talking the lingo in *Roma*. I don't know if my not feeling 'personal', in the sense that this is the 6 o'clock news & this is Bruce Belfrage reading it, is my fault, your fault, or the fault of who or what we are. To be personal in sex is surely to be tender. To be tender is not to be lustful, or whatever one can call it. If you don't feel non-personally lustful too, then clearly a large gap remains to be bridged, as by the M & B stag (Ansell's?). I don't say it doesn't matter, but it's all a question of luck, isn't it?

I don't reckon you're *inarticulate*. I shall go to the grave thinking you talkative, just as you'll go to the gr. thinking me dominant & careerist. [...]

My late secretary's engagement is off: I rang her up yesterday having just had a resignation, but I don't imagine it wd be possible for her to return, either from her point of view or mine. People are so expensive at her age, NALGO scales etc. The whole thing is the hell of a confusion, really: and I can't grumble for fear of upsetting the present incumbent, who is very nice really & seems to worship Trueman.[2]

Incidentally, *that chucker-out cat* has a look of Trueman. I studied him again on Sunday. [*drawing of cat*] I won't say he looked round in quite the same way, but there's a certain malevolence that reminds me of the Yorks & England figure none the less. [...]

I liked your clothes business, not only the APHRODISIAC qualities of the French rig (you shd know by now what an old fetishist I am) but for the satire of the rest: the drawings were funny. I don't think I ever dress for purposes of satire – dressing at all is hard enough for me. [...]

When do you think you'd like to come here? Before August 10 (arrival of Mother)? Give it some thought. My best love   Philip

1 Robert Langbaum, *The Poetry of Experience*. Reviewed by L. in *Manchester Guardian*, along with Frank Kermode's *Romantic Image*, 23 July 1957; reprinted in *Further Requirements*.
2 Betty Mackereth; Fred Trueman: Yorkshire and England cricketer.

26 July 1957

32 Pearson Park, Hull

[...] *Truth* printed my jazz review today, rather cut. Thom Gunn calls me the best younger poet, in the *Spr*. A dreary cove – combination of Anthony Flew & Leo Butler – from T.C.D. informed me that Davie was on his way to California, as exchange for Hugh Kenner for a year. After that he's going back to Cambridge – not attached to a college, this sublime ass explained: DOESNTWANTTOBETIEDORHAVEANY-TUTORINGYOUSEE: his idea is to 'live outside Cambridge some-where' and come in to lecture TWO DAYS A WEEK – during the 26 weeks out of the 52 when he's SUPPOSED to be working. And he'll get it, too. Apparently his fatuous 'imaginary museum' talks – which led to my being publicly insulted ('sturdy philistinism') in the TLS leader – were just for money for the passage. I'm getting a bit tired of Davie & his book-fuddled pontificating. He's so wrong. He's like a chap who thinks you'll improve the quality of manure by feeding your animals on manure in the first place. It's a nice theory, but breaks down in practice. Still, I wouldn't mind trying it on him. [...]

Monday Am propped up on my studio couch, having at last found a way of 'sitting comfortably' – one end pushed up against the wall behind, &, not a carrot, but a bottle of Riesling, within reach. What makes me search the telephone directory (London) to see if there is anyone called Rabbit? There isn't, but there is a K. Rabbitt in S.E.19. And there is a Rabits. Then a host of crypto-rabbits, Rabinovitchs & so on. Rabbis.

I feel better today: there's no doubt *working* does me good. Spent most of the day conferring with the Asst. Reg. about furniture for the new Library. Nobody much about except *Wood*, & 'Espinasse with his daily rose in his buttonhole (self grown), & I-knew-Julian-Huxley line. I've been reading Corvo's *The desire & pursuit of the Whole* since sup-per, & enjoying it no end. I love Corvo: *on paper*. [...]

Don't you adore Carol Grey's voice when Tony S. is making love to her? It quite broke me up over my leathery tinned tongue tonight: she goes all small & unconfident. She's the only woman on the programme[1] I've ever liked. I'm getting to the point where I want to bang a skillet on Prue's head. Most of the cast seem on holiday: haven't heard Walter for weeks, & the programme staggers on by means of Carol, Tony, Prue, John, Laura, & of course Doris-and-Dan.

Regarding the Other Town,[2] I think it's striking because they were two such very sophisticated young men & cd bring it so near the borders of literature. *The Railway Accident*[3] was actually pub. in U.S.: I must try to get hold of it. But it's not only that that makes the book[4] interesting. I'm fascinated by 'my friend Eric' – one never quite gets who he is, or what he's doing in the book. I know every inch of it, & can't criticise it any more than one can criticise a garden one played in as a child. [...]

Tuesday I know I can't be said to present a consistent front to you on the subject of visits, holidays, etc., & I don't at all resent yr questioning what I mean, or what I feel. I know I say one thing one time & one the next. Recently I've felt that we have grown slightly stale, like a good show that needs a break or a rest – does this sound very rude? – I mean myself as much as you: same jokes, same attitudes, same prejudices ... I don't mean the rabbits, I like them, or our friend from Poules,[5] he's all right, but all the other gags seem to be ossifying a little and not being replaced. Again I feel that they exist because inside them we agree or agree to agree, outside not. I hadn't meant to knock the holiday on the head so decisively, but – but – I don't know, dear: last year made a great impression on me, as about the first *failed* holiday we'd had. And I think perhaps your lack of enthusiasm for a return to Sark, or a visit to the Scilly Isles, meant that there really wasn't much enthusiasm in me either. Sark pleased me & I'd like to go nearer the season: that is the kind of place I like. Perhaps I'm a Mediterranean addict without knowing it! Anyway, perhaps I didn't say so clearly enough, but if it was 'my choice' this year, I'd have chosen Sark or something like it. [...]

1 *The Archers*, BBC radio.
2 Invention by the young Christopher Isherwood and Edward Upward.
3 Edward Upward, *The Railway Accident*.
4 *Lions and Shadows*, fictionalised memoir of 'an education in the Twenties' by Isherwood, another of L.'s favourite books.
5 Sir Pussy – whimsical invention by L. and Monica.

16 October 1957

32 Pearson Park, Hull

[...] I have a few moments ago identified my feelings on Sunday regarding your U.S. offer:[1] 'Toad ceased his frivolous antics at once. He became grave and depressed, and a dull pain in the lower part of his spine, communicating itself to his legs, made him want to sit down and try desperately not to think of all the possibilities.' It's impossible for me to start from any other point than this apprehensive depression, though it's not easy to account for it. Of course it might be that I didn't want you to go! but perhaps it's alarm at being forced to choose. In a way, the immobility of our relation suits me fine, & it may be that the prospect of being hoofed out of it is scaring the lights out of me. Yet, as I said on Sunday, it seems to me that I can't say 'Don't go' unless I'm prepared to marry you; and I suppose I might have gone on to say that if I'm prepared to marry you it shouldn't need an American invitation to precipitate the proposal. I wish I could describe how I feel without going on & on. I am simply terrified at the prospect of us going on year after year & not getting married – so terrified that it may almost be something else I'm terrified of but don't recognise: but equally there is something missing in me – or in the way we get on – that wd precipitate it. As you know, I think we are very queer – queerer than you do – but I can't swear that if we were better at 'the physical side of things' ('= love in a bad sense') I shouldn't find some other excuse for not marrying. But if I don't want to marry you then I don't see why I should mind not doing so, & if I do then I don't see why I don't. You'll say Mum is at the bottom of all this. Well, if she is, I don't know what to do about it, though I wish I did.

All this isn't very near the problem of you & U.S.A. You're right off the track as usual about my liking 'fascinating' people – at least, I think you are – I like you as you are, you're quite fascinating enough for me, *avec vos hanches galbés, vos serris rebondis*,[2] etc. etc., and who else has read a quarter of what you have? Should I swop you for a quacking bitch who knew 'Stephen' & 'Tom'? (Cf. 'Len'.) I don't think a trip to America wd make you in some magic way 'sophisticated' & attractive in some extra dimension.

But you'll want some impersonal advice as well as all this raving. I can't deny that a lot of what you say sounds true, tho' I don't see why ARH should like you any better for going to Yankland. Could be he thinks he is recompensing you for being held at the bar! Don't mistake an olive branch for a club, as K.[3] did when he accepted what seemed his Prof's directive to do a course of extra mural lectures at Neath, only to realise some weeks later that the Prof clearly thought that he had to some extent exonerated himself for having tried to hold K. at the bar. However, it sounds as good a chance as anyone could get: I wish I knew *where* it was, then I could look it up. Personally I shd be unwilling to go to *work* in U.S., partly because they work you hard, partly for fear of being found out as No Good, but if you feel you *ought* to go, if by going you'd rise in your estimation, and, by not going, fall, then I suppose *that* is the strongest of your arguments. Oh, I can't write on the subject: I want to retreat up to the end of the burrow, as I described them doing, & lie there till it's all over. My pen is quite heavy. Do I think it wd part us if you went? Not necessarily, but it's possible. Equally it might bring us together! A year apart might prove to be just what the doctor ordered, or it might be so dreary that we shd meet to part no more. But I'm sure I should hate to think of you out there in the bog with no one to help you, being 'dated' by octagonal-spectacled PhDs who were in Rome last year, & think W. S. Merwin a real pawut. [...]

1 Suggestion by A. R. Humphreys to Monica that she take up a visiting appointment at Queen's, New York.
2 Evidently L. trying out some Verlaine-like erotic writing.
3 Kingsley Amis.

2 December 1957

32 Pearson Park, Hull

My dear bun,

I am just opening a letter after telephoning you tonight: tomorrow I go to filthy Needler party, arrive 10, leave 10.10, after drinking 9 drinks & pinching 8 behinds (you'll be lucky), insulting 7 guests, telling 6 jokes, licking 5 fingers, turning all 4 cheeks, going down 3 times, giving 2 cheers, and looking after dear old number 1 – and on Wednesday I dine with the Publications Committee & an O.U.P. representative – so the few sentences I can write now will be all my care.

Do read Bradbury's article in the current *Punch* on teaching in U.S. – it's a killer, really wonderful, almost as good as M. McC. I know you won't believe me, but do read it. It should confirm you, if you need confirming, in turning down that sweat-shop job in N. York. [...]

I have great pleasure in Master Handel his Water Music, ay and his musick for ye Royal Fireworks. He is very good, you know: he writes short movements for the kittens, as well as the larger sonorities in wch a great D.Mus. can properly delight in. You will hear the kittens' movements when you come. What splendid pieces they are! He sounds quite different to me from other composers: there is a kind of urgent excitement in him, as well as the voice of angels, that marks him off: do you think that my love of Hardy, and Handel, & certain jazz players, is just narrow mindedness – 'mere' personal predilection – or will it all be 'explained'? I am glad Butler thought so well of Handel: 'As a boy, from 12 years old or so, I always worshipped Handel ...' He says that if George I and George II had not given H. royal pensions he wd have starved. 'Jones & I went last Friday to *Don Giovanni*, Mr Kemp putting us in free. It bored us both ...' Apparently Handel is buried next to Dickens, in W. Abbey! B. disapproves of this. Of course, B is rather a nasty old woman in some ways, but I have always liked him, or felt him sympathetic, though I may be wrong. Isn't it strange to think that he died after Oscar Wilde? And yet the year Wilde was born Butler went up to Cambridge. I was reading Oscar Wilde's trials last night, & *Dylan Thomas in America*, in an effort to convince myself that fun-having does you no good. Felt convinced *in re* Thomas, but less so *in re* Wilde. Apparently the one thing that threw him into a rage after his release was people coming up & saying they never believed all those monstrous charges against him. There is a pathetic story in Harris about his giving Wilde a cheque for 100 f at the beginning of dinner, & Wilde asking for 100 f at the end of dinner, having forgotten the earlier gift, & coming & apologising next day, after finding the cheque in his pocket. Funny how we have our troops of authors! You & yr Scott & Thackeray & Wordsworth: me & my Wilde & Butler & Shaw. I see yours & approve them: mine are what I pursue, & I suppose *vice versa*. [...]

Tuesday Horribly cold. Ghastly Needler 'Christmas party' tonight, God damn & blast it to Hell, I say meekly. 'Mem: Always go to the best hotels. Life too short for bad ones.' (H. Beerbohm Tree.)

11.30 p.m. Back! Caught the last bus with the shabby Xtian ferret,[1] good, good, good, but bad, bad, bad, he told me that Guzzling George[2] had got the job. This is very tiresome news – *tiresome*, that odd squiggle is. I am sorry & annoyed. The s.X.f. said that Hoggart 'got the impression' that Arty Rubbish[3] was rooting for G.S.F., & that the latter might have been cheaper than some others. Hum! Well: as I said, I don't suppose you'll see much of him, & nobody has ever found him *disagreeable*, quite the reverse. Like most situations, it will probably be worse than one hopes, & better than one expects.

Well, I am sorry. You'll be tired out when you arrive – you can spend a quiet evening here in the flat. You shall lie on dry straw, with a carrot within reach. [...]

1 Donald Charlton, lecturer, Hull University.
2 G. S. Fraser.
3 A. R. Humphreys.

18 December 1957

32 Pearson Park, Hull

My dear bun,

Well on into the *Messiah* now – *Why do the nations* – finished the Riesling – splendid old Hanoverian curlywig, patron of The Foundling Hospital ('he was liberal even when he was poor, and remembered his former friends when he was rich') who stroked the head of the infant Geo III and said he was 'a good boy', and had come to England & London the year St Paul's was completed, what a – ah! just starting the *Hallelujah* chorus, & the shade of Geo. II is starting to his feet in my mind – that is the most wonderful thing any king has ever done, don't you think – by the gov, all over Hull the large yellow placards of Hull Choral Society's *Messiah* have the words *sold out* plastered across them: the tide of English cloth caps cannot be diverted from *what it likes* – isn't the solid allegiance of the amateur choral societies to the *Messiah* JUST THE VERY REVERSE – of all that the Glyndebourne shower say of it – is it not a sign that *it* is good, & *they* are good, & that like goes to like, & that everyone who doesn't agree MAY BE DAMNED? I wd sooner sit in Huddersfield Town Hall than go to Glyndebourne on the arm of Desmond Shaw-Taylor – ay and eat cold beef and baked potatoes – oh, the trumpets! how wonderful of him to keep them nearly till the end – till *The trumpet shall sound* – there are none before – and was there ever a fitter equivalent of St Paul's epistle? 'Some bars of the score seem almost impossible of realisation except by a celestial choir ...'

It's over: great stuff. Good lord, yes. This is the first year I have heard it attentively & alone. I almost think I'd like a set of *The Messiah*!! How it *gets better towards the end* – this is almost a *sine qua non* of good art ... The sky is clear tonight, & milder, & full of great snapping stars, & I am dizzy with emotion & Riesling – I upset a glass, as Geo. II might have done, at the New Oratorio Compos'd by Mr Handel. [...]

26 December 1957

21 York Road, Loughborough, Leics

My dearest bun,

Well, I suppose this is the kind of Christmas most people have – kind, not degree, for of course one aunt doesn't counterbalance Ernie and Perce, and Gordon and Mae, and Stan and Doris, and Auntie Bea and Grampy and Sid and Flo and Arthur, and Mr & Mrs Ingleby and Eileen, and the Sopwiths, and Dadda Wilks and Irene and Wally – for really she's quite a quiet aunt, given only to constant cups of tea & monologuous anecdotes that all sound like something out of Stanley Houghton. Of course it does mean an increase of 100% in competitors for the best armchair, but on the whole I think the visit is a success. Mind you, I don't like home & never have. I am sent into furious rages about every 3 hours that make me want to smash things and shout obscenities, & sometimes smash things and shout obscenities. And it's awfully *boring*, too: I am quite sick of it by now. 'Till Thursday' – I can stand a week of almost anything till then. I am going back on Saturday, determined to have 24 hrs holiday at least. At the moment I feel full of ideas for sneering bad tempered poems. I'd like to do one on Christmas generally. I think the reason we make so much of Christmas is that we can credit anyone getting born. No one's seen anyone rise from the dead yet. There have been one or two fine spells of solitude, however – I walked to Nanpantan, absurd name, like some Red Indian town, on Christmas morning, where I drank a pint of mouldy beer before returning, & this afternoon I indulged in a last-hour-of-daylight prowl round the silent brick streets of Loughborough, coming upon Taylor's bell foundry & thinking of Dimity & Jubilee – and of course of Dorothy Sayers (she, & John van Druten – we could have spared many sooner).[1] I'm quite enjoying *Northanger Abbey*. If I've read it before, I've quite forgotten it, though the impression it makes on me is no deeper than the others: it's that I like the heroine better. [...]

Friday [...] The weather is really awfully fine today. The aunt & I walked out briefly before lunch – I am sending some parcels to Hull, parcels of books – & saw a goose in the Park that ate bread from people's hands and talked to them confidentially – you wouldn't like it, but it is most unusual. I've finished *N. Abbey* – a poor bundled-up conclusion, but all right otherwise. [...]

1 The novelist Dorothy Sayers and the playwright John van Druten both died in December 1957.

29 January 1958

32 Pearson Park, Hull

[...] Since getting in, I've read Dacre Balsdon's *Oxford Life* wch as usual has left me with a desire to go to the place, for his account bears no resemblance to the three shivering underbred years that the reference books assure me I spent there. The complete absence of dons in my time makes a great contrast: I had a moral tutor, but never saw him (the only words of his I remember are 'The three pleasures of life – drinking, smoking, and masturbation') – he is now President: nor did I get one sniff of the gay coffee drinking social life, girls & acting & concerts with recorders. Nor did I like the servants better than the undergraduates: thievish incompetent gossips, bullying and cringing. Actually, his book underplays women noticeably – is he a b—r, or what? The Mediterranean crops up now and again: a scrum-half is likened to a young panther. Pal of Coghill's, I expect. Ha. Hum. Ho. Actually, I think certain people take to Oxford, as they do to other things like the House of Commons & clubs. I don't say I didn't enjoy it, but I saw that the things I was enjoying were not endemic to Oxford. As for the fine old traditional life, *wpwpwp* (symbol of curious quacking noise made with the lips). Ah well.

No, I don't know *what* you ought to wear at ARH's: the sort of thing I see people in is 'smart dresses' – have you any of these? Perhaps they are like proper suits and collars in my life: something never actually purchased. I expect lots of people will be there – all the literary set, what? Scenes from provincial life – look, do try a Chuck McCreary gambit on Fraser, or Mrs Fraser: 'Of course, it's very different from Town' – 'Ah, there must be a great crowd of people there' – 'Yes' – 'All walkin' up an' down in fine shoes, none of um barefoot at all' – Or something along the lines of 'And do they have lights you put on with a wee button' or some such fancy. Get them to tell you more & more until they suddenly realise they are *describing the Underground* and fall silent, unable to recollect where they first went wrong. At least that's the general idea: to enable them to realise retrospectively that *you must have been pulling their leg.*

Elgar's daughter Carice had a rabbit called Pietro d'Alba, to wch he dedicated a part song. Puzzlingly, the name of dedicatee is given as 'Yvonne' in the appendix, & P. d'A. as part-librettist! Don't understand this. Perhaps Yvonne was the rabbit's home name. It is difficult to see how it cd have helped to write the words. Elgar was a funny old bird:

an R.C., did you know? He was always hard up. A great backer of losers at Worcester races.

I expect you were cheered as I was by Charmley's win, more convincing than Waterman's by the sound of it. What a long commentary it was! It quite filled my evening. Then I tried reading some Hardy poems into the recorder, & wasn't impressed by the result: more & more I think poems are better read with the eye. *Unhappy summer you*, one I like, is very soggy in the middle. One that went unexpectedly well was a sad one that I can't find now – about a lonely woman moving to a town & dying there. And how in the middle of quite a slight poem – *Raking up leaves* – there comes the line *Earth never grieves*,[1] wch if *Goethe* had said it ('Die Erde geweine nicht' or something) would have been elevated to the ripeness-is-all status. Earth never grieves, I thought, walking across the park, watching seagulls cruising greedily above the ground looking for heaven knows what. Don't you think it's a good line? A very good line. [...]

Thursday Heard Kingsley's programme tonight: EVERY SINGLE RECORD he played I had taken up to Oxford, & introduced him to in 1941: well, almost every one. He admitted that it was the jazz he had first heard. I expect I am getting like the character in one of Connolly's skits,[2] who introduces Betjeman to Victorianism, etc. He spoke quite well, but not entirely accurately, & showed rather a denseness, almost an insensitivity, towards his subject. Oh well.

I see 'W.' John Morgan is interviewing Kingsley next Saturday – *Get Kingsley Amis to sleep with your wife, You'll find it will give you a bunk up in life*, haw haw. Am going to London tomorrow to do this recording,[3] brrr, & shall see him there, pasty-face and all. There are some rumours of a literary party on Saturday, wch could be very nice but is much more likely to be very nasty.

I can quite honestly say I don't think nearly so much of qualities lacking in you as qualities lacking in *me*. It seems more to me that what we have is a kind of homosexual relation, disguised: it wdn't surprise me at all if someone else said so, only there's no one in a position to do so, except you. Don't you think yourself there's something fishy about it? Perhaps not, or not in that sense. But I sometimes think that what you have isn't a spiritual relation but a perverse one. I don't know. It's hard to say anything in letters if one isn't to write a 2 volume treatise. It seems to me I am spoiling yr life in a hideously ingenious way. I avoid thinking about it, as far as possible. I mean I like you and think you are unique & enjoy being with you, but not in the way commonly associated with girls – I mean, I seem entirely lacking in that *desire to impose oneself* that is such a feature of masculine behaviour: by marriage, by 'sexual intercourse'. Bothering people. Inflicting oneself on people. I'm devoid of all that, & it leaves a sort of central motiveless vacuum. I remember Winifred[4] saying in what was probably exasperation 'I've never met anyone as undemanding as you!' I used to cackle at this, but I'm not sure if it really is so funny. Anyway, I enjoy your remarks such as the deformity of your sack ('looking away from it'), & your baby-saga of the Evanses. I must say I used to think of them as utterly conventional, with what virtues & vices that implies, & I think I was right. [...]

1 Hardy's poem 'Autumn in King's Hintock Park' has the refrain 'Raking up leaves'; 'earth never grieves!' appears in the final stanza.
2 'Where Engels fears to tread', in *The Condemned Playground*.
3 Presumably for the British Council (Recorded Sound Section), of 23 poems.
4 Winifred Arnott: see Appendix B.

9 March 1958

32 Pearson Park, Hull

My dear bun,

Really, I do delight in side 2 of *Solomon*! After the first tender introductory chords, Solomon, whom I now envisage as a large white rabbit, advances in sky blue silk (& a white silk waistcoat) for *What though I raze*, the most appealing, firm, & humble song for such a great rabbit: then his Queen, a much livelier Mopsa, sings *Bless'd the day* when they were married, very gay and frisky: then a duet, & lastly she sings *With thee the unshelter'd moor I'd tread* (!) wch Beecham says is like an old English ballad 'but is none the worse for that.' Indeed no. Then the chorus sings them to their rest, accompanied by nightingale noises on the flutes. The whole thing is so 'sweetly pretty' it is a miracle & 'bless'd the day' when I found it in the Public Library. Each time I put it on I fear the magic will have faded, but no, not yet. When you linked Handel & Hardy in a recent letter it occurred to me that what they have in common as far as I'm concerned is that they make nearly all other essays in their respective arts seem just playing around: they alone are writing real music, real poetry, that can be taken seriously. Don't you feel that? Even Bach seems a dull codger to me beside Handel, & what's more to be writing 'music', just as Shakespeare is writing 'poetry'. Hardy & Handel are the pure & proper utterance. I expect you'd like to add Hutton![1] [...]

Monday 'O that I were winged and free, And quite undressed just now with thee'[2] – I doubt if Vaughan means quite what I mean, or if you'd like me if I were winged. But it's a nice thought. Oogh, Monday night, post-Committee: there are only five a year, but I always seem to be either preparing for one or getting over one. Today was a very narrow corner, wch I should love to describe: we came out of it, but I feel rather dubious about the future. It's all to do with seating in the new Library, & how much of it there ought to be. I wonder how Leicester gets on? Is your Library always crowded? You see, there is a formula that says one ought to have 1 seat for every 4 students [*drawing of two rabbits*] but I don't believe it works for our kind of university: I fear we need much more – 1 for 3 or even less, in the absence of things like engineering & technology, agriculture, medicine, &c. We're too library-centred. [...]

1 Len Hutton: cricketer, 1916–90.
2 From Henry Vaughan, 'Fair and young light!' (*Silex Scintillans*, 1655).

17 March 1958

32 Pearson Park, Hull

My dear bun,

Late – 11.25 p.m. – I cocked an ear to my programme, snapping it off as *Church going* started to drag its weary length along. The programme badly missed *Coming*, to separate *Bleaney* & *I remember*. Still, can't have everything, I suppose, though I don't know *why* not as I'm sure C.G. wdn't occupy the *8 mins* remaining, unless the needle stuck in a groove. Silly incompetent swine! Well, now I shall have to put away those poems for good. I'm sure everyone's sick of them.

I wrote to Collins[1] yesterday: whether it's the sort of letter he'll want to receive I can't guess: much of it was culled from Sir Pelham Warner's *Long Innings*, wch won't really interest him, will it? P.F.W. is oddly like P.G.W. to look at – & they're both called Pelham. Odd, that. Perhaps they're the same person. I do hope Collins pulls round. I tried to sound cheerful yet sympathetic: not easy. Your pencilled P.S. wasn't encouraging, but I hope he is better now. These illnesses, hospitals & such, at sixty bode no good to man or beast. [...]

Thursday Overslept today, no breca in consequence. It's snowing again, but not settling – *so far*! Thanks for your letter this morning: I'm so sorry about all the annoyances – who was it the Frasers wanted you to meet? Certainly your list sounds like Hell on earth: I'm writing this at work & so can't make up my own, but the dislikes wdn't differ from yours – *architecture*, Christ: I don't even care about architecture 'in good sense'. I'm surprised they're so conventional as to worry about Summer Schools – my God, the eager eyed literary scavenger seeking fodder, always on the scrounge for 'jobs'.

Nice	*Nasty*
Rabbits	Ferrets
Pints of draught	Halves of bottled
Men & women	Children
Fires	Convector heating
Books	Talk
Readers	Writers
(some of them)	(all of them)

My train arrives 8.28, Midland. Don't bother about food much. You know it's just discomfort of one sort or another to me. Indeed I am worried abt Collins   Very much love   Philip

1 A. S. Collins: Monica's first head of department.

9 August 1958

21 York Road, Loughborough, Leics.

[...] What I have done most of the day is read the *Letters of JC Powys*, my present from Mother: quite all right, though I don't feel I shall re-read it in a hurry. T. F. Powys thought those funny baggy trousers were called 'all fours'! I'm glad you are enjoying the Agate. He is a remarkable *pot-pourri* – *M. Guardian* & cricket & homosexuality & hackneys & theatre & so on, and all this Dickens & Literature as well. Sometimes I disagree with him & sometimes he irritates me, but in the main I enjoy him. I was rather pleased by his *labouring* at journalism.

But how late he went to bed! And how awfully he wasted his life towards the end! *Films*!

I'm sorry that our lovemaking fizzled out in Devon, as you rightly noticed. I felt so tired each night through the relaxing air &, I suppose, *being on holiday* that the grasshopper became a burden very easily. And of course, qualify it how I may, I am *not* a highly-sexed person, or, if I am, it's not in a way that demands constant physical intercourse with other people. (My handwriting is awful, unpractised.) I tire very easily & am always more prepared for sex in the morning than at night. I think sex is a curious thing, a kind of symbol of things we should like to be true & aren't, like 'being together' and 'losing oneself'. At least I suppose we should like them to be true! A kind of double symbol that we aren't alone & that we aren't selfish.* I suppose the fact that I can imagine these things is a clear indication that I don't appreciate the attraction of sex, wch is, what it *feels* like. Anyway, I'm sorry to have failed you! That is what always depresses me: the enormous harvest-homes you deserve, the few stale, shabby crumbs you get.

* whereas of course we *are* alone & we *are* selfish.

I suppose one's birthday is a fit time for reflection.[1] I find my life very *scrappy*: I write no letters or diary, let alone anything else, I am always tired or bored, I never *get out* (why don't I live in the country?), I am completely selfish without achieving anything. And my time is taken up so easily! Next week I have to zig-zag all over the place – Durham & Cambridge – all on *business* – hours & hours spent yawning on trains – this life, unambitious as it is, is too much for me. I feel I am on a dry dull stony road with nothing on either side but rubbish-dumps & filling-stations: life has no depth or colour now, I don't notice things, I've no strength to. All my strength is hugged close to keep going: there's no unselfish impulse outwards in any sort of action or writing or feeling or – oh well. [...]

1 L.'s thirty-sixth birthday.

7 September 1958

32 Pearson Park, Hull

My dear bun,

Have just played Elgar's *2nd Symphony*, & am now running through the second side of the *1st*, wch is almost my favourite piece of music.

The 2nd is not so enjoyable to my mind. It's about like the theme music of The Barlowes of Beddington – quite nice, but nothing to suggest genius. Dr Pussy had to be very diplomatic when it loomed above the conversation, & usually managed to turn it onto the 1st wch he thinks pleasant Gloucester kind of music.

I have also washed my hair & sit wrapped in a towel like Ali the Herbalist – this not because it was dirty (though it was) but because it was full of sand. I cycled to Aldbrough this afternoon: didn't mean to, but the wind almost blew me there. God! It's a dull graceless hole! The bungalows are indescribable: one's called ERSANMINE and another IZZE – IN. The ride was nearly 30 miles & in the course of it 6,000 turned up on my mileometer. Not far, since 1939! All that one can say for Holderness is that it's *flat*. [...]

I think it would be quite reasonable to work in something about swallowing minority 'lines' (or toeing them) uncritically – of course, you wd have to be ready with an example or two of how minority lines *are* wrong.[1] Do you think another thing would be that the object of the game is to *like* literature, not *dislike* it? I had another very subtle notion about how literature differed from science, but have now forgotten it. Oh, and another thing you might attack is Because A is good, therefore B is bad. These are very simple notions, but wd be useful to a student. If I were you I should just say you're going to tell them of a few dangers, tell them, then *perhaps* say something general about literature & its relation to 'life' – how much less important it is except insofar as ... ah well, that's up to you. I shouldn't like to have to give this blessed lecture *at all*. [...]

1 Monica was trying to prepare an introductory lecture for new students.

18 October 1958

32 Pearson Park, Hull

Dearest bun,

I have spent nearly all evening trying to finish this poem: I've never known anything resist me so! Not even *Church G.* wch I find I abandoned once. It's called *The Whitsun Weddings*, unless I can think of anything better. I have just hammered it to *an* end, but really out of sheer desperation to see this fiendish 8th verse in some kind of order. Verses 7 & 8 have taken since about the beginning of August. I wish I felt that such intransigence was a good sign, but I don't.

240

Hardy never made more than 2 or 3 drafts! *I remember* was written in the first *week* of January '54, when I expect I was travelling (with 'my friend') at least part of the time. 'If poetry come not as naturally as leaves to an American professor,' etc. The swinkers – Graves & Yeats – I hold in particular scorn: I think it shows in their poetry, not always by pedestrianism, but by a kind of *absence of bloom*. [...]

Today a degree (honorary) was given to the President of Rochester: there was a free lunch, wch brought Wood blinking in his Glasgow gown, & sent me scuttling into town to lunch at a quiet bar I know with a pint. Wood looked aghast at this, like Empson confronted with a poem. He just couldn't grasp it! *Coming* to the ceremony ... but *not* having the *FREE LUNCH* ... I fear the eccentricities of my behaviour will be too much for him one day: he will convict me of insanity, an academic Mr Deeds.

Mad rabbit, there are plenty of quotable things in *A.S. Attitudes*:[1] I *like* it all right, but as with all Wilson, except bits here & there, I feel (a) he has a rather too theoretical-nasty view of people: they don't seem at all like 'real' people to me, or say that it is only after a time that I see, why yes, this could be a quite credible person if someone else were writing about them; and (b) I don't think he is a *natural* writer, as I think, shall we say, Powell is: he's not unlike Snow in this. How you can be 'interested' in the plot beats me: I read it only for the isolated scenes, & didn't care 2d about who edited the book, or what happened to Danny Boy & John, & the fake was so agonisingly slow & dull in being 'revealed'. He is good at frightful girls like Elvira – but that French stuff I found tedious & repellent, bar perhaps Yves. Well, well. I expect you liked it because some of the characters were called Salad. Very, *very* sensible, yes yes yes yes. [...]

Monday 20 Oct.

'While all my pipes inspir'de upraise
An Heavenly musick, furr'd with praise.'[2]

– Have I quoted that to you before?
It is on p. 176 of the *Penguin Book of Eng. Verse* – how can it have been written, without knowing our friend? By Jove, he thinks it is fine understanding stuff – he *likes* it more than Shakespeare, though of course he can see it isn't as good. Still! ... As he purrs & growls at the organ

(he often reinforces the pedals under his breath) he thinks of it, and possible alternatives – *whiskered, pawed*, no, this is the *mot juste* all right. Isn't it? [...]

I'm sorry you feel so much against the *Catcher*[3] (Dr Pussy doesn't like it either: he thinks the title unpleasant, somehow) – I found it rather 'disgusting' at first, but after that it began making me laugh & I enjoyed it a lot. It's hard to defend it without seeming to 'think it good', but it seems to me *moderately* lifelike, I mean more lifelike than say *Lord of the flies* ('nay, if you are to bring in *gabble*) –' & certainly more lifelike than his own *Zooey* in the *New Yorker*, & that's something, even if his feelings & conclusions about life aren't your/my own. It's utterly artificial, a book with no proper plot, but the language & conversation seem real enough to me. [...]

1 Angus Wilson, *Anglo-Saxon Attitudes* (1956).
2 'Upon a Wasp Chilled with Cold': Edward Taylor (?1644–1729).
3 J. D. Salinger, *The Catcher in the Rye* (1951).

29 October 1958

32 Pearson Park, Hull

Dearest bun,

I feel I have been in constant touch with you by means of your waiting letter & lovely postcard this morning. The hedgehog comes in to do washing & odd jobs: the rabbit just comes in. The Siamese look strangely business-like and efficient, don't they? Their families feared at first they wd catch cold.

Since coming back there have been one or two minor upsets – well, the chief was almost a major: *George* (funny how that name reverberates horribly to both of us: George Westby is a nuisance too) rang up to say that *a lot of outside noise* had got onto the tape at the recording, & it shd be done again. As you can imagine, I blew up at this, especially as I had pointed out all this outside noise at the time, and generally rehearsed my ever-wakeful sense of being in the hands of an incompetent ape who learns his job at my expense. Now further information makes the position less definite: the tape editor thinks it of no account. But is it? I don't want another shoddy version like that of the B. Council. On the other hand I do *not* want to go through it all again.

'Allied Records', a shadowy firm who are making & distributing the records to the Classics Club ('your 4th programme'), are going to see what they think. God! All this makes me sweat as with an ague.

The other upsets were not worth mentioning except for an article in the *Sewanee Review* called 'The Wain–Larkin Myth' by Mr John Lehmann. Gibber Gibber.

I hope you are better now – I fear I didn't treat you very considerately! We had a fine large cavalier time, though, and I look back on it with delight [...]

I feel empty at present, but there's nothing much to eat – wait! some cheese – a selection from *The Cheeseboard*, in fact. You'd be surprised at the morsels I eat: not at all the fare of a big fat rabbit, 'juvenile-tummied'.

This cheese is rather hawrubble. Ugh.

My journey back was slow & dreary & I read most of *The Laodicean* during it: it's quite a *readable* book, but not like Hardy really: more like a talentless provincial *pastiche* of the Young James. The characters spend much time roaming round Europe and are aristocrats, at least some are. I don't recommend it unless you are v. hard up. What a good game we had with the poems. I feel Auden might do *Maud* if not *In Memoriam* & Britten wd set it. I feel as if I have actually *read The Prelude* by D.T.! I've been trying to think of others, but failing ... Betjeman might do *Modern love*, that wd be good. Novels too: there's a rich field. One must pick works & authors that, but for the grace of God, actually could have coincided – *Tristram Shandy*, by Joyce, perhaps.

Thursday [...] Allied Records say the tape will 'do', but they sound as if they think it sounds 'intimate' and home-made, wch isn't our idea at all. However I am so relieved I haven't to do it all again that I don't care. Poor George, sounding utterly wretched & miserable with a cold, didn't know whether or not *he* ought to go down and listen to it. Really he ought to! but I so little wanted to have to repeat the gruelling business that I am laissezfairing. Hope it's not too awful.

Tonight I am going to the Ferret's to meet some superannuated old French professor from Manchester, so I must pack up this short screed. This headline[1] caused much excitement along the burrows! And it will cause the Building Societies much trouble, having their offices filled with furry long-eared customers all with plausible tails & almost identical names, & their children getting into the files & upsetting stacks of printed circulars & the umbrella stand . . .

Goodbye just for now, dear lovely one – I hope you are better & recovered. Was George sorry to have 'missed' me? 'Oltra & Ai were vaira deesapointed . . .'

Love & carnal embraces
Philip

1 Newspaper headline taped to letter: 'ADVANCES TO BUY SMALL HOMES'.

3 November 1958

32 Pearson Park, Hull

Dearest bun,

I'm so sorry you had no word from me last week – I did try to get the photographs off on Friday, but I *felt* that the university collection at 6 wd be too late – I went to the sub-postoffice in the lunch hour, but it *closes* from 12.45–1.45, with supreme annoyingness. They wdnt go in a box, of course. This week was a testy one, as you probably gathered. We have decided to let the recording go, wch is fine as regards not having to do it again, but not so good as regards putting out an amateurish performance. I feel disagreeable about the whole thing.

I'm sorry too that our encounter had such unhappy results for you! I really didn't expect such a thing, though I suppose it might have been predicted. I am sorry. It does rather spoil the incident, even at best, which was very exciting for me anyway. Let's hope all rights itself soon. I'm glad you felt better when you closed your last entry on Sunday.

Supper & gas fire have combined to get *me* down & I am scarcely human, though perhaps no more than too heavily dressed for a mildish day. Didn't you enjoy the picture of Guy the Gorilla in the *S. Times*? and the article? I felt considerable kinship with him, & took the paper 'in' so that his huge face could glare benignly at me all day. Fine fellow.

I could kick that filthy Greek[1] all the way from the British Museum back to Soho Square if he says Barnes is 'clumsy' – the oaf! How dare he write so about one of the most scrupulous metrists, vowel & consonant balancers, in our tongue? I'll give him clumsy: *what* does he call clumsy? 'Do lean down low in Linden Lea'?[2] What does he call not clumsy? Why, as I've often reminded you, *Hopkins* admired Barnes, wch surely indicates that whatever he was he wasn't *clumsy*. Fat greasy garlic-slicer! Let him get back to his farced goat cooked in vine leaves and expense-account bills cooked in the stinking 'office', and take his filthy maulers off the class writers. Actually I've always thought *Look stranger* clumsy: I wdn't have left *light* & *delight* so near, & doesn't he do something slipshod like splitting a word to find a rhyme, further on? I think that selection very dreary & a complete show up of his utter failure after 1940.[3] [...]

Wednesday. I hope you liked the music tonight, but it distracted me from you, & wasn't really a good idea. I felt as if there was a distance (as there is) between us, only a physical one, but a distance. Funnily enough, I settled to write a short 'comic' poem[4] *à la Toads* – not very good, wanting a last line. It's based to some extent on Wood, horrible cadging little varmint.

I've bought a briefcase (not to carry briefs in): I spent a long time down at Carmichael's, finding fault with all of them, & I near as dammit bought one of those elegant flat *attaché*-cases like some architects carry. All that stopped me was the thought that I couldn't get a *loaf* in it! Sensible mole! So in the end I 'settled for' a Gothic black, with plenty of straps, & a window for a visiting card, wch looks rather like the case of a minor *Reichminister* in about 1931, full of documents bearing the Imperial eagle & flagellant pornography covertly purchased on the *Alexanderplatz*. It cost 6d short of £11, so is no cheap trash. I avoided the kind that you can put your pyjamas in – the Hoff kind. Nasty, I think.

I wonder why you're finding your work hard. Is it because as you grow older your standards (kwkwppls) get higher, or is it because as you get older literature seems a paltry affair compared with life? That wouldn't surprise me – I feel it, I think. My own kind of literature gets realler & realler – Hardy, Barnes, Praed, Betjeman (and you'd add Wordsworth) – the rest gets further away. Who cares about asses like Blake or bores like Byron!

I forgot to say that my 'overseas' broadcast[5] went out on Sunday, with some waggish echo-chamber stuff in *Ch. G.* so that I sounded as if I was actually in a church. But I read awfully. I think I'll send this on Thursday. You sound as if you want comforting Fat rabbit lovely pretty rabbit.

P.

1 Evidently G. D. Klingopulos, who in the *From Dickens to Hardy* volume (1958) of the Pelican Guide to English Literature wrote of 'the clumsiness of Barnes or Hardy'.

2 William Barnes's 'My Orchard in Linden Lea'.
3 *W. H. Auden*, selected by the author, the Penguin Poets (1958).
4 'Self's the Man'.
5 Recording of L. introducing and reading 'Church Going' for the BBC European Service, October 1958.

18 January 1959

32 Pearson Park, Hull

[...] I was down at the ponce's signing record sleeves[1] – the thing is ready & will shortly be sent out. No subscription has been entered from G. S. Fraser! I thought his generous assertion sounded a little unlikely. Do you want one? I have three, one for myself I suppose. I shan't give them anyone else, I mean not automatically if you refuse – & I don't *mind* if you refuse. The sleeve is nice, 'in a way', but the readings are amateurish to my mind, & I'm afraid they don't sound appreciably different from the B.C. one, except that in the place of background music there is poltergeist activity, drawers being shut, doors slammed, heavy rulers put down on desks, feet climbing stairs. Strange vowels bay out at times, chiefly ow sounds, but others effloresce like fungi in inaccessible spots. There are few hesitations: greater damage is done by a sort of tired dullness that must be my natural voice when I'm not 'putting expression in'.

Looking in Hackett & Laing's *Dictionary of Anonymous and Pseudonymous Literature* for *Nova* something or other, I came across: 'November Nights; or, Tales for Winter evenings. By the author of *Warreniana*. London, 1826.'

Now there's a burrow book, found backless & coverless in many a rabbit shelf! Tales to be told round the fire when ways are foul, and the ditches full of leaves, and the nights misty, and all very sleepy: tales of old Autolycus-rabbits at country fairs, and seagoing rabbits, all with rabbit heroes who come out on top in the end, and are, taken all round, pretty brave smart fellows: tales full of rabbit lore – *A burrow hard dug Is a burrow safe and snug* and *A carrot saved is a carrot lost* – very true, often! Tales full of snatches of rabbit song, *Green grow the lettuce, O!* and rabbit poems and receipts (*Take seven carrots* – 'take' to be interpreted rather literally) – oh, a fine book, all in all. 1826! It has some serious history in, about filling in the ears and that, as well, don't you think? Rather cloudy stuff about rabbits' rights. There were rabbit Chartists. [...]

1 Of the Marvell Press recording of L. reading *The Less Deceived*. This was a limited edition (100 copies) of a 33⅓ rpm disc.

12 February 1959

32 Pearson Park, Hull

My very dear bun,

We are a busy pair now – you enforcedly, me at least through my own doing – and letters seem melancholily few: anyway, I hope *you* are writing *me* one e'en now, and I am at least scrawling this page and perhaps another before toiling afresh at this awful Betjeman article.[1] I'm *sick* of Betjeman: cosy secret Tory weapon, for all I care, nostalgic & snobbish & that. And other articles are lining up behind one for the students' mag, & then the *M.G.* ... I HAVE NO TIME: it's awful never to have any large free evenings like I used to. I feel dull & stupid & tired.

Anyway, news of *The Boy Friend*:[2] when I looked in at the box office yesterday there were *no bookable seats* left, so I bought one for the *matinée* today. Some girls from the Library had been earlier in the week (gaining the gift of a Penguin copy of the book from me) & enjoyed it. I went alone & sat among a sea of felt-hatted mums, an extraordinary audience of dull aged Hull people. Do you know they actually ran out of programmes! it has been so successful, the houses so large. What was it like, well, it was *lovely*, just as good as ever; it seemed hardly believable that around all this fizzing popping bursting charm pathos and delight lay the gaunt thoroughfares of Hull. I couldn't get a programme, so I can't give names, but there are not so many changes as you might imagine. The best are a new *Maisie*, Roberta Huby, who gets star billing, and while perhaps not *quite* 'period' enough – the hair seems rather modern – is so full of beans she steals any scene she's in; & at last a new *Lord Brockhurst*, a youngish chap made up to look exactly what he ought to be, a jolly old buffer, not nasty at all. (*Question for addicts*: What is Maisie's surname?) Anthony Hayes looked better from Row G. I *think Polly* was Patricia Webb, but the whole take-off of her character was rather beyond the audience. Larry Drew was still *Bobby*. *Percival Browne* was the same as last time. As it went on I found it affecting me more than ever: when *Polly* is alone in Act 1, & tears up her letter, just before *Tony* looks hesitantly in through the french windows, I felt as if I were watching a great moment in drama ('No one who saw Rachel take the dagger from Cesare will forget ...' *etc*); when she ended the act with her terrific 'Oh yes, he's arrived! He's really arrived!' I thought it ranked with '*Kill Claudio*' and 'I'm a seagull' and Molly Bloom's last soliloquy. *Room in B.* is still done just the same, & Tony's dance with the box is still charming, as is Maisie's absurd butterfly (dragonfly?) costume & her wing-flapping run to sit down. And when the audience was moved to applaud *through* the *finale*, & all the girls raised their hands above their heads fluttering like mad, & the balloons came down, I could have wept with emotion at there being anything so wonderful *in a theatre*, of all places. My only regret was that *you* weren't at my side, as at the other times. One innovation – or so it seemed to me – was at the very end of Act II, where Polly sings half 'I Could Be Happy', then breaks down & the chorus *turns* & sings the last half (look at the text): well, now Polly sings the line 'skies may not always be blue', ending with a heartbreaking sob, *then* the chorus turns. Is this new? Or did they always do it this way? It's fearsomely effective.

Well, all this about the B.F., but you will understand, won't you? If it comes to Leicester, do book *instantly*: you won't regret it. But mind you get in. *Use your feet*. It is so much the greatest theatrical work of our day. [...]

1 'Betjeman En Bloc', a long review of Betjeman's *Collected Poems*, in *Listen*, Spring 1959. Reprinted in *Further Requirements*.
2 Musical by Sandy Wilson.

14 April 1959

32 Pearson Park, Hull

[...] This morning I had an enquiry from the U. of Cincinnati asking if I wd like to go & be their Something lecturer for six weeks in 1960 for 200 gns A WEEK and expenses. Sounded pure hell to me. Betjeman was it in 1957. Can't help feeling flattered, but am refusing, of course. [...]

7 May 1959

32 Pearson Park, Hull

[...] Next Tuesday I go to the opening of Sheffield U. Library. Any hopes I had of sitting next to T. S. Eliot were dispelled by the table plan for 'the lunch': I'm on the outer edge next to the representative of *The Star*. Haw! Hum! I say, jolly good about the reception of that tripe of John Osborne's,[1] 'the Christopher Logue of the theatre', as I feel inclined to call him: perhaps we could find someone to call the Christopher Logue of poetry. It got a bashing in *both* the *D.Telegraph* & the *M.Gardener* this morning: a long time since they were in accord, except about Betjeman perhaps.

Tuesday Back again – I left early so Eliot didn't get a chance to talk to me. Quite a nice day, but Sheffield is too far for comfort. I wore my new suit, Bengal shirt, white shantung tie, green hat, *Times* & rolled umbrella & looked all right, except that my socks were wrong. Eliot looked all right: he's a big man, you know: it's never said, but he must be well into 6'. The cast of his face is not literary at all. His hair is plastered down on either side of his head like Toad's, & he looks almost like an old storekeeper or engineer, or I suppose an old lawyer. Mrs Eliot was sitting two rows in front of me: she was dressed in a white straw hat with navy festoonings, a navy silk $\frac{3}{4}$ length coat with embossed flowering, & white shoes, not very nice. She reminds me of Rachel Trickett in the face, if that tells you anything. [...]

I was saddened to hear of the death of Bechet tonight: of course, he hadn't produced much lately – living among the French had brought out his Creole side musically – but he was a wonderful player in his day, as exemplified by the 2 choruses of *Nobody Knows the Way I Feel This Mornin'* they played on Radio Newsreel tonight. At least one could understand his music: not like this modern stuff ... cacophony (mumble mumble), deliberate atonalism (mumble) etc etc. Of course one wanted to take him back to New York and put him behind a good blues singer & in front of a good guitarist for a session or two, but I suppose now we shall have to be content with what there is. I've always wanted to hear a 12" *Summertime* (c. 1940)[2] on which 'the musicians burst into spontaneous applause' at the end of the record. [...]

1 Osborne's musical play *The World of Paul Slickey* opened on 5 May.

2 'Summertime', recorded 1939, for the fledgling Blue Note label, as a farewell to Tommy Ladnier, a trumpeter colleague of Bechet's who had died four days previously. It was Blue Note's first hit, and laid the groundwork for what followed.

8 June 1959

32 Pearson Park, Hull

[...] I felt awful yesterday, dull & feeble & bored. It strikes me I am extremely *lonely* here. I don't think I have ever had so few companions anywhere else. There were Ruth[1] & Bruce at Wellington, you and Peter[2] at Leicester, a variety of people at Belfast, but *here* there's only old Covers,[3] gaily going over the Niagara of marriage in the barrel of 'maturity', and I don't see him often. I expect you imagine I am always going out & about, but I don't, nor do I want to, but a few kindred spirits wd be no bad thing – to drink pints of beer with, as your man wd say. What wd be a bad thing are the available people, sad bunch of stupid sods. Or perhaps it's the set-up. Here social intercourse can only take place within the 'pattern' of you-come-round-to-me-and-I'll-come-round-to-you, plus wife & with nippers to get back to, & I don't really know anyone here worth cutting a plate of sandwiches for. The 'pattern' I prefer is the public house one, but there's no sign of it here.

This port is quite nice!

Of course you're equally lonely, if not more so, though you do have 'departmental evenings' – I don't! My life is really desiccated. Without my work – my filthy salaried employment – I am incapable, flat, aimless, pointless. That's a fatal admission. My individual life has, like the state, *viderdt avay*. I suppose in my place you wd do something at the garden. I think you have greater inner resources than I. I think of you as possessing a great deal of will power: I have none of that. Perhaps you have more to do! When you're *at* Leicester, you have more to do ('*Cer'n'ly* I have more to do'): then you're back at the burrow with house & garden. Anyway, I have been feeling increasingly that my dependence on my job to make life bearable is much too large for self respect.

– There I rang you up, & feel much improved thereby. Contact with my fellow men does me what Isherwood called 'medically demonstrable good.' Oh, & now I've forgotten to tell you that I read some *Noctes Amb*.[4] & found it *quite* funny, only I kept wanting to do one in terms of G.S.F. – 'Me & Eliot are aboon the age we live in – it's no worthy o' us'.

Tuesday More Eddie Marsh & sofa – no more port, at least for the moment – and Purcell's *D & A*,[5] edited by Dr P's quick young friend. Still feel lonely, & as if I ought to put in for the most interesting-looking job going. The appalling ninth-rate-boarding-house common-room faces. The loutish students playing soccer on the lawns on Sunday afternoon. The thuggish members of council. The awful trains. Perhaps in Graneek's phrase I 'need a holiday'. It's just a phrase I'm going through, as Mrs Browning might have said. [...]

– Now *A & D*[6] is on: it's just like the record isn't it? so far anyway. The mocking military mice are never far away in the first few arias! I didn't think he really did it justice in his few words, did you? It is a remarkable piece of work, with a kind of red cheeked innocent self-confident freshness: it reminds me of certain renaissance paintings, like that one of the fellow with the fish – *Tobias* – & the angel, walking along.[7] – Now here is the white rabbit in the garden – but O! much too fast!!! positively racing round the garden!!! not proceeding in stately rabbit state as on the record. God knows what they'll do with *Come rosa*. I'm glad I have the record & a slow version. But isn't she taking an extra repeat? with frills? Now the duet seems too slow. – Here is the big piece; again, too quick & light, yet recognisable as some bloody sort of *dance* rhythm, isn't it? I don't like it at all: seems to have lost all the firm unchallengeability of the record – no! & it's short, isn't it? Clearly they haven't thought to make it the marvellous set piece of the record, the rose of all the world. And what's this aria by D? Quite a nice one, but new to us, isn't it? *Piu tosto moriri* is still to come, surely. Yes, here it is, not so funny as the record: but Apollo's bits are nearly as good. I always like them. – Nearly over, now: rabbit-in-the-snow ending. Very nice & wintry.

[*drawing*]

Applause! Well, well. The applause in our hearts for the record can't be measured by such means, can it? [...]

1 Ruth Bowman, for a time L.'s fiancée: see Appendix B.
2 Peter Oldham: see Appendix B.
3 Peter Coveney, Warden of Needler Hall, Hull.
4 *Noctes Ambrosianae*: dialogues in *Blackwood's Magazine*, 1822–35. They 'present a romanticised and whimsical view of Scotland' (*Oxford Companion to English Literature*).
5 Purcell's *Dido and Aeneas*.
6 Handel's *Apollo and Dafne*, secular cantata (1709–10).
7 *Tobias and the Angel* (1470–80) by Andrea de Verrocchio, in the National Gallery.

4 July 1959

21 York Road, Loughborough, Leics.

[...] In the evening, I went out a walk round the park, and had another look at the war museum in the bell tower. It needs taking in hand. The faded litter of field postcards and armbands in glass cases looks very uncared for. I've been reading the book on Passchendaele,[1] which was the reason I went in. It's a harrowing book, partly by reason of the deaths, but partly, probably mostly, because of the disagreements & lack of cooperation between Govt & Army, & between Britain & France, and because the Army seemed incapable of seeing what was going to happen, even in the simplest things like sending tanks to fight their first battle in mud! After Passchendaele, when there was no one to back them up, they gained more ground in hours at Cambrai than the whole Ypres campaign had in weeks. On the other hand, one feels that we were close to defeat in 1917, & that some kind of action was needed if the Germans were to be prevented from attacking the French, who wd have given way at once. Whether Ypres & Passchendaele were the only answer I can't tell. But it leaves you stunned at the awfulness of it all. [...]

1 Probably Leon Wolff, *Flanders Field: The 1917 Campaign* (1959).

11 August 1959

32 Pearson Park, Hull

My dear,

I'm back in my customary dazed doze: any thoughts of 'seriously getting down to some writing' provokes merely a round, or canon, of *Who are you kidding*, etc. I sit in my chair, hiccuping distractedly, staring at a few lines of verse written two months ago, & trying to summon up the faintest interest in them. [...]

Nothing has happened since I went away: the building is nearly finished and can be seen for what it is – the ideal setting for an exhibition of decadent bourgeois art. Some bits are awful: others are not bad. Others again have still to come and be seen. It is a clumsy, rather graceless building, lacking intelligence at all levels, but not without a certain needless opulence in parts.

Wednesday Again a dumpy evening. I have faint notions for poems, but they aren't strong enough to find words to dress themselves. My mind has gone colourless and watery: I feel little, and when not working have no incentive or desire to do anything. Sometimes I am restless and jumpy, but not especially *depressed*, just at present anyway. The limit of disagreeable sensation is a mild apprehension about nothing in particular; the most perceptible symptom a refusal to pursue any train of thought. Last night I read a number of chapters of St John, and was somewhat repelled by the 'literary' nature of some of the passages: it was like a life of Dylan Thomas by Kathleen Raine, in the sense that the central figure was rather theatrically presented, & of course every literary bum with a flair for religiose aggrandisement has adapted the style for his own ends. On the other hand, much was very fine. I especially liked the sentence 'Your fathers did eat manna in the wilderness, and are dead.' Naturally the more famous ones are stirring. I was interested to see how much emphasis Jesus continually puts on God the Father, as I hadn't realised this before – since writing that I read to the end of the gospel with more enthusiasm than for the rest, and am rather inclined to read the others. Do you think I shall turn into a coneyite? [...]

I have at last had a letter from Kingsley, speaking of America with pretty well unqualified enthusiasm, but not saying an awful lot about what it's like to live there.[1] He just says he worked & drank v. hard & had lots of women, & that Americans are very nice & not at all as the intellectual English press depict them. Of course he wouldn't notice things like noise or no draught beer. Perhaps there is draught beer, though. I bet it's hard to find. He seems to have encountered most kinds of celebrity, including Mary McCarthy, 'who beamed all the time'. I hope there was something behind the beam! Also Eddie Condon. Also John Wain, who, on hearing he was writing another novel, winked and said 'Make it a good one this time, eh?' This annoyed Kingsley, seemingly. His letter contained a proper amount of reasonable apology, but even discounting my envy inspired rancour (& irritation at his uncalled for scorn at hearing I was in Orkney etc) I'm not sure I find it all particularly sympathetic. I only wish I felt any confidence that I was the tortoise to his hare, but the way I feel now (& now = about 9 months) I'm certainly not: I'm not anything to anybody's anything. [...]

I'm sorry you're low, & hope the worry abt yr father is dissipated now. If I hadn't my work I should feel low too. The move[2] starts 31 August – now I am *planning the move*.

As usual when you aren't here I should like to scramble to bed with you!!! How to reconcile this with my apathetic exhaustion in your presence is more than I can fathom. Anyway, many kisses.

1 Amis was on an invited appointment at Princeton University.
2 Into the new library.

19 August 1959

32 Pearson Park, Hull

My dearest,

It's about 10 p.m. & I've recently got in from the Library where I've been working late, trying to 'see my way through' the planning of the move, & also reading 50 applications for the post of porter – 'my friends tell me I am smart and I have never been in trouble with the police.' *Apollo & Dafne* is playing: 'As a rabbit to the larder' – no, it's the pursuit by now. How lovely that song is! I am glad something can slide easily into my esteem at the age of, Xt, 37 – makes me feel my mind isn't so impervious as I'd begun to suspect, not to good stuff anyway. Now the final sad rabbit-across-the-snow section is being played:

Homeward, rabbit, homeward go
Leave your track across the snow
Winter evening settles round
Homeward go without a sound

Actually, I saw a rabbit today! It bolted right across the lawn as I was going home!

I bought '3 farm eggs' today (not from that oily sod) & thought of you, because they had no stamps on & one had a feather sticking to it.

Today at last I got *Vote for Soarker*[1] & the other one, wch I enclose. These have been done rather better than the rest, haven't they, & do more justice to the negative. On the second one you look like Susan! It is a very nice recession of distances, isn't it?

My life is a little unusual at present as I go out these fine evenings, at least I went out on Sunday to the ponce's & we went down to the river with Jean & the children² (I carried them home; at least, one at a time); on Monday I went to the Fawsett Arms at Walkington, & a crap-haunted bar it was, though serving Worthington E, last night I invited the Rexes in, who'd come to look at the flat below (Johnson's). I don't think they'll take it. Don't blame 'em. And tonight I was working. [...]

Thursday 11 p.m. Am really very tired & worried by the task of plan-ning the move – was at it till 9 tonight. Rather sillily I have arranged to go to London tomorrow to say goodbye to Bob, who goes to Buffalo in a week: this *may* be a rest but I doubt it, & I can ill spare the time. Shd have thought of that before, I suppose!

My fears about the move are that I'm making it too complicated, and yet I feel it is *bound* to be complicated & all I am doing is schematising it. The difference between me & Gen Montgomery before D Day is that his plan mattered & could be affected by the weather, & he was on top of it. And presumably he had *a few competent subordinates*; I forgot that one.

I do feel I want to lie & groan a bit!! Still, it will all pass. I've never been so busy, though. [...]

1 Allusion to 'The Peace of Mowsle Barton', a short story by Saki.
2 The children were Laurien (7) and Alison (4).

25 August 1959

32 Pearson Park, Hull

My dear bun,

Just a line late at night. I have started having a bath at night during this hot weather, for something to do, as I feel inactive – the sort of inac-tivity people had in the army before a big operation, perhaps. It's still not altogether certain that we shall start on Monday: I think someone isn't facing facts somewhere. I went into the upper floor of the stack this afternoon and there wasn't a single switch, a single socket, a single bulb. Or a single —ing workman. And they are supposed to be out by tomorrow, & if they aren't I can't put the cleaners in, like ferrets. And if they don't get in, I'm sure we can't load dirty shelves.

At the other end, workmen *start breaking through a wall* into the *old* library *tomorrow*. There is a screen to 'prevent dust', ha ha. Mind you, this is o.k. by me. I'm all for taking a pick axe at the place myself, and have been these many years. I saw a van in Newland Avenue called Mobile Butchery Service today: felt like giving them a ring to come and deal with Wood. [...]

The weekend – it was very short really – was two sauna-baths of train journeys enclosing a Saturday spent entirely with Bob & Kingsley, who happened to be there, & on the whole enjoying myself, though acutely aware, once more, of the difference in the lives of us – their lives are to mine as mine is to yours, as regards incident & sensation. Kingsley, so far from being D.T.'d, seems thinner & less bloated, & clearly is extremely pro-America. Bob is just the same, but very nice & kind & thoughtful, wch is a contrast. We spent most of the day drinking, & finished up in the Nicholsons' flat with sundry other persons of Welsh extraction. As usual. Everyone is having affairs with all the old people & lots of new ones.

I rather surprised Bob[1] by getting up early on Sunday & doing all the accumulated washing up – I get great satisfaction from washing up, given hot water & Daz. He was in a flat in St George's Sq., rented from 3 school-mistresses. He prepared fairly eatable brecas, just what I have myself. 'Will you have fruit juice & bacon? I should perhaps warn you there's — all else.' He had his usual litter around him – *Astounding Science Fiction, The Polish Revolt, London Magazine, Frolics at St Freda's*. He *is* an odd chap. A real character, like Martin in *Tom Brown's Schooldays*. [...]

1 Conquest.

2 September 1959

32 Pearson Park, Hull

Dearest Bun,

Autumn is with us up here: I must add a third blanket tonight, and the cobwebs are very heavy with dew in the mornings. Well, The Move is on us: alarm at 7 a.m., start work at 8.30 a.m., everyone, except perhaps myself, working like beavers, keyed to a kind of hysteria reminiscent of wartime gun-sites. It is of course *fun* (of a kind), & delightful to have one's foot in the door of the new building, but it is awfully hard work because, although in theory the movers do all the heavy work, in practice full boxes have to be lugged to doorways and so on, which is tough on the girls. They keep going by a kind of nursing-hostel facetiousness, conversing entirely in glottal stops, etc. Wood hasn't seen much of the soft side so far: 'leading' the blue team, he has so far not done anything silly, but has been kept *hard at it*. I put the ferocious Wendy on his side, & am content that she'll give him hell. Sheldon has started: seems all right, but nothing to write home about.

Today I transported our set of *Scrutiny*[1] over & locked it away in the new building myself: this sounds intentional, but in fact was part of quite an ordinary decision. We treat our *Scrutiny* very carefully, to avoid having it stolen, but this isn't proof against asininity (= 'loss'). Guilding has a set himself, & has insured it. These Downingites!

[...]

1 A set of the journal, 1932–63, founded and edited by F. R. Leavis.

15 September 1959

32 Pearson Park, Hull

My dear Bun,

The first week was exciting, the second exhausting, the third merely boring. We shall finish tomorrow, or the next day; at least we shall lock ourselves in & close the doors (reverse that). The sun has gone & the days are grey & chilly. Professional demolishers are breaking up the old library shelving and it is a strange wrecked string of rooms, like an air raid. At last I am free of that foul futile mockery of a library, fitting for Hull, a libel on me.

Just at present I am listening to Bantock on Snow!

Actually, the break up of the library meant a good deal of wooden shelving could be had cheap, & strange sights were seen – *Wood in on Sunday*, gaping speculatively round, people who never set foot in the library between end of term & beginning of term (and not often otherwise) were running in as easily as rats. The intoxicating spicy Trade Winds of Something for Nothing bring our jolly mariners out of the hold as limber as weasels – my God! I've never known a safer bet than that academic people will be round you like wasps round a jar if you so much as whisper 'no charge'. They will carry off anything no matter how useless. There were people bearing away mouldy spars on the grounds that it wd be 'cheap even as fire wood', like some crazed medieval yokels. Don't you think that in the academic nature flithy meanness reach a pitch of when it is a streak of pure romanticism – as if the famished search of these sandalled swine for the Lost Teat of the

World were some Grail-Quest instilled in childhood? It is the one common factor of them all – commoner than *The Observer*, *The Guardian*, left wing politics, *Which*. [...]

Thursday Feel very watered-down tonight: we are at last moved: the last load came over shortly after lunch and the rest of the day – like the first part – was spent in feverish direction and discussion. During the morning there was a light shower – the first all the time we were moving. I must say the capacity of the stack doesn't look much now all our stock is in. My room is enormous, & its white furniture blinding: it looks like the work room of a Brighton bookmaker – like that chap in *Brighton Rock*, what was his name, the Italian. Colleoni. [...]

29 September 1959

32 Pearson Park, Hull

Dearest bun,

I was sorry to hear about your mother being ill from your letter this morning. What an awful year you are having, nothing but people close to you suffering illness. I do hope this is not serious and you are able to leave home with fair peace of mind. One ill parent is bad enough, but two! And only you to look after them! A few sisters or near cousins – or anybody, really – would be a godsend, at least just now. I suppose there is nobody. But it is too much worry for one: do try to keep your strength up by eating *and drinking*, and get plenty of sleep. I do hope things soon improve. If you wanted to ring me up (41719) you cd always reverse the charges. I'm usually in my sitting room after 8 p.m. (before that I shouldn't hear the telephone).

It wouldn't have occurred to me that you weren't grown up! I don't know whether you mean something different from being put on, or disregarded, or overruled: these things happen to grown-ups, sometimes exclusively so. No one 'puts on' a child, do they? What people do for children is *make allowances*. I suppose 'eventually', as Fritz Wendel[1] would say, no one is quite grown up. It might be said that anyone not bearing a full load of 'adult' responsibility (e.g. marriage, property, nippers) is often taken to be incomplete, wch is nearly the same, but I don't think you are less grown up than Hilly, say. I'm sure one is more likely to be treated like a child at home than anywhere else: stands to reason. They're just in the habit of doing so ('Well, get out of the habit, then').

As regards the rabbitry (did you know there is a legal term *bottomry*?), well, it is deep, and perhaps fishy, it might just as well be infantility on my part as recognition of it in you. Indeed, although I know you are living there a normal girl I do deeply feel 'somehow' there is a rabbit there too, doing the things you do; even lecturing on Hopkins. It is a strange fancy. I can't explain it. I think perhaps the rabbit takes your place at times, or stays behind when you go out to an evening at the Frasers. Of course I know it doesn't really! but I feel loth to say 'there *is* no rabbit'. It must be deeply fixed in *me*, & therefore the fault, if there is one, is mine. [...]

1 In Isherwood's *Goodbye to Berlin*.

7 October 1959

32 Pearson Park, Hull

[...] I began writing a passage beginning

'A LECTURER, in drip-dry shirt arrayed,
Rode with us, his expenses nicely paid
To teach creative writing in the States
(Plus a few summer schools and lecture dates) ...'

This is 'no accident': I have decided that G.S.F. & his kind are THE MODERN PARDONER – & my Protestant soul revolts at the self-imposition of this mangy crew between the simple reader & the Word. Don't you agree? But don't spill it: I've a mind to work it up into a satiric dialogue. One speaker could recite the above:

Where'er he went, it was his common caper
To steal some sheets of headed letter-paper

– all right, eh? *All right.* [...]

11 October 1959

32 Pearson Park, Hull

Dearest,
I was very upset to get your telegram & did feel for you strongly.[1]
I didn't pick it up till I got in about 6. Of course I realised yr mother

was seriously ill, but (like you?) I fancied she *might* weather this new attack as she had others. It is comforting to know that she was normal & happy in her mind so near the end: I wish I'd felt the same about my father, who'd drifted away many days before, or so I felt. To die with Conservative gains coming in is not the worst of ways!

Meantime I hope you are looking after yourself & getting some help from the doctor in the way of the upsetting arrangements that need to be made. Is some care being provided for your father? I'm not forgetting him & indeed think he is of those involved most to be pitied now. If you think it wd give him any comfort to know I have a particular sympathy for him then do tell him.

Of course I shall think of you tomorrow. Your letter suggested (perhaps wrongly) that the funeral wd be an 'almost –' exclusively family one & so I haven't even ordered flowers, but I shall be sympathising with you & thinking of your mother. I'm sorry we met only twice(?): she sounded a very brave & lively person.

There's not much to report here. There were some long faces in the University on Friday, haw haw. Old Covers hasn't surfaced yet! He was by all accounts in that state of stuttering euphoria Gallup increases on the left invariably induce in him, making his wife drive voters to the poll in 'the' car. John Saville,[2] normally (to give him his due) one of the few people in the place to greet one first, strode past me like a dance-hall usher on his way to stop some jiving. I was particularly glad N. Hull stayed C. after that interfering Yank Yid Liebling's comments in the *S. Obs.* about 'university intellectuals'. Oh well. How singularly unfunny & inept Feiffer is once he leaves The Village! Yankees Go Home.

I'll be going home next weekend. I know you'll have lots of letters to write, but perhaps you'll send a card saying whether you'll be in Leicester & if so whether you'd like me to call.

I have at last bought a second hand mirror (15/-) for the bedroom: not exactly a work of art, but decent enough. Hope it doesn't disintegrate when I try to hang it! It has a signed painting on the back of what looks like the Humber ferry coming in at night. Quite nice too!

Sun still shining here, but 'not for long' I feel.

My very best love
Philip

1 Monica's mother died on 11 October.
2 Marxist Professor of Economics at Hull University. He and Larkin were on good terms, sharing their passion for jazz.

13 October 1959

32 Pearson Park, Hull

Dearest,

Are you really going back to Leicester tomorrow or Thursday, I wonder? I expect there's much to keep you and yet much to take you back. I do hope you are having help in the sad and difficult business that must result from your mother's death. Really, I can hardly believe it is all true, and wish it weren't. It shows, or seems to show to me, how thin the surface of life is that we scuttle over like water-beetles. I thought of you yesterday, and deeply hoped you were not being simultaneously ravaged & numbed by it all. I think it is affecting me by making me peevish and unwilling to undertake the increased bothers of a new term. Of course I might have been peevish anyway. More than likely! [...]

26 November 1959

32 Pearson Park, Hull

Dearest bun,

I have four rolls of pink toilet paper on my low table, more or less at my elbow, but their only significance is that I've been too lazy to put them away. Pink is a new departure for me – only just discovered Bronco (why *Bronco*? Talking Bronco) makes it. Well, it's curious to begin a letter in this way. I have been alone to the cinema to see some Italian film called *Girl in a bikini* (remember Maria Allasio) and didn't much enjoy it. I do think foreign countries look vulgar & ruined. Coming in I ate two buttered pikelets and drank some milk (I'd previously had a Chinese dish at the Red Lion Restaurant. The Chinese are marvellous at making you feel you don't want any more, without satisfying you.)

I had a card from Hoggart, as I said – *then a letter from Grigson* giving complete bibliographical details down to the arrangement of the t.p. & the pagination of the original GPO leaflet.[1] There's scholarship for you. I've always had an admiration for Grigson. His anthologies show wider reading than Hoggart wd do if he lived to be 90. *And* he's a significant editor (*New Verse*) into the bargain. So tell R.H. that *Grigson* fixed me up: actually it's included in a Grigson anthology for children called *The Cherry Tree*, too. It's a nice poem. 'Everybody' knows about it now (hence my enquiry), as the original documentary was on TV, or part of it. How little people know, without having it stuffed down their throat by mass media.

I have now hung up my vast heavy mirror in my bedroom, & am fearful of the screws giving way & it crashing down like something out of the Castle of Otranto. It wd scare the living daylights out of me if it fell down in the middle of the night. I bought special screws & a chain, but the screws were so hard to get in I'm afraid I used a Brummagem screwdriver (hammer) some of the time. It's the sort of job you'd think needed a man: *so do I*.

There is not much news. The SCR politely passed nem. con. a motion of mine that the food needs improving, then (also nem. con.) one proposed by the other side saying that we were quite satisfied with the food at present & thought it good value. We're in 1984 already, boy: double-think while you wait. A Kitchen Committee was in fact set up, though, & I was put on it. We are still waiting for the 'varieties' of beer. God, it's a farce. Something tearstained seems to be clutching my lapels and urging me not to let it get me down. It isn't the *food* that gives you ulcers: it's getting angry while you eat it. [...]

Well, this is all about me & my doings. I do of course think about you, & wonder if your bed is aired. A pity you cannot arrange for it to be 'switched on' as required. How is your father this weekend? You will be feeling the awful mixture of regret & sorrow, & joy at getting away, when you leave. I did sympathise abt the food. Tell him our caterer is an ex-hospital caterer & is so bloody awful I am protesting – if you think he will care. I do sympathise with you, but I'm sorry for him, too.

All best love

Philip

1 L. had been asking various people about the history of Auden's poem and film commentary 'Night Mail', including Richard Hoggart and Geoffrey Grigson, the poet, critic and editor.

1 December 1959

32 Pearson Park, Hull

[...] I met the Registrar's secretary at the bus stop, who said 'I didn't think you'd know me with my clothes on!' This is the kind of verbal gaffe she's given to making. As a matter of fact I didn't.

Wednesday The slow movement of Elgar no. 2 is on the wireless, & reminds me of long Edwardian Saturday-to-Mondays of Dr Pussy, the rich cigar smoke, the mist over the woods at the bottom of the paddock, the muffins & Gentleman's Relish, the guns and gossip, and the young Pussy stealing away to do some scoring that he must have ready by Wednesday – rather cold up in the stable-loft, but he often has sport there of an unexpected kind, that perhaps the others wouldn't appreciate … My eyes are swimming with tears!

Half an hour later, the end resounding, receding, splendid, sunset-like – is it Dr Pussy in the Pullman on Monday running rapidly through Surrey woodlands, 'Oh', what a splendid time the rabbit has! But how awful my medium-wave has become – awful interference all the time, can't hear anything really. Has yours gone worse? Is it my valves? Elgar always makes me think of Dr P., & you, & fills me with a terribly strong loving yearning, for wch there seems no proper target or expression, & wch no one will ever understand – it is like some land where we are together for ever, beyond the reach of time and change and small selfishnesses and the burden of scrabbling from day to day. [...]

9 December 1959

32 Pearson Park, Hull

Dearest Bun,

A drowsy evening: last night I finished a review and the poem, so I am resting before the next review. Damn me if I know quite how I am doing so much. *Facilis est descensus in Averno*??? (– your Brewer gives *Facilis decensus Averno*,[1] so I wasn't far wrong) – so much reviewing, I mean. Not so much poetry.

Well, I was glad to get your letter, very long in the circumstances. I do feel sorry for you, & for your father. I sympathise with him because I am one of the mice who give up & drown, not the kind who go on swimming until the milk turns to butter & they can hop out. Particularly as it won't! I shouldn't have the heart to make him do anything. But I'm not the kind of mouse who tells other people they can't boil eggs. I'm sure it is all a fearful strain on your strength and patience. I wonder if you managed to get the nurse. [...]

1 Virgil's *Aeneid*, 6.126. (Dryden trans. 'The gates of hell are open night, and day; / Sweet the descent, and easy is the way').

13 December 1959

32 Pearson Park, Hull

My dearest,

Much saddened to find your postcard here on my return.[1] I sent a card to you at Leicester from London, lamenting its usual dirt and chilliness, but that will lie uncollected now – doesn't matter. I only wish I could get a word to you quickly. It is good that there is some friend there – will he remain within call?

If there is any way in wch you think I could help, let me know.

The conference was stodgy: I didn't see your man – Wight was there, getting and passing to me the jugs of draught beer that were served at lunch, wch was a nice change. Graneek says he is being offered Edinburgh, & if he takes it wd I like Belfast? I said I didn't think I could retrace my steps. Never return to the scene of the crime, as Frances says in *The Disguises of Love*.[2]

Regent Street looks very pretty with a central row of chandeliers much prettier than those lolling lumpy figures last year. I didn't get time for any shopping, not that I cared. Lugged Rollei all the way there only to find the shop shut – I was going to have it overhauled.

I asked Wight what happened when all the English Dept were on TV on the same day. Ogh ogh ogh. My dearest bun, this drivel won't divert you – I am sure Dr P. is sorry for you: he misses his friend Ld Catto.

I will try to send more frequently. All love   P.

1 Monica's father had just died.
2 Robie Maculay, *The Disguises of Love* (1952): American campus novel about the seduction of a college professor by a student.

20 December 1959

32 Pearson Park, Hull

[…] I think there are some very pleasant things in *Altar & Pew*[1] – would you credit John Meade Falkner with the skilled anticipation of Betjeman on p. 42?[2] Verses 3 & 4 seem to me almost better than Betjeman – and the idea is such a nice one, almost like Hardy – he used to have feelings about the Christian year just like these. And Jane Taylor[3] – p. 25 – is excellent too: real changeless verse. Who was she? […]

1 *Altar and Pew: Church of England Verses*, ed. John Betjeman (1959).

2 'After Trinity': L. included J. M. Falkner's poem in *The Oxford Book of Twentieth Century English Verse* (henceforth, OBTCEV).
3 Jane Taylor, 1783–1824. With her sister Ann, author of children's books and hymns.

9 January 1960

32 Pearson Park, Hull

[...] The problem of what to do in the evenings has reappeared – of course, there are plenty of odd jobs, and I *could* write a review or two, but I wish I felt more inclined to write poetry. The poetic impulse is distinct from ideas abt things or feelings about things, though it may use these. It's more like a desire to separate a piece of one's experience & set it up on its own, an isolated object never to trouble you again, at least not for a bit. In the absence of this impulse nothing stirs. [...]

9 March 1960

32 Pearson Park, Hull

Dearest,

I'm back and somewhat rested, certainly more cheerful – I'm not going to Reading: didn't care for the looks of it: withdrew my application what.[1] Just withdrew what. Not very courteously actually, but effectively enough. I have lots of good reasons for this, but I was certainly in a funk too, and I shouldn't wonder if it was just that. Actually the principal thing was the Librarian's room, a dank hole about 8' × 8', no carpet, generally resembling the station-master's room cum ticket office at Llanberis Junction (with Tydgogogoch). I felt it was IMPOSSIBLE for me to work there. [...]

1 L. had applied for the post of Librarian at Reading University, but withdrew before the interview.

16 March 1960

32 Pearson Park, Hull

Dearest bun,

Thank you for your nice card. I've had an extravert sort of day, meeting W. G. Moore, my old Dean, then giving Farrell his weekly chivvying, then lunch with the works manager of our binders, then Senate, wch was all right but a bit frightening. I don't know when I shall stop being nervous at Senate! – never, I dare say. Stage 2 of the Library is provisionally fixed for 1966–8 at a cost of £600,000! I doubt both these figures. Fortunately I had nothing to do with them. But ours is a slack sort of joint in many ways.

This reminds me that I found Sir Leslie Martin & his italianate side-kick St John Wilson sneaking into the Library at 6.15 p.m. yesterday so I gave them a brief tour.[1] It was rather embarrassing, like showing two conscientious objectors round the Imperial War Museum. The only thing they fell on with glad little cries was an exhibition of filthy modern paintings on the landing. Of course, they didn't criticise anything: it was just their miserable silence that underlined their response, or lack of it. It left me feeling like the proprietor of a Victorian music hall. Not that I mind that in theory – but for an hour or two it did seem rather garish, those reds & pinks & blues, & my room appeared like the madam's room in a high class knocking-shop. Anyway, I made them sign my book. I almost expected them to add 'Weather unfortunate', or 'Meals monotonous'. The Library will be the swansong of the old style. After this it will be all Danish butter-factories.

I'm glad to hear your dept. is getting into a mess – that'll teach your man to go gallivanting off to the Land of the Free and leave you to educate each other. He needn't think he is older than the Bourbon-on-the-rocks by wch he sits. [...]

17 March. Saint Padherick's Day. And rather a dull day too. I'm scribbling this between 6.15 & 7 p.m., as I am having to go out then to meet & entertain a librarian called Hoy, a tough character from Oriental & African Studies. Probably 2 or 3 nicker down the drain *plus an evening*, ay, mark that, Cesario. [...]

I have had a copy of *The L.D.* bound in green leather: it looks quite nice. What a curiosity the subscription list is! Talk about social history. Dig the latest *Listen*, with 'Patricia Avis' saying how dull life is, & Richard Murphy lamenting his island girl's maleficence, in consecutive poems ogh-ogh-ogh. Also one from me about nothing in particular.[2] [...]

1 Leslie Martin, St John Wilson: architects of the new library.
2 'Before Tea' (later 'Afternoons').

12 June 1960

32 Pearson Park, Hull

[...] I hope you got my card from Pocklington,[1] I gave it to one of the boys who met me to post – expect he read my prospective opinion of my evening there. This was quite pleasant, but an awful bore when it came to talking about 'poetry' (ugh! the very word makes me spew). The master who entertained me was a Cambridgey kind of Trevor-Roper kind of person: *grace* was said, rather disconcertingly. But the meal was quite good, though tinned raspberries in the complicated pudding fermented dismally in my stomach all night. One smaller boy with a white, criminal face contradicted me unsmilingly quite a bit – I should say he was the best of them. The rest were quite decent chaps or fly general-paper finessers. Next morning I felt in fine fettle to refuse the morning's invitation – from Kings School, Canterbury. [...]

By the way, at Pocklington someone began a sentence '*Hoggart himself* says ...' (my italics). Our friend is becoming a kind of religious figure, isn't he?[2] Confucius he say. By the beard of the Prophet. And there was a certain man dwelling in East Riding, in the town of Hull. Roll on that *News of the World* case: 'Lecturers sentenced. Well known TV personality sent to prison. Judge on "amateur sociology".' Ogh ogh ogh.

And my contribution to *Sayings of the Week* is from the *Obs.* review of MND:[3] 'It is easy to see what led Britten to cast the fairies as small boys.' Oghoghogh ogh ogh ogh. Ogh.

I have had my lunch now – a tin of salmon – and when I finish this shall take it to post, & perhaps go a walk round. I look forward to yr visit on Friday, and I'll try not to be too distraught. Mother will be arriving on Sunday night. I feel a bit better now than I did earlier on, though still unhappy at the prospect of DEATH and of wasting my life, or of having wasted my life, worries familiar as bailiffs, sitting constantly in my hall. I ought to get away from this reform school – but to do what? a general shop in Beaminster? Gibber gibber. Anyway, there's heaps to do today: laundry & so on, & all the papers to read for a 'project committee' tomorrow. I've got a new pair of sandals, Lotus, like the others but light-coloured leather. How vulgar shoes are becoming! It's hard to find anything that doesn't make you look like a ponce or a professor.

Much best love, dear one   Philip

1 L. made a rare visit to a school, Pocklington, an independent boys' school near York.
2 Richard Hoggart, who had immediately become well known with the publication of *The Uses of Literacy* in 1957, and was a source of wry amusement with both L. and Monica. See Appendix B.
3 *A Midsummer Night's Dream*: Britten's opera premiered the day before (11 June 1960) at the Aldeburgh Festival (Peter Pears played Thisbe in comic drag).

4 August 1960

32 Pearson Park, Hull

My dear,

You'll be surprised to hear I've just torn myself away from Bradbury's novel:[1] I began reading it in the bookshop again this afternoon & couldn't help buying it, it seemed so funny. Brain must be going. I hear all the Wain sentences in J.W.'s voice wch vastly improves them, & it seems pretty well sewn with good things – after all, it's considerably better than even the best of J.W.

Before that I was sponging the sitting room walls: antidote to being fed up. They're now all smeary like endpapers. I dreamt I dwelt in marbled halls.

Well, the Gatwick train & that purple vested charlatan seem further away than a week. Home was pretty awful by contrast: mother was in a low mood because of real and imagined thunderstorms, wch means manic grumbling and selfcentredness, & there wasn't anything to do, except verify the time of my train. I did some white painting, & chopped up a box for firewood, & read *Persuasion*, wch seemed to me novelettish, & gloated over my shirt. Of course I hate hating home: it makes me feel a rat for not providing mother with a better life, & for being so unsympathetic.

Returning here wasn't much better. On Wednesday I had an all-day visit from one of the elder librarians and his wife: today it's been suddenly & disagreeably hot, & I found myself completely uninterested in my salaried hemployment look you. I miss the drink and the laziness of our holiday, & your company & readiness to trade chuckles and gull cries. [...]

We didn't get around to discussing your will, or my will: I freely admit such things give me the creeps, & a leaden weight of fear in the stomach. But we ought to have done, because I didn't find your letter

268

clear – I wanted to ask you exactly what you want me to do: you want me to make a will, & tell you the provisions of it, is that it? or is there some special provision you want me to make? I don't know that I have any ideas on the subject. I suppose you & mother & my sister are the only people I need consider, unless I want to leave funds to provide a bottle of Guinness on my birthday for anyone who calls at Hardy's birthplace. My birthday will be a grim day – I think the house will be empty after it for the rest of the week. I may have a few library people in, or go out. What do you think Paul[2] is up to?

Much love xxx
P.

1 *Eating People is Wrong* (1959) was Malcolm Bradbury's first novel. His portrayal of Carey Willoughby, a visiting writer, was not surprisingly seen by L. as a version of John Wain.
2 In *The Archers*.

15 August 1960

32 Pearson Park, Hull

Dearest bun,

Feel irritable these nights: I have an urge to do a poem, but can't get it going. I suppose basically it isn't a real poem. Often one spends weeks trying to write a poem out of the conscious mind that never comes to anything – these are sort of 'ideal' poems that one feels ought to be written, but don't because (I fancy) they lack the vital spark of *self-interest*. A 'real' poem is a pleasure to write. I have been trying this poem on and off for some time. [...]

I must say I feel sorry for Paul: to be an errant husband married to an Archer must be the end. They don't seem inclined to rely on their philosophy of letting things sort themselves out, do they? They seem more inclined to sort Paul out. I can't – as yet – feel much interest in Marianne, but perhaps it will grow. His idea of being a traveller struck me as pretty thin! They cut all that long talk with Phil in Borchester, so you see one can miss quite a lot that way.

Tuesday. Got boozed tonight, by drinking a bottle of Bow Joe[1] along with spaghetti, a rare dish these days. The drink made me feel pretty cheerful, & disinclined to sit staring at an empty page, *comme d'habitude*. I played jazz as loudly as my player could manage, reading the end of *D.T. in America*. I'm jolly glad they got Caitlin in a strait-jacket. Serve her bloody well right. Pity they didn't forcibly feed her with emetics into ye *Bargaine*.

I am distressed to hear about your upset state. TAKE IT EASY. Bird or no bird, you must preserve yourself, & not have seizures, except such as the badger deals out in the field of play. I know birds upset you, but they're not like Teddy boys, they don't mean to. Baron Corvo used to have seizures at the sight of 'reptiles' i.e. toads, lizards, etc., so you have good precedent, but don't be alarmed, don't get into states: they are more afraid of you than you of them.

I have to keep describing Sark to persons in my daily life: I call it 'a village surrounded by sea'.[2] That is really how it struck me. I now have the print of the clubman duck: not very good but very recognisable. 'Takin' snaps without so much as a by-your-leave ... Board School products.' He looks wan without his fine red wattle.

Wednesday. Empty-page staring again tonight. It's maddening. I suppose people who don't write (like the Connollies) imagine anything that can be thought can be expressed. Well, I don't know. I can't do it. It's this sort of thing that makes me belittle the whole business: what's the good of a 'talent' if you can't do it when you want to? What shd we think of a woodcarver who couldn't woodcarve? or a pianist who couldn't play the piano? Bah, likewise grrr.

I wonder very much how you are getting on. Are you aiming to get everything stored or sold by the end of September? When are Pickfords going to appear? I expect you wish you had a telephone to do these pieces of business on.

I wish I could get something going in the poetry line. Sorting over my papers at the Library I began a file called *Refusals*! I find I've already turned down the Poetry Book Society without remembering it. Good show, good show.

Thursday Just ten. I've spent the evening boiling down my Annual Report & doing the silliest sort of figure-computing, giving myself a slight haddock. [...]

1 L. and Monica's name for Beaujolais.
2 L. and Monica had recently returned from a holiday on the island of Sark.

22 August 1960

32 Pearson Park, Hull

Dearest bunny,

It's warm again. This makes me more aware of my unwritten poem. Every night I sit & can't write it. On Friday I wrote a disrespectful little *jeu d'esprit* called *A Study of Reading Habits*[1] ending 'Books are a load of crap'. It needs a little polishing, then perhaps the *TLS*. I've never had a poem in there. This would be especially suitable. But the poem I have in mind remains obdurate. [...]

Wasn't the cricket exciting today! Though I thought they overdid Pullar's 'understandable weariness' after scoring 175, was it: after all, there was a man named Bradman, & a certain day at Leeds, eh? and probably against better bowling than this. And why that fellow Dexter couldn't hit a few I don't know. I don't expect anything of *Smith*, God knows, or *Parkes*, but Dexter & Barrington ought to have flayed them, simply flayed them – what wd Compton and Edrich have done at their age? I had the wireless in the Library and sat beside its mutter all afternoon. I can't imagine England forcing a draw. If a Compton–Edrich pair had put on 150 after 5 p.m. there would be a better chance.

And what is *Benaud* doing in the Press Box? I view him with as much pleasure as I should Göring at Farnborough Air Display. The bastard will learn all our tricks. I think it pretty rotten for a playing captain to go snooping round disguised as a journalist, & should have thought the M.C.C. might have objected. [...]

Tuesday Haven't done much tonight. Ate bacon & *three* scrambled eggs, a pear & a piece of cake & a few spoonfuls of honey & a can of Bass (!!) & a glass of milk (not necessarily in that order), & then fooled about with a tape recorder, borrowed from the Library for a joke. Recitations of poetry, gull-noises, a passage from *Any Questions*, with jeers by me, all served to idle away an hour. I then sat down in front of my poem, or non-poem, & promptly fell asleep. Escape mechanism. After I woke up again I wrestled a line or two out. [...]

Wednesday Rather wasted this evening, fooling about with the tape recorder wch then proved to have picked up as much atmospherics as *vox humana*, heaven knows where from. Then looked at my poetry-book without success; I'm quite fed up & jaded with this particular idea, which seems to have got tangled up so that I can't even write grammar on the subject. I suppose people who can write when they want are people like Humbert Wolfe & Austen Dobson. Yeah, & Shakespeare & Milton. Ogh ogh ogh. Ugh. Silly bugger, silly bugger, old boy. What?[...]

1 'A Study of Reading Habits' first appeared in *Critical Quarterly*, Winter 1960.

4 October 1960

32 Pearson Park, Hull

Dearest bun,

I'm hoping to enclose a couple of prints of Sark with this – the yard, and the one of us on the headland. I got myself a print of Tabitha & children, but they are in fact out of focus. Very pretty, though. She looks just as if she is telling them off. But I don't see much future for me as an animal photographer. [...]

There isn't much news about D. J. Wilks,[1] Esq., c/o British Council. Last night he got his player limbering up, and gave us a piece of atonalism. Twenty minutes or so. Sounded like a ferry boat trying to get out of a piano factory, & horribly large & loud. After a bit I gave him one side of *Blues Fell This Morning* – gallant little Belgium. Repeated the dose at 8.45 a.m. this morning, same side, a bit louder. Later in the morning I heard he had expressed himself a bit worried to Campbell about the disturbance from the jazz music of the man upstairs! I'll disturb him. Ogh ogh ogh. *Blues Fell* is a pretty good bit of monotonous nigger yowling to the untutored – fine example of primitive negro art really, of course. Think I'll try *Ellington – The Big Sound* next. Of course, this is just to make him come to terms: I couldn't endure a free for all.

Wednesday night. Groogh. Battle is still not yet joined, but skirmishes continue. They were out last night but contrived to wake up the Rexes[2] in the small hours, presumably by coming in and clumping about on their bare boards in shoes. Tonight we have had a nice little half hour of Bach, & now he seems to be limbering up on some louder stuff. The Rexes have invited them to coffee tonight at 8.30, but as Rex says, 'I don't want to invite him to coffee, I want to kick his backside.' I am to go too, with a hope of effecting a pincer movement about things that go bump in the night, not to mention saw and grind and yelp & jangle. I doubt myself if I shall ever be as comfortable here again, now, thanks to this sod. [...]

Late at night. Back from the coffee. It appears that the man intends ultimately to shift his killer player into the back room – the one that sticks out beyond me. May it be soon. I didn't care for him much, but he didn't give any overt cause for offence. He 'likes jazz' but not my kind, the fool. *Blues Fell This Morning* had obviously gone home. Gallant little Belgium. *Mais il gagnera parce qu'il est le plus bloody insensitif.*

It's full moon tonight, misty yet clear. Just midnight. I am thinking of you and wondering if you are in bed & rested. I do hope so. It was nice your bolting here: I hope you found it cheered you up. You are such a nice rabbit – really thoroughly nice. Much love – goodnight.

Thursday. Just given the bastard a dose of the old 4/4, without retaliation so far. Maybe he's out. I took a tape of part of the *Scrapbook of 1940*, & am playing it now. Did you hear it? What struck me most of all was how funny Jack Warner's *Garrison Theatre*[3] sounded. I never used to listen to it at the time. And that gruesome German parody of *Stormy Weather*!

I feel rather like you, with aches here and there due to the restart of filthy term. Are you better? I do hope your back is not keeping you awake, but even if it hasn't, the weather has been very erratic, warm then cold. The leaves are falling fast in Pearson Park, and it was quite misty in the morning. Pretty foggy over Scarborough too what. The rancorous vindictive socialist voices are heard on the air these days, too, aren't they? I haven't heard Mrs Castle[4] yet.

Now I hear footsteps moving about below – I don't think they've been in tonight after all. Goodnight, my dear bun.

xxx Love

P.

1 L.'s downstairs neighbour at 32 Pearson Park.
2 Also Pearson Park neighbours.
3 Popular BBC radio entertainment show during the Second World War.
4 Barbara Castle, Labour MP for Blackburn at the time.

11 October 1960

32 Pearson Park, Hull

[...] Had a long letter from Bob Broadbeak[1] this morning. 'Did you see that Wallace Stevens says that French and English are the same language? *Cor pierrez les corbeaux.*'[2] The very existence of people like Stevens, Pound, Eliot & Yeats seems to fill him with dancing fury: he has written denouncing them all to the *Obs.*, but they refuse to print it. He is going to Swansea with a girl this weekend: that's what I mean about people like him (not that there are any others) always being on the lookout for flats etc. I congratulated him on replacing me as chief unpaid unacknowledged gagman to Amis Inc. Trust the shaft goes home. [...]

1 Robert Conquest.
2 Franglish for 'Cor stone the crows'.

10 November 1960

Sorry there's so much about *Lady C* – it's as bad as *Lucky J*.

32 Pearson Park, Hull

Dearest Bun,

Well, I have had my *Lady C* exhibition.[1] I bet few university librarians had a signed copy on show the day after. The Ferret & Saville were appreciative: others less so. 'Bad taste.' Our bookshop has had and disposed of 50 copies of the Penguin first printing, so I have one of those too now. It looks more natural in the Penguin format. But it still seems a very odd book to me. I can't see it as a tract for beauty and openness; if it were, it would be less interesting, like something by Wm Morris. I think it may have been meant against industrialism, but I don't find that convincing. 'The fault lay there ... in those evil electric lights' etc. – I don't see why. No, it reads much more like a personal daydream, a return back beyond Frieda, Helen Corke & Jessie Chambers, into a wood, though not far from home and mother, and finding a really sympathetic woman at last, *physically* sympathetic (reading it through I'm struck by the number of resentful references to women who don't achieve orgasms simultaneously to him). But it isn't especially happy: either he can't believe it, or else he can't believe his own advocacy. One could make a list of all the times Mellors dodges or parries Connie's endearments: p. 183, 221, 235, 261 at least. And even the end is half hearted. 'A hopeful heart'! Is that all this vindication of love can offer? Then again, one doesn't *like* either of the chief characters: Connie treats her husband badly, and is rather tricky and gushing and awful, while Mellors with his Derbyshire-cum-Officers Mess accent is much too much of a piece of self indulgence: he has bronchitis (like D.H.L.) despite being a blacksmith!

Yet all the same one has to acquit it of indecent – or at any rate pornographic – intention: Mrs Bolton is good in a *Lost-girlish* way, the sense of spring in the wood is very fine. One finishes it feeling sad and sorry, but far from angry or uplifted. And far from Christian! Well, enough about this. I'm as bad as you about George Eliot. [...]

I have given my 'Books are a load of crap' poem to Cox for 5 gns. I hope it will upset people like John Wain ('I wish you wouldn't copy Kingsley'). Talking of the last named, TAGLY[2] is hitting the jackpot – over 20,000, film rights gone. Can't stop him now. He's there. He's arrived. Not down here with me & John Holloway, but up there with Arnold Bennett. [...]

1 At his own initiative, L. had organised an exhibition in the Library concerned with *Lady Chatterley's Lover*, timed to coincide with the legal clearance of the novel after the famous Penguin Books case. The 'signed copy' was L.'s own.
2 Amis's *Take a Girl Like You* (1960).

27 November 1960

32 Pearson Park, Hull

My dearest,

I didn't have time to put anything in an envelope to you this week, thanks to this review (wch thank God is now in the post), so I wasn't able to say anything very loving – but I did love being with you last weekend. I treasure the memory of your lovely looks, really as I say lovelier than ever. Beautiful handsome girl! You're really horribly attractive, especially your legs, as you know. It must be all this milk you're drinking, don't you think? I wish you had put on the silk dress, but as you said it would probably have come to grief. [...]

10 January 1961

32 Pearson Park, Hull

My very dear bun,

I saw your white furred face turn to go back in the station,[1] as if you were quick to get on with the next thing. In fact I then saw the best view of the cathedral I had had all day: straight up the High Street, floating as if in mid-air, its four red lights on. This is the view Paul Morel and his mother must have had, emerging from the station after coming from Nottingham. (I don't wonder Lincoln strained her heart, by the way.) It's a pity we never turned round; did you see it?

All in all it was a good and thrilling visit, wasn't it? Very rich in experience. The only parts that might have gone wrong were due to the Evanses – searching down that wretched dock for anything worth looking at. And the hotel wasn't worth '5/- more than anywhere else'. The cathedral & general air of Owlby & Scratby were fine, though I have given the Library my catalogue – it was great news to Cox, who comes from Lincoln, or Grimsby, or somewhere. [...]

1 L. and Monica had been visiting Lincoln and Lincolnshire. He is remembering Paul Morel and his mother's visit to Lincoln in Lawrence's *Sons and Lovers*.

11 February 1961

32 Pearson Park, Hull

Dearest bun,

Here is *Naturally*.[1] You know, I don't think Cox really got it. He said something that suggested he thought it was a bit hard on the Queen. What do you think of it? Seriously? Shd I try it on Alan Ross? Or is it just not good enough? It 'came to me', I think, when washing up after listening to the Cenotaph Service last November & thinking how much sooner I'd be there than going to India – in fact the two situations presented themselves so strongly in opposition that I was greatly *stricken*, and dyd Seek to Compose vpon Itt. [...]

1 'Naturally the Foundation will Bear Your Expenses': completed February 1961, published *Twentieth Century* (July 1961). L. evidently did not 'try it' on Alan Ross at the *London Magazine*.

2 March 1961

32 Pearson Park, Hull

Dearest bun,

I meant to start a letter to you last night, but my eyes went peculiar about 4 p.m. & I couldn't see to write or type. In the end I went to bed! This was awfully disturbing but seems to have cleared up now. Just at present it's 4.15 & I'm not 'in' being 'on' tonight: I ought to set about getting some tea.

I had a letter from Barbara Pym this morning, quite formal but friendly. She says she has done 4 chapters of a new one, 'wich is good', as the Sweep would say.

Isn't it a scream about Kingsley,[1] a scream of laughter or rage as the case may be? Guilding & Coveney are white with fury – & I must say I'm glad it's Cambridge & not Oxford who have done it. On the other hand, I don't mind really as if anyone is going to get it I'd sooner it was Kingsley than John or Enright or John Press (God) or Chas Tomlinson. Queer College to have done it, though – all historians.

Saturday. A wasted sort of day, in that it's spent going to Leeds. I see the old VC in the morning, still rattling out his litany of 'good … splendid … how charming … I'm so glad … good …' at everything I showed him. Then, since he goes fairly close on noon, there doesn't seem any reason why I shouldn't go to an annual general meeting at Leeds, as one or two from Hull are going. So I go, & damned dull it is too. Information retrieval if you don't mind. Then most of the evening gets wasted eating & drinking.

Sunday. Very fine morning: I am wearing my trendy trousers & the purple jumper. Bunny news is that there is beetles & woodworm in the church roof. I bet! Beetles with long ears, etc.

How are you feeling? It's funny you should sleep so long, but it isn't likely to do you any harm, is it. I should find it hard to *walk* as far as you do, but I suppose it seems natural to you by now. It *is* a long way, though.

Now I have had lunch & shall go out on my bike for a bit, though I have endless things I could do. You'll be amused to hear that my sister, ill in bed so that my mother had to be fetched to get food for Walter & Rosemary,[2] nevertheless managed to rise from the sickbed to attend a dress rehearsal involving the last-named. God, that my skirling laughter were a flame-thrower to extinguish such a nest of stupidity.

I'll put this in the post now. How did you like Wm Cooper? I wonder
if you are in York. I hope not, really, just for my own sake. Though
you'd have a fine day if you were. Very best love, dear.

xxx
Philip

1 Kingsley Amis had just been elected to a Fellowship in English at Peterhouse,
Cambridge.
2 L.'s brother-in-law and niece.

11 March 1961

Ward 6 [Kingston General Hospital, Hull]

P.S. – I'm afraid this becomes rather a 'frightened' letter, & isn't much
fun to read for that reason. There's no news.

Dearest,

I have got a ballpoint pen now, as likely to last longer & be less
trouble than a pen, an ink pen I mean. It is Saturday & I've just had
some lunch: it's 10 to one. There is nothing much to report. I haven't
been x rayed yet, or brain-waved, as I believe they intend to do.[1]

I *feel* about the same – that is, there is something wrong with my
vision, wch makes me have to focus specially sometimes, & I feel rather
distant from my feet: this is all summed up by being *aware* of my right
eye. In addition to this, I am out of sorts in a 'flu-y kind of way – no
appetite, coated tongue, bowels sore, & ready to sweat easily. This last
symptom seems to interest them. The nurse noted me sweating after
lights out last night, & fetched an orderly who took some blood.

Today the doctor came round and said there were many more tests still
to be done, but that nothing had been revealed up to now. It *isn't* heart,
anyway. Of course I can't help worrying a good deal about it. I dread
hospitals, & the very fact of being in one is enough to frighten me. The
very phrase 'results of the x ray' makes my blood run cold. Some people
are at home in hospitals, but I'm not one of them. What the hell is wrong?
I suppose I could have picked up a virus, but this wouldn't explain the
persistent sense of strain in the eyes – & one instance of lack of focus –
since I had these new lenses. It could be this eye strain, perhaps, though
this wouldn't explain the temperature & being out of sorts. Or it could
be something wrong *in the brain*; needless to say that's one of the things

278

I dread. To me there seem two diseases, really: the 'virus' that brought temperature & lack of appetite & coated tongue & sore bowels & eye-ache, & the longer-term focussing trouble centring on the right eye, & wch isn't accompanied by any other trouble except slight ache – only very slight – in the right eye. How can one fit the two diseases together? And why should I have fainted? I suppose the whole thing may tie up in some way I don't know about, like Walter Gabriel & his diabetes.

Anyway, allowing for the fact that I'm ill & writing on a too-high surface with a ball-point pen, this writing isn't so bad, is it? But I'm not getting better, I'm afraid, not as far as the focussing trouble goes, or sense of unreality.

I must thank you, dearest dearest love, for coming to see me so quickly, and for sending me cards & letters. Our meetings were pitifully short, even on Wednesday, & I don't know what I said – I was quite muzzy on the early days of the week. One thing that makes me ashamed is my refusal to let you use my flat. This has been a worry all through, & springs from the fact that I had left a few private papers & diaries lying around. Such things, which I suppose I keep partly for the record in the event of wanting to write an autobiography, & partly to relieve my feelings, will have to be burned unread in the event of my death, & I couldn't face anyone I thought had seen them, let alone being willing to expose you or anyone else to the embarrassment & no doubt even pain of reading what I had written. This is just the kind of situation I feared might arise. Let me say how ashamed I am of it & of having to explain something of my reasons to you. What this will lead me to do about such things in the future I don't know – assuming there is such a future. Perhaps destroy them right away.

I've been writing for an hour now, partly because I like talking to you, partly to see how my eyes & brain stand it. If this looks legible & makes sense I suppose I'm not too far gone yet. It's 2.5, & I think I might rest a bit. Oh darling I wish you were here! I don't know if things like x rays & so on go on at the weekend. What do you think will be the outcome of it all? I'm caught up in another backwash of apprehension.

Wood is coming tonight, & Maeve. People come every night, very kindly.

I think I may be getting better, because I don't like the grub! But better appetite wd be fine sauce.

Later on. I ought to write smaller if I'm going to keep on – not that I expect I shall write lots if I get worse, but I might if I get better. Just now there's nothing to do but lie worrying. Defective *vision* can be a symptom of all sorts of things, can't it – not necessarily eyes, or even brain. I mean, it could be *liver*, couldn't it. That wd tie up with the coat on my tongue. Yet I don't think I look very yellow, allowing for the fact that I'm ill anyway. A slight focussing disability – wch is really how this began – is a wonderful symptom for something terrible. Oh dear, I'm really a horrible coward. Can you imagine all the fearful things that are passing through my imagination? In a time like this one has to keep all the fright and anxiety to oneself – there is no point in expressing it, yet one, I – think things, & construe things, & imagine things, & all to the very blackest end. I shall be TERRIFIED of seeing the doctors after the x-ray!! Terrified lest they employ some guarded formula as an approach to an operation! The doctor said this morning 'It's nothing common' – this is the Cypriot (?) houseman – wch was at first cheering, I mean all the things it *wasn't*, & then rather daunting, in the even more things it could be. Shall I end up in a London brain clinic? I have a nervous dread of x rays – in fact I'm so unhappy altogether, I can't bring myself to do anything but lie either whining to you or shuddering to myself. I am not finding it easy to read, as I suppose I should if I were getting better. I'm not getting better, at least as far as my sight goes. I know that. And it's a long time now – six days. I shd be getting over anything *trivial*, shouldn't I? Oh dear, does this read like the contemptibleness of a very fainthearted kind of person? You'll read it on Monday, the day I expect when I am x rayed. My sentence. My dear, I'm sorely afraid at the thought of all I have to go through. I can only tell you so over and over again with variations.

Later. I've tried to read, but I can't seem to take it in. The bloody TV is on – it's 5.20 – & this doesn't help. But of course the real trouble is I'm rigid with funk. The doctor felt the bottom right hand corner of my stomach (wch is slightly sore: it became much more sore during Thursday night) & made a grimace to his fellow, not really construable as anything, but it was then he confirmed I hadn't been x rayed. Do you think he felt something? Is it liver there? You can imagine my dreads. You'll say I don't look livery – at least I hope you will! – but oh dear, oh dear, I do feel frightened. They seem very interested in my sweating but I don't take much account of that. If I have some kind of virus or germ I should expect to have to sweat it out.

I hardly know if I ought to send letters like this. You see, darling, I'm afraid I'm *seriously* ill, & really this is all that's in my mind, and nobody can give me any comfort. It would be comforting to have you here to talk to, if you could stay all the time, but it wdn't be any *ultimate* comfort, wd it. You know, when I first came in here I didn't worry at all: I just thought I'd fainted & my specs were too strong. But now after six days, or 5 days, during wch I know I've been recovering from my sort of fever or virus, but at the end of wch I'm no better at focussing – if anything I might be a bit worse – and at the same time nobody pays any attention to my specs story – and I've lost my appetite and just lie shuddering with terror. You can imagine the situation where someone is ill & no explanation is forthcoming *before the x rays* is pretty fraught with terror for me. Oh dear, oh dear. If you were here I'd hold your hand very tight. I'm feeling dizzy as I write, but this may be due to smoking a cigarette, or funk, or what? I've also gone deaf in the left ear, wch I do sometimes, I suppose, though not lately. Darling, I'm very scared. I'll lie back a bit & see how I feel.

Sunday morning 8.15 or so. Well, I had a number of visitors last night & they cheered me up, & I also stopped being deaf. This morning I feel just about the same, perhaps a fraction better in the 'virus' group of symptoms – a trifle less fur on the tongue – but there's no change in the 'vision' group. Morale isn't too good either! All the things I mentioned yesterday continue to gnaw away at my vitals. But talking about them won't do any good. Or at least I suppose it eases my feelings to a small extent. It seems to me that I have either some organic trouble – something begun to *grow* wrong, or *work* wrong – or else I have picked up some virus wch in due course I shall get rid of. Or the third chance is the specs, but I can hardly see these giving me a blackout or a temperature.

I'll write one or two other letters now – last Sunday seems so far away! & close this later in the day. Oh darling, please have patience with me – I'm so low in spirits.

10.30 a.m. The time drags by. I'm afraid I'm due to spend it worrying from now until – I hardly dare think of what the conclusion of my worry will be. I just lie here thinking of all the things it might be – I'm obsessed by this liver idea at present. My inside is certainly upset – coated tongue, not much appetite, for instance – and the liver *can* affect vision, can't it? You know what horrors are associated with livers for me, through my father. You know the kind of thing that's passing through my mind – well, I wish it *were* passing through: it's settled down to stay, I'm afraid. I lie remembering all the details of the past few weeks that might be relevant – I *have* had a *little* less appetite, especially at breakfast, but I honestly can't remember anything else. The failure to focus my eyes occurred too, some weeks ago – I *could* find out when, but I don't suppose it matters. What alarms me is that – well, at least, from this point of view – my head & eyes don't ache, just feel a trifle giddy – and if it were *chiefly* them, they would be claiming more attention. Oh darling, I'm so frightened of what it may be. Am I silly? I long for someone to reassure me. I wonder if anyone ever will. I have really only begun to 'go through it' since I thought of the liver, on the back of page 4, but I've been going through it since then all right. And there's so much more to endure: the x ray, the verdict on the x ray, & all after that. I am so afraid of 'uncommon' things – things that are only revealed by x rays. I'm so afraid of not having anything obviously wrong with me for fear what is really wrong will be all the more serious. Oh darling, how awful all this is! Do you find it shameful of me? Just think of me as a very frightened person lying a prey to all kinds of imaginings, and *knowing* that *something* is wrong, and *fearing* it is something BAD. Oh darling, do have patience with me, and send me some comfort, but there can't really be any comfort except from the doctors.

1.20 p.m. After lunch. I have shaved and propped myself up in bed again Visitors will come at 2.30 – Betty & Wendy, I believe, perhaps others. Coveney is being *very* good all this time. Dickens called last night, & was cheering in a pompous kind of way. (There is a funeral on the TV screen just now.) Also Rex, who went to the wrong hospital first.

I keep thinking about the doctor palpating the lower right hand corner of my stomach – what is there? His grimace could have been 'It's all yours' (his fellow prodded me similarly afterwards) or 'search me', or of course something much more serious. It was funny how my stomach, or what I think of as my bowels, got sore on Thursday night, just as if I had gastric 'flu, or as if I'd eaten unchewed tomato skins. He was prodding the remnants of the soreness. I wish I had more confidence in the medical profession! They're still slightly sore now.

My dear, this is a rotten sort of letter to send you. Do you mind? You are all I have to talk to, to ease my mind. If your ideal man is strong & silent then I am a long way short of your ideal: I am weak & babbling. I shall give this to the visitors to post, & probably start another one pretty quickly.

I remember smiling a sickly smile about Dick Diver: but there you are. If I'm ever in a position to repay old Covers' kindness I shall want to do so.

You know my sister's telephone number, 4160, in case you shd want to telephone her. I don't know why you should at present, but it's as well for you to be prepared.

A new inhabitant has just been wheeled in – he 'looks healthy enough', wch is what one immediately asks oneself. Mr Cooper.[2]

It's 20 past 2, & I will seal this up. Once again thank you, my dearest, for coming so quickly to see me, & for cheering me up. I wish I could be more spirited for you, but just now I feel very low & frightened, & afraid of what the future may hold. xxx Love Philip

1 On 5 March 1961 L collapsed during a Library Committee meeting and was taken by ambulance to Kingston General Hospital, Hull, for 'neurological investigation'. When he was discharged, he was looked after at Needler Hall by Peter Coveney. In April he spent two weeks in Fielden House, London, being examined by Russell Brain. The diagnosis was 'epilepsy of late onset' with 'no positive evidence of an organic cure'.
2 The final words of Anthony Thwaite's poem 'Mr Cooper' are: 'And Mr Cooper dead'.

11 June 1961

32 Pearson Park, Hull

Dearest one,

Have had a proof of *Naturally*.[1] Betty, who opened it, said 'They'll say, "Well, we know he's been ill" ' – not that I think she gets it any more than Cox did. How to read a page. Ogh ogh ogh. I keep thinking of people it applies to. Madge. Spender. Holloway. Jeffares.[2] Oghogh. Well, it may not be a good poem, but it's a good title.

How are you? I can remember of course that you were here, & what we did, but you slip so easily into my life, making no disturbance, it's almost like trying to pick out a rabbit among bracken. Not that rabbits have lovely legs like yours. Your legs are the only legs I ever see the point of, except for walking about on, of course. [...]

1 'Naturally the Foundation will Bear Your Expenses'.
2 C. B. Cox; Charles Madge; Stephen Spender; John Holloway; A. N. Jeffares.

9 August 1961

32 Pearson Park, Hull

[...] I wish you could have raised this money business when we were together, though, rather than write bitterly about it.[1] I quite *see* it's wise to settle such affairs; unresponsiveness on my part isn't due to ingratitude, or to whatever it is you're suspicious of: it's due, without being deliberate, to funk (hate the thought of making a will) and genuine puzzlement. You seem to be wanting me to do something & I don't know what it is: you seem to be saying Make a will, & tell me what's in it, and if I like it I'll leave you some money. Remember I don't *know* anything about wills, though I'm willing to learn. Do you mean you want me to make a will saying that in the event of my receiving a legacy from you it should be disposed of on my death in a particular way, e.g. to UFAW or back to your people or to my college or your college? Is this customary in wills or legacies? It may be: I just don't know. As for Rosemary,[2] I only mentioned her (along with, as I recall, yourself & my sister) because she is the kind of person a solicitor wd remind me of, I suppose. I don't want to leave her *all* my money, such as it is. But if we are contemplating a time when you & I & my mother & sister are all dead, I don't know what other *person* at present would have a claim of *any* kind on *my* estate, bar remotish cousins.

If I were to make a will here & now I suppose I should have to think of a literary executor – say, Bob – leave him something, leave something to Rosemary, and divide the rest somehow between you and mother. I suppose there are a few institutions or people I might remember in a small way. But it isn't a topic I relish thinking about. No doubt I ought to follow the advice 'If there's something you *have* to do, do it from choice while you are strong.' But I shd quite genuinely be rather at a loss to know what to do. And I'm also uncertain as to how far a legacy can be isolated from the rest of one's estate, if it is in cash & not shares or property, for testamentary purposes – I mean if I have £5000, & am left £5000, and spend £5000, & leave £5000, whose £5000 is it? However, tell me more about what you want. I do see that it is a serious matter and ought to be settled. I also see that you are offering me a great kindness, and I'm properly grateful. I'm sorry I'm not naturally adept at wills. They are one of a long list of subjects that never seem to have been discussed much in my life. Don't please think of me as being deliberately stupid or obstinate. [...]

1 Monica had written to L. on 8 August 1961: 'You refuse to talk about money, I've tried you several times. I gather that you want anything I have to leave to you to go to Rosemary, since you refuse to say otherwise [...] I think any of us might be run over or otherwise die at any moment – *I* am very anxious to make a Will – I *don't* want my relations to inherit all that I have ... I'd like to leave you something considerable, but I've said this before & you retain the same position I can't meet. You can hardly blame me if it makes me uncertain, even amazed, even suspicious. It's a pity to send you this on yr birthday, but I have asked you plenty of times more. I shd appreciate a straight answer.'
2 L.'s niece, b. 1947.

17 August 1961

Pearson Park, Hull

Dearest,

Tonight I've mown half the back lawn, burnt the TLS for 1960, and read two books by Thom Gunn. I really don't know what I can say about him.[1] And the worst is that one fears he wouldn't be above beating you up for a bad review. There isn't really anything wrong with his poems except that they're dull. And one doesn't expect a 'tough' poet's books to be full of Julian the Apostate, Rastignac, the BVM, Baudelaire, etc etc.

It would be pretty dreary for you to have to go back through Birmingham as in the old unhappy not so far off days. I don't think I realised you were going. But doesn't your pulse quicken at the thought of exhuming your belongings, of arranging them into rooms again? Of getting away from the bag? How does the flat seem as regards noise – are there people overhead? I hope it won't be too much to keep clean – the passage is long, isn't it? And as regards Hexham, are you going up with the luggage next week?[2]

Guy Mannering must be a good book if it can entertain you in such circumstances. I don't know what I'd want – *The Rock Pool*, perhaps. I suppose I might try. I don't think I recovered from being advised to read *The Heart of Midlothian* – was it? At different times I've tried that, and *The Antiquary*, and *Old Mortality*. All fell from my nerveless fingers. I *want* W.S. to be good – heavens, one wants anyone to be good, especially a nice voluminous chap like Scott – but I don't know, there seemed nothing in his books, no imagination, humour, malice, style, perception, story even. Talking about books, I have your *Anglicanism*. I finished it here, skipping all the overseas stuff. I'm now going through the bibliography. I shall order what we haven't got for the Library – we haven't got quite a lot. Give Farrell something good to catalogue ogh ogh ogh. Then you may have it back. I hope you don't mind my having it a little longer. [...]

1 In the end L. sent back the Gunn books to the *Guardian* and did not review them.
2 Monica was moving into a new flat in Leicester, and had bought her cottage in Haydon Bridge near Hexham.

11 September 1961

Hull

[...] *Thursday*. Feel rather better tonight: have been brooding on my verses again, and have done in all 2½ stanzas, not very good.[1] Karl Miller rang up & gave me the choice of the Twitnam Pope or Ogden Nash: I chose the latter. He said that the 'Mr O'Brien', UN's man in Katanga, is Conor Cruise O'Brien, *pseud* Donat O'Donnell, Patsy's erstwhile flame, wch was news to me. He's an Irish diplomat, I thought. Anyway, Karl lamented his absence, wch he said partly explained his badgering of me. I don't understand what's going on there, but I don't suppose it's any better for a literary critic's being mixed up in it. [...]

1 'Here', completed 8 October 1961.

2 October 1961

32 Pearson Park, Hull

[...] I wrote 3 letters to B. Pym[1] before feeling satisfied with it, becoming progressively more impersonal. Do you think she has many admirers? I have looked at *Exc. Women*[2] again, & think it very good: that has the large white rabbit thrust suddenly into one's arms in it.

I was not surprised to hear Ruddick has been to see you: you are only as far from him as, well, Selby wd be to me. I'm glad he was useful, & he'd be company for you. I shall be jealous if he comes very often, though! Envious, anyway. I'm less jealous of the cat. I hope its owners don't turn it out on the assumption that it has a new home. Is it a nice cat? I forget what colour you said it was. [...]

1 See *Selected Letters*, 1 October 1961.
2 Barbara Pym, *Excellent Women* (1952).

8 October 1961

32 Pearson Park, Hull

Dearest,

I'm sitting down after a quite busy though fairly enjoyable day – didn't get up till 10.40 ogh ogh, then, it being a fine sunny morning, I got on my bike & went out eastwards: had a drink at Paull, a village on the Humber, & round through Hedon & home. About 30 miles in all. On the wall of the Paull pub there was a notice saying 'old golfers never die, they simply lose their balls.' Bucolic humour. A dull ride on the whole, but I felt in better physical shape – isn't it odd that on Friday I was so feeble, just going to town tired me, yet today I could cycle a long way without feeling exhausted. And do the bed & laundry & wash socks & make a proper supper of two very nice lamb chops, rice and onions. This sounds like boasting, but when I feel low I tell you, so when I feel well I might as well tell you that too. [. . .]

Monday Wet day. It is a bit of a rush to get this finished, as Mitchell[1] has turned up and I want to talk *D. Telegraph* with him, & then there is a Refec. Comm. at 2.15. Last night after finishing – sorry, not finishing, writing – this to you I finished a dull poem called *Here* about ye Eastern Thridding, wch I'm now trying to flog to Thwaite.[2] [. . .]

1 Donald Mitchell, musicologist, engaged L. as *Daily Telegraph* jazz records reviewer.
2 At that time a BBC Features Department producer, who had broadcast 'The Whitsun Weddings' and 'Ambulances' (and earlier L.'s Overseas Service programme in 1958). 'Here' was not broadcast, but published in the *New Statesman* (24 November 1961).

2 November 1961

32 Pearson Park, Hull

Dearest,

Gob but this week began badly, with the annual coming of Vernon Watkins – sherry party & dinner on Monday, *after a day's work:* then the sodding talk, with me in the chair & nervous; then coffee party – *standing* – & like a fool I asked the Hartleys back: gave them about 16/- worth of gin & got them out about 12.40 a.m. Then next day cleaner coming & another V.W. talk, in the *Library* this time, and *me in the chair*. Then *lunch with V.W.* & gas & *talk*. I was absolutely beat, & then I had to go down & see Rex[1] in hospital – felt like stayin' there myself what. By now I feel pretty well recovered, no thanks to anybody but me. God these absurd Watkins visits are the end – this is the fourth –

Otherwise there hasn't been too much to worry me, *this* week: next Wednesday is the interview for Farrell's successor: two dull men &

two women from Cardiff and Sheffield. My money is on the Sheffield woman, but we'll see. One of the men is from Aberystwyth! though not a Welshman, or BJ[2] wd address him in Welsh, a favourite gambit. No doubt saying 'I'm verree worreed' in Welsh. Runnin' this University gives me'n 'eadache. This coming Saturday is his annual sherry party, a tiresome affair that always leaves one feeling drunk, ill & exhausted. Shall take it very easy, I reckon. [...]

I've sent a poem to the NS about these parts, so look out for it probably next week or the week after.[3] Laughing Boy Cox tells me he is printing a long rambling article (review?) on Gunn by G.S.F. wch gets on to me with no great friendliness. Fat squinting blinking drunken swine, kick him downstairs from me. This reminds me of A. Wilson's new vol,[4] wch I'm reading by courtesy of L. B. Cox and wch has an odd sort of hero, rather 'modern', as if A.W. had tried to imagine one of us grammar school louts having aged in the Civil Service by 1970. There are outcroppings of crudity that make me laugh rather, but on the whole the book's rather dull. Just a dull story about what it might very well be like running a zoo.

This reminds me that Bob's new book (!), 'The Pasternak Affair',[5] arrived this morning. It's dedicated to *me*, wch will no doubt mean a new file in the Kremlin. Yesterday from the same source came two copies of an indecent magazine called 'Swish' and a letter saying he'd been badly scratched by a girl of 22 the previous evening. He makes me feel about as protean as a flatiron! The book looks a typical Conquest exposé of life in the U.S.S.R., full of appendices giving verbatim translations from Russian sources. [...]

1 David Rex, a neighbour at 32 Pearson Park.
2 Brynmor Jones, Vice-Chancellor of Hull.
3 'Here', *New Statesman*, 24 November 1961.
4 Angus Wilson, *The Old Men at the Zoo*.
5 Robert Conquest, *The Pasternak Affair*.

18 January 1962

32 Pearson Park, Hull

Dearest rabbit,

I have got round to writing you a few lines after having had to go to a lecture – sherry, dinner & lecture be gob – by one Michel St Denis,[1] who may be known to you but wasn't to me. A big theatrical bug, very amusing inasmuch as he acted his lecture, with lots of funny expressions chasing each other across his features.

Dinner was pheasant, with fried counters & a whole dish of gravel handed round separately. I found a pellet of shot too.

There is another lecture by the same man tomorrow wch I *ought* to go to, but ... but ... but ...

Well, dear, how have you been this week? I should like to stroke your little rabbit brow & large rabbit hindquarters. I do hope you aren't getting influenza or a cold. Everyone here seems to have had a dose at some time or other. Not me so far: cabbage & carrots. Virginia[2] is v. enthusiastic – well, not exactly that, because it's so obvious, isn't it? but she thinks she has come to a *sensible ménage*. I can see her ears over a pile of books as I write.

At 'the dinner' I sat among some Richard-fans,[3] not Cliff Richard as you may well imagine. One had had a letter from him – 'oh, good' cried the others, as if the first had reported a win on the pools – written partly in the 'plane, partly on land. I don't know which way he was going. The one I sat next to had met you 'at Richard's' about seven months ago, she said: one Muriel Crane. Drama. Theatre in the – yes, you've guessed it.

Wch reminds me I went to see *Nudes of the World* after work on Tuesday, and sat among giggling Chinese for 4/6 feeling terribly humiliated to be watching such stuff: it was such a terrible *film* apart from anything else. Full of lines like 'But how can we overcome the prejudice of the villagers, Gerda?' made only slightly better by the speakers having no clothes on. It was as if it had been made by the staff of a large store, nothing to do with films at all.

Otherwise it hasn't been a very interesting week. I spent *all day* on Tuesday in the Council Room with the Building Committee, & Wednesday pm there on Senate. If we had $\frac{1}{4}$ as many buildings on the ground as we have on paper we'd be all set. Ogh ogh. Was *furious* to find that a new *men's* hall had washbasins in *all* rooms, whereas *mine*, reputedly for *either* men *or* women, had *sets* of rooms to a *bathroom*. More about this when I see you. Imagine BJ *explaining to me* that the former arrangement was *more flexible, see*.

Today my head cleaner who has been off for a long time came in & resigned. Nerves, & quarrel with the rest of the cleaners. Shall have to promote the chief quarreller, I'm afraid.

For my next jazz article I think I shall do Johnny Hodges, who has just come out on a new LP, so watch out on 10 Feb for 'Jazz Rabbit'[4] – if I can find enough to say. Records aren't coming through because of this parcels business.

Are you still remembering your time here? I thought it was a great improvement on anything we have done before, except that the bed wd take a bit of getting used to, from a sleeping point of view. It was so nice of you to be grateful for breakfast wch I should have got anyway! These mornings I'm not having bacon every day, as a matter of fact – don't like a big meal at the beginning of the day. A man doesn't need bacon.

Saw Brett casually tonight but he didn't say anything about papers. He is more concerned about the Future Developments Committee wch he thinks is killing him. Since it cut down people's staff requirements for next year nobody much will care if it does, an' the rest of the crowd inta the bargain. There's about 15 adumbrated for next year, in all. Do you know how many your lads are getting? Not that I care. This is the hell of a hole. Leo Japolsky[5] wrote to ask if he should put in for a job here (God!) – a p.c. came today saying he had abandoned the idea, but in the meantime I'd said I didn't advise it. Well, can you, really?

Dear bun! I think of you many times a day. Only you wd understand so much I see.

Friday Today is sunny & mild, wch is good, as the sweep says. Letter from Bob saying Alan Ross has had ECT (convulsions, you know) & that he (Bob) has just had two girls – a blonde & a brunette. Honestly, I don't know whether to believe him! Love   XXX   Philip

1 French actor and producer, a director of the Royal Shakespeare Theatre Company.
2 A miniature figurine of a rabbit, given to L. by Monica.
3 Fans of Richard Hoggart, at this time at Leicester University and a colleague of Monica's.
4 L.'s *Daily Telegraph* article actually carried the title 'Ellington minus the Duke'.
5 Lecturer in French at Queen's College, Belfast.

23 January 1962

32 Pearson Park, Hull

Darling,

I've just switched on the Cooper fight,[1] setting aside my typewriter to do so: I am trying to finish off my Emma Hardy review,[2] curse it. The fire is too hot, but is so blocked up that I daren't turn it down or it will 'pop'. I seem to do nothing but reviews these days: I had to read a book by Francis Berry[3] & compose a summary paragraph to insert into my NS review: crazy tripe. [. . .]

It was lovely to have such a long letter from you yesterday: I read it drinking sherry after I got in at night. I grinned at your 'lecturing to rule', and applaud it, only it's a miserable situation (fight just stopped) that produces it. It's hard for me to tell what lecturing well & lecturing badly is, really: plenty of simple boiled-down takable notes, plus a bit of inspiration-cum-cleverness at start and finish is how I'd do it, I suppose. Thank God I don't have to.

This afternoon (Christ! that devil Wilks:[4] *Music Who's Who*, or something, gives his recreations as 'motoring': BANGING DOORS'd be more like it: STEALING OTHER PEOPLE'S SUNDAY PAPERS), being in my bank, I enquired about what I could do for my money to ensure capital appreciation as money values fell. This ended with my giving them £1000 to invest on my behalf! I hope it's sensible. This is because I don't really want *income*, as it is taxed so heavily. The manager accompanied me to the door & shook my hand, leaving me with a sense of having bought the Humber bridge, or part of it. Have I been silly? I hope not. LLOYDS CRASHES. BIG FIVE NOW BIG FOUR. MILLIONS LOSE SAVINGS. Oh well.

On Saturday I bought a pretty pillowcase rather like your nightdress. I should say, really, that you could always stay here: the Wilkses, I now find, have their bedroom under my sitting room & *vice versa*. They don't strike me as being a very noticing pair, being, like most musicians, completely wrapped up in themselves. I don't know. It's so much better all round, isn't it? – *cheaper*.

Back to Emma.

Wednesday Gob, pretty enfeebled by evening: I'm sitting in my chair, deliberately ignoring the inaugural lecture by the Dublin philosopher due to start in 10 mins in the University. After a week of feeling not so bad, I am now subject to heart-failure & brain-boiling. Anyway, devil take it. I am invited to a Students' Union sherry party tomorrow – don't want to go out two nights running, & anyway I usually write to you midweek. I suppose a lecture would do me less harm than a sherry party. Hum.

I didn't quite twig where F. Berry had been making sure we all knew about WK:[5] the latest I have seen is John Sparrow in *Enc.*[6] – well! All

Souls becoming interested in women! It wd take this particular aspect of it to effect such a transmogrification – gob! just 'come round' after about 30 mins daze, coma, brain boiling – oh dear!

I feel a little irritated that this particular sort of sexual intercourse should be attracting attention in the weeklies, for while I can't claim any personal stake in it exactly, and while it seems much too difficult technically, all things being equal it would please me to share it with *you*, as fit expression of a feeling you're well aware of, and I regret finding myself in the van of intellectual progress along with the boys. I can't imagine there is much in it for you, though. I imagined it was the custom in Catholic-ridden countries where it was the only way girls could keep their fiancés happy & the priests at the same time. I never supposed what they wanted was this piercing, rather awful sensuality. Ogh ogh. Hagh.

Anyway, god, I don't feel well enough just now. Do you think my nervous system is 'frayed', like a rope, & as unlikely to mend as a frayed rope, & as likely to *snap* as a frayed rope? I take two phenob.'s at night, & tranquillisers during the day if I feel awful: the former *might* do some good, I doubt if the latter do. I feel better now than I did an howre ago, yea, or even half an howre. [...]

Oh dear, I don't know what to say about – well, Bill:[7] I've forgotten his surname ('My God!! Freudian!!'): I imagine he *is* attracted to you, in that you are about 200 times more interesting and amusing than anyone he is likely to meet, leaving aside the tremendous physical attraction you have (I say, I am piling it on, but you know what I mean – legs & body); but whether he is attracted in a straightforward way, or whether you give him the pleasure of being with a woman without the strain he would find a girl of his own age I don't know. I mean he might think a girl o.h.o.a. wd expect him to make advances to her, wch he might not want to do, because of being too shy or not wanting to get involved; and that you don't expect this. (Of course, if he is just doing so as I write I am mistaken.) This doesn't really explain what sounds like a pretty doglike devotion – very decent, too – and wch argues either strong feeling or a kind of simple-minded inability to think of or do anything else. I should have thought it might have occurred to him that he was risking comment, either on himself or you, but perhaps he isn't. If his thesis turned out to be no good, it wd be important that this shouldn't be attributed to his running after you, wouldn't you say? From both your points of view? [...]

Must end now, dear, as I have a – guess what – Committee. Was I perhaps rather outspoken earlier in this letter? You know I don't mean any harm. Or, if I mean it, I shan't do it. Anyway, my dearest love to you, bun. XXX P.

1 Henry Cooper, boxer.
2 'Mrs Hardy's memories', *Critical Quarterly*, Spring 1962.
3 Francis Berry, *Poetry and the Physical Voice*, reviewed by L., *New Statesman*, 2 February 1962.
4 L.'s downstairs neighbour in Pearson Park.
5 G. Wilson Knight.
6 An article by Sparrow in *Encounter* on his supposition that in *Lady Chatterley's Lover* Mellors penetrates Connie from the rear.
7 Bill Ruddick: student of Monica's, later lecturer in English at Manchester University.

8 February 1962

32 Pearson Park, Hull

Dearest,

Thursday night again, & the week gone jolly quickly. I feel irritated at present over two minor work things, not worth retailing (Dr P. about his Manx friend's stories) but nagging all the same. A varied day as far as work went, writing a reference for one of the girls appointed during my illness who now wants to go to Swansea to be near her boyfriend who is in the National Library of Wales; correcting the style of the mad Irish professor of Philosophy's inaugural lecture for the printer – he said 'e.g.' about everything: 'leaving the University, I caught e.g. a bus', almost – and after lunch to a Hull church to look at a polyglot Bible, reputedly valuable. Very funny to hear the clergymen talking – two very intelligent ones, one shortly to be Prof. at Leeds, the other from TCD[1] – 'So now the whole thing's in the lap of the gods?' 'Well, of the Diocesan Council, if you count that the same thing.' The way they talked about 'Hull' was rather like I talk about B.J., minus the imitations.

I have thought a lot about our nice Sunday, wch *was* nice, but left me ashamed of myself for causing you embarrassment *vis à vis* old Charity-Boots,[2] & feeling let down in general. I don't know that it's worth saying anything except that my delight in you isn't pretended: you blot out anyone else. This was the first 'love' poem[3] I've written since *Maiden name* in about 1954, & I shd think both are pretty tenuous, pretty remote, as far as general approach goes. In fact I think this one just a shade ludicrous! No one here seems to have noticed it, except Cox, who like a dog sees but doesn't understand.

Talking of poetry, 'Bill' Empson[4] is coming here tomorrow night – I suppose it wd be interesting to go. Dig the mugs in *Lond. Mag.* – they didn't correct my mispunctuation,[5] the sons of sods, as Ll. Powys wd say. I quite like the poem – 'it doesn't rhyme, but it's true,' like George Green's remarks. Such absences! Wain, Davie, Holloway, Moraes, Cronin, Heath Stubbs & Uncle Tom Cobley & all – not Uncle Thom Gunn, unfortunately. Handsome, he looks, doesn't he, beside me. Nor Uncle Ted Hughes.

I've had a good week in, fiddling about with a poem – a wonderful relief after all those sodding reviews. Attempts to buy salmon fishcakes result in being told they are 'rather pricey' & so not sold. Wherever there exists a demand there is *no* supply.

My mother is preserving the photograph of you, though; as she says, you are not as *thin* as A. Hepburn. Jolly good, jawley good. It seemed romantic to be doing that long dark wet 'bus journey again.

Friday. 'Nothing to be said', except that tickets for the International Smallpox Congress at Lord's on June 21–23rd have arrived safely.

Best love & kisses
Philip

1 Trinity College, Dublin.
2 Maeve Brennan, the subject of L.'s 'love' poem.
3 'Broadcast', published in the *Listener* on 25 January 1962.
4 William Empson, poet and literary critic.
5 The February 1962 issue of the *London Magazine* carried poems and a symposium to which L. contributed, along with photographs of several poets. L.'s poem was 'Nothing To Be Said'. The mispunctuation was an extra comma in the first stanza.

11 April 1962

32 Pearson Park, Hull

[...] I thought your little house seemed (how fond I seem of that word!) distinguished and exciting and beautiful:[1] clever of you to have found it, bold of you to have furnished it in Rabbit Regency: it looks splendid, and it can never be ordinary with the Tyne going by outside. Others may have Swedish glass, or Swedish forks, or Finnish clap-boarding, or theatre in the round round the corner, or a Picasso, or stereo hifi, or a split-level living area – *you* have a great English river drifting under your window, brown and muscled with currents! [...]

We have *Critical Q* in our building now: Cox's secretary gave me a practical criticism quiz that is to be presented at their coming Scarborough weekend. I spotted 7 authors out of 19, plus 2 halves (e.g. 'translation from Chinese?') – but some frightful bloomers – I *missed* a Hardy (*T. Major*), and a Forster: I thought Fielding was Henry James and Peacock G.K.C.! Can you imagine it? And they had dug up a *poem* by Jane Austen: never knew there was such a thing. Cox is slowly moving into the Library, I fancy. He uses our lavatory constantly – I tell him I'm glad he finds the Library such an essential institution. [...]

1 Monica had bought her terraced cottage in Haydon Bridge in late 1961. The River Tyne flows alongside the back of the house.

20 April 1962

Norfolk Hotel, [Bournemouth]¹

Dearest,

The place is filling up now, reminding me of *Brighton Rock* as much as anything. Mr Colleoni² sat next to us & sent his salmon back at dinner. I don't blame him if it is anything like the salmon I had for lunch. In fact the food is pretty moderate, & in addition to that pretty scarce. This doesn't bother *me*, but mother feels deprived.

There is also a character I call Aragon, who looks French & sits by himself reading books & the N. *Statesman* except when another Frenchman in a raincoat comes & seems to interview him. [...]

Between tea & dinner I went out into a kind of garden-cum-carpark, and to my astonishment found a small hutch *full of rabbits* behind some bushes. One huge white contemptuous doe: perhaps eight Peters & Benjamins who fled with exaggerated terror into the side-quarters at my approach, and soon reappeared, having forgotten why they were scared. I was astonished at finding them. I don't know what they are doing there. [...]

I'm pressing on with *Moby-Dick* (it appears to be hyphenated) – it's a kind of fishy Dickens, so far. I wonder how much of it is sublimated liking-to-talk-to-sailors, though. 'Oh, I do like to be be beside the quayside, I do like to meet chaps from the sea, I do like' – well, anyway: I can see plenty of good ways it might develop. [...]

After lunch today I nipped out to have a look at a 'Museum & Art Gallery' in the hope of finding a Brett[3] or two, and it turned out to be a really rather fascinating old private house, built just on a vantage point of East Cliff & commanding the bay, and full of all the junk of a Victorian-Edwardian lifetime of someone called Russell-Cotes – endless cases of stones and stuff, & Burmese & Japanese rooms, but a lot of worthless pictures of a kind I quite like (Sir Edwin Long in particular), and one or two far from worthless ones – Frith's 'Ramsgate Sands', a Millais, Landseers, a Rossetti (unusual one of That Girl stripped to the waist), an Etty or two, and Lawrence & Gainsborough in minor forms. [...]

1 On holiday in Bournemouth with his mother.
2 Character in Graham Greene's *Brighton Rock*.
3 *The Stonebreaker* by John Brett (1831–1902) was one of L.'s favourite paintings.

3 May 1962

32 Pearson Park, Hull

[...] I don't know that I have the energy to go over both sides of this sheet – I have temporarily given up the little smoking I did, & each night miss it so much I say, well, you can buy some tomorrow, but since it is in the evenings only I want them I forget till it's too late again. The 'Espinasses'[1] have both given up the lot of smoking they did, and are now aware of how frightful their house smells – are sending to London for potpourris. Ogh ogh ogh. Their doctor says cancer of the lung is better than cancer of the stomach. Their tobacconist's receipts have fallen dramatically. Social history.

Brett[2] had a Rochester hag in today called Rauschenbusch, who lectured on *Lear*. Did I say Brinnin[3] had asked me if I wanted to visit U. of Connecticut next spring? I've said no, though whether it's wise to go on being so negative I don't know. 'Nothing will come of nothing.' On the other hand, I just don't see myself lecturing there, do you, if I don't lecture here. It wd give me a nervous breakdown.

Have just broken off to make some Horlicks, the first for ages. Was delighted to see the 'two schools' (why are there always *two* schools?)

of poetry described in *T & T*[4] by some smart Alec-ess as 'beat' and 'bicycle-clip'. [...]

1 Paul 'Espinasse, Professor of Zoology, Hull.
2 R. A. Brett, Professor of English, Hull.
3 J. M. Brinnin, American poet, author of *Dylan Thomas in America*.
4 *Time and Tide*, weekly journal.

6 May 1962

32 Pearson Park, Hull

Dearest,

After all my searching for something that stood up & said your name (one handbag was labelled 'Monica' but I didn't think you'd like it) I didn't buy anything – at least I did, but it's a silly dull thing – you'll probably get it on Tuesday.[1] You'd some narrow escapes, though. I lingered over a tiny brooch-watch, enamelled, but thought it wouldn't survive burrow-life long. Then there was a watering-can, & a 'George II silver spoon'. It isn't till one really searches the shops that their paucity is laid bare. Or perhaps mine. A silver corkscrew & bottle opener might have been sensible – and I also turned over some Wedgwood candlesticks, but 'clutterin' yerself up' came to my mind. Anyway, if any of these things please you, do let me know. I did really *search*.

Well, spring comes with your birthday, and I love to think of you as somehow linked with the tender green shoots I see on all the trees and bushes [*drawing of rabbit*] – linked in one practical way, perhaps – but also by your ever-fresh love of the real stuff of life, the beauty and *comfort* of it. I wish I could be with you and we could plunge into bed – I wished it yesterday *very* much. Do you remember putting on your red belt & open-work stockings? I shall always remember *that*, a cataclysmic spiritual experience, like somebody's *Lear*. Ogh ogh ogh. You are really terrifically attractive, the sort of thing David Holbrook wd try to stop. Well, what a funny letter, watering-cans & open-work stockings, but my dear you know I'd like to kiss you all over and give you a good mauling   xxxx   P.

1 Monica's birthday present.

10 May 1962

32 Pearson Park, Hull

[...] I do think it sounds funny when you talk about the Terrible Sonnets[1] – there's quite a lot of them about, also Terrible Poetic Plays, Terrible Novels – the Terrible Novels of John Wain, for instance. I have been reading Statham's autobiography,[2] wch is much more fun. He says he never knows what his deliveries are going to do, so he knows the batsman can't know either: he just bowls at the off stump with the seam between first and second fingers. Odd, isn't it? Perhaps he is just kidding.

I had a surprising invitation yesterday, in wch I detect the hand, or paw, of Dr Pussy – *an invitation to the Mansion House* on June 6th, to the Lord Mayor's Midsummer Banquet! Isn't it strange? Wouldn't I love to find myself sitting opposite the fine-whiskered head, the vertical brow-markings, the alert ears! 'Very pleased to make your acquaintance ... George Grouse spoke of you ...' I expect I shall find myself sitting opposite David Holbrook, or Kingsley, or someone who will take all the thrill away from it. Or of course Sir Wm might be there. 'Left a pair of scissors, six swabs and a ticket for the Centre Court in the poor devil ogh ogh ogh waiter, some more of that brandy, no, not the surgical spirit you're giving the lower tables, the pale stuff by the Sheriff.' Oh dear, I'm sure it won't be as exciting as that. Still, it *is* exciting, in prospect.

I wonder what you have bought yourself! and fancy having a roast turkey. Jolly good, as Robertson would say. I don't regard the advent of 40 with much cheer, but there's nothing to be done. I feel very much with T.H. that I was 'a boy till 25, a young man till 40' – was it? It seems hard to be no longer young when one hasn't done many of the things young people are supposed to do. Anyway, I don't think I'd *mind* being no longer young if it didn't mean being nearer death. I dreamed last night that T. S. Eliot was dead. [...]

1 Description of some of Gerard Manley Hopkins's poems of despair.
2 Brian Statham, cricketer.

12 May 1962

32 Pearson Park, Hull

Dearest,

Very late – don't know what I do with my time; well, I do in a way: last evening I was out to a ghastly 'at home' in the country (took me 1¾ hrs to *get* there), tonight I went to the ponce's after shopping, & it was about 9 before I'd suppered. After each I fell asleep, then prodded at a poem[1] G.S.F.[2] wd no doubt regard as displaying a disagreeable *persona – pairsona*, he wd say. The ponce gave me £99 in used notes: a year's takings, or 50% of a year's takings.[3] This will pay for my clothes, almost. [...]

1 'Wild Oats', completed 12 May 1962.
2 G. S. Fraser.
3 L.'s share of the sales of *The Less Deceived*.

23 May 1962

32 Pearson Park, Hull

Dearest,

Feel a bit better tonight, less dowsed with utter fatigue, though I may have snoozed earlier. Have added about 2 lines to my long no-good poem[1] – I really think it could have been good if I had the talent of, say, Swinburne, put to my own ends. As it is, it is just dull, like a mixture of John Holloway and bad Dylan Thomas. [...]

I have finished Kennedy's election,[2] & am now concentrating on Stanley Spencer[3] – an odd little bloke, resigning from the RA when they turned a couple of his pictures down, and now he has just started this incredibly short sighted wife-wangling. But I like his adherence to the commonplace and near-at-hand, and even his less appealing qualities are better than those of sods like – like – Well, I don't know.

How pretty you looked on Sunday in your blue smock frock (funny word, like *Hausfrau*), or whatever you call it; ay, marry, and out of it (with a Pox) – it was a splendid meeting, day, encounter, & I hope you were as happy as I was. I had meant to say something about holidays, but never got round to it. What does the future matter when the present is so fine? I wish holidays didn't need so much arranging. It is all right taking them, but arranging is the devil.

I forgot to say that Stanley Spencer always put his clothes on over his pyjamas, not a bad dodge for (a) warmth and (b) saving time at both ends of the day. Also that Kennedy's desk in the White House is smaller than mine.

Thursday now, & a less agreeable evening – have crossed out all I wrote last night and more, cursing & bored and raging. I am no good, all washed up, can't even write a *bad* poem, let alone a good one. Thank you for your Worcestershire card this morning: I am sure you are *loving* the hamster, it sounds heavenly.[4] Where do you keep it when you are out? Is it in a box, or cage? Or do you find it in your slipper when you come in? What do you give it to eat? Do you think it misses the Craiks, or 'knows' you? [...]

I've finished Stanley Spencer: a fascinating book, do read it if you have a chance: perhaps I'll save it for ya. Although he was something of an ass in practical affairs, & wd have been hell to deal with, I find him very sympathetic with his genuine indifference to success and love of solitude & 'low' things like weeds and kitchen chairs. I never realised he went to China once! It had no effect on him. He wrote that after a session at Cliveden with Lord Astor, saying 'Yes yes, very interesting, yes' he was relieved to get back home where all his selves could reemerge 'like children let out of school'. Don't I know it! Don't you! 'Oh! What a *good* idea!' Band of elastic. [...]

– Rushed out to the kitchen to retrieve my white tie, boiling for nearly 3 hours! Luckily the water hadn't boiled away, so I could rinse it and hang it up to dry. I last wore it on Queen Mother day – such bits of clothes must get a very exalted idea of one's daily life. Ideas of one's dancing-shoes, one's black mourning tie, one's swimming costume. Oh, curse this poem, I think I shall chuck it – I am no booldy good.

Friday Must get this in the post – dull day, bucked up by kind words in the *Spr*. Much love, darling. I kiss you from head to foot.

Philip

1 'Essential Beauty', completed 26 June 1962.
2 Possibly James MacGregor Burns's *John F. Kennedy: a Political Pro*file (1961).
3 Maurice Collis: *Stanley Spencer: a biography* (1962).
4 Monica was looking after the Craik family's pet hamster while they were on holiday (see *About Larkin*, No. 11, April 2001, for 'Presents from Monica' by Roger Craik).

6 August 1962

21 York Road, Loughborough, Leics.

[...] Isn't it a sad shock about Marilyn Monroe?[1] *The People* made her sound very dopey, but I was shocked all the same. *The Mirror* said her fan mail had shrunk from 8,000 to 80 a week! I'm sure Hollywood is a ghastly place to work in for anyone like her, everyone wanting to screw you and get a cut for doing it, nobody *really* helping you. Did you see, by the way, the story in *Time* about Cary Grant receiving a telegram from a paper asking 'HOW OLD CARY GRANT' to wch he replied 'OLD CARY GRANT FINE HOW YOU'? Ogh ogh. How old Wm Gull. How old Dr Pussy.

I am reading my 'home' books, like S. Sassoon, Saki, & J.C. Powys' *Autobiography*: also had a shot at G. Eliot's *Scenes from clerical life*, but got bogged down in 'Mr Gilfil'. I see the TLS review of Barnes was like mine in criticising the scholarship & production of the edition – they'll think I cribbed it. *The Listener* will sit on my review till September ('Autumn Books') by wch time it will be thoroughly *vieux jeu*.[2] [...]

I can't say I feel on top of the world here – Mother's friends all seem to have just died, or had a stroke, or a fall, or been widowed, or be having 'deep ray' treatment, or in the mental hospital – no reason why they shouldn't, in the driving rain of time that will bring us all down in the end. A few more years shall roll. Still, it is a sad atmosphere – don't know what I should do if it weren't for *The Archers* & other forms of unreality. [...]

1 Died 5 August 1962.
2 The *Listener* published L.'s review of *William Barnes: Poems*, ed. Bernard Jones on 16 August 1962. It is reprinted in *Required Writing*.

12 August 1962

21 York Road, Loughborough, Leics.

Dearest Bun,
Just a few words before bed – I don't know how it is, but I seem to have very little time here – it's all eating or washing up. I must say that after a week of it I begin to feel for my father in his retirement – it is a

dreadful life. I remember him holding up some implement or other at the sink and saying 'That's the third time today I've washed this!' And it was, and I expect I've washed it three times a day myself, 15 years later. I wondered what he would have thought, to see me washing the same old colander, the same old saucepans, the same old cooking knives and forks – laughed, I should think. You may say there's nothing very awful about all this, but all the same I think there is – I *feel* it as awful, anyway.

Home is a sad place, anyway: I find so much from the last 20 years, and before: your letters, other letters, back to the telegrams about my Schools results, letters about *A Girl in Winter*, school magazines – I feel I've done nothing with that fat fillet-steak part of life, 20 to 40, and now it's gone. And I haven't done anything with it because I'm too spiritless and cowardly and talentless. People live a lifetime a year compared with me.

We went to church tonight, wch was all right in a way – 'the passion-less Sundays after Trinity'. (What a lovely poem that is! The only good one in the book, I'm thankful to say, since the book is ungettable.)[1] A sermon on 'Beware false prophets', but a dull one. I thought he was going to start on Bertrand Russell, or the Dean of C.[2] [...]

Tuesday Last day here – feel consumed with boredom and irritation. There is an Irish-Polish family moved in next door, with several tod-dling children who take it in turns to maul the kitten. Every time I look out of the window I see one of them pulling it about – I would forbid all pets by law, & all pet shops: licensed suppliers of torture-material. Why doesn't it scratch their stupid little eyes out.

Oh dear, I really haven't time to finish this, if I'm to get it off this morning – I think my life at Hull is almost totally *unreal* – playthings like telephones and committees, & of course I live alone – so any prolonged contact with things & people such as only home provides sends me into a frenzy of irritation. It was always so, especially when I lived at home – I was really only happy either out of it or in a dream world of cigarette cards, i.e. poetry. Of course, one may have to *stick* it, but should one *embrace* it? I don't think other people embrace what they hate. [...]

1 'The book' was John Meade Falkner's *Poems*, published posthumously (*c.*1933) and hard to find. Falkner (1858–1932) also published novels, including *Moonfleet*.
2 The Dean of Canterbury, Hewlett Johnson, known as the Red Dean.

29 September 1962

32 Pearson Park, Hull

[...] I wish you could see yourself in the centre of my mantelpiece, standing by the hydrangeas dressed for Bunny United, in your delinquent stockings and shoes, a handbag hanging from your hand. It has come up quite nicely. You look like a poster for an X film, but basically innocent all the same. I have put you-in-the-water into my album.

Well, of course, I do understand and agree with what you say, when you say how we are wasting our lives.[1] When I say I wish we could talk more easily about ourselves, I mean just that; I mean it seems strange not to, and I think it's something of a barrier between us, or a failure between us – it's difficult to know precisely what I mean: I don't say I want to bore you with my feelings, or be bored, so to speak, by yours, but I have a curious feeling that in some ways we are not in sympathy & this keeps us off any kind of discussion that might reveal the fact. I have the continual feeling that you either know me too well or don't know me enough. Again, I suspect my own motives in 'talking': some holidays I have felt as they ended that I *must* get closer to you, that it was absurd, almost wrong, to be like this, but this time I felt it was that I simply wanted to get rid of my guilt feelings to enable me to carry on in the way I felt guilty about, which isn't fair. Anyway, I feel you shrink from such talk, as from hens – indeed, I do myself unless I can feel a sympathy in you to encourage me. But then what is the point of talking if there isn't anything you particularly want to say, or feel you can say? – by you, I mean either of us, of course.

I can't say how badly I feel about the way we are wasting our lives: it terrifies me, and gets worse every day. [...]

Sunday High wind during the night – woke me up, rather frightened. Today the Park is strewn with brown leaves. I see *The Obs.* hasn't printed my poem,[2] nor have they said anything about it – it's not a particularly good poem, I suppose, but I am fond of it. Doubt if it will please El Al,[3] who I understand does the picking, though. On the other hand the *S.T.* gives *Triple Time* a run – didn't they include it before, years ago? Quite a nice poem – 'the thought's good.' Expression less good.

My dear, I don't think you are incompetent, or whatever you said you were in your letter: I think you are very good at knowing what should be done, very good at not being afraid of doing it, and pretty good at doing it. Big things, I mean. In little day to day things I don't know – you seem to *drag* rather, represented by your unwillingness to have the right time anywhere about, but I do realise – fully, really & truly – and lovingly and sympathetically – that you have, at Leicester anyway, *too much to do*. I understand, in a way, about not wanting people despite being lonely, but of course I behave badly about people. While I was writing this page Binns[4] rang up, compelling me to dinner on Thursday – now, earlier in the morning I was thinking how I had put the Binnses off, at last, by seven years of non-return of invitations, despite some open hints on their side. Seems I haven't, quite. And I do think you dislike people more than I do, not that I like them enough to have them in the house, ogh ogh ogh.

After lunch, & getting on for post-time. I don't seem to have said much. Of course I am grateful for your openness and assurances about Bill,[5] but if you feel like that, the way you said at first, then it's my fault rather than yours and I shouldn't have any legitimate grumble, though plenty of illegitimate ones, probably. It gives me a queer disagreeable feeling to think of you with someone else: I don't know how I shd feel if instead of Bill it was a 40 yr old professor with a sports car – well, I *do* know how I shd feel, the question is how strongly I should feel it. I am not, for the record, feeling attracted by Maeve again. [...]

1 In a letter from Haydon Bridge dated 26/27 September 1962, Monica had written: 'You know how you are often trying to talk to me about us, & I always start to cry so you can't; I wish I didn't, but it just makes me cry to think of it, so I try not to think of it – all the same, I'm sorry, because I think you ought to be able to say something without tears from me, & indeed I wish I could talk about it without tears. Nevertheless I do think abt it sometimes, and today is a day that has made me think of it – the summer going, unused, the beauty of the scenery, unused. It made me very conscious of what a short time we are here for, & how little of that time we have left, you & I; it isn't much, and for all we know it might be very short, & I wish I could spend what is left with you, or more of what is left than I do spend. I can write this, just, but I'm sure I couldn't say it – I am not in tears, but tears are behind my eyes, making eyes & head ache. If once I start thinking of reality, *all* the sad things lock to mind at once, & all the impossible difficulty of life, the way I just scrape along, never, never being in control of the situation, never doing anything properly, & I can hardly bear it. I live so foolishly, too; wasting hours in lazy inertia, doing *nothing*, or thinking sadly & pointlessly, always worried abt things undone & my inability to get on with them; and I do rely on drink more than I like, I really have to have my tipple, now, & *sometimes* I drink a lot, tho' not, I think, as badly now as I did just after my parents died.'

304

2 'Send No Money'.
3 A. Alvarez, at the time poetry editor of and reviewer for the *Observer*.
4 A. L. Binns, Lecturer in English at Hull: see Appendix B.
5 Bill Ruddick: see Appendix B.

4 October 1962

32 Pearson Park, Hull

Dearest,

You must think me awful, as if I deliberately set out to upset you – I'm so sorry: it isn't that.[1] I am *always* oppressed by guilt-feelings about the mess I have got you in, and my own behaviour seems so bad anyway that almost anything else wd seem better, in the way of behaviour I mean.

I got your letter only this evening, & now I have to change & go to loony Binns right off – I'd sooner write to you. Oh, how tired term makes me! It was lovely talking to you last night, & made me feel happier. [...]

You know, I expect you do want to be reassured, but I always fall into the habit of thinking you are more assured than I am: you have such a strong, seamless character – not vague, shifting and gullible like mine – and you have a – really, I wd swear it – stronger personality than mine: you aren't given to bursts of temper or vindictiveness but are much more level and firm than I. For this reason I am always feeling I deserve a denunciation from you – I always feel morally inferior, not only relatively in the way I have behaved but absolutely in comparing ourselves. And of course I do feel terrible about our being 40 & unmarried. I fear we are to turn slowly into living reproaches of the way I have dallied and lingered with you, neither one thing or the other. This leads me to spells of wanting to explain & defend myself, wch appears like brutal & gratuitous attack to you, but wch are really products of miserable self accusation – I feel like Murry, always my *bête noire*, without your being KM. And then again I hope if only we could achieve, I don't know, a kind of *self-encouraging intimacy*, it wd be so easy for us to marry. But this may be a fancy on my part – people *are* different, after all. [...]

1 Monica had written in a letter dated 1 October 1962 from Haydon Bridge: 'I wish I were better – I'd *like* to be able to talk more. I think I could have, when we began, perhaps; but I never know what you are thinking, and thinking of

me – & you must admit, with some reason, you *have* been attracted to various people & haven't told me. I don't think I'm *too* much to be blamed for being so tiresome – I do not behave reasonably, I know, & I wish I did; but it is not an *easy* situation, as you know & wish to say, I suppose, & I think it can be understood that I am very easily upset abt it [...] Anyway, I accept, don't I, & *without* private reservation or grudge, that you don't like me enough to marry me; then it seems rather unkind for you to want to *tell* me so, & perhaps tell me all the things that are wrong with me.'

7 October 1962

32 Pearson Park, Hull

[...] No poem by me in *The Observer*, but the Hoggart one in *The Spectator*.[1] On reflection I find it gets into a long skid towards the end, but the last line seems to me to 'stand', as Vernon Watkins would say. J.C. Powys 90 tomorrow! Dear old chap! Think of him burning 'Pray for the soul of John Cowper Powys' on the beam of his room in Corpus in about 1890! And living on weak tea and Woodbines in Wales! He never *worked* ...

1 'Essential Beauty', *Spectator*, 5 October 1962.

23 October 1962

32 Pearson Park, Hull

Dearest rabbit,

The nights are fairly dark now, aren't they! I am home in the dark, clutching my bottle of gin and my lemon. After drink, supper, & a bemused gassed doze I sit up and try to improve, or make less bad, my two current poems, *Toads Revisited* and *Sunny Prestatyn*, about the poster we saw at Tweedmouth. Neither is very good, or very elevating.

I did go out on Sunday, & for the brief time I was free of cars and motorbikes enjoyed myself a lot. The cottage gardens are all purple and red & gold, & the hedges full of hips & haws & elderberries, & now and again a pale pink wild rose. I stopped at Wawne & poked about in the churchyard, turning up chestnuts in the grass, & noting George Beulah, who had outlived two wives before dying in 1909. All three have identical tall stones. When I was there, a woman called that if I was going into the church, wd I be careful to shut the door, as the heating was on. I hadn't really intended to, but thought I would, as the heating was on! I was glad I did, because it was all decorated for Harvest Home! Really *very* thrilling, & funny, the lines of cabbages and cauliflowers, piles of tomatoes in little stone niches, a box of dates (!) on the harmonium, celery up the aisle, chrysanthemums everywhere, a big sheaf of corn, then on the table a bunch of black grapes, a pot of honey (homemade), and a loaf, specially baked I should say. I don't think I have seen a church so decorated for years, and the shock of it was tremendous – of course I thought of you, although rabbits would be unlikely to take part in such a ceremony, or at least not in the way intended. You *would* have liked it. I left them a pound, and shut the door carefully – all *I* harvest is money, but they were welcome to some of that. [. . .]

4 November 1962

32 Pearson Park, Hull

Dearest bun,

The time when I shall be able to write you long Paston-like letters seems as far off as ever. 'Yisterday Wm Turnip carter dyd pay iiij pence rent. Ij ewes fownd in long Meddow, sore afrayd, I doe thynk Lord Bullman's maftiff bee at fault' and so on. 'Bd of ye Faculty of Social Studies hath denownc'd Mee. Ye Father of Lies bee with yew & yr children – bastards, rather say I. Lord Brynmor-Jones home from foren parts – v. affable. Ye Treas^urer My Lord Leslie Downes hath denounc'd Peter Cocke, Architect, for gross mifspending on ye Pallas of Physicke – Bee allways in my Memmory ye Great Architect from wh^m Grace & Bownty flow Amen.' [. . .]

13 November 1962

32 Pearson Park, Hull

Dearest,

Having somewhat recovered from a trodden-worm feeling, I have had to spend the evening planning my jazz recital (Thursday lunchtime) about Pee Wee Russell, who now seems to me devoid of ability. Funnily enough, I walked up the road with a girl student who was saying that she enjoyed the previous one. When we reached the Arts Block the following conversation took place:

Me: 'Would you mind telling me your name?'

Her: 'Sugar.'

Me: '?'

Her: 'Serena Sugar.'

It's true, I looked her up when I got in. [...]

Well, dear, I got back in good order, rather trodden-worm, and lasted out the day. I hope you managed to get another little snooze after I went. How you'd enjoy diving back into your bed! and stretching out! I thought it was rather romantic, being seen off, you trailing in your nightgown. You wd have looked well with a candle. It was a nice visit. [...]

Wednesday. Late – back from Angus Wilson,[1] sherry, dinner, lecture & pub. Sat next to a girl at dinner who lived between Penzance & Land's End & just longed for Hull! Corstopitum. A. Wilson a small bunchy little man, looking every minute of his 60 years (he is 49), full of *energy* (the ineluctable quality), & full also of the kind of crappy theorising about novels I seem to remember your reporting from Charlie Snow. Attacked the idea that England/country good, abroad/towns bad he professed to find in novels from J. Austen up to Alan Sillitoe[2] (must admit it had changed a bit by then – Waugh wd be a better example). Great desire to 'talk to students'. Ogh ogh ogh. He said he was trying to turn *Totentanz*[3] into a musical. Cor! Coaargh! Cuh! He asked me to go & see him in Cambridge, in rather a nice way too. I asked if it hadn't occurred to him that what people had said since J. Austen might be true. That shook him, though perhaps only because he couldn't think of a *polite* answer. He said *The Queen* was full of pictures of balls. He is more like Harry Hoff[4] than anyone else I have ever met. So there you are! I have a good mind to turn queer, & cable the decision to my parents. [...]

Thursday. I ought to be out at a lecture tonight, but aren't. There's a limit to what flesh & blood can bear. I may have to go to another one tomorrow! Hell! My own recital went off, I can't say well, but anyway it's over now. I feel rather trodden-worm again. [...]

It's rather cold here, though dry enough for the time being. The moon has been enormous about 6 p.m., like a huge low luminous saucer. I think I shall add another blanket to the bed.

Cox is planning a *Critical Quarterly cruise* – the mediterranean, like the classical boys, Cyprus & Capri here we come, seeking the civilisation of rain-washed bum. Think of being shut up with that crowd for 14 days! 'How wonderful!' [...]

Friday. Jolly cold – freezing. I hope you are keeping astride your toad, and haven't been wondering why I haven't let you know whether I got back Got back, got back! Well, I did, but as you see I have had the chance to scribble only occasionally. Thank you for all your cooking & kindness – you wd like to get into your bed again. It was kind of you to give it up.

Love xxx
P.

1 The novelist was giving a talk at Hull University.
2 Alan Sillitoe, novelist and short-story writer, at this time best known for *Saturday Night and Sunday Morning* (1958) and *The Loneliness of the Long Distance Runner* (1959).
3 Short story by Wilson.
4 Real name of the novelist William Cooper.

18 November 1962

32 Pearson Park, Hull

[...] Your account of Sutherland[1] makes me feel like Huggins or whoever it was in *Off the Map*, with S. as Kenny:[2] 'I got to hear what this bloke's saying, see' – you know. I thought he himself seemed nice, though clearly not one to put his goods in the window – not willing or not able. This reminds me of Angus Wilson, who as I said was nice, in a Hoffish way ('how *can* he be?'), but a colossal fool, as Baudelaire put it ('Not only a colossal fool, but demoniacally possessed' – he was speaking of George Sand) – Wm Golding the *only* living novelist (is he homo? I didn't know), & the like. [...]

You must look a wonderful sight in fur hat & boots – nothing else? Holding a rawhide whip? (You see how naturally my imagination composes aesthetic *montages* for you.) I'm sure Miss Richardson retires like ye moon when ye Sunne doth appear. I don't remember you being drunk especially, but we do drink rather a lot – I know I urge it, but it leaves me feeling slightly ashamed afterwards: progressive decline in self-criticism. And a bit liverish into the bargain. [...]

1 Monica had written in a letter dated 15 November 1962: 'Sutherland was, according to Bill, utterly thrilled by meeting you: he went off saying he was going to re-read all the poems at once, in order to have them and "the man" close in his mind.' John Sutherland was a student of Monica's at Leicester.
2 Kennie Huggett, in Angus Wilson's *A Bit off the Map* (1957).

22 November 1962

32 Pearson Park, Hull

[...] *Wednesday* Just looked through my poem again, and made a few alterations for the better, though possibly not for the best.[1] 'The toad work' is a nice personification. It's in a different metre from *Toads*, slightly – AA/BB/ instead of ABA/B/ – I use the '/' sign to indicate dissonance, or half-assonance as Peter de Vries calls it. [...]

1 'Toads Revisited' completed.

26 November 1962

32 Pearson Park, Hull

[...] I felt deprived of you, & the love making that hadn't really been concluded. I was a fool to bring those pants – I can't think where to hide them. My cleaner will think I am robbing clothes lines.

Maeve apparently met the mother & sister of her ex chap in Boots' on Saturday, who told her he was 'looking for a house' & wd get married as soon as he'd found one. They dislike his new girl, according to Maeve, but he doesn't. She rides a motorbike & is seeming v. bossy & a super-woman. This has depressed Maeve who felt that after 5 years 'things wd come right again.' Seems they won't. I mean they knew each other 5 yrs.

Do you think Dawn[1] is going to have a baby?

Must bend my mind to jazz now. Ted Hughes tomorrah. Sodom & Gomorragh. Compulsory poetry-reading. Ugh. Goodbye for the moment, dear – I loved seeing you. I hope you'll come here. Ogh. *Awgh*. Philip. [...]

1 In *The Archers*.

6 December 1962

32 Pearson Park, Hull

Dearest bun,

I have sat listening to the broadcast of Britten's *War Requiem*[1] after supper – for the sake of Owen, not old B.B. It hasn't seemed to me any good at all, but I thought I would listen. Old B.B. has good literary taste seemingly, though I still await The Roasting Music from *Tom Brown's Schooldays*. I feel in a squashy emotional mood, much upset by Owen & all he denotes, or nearly all. If only it were someone else, not Britten! Elgar, for instance. It wd be unbearable.

We haven't had much fog today. I am glad you aren't in London, it sounds so dangerous. Is your flat warm enough? I expect you are sitting in your bedroom. The winter is wretched.[2] I get few imaginings of frozen ponds, low red suns, bright lights down long passages; I have a sense of melancholy isolation, life rapidly vanishing, all the usual things. It's very strange how often strong feelings don't seem to carry any message of action.

I have put on the Enigma, now Britten is over. How often Owen evokes 'dark' and 'red', dusk and crimson, like dreadful sunsets on winter afternoons in 1916 & 1917. [...]

1 The premiere of Britten's *War Requiem* was in Coventry Cathedral, 30 May 1962.
2 The winter of 1962–3 was the worst for many years.

Poultry.
E.C.1.

Christmas Eve 1962

My dear Miss Jones,

I fear you will think I
have forgotten you this year! But
so few "cards" have proper reference
to the Festival we are about to
celebrate that I decided to send
my good wishes in the old way.

It is very ~~and~~ quiet
and cold here: I attended
Evensong but shall not go to
the Midnight Service — many
I fear make attendance at it
an excuse for sloth on Christmas
Morning! which I deplore. Sir

Lionel will be there, I believe.

Christmas Day is very busy for me as I shall be at the Orphanage as usual. They are very kind and make me very welcome.

On Boxing Day of course I "go north" — further north even than you!

I was at the Club the other night and met some of our friends. I do not think Sir Tom will stay in England long as he finds living very expensive. Sir George advised him to return to S. America. Sir William spoke of what he felt to be unavoidable expenses, connected with his profession as surgeon — or physician perhaps. We all spoke of you + send our good wishes.

As my Uncle Simpkin used to say, one feels talkative on Christmas Eve! but I must end. Yours very sincerely, G. F. Pussy.

26 December 1962

21 York Road, Loughborough, Leics.

Dearest bun,

Well, though I don't doubt I shall speak to you before your eyes light on these pages, I must say thank you for the handsome box of forks – wch I might very well have guessed, but wch in the end came as a complete surprise. I don't know what I expected! They are a beautiful luxury – I shall dispense with my awful poorhouse ones now. Or I could pass them on to the Hartleys, whose forks are almost as bad again. I was amused by their freedom from any hint of the Scandinavian! Perhaps they might have been even better without the slight decoration they have, but the shape of the handle is a delight.

Thank you too for your nice cards, I also had a card from Dr Pussy, depicting a shooting scene, and there was another one from some anonymous friends – anonymous friends with long ears and vurry Bellies, I reckon. Your card of old style greetings was extremely stylish – a Karin Press card, like those I found in Heal's, and designed by Robin Jacques, Patsy's pal. Well, he can design a Christmas card all right, I'll say that for him.

I suppose I can look back on Christmas day without rancour by now, but it *is* a trying time and no error. All went reasonably well until tea as you can imagine – except that I did the entire washing-up, saucepans and all – but from then on it was a question of down, gorge, & to some extent down, spleen. My lady sister, spurred on by my hints of expectation of supper, produced *the left-overs from tea* about nine. No coffee of course. The glass-dish was up to standard – it seemed to incorporate cubes of sponge bathmat at a lower stratum. Rosemary was interrupting and correcting everyone, and (at the age of nearly 16) insisting on her usual childish games. Honestly I don't think I did anything I wanted ALL DAY except go to the lavatory. Their presents to us were miserable, average cost 10/3d. Mine were opulent, average cost 27/-. I gave Walter[1] *Life At The Top*,[2] hoping to annoy Kitty by giving them *a book* to keep, and a *novel*, and *not a very good one* – ogh ogh ogh. Anyway, he seemed to like it. I like Walter.

Life has otherwise been much as usual, made ghastly by the *medieval* cold – honestly, I believe it is worse than *nineteenth-century* cold: the fire is all very well, but there needs solid accompaniment of two-bar heaters – and there's only one, awwrrghgh! only one. My bedroom is like a refrigerator. Mother's electric blanket broke, & I have 'mended' it, so she may be practising suttee involuntarily before long. I get the coal in, damn & blast it. Today I went a walk in the snow. A young chap tried to give me a lift, but I declined, on the grounds that I was walking for exercise, at wch he broke into great guffaws of laughter: 'Lovely! Jolly good!', slamming into gear, quite pleasantly though.

Loughborough seems *good* after Hull: on Christmas Eve there was a Stilton in the bar at the Kings Head, at lunchtime, for all comers. I met Rex there on the Sunday night – he had kindly come in, though he wasn't well, nor was Liz who hadn't come – and we were the oldest people in the packed bar by a long way: but all well dressed and well-behaved. Youth! Why didn't I have one? I've always been aged about 65.

Mother asks me particularly to send thanks to you for your pretty card – holly & the ivy. I think she sent you one.

Judy has had an article turned down by *History Today*. Bridget says half the girls at Benenden are doing bust-reducing exercises, and the other half bust-enlarging ones.[3] That seems terribly symbolic of life, really, doesn't it? There is no news of going to Mo – I suspect this is on the way out, like Max in the Archers. This is a short self centred letter – see you soon. Love dear xxx Philip

1 Walter Hewett, Kitty's husband.
2 John Braine, *Life at the Top* (1962).
3 Judy Egerton and her daughter Bridget, who was at the independent girls' school Benenden. Mo was an American friend.

13 January 1963

32 Pearson Park, Hull

[...] I have been reading some of Butler's[1] letters to & from his father – I must say Butler sounds an ass when young. His only clear idea is not wanting to work. Pity Majorca hadn't been discovered then. He'll do anything but work – go to Canada, join the Army, go to N. Zealand: the funny thing is that he *did* do the latter, & *did* work, and made a success of it as far as one can tell. But since he lost all the money he made by being an ass it wasn't much use. You remember it was in N.Z.

that he made a practice of doing the forks last when washing up, on the grounds that he might die before he got to them. This is very much his principle of 'eating the grapes downwards', so that however many grapes you have eaten the next is always the best of the remainder. [...]

1 Samuel Butler: *The Family Letters 1841–86* (1962).

17 January 1963

32 Pearson Park, Hull

[...] John Wain has sent Cox some of his 'Niagara of verse'[1] – it is pretty bad; poor old John; Cox is going to shoot it back to him. It's Pound & what we will by courtesy call water: all about *Henry Ford* and *Stalin*, God help us. [...]

1 These were parts of what eventually became Wain's *Wildtrack* (1965) – as the blurb described it, a 'long, wide-ranging single work'.

19 January 1963

32 Pearson Park, Hull

[...] Last night I tried some *In Memoriam*, but wasn't much pleased. I wanted to like it, but time and again some point of *language* broke my attention – there is a certain lack of reality about his choice of words – he will suddenly talk about harps when he means writing – and the *colours* are bad – whenever he mentions a colour it is like a seed packet. And the whole thing is pretty out of proportion anyway. Funny fellow, Tennyson. Must try the *Rubaiyyat* next – that at least is *sense*. Compare

That God, which ever lives and loves,
    One God, one law, one element,
    And one far off divine event
To which the whole creation moves

with

    Ah, make the most of what we yet may spend,
Before we too into the Dust descend;
    Dust unto dust, and under Dust to lie,
Sans Wine, sans Song, sans Singer, and – sans End!

316

Still, the second wouldn't have kept the mills turning or dividends up. Philip Larkin: The Marxian approach to the Muse. 8 p.m. All are welcome. (Entrance in King's Road.)

I feel full of poetry myself, except when I sit down with pencil and paper. Am currently doing one[1] from the death of my mother's friend before Christmas. [...]

1 'Long Last', in 1988 *Collected Poems*.

10 March 1963

32 Pearson Park, Hull

[...] I had time only to scribble you a note on Thursday, was it, before going to London – my spirits didn't greatly improve there: what an old bore Bob is, with his girls & unretouched nudes and threadbare verbal jokes. And squalor! His flat seemed particularly bad this time. I hardly slept at all, not for that reason. I won't bore you with what I did – lunch with Romantic Mitchell,[1] meeting, no Pullman, home by *eleven*, slack sodding railways, Leeds on Saturday, lunch, AGM of some lousy librarians & a talk of stupifying dullness on renaissance Basel. Home & got drunk, or half drunk, alone in the flat. Heard little of interest, except that Mitchell contemplates leaving the *D.T.* – awgh! awgh! I give myself 7 days after he goes – and that S. Plath gassed herself. She had had a mental breakdown once before, & is supposed to have feared another, while, as far as I can see, making certain of it. Ted had cleared off, not enjoying the symptoms. [...]

I still feel pretty depressed, I must say. Every now & then I open the little trap door in my head & look in to see if the hideous roaring panic & misery has died down. It hasn't, & I don't see why it should – I mean, the only change in my life wd be to have something to be miserable about.

Thwaite showed me his proofs[2] – he seems better than me now, at least in my way. Not that I'm miserable about that. [...]

1 Donald Mitchell, music critic and musicologist.
2 Of *The Owl in the Tree* (Oxford University Press, 1963).

9 May 1963

32 Pearson Park, Hull

Dearest bun,

Just hearing the wild ravings & quarrellings of Bob, Fraser & Goacher about Pound on the Third.[1] What a clamour! What larks! I didn't get in at the start, but I don't think it would have been any clearer if I had. Are you listening? Quite good fun, so I hope you are. Nobody criticises E.P. for being literary, wch to me is the foundation of his feebleness, thinking that poetry is made out of poetry & not out of being alive. Bob was very funny in a letter recently, quoting Tom Scott[2] in a recent issue of *Poetry*, saying to USA 'Tak' awa yer Polaris, an' gie us *Poetry*.'

I went up to London on Monday, back on Tuesday, and had the worst of nights at that hotel in a room folded lovingly round the lift. Slept c. 4.15 a.m. – 6.25 a.m. – *and that's all*. Felt I would never stay another night in London again if I could possibly help it. Gave Bob & his new girl dinner. She is not really as nice as Linda, though *born on the same day*. This gives point to my proverb 'I grow old, but the girl in Bob Conquest's bed is always the same age.' Linda married someone she had known for 3 days. According to Bob, he is five foot high & everybody hates him. Later he revised this verdict, saying he was three feet high. [...]

If you see a thing called *The New Horizon Concise Encyclopaedia of World Literature*,[3] look at the nice picture of me in it. Compared with Kingsley, anyway. [...]

1 BBC Third Programme discussion on Ezra Pound between Robert Conquest, G. S. Fraser and Denis Goacher, actor and a former 'secretary' of Pound's.
2 Tom Scott, Scottish poet, advocate of 'Lallans'.
3 Ed. Geoffrey Grigson (1963), plate 71, p. 227.

13 June 1963

32 Pearson Park, Hull

[...] It's duller today, and cooler: a kind of fine rain-mist blowing. The chestnut candles are dying, and the huge trees shift in the dusk. For once this has been a fairly empty week, but I haven't felt any inclination to write poetry. As a matter of fact I sent off my collection to Faber's on Tuesday. Provisionally called *The Whitsun Weddings* (TWW) it comprised 33 poems. Some are *very thin*, in fact I might knock out 2 even now. It's a poor harvest for 9 years, in fact I think it's definitely *worse* than the L.D. It has nothing like *If, My Darling* or *Maiden name*, poems that give the impression of *having plenty in hand*. The poetic quality is diluted. Too many depend on mere sentiment. It's all very depressing. But then, what isn't? [...]

31 August 1963

32 Pearson Park, Hull

Dearest bun,

It's nearly 10 – evening eaten away by bath, supper, washing up, bedmaking, tidying. I was at the Hartleys till 5.30 after shopping – I try to keep in touch with them. They hadn't any real news, except showing me a satiric exchange at the end of the August *The Review* between 'John Strain' & 'B.F. Razor'¹ – not unfunny but a bit cruel. All about John's poem *Wildhack*² & longing for recognition, & not getting it except from 'Pox & Bison'.³ 'Razor' kept saying 'I'll stake my critical reputation on it', with obvious implications. Poor John. I gather he had done a rather silly & vainglorious broadcast about it.

Still, I may be next: I sent off *Jill* today. The introduction is mostly *Lions & Shadows*⁴ stuff about Norman, Kingsley & Bruce. God knows what they'll think – I've cut out Norman's surname,⁵ but in a way this seems to make it worse. Wain & A. Ross have been dragged in by the scruffs. I don't know how it will read. It was really designed to counter the gloomy atmosphere of the novel. I used a number of your corrections (some had been noticed, but not many),⁶ and laughed at Eddie wearing a tweed cup, which I'd never noticed, also the game of darts with the pies. I felt unable to do anything about Crouch or the dialect, though I agree they sound wrong, C. in particular. The fact is, I know nothing about even schoolmasters. Some points I had deleted – including the rabbits! but I put them back for your sake. I left *MND*, & the talcum powder, not wanting EMF in my pages – anyway, it's out of character for John to read anything modern or readable, not that you'd agree there, wd you? I was surprised at your eye for grammar &

construction – I cd read these things a hundred times & not see they are wrong, but as soon as you point it out I see it. Perhaps a *bit* of the awkwardness you object to is my *style*. Leave it alone, now. [...]

Thwaite has sent me a complete Owen to do, plus a remark that *Send No Money* is the best poem since *Kubla Khan*. I hope to do an impassioned oration on the text 'Above all, I am not concerned with poetry.'[7] Isn't that a marvellous thing to say, beside TSE & Ez & WBY? Then Karl M.[8] rang up, seeking to heal the breach with a complete Eliot, wch (he said) had new poems in. On cross examination he reduced this to 'poems he hadn't seen before' – poems like *Little Gidding*, perhaps, or *Ash Wednesday*. Said yes to O, no to E. [...]

I wonder if you think the title will do. I feel I'm getting a bit old for *The Way Things Go* or – well, what? I want to put that poem in the shop window, as it were. Give my thanks to Sutherland for his support. Dig that ass Silkin in *Stand*, going on about *Church Going*. People don't understand poems, do they? And dig Empson's dig at G.S.F. in the latest *The Review* (Empson Number).

So much for my craft and sullen art. As for my profession, I feel like Pearl White tied to the railway line of dinner with E. Sitwell on 28 June – can I fix up meeting with Sir L. Martin[9] in Cambridge & so escape it? All hangs in the balance. [...]

I am very sorry about your work. I can't imagine you are as bad as some of the zanies and layabouts we have here – I mean, you are bound to talk sense, even 'at that level', and have a sense of proportion. No more than you should I be capable of mugging up the criticism, but my aim wd be to tell them a nicely blended *story* of life & work about each man, rather à la Middleton Murry. As for Shakespeare, well, in the depths, on the heights – Christ! they don't know. You set the papers, anyway. I can see just how annoying the question-pinching is, by our wandering friend. And God, does *George*[10] read anything? You can't tell me he knows it arl. I'm sure you are a much better teacher than $\frac{3}{4}$s of the shower who haven't heard of the good stuff – look, I'm not flattering you: you may be an *incoherent* lecturer, I don't know, but you're incapable of being as bloody wet as *Cox*. *Cox* isn't clever & knows nothing, & hasn't any natural taste either. Think of Cox when you feel depressed. The great editor, laughing like a dog about to puke. The senior lecturer, thinking *Naturally* was 'hard on the Queen'. Don't you feel better already?

I bandy my new cigarette 'Profumos ... for the hell of a stink' at lunch these days. This replaces my other brand, 'Early Grave', where you saved coupons for shrouds, coffins, mortuary plots. Profumo coupons bring you Keiler's jam, ogh ogh ogh.[11] Actually, I'm rather sick of it all. [...]

1 *The Review*'s mocking versions of John Wain and G. S. Fraser.
2 i.e. *Wildtrack* (published 1965) by John Wain.
3 Similar jesting versions of C. B. Cox and A. E. Dyson, editors of the *Critical Quarterly*.
4 L. thought that his introduction to the reissued (by Faber) *Jill* was influenced by Christopher Isherwood's *Lions and Shadows: an Education in the Twenties* (1938), a lightly fictionalised memoir much admired by L.
5 Norman Iles, L.'s former tutorial mate at St John's in the early 1940s.
6 Monica had written, in a letter dated 29 August 1963, from Haydon Bridge: 'Dearest, I must be quick, because I want you to get the enclosed *Jill* stuff at once. I wanted to read through the 2nd half of the book again, because the clumsinesses seemed thicker in the 1st part & I wondered if I had grown negligent; but I hadn't, it is simply that once we *get* to Jill the writing becomes more confident; most of the 2nd $\frac{1}{2}$ are misprints or mis-proofreadings.' There follow nine pages of questionings, corrections and comments, products of a very close reading.
7 From Wilfred Owen's preface to his poems.
8 Karl Miller, at that time literary editor of the *New Statesman*, while Thwaite was literary editor of the *Listener*.
9 Sir Leslie Martin, architect of the new library, Hull University.
10 G. S. Fraser.
11 The John Profumo/Stephen Ward/Christine Keeler scandal was at its height. Ward committed suicide on 31 August.

16 October 1963

32 Pearson Park, Hull

[...] I've just finished reading *An Unsuitable Attachment*[1] – very much the mixture as before, except for a large cat called Faustine and a clergyman's wife who is besotted with it. Reminded me of you a bit! A rather watery 'nice' heroine called Ianthe, & an excursion to Rome (first foreign parts in her books, I think), and a girl called Penelope, described as 'a PreRaphaelite beatnik', who again reminded me of you in an intangible way. She is sexier than Ianthe, whom I got rather sick of, all this English gentlewoman crap, & sherry rather than gin & tonic, and 'good' furniture. Perhaps you are thinking you sound like a mixture of the two? Ogh ogh. I don't know why Cape should have refused it: perhaps it is just insufficiently original to compensate for the slightly-cloying flavour. Originality is being different from oneself, not others. [...]

Did I say that Fabers have *lost* TWW? Jolly good. Large efficient publishers. None of this Marvell Press touch. My God. [...]

1 By Barbara Pym. L. was reading the typescript, not published until 1982. See *Selected Letters* (1992).

28 November 1963

32 Pearson Park, Hull

[...] Senate dinner last night was woundy dull – 40 min. speech from some crap called Sir Christopher Cox, during wch I smoked a fat cigar, feeling like one of our friends (Brazilian cigars for Tom). Later the secretary of the Gull-benkian Foundation exchanged tired literary conversation & asked me to call on him ('... want someone to answer letters ... hate answerin' letters ... no screw, just three and a half thou. and exes, but there's a rather jolly little flat overlooking the Park' LIKE BOGRAY). Next to me was an ugly little man, supposedly Drama Critic of *The Guardian*. Very guarded. I asked him if he didn't think Agate was good & Tynan less good, & received evasive replies. [...]

Actually I was astounded by K's assassination[1] – I doubt if I experienced great personal *sorrow* – but this feeling was succeeded by *disgust*. I'd like to have seen the *D.Express* leader that said 'The shame of the Dallas police is now complete.' It sounds like the Wild West again, lynch law, crooked cops, everything we expect of *Russia*. As there were 3 Yanks present at the dinner BJ[2] made us stand in silence in memory of 'that excellent young man, John F. Kennedy', as if he were a student who'd got a research schol to Oxford. The Yank opposite me was a 'Professor of Television'. I don't think it was commies. I think it was *Georgia crackers*. [...]

1 J. F. Kennedy was assassinated on 22 November 1963.
2 Brynmor Jones.

10 February 1964

32 Pearson Park, Hull

My tongue is covered with curious yellow lichen

God, that foul cow is on the horn now twice a day – three times a sodding day.

Dearest,

Well, I am still at home – my cheerfulness of yesterday was followed by a feverish spell. Today I felt better, but stayed in: Betty came for an hour both morning & afternoon & I prepared papers for my higher-pay sub-committee tomorrow week. After she'd gone I had supper (does 'supper' derive from 'soup'? It ought to) & washed vest & pants, but this sent up my temperature & made me feel rotten. I don't know what I shall do tomorrow. With all this I have no *cold*. It must be some inner germ. The bloody B-H's[1] have contributed to the day with long horn & piano sessions afternoon *and* evening – sometimes they seem to play both simultaneously *and* bang doors. Splendid. I can't really grumble, because it's under my bedroom, but if I wanted to go to bed it would be fearful.

Your two letters – pm'd 7th & 9th – came this morning: how bad the GPO is, it just isn't worth trying to get anything delivered on Saturday, is it, for you clearly didn't get my note either. And as for where my book had been![2] – Anyway, I'm glad it turned up at last, though it's not bringing me a great deal of pleasure so far: I hated it *on sight*, as you can imagine. And now I am distressed about your reaction to *Broadcast*.[3] My excuse – or if it isn't an excuse, my answer – is, as you might expect, a complete forgetfulness: I didn't hesitate a moment about including it, because I didn't think it wd bother you, and it seemed good enough. My regrets and promises that you remember I had – have, even now – forgotten. About the only defence in this is that I didn't do it deliberately, but that doesn't go very far, I know. I just didn't think it still held any power to disturb you.

By the same post came an unexpected letter from Isobel, Ruth's cousin, saying that Ruth's husband had died about 3½ years ago, after less than a year of marriage: *that* made me think well of *Wild Oats*. I wouldn't have printed it if I hadn't believed she was all settled & happy. And a note from Bob, having had his copy, opines that apart from Ted H. & R. S. Thomas I've no equal ... I expect that's about it: one hurts other people & exposes oneself, & then gets told you aren't as good as R. S. Thomas.

I'm sure you're right about *liturgy*,[4] and now you mention it I believe you mentioned it on Sark, but I didn't take it in. *Litany sounds* nicer – a lighter word – but sense should take precedence, I suppose. The grammar mistakes alarm me: tell me the worst. 'Lambs like what learn to walk ...'

I wonder if you managed to go in today – I do hope you went only if you were well enough, or strong enough since I'm sure you wouldn't feel very well. You *have* had a bad spell of it – and it's self perpetuating, isn't it: you feel ill, so don't eat, then that makes you feel ill too.

Alun Jones, back from Rochester, says GS Fraser is already 'a legend' there. When pressed he said he was last heard of sitting on a grand piano (at a *party*, of course) playing pat-a-cake with a female student. Hence his failure as a correspondent, I suppose. Pat a what?

I see in 'Spanish for Beginners' at 6.40 tonight Antonio Lopez played 'Senor Alvarez'. 'Waiter, there are no moral values in this poem.' 'Tell me, please, how many times you have been confined in a mental hospital/ nursing home/psychiatric ward/straitjacket?'[5] 'The position has been struck by New Mexico.' And while on literary matters, what about Fanny Hill?[6] Can't say I care. One in the eye for Miss Laski,[7] whose *name* was bandied about in this connection *vulgarly* by a lunch-time comedian today. Backed a loser, what.

I'll leave this open, in case of any news tomorrow.

11 February No news, except that my temperature is still up and I feel worse than yesterday. That great big bouncing bloody bitch Mrs Burnett Hall is punishing the piano after playing with the poodle. *Sod* her. Have started reading *Little Dorrit*, dreary tack it is too. Shall I stop? Thwaite writes, saying he hates the jacket (not straitjacket) & is giving it to Betjeman for *The Listener*.[8] Bit *hard* for him – hope he doesn't do one of his slapdash pieces: 'Mr L's 1st book *A Sense of Movement*' Feel low, low, low.   Love xx P.

1 The Burnett-Halls, L.'s neighbours at 32 Pearson Park.
2 *The Whitsun Weddings*, 'lost' by Faber: see letter of 16 October.
3 *The Whitsun Weddings* was published 28 February 1964. L. had had advance copies and sent Monica one. Monica had first been upset when she read 'Broadcast' (clearly based on thoughts about Maeve Brennan) in the *Listener* (25 January 1962). On 7 February 1964 she wrote to L.: 'Well, I have sat and stared, absolutely incredulous that you have published *Broadcast* after all your crocodile-tears expressions of regret at its appearance before ... I suppose it's not so much the poem itself that I mind so much now, I *had* shed all the tears I'm going to shed about that, and I had, with difficulty, forgiven it, I mean its appearance and the way you never warned me of its appearance.'
4 When L. first published 'Water' (*Listen*, Vol. 2, Summer–Autumn 1957) the first line of stanza 3 was 'The litany would employ'. Evidently Monica pointed out the inaccuracy of this when they were on holiday on Sark; but the first edition of

The Whitsun Weddings carried the line 'My litany would employ'. On 7 February Monica wrote: ' "Litany" is too specific – how often is the Litany said, anyway? very seldom – "liturgy" *I am sure* is the word that ought to be there. I shd have said this before, you'll say, but I did not know what the book was to include, you were very cagey abt it so I stopped asking [...] I'm naturally not happy abt *Talking in Bed* because it will cause so much talking here, in & out of beds, & indeed elsewhere – what do you think yr Mother & relatives will make of it?' Later impressions of *TWW* and the *Collected Poems* have 'My liturgy would employ'.

5 Parodic versions of A. Alvarez's supposed critical responses.
6 John Cleland's erotic novel, published 1748–9.
7 Marghanita Laski: novelist, broadcaster, opinionated critic.
8 Betjeman reviewed *TWW* in the *Listener*, 19 March 1964.

18 February 1964

32 Pearson Park, Hull

Dearest,

Many thanks for your letter – I'm sorry I haven't sent one. I have 'no letter and no time to write letter'. This is just an interim note to say I am pretty fairly recovered, I think. I have Senate dinner tonight anyway, curse it. Snow is falling. Romantic Mitchell is coming.

B. Pym wrote acknowledging *T.W.W.* – she says *she* was a WRN[1] officer in Italy during the war! I thought there was something a bit plangent about that Rocky Napier[2] stuff.

Thank you for your young fifer that arrived on the right day but wch alas produced no results comparable to the card I sent you! Perhaps the Burnett-Halls are too gentlemanly to read other people's post-cards. Too busy blowing foggin' horns & banging doors, the *fools* and *swine*.

I'm sorry about *Broadcast*, and I'm sure my distress was real. I suppose I don't really equate poems with real-life as most people do – I mean they are true in a way, but very much dolled up & censored. Anyway, more later – must to work!!

Love
Philip

1 Women's Royal Naval (Service).
2 Character in Barbara Pym's novel *Excellent Women* (1952).

20 February 1964

32 Pearson Park, Hull

[...] This has been a tiring week. I have gone back & read a classic Gladys Mitchell or two – how good she is when she knows her background, as in *Laurels Are Poison*. I'm on *Death & the Maiden* now, and remembering our freezing time in Winchester. Just now I am playing a *delicious* record, old ragtime of 1900–1916 era; I wish you could hear it. It's not the piano rolls I did play you once, but band & banjo pieces as well as piano rolls. So gay & insouciant, & yet so sad under it all. It's like the band playing on some pre 1914 prom or pier – sun, straw hats, sovereigns, the pubs wide open all day, and a heat haze – or is it a cloud? – over the German Ocean ... I long to play it to you. Not at all jazzy – more the cakewalk, the syncopation of the plantation forcing its way through Gilbert & Sullivan. And so *musical*, tuneful, agreeable. [...]

3 March 1964

32 Pearson Park, Hull

Had a good journey back – 2 people asked me to autograph *TWW*'s in the train – the Ringo Starr of contemporary verse.

Dearest,

Groogh, what a day. I get my first driving licence & my first car in it, six months less three days after I took my first lesson, creeping petrified round the Park in low gear. Now I creep petrified along the roads in no gear at all. Oogh, groogh, uuurghgh. Instead of the cross, the Singer Gazelle about his neck was hung.[1] Oh dear, what have I done.

I think the most characteristic thing about it is the *fearful reek of the upholstery* (a blinding scarlet, anyway) wch tends to make me feel sick. I suppose it will wear off. It's a horrible solidified-peardrop kind of smell. I am acutely *aware* of it shining, complicated, *weighing over a ton*, sitting out in the Park, & its incredible routine – every week do these, every 3,000 miles do those, etc. Money will flow away into its maw. I feel I ought to go out & see that I have locked the boot & that no one can steal my jack, spare tyre, etc. Oh dear! Isn't it all *untypical*! I feel as if I had somehow slipped through into a different character. Phew. [...]

1 Parodic reference to Coleridge's 'The Ancient Mariner'. L.'s first car was a Singer Gazelle.

29 March 1964
(Easter Sunday)

21 York Road, Loughborough, Leics.

[...] I'm awaiting the Critics' onslaught at present – bet that Irish hoodlum Craig[1] will lam me as unswaggering & unpassionate, with his 'fillum' ... Ogh ogh, hear Karl bashing the Oxford crap, good show. And talking of the older universities, good old Oxford distinguished themselves on the Thames all right, didn't they. It's always like that when I listen (or look!). I thought they were supposed to be favourites – strange favourites!

Kind notice for *Jill* in *The Obs* – very pleasant surprise. See K. is reduced to fill-in for Pen Gilliatt – twenty years ago he was borrowing from me – well, fifteen, – fifteen years hence he'll be borrowing again, poor old hack.

Here we go ... K.M. apologising in advance, isn't he! God, he's not leaving much anti for the rest to say, is he. I can see that Bechet line[2] is going to be my albatross, like 'sex, but what is sex' from the other one. Well, old Craig comin' down on my side – must think I'm Irish, mustn't he? Good old Hobson – big poems about small things – hope my publishers are noting quotes for use in the unlikely event of their ever advertising ... Craig mentioning *Lambs*! Good lad, I'll send'm a crate of Guinness. And a coupla blawnds. Oh well, good on the whole, eh? Well, almost unreservedly good. I do feel defensive about that Bechet line: have they never heard the Beatles singing 'She loves you – yeah, yeah, yeah—'? Or read the end of Molly Bloom's soliloquy? Why is it so bad? I thought when I wrote it that it just 'got' love & Bechet & everything. Perhaps that's what's wrong with it! [...]

1 H. A. L. Craig, Irish critic and broadcaster, taking part in the radio programme *The Critics*, in which each week a new play, film, art exhibition, radio or television programme and book was discussed by a panel. In this case, Craig appeared alongside Karl Miller, Harold Hobson and others, discussing *The Whitsun Weddings*.
2 'Like an enormous yes', from L.'s poem 'For Sidney Bechet'.

30 March 1964

21 York Road, Loughborough

Dearest,

I have done up your little gift – hope it reaches you. There is a poem inside[1] wch I hope you won't throw away with the wrapping. It is absolutely unique – I have burnt the draft & forgotten it already. I am reading KM's letters to JM[2] – she calls him 'the Great Poet of our time ... I whisper "Oh, my *Wonder*" ...' Awgh. You don't say that to me. Ogh ogh. Shuold lock yuo in the Scurley if you did.

Now it's Tuesday, and I suppose this can't be any more than a note if it's to go today. Awful weather, fit to make you cut your throat. Why do I at 41 have to spend my 'holidays' at home? Why can't one stop being a son without becoming a father? Why is my life so devoid of active grape-bursting enjoyment? [...]

1 Poem missing.
2 Katherine Mansfield to J. Middleton Murry.

22 April 1964

The Library, Hull

Enclosed is £5 for food – I meant to give it you.

Dearest,

It's just about three o'clock, and I have absented myself from my visitors for a few minutes. I have really had little time to reflect since you left, but have felt extremely remorseful & upset & appalled at the situation I have created.

I can only say again that I didn't want to hurt you because I thought it wasn't 'serious' enough, but anyway I am ashamed of it all. Perhaps it was a good thing to bring the affair into the open[1] – I certainly feel closer to you now than I have done for some time.

I was heartwrung by your sickness. Please take great care of yourself & see that you don't get ill.

I hope the journey was tolerable & that you found things were all right on your return. I look forward to getting a word from you, and will write again very soon.

With dearest love
Philip

.

1 This short letter from L crossed with a 20-side letter from Monica to L., also dated 22 April 1964. Both letters followed a traumatic weekend in Hull, when Monica in her anguish over further revelations about L.'s affair with Maeve was physically sick. Monica's letter, completed on 24 April, ends: 'Well, I thought I was being very calm & sensible last night, but the letter gets more raving & hysterical, it seems, read today, as it goes on. Well, I will send it and believe that you will be able to forgive its faults of raving and of boring going on & on about the same thing; I think *what* it says is true, but the way it says it is tiresome, droning on and on.'

25 April 1964

32 Pearson Park, Hull

Dearest,

I do wish I could ring you up. It's Saturday, about 8: I've had Judy's Australian, rested, had a bath, & ought to have supper, but don't want it at present. I'm not 'not eating', exactly, but I think of you alone & want to get in touch with you. I feel alone myself, of course! not that I'd mind normally, but the general shock & unhappiness weigh heavily. Oh, I do wish I could get in touch with you & cheer you, as I know I could, or at least comfort you.

I had your long letter this morning – it's in the kitchen at present: I almost avoid it because of the pain it contains. Darling, I *don't* think you're mad or odd. I shd tell you if I did, no doubt giving you something more to swallow. I think when I first knew you you were (irritatingly) frighteningly sane. Now you are labouring under the burden of too much solitude & my cavalier treatment of you, & your domestic misfortune & unhappiness. But who thinks you're mad, or odd? Only you, surely. I think you have, through no fault of your own, an unhappy life – I'm afraid it is through some fault of *mine*.

Anyway, put out of your head any thought that Maeve & I did that party note between us – now that *is* an odd thing to think. It makes me realise how you must be upsetting yourself by imagining things that aren't so. No, it was her own innocent work, & I shouldn't really have shown it to you to laugh at, but it was such a perfect & extraordinary example of that kind of language I felt you wd marvel at it. Dear, I can tell you are thinking Maeve is 'better' than you – I mean you are instinctively thinking 'I'm awful, dull, mad, unsophisticated etc' – but really that's not so, & you know it isn't. If you wonder how I can be attracted to someone who in all sincerity thinks like that, well, I suppose it's just that she's got other, nicer qualities. But it doesn't blind me to her – well, I won't say deficiencies, because there's no law about calling jam jam. Differences. Well, hell, deficiencies of taste. *Her* 'Whitstable oyster' is serving home made cakes (by her) with cornflakes & grated coconut on top. And if you think I'm just pretending to denigrate her to comfort you, & am being insincere, well, I'm trying to preserve the balance, wch I think is in danger of being lost.

And I'm sorry about that oyster. I thought you were deliberately refusing to commit yourself in case I turned on you if I didn't like it. I'll never mention the incident again – I'm sorry, I do understand. In return, will you exonerate me from battery eggs? I was silly & ignorant in those days: I always (except when *absolutely* forced) buy fresh eggs now. I've found where the shops are, round about.

This is the end of a pad – I buy pads & pads, & lose them, either at work or here. Somewhere there are about a dozen pads. Ah, found one.

Judy's Australian was bearded and a bit of a dope. He said he thought Judy was like a Henry James heroine. I don't think I've seen the last of him.

I do hope you are better. No tears, no reproaches could have shamed me more than your being sick. I feel quite awful, as if I had, well, kicked something to death – I'm not, I hope, being melodramatic: kicked something & seen it vomit as a result, perhaps. You know I feel I ought to take care of you – I have always felt this since your parents died, and it has caused enormous conflict & worry in me, that from time to time I've tried to explain, in that I did not ask you to marry me – I think I am mad & odd too: sometimes I am tempted to say how much I'm affected by sex fear & auto-erotic fantasies, & how I feel normal emotional relations & responsibilities a terrible strain, I mean a big tiring strain. I don't want to bore you with such things – only don't assume that I'm wise & 'mature' compared with you: I'm infantile & cowardly & selfish, too frightened to make a will even. I've been afraid that my 'support' of you was in fact a covert weakening of you, a kind of paralysis, & a cheating you of a happy life. I engaged your emotions & refused to satisfy them – an action, as G.B.S. says, for which I know no polite name.

It's ten past nine now – I ought to go & clear up the kitchen, any-way. Oh, I do wish I could get in touch with you. Not, I suppose, that I could say anything immediately comforting – I mean, the harm has been done, by hurting you.

Suppered. Have re-read your letter & also one from Bob wch arrived with it. (I think there is a poem to be made out of the letters that arrive together.) *Do you know*, he is *spending his honeymoon* in something called The International Cultural Center, in Tunis, *FREE* ('free bed, board & sun'), & lecturing for his keep IN FRENCH – the place is empty at the moment, but *there might have been other writers there* – can you bloody well beat it? His *honeymoon* – even if *he* didn't care by now, he might have thought of her. *Her honeymoon! Among writers! In Tunis!* I do frankly think this is *amazing*. Don't you?

Your letter is sad and some of it is sensible – well, yes, it has been a relief, in a way, to behave like everyone else, bloody ass though you feel sometimes, but Maeve isn't as young as all that. Thirty four, thirty five next autumn. About love, if I could have said last September 'I'm in love with Maeve, goodbye', I wd: as it was, I couldn't – perhaps too fond of you, perhaps not fond enough of her, perhaps just too cowardly all round. So don't go thinking I am skipping like a young ram in a rosy haze, 'in love' – I think I get some of the emotions with her. But I get some of them with you.

Oh God, burbling on—

More tomorrow, dear. I really do regret all this, and wish I could be there to console you. I'm glad you have Noggs & co. Do tell me *people's reactions – all* people.

Had a Swedish cutting today with 'Philip L. – ingen arg ung man' under my picture. Sounds funny. Cheeky devil.

This page sounds a bit insensitive – I'm sorry.

Sunday, about 3. Dull day, not the weather which is painfully spring-like. I got up, etc., wrote home, cleaned the car after a fashion, went for papers and a pint, had lunch – all rather like last Sunday, except that the sun is shining. Actually I keep falling asleep!

I thought I might add to this, but I feel a bit weary of my explanations today. I'm sure my letters *were* all right – I can always *write*. *Doing*'s what I'm bad at. Not that they were insincere – why should they be? I'm always very fond of you, and you are easier to write to than anyone.

I have been thinking I might come up to L'boro' from Cambridge on Sunday, stay the night, see you a bit on Monday, & return to Hull on Tuesday – Tuesday is a non dies, Founders' Day. The only trouble is that Monday *isn't* a non dies! Otherwise I should be presumably coming home at Whitsun – I shall be in Reading on 15 May for their opening – I don't know if anything is obstructing 9 May, but as you know I don't like going away two weekends running. If I did manage to keep Monday 4 clear, wd you be able/willing to see me? I shouldn't especially want to go 'in' – Simmons[1] is eager for me & proposes coming here on 23 May for this purpose, & in consequence I'd sooner keep out of his way. I shd – I hope – like to see you: I mean I am afraid to, in that I am ashamed of the hurt I have caused you, & of my own frittering away of your life, but, well, I feel concerned for you and – I don't feel able to face losing touch with you.

Getting on for post time. Gay, sunny Sunday: painful Spring. Those she has least use for see her best.[2] I wish you were reachable at Leics.

Hope you are feeling better. Best love, Philip

1 Jack Simmons, Professor of History, Leicester.
2 Line from L.'s poem 'Spring', written in Leicester, May 1950.

27 April 1964

32 Pearson Park, Hull

[...] I asked Maeve about the time *Broadcast* was published, & she said that at that time we had quite given up seeing each other as she was trying to recapture Philip (her other chap was called this). This relieved me, as I didn't like to think I'd said anything that wasn't at least fairly true. Of course, I'd forgotten all about it – boiled as an owl when he wasn't working. We then had a remote kind of year (1962) wch ended with a sort of resurgence of feelings on my part in about March 1963. I forget when Philip faded out – late in '62, I think. [...]

29 April 1964

32 Pearson Park, Hull

[...] I wish I *were* more open with you: we are now, but I'm rather like Sir John at the beginning of *The Crooked Hinge*,[1] not knowing whether he is an impostor or not. Sometimes I think Maeve is a kind of 40-ish aberration of mine, and her family & religion & desire for marriage & children & all that wd scare me out of the country if I were left alone with them. At others I think we have – that's you & I have – got into a sort of rut that will become increasingly ludicrous and painful as the years waste by. In a way you reflect what I am, she what I might have been – manager of a local insurance branch, I should guess. But you know how potent what one isn't can become! You flatter her if you think she wd have heard of either Barnes, but she once told me that her previous chap had never heard of D.H.L. This gave me a *ils-sont-dans-le-vrai* feeling, silly swine. I mean, quite an achievement not to have heard of him. [...]

1 Detective novel by John Dickson Carr (1938).

10 May 1964

32 Pearson Park, Hull

Dearest bun,

I'm sure you won't be surprised if I say the card is the most beautiful I've ever seen – it's almost like a rabbit Ingres. What a terrible shame it couldn't come with a happier message – I'm very depressed to hear you had such a sad birthday, but surprised too, as I left feeling I had really assured you that I liked you better than Maeve & that if I felt I was cheating anyone it was *her*! Not of course that I feel happy about it all anyway: as I say, I think sometimes I am ultimately an auto-erotic writer case incapable of love for anyone but himself. (How my hand trembles! I've been cleaning the car.) [...]

12 May 1964

32 Pearson Park, Hull

[...] Well, I was a bit saddened by your fat letter, but no need to apologise, no reason why I shouldn't be saddened. I thought your letter quite sane & collected. I wish I could reply more fully, as you deserve, but I know I have only about 2 pages in me: in a way you make me sound more romantic & dramatic than I am, wch is almost more crushing than deflating abuse. My situation seems to me a little squalid, a little contemptible, more than a little infantile, on one side of it, & a bit pathetic & frightening on another – I suppose so much of life really has gone, the 'young romances' I never had at the proper time, the normal-age marriage, house, children, laying hold of life as you might say: I still don't want them or am frightened of them or something, but they haunt me, the fact of their being irrevocably lost is unsettling and probably lies behind some of this. How silly it all sounds! But as I may have said, earlier, our great bond is at present the part of my life I am *at times* – just at times – not even *most* times – in revolt against. Or, if revolt is too strong a word, then a bit tired of. In theory, at any rate! Doesn't sound very impressive, does it? It doesn't impress me, anyway. I don't know why I go *on* about it, when I feel so dispirited. And I do know that I am very lucky to have you & your patience instead of some less generous person, less funny & individual person.

BJ read out my summary of CDL's[1] claims on our attention – 'sensitivity of Hardy & intellectual stress of Meredith' – then ascribed it to me, wch was unfair I thought! CDL is really awfully charming. He asked why I mentioned Chatto in *Naturally*[2] (he is a director) so I told him ogh ogh. He agreed, with just the right amount of ruefulness. [...]

1 C. Day Lewis: proposed for honorary degree, he became the first Compton Poetry Lecturer at Hull.
2 Chatto is mentioned in stanza 1 of 'Naturally the Foundation will Bear Your Expenses'.

19 May 1964

32 Pearson Park, Hull

[...] The TV men[1] are after the Arundel tomb in Chichester – I hope to God it's there & I didn't dream it. They want to know if it's free-standing, or against a wall. I hope all my descriptions are accurate – jointed armour, stiffened pleat, little dogs. I'm quite likely to have invented them. Do you remember it? I expect you do: total recall. [...]

1 From Patrick Garland's *Monitor* film of L.

22 May 1964

32 Pearson Park, Hull

Dearest,

The London trip was as predicted: I saw the MS. sub-committee[1] receive the £600 Auden notebook (all the best poems cut out & no doubt sold separately) before handing over my own notebook no. 1, 1944–50, FOR NOTHING ... Christ! jammed with unpublished poems etc. I must say they are all fearfully dull, stodgy humorless (?) thin Yeats-&-catpiss. Still.

Judy & Ansell[2] were as usual, Judy having to be persuaded that it wd be nice to accept an invitation to someone's box for the Derby, & asking where it was run. She lent me the new De Vries (U.S. edition), wch is all right without being good. 'We want you to feel a member of this congregation' – 'Fine, who is she?'

The TV film is very much in the air, but I wd prefer it to be more down to earth. They are going to try to make it in time to *put it out* on July 5 (I believe), so there won't be much time for calculated effects. Betjeman is still due to be included, wch *I* rather deplore – I shall be typed as just another Betjeman. [...]

1 Of the scheme initiated by L. to acquire writers' manuscripts for a national collection.
2 Egerton.

23 May 1964

32 Pearson Park, Hull

[...] I had your letter this morning: I am ashamed to have behaved so inconsistently. I wasn't angry with you, just miserable. What happened was simply that Mother quite innocently asked if I could spend a week at home in August to facilitate her own holiday arrangements, & this threw me into a fury of despair about the way I do the same things every year, & not adventurous things either; every Christmas, every Easter, every Whitsun, when other people are enjoying themselves I am stewing at home in a rage of irritation & boredom. I needn't elaborate. We had the usual 'home' scene – tears etc. – Where you came into it was that my unhappiness about ourselves got caught up in it, but I didn't feel able to say anything because I thought you wd promptly say what in fact you have said about Lords. It's not so much doing the things I mind, it's the way they underline the emptiness & indecision of my life; not to mention the incompetence, when I think of Betty with her car passage to Corsica booked & even the women at the off licence just back from Greece. And so on & so on. Even Brenda[1] spent 2 days 'walking in Swaledale' – how? where did they stay? how did they get there? who were they, anyway? Anyway, I've said enough to recreate the mood in wch I was last Sunday.

It's nearly half-past nine. I am trying to do a BBC progr. of my poems[2] – 'only the links', as your friend wd say, & ought to get on with it. I'm not finding it easy. But I don't find anything easy these days. No poem done since March 1963.[3] [...]

1 Brenda Moon, at this time chief cataloguer in the Brynmor Jones Library.
2 *The Living Poet: Philip Larkin*, Third Programme, 16 December 1964.
3 'Dockery and Son' completed 28 March 1963; L. abandoned 'The Dance' in May 1964. See *Collected Poems* (1988).

6/7 June 1964

32 Pearson Park, Hull

Dearest,

This is *exhausting* – the pattern is one of fatigue & boredom, *standing about* while they 'set up', then short periods of intense fright while they film. So far it has been Wednesday in the Library; Thursday in the fish dock (up at 6), a ruined chapel, & my flat; Friday over the river at Barton; Saturday in my flat with Betjeman; today we are supposed to be on the ferry, but the weather looks unpromising. Betjeman is very nice: he was much taken with Virginia, & has brought his teddy bear Archie, also a girl called Lady Elizabeth Cavendish.[1] He thinks Uncle Alfred's water colour is a De Wint! I let him find an enlargement of you in King's Norton wch I had got that morning & he identified it *instantly*. [...]

1 Betjeman's long-time companion.

8 June 1964

32 Pearson Park, Hull

[...] I'm writing at 9.15 a.m. – they are 'coming for' me at 10. Today we 'work the graveyard' – i.e. shoot about 2 mins of B. & I talking among the graves. It will take about 3 hours, I expect. Then this afternoon I have a Library Comm! Never have I prepared less for one. My rabbit, my burial ground – I suppose it *is* nice to have them filmed, but I know you'll understand that they seem less mine now. In fact *I* feel less mine now, if you follow me. I shall be glad when I see the whole caravan of sound, lights & cameras disappearing up the road towards London.

I had your letter this morning – I'm sorry you had such a wretched weekend. The thought of being the cause, or partly the cause, makes it worse. I think we both have very curious characters or upbringings or something, that render us quite incapable of managing life – what is *Dockery & Son* but what you're saying? Funnily enough, it isn't our bond – our bond is more the things we like, and our friends, &, I think, the extreme gentleness of our natures (you may not think I am g. but I do). I wish it did bind us more in one way. Well, scripts for you, graveyard for me. Please try to keep more up, dear – I wish I could come & see you.

Many kisses
Philip

Later – Everything cancelled! No graveyard today. This is turning into a film about Betjeman.

9 June 1964

32 Pearson Park, Hull

Dearest bun,

Again I write before 10 a.m. – I ought to write at night, but I felt so corpsed last evening I could face only Stevie Smith, who had sent a note expressing regret for not having met me at the Poetry Panel when we were both there (we have in fact never both been there). The Library Committee took it out of me more than I expected – after asking for & getting £1 m. *for the Library*, BJ is now thinking of all the lovely halls of residence & social science buildings he could have for the money, like a boy who, having been given 6d to get his hair cut, passes a sweet shop on the way. And of course I felt terribly sad & remorseful about your letter & your sad state. If you were whooping it up with some plausible sod in Leicester I should be *shattered*: why then do I so lightly shatter you? You are a much nicer – well, more selfless – person, but is that any reason why I shd trade on it? *Of course* you are upset & it is I who am upsetting you. Blame me.

Betjeman is really very funny – a running monologue from the back seat in Yorkshire dialect – 'Ee, they've got a compre'ensive ... ay, well, you've got to keep up with the times – we've no place for the dreamer ...' Lady Elizabeth bought 3 fake breast-pocket handkerchiefs for 1/- in the market, & gave them to myself, Garland & the camera-man, Charles. They are incredibly debased things *on card*. She is a friend of Eliz. J. Howard, so my image of the English aristocracy is somewhat tarnished. I don't think there's much of the repose that stamps the cast etc. left today, do you? [...]

31 July 1964

21 York Road, Loughborough, Leics.

[...] You mustn't apologise for crying – cry all you need. It is not right to think you have to spare me the pain of remorse caused by my injuries to you, is it? I don't at the moment feel like going on with the subject – I'm sorry to cause you pain, especially in this half & half way. Anyway, I liked the weekend, except as I said I feel 'the situa-tion' hanging over our happiness rather, and, as I also said, I'd as soon start referring to it the moment I arrive. But then I wonder if there *is* 'a situation' – do I *really* want an R.C. wedding with Maeve & 'a recep-tion' at somewhere in Hull, &c. – I don't, of course, not really or even unreally. So then I begin to feel guilty about Maeve & that I ought to confront her wearing a sandwich board bearing a resumé of these remarks.

Anyway, dear, I wish I were with you now, especially if you are wearing your mauve dress. I really do. I hate my own behaviour these days, and yet, God, it's pretty moral compared with some. I do send you kisses, & would wash *your* dishes, on any shift. This is a silly conclusion – perhaps I'm dizzied by the sun. Love & kisses Philip

5 August 1964

21 York Road, Loughborough, Leics.

Dearest bun,

Back from Lichfield,[1] wch was pretty hellish – hacking long grass away from graves in a temperature of about 80°, and flies ... And even on early closing day the town is rendered HIDEOUS by cars, lorries & motor bikes: it's quite the foulest cathedral city in England. We went into the cathedral & got turned back on account of there being an invisible inaudible service on somewhere. The tea at Angel Croft Hotel was dingy & doughy. The drive there and back took about an hour – hardly any frights, but so *hot*. When I got back, I watered some flowers in the garden, wch were looking limp, then I sought out two bottles of Guinness as I thought I was looking limp myself. My father's parents' house has been divided into two – *hair stylist* & *turf accountant*.

I thought duck three times running was all right, and in fact in retrospect think you might have done even better with ordinary duck, not with orange. I hawked a bit at pal Bill's[2] gastronomic tastes – what does he *like*, then? Lyons' individual fruit pie? Cod and two veg., free pepper, salt & mustard, followed by nice hard plums and lumpy custard? I think I should tell him to learn to eat all sorts of food, as he'll probably have to. As regards advice, he seems to be *doing all right* – he sounds as if he has charm & disponibility, & will get on up to a point – the point at wch he has to do some work, I suppose. Still, don't think I wish him ill, ogh ogh. (I love ogh ogh. It expresses so much. Ogh.)

I was terribly hot last night. I lay thinking how nice it would be to have you beside (or under!) me, & not to be *drunk*, or *tired*, or *watching the clock*, just gathering your great smooth hips under me & shoving into you as I felt inclined. How rarely this has happened! It didn't happen last night, either. At least not for me, & I hope not for you – I'm not thinking of pal Bill as much as someone who might invite you out to dinner. They won't be doin' it acos they think you look hungry, y'knaow! You'll ave a bill at t'end of it an' all! [...]

Friday I feel out of spirits this morning partly because my mother seems to be resuming her normal whining panicky grumbling maddening manner which infuriates me, partly I am just tired of being here I suppose (everything gets boring after a week), & partly I was sickened by an article in the D.T. announcing prospects for the grouse season. Am meditating a letter to the editor[3] – it would be a good occupation for my birthday. [...]

1 Where the Larkin family graves are.
2 Bill Ruddick.
3 L.'s letter to the *Daily Telegraph* was published 13 August 1964.

14 September 1964[1]

32 Pearson Park, Hull

[...] Dear, don't, please, be miserable over this Maeve business. You've been extremely tolerant all the time, and I shall be glad to have your sympathy, but I think we both feel this is the best thing at present – she is perhaps more upset than I, because it is she who has been rebuffed. I felt bound to say that I had not finished with you, nor did I seem likely to, & she just said, Well that doesn't give me much alternative, does it, & I couldn't honestly think of one. We are quite friendly & have to see each other daily – the *real* breach & dismay is yet to come, I feel. And I suppose it will come. This is like the interval between Sept 3 1939 & the first air raids. [...]

1 In the margin of this letter Monica has scrawled 'For 5 minutes' against L.'s 'at present', which she ringed. In the margin alongside 'We are quite friendly' *et seq.* she squeezes an indignant critical analysis of L.'s tone: 'Note the style, the irony of style, & no intention of doing anything like what is said – perhaps style indicates'. She begins again where there is more space in the opposite margin: '& both of you had my sympathy – what a good giggle for both of you too, later. I was terribly upset for *both* of you while you were giggling together*' The asterisk directs the reader to the bottom of the page: '*I learned a good deal more later'.

13 October 1964

32 Pearson Park, Hull

Dearest bun,

In hurriedly acknowledging your letters yesterday I omitted to mention the two most important things – the ten shillings & *The Boy Friend* ogh ogh ogh. Thanks very much for the former: I don't think you should have troubled, but it was very kind of you. *The B.F.* sounds very nice, & I should like to see it, if you don't think it wd be too painful – isn't it *early* in January? I see you say it'll last into term. I'm pretty sure that would be all right. Yes, you'll have a lot to put up with ('it was a copy of Salad Days') ('By Angus Wilson'). *She Stoops* sounds a rattling fine production – starring Miss Greatheart Montague.

I've heard the name Paris Leary[1] before – isn't he some vile expatriate littérateur from the old *rive gauche*? I seem to remember him asking me for poems about 10 years ago. Some no-good bum, desperately leaping from log to log in the Fulbright timber river. Where did ARH pick him up? Should think he approached him somewhere in Montmartre with a fistful of infamous Camera Studies. Still, perhaps I've got it wrong – maybe he is a nice reliable Ivy League character. But I can't imagine he'll do much of your work. Ray's report to Senate begins sadly 'The links between the Department and North America grow firmer each year' – yes, poor bugger, always someone on the lam over there, leaving his work to be shared out among the mugs remaining behind. I'm glad you put that question to ARH – I can just imagine 'Espinasse quibbling on Senate or Faculty 'I-may-be-very-stupid-but-I-think-we-must-*decide*- ... *whether* we are over-*staffed* if *no*-one goes away ... or over-*worked* if they *do* ... I've-given-it-a-great-deal-of-thought-and-it-does-seem-to-me-that-this-is-quite-crucial-to-our-planning' etc. etc. No more news of Kenyon & his £750 p.a. for being Dean.

I'm sorry you are feeling so awfully low – it is silly for me to express sympathy when it is my fault, I suppose. How utterly unsatisfactory life is. I think this is a grim time of year. In theory it is beautiful, and is I suppose, but people are so full of energy after their summers of foreign travel & doing nothing. I don't mean I'm not sympathetic, of course, dear – it's just that I feel hypocritical, talking as if you had an attack of 'flu, when really *I* am denying you happiness & have for over 10 years. Of course your life is very unhappy anyway. All alone, & not able to go to the Clarendon! Not that I go much, or have one to go to. My dear, I do wish you felt *well*, let alone happy: I don't like the sound of your rheumatism and paralysis.

I have got two tickets for Pee Wee Russell at the Conway Hall W.C.1. at 7.30 pm on 30 October (Friday) – could you go? It would mean staying the night in London – you could pick a Ronay hotel. They aren't 'Press' – wish they were – but *paid for by me*. It would be nice to have your company, but I don't want to force you if you feel it wd all be too much. This weekend is Oxford, next Swansea. Russell has never been to England before & of course this will be a great thrill for me, though I expect he's gone off now. He's 58. It's a long time since we've heard any jazz together – it is row E, I see – perhaps a bit loud. I bought the extra one with you in mind – rather blackmail, really. What do you think? In retrospect it seems a mad thing to have done, but he is such a legend of my youth I couldn't resist:

I would I were where Russell plays
Through a foul tobacco haze
I would I were where Russell plays
   And Condon calls the key

as I used to say – Condon won't be calling the key of course, but Russell will certainly be playing.

I feel drowsy now, having turned up the fire – must I be either cold or dopy? This is really a serious problem. Do you feel all right with your coal fire?

I've finished my little poem about the sun:[2] it's the sort of thing anyone could write, and indeed it ought to be much longer & deeper & altogether better, but one can't be on one's high horse all the time. Nay, nor any of the time, an yr name be *Hughes*, or *Gunne*. *Arp*[3] knows *Gunn*. He seemed surprised I didn't – I expect all Americans expect all English people to know each other. I explained he was much younger than I, & had been at Cambridge. Arp said Gunn was suffering from hepatitis – who he? – & was in England, I mean is in England: he would try to get him up. In vain I tried to suggest that I have got on without him all right for 40 years – we'd not been together now for 40 years & it didn't seem a day too much.

(Wed.) There ain't a lady living in the land That I'd swop for my dear old Butch ogh ogh.

Well, first Senate meeting – I went to sleep. Woke up with Kenyon kicking me, to hear the raising of the retiring age being debated. Why not lower it? Surely the trend today is shorter hours, not longer. Brett quipped that he wanted to sack people at 35 not 63 – yes, & I know who: Alun Jones for one.

Nimrod is just coming on, on the wireless.

I wonder if my eyes need re-testing – there is a slight sense of strain in the right one. Shades of 1961!

Friday I drive to Oxford for big deal on Saturday – Congregation in morning, lunch in All Souls, opening of Law Library. Staying in St Johns; I have also got a bit embroiled with Wain, whom if I see it will be on Sunday a.m. I feel very doubtful if I can manage to call at Leicester on the way back, though of course I'd like to: I don't want to be racing the clock, and in any case it would be for so short a time it would hardly be enough to recognise ourselves in. I am rather frightened of driving in the dark, after that first essay, as well. I can't see Wain on Saturday as it is *Critical Q* dinner in London ogh ogh. And he reveals he *isn't* a member of the Johns' SCR ogh ogh. Not even after being a Fereday Fellow! I gloat, hear me. What all this means, I suppose, is that I don't feel I can commit myself to diverting myself to Leicester on Sunday. If I shd have time – though I honestly feel it's unlikely – of course I will. It rather depends on how easy it is to get away. But I do hope you can fulfil the London meeting – or will it be the *Motor Show*, Christ, all hotels booked? I shall be in London all that day, Friday 30th I mean.

  I enjoyed your letter: it had lots of small interesting passages in it, as if you were trying to amuse me. 'Small interesting passages' – naturally, in a rabbit letter! [*drawing of rabbit*]

Thursday Mother sends a cutting of 'Bunny Garage' – lots of Landrovers for sale! And thank you for your card. I like the way the track disappears into a tree, & the ticket office in another tree, dimly supervised by a mole. You sound as if you are having an *awful* time, with all these sods. You are reported as having better students than usual this year – hope you get fat on them.

  As regards weekends, then, this one is unlikely & next is impossible (Swansea) – all I *might* do is look in on Monday 26th, but even that is difficult unless I stay the night. So that might be a good weekend for Sutherland. Actually *I* have a meeting in Edinburgh on 27th & cd go straight there from Swansea! but feel I shall have to excuse myself. After all, it's either me or them. And it ain't gonna be me.

  Harpo Marx, Eddie Cantor – oh dear! Well, polling day today. Ray & Garnet are going to vote Liberal. I gather *The Times* told them to. By the way, I did laugh at 'my' 'introducing' in your letter – I think this is a kind of humour we have invented, & bloody funny it is too. Have told *Observer* to stuff it. Do let me have a line in due course – wish I had that pie here, & you   xx P.

1 Newly appointed American lecturer in English at Leicester University.
2 'Solar'.
3 Thomas R. Arp, visiting fellow at Hull from University of California at Berkeley.

2 December 1964

32 Pearson Park, Hull

Dearest bun,

Many thanks for your letter – I'm so glad you enjoyed our day. I was especially interested by your comments on Patrick[1] and Anne[2] – I suppose I had taken for granted that PG was some corrupt theatrical layabout: the notion of him being a church worker is rather odd, but I can see what you mean. Anne I always admired, she was so good at her job. I wrote to Patrick thanking him for the lunch on our behalf, and saying cut anything but the H-bomb bit, & he writes back today to say that he hopes he will see us both again, & that arguments about the cuts are still going on, but that the programme is definitely on, 10.15 p.m. 15 December: O bun where will you see it? 15th is deep in vacation here: is it at Leics? Will you be in Leicester?

I didn't think you seemed pushing or awful, in fact I didn't notice you except for taking an interest in Patrick's religious film, or refugee film, or whatever it was – I was glad you did, I couldn't. I hear that there was a bit of the film on *Monitor* last night – Campbell's ex-secretary saw it, & a Geography lecturer. Apostles of culture! Just me walking about. [...]

1 Patrick Garland, producer of L.'s *Monitor* film on BBC TV, 15 December 1964.
2 Anne James, Garland's assistant and stills photographer.

13 December 1964

32 Pearson Park, Hull

[...] Well, all aboard for Monitor. I see good old *Obs.* gives space to this joke Yank charlatan & not to yuors turly. In retrospect I hate the film: my comments seem silly or uninteresting, Patrick's direction 1958 Tony Richardson-&-water. *Hull D. Mail* rang up to ensure it actually showed Hull people in Hull! [...]

16 December 1964

32 Pearson Park, Hull

[...] I saw the film, as I hope you did, & wasn't slain by it, but it was interesting to note the cuts, wasn't it? I see our H bomb bit went. 'Ay, well, naw use lukin on't dark side.' Sods. Glad the 'another evening gone' bit was kept. The general opinion here seems to be of disappointment – I'm thought of as funny, you know. Still, you don't get taken seriously by arsing about, do you. [...]

28 December 1964

32 Pearson Park, Hull

[...] Have now recovered the post & find one or two letters – even *Vernon Watkins* saw Monitor! He adds that he shut his eyes while the poems were being read – this is so typical of him! Also from N. Iles, who thinks he could have written my poems (not disparaging them thereby, of course), who says my voice frightens him. Heighho. Also Patrick Garland, regretting the 'nuclear' bit (ass, it was the *death* bit), but saying it has been judged a great success & lots of people have bought copies of *TWW* in consequence, including Mr Big himself as PG terms Kenneth Adam;[1] is he D-G? This is a revelation to me of the power of television – it's like *The Guardian* compared with the *Telegraph*. [...]

1 Director of BBC Television.

31 December 1964

Loughborough, Leics.

[...] If I were in Hull I should probably be at a party given by my dear old pals David & Jean (Burnett-Hall), so you see family duties serve their purpose. Maeve is going. I told her that on N Year's Eve Scotchmen are honorary sociologists. Peel's research is being assisted by a grant from 'a firm of rubber manufacturers' ogh ogh ogh. Managing durexer. I can't imagine what the party wd be like – *reels*, I shouldn't wonder, whisky & Auld Lang Syne. 'First bangers', too – not the first sausages of the year, the first door-closers. [...]

Later – within half an hour of 1965. I had to wash up & then slept in the armchair a bit. I suppose we can wish ourselves a moderately happy New Year! It would be very wrong to say 1964 had been anything but a good year for me, materially, but as you know I have a very deep sense of unhappiness, or something, that seems more convincing than literary success. I suppose if one isn't actually dying of cancer or angina one is in fact riotously happy. Let's settle for that!

I've got your card out & got it out on the mantelpiece – what's the rabbit doing? fondling his own harmless face?[1] Eating something, more like. I don't expect rabbits have much sense of New Years – they haven't a sense of occasion in that way. I've put the wireless on & found a curious unhappy waltz I know but can't give a name to. Now the Watchnight Service! From *Scotland* would you credit it – why is this all a prerogative of the Macs? [...]

1 'The rabbit fondles his own harmless face' – in closing lines of Tennyson's 'Aylmer's Field'.

23 April 1965

In train Hull–King's Cross   St George's Day

Dearest bun,

I am reduced to writing in the train, wch won't suit my hand, as I've always found it difficult. Sometimes I wonder if I really hear all I fancy I hear. On the radio yesterday I fancied I heard

Ring a ring a roses
A coronary thrombosis
A seizure! A seizure!
All fall down.

This was at breakfast ... soon after I was reading that a symptom of an approaching stroke is 'inexplicable tiredness.' Oh hadn't we the gaiety. Today I doddered up at 7 to get this 8.50 train, feeling as if my heart were in the grip of a giant hand. Perhaps I was nervous of the *Weekend Telegraph* wch looks to me nothing to be ashamed or proud of.[1] The paragraph on post-Parker developments is ludicrous,

I'm afraid, & more stress ought to have been put on the beat craze. And were the Border ballads the product of a unique set of sociological factors? Are there no ballads now?

> O wha will o'er the downs with me
>> O wha will with me ride
> To a lectureship in Psychology
>> In the University of Strathclyde?

Anyway.

It's been a busy week, of course – I sometimes think I should take a day off a week to catch up with things like Tax returns. I suppose if I didn't drink when I got in it wd save time, but life is very narrow without glasses OF GIN AND TONIC. The thought of the situation at home is also depressing. I shouldn't mind Mother being left alone if I thought Kitty wd visit her regularly & ring her up, but I'm extremely doubtful if she would. It is this attitude of 'Well you can ring us up if you get a telephone & there's a bus if you want to come & see us' that I find so graceless & unkind. I don't know where the justice of it is. It's no use blaming Mother for having produced children who can't live with her: she has always done the best she could, considering *her* ghastly parents. I can't blame Kitty for finding Mother impossible to live with – I do myself – but I do think they might regard it as a duty to go to see her regularly and even take her out. I do. [...]

1 L.'s piece 'Requiem for jazz', *Weekend Telegraph*, 23 April 1965.

25 April 1965

32 Pearson Park, Hull

Dearest bun,

I am just consuming the last of my Lindt rabbit – a v. emotional Sunday, in that two large gins at lunch were accompanied by *good* jazz, then tapes of *Scrapbook for 1940*: now I am letting *Solomon* roar out (buggers below away) – 'Ye harps & timbrels sound!' ... The *Scrapbook* completely destroyed me – I think under this unemotional frustrated frustrating exterior there is all the emotion I have never expressed, ready to be released by alcohol & the cheapest possible appeal, like AEH[1]

& 'Soldiers of the Queen'. But I must get the record of *Scrapbook for 1940 – it's not that I remember it* – you know? I don't feel 'I lived through that'; I feel just 'How wonderful!' ... Do you remember the noise of the trains, supposedly bearing the wounded from Dunkirk, & everyone turning out, not to cheer, not to wave, just to watch? Heaven knows if it is true. Oh dear, I must stop indulging myself like this, but I feel like the Walrus and the Carpenter. Very fine speech of W.S.C.[2] – 'We now stand *alone* as champions of the free world, and if we fail, everyone, *including America*, will—' A kick in the arse for that old sod Kennedy.[3] And I wd dearly love to know if 'the announcer' who, presumably on his own initiative, put on the Trumpet Voluntary after the 'finest hour' broadcast was Grisewood himself, and if this is why he included it in the programme.

Now the blessed second side – 'How vain were all I knew' – oh, dearest bun, you are the only one who appreciates what I am on about!

God. [...]

1 A. E. Housman.
2 Winston Churchill.
3 JFK's father, US Ambassador to London in the early days of the Second World War.

15 May 1965

32 Pearson Park, Hull

[...] Agitation on the part of the acquisition dept for the return of Adriaen Brouwer has led me to look at it again – fine stuff: a comforting world of its own – you are a great fat oaf, three quarters drunk, sitting on a bench with a jug of beer in your hand, surrounded by cronies as ugly and disgusting as yourself.[1] You are all smoking clay pipes: there's a good fire in the hearth. One man is flat out on the floor, having spewed (dogs are licking it up), another is pissing out of the back door. The candlelight shows patched clothes, broken cupboards: outside is wind, mud, winter. *But you are all right*. Did you get that impression from it, the book I mean? Shall have to take it back tomorrow before I leave my car in for service (wish I could leave myself in for service) & go away. [...]

1 Cf. 'The Card-Players', completed 6 May 1970.

21 May 1965

Belfast

Dearest,

Many thanks for your lovely card, wch brought you very close in spirit (I sound like a Methodist youth club leader writing to his affianced girl) – a lovely picture. The Bayleys[1] have arrived – IM is obviously regarded as the *clou de la saison* & everyone fights to sit by her. I walked over to the lecture with her yesterday & was amused when we got to the hall that she whipped out a comb & gave a few vigorous tugs to her 5" locks. She has the look of a plump unhappy little girl. [...]

1 John Bayley and Iris Murdoch.

undated (22–24 May 1965)

Hull 7 pm

Dearest,

I'm terribly shocked by yr bad news – the fact is I hadn't *got* your first letter: it never occurred to me to look for post, & I didn't have any bill to pay, so nobody told me – anyway, I gather you've had a burglar: this is awful & upsetting & I know how shattered you must be feeling. Oh, dearest, I *do* feel upset by it all, the more so for not knowing what happened – did it happen on *Friday*? Did you lose anything? The whole thing is so shaking I feel quite sick – I wish I were with you, or you with me – wd you like to come here on Friday, till Monday? Perhaps you wdnt want to leave the flat. But you'd be very welcome of course.

Of course this kind of thing is terribly common these days – I mean people do it just for a lark, I don't think they'd be *watching* you, but there, you'll know more of this than I. For some awful seconds I thought they'd molested *you*, but your letter sounds more as if a break-in was made at the back door. Bad enough.

I haven't had a decent meal all day & feel unhungry & unhappy – darling, the fedder up I got the more I thought of you. Do think if you'd like to come *here* you wouldn't be alone – not much help, I know, but if you feel you'd like to get *away*, come, or should I, could I, come to you? I have an article to do sometime. Dearest bun, please be comforted by my love. xxxxx Philip

30 May 1965

32 Pearson Park, Hull

[...] *Faber Bk of MV*[1] turned up yesterday – you know A. Ridler 'extended' it: now D. Hall has redone it, putting in a lot of Yank stuff & 'letting fall certain unfashionable names as a cat lets something unchewable fall onto the carpet' – e.g. Peter Quennell, S. Sitwell, *James Reeves* (he'll hate that), C. Dyment. Ogh ogh. My turn in 1985. The ponce of Hessle says about 120 copies of my record have been ordered. Do you think it wd be a gracious act, or just a silly one, to send one to HM?[2] Probably the kind of thing Philip Hobsbaum[3] wd do. It was unnerving in Belfast to hear people saying 'As a poet, Philip, do you feel' – and have PH's eager voice replying. [...]

1 *Faber Book of Modern Verse*: first edition by Michael Roberts (1936), then revised by Anne Ridler (1951), then again by Donald Hall (1965).
2 The Queen.
3 Philip Hobsbaum: see Appendix B.

20 July 1965

32 Pearson Park, Hull

[...] I don't know what to say about Maeve – your letter to Loughborough depressed me, the one here on Monday continued the process, the one today was more cheerful and forbearing, wch has lifted my gloom rather, but I still feel that I am shown up at last for something rather low. I've always tried to get you to see me as unlikable, and now I must be getting near success. (Do you remember what must have been an early letter to you, certainly early in our affair, incoherently saying I was no good? I always feel I tried to warn you, insofar as a no good person could.) I feel that as long as I was faithful, you could somehow accept the unsatisfactoriness of our relation – we might not be married legally, but we were different & perhaps superior – at least your sacrifice of yourself to me was superior to frogmarching me or anyone to the altar rails. But when I am unfaithful – not technically but spiritually – you can only feel duped and made light of, quite apart from the awful upsetting emotion, and you are wondering, I suppose, just how far you can put up with it, from all points of view.

Not telling you of the affair in the first place, or of its wan latter recrudescences, was just infantile precaution – I didn't want to hurt you, & I didn't want to give it up. I had in consequence more trouble with Maeve, who had to accept my departures & your arrivals, & our holidays – usually she did so resignedly, but she occasionally told me off. You can see what a dislikable & discreditable position it was. It could only have been accepted by someone as weak & selfish as myself.

This is beginning to sound like Middleton Murry! I say this last bit to deny your suggestion that I enjoyed deceiving you. Of course I didn't, but I don't enjoy not deceiving much more. And I certainly wasn't purposely hinting at things at Whitsun. I should think I was trying to tell you & failing to pluck up courage to do so. I'm sorry I upset you thereby.

Otherwise I don't think that letters are a good medium for this delicate exchange, I don't mind your allegations about Maeve, though I don't think they're true – they are your hated image of the 'real girl' (comparable to my envied image of the 'real man') rising again. I think there's something unreal about my relation with her, as indeed there is with ours & with mine with Ruth – in that it isn't 'serious' in the world's sense of the word, i.e. leading to marriage & children. I don't say this is particularly comforting, but I think it's my fault. Oh well. I think this gloomy kind of oration is also unreal. Theorising is flight. Ratflight at eventide. Rats' songs at eventide. [...]

24 July 1965

32 Pearson Park, Hull

[...] It amuses me to think that the 'cricket match at Taunton' the wireless says Maudling[1] is attending instead of 'sounding opinion' in his constituency is the one Ansell asked me to umpire! I'd've been in the swim for once, shouldn't I? How inconceivable! What should I think of anyone else doing it? Climbing sod, frivolous sod, back-to-the-Georgians arse-creeping sod. Oh well. How marvellous to have had a few hints to drop around the SCR about Reggie & 'Edward'[2] (what do they call Duke, I wonder?) when we met at – I don't know where we were to meet at – though, wouldn't it? 'Maudling told me himself, Vice Chancellor, that the Conservatives—' ''ow d'you know Maudling?' 'I know one or two in that set.' Almost worth doing, really. [...]

1 Reginald Maudling, Conservative Chancellor of the Exchequer.
2 Edward du Cann: 'Duke', L.'s contemporary and friend at St John's, Oxford, 1940–3; he later became an MP and prominent Conservative politician.

10 August 1965

21 York Road, Loughborough, Leics.

[...] I had a strange dream about you last night – I dreamed you were playing cricket for England![1] And very well. I saw you hook a boundary. The TV commentary played tricks with you, making you very small & Alice-like before enormous stumps. It was all very exciting, but I couldn't get near you – there was a *supper* interval, but you were with the teams. I believe you'd been asked to the *Snows* afterwards. Then there was your picture on the sports pages, in your white shirt. I woke feeling tremendously proud of you & in love with you. Isn't that strange? I hardly ever dream of you, or anyone else, but this was very strong. I can remember now the sense of seeing you 'out there', wanting to help you, then as you cracked the ball to the boundary realising you *didn't need* help. It was all marvellously romantic.

It looks a fine day here – I don't know what to do. Perhaps I should wash the car. It's choral evensong day, of course, wch I always carry in my mind as a symbol of rest & retirement & holiday – listening to choral evensong in winter before the fire, then having tea. Second-rate image! Or I might take mother out. She has come back full of a desire to live in a hotel or an old people's home – to be free of work & responsibility. I suggest she tries it, though financially it wd probably be more troublesome. But she could try it, & see how she liked it – I don't think she would, of course. Anyway, she wants me to look at (from the outside, I hope) a 'home' in Loughborough. [...]

1 Monica wrote in her next letter: – 'Oh, I wish I *could* do something to make you proud of me like that, it *would* make you love me more, just as in the dream: if "my book" were coming out or something. Dear, you have to put up with someone who will never distinguish herself.'

14 August 1965

21 York Road, Loughborough

Dearest bun,

Dull evening – wet. Have written to *The Queen*, refusing to be their jazz critic for £5 a month more than the *D.T.* pays; to P. Oakes,[1] continuing to haggle about the *S. Times* interview; to the BBC, agreeing that the Monitor film shall be shown in theatres where people pay to go in! Wonder wch they have in mind? Evening of a successful man. Well, enjoy it while it lasts. Ogh ogh ogh.

Bill[2] will feel my boot on his bottom if he keeps his eyes on yours. I'm glad you had a good day – he still reminds me of Horace Walpole rather. Mother was amazed to hear of your breakfasts – she was just struggling with *one* kipper – she had bought two & I had had one the previous morning. Not two! Today I bought two more & hope to get them both tomorrow. We'll see. It sounded a wonderful idyllic breakfast – I don't think I could take fruit in quantity, but Lapsang is lovely. Perhaps I ought to switch.

Oh, that reminds me of a less happy piece of news – Fabers don't want *An Unsuitable Attachment*. I discussed it with Charles, but he was adamant – he clearly didn't think it was good, not as good as *E.W.*,[3] & really not any advance. I don't know that I danced up & down in its defence – it's difficult when it's a case of someone else spending money – but I tried to convince him that it was suitable to his list – not successfully, I'm afraid. Oh dear. I can see what he means – it's not a really good book of its own kind, even. I'm afraid she will be disappointed. So am I.

Eric White was very nice about the Arts Co. prize:[4] he loves breaking confidences. He said the judges began with a long list of books wch on his invitation they reduced to about 20. Then he told them to try again & got them down to 12. Then he said: 'Well, this is taking rather a long time, is there any one book you think clearly merits the prize?' They all thought mine did, but hadn't liked to say so! Oh dear, how conceited I sound. Forgive me. I'm written out now – shall never write anything else.

It's misty tonight, like autumn. You notice round the street lamps. It hasn't been a bad week, though Mother slid quickly back into her old depression. Home too is a wonderful place for realising the awful perspectives of time. How different my life is from everyone else's! as if it ran on a different mainspring. Loughborough is a dump. I think of

353

myself 'coming home at holiday time' just like the aimless undergraduate of 25 years ago – I am more aimless, really. He at least had his head full of 'wanting to write'.

I can't think what book I gave you! 'Burrow Construction and Maintenance'? 'How to Live on Two Lettuces a Day'? 'Some Rabbit Songs'? I didn't mean to leave the Salinger, but I'd finished with it. I bet you're engrossed in it. I think *Seymour: an Introduction* is almost unreadable, & a complete flop. It tells me nothing about Seymour – is it meant to conceal, or reveal?

Yes, that Abbey shop is fine. I went to it at least twice but it was always closed. I don't know that I wanted anything, but I should have liked to look round. How kind of you to send me the Newcastle songs![5] Mother is highly amused at the sack of sawdust concept. The laylock nightgown is very appropriate too. I wish I could read the tunes: I like such of them as I know. We used to sing *The Keel Row* at school, so that's well rubbed in.

After some preliminary self encouragement I rang old Covers[6] tonight & got landed with tea *&* dinner tomorrow. I knew we shd – they are so hospitable. It's especially unsuitable as his mother is there convalescing after a serious post-fall illness. But I felt I couldn't go without making some sort of contact. I'll remember you to them. Romantic Mitchell,[7] who works at Fabers now, says M. is having another baby, or not having one, I couldn't quite gather which. I don't really want to go.

Today on an impulse I bought Elgar's *Violin Concerto* – the 1932 recording conducted by him with the youthful Y. Menuhin. God knows if I shall like it.

Dear bun, I hope you are not too badly off by your river. You treated me to a lovely few days – for your bounty,[8] there was no winter in it, to quote your favourite play. I rather wish we'd seen L. Castle.

Very best love & kisses to a dear rabbit.   Philip

1 Philip Oakes: *Sunday Times* interview, 'The unsung Gold Medallist', 27 March 1966.
2 Bill Ruddick.
3 Barbara Pym, *An Unsuitable Attachment* and *Excellent Women*.
4 Given to L. for *TWW* (£250 for 'the best book of original verse by a living poet published from July 1962 to June 1965'.) Subsequent to its publication, on 5 May 1965, L. was awarded the Queen's Gold Medal for Poetry.
5 In his *Desert Island Discs* (13 July 1976), L. chose a Newcastle street song, 'Dollia'.

6 Peter Coveney.
7 Donald Mitchell.
8 'for your bounty': *Antony and Cleopatra*, Act 5, sc. 2.

10 October 1965

32 Pearson Park, Hull

My dearest,

God, I am just recovering from an ill few days. John's[1] visit was far from restful: after the 'dinner' I asked him & the Hartleys & a few of the previous guests back to my flat. John, who appears to be trying to inherit the mantle of Dylan Thomas & J. B. Priestley simultaneously, had drunk an enormous amount of brandy after the 'dinner' (I wish I could remember what the main dish was called – something like *entre-cote université*), now drank a great deal of beer & after a long disquisition on Europe staggered out into the Park for 'fresh air' i.e. to spew, wch he continued to do all night, even on the way home. Still, he was very good about it, taking great care not to spoil the car or embarrass me. What a nice man is somewhere hidden among all that posing & ignorance & lying & boasting & corn & crap an'all! Brian Cox drank scotch & laughed like a maniac & broke a plate, then drank more scotch & laughed even more & broke a glass. He drove the Hartleys home & George said he nearly knocked down nine men on the way. Brian denies this.

The next day wasn't any better – his lecture (*wch I chaired*) was a furore of embarrassment, because his bag-act revealed he hadn't got his notes – they were later discovered on a window sill outside, but whether he'd purposely left them there or not I don't know. Anyway, he ad libbed with painful thinness though great fluency. What a dead loss he is. But the only time I really disliked him was when he was telling me how bad Hardy's poems were – he is, of course, making a selection for publication. Why the hell Macmillan's can't ask me I don't know. Silly sod. *He* is doing jazz records for *The Queen* ogh ogh £25 he says. They offered *me* £20. Ogh. Still, his agent takes 10%. He'll pack it in when he realises it means regular work.

Anyway, then it was 'seeing the docks' & off, leaving me to collapse, only to be kicked to my feet the next day by 'opening the exhibition', VC's sherry party, & lunch with the artist Sillince.[2] God. Afterwards I bought a pair of kippers & some *Twinings* Lapsang in Beverley, hanging on to the idea of you like a drunk clinging to a lamp post. Oh oh oh [...]

1 John Wain, in Hull to give a lecture.
2 William Sillince, painter (1906–74), Lecturer, Graphic Design, Hull Regional College of Art, 1952–72.

16 January 1966

32 Pearson Park, Hull

My darling,

Fifty minutes to post time – I wish I could find longer to write to you, because you are always in my thoughts. Today I think I'm not very well – I went to bed with a headache last night (most unusual for me) & couldn't sleep: ultimately took aspirins & went to the lavatory, & stayed in bed till noon, when I got up, looking worse but feeling better. I think there's a lot of infection about these days, upsetting one's insides: with all these foreigners about, one is never completely well, as when abroad. When I post this, I shall go for a walk round. The ground covered with snow & slush.

Dear one, you *are* always in my thoughts – I love you & don't want you to be in any doubt of it. How was the trip to Harlaxton?¹ I thought of you all day, & sent the telegram. I do hope it wasn't too upsetting – *tiring*, I don't doubt: *poor* bun.

I feel rather low: *work* has a number of nasty angles at present, the OBMV² seems a fearful burden, & in general I find things depressing. Our last Sunday was very nice: we were in good form, not too tired, very friendly & loving. I am beginning to feel I need to lead the life of a semi-invalid: *much more rest*. I had a ghastly day on Friday: an awful inaudible Yank talking about computers with Brenda & Burnett-Hall, the two chief inaudibles in Hull. After lunch I went back to my room & lay in a chair for an hour, doors locked, curtain drawn. People, as you say, are exhausting. Oh God! they are.

It is peaceful sitting here in the dreary afternoon light, both fires on, sky outside grey & drab, but I wish you were here. I was very touched when you said you thought of me when you saw a picture of a beautiful landscape! I too think of you when I see or experience anything particularly nice (or nasty, as the case may be!) – our spirits are joined, I think, in a way it wd be impossible to separate. Did you notice the de Vries remark about lotus becoming lettuce? I thought you wouldn't mind that.

Have you bought that in paperback? Imagine my scorn. Never mind, you buy things in hardcovers, don't you – books about mountains, perhaps. Ogh ogh. I'm not really getting at you, except in the mildest & friendliest way.

I had a letter from Betjeman, acknowledging the picture & being very kind about it. He says he & Elizabeth (Cavendish) met Kingsley & E.J.H. & had a long chat or some such nonsense. Grr, brr. They're all the same really. The only good life is to live in some sodding seedy city & work & keep yr gob shut & be unhappy.

Well, I feel a bit better for talking to you, darling – I wish we were in closer communication. I'll send you short notes if I can't send long wans. Do the same, my dear, my coney, my love! xxx Philip

1 Residential course for American academics to which Monica had been invited.
2 *The Oxford Book of Twentieth Century English Verse*. L. was approached by Dan Davin at the Oxford University Press early in 1966 (see letter to Davin, 20 January 1966, *Selected Letters*) about editing the book. It preoccupied him for the next several years, until its eventual publication in March 1973.

17 January 1966

32 Pearson Park, Hull

Darling,

God, what a grim day you had. I had visions of central heating, Martinis, perhaps even a distinguished Virginian greying at the temples to suggest dinner at Stamford ('Let's shore a fragment or two against our ruins') in his Oldsmobile or whatever. Who *are* all these silly sods? *Why* are they isolated in such conditions – is it a sort of reform school, a punishment for flunking? What about the American passion for heat? Anyway, I'm awfully sorry you had to get mixed up with it, dear. It sounds like an excursion into summer-school land, especially the tongue & salad. Let them as wants the money do it – is ARH going? I'm very sorry about your throat, too – I'd hate lecturing, everything about it. Do gargle, dear, & rest. 'Miss Jones is unable to lecture today.' Yeah, team, let's see a home bun.

I took my walk yesterday along the Avenues[1] – between 4 & 5, dusk, dirty snow, Victorian houses, silence, lighted interiors. Fascinating!

Jessel posters predominated, then Millward. Lots of television watchers. I crossed the new, or newer, cemetery and bought papers from a tiny kiosk heated by an oil stove – *Express, N of the W, People & Sunday Mirror*. When I got back I had a large gin & began clearing the place up. Supper was a foul mess of stuff – not the chops I'd bought, couldn't face 'um. Faced um tonight. Then tried to write to the Clarendon Press, and finished earlier this evening. Damn silly letter: betrays great want of ideas. This is the end of me as 'a writer'. Well, 20–40, not a bad stretch, though little enough done in it. After this it'll be God knows what – those Harvard lectures, Laureateship, OM ... ogh ogh. CBE, annyhway. Still, I see no reason for turning it down, except feeling it will be an awful burden. I've lost *their* original letter: wish I could find it. Searched & have found it! Felt my letter may have to be revised. I'd like to include *Whitman*, but he's out of the period really. [...]

1 Residential area of Hull.

28 April 1966

32 Pearson Park, Hull

[...] Well, Leavis was no great strain, no more than anyone else, but what a ghastly little man! He seemed to me rather like a Beckett who'd read Lawrence & wasn't Irish: a compulsive talker – one of the bores of the century, I'd say – and really a typical Oxbridge don, cocky, smart, full of petty cattiness. Oh dear. And what a *bore*. 'I live on my nerves,'* he told me   *cf JBW[1]   early on, then later in the afternoon round it came again: 'I live on my nerves.' I don't wonder Cambridge, or Downing, can't stand him at any price, except for electing him to Faculty & asking him to give the Clark lectures. I've never met a man so full of himself. Stupid little sod, the ideas rattling in him like peas. No, a typical don, one who *likes* being a don, full of tricks to make the students laugh, and venomous enough to make A. L. Rowse sound like Hotspur. God. I've not met a *sillier* man for many a long day. Didn't you think he was *silly*? I'm awfully glad to reflect that I don't possess a single book by him. Not a *single* book. [...]

1 John Wain.

30 April 1966

32 Pearson Park, Hull

[...] I had a further dose of Leavis on the Friday – 'Ray'[1] rang up and collared me for the lunch, wch I must say was a lot better than the York one – salmon, cold. Blackcurrant tart & cream. U of Hull Shabbily. Leavis was much as before, happier with university people I thought: he was nasty about Kingsley in a sort of old woman over the garden fence way – the bad state he'd left his house in, broken windows, & so on, & I wondered if I ought to get up & walk out, but reflected that I knew nothing about Kingsley's Cambridge years. Still, I must say that Leavis's resentment at being attacked is a bit ingenuous in view of his own continual stream of adolescent venom. I didn't go to the lecture. At lunch Alun Jones & Armstrong sat opposite me & talked solidly for about 35 mins on domestic heating. [...]

1 Ray Brett.

21 May 1966

32 Pearson Park, Hull

Dearest,

A *dull* evening, too cold without a fire & too warm with one. My disappointment turned more to peevishness: the town seemed particularly oafish and tiresome this afternoon, & hot ... I started out well prepared against a chilly wet day, so that by 3 pm I was sweating & itching. Couldn't get served at lunch, couldn't buy a mouli cheese grater, all shops seemed utterly cheap or bourgeois, no High & Dry, no crystal heart lettuces – I felt all I wanted was small tins of baked beans. *No* books in *any* shops – *Smith's* all guide books, *Brown's* all novels called *Peg o' my Heart* or *My Panda Chums* – no Beverley on Maugham[1], or any novels I have recently seen reviewed along the lines of 'the constant pornographic titillation becomes wearisome', such as *The Nightclerk*, or *The Microcosm*. [...]

1 Beverley Nichols: *A Case of Human Bondage (A Memoir)*, 1966.

24 May 1966

32 Pearson Park, Hull

Dearest,

I don't often write in bed! and shan't, really, now – I'm not ill: it's just that I thought I wished I could be in touch with you. Nicer of course if you were here with me. I love the way you prepare very carefully with brush & cream & scent, as if I weren't there.

I had a dubious hour with Jane Bown, being photographed with ambulances – after *The Q.*, I distrust all these efforts. Much to my annoyance she said Ted wouldn't cooperate, except to *be* photographed – this made me feel very commercial and eager. Bah. She was a funny little woman. She carried, but didn't use, a Rollei: I sneaked a look inside at the lenses & they were filthy. So much for professionals.

I have been doing my jazz article last night & tonight, so that's off my chest. Also finished reading E. Thomas, for the OB. I picked out about 10 – I'm deliberately assembling much more than I need, to give myself choice later. I still think he's good. A poem *Celandine* seemed moving – I've never noticed it before. Do you know it?

Darling, I hope you feel better about the lost weekend. I didn't realise you had things to do when I suggested you came. I expect I shall be with you almost as soon as this, all over you like a dog. I hope the traffic isn't delaying – I shall have not to be impatient: truly. I suddenly found today I hadn't licensed my car – am liable to jug, fines, God knows what. It ought to have been done in March!

Well, that was just a word – must settle down. Goodnight, dear bun – much love as always; very tender. [...]

2 June 1966

32 Pearson Park, Hull

[...] Have spent the evening reading the first 200 or so pages of TH for the book[1] – well, reading and skipping. I have marked a good many, though one or two, that I consider almost too much mine – or yours – I have left unmarked. It's a strange experience: old TH can tweak the heartstrings more unerringly than anyone, yet I haven't actually been tearful tonight, as I so often am. Perhaps the best ones are later, or I am insensitive. Of course it brings you close to me, as you always are, dear, though to be close in such a context is rather a bittersweet experience. Aren't I writing cornily tonight! Perhaps I should scrap this sheet. No, I'll stuff it in. It's just that when I read Hardy my thoughts turn to you, in love. Wasn't that article queer! I'll be sorry if he really had a reason to be sad. I thought he was good precisely because he saw the sadness of life in the abstract. [...]

1 Hardy's poems for the *Oxford Book of Twentieth-Century English Verse*.

4 June 1966

32 Pearson Park, Hull

[...] I am putting in the markers thick and fast now – the book would be half Hardy if I had my way. 'Crocus root', 'Hack of the Parade', 'Sally I see thee', 'Everybody else, then, going', 'Pet fowl come to knee' – they come crowding in. I don't know how I shall ever sort them out. Do you know 'An Anniversary'? Page 441. Very powerful. [...]

Sunday It's about 1 pm, and I've just poured out the Sunday gin. Do you like the photograph? It's a good example of a novice's error – exposure geared to the background instead of the subject. It makes you look like something out of Moberly & Jourdain.[1] Doesn't the background look like a different picture, stuck on? 'I became aware that a rabbit in a flowered dress was looking busily at a bed of lettuces a little way to the right – it wore what appeared to be sunglasses, as a kind of disguise, but these did not impede its swift working. Curiously, when I glanced again in a few minutes, I could discern no rabbit, and no lettuces ...' This is ye onlie trewe coppie, so if you want one, send it back & I'll have one made. I do: want one, I mean.

Well, dig the Tryphena stuff[2] in ye day's Publick prints. I look forward to seeing the book. Joo think iss troo? as Kingsley's joke used to run. A lot of it sounds pretty conjectural. Mind you, I'm prepared to consider that TS was the model for SB[3], who is really too irritating not to have been a real person, but further than that I don't go. I do feel they ought to produce more evidence than a family album photograph that the son existed. After all, I've seen a photograph of some unknown N Orleans trombonist labelled Kid Ory! But it would be disappointing to me if it were true – first, because I've always thought TH a non bastard, & secondly because I should hate him to have some *reason* for being gloomy – I thought he & he alone saw the inherent misery of life. If it *is* true I shall have to fall back on Barnes for the decency, & who for the second? Myself, perhaps. Still, there *are* some odd poems in the Hardy canon – autobiographical stuff one can't account for. I don't think I could ever write poems like that – one must make everything clear, present a picture or a story, not mutter about things you don't want known. I can't quite swallow that *Midnight on the GW* is about this son, either. It just isn't the kind of poem one wd write about someone one *knew* anything about, do you think so? Hutchinson, 40/-. Awgh. Nice rabbity publisher, anyway. [...]

1 In *An Adventure* (1911), Charlotte Moberly and Eleanor Jourdain claimed to have seen Marie Antoinette while visiting the Palace of Versailles in 1901.
2 'Concerning Tryphena Sparks', in *Providence and Mr Hardy* by Lois Deacon and Terry Coleman, a book that floated many conjectures about Hardy's life and relationships.
3 Sue Bridehead.

11 June 1966

32 Pearson Park, Hull

Dearest,

11.20 pm – have just upset a large tumbler of white wine over the carpet – all I had left, too! Awgh! Awwghgh! Have got out the Glenfyddich, or however you spell it, in compensation. I'm sorry you are slaving away at scripts. It must be a foul job. Let's hope from teaching machines we proceed to examining machines – well, why not? Bloody sight easier to arrange, I'd say: Name the 'odd man out' of the following—

Oscar Wilde
E. M. Forster
John Galsworthy
Christopher Isherwood

(Answer: Oscar Wilde, he was b. in Ireland ogh ogh ogh fooled again) [...]

Misprint in the CQ proof of my Hardy review[1] – *Far From the Madding Crows*. Dr Pussy thinks, well, yes, they can be very irritating, standing gossiping when you want your next course.

362

Sunday Dull morning; I feel dull, depressed too, I suppose. I read the Hardy book yesterday & it depressed me rather, seeming to show as it does the shortness and sadness of life. There is a lot in it. I don't know whether to buy a copy for myself – rather dear at 2 quid. Much time is taken in parallelling plots of books with suspected events – Elfrida & Knight & the other chap in *A Pair of B. Eyes* as Tryphena (not EL, despite the hair & riding), Hardy & Moule, for instance. It's all rather a *tour de force*, with little concrete at the centre, but no doubt there is something there. [...]

I do look forward to seeing you. I have been very unhappy all this year & still am – all this Hardy stuff seems to underline it. I agree about camels drinking.[2] With me it's rather different – I feel this isn't natural to me, or kin – I don't know why we can't live our lives like everyone else. Reading abt TH binds me to you deeply, yet if the story is true he is just another writer – I find this depressing. Almost like DHL, really! 'One sloughs one's sicknesses in books.' i.e. one retells real events to one's own advantage ogh ogh. Darling, will you write again? If not, I'll meet the 4.33 at 6.13 at St P's. You'll be in plenty of time. I love you, dear rabbit – Philip

1 L. reviewed Roy Morrell's *Thomas Hardy: The Will and the Way* and Carl J. Weber's *Hardy of Wessex: His Life and Literary Career* in the *Critical Quarterly* VIII, 2 (Summer 1966). The review was called 'Wanted: Good Hardy Critic', and it later appeared in *Required Writing*.
2 Monica had written in a letter dated 5 June 1966, from 1A Cross Road: 'Are you writing to me? As you wrote a fortnight ago, how silly our lives are. Darling, I do feel lonely & wish for you. We had a nice time last weekend, but no, I can't say I do feel the happier for it; why should I? Well, I suppose I do in that it is one more nice time to add to all our nice times, but it's *over* now & *that* doesn't make me happy; it isn't like camels drinking, is it?'

8 October 1966

32 Pearson Park, Hull

I *never* got a reply from Terry.[1] Haw haw.

Dearest,

Buses run lighted down Princes Avenue like school reports. 'Fair Only.' It is a misty evening. The flat is full of the smell of another lamb stew, smaller this time, & simpler (no kidney, I found them difficult &

363

revolting to cut). Apart from it being later than I shd like, it's a nice moment of time.

I was much relieved to get your letter this morning and to know you felt less distressed. I slept very badly last night thinking about it all. I don't take any credit for this, for really my thoughts were mostly selfish, I suppose – dread of being forced into action. There isn't any need to make my situation any better-sounding than it is: a self-centred person conducting an affair containing almost no responsibilities with one girl getting mixed up with another, heedless of the feelings of either. Well, not heedless, but not heedful enough to do anything about it, anyway. I suppose one reason I don't find it easy to talk about it all is that it doesn't bear talking about, if I'm to keep any self respect. I also find it painful.

The incident in July I half mentioned wasn't really epoch-making: Maeve suddenly got very cross at my evident preoccupation with you & said she was going to clear out for 6 months, & if I decided I wanted her I could see if she was still available, and in the meantime she wd do what she liked & so on (as far as I can see she does that anyway). I didn't really respond to this, & she found the separation so upsetting that she called it off, but it has left its mark. Then her holiday came, then mine, then hers again, then you, then this week we really haven't had any coincident time free. I suppose we are wondering 'how we stand'. You may wonder why I don't end it, in my own interest as well as yours. Partly cowardice – I dread the scene. Partly kindness – if I've encouraged her to depend on me it seems cruel to turn her away. If she wanted to be free it wd be different. I could lose her completely easier than I could have her half-dependent. And it's painful in a way to end something that however silly and inconsiderate did at one time seem a different kind of experience from anything hitherto. All the same, I think we are going in that direction. I only hope it can be done friendlily, because we do have to have a lot to do with each other anyway. Never have the Gods of the C. Headings[2] been better exemplified: Don't Touch the Female Staff.

I don't expect all this seems particularly endearing to you – I say it because I never seem to say anything, & I sometimes think if you knew more you'd worry less.

Sunday. Well, I wonder. *If* I send this, dear, it is because I want to say *something* to you, & not seem to be trying to pretend the situation doesn't exist. I wish it didn't now. I was ashamed on holiday when Maeve's letter or letters came, not because there was anything especially amorous in them, but for seeming so careless of your feelings & so bloody bad mannered, even. It was incredibly stupid & vulgar of me to spoil our holiday in such a way. I could quite easily have said I didn't want any letters.

Darling, this seems far from the 'nice' letter you ask for: I *am* at home with you, & think you are delightful and irreplaceable: I hate it when you go, for the dreary failure & selfishness on my part it seems to symbolise – this is nothing to do with Maeve, you've always come before her: it's my own unwillingness to give myself to anyone else that's at fault – like promising to stand on one leg for the rest of one's life. And yet I never think I am doing anything but ruin your life & mine. I suppose one shouldn't be writing letters like this at 44, one ought to have got it all sorted out twenty years ago.

Let me try to write nicely for compensation – dear lovely rabbit, my large white, my lettuce-eater ('Courage!' she said, or Courrège I suppose). I ate the lamb stew for lunch: it was simpler than yours, but quite all right. I'm not in much of an eating mood, though. I am persevering with my no-gin & little milk campaign, & have lost about 3 pounds, but don't see any progress beyond this point. One splendid morning I was down nearly to 13st 7 lbs again, but it didn't last. How are you getting on? I think of you padding about, leaving the bathroom strewn with powder. The bed continues, but I couldn't say it was a dream of comfort: dream of your granny. I wake up & lie wretchedly as of yore. I feel quite tired *now*, sleepy: I really need an after dinner sleep regularly. Are you sleeping all right? [...]

1 Arthur Terry, Lecturer and eventually Professor of Spanish at Queen's University, Belfast.
2 The Kipling poem, 'The Gods of the Copybook Headings'.

13 October 1966

32 Pearson Park, Hull

My dear,

It's only with difficulty that I bring myself to lay down C. S. Lewis's *Letters*, & write to you. You know I meant to bring them on holiday. They are really most interesting, (a) because of his odd private life (b) because he is an English teacher (c) because he is of our time. By the first I mean only that at an early age – about 25 – he took to living with the mother of a friend of his who had been killed, & her daughter – Mrs Moore – and referring to her as 'mother' & the house as 'home', although he had a home & a father (not a mother) in N. Ireland. He kept this up till his early 50's, doing housework & putting up with Mrs Moore, who was not bookish or clever or even particularly agreeable. There is no hint that the daughter came into it. What can have led him into such a strange association?

It's a nice life, being good at being fond of books. You watch him golloping them down, & getting a living out of it, & finding more books to gollop. I wish I could have done it. I don't think I really liked books, not old books anyway. I could never feel that Chaucer was as real as the *Daily Mail*, & so I was never an academic. He became a Fellow of Magdalen at abt 27. The President said a lot of Latin over him (him kneeling on a red cushion & everyone standing round) for abt 5 minutes, then stopped. *No one had told him what to do*. After a moment he ventured 'Do fidem', wch seemed to go down all right. Of course he'd understood $\frac{2}{3}$rds of the Latin, but even so I think it was pretty sharp of him. I have got about halfway, just up to 1940: not too much religion so far.

I'm slowly getting to like my bed (perhaps I'm hollowing out a place in it – I don't think so): I slept beautifully last night till about 7.15 a.m., very good. It isn't in my nature to like it immediately. As you say, the not-having-to-make-it is a joy.

I got 10 gns for that *Urban blues* review. Also Fabers sent a 6 months' a/c up to 30 June – *Jill* doing poorly, only 70 copies or so sold, *TWW* doing well, 543 copies, almost 3 a day. In all, 7210 copies (& 3225 in U.S.), total takings about £520, leaving US out. That's success in poetry. Of course that's just royalties, not anthology fees. Still. Pardon this excursion into Arnold Bennett land. [...]

I have been worrying lest my Sunday letter has antagonised or upset you.[1] It was written in some stress. More probably it just repelled you: I'm sorry. These personal letters aren't really a success. I have said to Maeve that I should like things to be cooler: not much consequence. We are all still too busy to see anything of each other even if we wanted to. Under C. S. Lewis's influence I feel attracted to the life of the study – I sound like Boswell. Anyway, don't let it trouble you – it isn't meant to – and don't refer to it if you don't want to. [...]

How is the work you weren't looking forward to, that 2-hour class, for instance? Is it this term? I do hope it isn't a bother. I look forward to hearing from you, dear: my efforts to bring us closer seem to have had less success than I meant, but you are always very near to me – I am surrounded by so many things you have a part in, & that I can't see without thinking of you. Even the dear caboc, now nearly gone – how easily it goes! Swiftly comes & swiftly goes. And the bed too: large & meant for your greater ease, mine too of course. I must go to it, with C. S. Lewis. Goodnight, dear. [...]

1 i.e., the letter dated 8 October 1966.

30 October 1966

32 Pearson Park, Hull

My dear,

I have put the mauve sheets on the bed, which means it's a month since you were here & the bed came. They look very pretty – I shall have to wear the mauve pyjamas to match. This has been an odd day: I went 'in' in the morning to clear up some work, and after lunch was about to dash off a short note to you when I was seized with a desire to *see* you – I leapt into the car (at 2.45!) and drove into the greying West. Well, of course, it was all very silly: when I reached Bawtry I realised I had only 26/- & needed lots more petrol – and if by any chance you *shouldn't* have been there ... It was four o'clock and mists were beginning to gather, so I turned round and came home. It would have meant six hours driving for 2 hours meeting! Yet if I'd had plenty of money I might have persisted. I got back here about a quarter to six, having spent the afternoon driving 100 of the dullest miles in the neighbourhood. A misguided impulse, yet I did want to see you: not *about* anything, just as a comfort. I wonder if I'd have found you in, if I'd arrived about 5.45? Perhaps you'd have been alarmed at a caller. Shall I try to call in on my way home on Thursday? It won't be for very long – an hour, perhaps. But I know I shall long to overshoot L'borough and come to see you. Will you be there, about seven, six or seven? Or will you be at some *theatrical production*?

I feel rather scared these days, of time passing & us getting older. Our lives are so different from other people's, or have been, – I feel I am landed on my 45th year as if washed up on a rock, not knowing how I got here or ever having had a chance of being anywhere else. Indeed, when I think of being in my *twenties*, or my *thirties*, I can't call up any solid different image, typical & unshakable. Twenties ... 1942 to 1951 ... Thirties ... 1952 to 1961 ... Of course my external surroundings have changed, but inside I've been the same, trying to hold everything off in order to 'write'. Anyone wd think I was Tolstoy, the value I put on it. It hasn't amounted to much. I mean, I know I've been successful in that I've made a name & got a medal & so on, but it's a very small achievement to set against all the rest. This is *Dockery & Son* again – I shall spend the rest of my life trying to get away from that poem. [...]

15 November 1966

32 Pearson Park, Hull

Dearest,

I was rather disturbed by the news of your freak wind this afternoon, that I heard on Radio Newsreel, or spewsfeel as I irrelevantly and irreverently call it to myself. I wish I could ring up and satisfy myself that you are all right. I *expect* you are ... Moat School, they seemed to say, was damaged. I hope you were snugly indoors. Ought I to send a telegram? They didn't say anyone was hurt, except these school people, though there was much damage to property.

It's half past (harp-arsed) eight (sort of Aeolian harp ogh ogh) & I am feeling rather exhausted. Patsy[1] cleared off after lunch on Monday, having rather corpsed me. As a visit it was as well as could be expected: not unlike one of yours, in as much as we didn't do much, just sat about and drank. The first day, Saturday, I met her at the Station & we had lunch, then a bit of shopping, then back to the flat for *sleep* (in chairs) & drinks & simple meal, more drinks ... I ran her home about 1 or so. Sunday I picked her up about 11, showed her the University, went to the Haworth, back for simple meal (one thing about her she doesn't bother about food), somnolence & letters, tea, drinks, simple meal, drinks ... This time things went rather less well: after finishing the bottle (of port) I was ready to take her to her hotel, but she suddenly reattacked 'her' gin (de Kuypers) & became rather drunk and quarrelsome & cried, all of wch was embarrassing and depressing – I couldn't make out what she was on about (I couldn't understand her very well at the best of times): she'd been blaming me for not being continental & so on: I suppose if I suggest it was pique & depression at my not asking her to stay the night you'll hoot conceited rubag & perhaps be right. It was rather complicated by her having nowhere to go until she collected her wards next Saturday from Downside.[2] No doubt she'd have liked to stay here, but I didn't encourage the idea. Anyway, I got her back about 2 a.m., & returned deeply depressed: it seemed a glimpse of another, more horrible world, quite a true world in a way, but one inhabited by people like Brendan Behan[3] & not yours truly. The next day she apologised for 'keeping me up' and all went well, gossipy lunch with Kenyon[4] & a Dublin historian named Watt: she can rattle off history chat all right. Anyway, you can imagine my exhaustion, & it's far from cleared up: I was doing well until this last week. Late nights & people!!! I really must go to bed early. [...]

1 By this time Patsy Strang had been divorced from Richard Murphy for several years (since 1959), and was living in Dublin. See Appendix B.
2 Catholic boarding school for boys; Patsy was guardian to two nephews whose parents had died.
3 Irish playwright, known for his drunken and self-destructive behaviour.
4 J. P. Kenyon, at the time Professor of History at Hull.

22 November 1966

32 Pearson Park, Hull

[...] My suit has come – v. dull. Haven't worn it yet. The button-holes are cut out & machined on one side only in best Monty Burton style. What am I paying money for? It is school-master grey, dull, dull, dull. Shall wear it at once: it needn't flatter itself it's going to be my 'best' suit. Shall wear it tomorrow at the departmental reps. tea party, & the Vernon Watkins dinner, & the Vernon Watkins lecture, & the Vernon Watkins evening after, *chez* Rees the French ... Then the Vernon Watkins lunch on Thursday, & the Donini presentation, & the Donini dinner, & the Donini lecture ... I feel like cutting my throat with a blunt cunt, as I find Dylan Thomas said. (I don't think that funny in the way most people wd, but I think it mildly funny all the same.)

I'm delighted you had such a good time in Lichfield, but it does all sound most uncharacteristic – a day not spoilt by no lunch, made by old books in an unheated library! Cor stone the crows. Pox got to yer bonce or what. I've never thought Lichfield *was* at all pretty – hellish unending mouth filling, nose filling, ear filling traffic, cathedral denuded by Cromwell (was it?), town all garages & tea shops & knocked down slums, not a single decent hotel. There's a sort of pond, isn't there, & an old-style bow-windowed double-fronted chemist. I wonder if the cathedral library is written up at all. It's a town of grim association for me. My first Oxford Christmas I spent there – well, no, I didn't: I went there, where my mother was, & where my father intended to come, but the Uncle & Aunt couldn't face it & tipped us all out, so we spent it at Coventry in perfect safety. I expect my mother had been irritating them, but they were pretty neolithic in their own way. I think it was insensitive of my father to send my mother there. In fact I stayed in 'lodgings', but ate there, a kind of silent Rosemary, only longing to get away & continue reading *Scenes from Clerical Life* & lurk near the Cathedral at dusk, to see the few people going in. I didn't dare go in myself, of course, not knowing how to act in the service.

Bought the new Auden *Sh. Poems* today.[1] Stupid ass, he's been mucking about with them again. He & Graves are a right pair. It's odd how these 'poetry-is-magic' boys are always the first to monkey about with it – just what you *can't* do, if it's magic. *Fee fi fo* – no, not *fum*; let's say *trouser-button*, that suits my ear better. *Fee fi fo trouser-button* – why, where are you all going? Oh, well, I've got my writers fellowship. *Fee fi fo writers fellowship* ... All I wish to preserve. *Fui.* Preserve your granny. [...]

1 W. H. Auden: *Collected Shorter Poems* (1966).

26 November 1966

32 Pearson Park, Hull

[...] I think I am feeling a little better today, though waves of sadness, fear, remorse, fear and all the rest of it wash over me periodically like the automatic flushing of a urinal (do these 'an hotel' wallahs say 'an urinal'?). I have started *Jane & Prudence*.[1] I wish I cd do something on her – CQ are having a 10th anniversary no. ('ah me, the years, O!') but I don't suppose they'd accept it – her work depends on such tiny lowly things ('Prawns (and other fish)') I should find it hard to erect a claim to such serious critical attention as is focused on *Lord Jim* or *Lord of the Flies* on them. Are there 'values' there? 'Real' values, not just M. Lathbury valuing Bone 'because he was a churchgoer'? And how about dynamism, Life, etc.? I must say I find her books absolutely pulsing with life – I never think 'O god, here's that dull chapter about –' as I do with, well, DHL for one. Yet there is a sort of woman's magazine quality there – a kind of cosyness – surely the best novels aren't cosy – reassuring, perhaps, but in BP all characters seems potbound, nobody's ever going to *do* anything, Harry isn't going to screw Wilmet, Prudence isn't *really* having an affair with Fabian, do you think, even, that Piers buggers Keith? I don't. I suppose in a way M. Lathbury is the best of the heroines because she doesn't flirt with action, just plugs on uncomplaining. Like, in a way, Mary Beamish. I do wish I cd isolate what, if anything, is *good* abt her. Can you help me?

Bit of a shock to see John Perree & that other chap & the rest of the Sarkese in the paper today, wasn't it? Yes, I expect Sark *is* being spoilt. Well, we knew it, it is our darling scenery, & it'll never be *quite* spoilt because there's no wonderful beaches for oil-soaked bitches. It is my ideal place. I wish we could go there again, just once again – those lanes! that sea! *The Mermaid*! The flowers! The cows! (The hens!) [...]

1 Novel by Barbara Pym (1953).

29 March 1967

Dublin[1]

Dearest,

Late, after dinner in Trinity, everyone else falling about but I thought there wasn't enough drink. *Or eat.* I was delighted to get your card & the v. Dr Pussyish scene it showed, & of course to know, as I shdn't have known if I hadn't rung you up, that your rings are safe – I *am* glad, I needn't say more.[2]

Well, the crossing was *all right* – very rough indeed, but pitching not rolling, & it be the rolling that do do for I. No puking: $2\frac{1}{2}$ pints in the bar (the ½ was to see what it was like) & then a cold, sleepless but otherwise untroubled night. All the same, conferences are hell. We are stranded out in some godforsaken suburb, no stamps, no pub, no papers, miles even from the hall we meet in – I have no stamps yet, but *hope* to find some tomorrow. Radio Eireann rang up tonight to do a short interview tomorrow: fame. [...]

Dublin is fascinating in its horribleness – I can look at it for hours: sat looking out of the window of some law library watching the nuns & begging children & broken fanlights. Meantime K. Humphreys found a backless 1st ed of *Endymion* on the open shelves. Dublin!

Love, darling – *wish you were here*. P.

1 L. was at a librarians' conference in Dublin.
2 Monica had earlier supposed her rings had been stolen.

2 April 1967

21 York Road, Loughborough, Leics.

Dearest bun,

Here is a note to greet you when you arrive[1] – you *will* feel out of your element, but you must remember that girl in *No Fond Return*.[2] Will you have a bottle of gin in your handbag? I've never been inside a York hall: hope they have washbowls in the rooms. [...]

I didn't evade Patsy in the end: the Conference had been reported in the local paper & I found a letter from her asking me to ring her up. So I did, & spent Friday evening with her. She had her two nephews there, but Emily (10) had just set off for a spell with her father. She seemed much the same, i.e. rather depressing – I had the same feeling, to a lesser extent, that I had when she came to Hull, that of being in a book by Edna O'Brien. However, she told me one or two things – Hilly is getting married, to an old (55) Caius don who is giving up his job & going with her to Ann Arbor, at no doubt double the pay.[3] A classics don, a bachelor. Patsy's own professor is booked for a year at Cambridge so she is going to spend term time there, though it seems rather an odd set up. I wonder if it will 'go down' – I didn't remind her that in Ireland you can do what you like as long as you say the same as everyone else, but that in England it's the reverse, & *vice versa*, but I thought it. Hilly's old don is called Shackleton-Shagbag, or something.

I hope you don't mind my seeing her: it was all quite harmless, though I certainly don't want to see any more of her than I can help.[4] We had a dear & not very nice dinner at the Russell Hotel. [...]

Well, I hope you'll like the *novelty* of being at York – I hope it's a 'good' conference, in the catering sense – have you just had strong Indian tea & biscuits? That's always a grim welcome, I find. Is there a lock or bolt on your door? You'll need it among all those men. I wonder if you'll ring up tonight. Apart from seeing you, and I suppose getting away from here, I don't really want to go back. I feel my spirits will sink, even at the sight of *Betty*,[5] let alone the mound of 'post'. Anyway, *all being well*, I'll show up around 5.15 or 5.30, room 214, C 214, Langwith Hall. Dear! can we go to The old store? Where your ancestors had their roots? Rotten bad beer it is there, as I remember, but never mind. [...]

1 Monica was at a conference at York University.
2 Barbara Pym, *No Fond Return of Love* ('that girl': see Viola, Chapter 18).
3 Hilly Amis's new husband was D. R. Shackleton-Bailey, a classical scholar.
4 L. was obviously sensitive that Monica would be reminded of L.'s intermittent affair with Patsy, 1952–4 (see *Selected Letters*).
5 Betty Mackereth, L.'s secretary 1957–84.

9 April 1967

32 Pearson Park, Hull

Dearest,

Well, what jubilation in the long archaic burrows under Petergate in York, & Fleminggate in Beverley, & in Conisborough and Earswick and all other subterranean candlelit communities! The years, the centuries even, of continual nibbling and sniping and gnawing and scraping bringing success at last! Can't you imagine them drinking and gorging, and singing all the old songs, *Down, down, down* and the like, in celebration of the Dean's announcement? What persistence! Rather unrabbity, really, but where the sense of true wrong burns, strength is found.

What a nice letter you sent, too: it arrived very splashed with rain, but still. I'm glad T & W[1] came back with you, if it 'settled you in', though the breakage rate seems excessive for such quiet people! Some celebration about York, perhaps on your part. I can't say I got at all a clear impression of the conference, wch is hardly surprising: everything seemed too fragmentary for me to take in, even if I could hear it, wch I often couldn't. They seemed a gayer & more intelligent lot than librarians, though – probably are. We are your failures, your aegrotats, the people the Appointments Board can't 'place', the stammerers, the twitchers, the 'unrelaxed'. I've *never* known a late night party at a library conference, for instance, on the Warwick lines. Still, I do my best to redress the balance, not with much success. Everyone has 'bad stomachs' or are just too mean to pay a round, or too scared of being 'caught at it', or else they 'don't like the taste of' beer &c. I'm not sure what I should think of Bill if he didn't come under your recommendation, but he certainly was nicely dressed, better than anyone. Tom seems like some small friendly unimpressive animal, a mole or vole, Wendy a fearful basking shark. Ellis² seemed a decent chap, good officer material: we got on well. I'm sorry Sutherland³ didn't appear – I suppose he *does* exist? I've certainly met someone you *introduced* as Sutherland, years ago. [...]

1 Tom and Wendy Craik; Tom was a colleague of Monica's, Wendy a former student.
2 John Ellis, colleague of Monica's at Leicester, 1964–6, then Lecturer at Edinburgh.
3 John Sutherland, former student of Monica's.

23 April 1967

32 Pearson Park, Hull

[...] I seem to have spent a rather fruitless week, spending the evenings sleeping or staring at an incomplete & v. modest poem.¹ On Friday I 'got drunk' – this is perhaps a theatrical way of saying I had two gins before supper instead of one – still, you know my gins! Now is the woodcock near the gin: they often quote that at the club, much to the annoyance of Sir Jeremy (Jemmy) Woodcock. I think it is funny the way my idea of happiness is to be listening, part-drunk, to jazz ... I mean, compared with other people's ideas: am I just an old *dérèglement*² boy after all, a Hart Crane?

The poem is four lines wch I thought all right, then four more lines wch are less good; now I really want four more about as good as the combined best of Wordsworth & Omar Khayyam to sort of lift the thing up to a finish.

Talking of poetry, have you ever come across these three enigmatic lines from Wallace Stevens?

374

And to feel that the light is a rabbit-light,
In which everything is meant for you
And nothing need be explained ...

Rather nice, isn't it? From *A Rabbit as King of the Ghosts*, complete bunk otherwise. But doesn't the extract sound deeply sympathetic to you? [...]

1 'The Trees'.
2 'le dérèglement de tous les sens' (Rimbaud).

10 May 1967

32 Pearson Park, Hull

[...] The Monday night dinner was rather curious. It was with a woman called Baily[1] who is in The Retreat[2] in York. I had known her very slightly at Oxford, & a year or so ago she sent me some poems she'd written, no good. Then she said she was coming up here & hoped I wd come over & see her, which I did, somewhat nervously: her letters hadn't been reassuring, broken marriage & suicide attempts & so on. However, we had dinner at Young's, & she seemed quite in control of herself, but you can never tell. She showed me some of The Retreat before we started, wch wasn't too bad, but it had that hospital smell – as well as the fitted carpets. The dinner was pretty rotten, I might add. She looked alert, dowdy & a bit toothy: a small woman. She's not *paying* at the Retreat: her sister is married to one of the governors. [...]

1 Penelope Baily, *née* Scott Stokes. At Somerville 1941–2, and played Viola in a college production of *Twelfth Night*, which L. saw and on the strength of it invited her to tea. 'So through that unripe day ...' (No. 30 in *The North Ship*) was the result.
2 Private nursing home in York.

13 May 1967

32 Pearson Park, Hull

[...] Well, poor Masefield is gone.[1] I read about it at the breakfast table, my own hold on life not feeling too secure. I hope they offer it to Betjeman: he is so obviously the only serious candidate, & it might revive interest in the office. C.D.L.[2] would be just a cypher. Peterborough[3]

mentions Plomer!⁴ Cor stone the crows. Do you think B. would like it?
I think he would: I think he could stand it, too. [...]

1 John Masefield (1878–1967), Poet Laureate, 1930–67.
2 C. Day Lewis: he succeeded Masefield as Poet Laureate in 1968.
3 Columnist in the *Daily Telegraph*.
4 William Plomer, poet (1903–73).

3 June 1967

32 Pearson Park, Hull

[...] I celebrated TH's birthday by *finishing* my sixteen year old's poem
about spring etc. Well, completing a draft.¹ It runs:

The trees are coming into leaf
Like something almost being said,
The recent buds relax and spread,
Their greenness is a kind of grief.

The faint reclothing of midair
That thickens into restless towers
Creates a different world from ours
Up to the edge of winter. There

A summer is a separate thing
That makes no reference to the past,
And may not even be the last,
And mocks our lack of blossoming.

PAL (VI mod), eh? First verse all right, the rest crap, especially the
last line. What do you think of it? I'd like to do one on Dutch tavern
scenes now. 'Jan Hockspew staggers to the door ...'² [...]

1 Stanzas 2 and 3 are quite different from what appears to be the final version of
'The Trees', dated 2 June 1967 in Notebook 7.
2 Cf. 'The Card-Players', not completed until 6 May 1970.

9 June 1967

32 Pearson Park, Hull

[...] Did I tell you I wrote to Betjeman offering him our Arts Co.
poetry lectureship?¹ £2000 + expenses, 2 nights a week in term. D'you

think he'll take it? D'you think he'll keep faith if he does? I shall be equally unsurprised if he accepts or refuses. Two thousand for sitting on your, if you'll pardon the word, may mean more to him than one imagines. On the other hand, think of trying to talk to our students! Or our staff! And coming up here, in the snow & in the wind! We'll see. [...]

1 Betjeman turned down the offer of the Arts Council (or Joseph Compton) Poetry lectureship at Hull, and it was taken up by Day Lewis, soon to be appointed Poet Laureate.

23 August 1967

32 Pearson Park, Hull

[...] Another fine day, after a misty start. It was nice to hear you tonight. After ringing off I went out to see George to tell him about Norman Jackson. He was alone, except for Laurien who made me a cup of coffee: Jean[1] was 'having a drink at the Liberal Club'. Eh, bé. She got a B in her A level English, but hasn't heard about her O levels yet. Not bad for someone who was in hospital and anyway had never taken an exam in her youth. The ponce showed me a blurb for a reprint of *Listen* saying 'As PL said, merely to read the list of *Listen*'s contributors is to call the roll of all that is best in,' etc. 'Where did I say that?' I asked, genuinely puzzled. 'In this very room,' he said. The bastard!! The bastard!!! [...]

1 Jean Hartley.

27 August 1967

32 Pearson Park, Hull

[...] *Evening* I feel rather upset tonight, after ringing you up & finding you so down. You sound *so* drunk on the telephone, it makes me wonder how much you've been drinking, knowing how you can outdrink me – not that I am grumbling about this, of course, only if it's in sadness, & if the sadness is my fault, of course I am upset. Perhaps I seem to shrink back a little – not through unfriendliness, of course, through embarrassment. I feel: 'He drove her to drink.' I don't know what to say.
– God, now I hear B. Epstein is dead.[1]

Later – Just as I wrote that you rang. Now *I* have been drinking, and feel happier, because you called & because of the gin I suppose. Thank you for calling.

Monday Another dull morning, & the sensation of being on my own is most unfamiliar. It makes me wonder how I should get on if I had enough money not to work. I suppose one would have to make up a timetable & obey it, or else one would 'go to seed'. I have felt rather seedy this morning, returning to bed to finish *Strangers & Brothers*[2] which is an appallingly dull & bad book: do you remember it is dedicated to 'H. E. Howard'? I remember him: hadn't there been some scandal about *him*? He was an English master at Peel's school, & Peel said something about him. I'm inclined to think Collins did as well. Perhaps *he* was the common archetype of these fictional figures. I met him once or twice: didn't he come to the Old Horse sometimes? Broad man. [...]

1 Brian Epstein, the Beatles' manager.
2 C. P. Snow, *Strangers & Brothers* (1940).

7 September 1967

21 York Road, Loughborough, Leics.

Dearest bun,

God, this is being a week. National Rage, Irritation, Boredom & Depression Week. Give generously. I'm all these things. Home, home, hideous home. Well, you know all these things. No point in going on about it. [...]

Today is the day of the 'big tea', for wch lunch & supper can be forfeited. After lunch I shall have to put on different clothes, go & fetch the car at 4.30, then heigh ho for Forest Road & sponge cake in glass, in at the mouth etc. I shall believe in the 'supper' when I see it. The idea of supplying coffee with the pork pie apparently appalled her. All that work! All that washing up. I expect I shall be forced to eat & drink alone in humiliation, male greed being pandered to by saintly sister, aargh –

Pause while I pour out a second Guinness. Aawwgh ... [...]

Had a form from 'Who's Who in America' yesterday – big deal. Expect everyone else has been in for years. Have filled up the form, describing myself as 'University Librarian' – as long as I get four times as much money for this role as for 'author', 'writer', 'poet' I shall go on doing so. Besides, the other roles send shivers down my spine. *Who's Who* changed it, after a few years, without asking me. Annoyed me a bit, but what the hell. Apparently one can be in *W.W. in A.* under either of two headings – 'Titular' or 'Achievemental'. I'm achievemental. Yare, yare. It couldn't be called ungentle. [...]

22 October 1967

32 Pearson Park, Hull

[...] I look at the world rather bleakly today – this trip to Edinburgh means I must clear things up, wch I must do anyway, so I was in the Library last night and shall be again tonight. And there are the usual household things to do. The day didn't get off to a very good start by my reading some stories by 'Flannery O'Connor' in the bath – horribly depressing American South things. I felt pretty depressed anyway, age, death, ingratitude, failure, all the usual things. Sometimes I think 'I wish I could tell Monica all this', but what's the use. You can look out of your life like a train & see what you're heading for, but you can't stop the train. [...]

28 October 1967

32 Pearson Park, Hull

[...] Digging out my 1953 audiogram led me to reread my diaries from then to 'the crack up' in 1961, a curious experience: they're very much what GSF wd call a 'persona' and an unpleasant one at that, but there does seem a noticeable sense of strain. I really ought to burn them: there's very little good in them ('I'm full of the cheese of human kindness – milk of h.k. gone sour'), though do you remember asking Hoggart whether the words 'Nigger', 'Wop' and 'Yid' were 'bad in themselves'? Ogh ogh ogh. [...]

31 October 1967

32 Pearson Park, Hull

[...] Cat. Lit is a very fine concept. Charlotte Mew. Uncle Tom's Cabin. Tabby or not Tabby, that is the question.

You know Mrs Cornford's poem for All Souls Eve?[1]

I dreamed my love came back to me
Under the November tree
Shadowless and dim
He put his hand upon my shoulder,
He did not think me strange, or older,
Nor I him.

I hope you like it – I do, & always think of you when I think it to myself, which is often. Bob wrote, signing himself Secretary, Caerleon-on-Usk Nathanael Tarn Society. He's a mad ass. See you Friday! London tomorrow! Love!! xxxx P.

1 Frances Cornford, 'All Souls Night', included by L. in *OBTCEV*.

12 November 1967

32 Pearson Park, Hull

[…] I enclose 3 more Bellingham pictures.[1] I love the one of the wrestlers – it absolutely has the scene as it was, the odd ritualistic stance & garb of the wrestlers, & the rural crowd in a circle. What a lovely day it was! It will stay in my mind for ever, it was lovely. The others are the *World* champion putting away his trophy, & the pretty awful one of you. You don't look like that! […]

I've been pegging on with the *Oxford Book of Mediocre Verse*, & took great pleasure in LAG STRONG, cor mate, syph got to yer bonce or what. Do you know him? One about a girl singing to seals:

Leave her alone,
She is the Islands' daughter.
Sleek heads, dark heads
Are risen from the water:
Leave her the company
Her songs have brought her.

And there's one about rabbits and a prehistoric site of a town – 'The white scut bobs among the stones That still are faithful to his bones'. I ploughed through E. Jennings with some boredom: what a lot she writes! And how sort of conventional it is! […]

1 L. and Monica had been to the Bellingham Show in Northumberland, which they often visited when staying at Monica's cottage in Haydon Bridge. This is the scene evoked in 'Show Saturday' (completed 3 December 1973).

23 November 1967

32 Pearson Park, Hull

[...] I gave my record recital at the Anglican Chaplaincy last night. Not so opulent as the RCs! And not as good an audience – only about a dozen. Aawgh!! They were very pleasant, however, except for one jeaned nuisance who kept on about Blue Grass – not the scent, some kind of music. I feel I should do more for them, but when I talk to students I feel entirely devoid of desire to educate or make contact. I quite like listening to them, & looking at their legs in the case of the girls, but can't always hear what they say, & certainly don't as a rule know enough to reply. Which side are we on – North or South Vietnam? Aawgh. However, perhaps I could give them some more money, or records. They weren't *badly* off, but it was a good deal less rich & large than the RC place. [...]

I think about Jan Hogspewer (flor. 1600) sometimes these days – I would write a poem about him if I believed poems about works of art were licit, but I can't think of any way in which it would be.

Friday. I am now sitting in the SCR opposite Pollard & Brett, so I can hardly withstand the tremendous pressure of steam-intellect coming across the littered coffee table.

Oh dear. I don't seem to be able to write you the interesting sort of letter I should like to – if I lived in the golden age of English letter writing, and had nothing to do but snuff the candles, draw the curtains, and lodge the kettle on the fire, I'm sure I could do much better. 'Past Turvey's Mill on my walk, dyd see a *Hare*,' etc. A pity we can't live in our imaginations! My kitchen wireless has gone wrong, so I eat my meals in silence – having heard the Archers in the sitting room. All being well, I shall see you next weekend. I don't know whether I shall appear by six – I'll let you know.

Great brains now slouched off, both after grumbling about the Library. Wanted to turn round & show them my bum, not for the grumbles but for raising them outside workin' hours, while I was writing a letter. Darling, I wish you were here & could see these people.

On my walk this afternoon I shall see the Ferens Fine Art Committee (2 pm) and the Academic Bd of S.E. Asian Studies (4.30 pm) OOYA BUGGER Love love

xx love x love to dear bun   Philip

28 November 1967

32 Pearson Park, Hull

Dearest bun,

I've just had that pair of swine from Loughborough[1] on the telephone, & it has left me in a rage, even more in a rage because I couldn't think *why* I felt in a rage & so formulate it while I was on to them. I'm not very good at taking offence! *Why* I was annoyed was that this bloody holiday of theirs was again shoved at me, without any hint of (a) sorry to be putting you out – presumably they don't think they *are* putting me out – this is all some private whim of mine, wanting Mother not to be left alone (b) thank you for letting us go away with a clear conscience – they wd go away anyway, they have no feelings at all. I was flabbergasted by their *sheer hoglike gracelessness*. I could hardly believe it was happening. Neither made any reference to any feelings Mother might have in the matter: I simply said I couldn't decide until I knew wch she preferred, & I also rubbed it into Walter about not leaving her alone at Christmas, wch he didn't like, & was scarcely civil about. The whole thing has been conducted on a basis of you-asked-to-be-told-we're-telling-you. God knows I'm obliging enough about putting myself out for people if asked nicely, but I certainly am not being asked nicely this time. The sons of sods. I wonder if you see why I feel like this? Anyway, I do. [...]

1 L.'s sister and brother-in-law.

10 January 1968

32 Pearson Park, Hull

Dearest,

God! I ring up my mother on her 82nd birthday, & in 10 mins am cursing and screaming at her. In retrospect it seems incredible. In fact it is my constant & immediate reaction to her in any circumstances. The call goes on for 55 mins at a cost of £2.5.10d. Long telephone calls are always unhappy.

The particular point at issue was that I *thought* she was suggesting that in the event of A. Nellie's death *I* should immediately drop everything at Hull (familiar pattern), drive to Loughborough, take her to the funeral, take her back to Loughborough, & return to Hull, all because she 'wouldn't dream of asking' Kitty to take her. In fact she says she wasn't saying this, but I don't know. I know my bloody family. However, it was an extremely unhappy call, & I feel fed up. Visions of years in America, jobs in Australia, swim before my eyes. Isn't it all hell? Everyone should be forcibly transplanted to another continent from their family at the age of three. [...]

14 January 1968

32 Pearson Park, Hull

[...] I don't feel too cheerful still: I didn't hear from you yesterday, wch always depresses me, & I haven't got over my extraordinary behaviour on Wednesday. (Of course I'm not grumbling about not hearing, but it always affects the weekend general colour.) It seems incredible that I can't exercise patience with my mother, but in talking to her I almost immediately start to feel irritated & angry, wanting to attack her. I never feel this with anybody else, really. I suppose it's a textbook case of something or other, but it isn't going to help in the years to come. Perhaps it isn't a textbook case, just the natural reaction of a supremely selfish person threatened with having to do something for somebody. It's all very depressing: I could pretend it was worth while being the kind of person I am if only I justified it in some way. God. Life doesn't bear thinking about. I met Thompson when his things were moving in, & said my usual piece ending 'I've been here since 1956'. I can already catch the note of pride in my voice common to silly old sods who're proud of having done or been one thing for ages – you find it in the *D. Telegraph* correspondence columns sometimes. Shall I end up like Despard-Smith in *The Masters*,[1] boozing alone & saying 'I've had a disappointing life'? Hell. Of course it's absurd to complain about what one has chosen to do or be, but all the same it seems increasingly frightening. Yes, frightening. That's the word. [...]

1 C. P. Snow, *The Masters* (1951).

21 January 1968

32 Pearson Park, Hull

[...] Oh, darling, I wish you were here & we could gossip & booze & back bite, & be cheerful: and talk about great writers such as me and B. Potter & Shakespeare. I'm reading *Corridors of Power*.[1] I never get any new books, & haven't the brain power to read Thickens & Dollope & Trackeray & Iris M., so I have to reread my old Penguins. It's *terribly dull*, & yet readable, whereas Dickens is fascinating, & yet unreadable. It's just a question of the number of words on a page, or something. I wonder if old CPS thought he was writing the great political novel. All he does is tell you what ninth-rate faceless craps run the country – at least, if they are anything like he says. [...]

1 C. P. Snow, *Corridors of Power* (1963).

7 February 1968

32 Pearson Park, Hull

[...] Listening to *My Word* over supper I heard them cite a bit of *Ver*'s song[1] from *LLLost*, & this sent me tumbling to the book-case for my New Temple – of course the *Hiems* is best, direct, real Jan Hogspewer stuff, but the other is nice – 'When turtles tread, and rooks, and daws, And maidens bleach their summer smocks' – oh darling! I can hardly write for tears, & only you can share it with me. Isn't it marvellous for there to be Shakespeare, & for him to be English! Or for *us* to be English! Suppose you were a Czech, cease-lessly grumbling, and I were a Yank, writing a thesis on water-imagery in Ezra Pound! I thought of you at Oxford, meeting 'the Printer', & being shown round the works after lunch – plenty of the Shorter Oxford being printed, and the Little, & a queer thing called *Dictionary for Advanced Readers of English* – 'What's that,' I said. 'Oh, that's a dictionary for "emergent nations",' he said, giving the inverted com-mas. 'How many do you print?' I said. 'Well, this is a reprint – I never do less than a quarter of a million.' 'Where do they all go?' 'Mostly Africa.' Well, I hope they do some good: I must confess I felt touched to think of them all winging their way there. Troops out, books in. I don't know. [...]

Dearest bun, I'm sorry I haven't time to write longer & more considered letters these days, but you are always in my mind. I was amused to see the two pigeons that live on the roof opposite my bathroom sitting together, very cosily, the one nibbling at the other in an affectionate way; and thought of my poem on pigeons, and how *you* told me about birds choosing their mates on 14 Feby, and all sorts of things – the *Ver* poem again, for instance. [...]

1 'Spring' ('When daisies pied and violets blue'), from *Love's Labour's Lost*.

3 March 1968

32 Pearson Park, Hull

[...] If the VC isn't careful he'll find the whole pass of representation has been sold by these irresponsible fools who are admitting students to departmental meetings. I told you I had a LC last Monday: I didn't come off too well, on this bugger-the-students question, but I may get in a few shrewd ones at Senate. My line is that I refuse to discuss Library administration with a student with a bad library record, just as (I presume) a professor wd refuse to discuss deptl. business with a student with a bad deptl. record, or a Warden etc. Theirs was that if the students elect a representative you've got to swallow him. I say that this means you must never let them have representation. They say they'll have your balls. I say, then you don't think I'm wrong, just rash. They say get stuffed. I say with onions. Academic life. You start off as a sensitive boy fond of reading ... [...]

But isn't it an *angry* time – how easily one gets cross, how when left to oneself irritation begins to ferment like some neglected juice! I can feel my mind digging up years-old slights and getting furious over them. Only drink releases me from this bondage. I'm not the sort that gets angry when drunk. [...]

24 April 1968

32 Pearson Park, Hull

Dearest bun,

I think I've just *finished* the moon poem[1] – if so, I'll send it. It's pretty unoriginal, just another moon poem. And now I look up *Shut Out That*

Moon,[2] as Scannell says he is going to have it in his programme[3] – it isn't at all the same sentiment, but I suppose all moon poems are the same. [...]

1 'Sad Steps', completed 24 April 1968.
2 Hardy's poem.
3 Vernon Scannell's BBC Radio 4 programme, *A Man Who Noticed Things*, broadcast 7 June 1968, included it.

18 May 1968

32 Pearson Park, Hull

[...] *The Trees* appeared in the NS today, looking all right except for the last line wch I still find rather much for these days. The moon one I am still brooding on: it doesn't really say what I want. [...]

I had meant to be a little more definite about the holidays when you were here: we did talk about it, I know, but apart from Gairloch I don't remember settling anything. Not for the first time this morning I wish I had my AA book here. Do you think a week there, & a week at some different place, & get up & down as fast as possible? Or a tour of say three or four places, a few days at each? The latter isn't so nice, not so restful, to my mind. If the first alternative, what wd the other place be? What's the east like? How about Skye, even? Perhaps I could bear those obtrusive hills better in middle age. I wonder if the car would stand it. Not very nice to be marooned in Sporranshire 50 miles from anywhere & night coming on! Awgh!

The ponce of Hessle gave me about £250 in used notes yesterday.[1] God, shades of the prison house. I am beginning to think I ought to take it up with the Income Tax authorities – 'undisclosed income'. Gob. Prisoner at the bar, you have heard the sentence, no, I mean the verdict. Or do I? Anyway, ten years in stir. We had a bit of a wrangle about Fabers' latest attempt to get their maulers on *The LD*. Not really fruitful. I take pleasure in pointing out to George that he's no longer an active force as a publisher, wch annoys him, but I can't stand the little sod sitting there pontificating as if he were John Murray himself. [...]

1 Royalties on *The Less Deceived*, paid by George Hartley.

30 June 1968

32 Pearson Park, Hull

Darling,

This is a funny Sunday – lovely day – so that I went out into the coun-try to write my letters, but was attacked by hay fever & had to give up & return to the flat & take stuff & Antistin & gin & rest in a cool dark room ... then have lunch. God, it's hell – you know happiness for me is a cloudless summer day (*High Windows* – out in CQ now): agreeable I shd have this built-in device to stop me enjoying it. Anyway, I've had my lunch, & it's pressing on for post time, so I'll be brief.

The worst news is a telegram from Torridon saying they've nothing now before 1 Sept. I sent them a telegram in return saying transfer our booking to then – 'hotel preferred' – and last night wrote to the six hotels you mentioned – well, five places, two at Poolewe. How I shall handle their replies I don't know. I asked for a period *ending* on Sept 1. To my mind we shall have trouble getting there & back – I don't think I shall bother about the car train, it'll clearly be booked by money-mad kiddy-hung swine from the Great Wen – but we shall have to do our best. I wonder how I am to keep in touch with you. Are you to be there for the next week? Or do you prefer to come here next Saturday (7 is it? 6th per-haps – yes)? It'd be *no bad thing* for you to be here then, but equally I'll be down in Leics 11–14 time & completely free on 12th. I cd bring you up. *Let me know*. Remember Friday is my ghastly sigh, Tay Shun[1] & the dinner in the evening. I think you'd have to come on Saturday.

God. Hay fever & drink. Still can't *quite* taste gin, but am certainly feeling drunk. How did you think the poems looked?[2] I like them drunk, prefer *Posterity* sober. It must be the title. It gets in Yanks, Yids, wives, kids, Coca Cola, Protest, & the Theatre – pretty good list of hates, eh? I long to write a political poem – the withdrawal of troops east of Suez started me, now I see someone boasting that in a few years' time we shall be spending 'more on Education than "Defence"' – this shocks me *to the core*,[3] & I seriously feel that *within our lifetime* we shall see England under the heel of the conqueror – or what *used* to be England, but is now a bunch of bearded layabout traitors & National Assistant 'Black Englishmen' – if I had the courage I wd emigrate – terrible –

(This is the Powys punctuation, not approved by GBS in the ST)

Darling! Your hair! and I was comparing you to Rita Hayworth! Radclyffe Hall, more like. Anyway, I can't imagine how you can stand that stuff flopping about all the time – like Mick Jagger – I quite sympathise about it. What a full week you've had, & none too good if the Evans evening was any guide. Did you abstract my *signed* copy of *Scott-King*?[4] A rabbit might have done that, nibbling unobtrusively along the books.

See that sod Tynan, pro-Milburn – I'd like to write, saying that 'my companion' said that the first Australian bowler to put a man on the mid wicket boundary wd get Milburn: Gleeson was the first, & he did – And then backing up Hancock – he was no good – *not funny* – bit of a handicap in a comedian –

Darling! What a Sunday! Hayfever ... gin – I was out beyond Cottingham, in lovely fields, but the allergy struck. Must 'grope to the bathroom', 'after a piss' – Love XXXXXXX

Philip.

1 L.'s citation of the City Librarian at Hull degree day.
2 'Posterity' and 'Sad Steps' in the *New Statesman*, 28 June 1968.
3 See L.'s poem 'Homage to a Government', completed 10 January 1969, which concentrates these sentiments.
4 Evelyn Waugh, *Scott-King's Modern Europe* (1947).

4 August 1968

32 Pearson Park, Hull

Dearest bun,

Sunday morning in the bedroom as usual. O, the blessed peace! though my stomach doesn't feel entirely at rest. I had slightly more for breakfast than usual.

I haven't responded well to your charges: retreating into a mumbling silence is neither graceful nor honest. (It's always my reaction to attack, though.) I should have been much more upset and affectionate: perhaps I should have come to see you, not that this would have been possible without treating it as a real emergency, for wch commitments cd be dropped – I *would*, only I didn't know till Friday that you were having a bad *week*: I thought you might have felt improved after writing your letter. Not that I mean it sprang from a kind of shallow vindictiveness that could spend itself like that, but since there didn't seem any immediate cause for it I thought it might have arisen from mischance and loneliness & so not be deep-rooted.

It's still difficult to answer, partly because of our parallel telephone conversations & partly because, well, I don't know, I'm not so confident about telling the truth as you: not so sure I can, not so sure I want to. I cling to pretence like the bathing steps at the deep end. Most of the time I don't want to be bothered, like knowing the medical statistics about lung cancer for my age group. You *see* this all right, but, I think, interpret it as deliberate and hostile deceit. It doesn't seem like that to me, more like making life livable. Of course I don't defend this for a minute, or expect you to give more than a snort, but at least I claim credit for trying to be nice. There's nothing more excoriating than the reverse, as I've learnt.

Anyway, I'm awfully sorry that I've caused you unhappiness, however unintentionally; I can imagine how easy it is to become dominated by painful thoughts, but, you know, most of them *are* imaginary, and not worth bothering about. In two weeks and a half we shall be together, & I'm greatly looking forward to it: I hope you are too. I'm sure it will scatter this miserable stretch.

Thank you for the letter, & also, dear, for ringing back on Friday – it was typical of you. I was in a rage over some small transgression – it appeared I was being DISOBEYED, wch sent me into a frenzy of teeth-grinding fury. I left an intemperate note for Hoare[1] (you know, one of the Hoares that went on holiday); crept in yesterday to retrieve it; found he'd already got it. Awgh! But there were signs that he had begun to rectify the point at issue: it wasn't his fault, anyway. That hag of hell Margaret Nicholson,[2] not to mention that Einstein of Acquisitions, Charlie boy.[3] I'd like to chop them into messes.

Your village certainly sounds full of action: frightening, almost. Like *The Devil At Saxon Wall*. Mrs Passion & Mrs Fluke. Well, not quite, with the main road from Newcastle to Carlisle running under the windows, but rather. As Baudelaire said, '—ing is the poetry of the people' (since he wrote in French, I don't know what kind of word he used, but it's very true.) Except drink, I suppose. I'm still not drinking: in a way it's a relief, not having the bother of buying it ('Pox got to yer brains?'), & I was still a tiny bit below 14 st this morning.

I've finished the Brian Howard book – a fearful, drugtaking, cruel swine. No good at anything. Remind me to tell you the story about his weapons being words, not fists. Edith S.[4] tried to take him up, & invited him to one of her teas – 'I got *one penny bun, and three quarters of a cup of rancid tea in a dirty cottage mug*' (his italics). Silly old cow, toadying to a young shit.

Yes, do keep your short hair. It makes you look lighter & younger & gayer: I like it very much. I wish I could find something to do the same for me.

I don't expect this letter reads well, but nevertheless with much love. Philip

1 Peter Hoare, Sub-Librarian (Cataloguing) at the Brynmor Jones Library.
2 An assistant librarian.
3 L.'s deputy, Arthur Wood.
4 Edith Sitwell.

14 August 1968

32 Pearson Park, Hull

My dear rabbit,

A dark chilly evening after a sunless wet day. I have the fire on, wch makes it seem like autumn, and have had a spaghetti supper. It's been a pleasant enough day, mostly work: Betty left at midday, leaving me ex BBC false-eyelashed blonde Judith, her stand-in to whom she seems to have taken a fancy. Alan Park[1] called me out for a hideous pub lunch – well, it wasn't hideous, but the sandwiches were damp wool bread. I drank $\frac{1}{2}$ pint. Afternoon spent with ma little concrete dove,[2] ma steel snowdrop, planning the Library for the next ten years.

I'm sorry I sent you such a (your telephone call) irritable letter from home, hardly worth reading. I wish I could avoid being so cross and irritable at home. I wish I knew what caused it. It's probably a stock psychological trait. Sometimes I wonder if I'm fond of my mother at all. Away from her I know that she's old, and hates living alone, and keeps on with it largely for my benefit; that she's extremely kind and considerate and conscientious; that she never thinks badly of anyone or says anything malicious about them; that she is my mother, after all, & it's my duty, yes, mah dooty, to look after her if she can't look after herself. But once let me get home and I become snappy, ungrateful, ungracious, wounding, inconsiderate & even abusive, longing only to get away, muttering obscenities because I know she can't hear them, refusing to speak clearly so that she can hear, refusing to make conversation or evince any interest in her 'news' or the things she says. All these traits are manifestations of a physical discomfort associated with intense irritation, and one caused by her: if I go upstairs to shave or do something in my room, I find in 5 minutes I am humming cheerfully and full of creative thoughts. How does one explain it? I suppose she arouses in me strong alarm & hostility because she makes me feel guilty for not looking after her. Sometimes I think she, and my being at home, represent to me my own failure as a human bean, to 'assume adult responsibilities' and all that, wch makes me guilty – and angry – in a different way. Or is it just that I resent the slightest demand on my unselfishness? There must be something in it to explain the violence of my feelings: it's not just being irritated with an old person, though of course she *is* irritating *and* boring, though not, probably, as much as countless other parents. And anyway, hasn't one a right to be boring at 80? And if I'm so clever & superior & a jewel in the crown of my age, can't I put up with it?

I don't suppose you know the answer to all this any more than I do: perhaps there are more pathological explanations that I haven't mentioned, that really my anger is a fight for emotional freedom against its enemy – you know all that. I suppose it links with my unhappiness at ties of all sorts, or not so much at them, but at having to do anything to honour them. [...]

How nice for you to savour the joys of daytime radio! Isn't it the height of luxury, to sit *or lie* with the afternoon programmes murmuring in your ear: designed for old dodderers in cathedral towns, as the rose sunlight moves down the wallpaper & someone comes in with a tea tray with a lace cloth on it, & makes up the fire. No matter how bad the programme: *you aren't at work*, as everyone else is, and that recompenses for all. [...]

This time next week we'll be taegither! XX P.

1 One of the architects for the Library.
2 Brenda Moon, L.'s about-to-be deputy.

12 September 1968

32 Pearson Park, Hull

Dearest,

Just a scribble – I'm not nearly back on an even keel yet, but am making progress. Was hindered last night by the arrival of *Jean*[1] (pre-announced by telephone) to say she'd 'left George' & was established, with the children, in Victoria Avenue! She had a long story of trouble, wch rather surprised me: she thinks George is barmy & getting worse. I was rather uneasy, but I think she just wanted to tell me about it: she's a curious creature. What's going to happen to my book? Awgh! Anyway, this deprived me of my promised early night. It rained terribly: *all* the basements in the university were flooded.

Of course it seems terrible to be back. Work boring & frightening, my flat dreary & sordid. Mess everywhere. I hated leaving you, even though I knew that the time to restart work had come. You were *so kind, so kind*! I kept thinking of all your kindnesses as I drove through the rain. I hope you enjoyed the holiday: I did, though sometimes unaccountable waves of boredom and irritation and anger swept over me. Perhaps I'm another George. I'm sorry. What fun it was, very rich. [...]

1 Jean Hartley.

1 October 1968

32 Pearson Park, Hull

[...] God! I tried making dumplings – was this some coarse, medieval, kitchen jest you were playing on me? I got both hands covered with the stuff, so that virtually none was left on the plate – then I perforce transferred it to taps, knife handles, pan-handles, flour bags, every damn thing. It was a nightmare.

I did eventually get enough into one unit to cook but hell! Rabbit joke, I suspect. I had the stew, & again tonight, having added a tin of game soup. It was all right. I also ate the stewed pears. The sausages had to go. I couldn't face them. [...]

6 October 1968

32 Pearson Park, Hull

[...] Good review of Kingsley by F. Hope.[1] He's a good lad. I told you it all went to pot at the end, but the beginning & middle are excellent.

Thank you for your nice letter received Saturday. So old Peel is dead.[2] I wonder how old he was. That was the address I went to for dinner. I remember his sexual maniac's smile, a property Kingsley duly appropriated – most inappropriately (that wd baffle a Frog) – for Welch. I thought he was a tremendously striking character, a horror story on two legs, a dreadful warning. I once began a novel in wch the central character was Peel in AS Collins' situation, but of course it never came to anything. Or was the central character Sam Wagstaff (= Shakespeare), a Norman Sharpe kind of person? He was a relation of *Gillie Potter*, was he, & an uncle or something of JHB Peel? He was certainly the most fearsome bore I've ever met. I wonder if he'd seem so now? I mean, one has met bores, one's been initiated & worn down ... no, I *still* think Peel was rather special. [...]

Yes, I did miss you, dear, & do: it's nice to be alone, & have one's strings slackened entirely, but you are very sweet & kind, & I miss the warm breathing shape in the bed, with its private grunts & whimpers, like a rabbit dreaming of Mr McGregor. [...]

I addressed the students yesterday, two lots of 600, in my gown (wch seemed to astonish the organisers: I bit back something about pretending I worked in a university), & got good response in the Middleton Hall, poor in the Assembly Hall. Having failed to 'get a laugh', as Peel wd say, at one point, I added 'That went better first house', & failed to get a laugh for that either. I expect they just didn't understand. [...]

1 Francis Hope's review of Amis's *I Want It Now* in *Observer*, 6 October 1968.
2 J. K. Peel: see Appendix B.

17 October 1968

32 Pearson Park, Hull

Dearest,

I've just written to Barbara Pym, to send back AUA;[1] the last quarter or so I reread before doing so. I think the *real* book shd concern itself simply with Leonora, James, Phoebe, Humphrey, Ned & the 'girl from Christie's' who doesn't materialise. Leonora should get James off Phoebe. Then the Christie's girl should get James off Leonora, through the Puckish intervention of Ned. Leonora falls back on

Humphrey. It could be a simple but strong book, depending on the pathos of Leonora. [...]

1 Barbara Pym, *An Unsuitable Attachment* (written 1963, published 1982).

20 October 1968

32 Pearson Park, Hull

[...] Friday night was boring, though all right otherwise I suppose. George[1] was his usual boring self. He has a maddening habit of thrashing his feet about, so that my rug stands up like quills upon the fretful porpentine: he lifts his feet alternately and lets them fall with a bang, very charming to people below, & scatters crumbs everywhere. The Dunns (Douglas & Lesley) were pleasant enough: she very ordinary, he amusing when he had 3 whiskies on board, but rather fond of the books. Indeed at times I thought I was presiding over a 3rd rate provincial literary soirée, as I suppose I was. [...]

1 George Hartley.

27 November 1968

32 Pearson Park, Hull

Dearest bun,

> Morning, noon & bloody night,
> Seven sodding days a week,
> I slave at filthy *work*, that might
> Be done by any book-drunk freak.
> This goes on till I kick the bucket:
> FUCK IT FUCK IT FUCK IT FUCK IT

Nice to be a *pawet*, ya knaw, an express ya *feelins*. Eh? The last line should be *screamed* in a paroxysm of rage.

This is just to say that I'll be coming home on *Saturday*, having decided I must go to the meeting after all, bloody conscientious fool. Clearly we are all set to sell the SCR out, and nothing I can do will stop it, but I'd better be there. Another 20 years of the *status quo*. I'm fed up.

Anyway, this means I'll be over to see you *after* lunch on Sunday, as soon as I decently can. Sorry not to be coming as usual, but I don't much want to delay things another week. I wonder some of you don't kick Dr Potter's arse, stupid little jumped-up cow: how tiresome she sounds!

Ghastly day here. Students by all accounts have had a 'moderate' swing, & accepted the parallel proposals. Library still hot news. Awgh.   Love, darling.   P.

23 January 1969

32 Pearson Park, Hull

Dearest bun,

The second little letter today – fine day it's been, I expect it has been with you, as Thwaite rang up & said it was fine in London. He wanted me to do the Ricks *Tennyson* for the *N.S.*, & I said I would, but I'll have to do some boning up on the old boy. I can't think of anything to say at the moment!

He also said (I asked him) he didn't care for the poem on Sunday.[1] 'If you believe them when they say you're good, you have to believe them when they say you're bad' (E. Hemingway). Of course, I shouldn't have asked him, but I thought as he rather makes a speciality of me he might be a good judge. [...]

1 'Homage to a Government' in *Sunday Times*.

2 February 1969

32 Pearson Park, Hull

Am drinking up a bottle of Bastille (you remember): pretty grim. Bottled by Quink Frères. Imported by Stephens Père et Fils.

After lunch Marvellous extracts from Paisley on *The World This Weekend* – pure Tom Teevan – recorded at a secret meeting – of course, it's frightful stuff, but one hears so much lefty nonsense it makes a pleasant change. I *did* wish you'd heard it. The drums in the background were thrilling. But 'There is always something peculiarly impotent about the violence of a literary man. It seems to bear no reference to facts, for it is never kept in check by action. It is simply a question of adjectives and rhetoric, of exaggeration and over-emphasis.'[1]

Guess the author of that if you can. £5 by return. 1850–1900. We both like him. Hay?

Love you always, darling XXX P.

1 Oscar Wilde, from his review 'On Mr Mahaffy's New Book' (on *Greek Life and Thought*).

5 February 1969

32 Pearson Park, Hull

Hilly has opened a chip shop in USA called 'Lucky Jim'. It was in the *S Express*.

Dearest,

No, Oscar Wilde! You'll find it in H. Pearson, about *Mahaffy* (another surprise). I was looking at HP because when in *Any Qs* they asked what book cheered you up, I immediately thought of that. It does, too. You remember Yeats always said Wilde was a man of action. [...]

19 February 1969

32 Pearson Park, Hull

Dearest,

Bite, frost, bite!
You roll up away from the light
The blue woodlouse, and the
        plump dormouse ...[1]

Brr! Foully cold today, east wind, ground iron-hard. I at last got my hair cut, & bought a pair of shoes, also a pair of Swedish overshoes, very odd, for use in slush. Brr! No slush now, though.

I am writing this because I go to London tomorrow until Friday night, & I don't know what chances there'll be of writing there – perhaps I could finish it there. Last night I went out to Paull, to loony Binns,[2] & found about a dozen people, hardly anything to do with the university – oafs and oafesses poor romantic Binns invests with the unearthly light of trade & navigation. I suppose they're all right. Stayed till nearly one & drove home well warmed with hot rum-infused wine.

He seems to be living with this hare-lipped German girl. We had pickled herring and reindeer meat balls & similar Binns delicacies.

I feel rather discontented and out of sorts – cannot get on top of my work –

I finished the stew, & had some slight quatermass experiences, but was more cautious & so more successful. The Sunday I had some indigestion again, but the Monday it went down better. On the whole, though, I think it doesn't suit me – too tough & fibrous. I think a lot about you, & *tibi cras*, & *Generations have trod*,[3] & my Tennyson line 'At the heart of frost love burns'.[4] Not a good line! but you know what I meant. A lovely great warm breathing rabbit.

I noticed that one of the assistants at Southampton is called Miss Rabbitts! Nice. One of the attendants is called Wasp.

It's eleven o'clock – I keep putting the news on, to see how the weather is. My record player has broken & been taken away, & life is very narrow. Did you see Pee Wee Russell was dead?

Friday a.m. I'm in my hotel room; Castle[5] is coming here instead of me going there, as he has had flu. I had a grim journey down yesterday, in almost continual snow – about ½ hour late. Lunched with Thwaite, then went to the exhibition,[6] & spent a bit over an hour there. Of course it's exceedingly interesting & enjoyable, but very big! I cut the sculpture & stuff, & most of the drawings, though there's a fine Palmer, chestnut-candles & sheep. Do go. Plenty of John Martin, a Grimshaw just like that one (how I *curse* myself) in Hexham, *Val d'Aosta*, *Pretty Baa-Lambs*, *Boulter's Lock*, and lots more. Tiring, but full of decent people, like Lords – only the occasional *au pair* girl. No *students*. I wished you'd been there. I've decided I don't like Constable: his muddy palette has no inner life.

In the evening I went to Bob's & had dinner, very pleasant. He showed me a cutting saying 'Latest book on Richard Nixon's desk: Robert Conquest's *The Great Terror* ...' & I showed him the rod room photograph, wch he quite liked, but in an abstracted kind of way. He is obsessed with the Eton man becoming head of a girls' school, & has written (but not posted) a letter to *The Times* signed A. C. Swinburne saying how much he wished the reverse had been true in his day, as a feminine touch would have made all the difference. Bluebell, the bassett (?) hound, is more of an obsession also than ever – really quite absurd. I don't like dogs. Bob is now a grandfather.

They have been to *Lemmons*[7] (K's house), & Caroleen says it has the biggest rooms she has ever seen outside Blenheim. Apparently the A's 'have to have' a car there, & so EJ has learnt to drive, *terrifyingly*, according to Bob. No news otherwise. They had a painting by the brother's boy friend.[8]

I hope you are cured of your cold. I felt your visit was too short. I never know whether you come to escape from worries or to discuss them: perhaps the former, since they don't arise. I hope you are keeping well & warm, dear dear bun. I do love you.

I dreamed of Russian tanks last night – terrifying. Today I read of our defence estimates. Huh!

Much love   Philip

1 'Bite, frost, bite!:' from Tennyson, 'Window, Winter'.
2 A. L. Binns.
3 G. M. Hopkins.
4 This indeed appears to be a 'Tennysonian' line by L.
5 One of the University Library architects.
6 Royal Academy Bicentenary Exhibition.
7 House in Barnet, home of Kingsley Amis and Elizabeth Jane Howard.
8 Evidently Sargy Mann, a friend (but not a lover) of Colin Howard, Elizabeth Jane Howard's brother.

4 March 1969

32 Pearson Park, Hull

[...] Why am I writing on *Tuesday*? Well, I'm not really: just that I have *finished* Tennyson,[1] thank God, whoopee whoopee whoopee: cheap smart journalism, but a good weekend read for the yobs. The only good things in it are *yours* – I feel I ought to send you the cheque. Isn't *The Spinster's Sweet-Arts* good: I had to force myself to bring it in, but I didn't quote from it – let them hunt for it. I loved the bit about the Tommies – 'and one of you dead' – as I've tried to say in the article it's just caught the eccentricity of the village character *who isn't going to get any madder* & is sane enough really, just a bit odd. [...]

1 L.'s review of Christopher Ricks's edition of Tennyson's *Collected Poems*, *New Statesman*, 14 March 1969. Reprinted in *Required Writing*.

16 March 1969

32 Pearson Park, Hull

[...] I'm glad you liked the review. Interesting to compare it with Holloway in the *Spr*! He's a dull bugger of course. Paul Johnson wrote to me saying it was one of the best reviews they'd ever printed, wch surprised me – but the credit is yours. I wish you could come out at them, dear, with a great scurry of feet: *Words From the Warren*. You have the ideas & the thenthibilitah[1] & the knowledge: just a few essays on treason & filth & so on. I'm the only person to have noticed that misprint ogh ogh ogh. I do love Owlby & Scratby, as you say: think what they must be like, a bit like the villages to the east of Leicester, that I used to cycle round: Hungarton, Scraptoft. I think Owlby is very dark & tree-y, don't you? and Scratby all stones and hens. [...]

1 Fancied as spoken by Lord David Cecil.

30 March 1969

32 Pearson Park, Hull

[...] I listened to *The Archers* with my hearing aid on this morning, rare occurrence, but even so failed to catch much of it – it doesn't *sound* interesting, does it? My old friend Colin Gunner's receipt for novel-writing ('have your heroine raped by a gorilla') occurs to me: wouldn't come amiss, as far as I'm concerned, for some of that crowd.

The weather seems to be cheering up: blue skies & some pale sun. Thursday was a fine day in Belfast: I wandered about the University area entranced with all I saw, nipping into the Dept of Spanish for a slash at one point, & noting how different schools were coming out, looking like schoolchildren & not the contents of the brothels of Paris (local tarts & teds). I pored over confectioners' windows & boards of small ads & religious bookshops.

Now have been out & laid in drink, forgot papers ('*Forgot papers ...?*') & went to Library, where I found a proof copy of Douglas Dunn's book *Terry Street*. It looks just as I remember it – hard to pin down, evocative, unsatisfying, yet individual – not *big* enough, but Xt who is? I want great Victorian novels of poems, great Academy pictures. Watch out for it. And them, for that matter. [...]

8 June 1969

32 Pearson Park, Hull

[...] I did wish you were here yesterday. After dreary & not very success-ful shopping, I went to Hessle but found no ponce, so got real cheese at Field's, and motored aimlessly on till I remembered my 14 yr old desire to go to Yokefleet. It was a brilliant day, so I looked at the map & made for the territory in question. Broadly speaking it's the land lying between the main road Hull–Goole and the river an absolute dead end. Well, I turned down rather late, at Balkholme; went through Kiplin & then down to Saltmarshe; then back & along to Laxton, Yokefleet, Blacktoft and Faxfleet, & then up to the main road again, and wonderful it was. *Very* quiet: lanes all lined shoulder high with cowparsley; huge trees in their first full freshness; & the villages – hardly more than collections of houses – made Clunbury & Clun seem like Manhattan. No inns – or hardly any – a church or two: I went into Blacktoft, but it was nicer out-side than in. It had a queer deserted church hall (?) by its gate (Erected 1851, Extended 1873) wch looked completely overgrown and neglected, but inside I could see trestle tables laid for tea, as if for some outing that never came. Some nice houses, some nasty ones: plenty of farms, & yard dogs who would have liked to get at me. The river mostly invisible, behind high banks, but sometimes a gliding ship appeared (the cottage walls all have flood-marks): Blacktoft is where Ouse & Trent join to form the Humber. O, it was beautiful! And always the rare *white* of early summer: may, hawthorn, chestnut candles, cowparsley, nettle-flowers, so soon lost (I expect they go on till autumn really), so exciting, so sunny & marvellous. I drove slowly home, arriving about six. If only I'd had my camera! It was a day among days: I'm sure it'll never be so fine again.

Getting back, I found Dickens mentions *none* of these places, Mee only Blacktoft. Yet there are plenty of 'halls': Empson's brother lives at Yokefleet Hall. There's a Saltmarshe Hall. I felt I'd found a new little country. I did wish you could have seen it. [...]

13 July 1969

32 Pearson Park, Hull

[...] I'm glad you liked Belfast. I felt overwhelmingly at Easter that, although nowhere is really 'home' to me, Belfast probably means more to me, packs a stronger emotional punch, than anywhere else, even Oxford. That was why I planned a longer stay. I didn't feel it quite as strongly as at Easter, but I did feel it. [...]

18 September 1969

32 Pearson Park, Hull

Dearest bun,

Quite a satisfactory evening: I did a verse after talking to you. Since they're nine lines long this is not bad! I now have two verses[1] – no good, of course. But I feel as if I should like to get some poems written. If only I had time! That ponce Murphy.

As I said, I did enjoy reading *The Land*[2] – some of it's crap, but there are three or four fine passages. I also read the Norman McCaig one about Stac Polly[3] – he's all at sea, isn't he? Doesn't know anything about it. [...]

1 Of 'To the Sea' (completed October 1969).
2 V. Sackville-West, *The Land*; L. included two passages in *OBTCEV*.
3 MacCaig's 'Dying Landscape'.

11 October 1969

32 Pearson Park, Hull

Darling,

'The Prot – est – ant Boys ... will carry the day' – oh dear, gin and Orange again, the songs are so thrilling, I can't let them alone. No reply from the Belfast record firm! Expect they've moved, or been burnt out, or think I'm getting at them ('Lark'n? *Lark'n*? To haill wi' annywan carled Lark'n!').

Well, I had my kedgeree tonight: made too much, but on the whole it was very good. I used 'natural' rice, having found some in Beverley, wch took a long time to cook: haddock fillet, very nice – nearly ate it as it was! But it was very nice, and I wished only that you were sharing it with me. [*drawing of rabbit*] I think you might have eaten it. Thanks for your kindness in telling me how to do it.

Nobody tells me these things, but I gather that York gave G. Barker a *filthy* press, & BJ has dropped him like a hot turd: D. Holbrook is the candidate now. I expect we'll end up with Thwaite[1] – not that I'd mind, jolly good show. I'm *bloody* glad about G. Barker. I'm *sure* he's a shit, a real layabout cadging ponce. We had to absolutely kick Ray into ringing up York, though.

Oh yes, more pictures, rather disappointing really. [...] A nice one of you at Wexford, but I wish I'd got one of you in the hat. Sicut bucketus erat, if I can quote Joyce. [...]

I wrote to 'my MP' last week calling on him to speak and vote against the Ministry of Ag's proposed Codes of Practice for the keeping of food animals: fat lot of good it'll do, but still. Why don't you write to yours? It's to be debated on Wednesday.

1 Barker, Holbrook, Thwaite: possible candidates for the Compton poetry fellowship at Hull. Barker was turned down, Holbrook withdrew, Thwaite never applied.

26 October 1969

32 Pearson Park, Hull

[...] Spent the evening writing angry letters (one at last to *The Spr* about their 'Hotel Guide'), checking my money, & reading the poems of J. C. Powys, wch *aren't bad*, funnily enough. Very Hardyesque. Try the one that starts

'I'll never forgive you!' I said,
As among the phloxes we went,
Where the orchard-rail begins ...

It's not really good enough for the OBTCEV – but completely unlike Jack Flint's flirtation in the Space–Time continuum with Stella Matrix, or whatever his novels are about.

I wish I could spend more time on the book. Later on I read some Eliot – silly book-drunk buffer though he is, he has *dignity*. Reverting to JCP, who wd you say wrote:

The wild owl over the madhouse knows
In what padded place
The loveliest form that ever breathed
Lies on her face ...[1]

Not only wd I say de la Mare, I'd swear I'd read it in the *Coll. Po.* of
same. Yet JCP claims it as his own (p.120). Good, isn't it?

Yesterday I called on the ponce & found him in – rather to my regret,
as he started bullying me to do a reading of post TWW poems for the
first issue of some poncing Poetry Record Club fantasy he is nursing.
God damn him. Got away at last, & shopped in Beverley, feeling like
a hunted animal. He now thinks Jean was only friendly with him after
their separation to keep an eye on his doings, & enjoined me to secrecy
on what he is now up to. Go it, old woman. He's living on National
Assistance, of course – living on you and me, dear, living on you & me.
(Auden's *Refugee Blues*). [...]

1 Powys, from *Wolf's-Bone Rhymes*.

10 November 1969

32 Pearson Park, Hull

[...] Thank you for a lovely lunch and afternoon: I did enjoy it. You *are*
sweet & kind. I know a lady sweet & kind, who also has a big flat off
Clarendon Park Road ogh ogh agh leggo my yowowow [...]

3 December 1969

32 Pearson Park, Hull

[...] 'Looking for something else', which is the only way I find anything,
I found the poem about our Alnmouth holiday,[1] & enclose a copy – it
isn't a good poem, far from it, hence it's never been published. I expect
you remember where it all was – different places, of course. [...]

1 L.'s typescript of 'Holiday' attached.

Holiday

Clouds merge, the coast darkens,
Sunless barley stirs.
The sloping field alters
To weed-ribboned rock,
Waders and lichens.
The sea collapses, freshly.

~~Inland,~~ A vacant park *inland*
Is roughened by wind.
Trees throng the light-oak chapel.
Storm-spots quicken round
A railed tomb of sailors.
The house is shuttered.

Embedded in the horizon
A tiny sunlit ship
Seems not to be moving.

O things going away!

6 January 1970

32 Pearson Park, Hull

[...] Enclosed (I hope) is my version of the Trimdon Grange Explosion.[1] *Don't tell a soul* where I got the idea from. I may send it to *The Listener*. Djoo think it 'does'? [...]

1 'The Explosion' (completed 5 January 1970), touched off by a musical arrangement by Thomas Armstrong of 'The Trimdon Grange Explosion', 1882.

11 January 1970

32 Pearson Park, Hull

Glad you liked the poem. I have reservations: what time of year do larks lay eggs? Would it be as sunny as that? I think I might put the verse 'The dead ...' in italics, to bring the reader up short a bit & show someone is speaking (the minister). On the whole I think it does, though. The emotions the song raised in me were very strong. The song is better, though – more coaly & local & shining – 'where explosions are no more'! Couldn't beat that. [...]

12 January 1970

32 Pearson Park, Hull

Darling,

Just a little note – there was a Handel programme on tonight, of wch I heard about half (watch for a repeat! it wasn't as good as Hassall's 1950 *Life*, though – it was called *The Late Mr Handel*), & wch 'broke me up' for the night – I am steadily playing through *The Messiah*, through laundry, through washing up – how marvellous! how splendid! I crawl at his feet – Handel & Hardy, & you & I, what links, what deep superiority!

I've never noticed before what a miniature climax he makes of 'His yoke is easy and his burthen is light'. Every note reminds me of our times together. [...]

22 February 1970

32 Pisson Park, Hull HU5 2TD

Dearest bun,

I'm afraid this will be a short wan – I emerged from bed at 20 to 11 (having read the whole of Russell Brain's pissy book on W de la M therein), brekkered (this spelling brings in Aristophanes,[1] & reading Jilly Cooper & Alan Brien), shaved & am now (20 to 1) sitting in dressing gown in sitting room, feeling as if I'd had a hard day. I think in fact I'm emerging from having the ponce of Hessle round on Friday – got him out at 1.30 a.m., but it's terribly tedious. However, he did go some way towards paying for the ½ bottle of Courvoisier he drank by assuring me (apropos of *W in Love*) that Lawrence wrestled naked with Gilbert Murray. Perhaps he was thinking of TE Lawrence – the old Greek fellow-feeling, you know.

Thanks for your card: hope you enjoyed the sausage & mash. It's a dish I've got to like rather. See me in Faber's rogues gallery this morning: still, you'd like Janet *Burroway*,[2] wouldn't you? A pity they're using Kingsley,[3] in a way – it'll repel all the people who don't like Kingsley. Still, a generation will be growing up who don't know we know each other.

'Sherry' or 'cocktails' at BJ's Saturday morning: boring affair, Kenyon there without Angela, Drinkwater telling me about Australia, wch they liked. Did you know E. Dickinson wrote 'I am a kangaroo'? A new theory. *Bolts* of melody (*bounds*?). I am deep in her, then W de la Mare,[4] are to be done by Mar 4; then Gregory Awards (the crap has started to arrive) & Day Lewis citation – God, God, God!! Roll on A'Souls, that long Sunday that goes on and on.[5] [...]

1 As in the onomatopoeic noise of frogs in Aristophanes' play of that title.
2 American novelist resident in England at that time, published by Faber and reviewing in the *New Statesman* and elsewhere. L. fancied that her rabbity name would appeal to Monica.
3 Faber were quoting Amis in reviews of *All What Jazz*.
4 L. was reviewing the *Complete Poems* of Emily Dickinson and of Walter de la Mare for the *New Statesman* (13 March 1970). Reprinted in *Required Writing*.
5 L. had two terms, 1970–1, on leave of absence at All Souls College, Oxford, while working on his *Oxford Book*.

22 March 1970

32 Pearson Park, Hull

Dearest,

A footnote to my Sunday letter – having read about the diary of the young man from Laxton in the *S.T. Col. Supp.*, I drove out there & walked about[1] – looked at the 'red brick vicarage' (yes, it *is* red) & found a curious graveyard on the opposite side of the road from the church, with graves from mid 19th century to present day, & a simple crumbling chapel, with pews, very crude furnishings, roof coming down, and one of those old-fashioned biers, with pram wheels, like a hospital trolley, & a canvas thrown over it. I walked among the graves, the snowdrops & what seemed to be fresh mole casts (unless they'd been digging for them), & went & looked at all the Empson monuments in the church. Spring very slow – no signs. I sat in the church for a few minutes, thinking of you & full of emotion of a kind not easily susceptible of literary rendition.

Coming out, I found a marvellous farmyard scene – dutch barn, haystack made up of rectangular blocks now reduced to an end only – on the blocks sitting seven cats – five black – green eyes – yellow straw – all staring at me – all at different levels – pure Eden Box – the most natural picture

I've ever seen –

Much love
Philip

1 L. went out to Laxton to see the graves of and monuments to the Empson family, apparently in homage to the poet William Empson.

6 April 1970

32 Pearson Park, Hull

[...] Have been reading the orig. version of *Tailor of G*[1] – just shows you how marvellous the later version is. Great tears roll down my face. A perfect work of art: I'd give all Proust – Joyce – Mann for it. [...]

1 Beatrix Potter, *The Tailor of Gloucester*.

1 May 1970

London

Dearest,

London hangover on my back, like a medieval hangman. Faber reception v. noisy & exhausting – George & Paddy[1] there, & lots of people I didn't know but felt I ought to. Who's Lady Gowrie?[2] Dowry? Sort of female skinhead in a purple velvet caftan. Mrs Eliot.[3] Lady Faber.[4] Et everyone except Al.[5] Dined alone with Bob & Caroleen.[6]

Lowell says he's going to visit me in Hull on 21 May. Why? There was so much noise I couldn't hear a quarter of what was said. He seemed a poor crazed creature. Liz Jennings looked like Dylan Thomas as usual.

I'm sorry my letters are so scrappy these days, but more when I have time. This weekend is jazz weekend.[7] *Around the world in many a pansy bar, From Aberystwyth right to Zanzibar*, mutters Bob.

Dear bun! I loved the rabbit card. See you next week.

Much love
Philip

1 G.S. and Eileen Fraser, evidently at a Faber & Faber party.
2 At that time Xandra Gowrie, woman of letters.
3 Valerie Eliot, widow of T.S.
4 Wife of the then Chairman of Faber & Faber.
5 A. Alvarez.
6 Robert Conquest and the third Mrs Conquest.
7 Writing his *Daily Telegraph* jazz record review.

7 June 1970

32 Pearson Park, Hull

Dearest bun,

God, eleven when I woke: sun high in sky. If I don't set the alarm, I just sleep on – can always do with it, not that I did anything yesterday. London was *boiling* & my all day drivel so *boring* that I *pissed off* at three & went to Simpson's & ordered a light suit, like Alan Brien. Mine will have the disadvantage of not fitting: trousers too tight. Then I bought braces & a wing collar – dare I wear latter on your degree day? I'd like to look as Conservative as possible. Got to Kings X & (on Pullman) ordered 4 Worthingtons, a ginger beer, & a gin & tonic.

Made a shandy & drank it, drank the g & t, & felt better. Found myself opposite the husband of a girl who left about 1958.

The Egertons seemed in good form, Ansell particularly bucked by his first 'big deal', involving millions of pounds: everything else seemed very small to him. I couldn't rouse him on anything – inflation, devaluation, balance of payments, anything. 'The amounts involved are so marginal.'

Judy has been to Italy & seen Bridget, & Bridget's boy friends, who don't sound encouraging – travelling salesmen, electricians, Lebanese students. It all seems a plain case of stupid English girl being bashed by low Eyties (on their side), and the old love-of-freedom, youth, youth, escape from home to romantic foreign countries on hers. I told Judy that in 10 years Bridget would be pouring out tea like everyone else, & that in any case she was an adult now & they've done all they can for her. And in 40 years she'd be alive & we'd be dead ... At least, I don't know about Judy: she has a sort of whippet frame that will see 90.

Well, my dear bun, I expect you are deep in marking – it must be hell. I didn't get anything from you yesterday. When I got back from London I found sundry *Dispatches* from North Britton – not reassuring. The one-nighters are coming in, in a variety of singles & annexes & things, but Ardelve says no & Uig hasn't replied. Have written to Invergarry ... I can see us sleeping out in the car for a week. If Uig says no, shall I continue to try Skye? If Invergarry says no, shall I try the Kyle hotel?

On Thursday I tackled Wood & told him I was going to propose Brenda for Acting Librarian. He took it very well, as he always does – even, I gather, went & saw her & promised support. Friday things were not so sunny, but I know the pattern: he goes home & tells Margaret, & she gives him gee-up. However, it's done now. Power slips from Larkin's hands. I've seen it happen before. Once you start not *understanding* things ... I don't understand the new ordering system. I don't understand the tape typewriters. It will grow ... However, six months is no time really. I begin to think I shall spend only the occasional weekend there anyway: every conversation I have seems to end 'Well, you can come back for that' – the second course on Library Planning, the Opening, the Estimates. Any small balance will be spent at Ashmansworth ... I feel like saying that I intend to spend every single second of the six months *at All Souls*, where I've never been before & shall never be again, & they may all FOG OFF ...

time enough for wasting when I'm booted back to sesquipedalian dreariness again. O well …

Had an odd dream on Friday, wch I transcribed into verse last night, or into *lines*, anyway.

Must start letter home now. […]

Much love dearest   Philip

11 June 1970

32 Pearson Park, Hull

[…] I've sent *The Card Players* to *Encounter*, together with the dream poem wch I've called *Dublinesque*. It's pretty thin, in fact pretty bad.[…]

28 June 1970

32 Pearson Park, Hull

The Explosion is coming on Monday: I have to sign 1000 copies.[1] They're a rum bunch to deal with. I've altered it slightly, not really for the better: '*Plain* as lettering … *Larger* than in life …' I don't think larger will do: I'll have to think of another word. They say I can keep three copies, so one for you, not that you'll want it – clutterin' y'self up with junk. It's hideous printing. […]

1 For the Poem of the Month club.

16 September 1970

Beechwood House

The mallard is everywhere, even a head in CRoom, in glass case, like some mangy exhibit in the Commercial Room –

Dearest,

Well! I *was* sorry to leave you – I could have stayed 5 mins more & been nicer – I get wound up on journeys, and a bag of nerves – I hated the journey out of Leics until I got onto the M1, then all went fairly well – arrived about 4.30, found the place with *some* difficulty, but was expected: man opened the door as I drove up.[1]

410

Doubts, horrors & despairs: *garage* completely unknown – 'they're all full, sir – you'll 'ave to see the manciple, sir—' *Heat* is off – electric wall fire in room but not in bedroom, and runs off *only* big plug so can't have jazz *and* heat. Rang Gibb: 'Afraid I can't be in tonight – *Leslie Rowse will take you in—*' Holy God –

Tom² is on mantelpiece, looking at *you* – he feels more at home. I brought your picture.

Quite a nice house, though not large. I have rooms (2) over the front door. House is painted pink – foully ugly. There's a lavatory next door, but I'm not very strategically placed for baths. I've unpacked – 3 miserable hangers – you were right – rotten towels—

Later – about 10.15 pm. College room nicer than this, really – Parker chair, antique desk. In sort of built annexe. Duly met Rowse, who was onto sex in *20 secs flat*, but he was very kind on the whole. Cleared off early. An old £50-er³ named Campbell showed me round after, very kindly – Scotch lawyer. A scatter of young sods at dinner. Dinner was fish, a kind of roast meat I didn't identify – veal? could be, & an extraordinary savoury, an egg in a bowl floating on brown stuff that tasted like marrow & mushrooms. ('Rayther hawrubble.')

Well, I don't know – I'm back in the empty, *chilly* house: nobody here yet, though there are signs of life in the flats – they are built halfway down the drive, in very much new university hall of residence style. Received a wad of papers wch I've not yet digested – seems to be all paying & privilege. Correspondence is stamped by the College, but *breakfasts are £17 a term* (that's news to me). Awgh.

Well, this is a short note from Damon in Iffley to Phyllis in Leicester (do you remember sending me valentines in those terms?) – a new situation for me. I must say I only wish you were here to share it all. It seems very unreal, but I expect I shall get used to it. Parking is obviously going to be a difficulty, in fact all the car stuff (the manciple!) I'll pop this in the post tomorrow, & write again. How beautifully you'd packed! You are the kindest of rabbits: very much love – XXX from Philip.

Later – after breca –   17.9.70
Market Bosworth division – letter from *Geoffrey Moore*⁴ – 'just missed you' – 'can I rent your flat' – ogh ogh ogh ogh shall reply on Mallard paper. It's the goods, eh? In a pig's arse he can rent my flat.

And your *very* kind card. How *very* nice you are. I did want to stay & help you get straight. Good about the garden tools! That's very good. But make it clear they're *yours*.

Breakfast alone with all morning newspapers – 2 boiled eggs – tea – shoes cleaned while I was at it. Less bad. Now off to the manciple ...

> The Manciple's Tale
> Whilom there was dwelling in this toune
> A MANCIPLE, well used to doing doune
> Visiting felawes in their owene righte
> Especially *cars* he liked left out all nighte ... [...]

1 L. was moving into the accommodation provided for him by All Souls for the two terms he spent in Oxford working on the *OBTCEV*. (see Appendix A.)
2 Figurine of cat.
3 All Souls term for someone who has been a Prize Fellow and who was paid £50 per annum.
4 Professor of American Literature, Hull University.

19 September 1970

Beechwood House

Dearest bun,

A few words late at night (Saturday). You wouldn't think I had been chatting with Lord Hailsham & Douglas Jay?[1] Well, I have, & the *latter* I thought a ponce. Had on a check shirt for dinner & filled both his port & his madeira glasses with port indiscriminately. The former was all right. Maintained Dean Inge had a tail. I said this explained his acceptance of evolution.

However, more remarkable features of the day were buying a pair of lemon braces, & walking back to Iffley along the towpath: this is quite possible, and very nice – you start from Folly Bridge. Had visions of doing it on frosty mornings agh-hagh-hagh. [...]

The Warden has not yet materialised. They said Lowell was hardly ever there during his term: Clayre[2] said he spent all his time making love to ____ (name supplied but not heard). The idea of Visiting Fellows doing anything seems to strike them as comic. Prince (F.T.)[3] wrote a long poem wch Sparrow didn't think much of: that was his valuable contribution. The TLS has crapped on it recently. I expect they will watch to see what I do. Sweat like a pig & not hear is all, so far. And boast about walking from Iffley, wch I must say is very nice, only cooler weather would be better. [...]

My proudest moment is when, under the eyes of loitering Yanks & coachloads of Frogs, I take out my fellows' key & open the door in the wall opposite the Radcliffe & disappear into the splendours of North Quadrangle. Vanity, all is vanity.

Much love, dear   P.

1 Hailsham: Quintin Hogg, Conservative politician, Lord Chancellor. Jay: Labour politician, President Board of Trade.
2 Alasdair Clayre, young Fellow of All Souls.
3 F. T. Prince: *Memoirs of Oxford* (1970).

8 October 1970

Set 3 BW, Iff, Oxford

[...] In my researches in the B. I found a vol. of poems by some woman called *In Wartime*, and one struck me as very good. Then later on I found another vol. by her, about 1919, and *another* struck me as good, good by accident, wonderfully evocative of the first war. May (or Mary) Wedderburn Cannan, she's called.[1] They probably aren't any good really. I've used up 200 sheets pasting up Hardy, Eliot, Betjeman, Auden, Housman & Hopkins. The whole thing will have to be reduced by about 75%. Found *In Flanders fields*,[2] then realised the author was Canadian! [...]

1 L. included May Wedderburn Cannan's poem 'Rouen: 26 April–25 May 1915' in *OBTCEV*.
2 John McCrae, 'In Flanders Fields'.

5 November 1970

Beechwood House, Set 3, Iffley Turn, Oxford

Dearest bun,

Late on Thursday night: have been to dine at 'my old college':[1] not bad. A bit strange, but in a way more congenial than AS. The port & fruit & nuts & tobacco and whiskey all take place in the same room, wch is good: all the same, not many people stay for dessert.

Oxford college life, in my view, is dying – if not dead. But I liked the intimate air – as if we were suddenly going to start discussing a living in Huntingdonshire.

Rowse is back. *Within twenty seconds* he was FEELING MY ARSE (demonstrating the frisking routine at airports) and asking me to read his poems. Oh God! Every Eden has its snake. I *can't have tea* these days, because *he's* always there. I thought there'd be strangers around me. [...]

1 St John's College.

8 November 1970

Beechwood House, Set 3, Iffley Turn, Oxford

[...] I now have the OBTCEV in my room at the Library, so that I can do a bit when I'm fed up with work. I've found a compromise about the 'popular' ones: if I've already taken a copy (e.g. Masefield's *Sea Fever*) I'll put it in; if not (e.g. *What is this life*), I won't. So *Innisfree* is in, *Leda & the swan* isn't. I should like to get it done. But there's plenty of work to be got through yet. I don't know what I think of it – whether it's good or not, I mean. And I can't *think* what to say in the preface, except that poets born before 1914 were better than those born after, & that they in turn were better than those born after 1939. I am longing to kick Geo. Barker out. [...]

15 November 1970

Beechwood House, Set 3, Iffley Turn, Oxford

[...] I really meant to start by telling you about Kingsley's visit but I suppose it wd take far too long to describe it all – he & Jane came up on Wednesday, or Thursday, & stayed a night at the Randolph & he gave a reading in Balliol Hall the same evening. He stood me lunch, *Martin* making up the party: *he* looked & behaved like Mick Jagger, but was curiously good about *offering his cigarettes round* & *standing up* when EJ joined/rejoined the company, so there may be some good in the lad. Am wondering whether to have him in to All Souls: stiff cocks wd upset the table. Kingsley's reading was very poor, I thought: got hardly any laughs, wch was absurd, but it was his own fault. He adopts an absurd AEH[1] sort of manner, wch as you may imagine didn't at once commend itself to the audience. 'The stronger brethren will recognise ...' 'The weaker brethren should know ...' [...]

1 A. E. Housman.

17 January 1971

Beechwood House, Set 3, Iffley Turn, Oxford

[...] No letter from you yesterday, but that's all right, you sent me one in the middle of last week. In any case the post is so absolutely rotten that the old rules hardly apply.[1] It is a grim prospect. On a day like this – I mean a Sunday: the weather looks dreary as can be – I want to get in the car and come to see you: why don't I? Well, I suppose it's the prospect of driving *back* in the dark, motorway madmen & so on, tiredness – and perhaps you wd be surprised to see me, though as I say one of the most lovely things about you is that you *never* make me feel unwelcome – and then of course I *ought* to get on with my so-called work, about wch I am worried. But I do miss you. Don't be surprised if any Sunday I turn up – don't order your life to expect this, of course, because I can go to see my Mother if you are out. Of course I want to see her too, in a funny kind of way: well, in quite a reasonable way, I suppose. After *not* going home for her 85th birthday in order to do my jazz piece you'll see the bastards didn't print it.

I am pegging away at the bloody OxBo. Trouble is I can't see *any* worth, or *hardly* any worth, in people like Roy Fuller, Day Lewis, Grigson, Gascoyne, Barker & the like, and want to leave them out. Secondly, I think *everybody* born after 1930 is no good. I can just about stomach 1929 Thom & 1930 Ted, but the rest, no. Now either I cut all these sods out, or I include poems I think worthless. It's v. difficult. My feeling at present is to get some sort of text as soon as I can, and see what they think of it. I must get a final lot of xeroxes from the Bodley, then I think take the whole lot up to Hull to get a second copy – cheaper, quicker. Then bring it back. This wd be about mid term, I suppose. Of course, I shall be continually finding fresh things: and all the editorial work is still to do. [...]

1 A postal strike ran for much of January, all of February, and into March 1971.

14 April 1971

21 York Road, Loughborough, Leics.

Little Easter poem – ought to be dedicated to D. Holbrook [enclosure][1]

1 Same version as sent to Thwaite on the same day; evidently written from 'home', Loughborough. See *Selected Letters*, p.437.

18 April 1971

32 Pearson Park, Hull

Dearest bun,

Thanks for the welcoming letter, very kind of you. I really don't know that I've much to report: the ponce of Hessle has just rung up, & is bringing an Australian girl for tea. This is all part of my getting money out of him, of course. (My money, of course.) O cursed spite! that ever I was bound to such a shite! Talking of pwetry, as Kingsley used to call it, I suggest

They fill you with the faults they had
  And add some extra, just for you.

I think this is better. Or do you think

  They foist on you the faults etc?

That might be better. *Causons, causons, mon bon.* 'Foist' is faintly farcical, wch is good – better than 'fill'. Shall it be foist? (The last shall be foist.) No: there is then too much emphasis on the two *yous*. [...]

Oh, in the paperb. *TWW* 'litany' has been replaced by 'liturgy'.[1] I rather wish I hadn't listened to you on this: it seems to wreck the whole verse, it's so heavy, as opposed to the dancingness of *litany* – *liturgy* anticipates *images* in the next line, too, the g sound. I don't think the meaning is sufficient gain, as no one knows what either word means anyway. [...]

1 In 'Water'. See pp. 324–5, note 4.

THIS BE THE VERSE

They fuck you up, your mum and dad;
   They may not mean to, but they do.
They hand on all the faults they had,
   And add some fresh ones just for you.

But they were fucked up in their turn
   By fools in old-style hats and coats
Who half the time were soppy-stern
   And half at one anothers' throats.

Man hands on misery to man:
   It deepens like a coastal shelf.
Get out as early as you can,
   And don't have any kids yourself.

25 April 1971

32 Pearson Park, Hull

[...] Yes, I was pleasantly surprised by old Kerensky-Hamilton's piece in the *NS*,[1] but I can't really agree with him altogether: I mean, granted the Movement wasn't *much* good, at least it was better than anything else at the same time, or immediately before or after it. I'd give all Terrible Ted for a few Kingsley poems. I expect he'll turn on me in the end, anyway. Wish I could write something to justify Master *Hamiltons* Regarde. [...]

1 Ian Hamilton, 'The Making of the Movement', *New Statesman*, 23 April 1971.

2 May 1971

32 Pearson Park, Hull

[...] I've had to give up Trollope unfinished in order to read Hardy books. I finished Southerington,[1] then reread Lois Deacon to refresh my memory. Now I must start on Millgate, Biswas's pal. I must say that the Deaconites carry their discoveries rather far. I can accept that Tryphena is the origin of Sue B. – I can accept that she's the origin of Tess. But I can't believe she's the origin of both! They're surely totally different characters. Southerington even tries to see her in Arabella! One curious point about Sue, or Tryphena, is that Sue is surely rather frigid, whereas T. (being a Training College student) is, as the evidence shows, *free* with her favours. That seems a contradiction, don't you think? As a story, it's all very sad and interesting. Deacon says she wasn't his cousin, but his niece, & hence they couldn't marry: hence, too, Hardy's interest in decayed & inbred families. The close of the Deacon book is stunning, reprinting deleted sentences from FEH's account of TH's death 'when a few broken sentences ... showed his mind had reverted to a sorrow of the past.' As biographical fact, well! The sorrow of the past might be anything – Emma, no children. There's no record of the son's birth or death. Ah, well! I found Southerington rather dull – there's a frightful lot about Will and *The Dynasts*. Can't say I can work up much enthusiasm about either. [...]

1 L. was reviewing F. R. Southerington's *Hardy's Vision of Man* and Michael Millgate's *Thomas Hardy: His Career as a Novelist* for the *Daily Telegraph* (3 June 1971); reprinted in *Further Requirements* as 'Hardy's Mind and Heart'.

15 May 1971

32 Pearson Park, Hull

Dearest bun,

I've just spent a not very profitable evening trying to finish off a poem, and making it bad Aldous Huxley, i.e. Aldous Huxley, and then putting my nose into a Society of Authors' Retirement Benefit Scheme, wch I'd written for details of. I just can't do money. Since being let down by Lloyds I really feel I ought to find some other source of advice, but who? What?

This afternoon I finally went to see the Elwells[1] in Beverley Art Gallery, & very nice they are too. There are one or two of the old Beverley Arms kitchen (you remember the one that used to hang there). Also on show was an exhibition by 'Friends of the Minster', which I looked round at a brisk trot – the oils were foul (why can't amateurs have a sense of harmony?), the w/colours better. Just as I was bounding out I saw a drab little picture high up – oils – it didn't look bad. A label on the back said 'Jenny's Shop 1950', 'Lilian Walton, £2' in a clear old fashioned hand. I went down to the Libary – hesitated – shied – cleared out – then in porch saw that this was the *last day* – so went back & bought it. Cluttering myself up with junk. But it seemed so humble & modest – and so much *better than the others*, wch were *much more expensive*, that I fell. A very drab, Hully picture. [...]

I've almost finished my crowd-of-craps poem – shall I call it *Vers de Societé*? How d'you pronounce it? Vair duh sōce-yatay? Don't want to have a poem I can't pronounce. [...]

1 Fred Elwell, RA (1870–1958), Beverley painter.

3 June 1971

32 Pearson Park, Hull

[...] It's bloody cold here – fine, but cold. Am trying to write an ethereal little song,[1] nothing like *This be the verse* or *Vers de Soc.*, about the time of year. [...]

1 'Cut Grass'.

6 June 1971

32 Pearson Park, Hull

[...] I've bought a collected Frances Cornford: one ought to have it. There are plenty of nice ones in that I didn't pick.

Come inside the swinging gate
And pay your pennies for the Fête,
Where once I strolled with all the rest
In my sash and Sunday best.

Dust and ash the eyes I sought
Where I strolled and strayed and sat,
And the rose my mother bought
To stick inside my shady hat,
His blue eyes and my bright sash,
   Dust and ash.

A sort of blend of AEH/TH, isn't it? I shouldn't be ashamed of it myself.

Big wedding in Beverley at St Mary's: I saw the bride arrive heavily veiled from a blue Daimler, with Dad in grey topper. Pretty scene. [...]

13 June 1971

32 Pearson Park, Hull

Dearest bun,

Back from 'that great cesspool into wch all the loungers and idlers of the Empire are irresistibly drained' (A. Conan Doyle) – peaceful journey down & back, first-class, empty uninvaded compartments. Read the new G. Mitchell, & got well on with *Could You Forgive Her*, wch seems better to me. I can't think why people don't film Trollope – Lady G. waltzing with Bungo Fitzgerald, Kate & George on the fell, it would be good. Alice is a bit of a bore.

The day was all right, in the context of being a nuisance: handed out bags of money to incompetent tarts and turds.[1] [...]

1 The Gregory Awards, for which L. was a judge. They are given to poets under the age of thirty. The 1971 award-winners were Martin Booth, Florence Bull, John Pook, D. M. Warman and John Welch.

15 July 1971

Puke's Head Hotel, King's Lynn, Norfolk

Dearest bun,

God – why do I always get this stupendous heat when Mother & I go away? It's murder. We set off about 11.30, & had lunch at Stamford; rested, then carried on through Thornley & Wisbech, arriving about 4.30. First impressions, as usual, were rather depressing, but I feel more restored now. Bad things: *fearful heat* (some of the hotel heating actually seems to be *on*); dull shoddy town, makes Loughborough seem like Washington DC; nowhere to sit in boiling hotel except the compulsory morons' twilight of the TV lounge, the *heated* nightmare of the public drinking lounge, or your own room; bedrooms *overlook the ballroom*, Christ (hope they don't have many balls); no morning tea (do it yourself), no shoe cleaning (ditto); *both bars still shut* at 6.15 – Christ!! In fact the Reist brothers have been much in my mind – 'Mike' (sports commentator), 'Bike' (keen cyclist), 'Ark' (believes human race can be classified according to whether you're descended from Ham, Shem, or Japhet), and 'Oak' (very anti-conifer plantation). Then there is one who never drinks anything but a certain Amsterdam spirit – 'My Fockink'. Still, apart from a new inhumanity (our passage is like part of a model prison), it doesn't seem too noisy (sharp noises-off *instantly* commence): dinner wasn't too bad (melon, cold salmon, lemon water ice); the town is very quaint in parts (fine sunset up the Ouse, very wide sky – sun appears to set in the north-east, very odd) – can't think of anything else at present. [...]

The three Norfolk towns I've seen so far – K's L, Thetford & Ely – have been exactly alike, nice stone towns *ruined* by main street developments. Really awful, like a Betj. poem. Ely however produced the weeklies – *Spr* preparing to sell out on Ulster. *NS* has some fulsome stuff about *Vers de Soc.* by J. Raban, who doesn't seem to have 'got' the poem too well. [...]

I feel depressed anyway – the prospect of life, or what's left of it, stretches before me (to use my favourite quotation) like an infinitely tiring staircase. One learns nothing and forgets nothing, like the Bourbons. It's ghastly. I wish I could forget things. Or, if I've got to remember them, I wish I could remember pleasant things as well as unpleasant things. I suppose pleasant things make no impression. [...]

20 July 1971

The Duke's Head, King's Lynn, N'fk

[...] I sent *Cut grass* to *The Listener*: they seem to like it. I wish some-one good would set it to music – that shows it's no good, of course.*

*I sing it to a sort of whine made up by myself, minor changing to major at 'Of young-leafed June', v. voluptuous. [...]

I'm sorry your degree day was depressing. I'm very sparing in my attendance, I can tell you: of course I've no students to see turned off. By the way, sorry to keep on about *The Times*, but the class lists for Oxford English came out today, and *no* mention of M. L. Amis[1] (Exeter)!! Isn't that odd? I'm sure he said he was sitting schools this summer. Do you think Martin Amis sat it & failed completely, or was one of the students who go into a drug-induced fugue ('What does FUGUE spell, Johnny?' 'Fug you.') at the prospect? He must have done *something* in Mods. Must write to Bob & get the inside info. We were pretty good, nine papers, one after the other, libraries closed at 5.30 & bloody cold even when they weren't, starved, blacked out ... The Brothers are dealin' very aisy with'm. [...]

1 See Appendix B.

1 August 1971

32 Pearson Park, Hull HU5 2TD

Dearest bun,

I had a go at my neck last night, trying to roll it between my palms like a cigar, & it seems to have done it good. The action was prompted more by exasperation than therapeutic knowhow, but the pain has sub-sided. The clicks are still there.

Weight is nearer 15 st this morning – bad, bad! Yesterday I was, *honestly*, nearer 14½ st than 15 st, a most marvellous thing. But now all is faded. I dreamed of food last night, a rare thing for me – dreamed I was at a special lunch at All Souls, where the food was much better than it ever is in reality. [...]

You Never Can Tell[1] wore quite well, didn't it? But like all BBC plays, twenty times too fast. I suppose they're deprived of the dilution of action, people hanging about preparing to speak, etc. They cut out the stuff about Mrs Clandon's book, did they, or did I just miss it? And the whip. 'Sadism in Shaw: a psychological quest.' Talking about that kind of thing, I see Ray Gosling is in the thick of it up in Burnley. Christ, why can't they just start their bloody club, if it isn't illegal any more? These fellows want it with jam on. I finished Ackerley[2] thinking it was like a farcical *Ghosts*, shot with *This Be The Verse*. It seemed to me full of *The sins of the fathers*, a kind of textbook case. [...]

I must have another go at the book: I'm typing the contents and source-list. It's all very shaky, scholarwise: I can see myself being taken to bits by someone like John Carter[3] – 'It is difficult to see why, with the 1966 edition of the enlarged *Collected Poems* easily accessible, Mr Larkin has taken his texts from the notorious selection of 1932 – and not even consistently, for at least one appears in the bibliographical motley that seems to have been regulation dress for Thomas Moult's "Best Poems" series ...' Oh boys yes, I can see it coming. Last evening I threw out Sir George Hamilton and R. Aldington. Bugger them. Boring old farts. Tedious old toads. Nor am I doing the entries, I fancy, as I should, not saying where things are from. Oh dear. I'm not much use at this kind of thing.

Enclosed is *Cut Grass* – I expect it still 'lacks impact'. Its trouble is that it's 'music', i.e. pointless crap. About line 6 I hear a kind of wonderful Elgar river-music take over, for wch the words are just an excuse. Dr Pussy could set it, but I daren't ask him. Do you see what I mean? There's a point at wch the logical sense of the poem ceases to be added to, and it continues only as a succession of images. I like it all right, but for once I'm not a good judge. [...]

1 BBC radio version of *You Never Can Tell* by George Bernard Shaw (1897).
2 J. R. Ackerley, *My Father and Myself* (1968).
3 Editor of Housman's *Collected Poems*.

15 August 1971

32 Pearson Park, Hull

Dearest bun,

Up bright & early, & the weather brighter too than yesterday, wch wouldn't be difficult, since after about five it was dark & rainy, plus storms of course: a storm was roaming round the East Riding like

O'Grady going down the bar room, knocking into things & occasionally switching the lights on and off (arberjays, I'll be gettin the Brendan Behan Chair of Poetry at the National when the ould IRA's settin' in Bucknam Pallas ... God: how revolting all things Irish seem to me at present. I chucked out Monk Gibbon last night, & shall be looking very hard at your men from now on. Should I perhaps put in WR Rodgers' poem about Paisley?[1] That wd please *Davin*[2] – gt pal of WRR & cross at his exclusion – and please *me*. Anyway, this is all too big a project for parenthesis). [...]

1 'Home Thoughts from Abroad'.
2 Dan Davin, L.'s commissioning editor at OUP.

16 August 1971

32 Pearson Park, Hull

Dearest,

Just come in from *B.Potter* – I couldn't wait, so crept off from the Library & saw the 4.15 showing. Well, it's *charming*, & thoroughly *decent*: all I would say is that there's too much foggun *ballet*. You *must* try to see it – is it on in Edinburgh?[1] Skip some canting balls & go & see it.

There isn't a *word* in it all, just an occasional miaou. Tab. Twitchett (I think) comes on in a beautiful dress, but her mask isn't nearly good enough. J. Fisher is a dream – not a bit like JF in Potter, but very touching: his spell of seeing he's all right after escaping from the pike is very good. The mice are good, some better than others: the pigs the same. P. Rabbit has a wild lettuce-dance, but otherwise doesn't appear much. Squirrels are a bore.

Well, I *do* wish you'd been here, but perhaps you'll manage to see it. It is really an honest job, worth seeing – too much bleddin dancin, but you have to put up with it.

Am cooking sausages & onions – less bad.

Hope you're enjoying yourself,
and much love & kisses
Philip

1 Monica was at a conference in Edinburgh.

16 September 1971

32 Pearson Park, Hull

[...] Another letter from Colin Gunner,[1] giving news of Coventry. He says he's turned RC! You can't imagine how extraordinary this is! I should have judged him entirely without interest in religious matters, except for his 'me velly Clistian boy' act, guaranteed to convulse. He was a kind of pre-Kingsley in my life: kept me in fits. Also that Jim Sutton has become a *pharmacist*! He was my painter friend. It all seems very odd. [...]

1 Friend of L.'s from schooldays in Coventry: see *Selected Letters*.

26 September 1971

32 Pearson Park, Hull

[...] Perhaps one source of malaise is my non-writing: I feel very much that my twenty or so poems aren't very good, & need good ones, all of *T.W.W.* standing, to buck them up, only I can't get around to writing them somehow. I don't really want to write about myself, and everything else seems hardly worth bothering about. I mean I can't write poems about Brenda, or Newlove's food. As you know, every writer has a book he wants to rewrite (Dylan Thomas said his was *Pilgrim's Progress*): mine is *The Seasons*.[1] Can't do it, though. Moan, moan, moan. Still, there's always drink. Perhaps I ought to have some, till I've drunk myself 'cheerful and loving-like'.[2] [...]

1 James Thomson's long topographical poem (1730) was not itself a source of L.'s envy; but several times he asserted that he would like to write a long poem on the seasons. There are some drafts in his poetry notebooks, and one might note such pieces (not published until the 1988 *Collected Poems*) as 'Autumn', 'And now the leaves suddenly lose strength' and 'A slight relax of air where cold was'.
2 From Shaw's *Pygmalion*.

14 November 1971

32 Pearson Park, Hull

[...] The OUP has woken up about OBTCEV: letters & comments fly back & forth. Isn't it awful: not only is May Wedderburn Cannan, my gt discovery, daughter of a Secretary to the Delegates: now they say 'Susan Miles' (Ursula Roberts) is aunt of the present Sec., old Colin Roberts of St John's! Though ye try to roll alligators, yet shall they prove to be logs. Still, Anne Ridler, Jon Stallworthy, out, out, out. [...]

17 November 1971

32 Pearson Park, Hull

[...] Had a cheque for £350 from the OUP today: advance & expenses. I think they are getting on with it. It struck me that my acknowledgment of your help in the foreword was rather distant, but in a way it was meant to be – sufficient that you are mentioned first and no one else is, except old Thwaite, who insisted on sending me lists of people who ought to be in, like Seamus Heaney. I've put 'constant' in before 'encouragement'. Or wd you think it better if I put in 'read through the selection in draft and made many valuable', etc.? Perhaps that wd be better. I wd like you to be sitting squarely in the credits, like a rabbit in clover. [...]

21 November 1971

32 Pearson Park, Hull

[...] Did I tell you about my discovery in Larkin studies? I was rereading *The Wind in the Willows*, & found within a few pages of each other 'long coats' and 'running' and 'over the fields'.[1] Isn't that odd? It's where Toad crashes the car & is chased. I'm sure I got the words from there – hiding places thirty years deep, at least. But perhaps I've told you before – perhaps I've *realised* it before. Brain going. Pox got. [...]

1 See 'Days', last four lines. In *The Wind in the Willows*, 'long coats', 'running', 'pounding across fields' all appear in Chapter X, 'The Further Adventures of Toad'.

5 December 1971

32 Pearson Park, Hull

[...] On Friday night I went to the Hull Library Theatre to see a programme of old films about Hull. Evocative as you might guess. Almost the best was 'Trams in Hull' (1902) (¾ min), the flickering monsters turning slowly in the sunlight, the bowler-hatted men snatching pipes from their mouths before they jerk across the road. But there was George V & Mary (1914), and lots about the blitz, & boring old VE day. There's something really too obvious about the past, but it gets you every time, or nearly every time. The war films tended to leave me feeling as isolated as the war itself did – d'you think people *really* felt as they were supposed to? all these parades of landgirls & factory workers (cf the Coventry tool shop agreement – how my father would have hooted): I don't know. They hardly seemed to have the unforced touch of Kitchener's army. It seemed a civil service war, a trade union war. I don't know.

Good old Enoch, chasing up that priest. More traitorous rot in the weeklies. To hell with the whole boiling. What do you think Paisley is up to? If Ireland reunited, Ulster wd probably get control, except for the Church of course. But it wdnt make any difference: the Irish will always have a grievance & want to fight someone, even if only themselves. [...]

9 December 1971

32 Pearson Park, Hull

[...] I sent the poem about 1929 to the *Obs.*[1] That'll teach'm. I'm trying to do one about Oxford:

Tonight we dine without the Master
(Nocturnal vapours make him wheeze):
The port goes round a good deal faster,
The arguers are more at ease –
Which advowson looks the fairest,
What the wood from Snape will fetch,
Names for *pudendum mulieris*,
Why is Juggins like Jack Ketch?
[...]

1 Part I of 'Livings'. This is stanza one of part III, and there are slight variations from the final version, completed 10 December 1971.

20 December 1971

32 Pearson Park, Hull

[...] I suppose I shall take *Dombey & Son* home to read – might even finish it there, I suppose. What a dreary-sad book it is, as if he was deeply depressed by things. I can't say I'm grasping it – Punch and the Patriarch and William and Frederick waltz round in my fuddled brain. What's he on about? What's he on about? So far it's readable. I had thought of taking home Browning – the thought of him appeals to me at present – but it's a bloody great fat book, and *poetry* ... (Don't forget me on Christmas Eve, reading that snatch of depressed verse.)[1] I don't like reading poetry as such. Another Gavin Ewart turned up today: one poem, *The Select Party*, starts 'Hands that wiped arses Are holding glasses'. He's a mad sod & no error. Still, I feel I might like some Browning just now – he might fit the mood of my more recent verses. [...]

1 'Home Is So Sad', broadcast on BBC Radio 4, 24 December 1971.

13 January 1972

32 Pearson Park, Hull

My dear bun,

Your letter didn't come till 2nd post Tuesday – I'd like to know where the hell it goes for all that time. Floreat GPO. Great Paralysed Oafs. I was beginning to get worried. What an *awful* journey home! Really, I can't thank you enough for coming. It's a terrible price to pay. My heart went out to you.

It's been a dull week here. I've stayed in labouring at this craft of LIVING OFF THE BRITISH GOVT WHILE CRYING UP THEIR ENEMIES verse. Finished the 'commissioned' poem last night,[1] but it isn't any good. I'll never be laureate. The other one has got stuck in consequence. Today I sent II & III *Livings* to the *Knob-server* in the hope that they'll print all three together. I think they're all good in different ways. Better than *Crow* anyway. Have also undertaken to review the posthumous Stevie Smith for them, crazed loon that I am. I can't think of any comment, criticism, interpretation, description, verdict, opinion or fact to put down, except that I don't much mind it, to use a half remembered construction of K's.

The car has started leaking again. God damn and blast it to hell. [...]

Not much food news. I eat upstairs now, frugally, at lunch, and then go to the bar for some non alcoholic drink. I'm asking Mary to get in slim-line! What a comedown. I've been 14½ again since I wrote, but no less. A chap said today you don't get any effect for a month, then you suddenly go down. I bet. I ate the leeks last night, and some of the swede, with a poached egg. I've decided I don't really want meat or fish in the evening, it's too heavy. Egg one night, grilled bacon the next, I suppose. Oh, the days of macaroni cheese!

I think you're quite right about Hardy, if you're thinking about the family face & Who's in the next room.[2] It would be interesting to make a list: poems not deriving from a given individual experience, poems with Hardy not there. I've started J. I. M. Stewart's *Thomas Hardy*: bit opaque, like the author.

I'd love to write more, but feel I must devote some of the evening to the craft of, etc. I thought the *It's Your Line* on Ulster a sight more interesting than the TV *sounded*, but of course one can't know. Someone in *The Listener* today says the IRA have put a united Ireland off for a generation. Wow. Much love, my dearest bun. Thinking of you.

P XX

1 'Going, Going', commissioned by the Department of the Environment, and first published in their *How do you want to live?* (HMSO, 1972).
2 Monica had written in a letter dated 9 January 1972, from 1A Cross Road: 'Not much time now – I'm trying to work at Hardy. One thing I am going to say is that one thinks perhaps at first that his poetry is, at its most characteristic & its best, extremely *personal* in its materials & its emotion – real people, places, precise situations & memories; & one thinks this is what he's best at, & one thinks of some of his best poems & they seem to bear out this judgment. And then one thinks again & sees that he's also much moved by & can move us by *impersonal* materials & emotions, and that *some* of his best poems are of *this* sort too – *Old Furniture* is not recollecting *particular* persons, events, memories, rather he's thinking of people he didn't know but just knows existed; tho' they are the possessions of *his* family, yet he is really being moved by a kind of impersonal sense of the past & all the forgotten people; & *The Year's Awakening* is again & even more a *general* meditation, & *just* as emotional & as moving to me. One doesn't need to adduce poems on public themes to carry the point – *of course* they exist too, but there is this other distinction & I think it ought to be stressed that he can be absolutely at his best with *both* kinds of emotion.'

16 January 1972

32 Pearson Park, Hull

[...] Nothing from you yesterday, so I shall have to rattle on about myself. *The Gobserver* has accepted the three poems[1] and will print them together 'when I have space' in a pig's arse. I still like them. The 3rd verse of the King's Lynn one isn't quite right: 'big' and 'great' clash, & the penultimate line has six beats. Awgh. Perhaps I can maul it about in proof. I am still pegging at my two poems but without much success. The non commissioned one is now called 'The Meeting House'.[2] It's the best thing about it. Only Connect in a pig's arse. Haw haw. [...]

1 The three-part 'Livings'.
2 Later, 'The Building'; completed 9 February 1972.

20 January 1972

32 Pearson Park, Hull

Dearest,

I write at intervals of telephoning Loughborough numbers, wch true to type fail to ring, or if they ring fail to be answered. The reason for this is that Mother is in bed & I am trying to get news of her. Apparently on Tuesday morning she was dizzy and fell, & summoned the doctor, who suggested she went to bed for 'three days', after saying, presumably after trying them, that her heart and blood pressure were all right. I got Walter last night and he said that they had been there on Tuesday night, & that K. was there at that moment, and that they would go again later that night; also that she looked and seemed all right on Tuesday. Anyway, tonight I can't get a reply from either number, so presumably they are in transit one way or the other. At least I hope so. I'll try again in a bit. Of course I am a little worried.

It's been rather a strenuous day with a visit from four Reading people, VC & 3 others, and having to show them round. Although it all went quite well it *is* a strain, talking all the time, and trying to hear what they say. One of them told me that the tomb in Chichester Cathedral now has a brass plate on it saying I wrote a poem about it! Think of our going there, & now a brass plate. I can't really think why we went. Winchester I remember, but Chichester has rather vanished – I suppose

I thought it wd be a pretty town. We went to a yachting place, didn't we – Bosham, the map tells me.

Have just tried both numbers again, but without success – no reply, I mean.

The Starvation Stakes proceed, but I'm not gaining any ground. I suppose I'm really a stone lighter than when I left Oxford – I didn't make a note then, but I do find an entry celebrating the return to 15 st. so I must have been more than that.

Cooper,[1] or rather someone in his firm, has returned Gunner's book, saying it isn't suitable. Pity. I suppose I shall have to send it back to him.

I scored a hit with the Reading people by offering them Indian or China tea!

I have sent off my S. Smith review,[2] not specially good: it leans heavily on what I said in the NS years ago. Anthony Thwaite has offered me a book of Hardy's letters to Florence Henniker, due out in April. It would be an easy passage for my annual chore, but Hardy's letters are not specially vivid, though I haven't looked at them yet. It's compiled by Barbara Hardy & that Pinion chap. I get mixed with these Hardys.[3] Wasn't there an Evelyn Hardy? Edited the *Notebooks*? And none of them related. It's an odd, Hardyish circumstance: I mean you don't get people called Dickens writing about Dickens, or with any other name.

Anthony said he'd been asked to join in on the birthday programme[4] – said Auden, Betjeman, & Fuller had been *asked*. Ay, and do they not give *a reply* from their *breech*, you Son of a W—e.

It must have been an ordeal to lecture on Hardy: I'm sure you did it well, though. What you said sounds quite sensible. Did I say I had another letter from Sparrow saying how good the Betjeman intro was? Ahum. Aha. I don't think it is really. It was just designed to make the Yanks feel they ought to read him. [...]

Still no reply, at 9.10! It's puzzling, and the possible explanations not v. encouraging.

– I left it then until such time as I did get an answer, wch was about half past ten at Mother's number, answered by Kitty in her least attractive mood. The line as usual was bad. She didn't give much news, except that she went three times a day, and that Mother had seemed all right today but was 'difficult' this evening. Still in bed. I suppose if there were anything wrong she would notice it. The cleaner has been coming again. All in all I don't feel very reassured. I am to ring tomorrow night at 9 p.m. Perhaps I shall get more sense out of her then.

I'm sorry this isn't a very cheerful letter, but circumstances make it so. I don't know whether to think of going home myself. If I did I would call on you, if that were convenient. Perhaps it all seems worse, my not being there. Anyway, there won't be any means of letting you know what I decide.   Much love, dear, as always,

Philip

1 Leo Cooper, publisher of military books, to whom L. had sent Colin Gunner's *Adventures with the Irish Brigade*. L. wrote an Introduction (see *Further Requirements*).
2 Review of Stevie Smith, *Scorpion and Other Poems*, *Observer*, 23 January 1972; reprinted in *Further Requirements*.
3 Evelyn Hardy (no relation of Thomas's) and F. B. Pinion edited Hardy's letters to Florence Henniker. See L.'s *New Statesman* review, 2 June 1972, in *Further Requirements*.
4 'Larkin at Fifty', broadcast on Radio Three, 9 August 1972.

23 January 1972

21 York Road, Loughborough

Dearest bun,

I don't like your not having a letter on Monday just because I've seen you so briefly! Though what there is to say in such circumstances I don't know. I've bought papers and looked at most of them without finding anything of interest: what a waste of money they are.

I've been wondering what on earth there is to say about my poems – only to help you, of course, not from self regard.[1] Some people say a favourite theme is the contrast between the ideal & the real, wch I expect is true enough. But there are other subjects. I don't think I have the humanity of either Hardy or Betjeman, but I have the usual poetic appreciation of pretty things or striking situations. I am always trying to 'preserve' things by getting other people to read what I have written, and feel what I felt.

Still, balls to that. I was amused by The Thoughts of Chairman Bun. Some were quite poetic. Darling, I wish I were some use to you. The daffodils have opened wide now. What a nice day it looks! The lamb is cooking away busily. If I had a pair of hex-ray eyes I'd know if it was done!   Love, my dear

Philip

1 Monica had been invited to run a course on L.'s poems.

27 January 1972

32 Pearson Park, Hull

Dearest bun,

I forget how much I've been able to tell you of the events of this week. The chief thing is that Mother fell on Monday night, and on Wednesday after x-rays they said she had chipped a bone in her hip, & so took her to Leicester Infirmary. Today she is due to have an operation. I expect she'll be there at the weekend, and I shall visit her on Saturday and Sunday. Visiting hours on both days are 2.30–3.30. I thought I might come & see you afterwards on Saturday, though matters can change from day to day. God knows where one leaves a car near the Infirmary! It will be all I can do to get there.

The students are sitting in over Reckitts shares. I thought BJ's message was too aggressive. I seem to be falling back in the Starvation Stakes, but my neck feels better. It still hurts, but in a different, nicer way.

Sorry not to have better news. I hope you are all right in this foul weather.   Much love

Philip

26 April 1972

32 Pearson Park, Hull

Dearest bun,

Feel a bit sunk – fuddled with sherry, sleepy, but knowing that time is short ... I tried my Hardy review last night again, & found I was quite out of touch with it, quite scaringly so. Plenty to say, but can't fit it together. Awgh.

It's been a busy week. There seems nothing between lying flat on one's back and sprinting at 10 yds a second. I expect you've found it the same. I had another letter from Norman[1] today: *his wife came into money*, £700 a year, wch he supplements by letting the house to summer visitors, and I expect by Nat. Ass. So, just like Kingsley, *Dunna thee marry for munny, but goa wheer t'munny is*, or however Pope[2] puts it. '*Marry some rich cow and — for a living*' (*Death of a Hero*).[3] Heigh ho. He writes quite affably. Seems to spend his time *going for walks.* ' "Ach, scheiss. Bei mir nicht". He made the curt, brutal

433

gesture of the streets' (*Goodbye to Berlin*). My mind seems full of Eng Lit today: do forgive me. I'm quite sober.

Today Gorgeous MacDeath[4] will have been doing his recordings (A Thwaite calls him that). I wonder how they've been getting on. I still don't know when I'll do my contribution – end of May or beginning of June. I'd like to couple haw haw it with a visit to All Souls, but no reply from Sparrow so far. Did I tell you I'd heard from OUP saying the OB wd be published in *March* 1973? We'll all be dead by then. Just two —ing years and one — month after I handed it in. Really, it's worse than the Fortune Press: this year, next year, sometime, never. I really just don't care any longer.

Tomorrow my car gets its radio back, so journeys will (I hope) be better again, assuming it really has been mended. Shackety boom, shackety shackety boom.

Thursday Car back, two new foggin tyres if you don't mind BUT I DO MIND. Radio funk–shunning. So all is well for the moment, until the next calamity. [...]

1 Norman Iles, contemporary of L.'s at St John's, Oxford,
2 Pope, in jest: actually Tennyson.
3 Richard Aldington, *Death of a Hero* (1929).
4 George MacBeth, BBC radio producer of 'Larkin at Fifty'.

30 July 1972

32 Pearson Park, Hull

Dearest,

I'm not getting on very fast this weekend – have done bugger all to date in fact. Did proofs drunkenly on Friday night (do you know we *both* missed 'Man, we're playing funerals now?'[1] Curious San Francisco flavour) & had hangover Saturday. Shopped feebly – got chops & steak from your butcher – here & in Beverley, then came back & collapsed – found my armchair springs broken – *hell* – had second bath, then off for quite pleasant but *time-consuming* evening at the 'Espinasses. Back for more drink & jazz: hangover prolonged this morning.

I really must get down to things today, though the weather looks lovely and I should like to look at some things described in Pevsner.

My sense of nausea wasn't diminished by EJH's[2] stuff in the *S. Times* – God, they wring every little drop out of it, don't they? And how *dull* it all is, anyway, and how vulgar. I hope nobody goes on about me like that. Poor old Cecil. As a man sows, so shall he reap. And her description of his work as Laureate didn't go unnoticed – no, a fearful life. Mr Poesy. The Frankie Vaughan of Verse. The Elvis Presley of English Poets. No, sirree. At the mercy of every fool/swine/bore in the British Isles.

'Espinasse has found the phrase 'Pride & Prejudice' in Gibbon, Ch. XXVII: I suppose this is well known? It was called something else to start with, wasn't it – I wonder if JA read Gibbon. Wendy[3] wd know, I suppose.

No, I've never read *Birds of America*,[4] it got such fearful reviews, though come to think of it the worst was by A. Waugh, wasn't it. Isn't it full of pissy continental travel, & crap abt Vietnam? You make it sound very good. Of course you like anthin abt food! You ought to do an anthology 'Great Meals of Literature', though I expect it's been done already. Ow wow stoppit.

Shall have to get in touch with *George*[5] over the text of his pissy poem – this is going to be a nuisance, may even land me with going to see him next weekend, since that is the only way to get sense out of him. He couldn't send me a xerograph of a page, I'm sure. As a man spews, so shall he crap.

A nuisance the test finishing early, it wd have been helpful to you while at your sorting. I'm sure it's a rotten job. Dear bun! I wish I were there to help. Things aren't very cheering. I think continually of age & death, and how we must help each other, but I do nothing for you. [...]

1 Evidently both L. and Monica, reading first proofs of *OBTCEV*, missed this misprint in 'Take One Home For the Kiddies': it should, of course, be 'Mam, we're playing funerals now'.
2 See Appendix B.
3 Wendy Craik.
4 Mary McCarthy, *Birds of America* (1971).
5 G. S. Fraser. His 'Christmas Letter Home' is in OBTCEV.

9 August 1972[1]

32 Pearson Park, Hull

Douglas D is going to be the GSF *de nos jours*, hein?

Dearest,

I am just playing the medieval record, wch I have saved till last. So far it's not like the Christmas one, & not as good, but quite nice – dreary fenlike stuff, *some* capering. The others are lovely. I *adore* the Magdalen one, *and* the Evensong – they are both superb in their different ways. In the Evensong the readers aren't 'on mike' so it's *just* like being in church – can't hear a foggun word, *awfully* good! On the strength of the Magdalen I've ordered a Tallis, same label.

Well, I have had some good cards – heard from the choir kittens & the warrens (their number seems to be growing – there is talk of parsnip wine now), and of course Dr. P. No club. I had a card from a complete stranger enclosing a limerick:

There was a young [thanks] fellow of Hull
Who found life distressingly dull
    He sat on the quay
    And stared out to sea
Crying 'O for the wings of a gull!'

Not bad. Letters – or notes – from BJ, Brett ('welcome to the over-50s club'), Mother, the aunt, greetings telegrams from Charles[2] & a local mad bint, cards from the usual.

I had a curious evening last night, writing to my solicitor to try to get my will moving, and listening to your records & reading the holiday diaries. It'll be funny to be at Torridon 'married' & with a big car – shall we get put by the window, as we didn't last time? The packed lunches were *vile*, I hope you remember. Worse than Altnach. Lots of midges too. But there was the black rabbit.

The music is cheering up.

You were very autocratic about the fire at Torridon. I expect you remember all this. Was that the place where some kilted clown blew the bagpipes before dinner?

No, I am not breaking training – have bought chops, though. No lemons! Awgh!

Later Mad *with rage* with the fucking BBC, *getting the time wrong in this* area[3] – people *rang me up*, asking what the hell. If I hadn't 'happened', as they say, to have been in the Midlands last weekend ... Shall write to the fucking Governor General, some RC prick called Curran –

Anyway, I loved Auden's U.S. 'a's. Bob's reading quite pleased me, Ted's too, funnily enough. I was/am a bit pissed on Smith's Glenlivet. Betjeman did his best – I was *so glad* he did *Toads Revisited*, a nice poem I think. Rather a lot of 'old friends', I thought: enough to annoy non-friends. I taped it O.K. Bob didn't introduce Suckowski, did he. Great self-restraint.

Well, darling, I wish ya'd been here – I hope you heard it. You can hear it again when you're here. And your lovely records, wch will really be the most lasting thing of today – except being 50 ooya bugar. Of course I am glad – do 'say' do. Love xxx P.

1 L.'s fiftieth birthday.
2 Charles Monteith, L.'s editor at Faber.
3 'Larkin at Fifty' had its time changed in the North Region from that posted in *Radio Times*. The contributors were: Kingsley Amis, John Betjeman, W. H. Auden, Robert Conquest, Douglas Dunn, Roy Fuller, Ted Hughes, Anthony Thwaite.

13 August 1972

32 Pearson Park, Hull

Dearest bun,

Sunday moaning ... no, not really. Up fairly early, & brekkered & dressed & bed made by 9.50 a.m. I find I can't stay in bed to any advantage after about 7.30 – seems too hot. There are plenty of things to do, anyway – hairbrushes to wash, and night-scented socks.

I feel almost bound to drink gin as I have got 2 lemons – all the little shops took a delight in telling me they hadn't got any, but the shop at the end of Princes Avenue had a whole basketful. God knows what they charged for them – didn't listen. Ought to give up drink though. It just wrecks my evenings. Wake up with the record player revolving in placid silence.

I had a drive round yesterday, Pevsner in hand, Test on car radio, lovely weather. Didn't go anywhere special – Bielby, Pocklington, Huggate, and so on. At least half the churches were locked. Pevsner says the best house in Pocklington is the Ritz Cinema – and when you look at it, it is! The ugliness is astounding. Wally's Fish Fry jammed into 200 yr old cottage fronts. Then I looked at rather a pretty Victorian cemetery in Beverley. Quite a Larkin afternoon, in fact. The Test wasn't very cheering, but I reckon England had it coming to them for that Leeds pitch. In the evening I had chops & peach, & took down bedroom curtains, & fell into drunken stupor.

Quite a kind account of the programme in *The Obs*.! Had an interim apology from the Director-General – nothing from Hallam Tennyson,[1]

437

whose programme I have directed him to stuff. I've a notion he's a rather high-handed character, not unnaturally I suppose. I told him I wouldn't cross the road for the BBC, let alone catch the 6.45 am Pullman, so he may conceivably have grounds for complaint. This doesn't get me out of lunch with Harold Pinter – you never told me abt his plays ow yow. Do you know that the prick is only 42 & has the CBE? I feel very dubious about meeting him. Must remember to book my Pullman back today – this is *Thursday*: you haven't said anthin about coming north, except that you might stay a night. I've a bottle of champagne waiting on you – joint Hobbs & Sutcliffe celebration. Any time will do, but lemme know.

I think the flat[2] is marvellous, and I'm glad you're feeling more enthusiastic about it – it *is* nice, & very splendid. The best policy is to get in, & this gives an added incentive to add things. No reason at all to rush things – aren't I writing badly, the Archers is on. And didn't Hull do well in *Any Questions*, booing old Feather![3] I've always thought Hull was a solid Labour place, quite the last place to boo dockers – but then of course we've got 'em on the doorstep. We'll probably starve up in Scotland. Hotels are all booked, AA says Strome Ferry is discontinued. I'm looking forward to it, aren't you? Hope the car behaves!!!

Have got Tallis now – quite nice, but not super. Dearest love,

Philip

1 Hallam Tennyson: great-grandson of the poet, BBC radio producer, who had asked L. to take part in another programme.
2 See Appendix A.
3 Victor Feather: General Secretary, TUC.

26 October 1972

32 Pearson Park, Hull

Dearest,

O what a week – not for *nastiness*, that is a low'ring buggerlie great cloud in the distance, but sheer *work*, going back every night to wrestle with this literature course. And on returning at 10 or 10.15 to have to do this Hardy anthology, or write urgent letters, or read piss for the Poetry Book Society. Just occasionally I fall insensible from drink.

Fucking the Library has now become *Union policy*, & a sub-committee has been set up to plan this. I told you it wd go like this. I think I *shall* have to debate, on 13 Nov, but in the evening, & perhaps on a smaller scale. I don't know. Isn't it ghastly?

See H. Gardner's book is out; the *Daily Mail* rang up to ask if I minded being excluded! Fortunately Betty dealt with them. I gather she has excluded *L'Allegro* & *Il Penseroso*! Bit more than W. R. Rodgers or Jon Stallworthy, what? There's something in *The Times* about her asking people on 'a Hellenic cruise' what their favourite poems were – she's a person of great unoriginality, I think. Typical female don. Oh well – likes *Macneice*, God on a bicycle. 'To the Makers' jumping Jimmy Jesus.[1] The corn grows tall.

This letter is really weak with fatigue. I would have telephoned, but a letter is more lasting, & I hope to have one from you. You are a brilliant letter writer. Nabarro & Beloff will brighten my board, *Daniels* was gleefully anticipating conviction of the former in the bar yesterday. Haw haw. Market Bosworth. But there hasn't been much of the terrorist-blows-himself-up calibre recently. Good letters in the D.T. defending Craig. We are buying a £75 lot of Belfast literature, collected by an intrepid bookseller – remarkable proportion of *Communist* stuff, along with IRA & Orange. Peter Simple is right. Douglas says he is 'asking the academics' about Snow & Hoff – that means you, I don't doubt, heh heh.

I've had my Red Hand tie cleaned: it looks fine.

O bun! Bun of property![2] I think of you, so warm & safe & luxurious, & am greatly sad & glad & envious.

See the Lemmons lot at the CDL memorial service. Jill in a very light suit – Betjeman in decent black. Wonder what Sargy Mann had on.

Punch printed my Cole Porter[3] on Wednesday: quite efficient stuff. Must remember to collect all these fees. Jean[4] is getting me into court to testify something or other – feel I ought to consult my own man. Money, money. – Love, my dear one!! P.

---

1 Helen Gardner's *New Oxford Book of English Verse* ends with MacNeice's 'To the Makers'.
2 Monica had moved into a new flat in Knighton Park Road.
3 'Supreme Sophisticate': reprinted in *Required Writing*.
4 Jean Hartley.

14 January 1973

32 Pearson Park, Hull

Dearest bun,

Oh dear, it does seem a long time since I wrote to you – sign we have been together. [...]

The first flush (of ye lavatory cistern) having died down, the *Ox Bo* lies about my room like a reproach – oh dear. It's awful. I shall get such a ballocking. I just want to go away & hide. Hopeless incompetent ignorant rubbish. It's *far* too loaded towards the 19th century – if you cut out all the poems written before 1900 I suspect about ⅓wd go. But they are the best, or a good deal of the best. But seriously, dear, I am in a fearful state about it, I almost regret associating you & Thwaite with it, for your sakes I mean.

Oh dear.

Biswas was quite right about the TLS – I was wrong, drunken fool. It was quite a good review, yes – I mean, laudatory. I must have been think-ing about the one in the Sunday paper. I wonder if I shall ever read it – the book I mean.[1] It's very long, and doesn't look too readable, if you know what I mean. Actually, if you gerrold (Gerrold Duffin, sixth wicket) of the TLS, read the leader on Auden, or start it halfway through & read to the end. Well, perhaps it's piss. I've just re-read it. But it offers a sort of expla-nation of how the bloke can have *gone on* writing such rotten poems.

You'd like the NS competition results this week – awful menus of decent components, except that you'll think that *Woman* does better. I'll enclose it. Some of them – well, all of them – overdo it rather. One doesn't have to say more than 'Poach oysters in bacon stock' – but how is this worse than bacon on trout, as in real life not 100 miles from here? In fact, the shorter the better – pilchard crumble, swede melba, not that I haven't had a pint or two of that tack in my time, or so I fancy.

Later in the day – pissed as all get-out: ½ bott. sherry & ¾ bott of white wine, reading the buik. Well – I must say it makes me cry & laugh, wch is what ART ought to do, innit? I *do hope* people see this, & don't piss on it because it doesn't exemplify the latest critical balls. The best poems in it are *Rouen*, *The Things that Matter*, & the Noel Coward one about his childhood.

Darling. Can't write for those idle things –

Philip

1 R. K. Biswas, *Arthur Hugh Clough* (1972). The Indian scholar had become friendly with L. at All Souls.

12 October 1982[1]

105 Newland Park, Hull

Dearest bun,

I have been keeping this for you, perhaps for Christmas, but here it is now.[2] It looks all right for roast meat & so on, but how about vegetables, and soufflés (is that how you spell it?)? Anyway the sheer heat wd drive you back. Think of making toast.

Am naturally *very* worried about your face & wound.[3] *Do* get doctor: think of all you've paid in tax for him. This is the sort of thing he *can* treat. Think of *boxers* – they are v. worried abt eyebrows.

Dreary day in London & back. Stupid meeting at wch I spoke *once* – what a waste of time & money. [...]

Foggy journey down – late of course. Couldn't do *Times* crossword. Slept a bit.

Darling, I am so worried about you. Why not ask Mrs Willis to help? You could ring her, & leave door open. We shall talk before you get this. Rest, but eat, and *tell doctor*. All love   Philip

1 Please refer to the 'Note on the Contents', p. xiv, about the dwindling of correspondence after January 1973.
2 The postcard sent by L. showed a reproduction of *The Kitchen at Christ Church* by Ackerman (1813).
3 Monica had fallen downstairs at the Haydon Bridge cottage.

13 October 1982

105 Newland Park, Hull

Dearest bun,

The hospital rang up at nearly six today, so I knew you were safe, but oh dear, how nastily you must have been hurt, and what pain and distress it must have caused. *Poor bun*! And what a shock to be swept out of daily life into Hexham General. I rang them tonight about 8. The line, Geordie accent & my deafness made it difficult, but I gathered I might have spoken to you if something or other. As it was, I sent love. I will come & see you on Sunday (2–4). I rang Dick, & he is very sorry, & he may come on Saturday. He will also tell Tom. The nurse said they expected you would be in 'over the weekend', but no doubt stitches take some time to heal. And you will be looked after, wch will save trouble. But I am awfully sorry that such trouble should befall you.

Those stairs are a menace. *I* have to come down them like a pregnant giraffe.

I remember Hexham General is good for something, so hope it is good for everything. What is the food like? Are you 'allowed up'? Can you hear the Archers? Or is it all telly? I do hope you can rest, and get a night's sleep.

I sent you a card-in-envelope to HB, but it will be waiting there. I had a stupid day on Tuesday – meeting over by *two* – no *need* to hold it in morning – I spoke *once* – good lunch though – steak onion & mushroom stew (pie filling?), baked potato & cabbage. Cheese, fruit. And ten botts. of wine between twelve. I bought *Scenes from Metropolitan Life*,[1] and it is *piss-poor*. What a mangy pair they were, Hoff & Snow. Their self-satisfaction makes you puke.

Charles M. rang up today, over the jolly old lunar orb about *Required Writing*[2] – 'may be too long – we'll do it in two volumes—' Clearly he has come to realise my worth, now it has been pointed out to him. Blake Morrison sent a copy of his 'report' – very kind, pointing out a few omissions.

Dear bun, I know how utterly alien hospitals are, but I hope this one is kind and friendly, and that you don't feel too shaken. Can you get a paper? And a pencil for the crossword? [*drawing*] Think if you would like to come here to convalesce when you 'come out'. I could fetch you away.

Judy writes briefly: has put her flat & car up for sale! She sends her good wishes to you. Dick's little daughter has broken her arm, how seriously they don't know.

My dear, I think of you all the time, but will *see you* on Sunday. Much, much love. Philip

1 William Cooper, *Scenes From Metropolitan Life* (1982).
2 Monteith at Faber had encouraged L. to gather his 'Miscellaneous Pieces', which were first published in book form in November 1983.

14 October 1982

105 Newland Park, Hull

Dearest bun,

Oh dear, I am not one of Nature's hospital-telephoners. Having finally got Ward 11 tonight, I couldn't hear a word they said. 'Was

I a relative?' No – well, gibber-gibber-gibber gibber gibber. I tried to explain that I was intending to come up on Sunday if you were still resident, but gibber gibber. I tried to send love. In consequence I don't know how you are, or what wd have happened if I *had* been a relative. Feel worried and cross with myself. I shd *say* I am deaf.

How wonderful it will be to talk to you again! It seems an age since we spoke. Are you finding it bearable? Do you miss drinks? I *do* hope you are all right, and not made ill by being in hospital. I expect it is very boring – that is the best it can be. Let it be no worse.

How are you finding the food? Perhaps that could be the worst. I went to the Club for lunch & had a vile cheese and margarine sandwich. Had spent the morning at home, trying to write this ghastly newspaper talk. Fat brother was there, the bookie one, drinking a half of lager. I really don't know why he bothers, except of course that one doesn't know how fat he'd be otherwise.

I do wonder how you are. Did you bring anything to read? Was it all very rushed, having to snatch up a few necessaries? Poor bun, I do feel for you. I wonder if you are all bound up over the stitches, and how long it will take. Are you allowed to walk about? It's so hard for me to imagine.

Pressure of public opinion has restored the collection and delivery of post to departments *without porters* – not us, of course. That's all the news here. The dustmen haven't been. I can't get into the Bank: it is jammed with students. Ideas of a new car have faded – no time to think about such things.

The 1st ed. of *The Whitsun Weddings* plus autographed typescript letter proved (the latter) to be to *Norman Jackson*, Hull's layabout non-poet. The book had Loten's signature imperfectly erased – he was chairman of council, you remember, & died about 94. Fancy him buying it. Probably Brynmor gave it him. £95 we paid.

I'm afraid this was an unsuccessful evening. Tomorrow I must assert myself! Unless I hear anything different I shall set out on Sunday morning after breakfast & hope to fall in when they open the doors at 2 pm. Have nothing to bring, unless you'd like *The Doctor's Dilemma*. Very much love, dear bun,

Philip

1 March 1983

Hull[1]

Dearest,

I have got Betjeman off the
ground tonight, thank God.[2]
Page and a half. Now watching Meo and Reardon. If we
ever get cable TV, there will
probably be a snooker
channel & you can watch it all
day. [...]

1 Written on paper printed with 'All Souls College, Oxford' letterhead, crossed
through by L.
2 L.'s review of *John Betjeman: His Life and Works*, by P. Taylor-Martin, appeared
in the *Observer*, 13 March 1983.

2 April 1984

105 Newland Park, Hull

Tues. Rather dismal night – and cold. No bun for breakfast! Please take
care. Write R. Trickett.[1]

Dearest bun,

Monday evening – safely back. Went Tow Law way,
& at Scotch Corner (stopped for piss), continued down
motorway, half meaning to turn off for Thirsk, but in
end turned off at British Library Lending Division and
back through M. Weighton and so on. Had car wash
before coming in. House 54° – regular greenhouse after Lord Crewe.

Of course I have thought of you constantly, wondering how you are
feeling and doing. Did you have your bath? I hope you did and feel
more restored and relaxed. Indeed I can't imagine you'll be any less
feeble but I hope you find some satisfaction in being among your own
things, and your own boss again. Be careful, dear, of *stairs* & *road
crossings*, and be sensible about eating & drinking.

Monday night is boxing night: Belfast lads beat Newcastle 5–4
(after 'trailing' 1–3) and so go through to the semi final, along with

Manchester, Liverpool & N. London. Later there is Sibson, Jones & ...
forget who. Great Fights, you know.

A.N. Wilson's[2] lunch cost £132 for 3. Quite reasonable. I'll save it
for ya.

Dear bun, thank you for your company and all your kindnesses. You
are courageous and patient. Hope you are finding it possible to manage.

Much love
Philip[3]

1 Rachel Trickett: see Appendix B.
2 A. N. Wilson, novelist; at the time, had recently left the *Spectator*, where he was
literary editor, 1981–3.
3 This is apparently the penultimate letter. There followed one further letter
(3 April 1984), and a Christmas card, 'Bun's Outing'. After that they were together
at 105 Newland Park, Hull.

[Christmas 1984]

<u>Bun's Outing</u>

Saturday morning
I go for the meat,
Body all aching
Likewise the feet,
Fools at my elbow
Gormlessly greet,
Shopping is hell
In Stupidity Street.

© Philip Larkin 1984

APPENDIX A

Beauchamp Lodge, 73 Coten End, Warwick: L.'s parents' house after their Coventry house was damaged in the Blitz. His father died in 1948.

172 London Road, Leicester: L.'s lodgings when he moved from Wellington (where he had been Librarian, 1943–6) to Leicester University as Assistant Librarian, 1946–7.

6 College Street, Leicester: L.'s lodgings, 1947–8.

12 Dixon Drive, Leicester: L. negotiated for this house for his mother after his father died and lived there with her from 1948 to 1950, when he was appointed Sub-Librarian at Queen's University, Belfast. It is supposed that Kingsley Amis, who visited him there, took the name of 'Lucky Jim' Dixon from this address.

21 York Road, Loughborough: the house negotiated through L. for his mother in 1951 after L. went to Belfast in 1950. Eva Larkin lived there (close to her daughter Kitty, son-in-law and granddaughter) until she was hospitalised in 1972. L. spent parts of university vacations and many weekends there over the years.

Queen's Chambers, Queen's University, Belfast: L.'s first accommodation in Belfast, October 1950 to July 1951: a hostel room with 'a nice view, but there's no *carpet, nothing* but that horrible rubbery green lino'.

7 College Park East, Belfast: L.'s lodgings in summer and early autumn 1951.

49 Malone Road, Belfast: another brief lodgings, 1951.

30 Elmwood Avenue, Belfast: L.'s main flat (no. 15) in Belfast, from October 1951 until he was appointed Librarian at Hull University and moved to Hull in March 1955. It comprised a pair of rooms at the top of the house, where L. 'nurse[d] stews like a candidate nursing a constituency'.

Holtby Hall, Cottingham, East Yorks.: a Hull University hall of residence; L. stayed in this 'penurious doss-house' in March 1955.

11 Outlands Road, Cottingham: his second digs, April to May 1955. Here the landlady's 'filthy radio floods the whole house ... gabble, gabble, gabble. I have the usual wool in my ears.' Cf. 'Mr Bleaney'.

200 Hallgate, Cottingham: May 1955 to March 1956. His landlady, Mrs Squire, was 'a nice old thing' who played her radio quietly.

192A Hallgate, Cottingham: L. moved into the top flat in April 1956. Its owners, Mr and Mrs Drinkwater, had a noisy daughter but also kept rabbits, which endeared them to L.

32 Pearson Park, Hull: L. moved into the attic flat in October 1956 and stayed there for the next eighteen years. He moved out only when the University, which owned the building, decided in 1973 to 'sell off its worst properties'.

Beechwood House, Set 3, Iffley Turn, Oxford: All Souls College accommodation in Iffley, near Oxford, at which L. spent two terms (September 1970 to April 1971) while working on the early stages of the *Oxford Book of Twentieth Century English Verse*. He took most of his meals in college.

105 Newland Park, Hull: L. moved into this, the only house he ever owned – 'an ugly little house, fearfully dear', with a garden – in June 1974 and stayed there until his death in 1985. At Easter 1983 Monica was severely stricken with shingles while she and L. were staying at her Haydon Bridge cottage and, after hospital, L. insisted she should stay with him at Newland Park and recuperate. She stayed there until her death in 2001.

MONICA'S ADDRESSES

44 Summerfield Road, Stourport-on-Severn, Worcestershire: Monica's parents' house, where she spent many vacations from Leicester. She sold the house after her mother's death in October 1959 and her father's in December of that year.

15 Carisbrooke Road, Leicester ('White House'): September 1950 to July 1951.

6 Westgate Road, Knighton, Leicester: September 1951 to March 1953.

71 Shanklin Drive, Leicester: March 1953 to June 1954.

67 Stoneygate Road, Leicester (c/o Mr and Mrs Evans): October to November 1954.

8 Woodland Avenue, Leicester: November 1954 to September 1961.

1A Cross Road, Leicester: September 1961 to September 1972.

18 Knighton Park Road, Leicester: September 1972 to March 1983.

1A Ratcliffe Road, Haydon Bridge, near Hexham, Northumberland: Monica's Northumberland cottage, backing on to the River Tyne, which she bought in the autumn of 1961 with money from her late parents' estate.

APPENDIX B

Hilly Amis: married Kingsley Amis in 1948. Lived in and near Oxford, in Swansea, where L. stayed with them, and in Cambridge. The marriage lasted until 1963, when Kingsley left her for Elizabeth Jane Howard. She later married again, twice; she and her third husband, Lord Kilmarnock, shared a house with Kingsley until his death.

Kingsley Amis: first met L. at St John's College, Oxford, in Trinity term 1941, at the beginning of L.'s third term at the college. Thereafter his closest friend and correspondent, though with some demurs on L.'s part, especially after the great success of *Lucky Jim*, beginning in early 1954. Monica probably first met him in 1949, when Amis visited L. in Leicester. They did not take to one another.

Martin Amis: younger son of Kingsley and Hilly, born in 1949. Read English at Exeter College, Oxford, where he was awarded a 'formal' first in 1971. First novel, *The Rachel Papers* (1973).

Winifred Arnott: born in 1929, she was working as a cataloguer in the library at Queen's University, Belfast, when she first met L. in 1950. The correspondence between them began the following autumn, when she was studying at University College, London. She later returned to QUB, and she and L. worked, walked and bicycled together until she left on her marriage to Geoffrey Bradshaw in 1954. The poems 'Latest Face', 'Maiden Name', 'Lines on a Young Lady's Photograph Album' and 'Long roots moor summer' concern her.

F. L. Attenborough: Principal of University College, Leicester, 1932–51; father of Richard and David.

J. C. Beckett: Warden of Queen's Chambers, hall of residence at Queen's University, Belfast. 'A small old-maidish historian with a passion for Jane Austen and chess.'

A. L. Binns: Lecturer in English and Admissions Officer, Faculty of Arts, Hull University. He was, almost inevitably, known to L. as 'Loony Binns'. He and his wife seemed to show L. much hospitality.

Ruth Bowman: first met L. in 1943 in Wellington, when he was in charge of the town library (his first job) and she was a 16-year-old schoolgirl. Later, between May 1948 and June 1950, they were 'unofficially' engaged. See Andrew Motion, *Philip Larkin: A Writer's Life* (1994).

Malcolm Bradbury: a pupil of Monica's in Leicester in the early 1950s, he later became a lecturer in English at Hull (1959–61), Birmingham (1961–5) and professor at the University of East Anglia (1965–95). He was also the author of several novels, beginning with *Eating People is Wrong* (1959) and including *The History Man* (1975).

Dennis Bradley: Lecturer in Latin, Queen's University, Belfast.

Maeve Brennan: born in 1929 and educated at Hull University, she joined the university library as an assistant in 1953, two years before L.'s arrival. She worked as sub-librarian in charge of periodicals. She took early retirement in 1985, before L.'s death. Her memoir, *The Philip Larkin I Knew* (2002), is a sensitive account of her relationship with L., including their love affair – the cause of much resentment, misery and sometimes anger on Monica's part. She died in 2003.

R. A. (Ray) Brett: Professor of English at Hull University, 1952–82, and instrumental in L. being appointed librarian in 1955.

David and Jean Burnett-Hall: neighbours of L. at 32 Pearson Park, Hull.

A. S. (Arthur) Collins: Professor of English, University College, Leicester. He appointed Monica in 1946. He died in 1959.

P. A. W. (Philip) Collins: Professor of English, University College, Leicester, 1964–82. Earlier, staff tutor in adult education and lecturer in English.

Robert (Bob) Conquest: first approached L. in January 1955, soliciting poems for what became *New Lines* (1956). He soon became a close friend and correspondent, encouraging L. in pursuit of 'men's magazines'. Four times married. Monica came to speak of him more affectionately than of any other of L.'s friends, with the exception of Bruce Montgomery.

Peter Coveney: Warden of Needler Hall (of residence) at Hull University, where L. recuperated after his hospitalisation in 1961. Author of *Poor Monkey: The Child in Education* (1957).

C. B. (Brian) Cox: Lecturer in English at Hull University and founding co-editor of the *Critical Quarterly* there. Later Professor of English at Manchester University. Co-editor of the 'Black Papers' on education.

Donald Davie: while working as a lecturer in English at Trinity College, Dublin, in 1954, he was in a minority of one when reading L.'s manuscript (later *The Less Deceived*) for the Dolmen Press. Liam Miller and Thomas Kinsella voted against it.

Elspeth Davie: wife of George, novelist and short-story writer.

George Davie: Senior Lecturer in Philosophy, QUB.

Alec Dalgarno: Lecturer in Applied Mathematics, Queen's University, Belfast.

R. W. Drinkwater: L.'s rabbit-keeping neighbour in Hallgate, Cottingham, in 1956. Head of Department of Social Studies, Hull University.

Douglas Dunn: born in Scotland in 1942, he took his degree in English at Hull University (1966–9) and then joined the staff of the Brynmor Jones Library under L., working there from 1969 to 1971. During this period he was given a Gregory Award for poetry and published his first book of poems, *Terry Street* (Faber and Faber, 1969), in both instances backed by L. He was Fellow in Creative Writing at Hull, 1974–5. His first wife, Lesley, who worked at the Ferens Art Gallery in Hull, died of cancer in 1981. He retired as Professor of English at the University of St Andrews in 2008.

Ansell and Judy Egerton: L. first knew them in Belfast, where Ansell was a lecturer in Economics at Queen's University. Judy, born in Australia, became an art historian; they had two daughters, Bridget and Fabia. In 1951, L. was deputed to 'show her [Judy] the library'. The Egertons divorced in 1974, after their return to England from Australia in 1956. L.'s *Selected Letters* (1992) includes seventy letters or extracts from letters to Judy over a long period, beginning in 1954, drawing from a total number of over 250.

D. J. (Dennis) Enright: he reviewed L.'s *XX Poems* in November 1951, and this was indeed the only review. He edited *Poets of the 1950s* (Tokyo, 1956) while teaching in Japan; it included several poems by L., together with a 'statement', and preceded *New Lines* by a few months.

P. G. 'Espinasse: Professor of Zoology, Hull University, from 1948.

Gavin Ewart: one of L.'s favourite contemporary poets. L. reviewed him enthusiastically in *Quarto* (May 1982; see *Further Requirements*).

G. S. (George) Fraser: Lecturer and later Reader in English at Leicester University. Earlier, he had been an industrious and widely published freelance literary critic, doing much reviewing (particularly in the *Times Literary Supplement* and *New Statesman*) and broadcasting, editing anthologies, and in general being a considerable panjandrum on the literary scene from the late 1940s. His widow is Eileen ('Paddy').

J. J. (Jack) Graneek: Librarian, Queen's University, Belfast. The son of Russian parents who had fled a pogrom, he was liked by L.: 'I get powerful sick of work sometimes, but never of Graneek.'

Thom Gunn: the youngest poet included in Conquest's *New Lines*; also published by the Fantasy Press.

Ian Hamilton: poet and editor successively of the *Review* and the *New Review*. His strict and often harsh criticism earned him L.'s label (in a letter to Conquest, 6 May 1969) 'the Kerensky of poetry' – though L. probably meant some more sinister Soviet character. He was Compton Lecturer in Poetry at Hull, 1972–3. He died in 2001, and his *Collected Poems* were published in 2009.

Anthony Hartley: poetry editor of the *Spectator* in the mid-1950s, responsible for publishing several of L.'s poems there, including 'Wires', 'Latest Face', 'Age', 'Skin', 'Myxomatosis', 'Times, Places, Loved Ones' and 'Church Going'.

George Hartley: born in Hull in 1933, he was for a time an art student and then worked in a shoe shop. At the age of twenty he launched (with his wife Jean) the poetry magazine *Listen* from their small house in Hessle, near Hull. L.'s first poem there was in the Summer 1954 issue. Later that year Hartley wrote to L. in Belfast, inviting him to submit a collection of poems, as the first full-scale publication by the Hartleys' Marvell Press. Until L. replied, accepting the offer, Hartley did not know that L. was soon to arrive in Hull. The book, finally called *The Less Deceived*, appeared in late 1955 with a list of pre-publication subscribers organised by the Hartleys in collaboration with L. In 1968 Jean Hartley moved out, with her two daughters, and Hartley went to London; he later married again and went to Australia, where he now lives. Early on, L. dubbed him 'the ponce of Hessle'.

Jean Hartley: born in Hull in 1933. She tells her own story with honesty, unpretentiousness and much humour in her memoir, *Philip Larkin, the Marvell Press and Me* (1989). She is active in the Philip Larkin Society, has been editor

of its journal *About Larkin*, is an accomplished painter and potter, and still
lives in Hull.

Kitty and Walter Hewett: L.'s sister and brother-in-law. They had one daughter,
Rosemary.

Peter Hoare: Sub-Librarian (Cataloguing) in the library at Hull University,
1967–72. Later Librarian, Nottingham University.

Philip Hobsbaum: poet and critic (1932–2005). For a time he was a lecturer at
Queen's University, Belfast, where he encouraged the young Seamus Heaney,
Michael Longley and Derek Mahon.

Richard Hoggart: he was a staff tutor at Hull University (1946–59), Senior
Lecturer in English at Leicester University (1959–62) and Professor of English
and Director of the Centre for Contemporary Cultural Studies, Birmingham
University (1962–73). Later he was an Assistant Director-General of UNESCO,
Chairman of the Pilkington Committee on Broadcasting, and held many other
senior advisory posts. Probably his best-known book is *The Uses of Literacy*
(1957).

John Holloway: his first book of poems, *The Minute* (1956), was the second book
publication by the Marvell Press. He was included by Conquest in *New Lines*.

C. H. Horne: Lecturer in English, University College, Leicester.

Elizabeth Jane Howard: novelist, Kingsley Amis's second wife. They married in
1965 and for some years lived at Lemmons, a large house in Barnet, north of
London, along with her brother Colin ('Monkey'), the painter Sargy Mann, and
(during his final illness) C. Day Lewis and his wife Jill Balcon. She left Kingsley
in 1980 and they were divorced in 1983.

Ted Hughes: Hughes's publication and acclaim began a few years after L.'s, with
The Hawk in the Rain in 1957. L. was always doubtful about him ('No, of
course Ted's no good at all. Not at all. Not a single solitary bit of good'
– letter to Conquest, 1967). But it has been argued that jealousy played a
part in this.

A. R. (Arthur) Humphreys: Professor of English, University College, Leicester.

Elizabeth Jennings: her Fantasy Press pamphlet was published in 1952 and her first
book, *Poems*, by the same press in 1953. Included by Conquest in *New Lines*.

Brynmor Jones: Vice-Chancellor, Hull University, 1956–72. He was knighted in 1968.

John (J. P.) Kenyon: Professor of History, Hull University.

Laurence Lerner: poet and Lecturer in English, Queen's University, Belfast. He was
later Professor of English at Sussex University and then at Vanderbilt University,
Nashville, Tennessee.

Claude Luttrell: Lecturer in Old and Middle English, University College, Leicester.

Betty Mackereth: L.'s secretary at Hull University Library, 1957–84.

Karl Miller: literary editor of the *Spectator* and *New Statesman* in turn, then
editor of the *Listener*, and founding editor of the *London Review of Books*. He
published L.'s poems and reviews in the first three journals.

Donald Mitchell: was a member of the music staff of the *Daily Telegraph*,
1959–64, during which time he enlisted L. as a regular reviewer of jazz records.
See his 'Larkin's Music' in *Larkin at Sixty*. Because of what they took to be his
handsome appearance, he was known to L. and Monica as 'Romantic Mitchell'.

Charles Monteith: L.'s editor at Faber, from *The Whitsun Weddings* until L.'s death.

Bruce Montgomery: contemporary and friend of L.'s at St John's College, Oxford. He began early as a crime writer (as 'Edmund Crispin'), with novels such as *The Case of the Gilded Fly* (1944) and *The Moving Toyshop* (1946), to which L. contributed some pages. He was also a composer: in 1953 he collaborated with Kingsley Amis on a Coronation Ode, performed in Glasgow. From the early 1950s to the late 1960s he produced music for films, including some for the *Carry On* series. He died in 1978. Together with Bob Conquest, Montgomery was perhaps the favourite among L.'s friends with Monica.

Brenda Moon: Arthur Wood's successor as L.'s deputy in the Library of Hull University. Earlier, Chief Cataloguer. Later became Librarian at Edinburgh University, 1980–96.

Richard Murphy: Irish poet, later married to Patsy Strang.

Peter Oldham: read Maths at St John's College, Oxford, 1939–42 and 1946, and later read Medicine. Friend of Bruce Montgomery and, through him, of L. and Monica. Moved to the USA.

J. K. (John) Peel: Geography teacher, Alderman Newton's School, Leicester, and 'College Visitor'. A notable local eccentric, devoted to the study of Romania (and a great friend of the pre-war Romanian Ambassador to London), he became the target of much derision from L. and Monica. He died in October 1968.

Jimmy Piggott: deputy warden of Queen's Chambers hall of residence, Queen's University, Belfast.

Garnet Rees, Professor of French, Hull University, and friend of Vernon Watkins, who stayed with Rees on his visits to Hull.

A. L. (Leslie) Rowse: historian, Fellow of All Souls College, Oxford. As an aspirant (indeed, published – by Faber and Faber) poet, he was eager to embrace L. as a fellow bard. Like John Sparrow, he was homosexual.

Bill Ruddick: a student of Monica's at Leicester, and a particular favourite. When he was appointed to a lectureship at Manchester University in 1964, she wrote: 'the first person trained up by me to get a university post'.

Norman Scarfe: Lecturer in History, University College, Leicester.

J. D. Scott: novelist, literary editor of the *Spectator* in the mid-1950s, and anonymous writer of the pioneering article 'In the Movement' in that journal (October 1954).

Norman Sharpe: a pupil of Monica's at Leicester. He originally went up to University College, Leicester, in 1940, but then joined the RAF and did not return to the college until October 1946. After Monica's death, he wrote: 'Briefly, indeed, Monica and I had a mildly romantic interlude – not entirely surprising, since I was two years her senior – yet not exactly the marriage of true minds, more a mind and a half' (*About Larkin*, No. 12, October, 2001).

Peter Sheldon: Sub-Librarian (Service to Readers) at Hull University Library, 1959–82.

Jack Simmons: Professor of History, University College, Leicester.

John Sparrow: Warden of All Souls College, Oxford, 1952–77, at the time L. spent two terms there while working on the *Oxford Book of Twentieth Century English Verse*, 1970–1.

Colin Strang: L. first knew him at St John's College, Oxford. Later, a lecturer in Philosophy at Queen's University, Belfast, and married to Patsy. After his divorce from Patsy, Colin Strang eventually remarried and became Professor of Philosophy at Newcastle University, 1975–82. From 1978, 2nd Baron Strang.

Patsy Strang (*née* Avis; later Murphy): born in South Africa in 1929, she was educated at Roedean School and Somerville College, Oxford, where she read Medicine. She married Colin Strang in 1948 and moved with him to Belfast; L. saw a great deal of the Strangs from his arrival in Belfast in 1950 until Colin Strang was appointed to Newcastle University in 1953, and had an affair with Patsy (1952–5). In 1954 Patsy studied for a time at the Sorbonne in Paris, where she met Richard Murphy; she went to Greece with him in the winter of 1954–5 and, after her divorce from Colin Strang, married him in May 1955. The Murphys moved to Galway, where a daughter was born in 1956. They were divorced in 1959. Patsy eventually settled in Dublin; she died there, of alcoholic poisoning, in 1977.

John Sutherland: a pupil of Monica's at Leicester. In May 1964 she wrote to L. of him that he was 'the *most grateful* student I have ever had, and the one who probably owed least gratitude to me – I mean, he was so good that I could hardly help him'. He later became Lecturer in English, Edinburgh University, then Lecturer at University College, London, where he was later Lord Northcliffe Professor of Modern English Literature. A prolific critic and reviewer, he is also the biographer of Mrs Humphry Ward, Walter Scott and Stephen Spender. For his reminiscences of Monica, see his *The Boy Who Loved Books* (2007).

Arthur Terry: Lecturer in Spanish, Queen's University, Belfast. Later married to Molly Sellar, who ran the issue desk in the university library.

Anthony Thwaite: first met L. when a trainee BBC radio producer in the Overseas Service, in July 1958. Later, on the Third Programme, first broadcast several of L.'s poems, including 'The Whitsun Weddings' and 'Faith Healing'. Later, literary editor of the *Listener*, then the *New Statesman*, and finally *Encounter*, in which he published several poems and reviews by L.

Rachel Trickett: educated at Lady Margaret Hall, Oxford, she became a Lecturer in English at Hull University (1946–54), then a Fellow and Tutor in English at St Hugh's College, Oxford (1954–71), and was Principal of St Hugh's from 1973 to 1991. Also a novelist.

John Wain: younger contemporary of L.'s at St John's College, Oxford. He published poems and reviews early, began the *First Reading* series on the BBC Third Programme (in which L.'s poems were included), and published his first novel, *Hurry On Down*, in 1953. He was a Lecturer in English at Reading University, 1947–55, and then went freelance. He was Professor of Poetry at Oxford, 1973–8.

D. J. Wilks: composer, one of L.'s neighbours at 32 Pearson Park, Hull.

Arthur Wood: L.'s deputy in the Library at Hull University, 1955–69. Often referred to as 'Charlie Boy', and other more scathing names.

INDEX

at Rochester, 324; at Faber party, 408; poem in *OBTCEV*, 435; other mentions, 117, 127, 299, 379
Frith, William Powell, 296
Fuller, Roy, 415, 431, 437n
Furbank, P. N., 75
Further Requirements: *Betjeman En Bloc*, 247n; another Betjeman review (*Late Chrysanthemums*), 119n, 144, 145, 146n, 147; engagement article, 217n, 218, 219; Langbaum and Kermode review, 226n; 'Separate Ways', 210n; Smith review, 432n

Gainsborough, Thomas, 296
Galsworthy, John, 13, 161, 362
Gardner, Helen, 439
Garland, Patrick, 334n, 338, 344, 345
Garrison Theatre (radio show), 273
Gascoyne, David, 415
Gaskell, Elizabeth, 29–30
Gaunt, William, 43
George V, King, 138–9
George VI, King, 80–1
Gershwin, George: *Porgy and Bess*, 185
Gibb (All Souls), 411
Gibbon, Edward, 435
Gibbon, William Monk, 424
Gibbons, Orlando, 209
Gibbons, Stella, 8n
Gilbert, W. S., 37
Gilliatt, Pen, 327
Girl in a Bikini (film), 261
A Girl in Winter, ix, 3, 4, 55, 61
Goacher, Denis, 318
'Going, Going', 428, 429n
Golding, William, 309; *Lord of the Flies*, 242
Gone to Earth (novel and film), 23–4
Good (Hull professor), 172–3
Goodyear, Frederick, 7
The Goon Show (radio series), 200
Gosling, Ray, 423
Gowrie, Xandra, 408
Graham, W. S., 178n, 218

Grahame, Kenneth: *Bertie's Escapade*, 220; *The Wind in the Willows*, 27, 220–1, 426
Graneek, J. J. (Jack), 451; socialising with PL, 10, 55; PL on, 16; and Strangs, 56; and PL's application to Hull, 120, 123, 130; offered Edinburgh post, 264; other mentions, 142, 143, 251
Grant, Cary, 301
The Grapevine (magazine), 120n
Graves, Robert, 69, 85, 203, 241, 370
Green, F. L., 14n
Green, Henry: *Nothing*, 217
Greene, Graham, 56, 62, 66, 258
Gregory Awards (1971), 420n
Grigson, Geoffrey, 261, 262, 318n, 415
Grimshaw, Atkinson, 397
Guilding (Hull), 223, 257, 277
Gunn, Thom, 451; PL on poetry, 121, 285, 415; anthologised, 129n; Fantasy Press edition, 138n; on PL, 226; Fraser reviews, 288; photo in *London Magazine*, 294; Arp proposes to introduce to PL, 342; other mentions, 150n
Gunner, Colin, 399, 425, 431

Hailsham, Quintin Hogg, Lord, 412, 413n
Hall, Donald, 350
Hall, Radclyffe, 71
Hamburger, Michael, 18n
Hamilton, Sir George, 423
Hamilton, Ian, 418, 451
Handel, George Frideric: PL on, 54, 230, 236–7, 405; Butler on, 54, 142, 230–1; music played at George VI's funeral, 80; other mentions, 75, 115
– WORKS: *Apollo and Dafne*, 251, 254; *Messiah*, 232, 405; *Solomon*, 236, 347; *Sosarme re di Media*, 142
Hansford Johnson, Pamela, 95, 96, 210
Hardy, Emma, 290, 418

Isherwood, Christopher, 122, 228n, 250, 362; *Goodbye to Berlin*, 259n, 434; *Lions and Shadows*, 319, 321n

Jackson, Norman, 443
Jacques, Robin, 314
James, Anne, 344
James, Henry, 16, 70, 72, 295
Japolsky, Leo, 63, 164, 165n, 290
Jarrell, Randall, 118, 121, 181, 200
Jay, Douglas, 412, 413n
jazz: PL's record collection, 23, 67, 118, 171; PL's articles, 201n, 226, 287n, 290, 346–7; PL at Condon and Lyttelton evening, 213; KA's radio programme, 235; start of Blue Note, 250n; PL's recitals, 307–8, 381; PL at Pee Wee Russell concert, 341–2; PL refuses to be jazz critic for *The Queen*, 353
Jeffares, A. N., 283
Jennings, Elizabeth, 452; anthologised, 117, 129n, 201; Fantasy Press edition, 138n; KA and PL parody, 206; PL on poetry, 380; appearance, 408
Jill, ix, 3, 319–20, 327, 366
John O'London, 4
Johnson, Paul, 399
Jones, Alun, 324, 342, 359
Jones, Brynmor, 452; PL's mockery, ix; attitude to potential new library at Hull, 161; becomes Hull's Vice Chancellor, 194; at Thwaite Hall dance, 211; and Kennedy's assassination, 322; at Library Committee meeting, 337; and Compton poetry lectureship, 402; drinks party hosted by, 406; other mentions, 214, 288, 289, 307, 334, 433, 436, 443
Jones, Monica (MJ)
– GENERAL AND VIEWS: and animals, xi; appearance, viii, 47, 122, 360; and birds, 270; and Conquest, 450, 453; on DHL, 109n, 143n; and drink,

304n, 309, 377; and KA, 449; on KM, 64n, 127n; on *LD*, 192–3n; lecturing style, viii; literary portraits, ix; literary tastes, ix, 231, 275; and Montgomery, 450, 453; and pessimism, 63; on PL's poetry, 178n; and politics, 105n; relationship with PL viii, x, xi, 7, 142–3, 143–4n, 145, 147, 151, 152, 154–5, 157, 159, 184–5, 186, 212, 215, 225–6, 228–30, 235–6, 239, 275, 303–6, 328–34, 337–8, 341, 350–1, 363, 364–5; and social life, 304; talkativeness, 86–7; on TH, 164, 429, 431; on *TWW*, 324–5n
– LIFE: background, viii; description of her Carisbrooke Road home, 10; visits Ludlow with PL, 26, 28; forced to move out of Carisbrooke Road, 32–3; visits PL in Belfast, 40; moves into Westgate Road, 63; holiday in Lake District with PL, 85–6; pregnancy fears prove unjustified, 89–90; holiday in Warwick with PL, 97; holiday in Scotland with PL, 102–3; visits PL in Ireland, 111–12; holiday in York with PL, 153, 154; holiday on Sark with PL, 183, 217; love-making with PL, 212, 239, 292, 297, 339; insecurity about whether good at job, 214–15; possibility of taking up visiting appointment at Queen's, New York, 228–30; holiday in Devon with PL, 239; introductory lecture for new students, 240; problems with work, 245; worries about father, 253; mother ill too, 258; feeling not grown up, 258; parents' deaths, 259–60, 261, 262, 263, 264; visits PL, 267; holiday on Sark with PL, 269, 270, 272; visits Lincoln with PL, 276; visits PL in hospital, 279; will plans, 283–4; moves to Cross Road, 285n; buys cottage in Haydon Bridge, 285n, 294–5; and Ruddick, 286, 292, 304,

birthday, 431, 434, 436–7; takes in MJ to care for her, xi

– AS WRITER: on achievements as writer, 368; attitude to own poems, 17–18, 432; on difficulties of writing, 270, 425; on effects that can be achieved in poetry, 45; frustrations about writing and how to lead a writer's life, 106–7, 109, 124–5; on inspiration, 69; on need for falsity in poetry, 205; parody of own poetry, 207; on the poetic impulse, 265; poetry notebooks, 335; preferred poetry writing materials, 196n; on problem of writing about his feelings, 73; on reading poetry aloud, 235; on symbolism, 221; on types of narrative style, 60–1; on why writing is important, 222; writer's block, 271–2

Larkin, Sydney (PL's father): first job, 150; love of TH, 106, 209; ; courtship with wife, 106; retirement, 301–2; PL's feelings about last illness, 73, 260; death, 5; in PL's poetry, 209–10; other mentions, 370

'Larkin at Fifty' (radio programme), 431, 434, 436–7, 437–8

Larkin at Sixty, 6, 453

Laski, Marghanita, 95, 96, 225, 324

'Latest Face', 120, 180, 449

Lawrence, D. H.: PL on his life and dislike for Galsworthy, 13; PL on difficulty of looking at him objectively, 14–15; PL on his lifestyle and character, 15–16, 108, 141; compared to Forster, 16; PL on his characters, 53; PL wishes could write like, 61; life compared to Wilde's, 95; MJ on, 109n, 143n; use of clichés, 113; on KM, 125; PL holds *Lady Chatterley* exhibition at Hull University Library, 274–5; naked wrestling, 406; other mentions, 31, 33, 37, 117, 126, 222

– WORKS: *Kangaroo*, 112; *Lady Chatterley's Lover*, 101, 179, 274–5, 293n; *Movements in European History*, 47; *The Plumed Serpent*, 96; *St Mawr*, 107; *Sons and Lovers*, 276; *A Study of Hardy*, 91n

Lawrence, Frieda, 16

Lawrence, T. E., 145

Lawrence, Thomas, 296

Laxton, 407

Leach, Alfreda, 76, 77

Leary, Paris, 341, 343n

Leavis, F. R., 66, 358, 359

Leeds, 59

Lehmann, John, 243

Leicester University College, viii, 5–6, 172

Leishman, J. B., 164, 165n

Leopardi, Giacomo, 182

Lerner, Laurence, 113, 121, 164, 170, 452

The Less Deceived: contents, xi, 120n, 137, 139, 143; dedication, 137–8, 139; jacket blurb, 189; PL's contract, 186–7, 188; PL's special copy, 266; publication preparations, 134, 137–8, 150; published, 192, 451; reception, 194, 195, 197, 201n; recording, 242–3, 246; sales, 194, 195–6, 299, 386; subscribers, 163, 164, 170; title, 137–8, 139, 150

Lewis, C. Day: becomes Compton Poetry Lecturer at Hull, 334, 377n; and Poet Laureateship, 375; PL on poetry, 415; Elizabeth Jane Howard on, 435; last illness, 452; memorial service, 439

Lewis, C. S., 38n, 365–7

Lewis, George, 123

Lewis, Wyndham, 112–13

Lichfield, 339, 370

Lincoln, 276

'Lines on a Young Lady's Photograph Album', 180, 449

Lisburn, 43

Listen (journal): establishment, ix, 451; PL poems in, 105n, 120, 143, 266;

Proust, Marcel, 407
Pudney, John, 193n
Punch (magazine), 53, 116
Purcell, Henry, 251
Pym, Barbara: PL corresponds with, 277, 286, 325; PL tries to help get published, 353, 370–1
WORKS: *Excellent Women*, 286, 353; *Jane and Prudence*, 370–1; *No Fond Return of Love*, 372; *An Unsuitable Attachment*, 321, 325n, 353, 393–4

Q (magazine), 119n, 146n
The Queen (magazine), 353, 355
Queen's University, Belfast, 9–11, 19, 21, 29, 399
Quennell, Peter, 350

Raban, J., 421
Rackham, Arthur, 29n, 220–1
ragtime, 326
Raine, Kathleen, 200, 253
Ratcliffe, Dorothy Una, 197
Rattigan, Terence, 174
Rawlings, Margaret, 92
Reading University, 265
Rees, Garnet, 343, 453
Reeves, James, 350
'Reference Back' (formerly 'Referred Back'), 191–2n, 195
Reid, Forrest, 88
'Requiem for Jazz', 346, 347n
Required Writing: Barnes review, 301n; Dickinson and de la Mare review, 406n; 'Hardy's Mind and Heart', 418n; *Poets of the 1950s* statement, 202n; publication, 442; Ricks's Tennyson review, 398–9; 'Supreme Sophisticate', 439n; 'Wanted: Good Hardy Critic', 362, 363n
Rex, David, 272, 282, 287
Ricks, Christopher, 395, 398–9
Riding, Laura, 200
Ridler, Anne, 214, 350, 426
Ridley, M. R., 45–6
Rimbaud, Arthur, 375n

Roberts, Michael, 350n
Roberts, Ursula (pseud. Susan Miles), 426
Robey, George, 218
Rodgers, W. R., 424
Roethke, Theodore, 178n
Rolfe, Frederick William *see* Corvo, Baron
Ross, Alan, 18n, 276, 290, 319
Ross, Robert, 95, 319
Rossetti, Christina, 46n, 92
Rossetti, Dante Gabriel, 296
'Round Another Point', 147n, 186n
Rousseau, Jean Jacques, 103
Rowse, A. L. (Leslie), 37, 63, 358, 411, 414, 453
Royal Academy Bicentennial Exhibition, 397
Ruddick, Bill, 293n, 453; PL's feelings about, ix; visits MJ, 286; relationship with MJ, 292, 304, 353; tastes in food, 339; PL on appearance, 374
rugby, 75
Russell, Pee Wee, 67, 307, 341–2, 397

Sackville-West, Vita: *The Land*, 401
'Sad Steps', 385, 386, 386n, 388n
St Denis, Michael, 288–9, 290n
Saki, 26, 255n, 301
Salinger, J. D.: *The Catcher in the Rye*, 242
Sand, George, 29, 309
Sark, 183, 217, 228, 269, 270, 272, 371
Sassoon, Siegfried, 87, 127, 209, 301
Savage, D. S., 22, 24n
Saville, John, 156n, 260, 274
Sayers, Dorothy, 233
Scannell, Vernon, 385
Scarborough Cricket Festival, 173
Scarfe, Norman, 143, 144n, 453
Scarlatti, Alessandro, 142
Schwartz, George, 118n
Scotland, 102–3, 386, 409, 438
Scott, J. D., 164, 165n, 194, 453
Scott, Tom, 210, 318